A Companion to Michael Haneke

Wiley Blackwell Companions to Film Directors

The Wiley Blackwell Companions to Film Directors survey key directors whose work together constitutes what we refer to as the Hollywood and world cinema canons. Whether Haneke or Hitchcock, Bigelow or Bergmann, Capra or the Coen brothers, each volume, comprised of 25 or more newly commissioned essays written by leading experts, explores a canonical, contemporary and/or controversial *auteur* in a sophisticated, authoritative, and multi-dimensional capacity. Individual volumes interrogate any number of subjects—the director's *oeuvre*; dominant themes, well-known, worthy, and under-rated films; stars, collaborators, and key influences; reception, reputation, and above all, the director's intellectual currency in the scholarly world.

Published

A Companion to
Michael Haneke

Edited by Roy Grundmann

WILEY Blackwell

This paperback edition first published 2014
© 2014 John Wiley & Sons, Ltd

Edition History: Blackwell Publishing Ltd (hardcover, 2010)

Registered Office
John Wiley & Sons Ltd, The Atrium, Southern Gate, Chichester, West Sussex, PO19 8SQ, UK

Editorial Offices
350 Main Street, Malden, MA 02148-5020, USA
9600 Garsington Road, Oxford, OX4 2DQ, UK
The Atrium, Southern Gate, Chichester, West Sussex, PO19 8SQ, UK

For details of our global editorial offices, for customer services, and for information about how to apply for permission to reuse the copyright material in this book please see our website at www.wiley.com/wiley-blackwell.

The right of Roy Grundmann to be identified as the author of the editorial material in this work has been asserted in accordance with the UK Copyright, Designs and Patents Act 1988.

Library of Congress Cataloging-in-Publication Data

A companion to Michael Haneke / edited by Roy Grundmann.
    p. cm. – (Wiley Blackwell companions to film directors)
Includes bibliographical references and index.
ISBN 978-1-4051-8800-5 (hardcover : alk. paper); 978-1118-72348-7 (paper)
    1. Haneke, Michael, 1942 – Criticism and interpretation.   I. Grundmann, Roy, 1963–
PN1998.3.H36C66 2010
791.4302233092–dc22

                                                                    2009054210

A catalogue record for this book is available from the British Library.

Cover image: Photo of Michael Haneke © Jacky Azoulai.
Cover design by Nicki Averill Design and Illustration

Set in 11/13pt Dante by Graphicraft Limited, Hong Kong
Printed in Malaysia by Ho Printing (M) Sdn Bhd

1   2014

Contents

Notes on Contributors

Janelle Blankenship is an Assistant Professor of Film Studies and Graduate Faculty in Comparative Literature and Theory and Criticism at the University of Western Ontario. She previously taught in the Department of German at New York University. She has published numerous essays on early cinema, film theory, and literary modernism in the journals *Cinema & Cie: International Film Studies Journal, Kintop: Das Jahrbuch zur Erforschung des frühen Filmes, Modernist Cultures,* and *Polygraph: An International Journal of Culture and Politics.*

Christa Blümlinger is Maître de conférences in film studies at the University Sorbonne Nouvelle (Paris 3). She was assistant and guest professor at the Free University Berlin and has worked as a critic and a curator in Vienna, Berlin, and Paris. Her most recent publication is *Kino aus Zweiter Hand. Zur Ästhetik materieller Aneignung im Film und in der Medienkunst* (Berlin, 2009).

Eugenie Brinkema is a PhD student in modern culture and media at Brown University. Her work focuses on violence, ethics, and sexual difference, and she is completing a dissertation on affects in film, film theory, and continental philosophy. Her articles have appeared in the *Dalhousie Review, Camera Obscura, Women: A Cultural Review, Journal of Speculative Philosophy,* and *Criticism,* with forthcoming work in *Angelaki: Journal of the Theoretical Humanities.*

Peter Brunette is Reynolds Professor of Film Studies at Wake Forest University, where he directs the film studies program. He is the author of books on Rossellini and Antonioni, and co-author or co-editor of several books on film theory. He is also a practicing journalist and film critic and reviews films for the *Hollywood Reporter* at major film festivals around the world. His own book on Michael Haneke's films will be published by the University of Illinois Press in February, 2010.

Barton Byg teaches German and film studies at the University of Massachusetts, Amherst, where he is founding director of the DEFA Film Library and a founding faculty member of the Interdepartmental Program in Film Studies. His recent research and teaching focus on such topics as Brecht and film, documentary, landscape, and color. He is author of the book *Landscapes of Resistance: The German Films of Jean-Marie Straub and Danièle Huillet*.

Michel Chion is a composer of *musique concrète*, a writer, theoretician, and researcher who currently serves as an Associate Professor at the University of Paris III. His translated publications include *Audio-vision: Sound on Screen*, *The Voice in Cinema and Film*, and *A Sound Art* (Columbia University Press) as well as *David Lynch*, *Eyes Wide Shut*, and *The Thin Red Line* (British Film Institute).

Tom Conley, Lowell Professor of Romance Languages and Visual and Environmental Studies at Harvard University, is recently author of *Cartographic Cinema* (2007) and translator of Marc Augé, *Casablanca: Movies and Memory* (2009). His *Errant Eye: Poetry and Topography in Renaissance France* is forthcoming (2010).

Timothy Dail received the Master of Arts in German film studies from the University of Massachusetts, Amherst, where he was also employed as translator and subtitler for the DEFA Film Library. He is currently a PhD candidate in German at the University of Canterbury in Christchurch, New Zealand. His research focuses on the *Ostalgie* phenomenon in German popular cinema, DEFA films, and issues of pan-German identity and historiography since reunification.

Peter Eisenman is principal of Eisenman Architects in New York City and the Louis I. Kahn Visiting Professor of Architecture at Yale. His award-winning projects include the Memorial to the Murdered Jews of Europe in Berlin, the Wexner Center for the Arts at the Ohio State University, and the City of Culture of Galicia in Spain, which is in construction. Also an author, his most recent books are *Written into the Void: Selected Writings, 1990–2004* and *Ten Canonical Buildings, 1950–2000*.

Thomas Elsaesser is Professor Emeritus of Film and Television Studies at the University of Amsterdam and, since 2005, Visiting Professor at Yale University. His most recent books include *Filmgeschichte und Frühes Kino* (2002), *European Cinema: Face to Face with Hollywood* (2005), *Terror und Trauma* (2007), *Filmtheorie: zur Einführung* (2007, with Malte Hagener), and *Hollywood Heute* (2009).

Monica Filimon is a PhD candidate in comparative literature at Rutgers, the State University of New Jersey. She has published articles on 1930s French cinema and post-1989 Romanian films. Her dissertation focuses on the implications of film melodrama in totalitarian regimes in France and Spain.

Robert Gray is a translator and interpreter. He lives in Canada and France.

Roy Grundmann is Associate Professor of Film Studies in the Department of Film and Television at Boston University. He is the author of *Andy Warhol's Blow Job* (2003) and of a monograph on the cinema of Michael Haneke (Wiley-Blackwell, forthcoming 2010). He is currently co-editing the Wiley-Blackwell *Companion* *to American Film* (2011). His writings have appeared in numerous publications including *Continuum, Cinemaya, The Velvet Light Trap, GLQ*, and *Cineaste* magazine, where he is a contributing editor.

Vinzenz Hediger is Professor of Film and Media Studies at Ruhr University Bochum. He is currently working on a manuscript about André Bazin's cosmological realism. His publications include *Films that Work: Industrial Films and the Productivity of Media* (2009) and *Nostalgia for the Coming Attraction: American Movie Trailers and the Culture of Film Consumption* (2010).

T. Jefferson Kline is a Professor of French in the Department of Romance Studies at Boston University. His publications include *André Malraux and the Metamorphosis of Death* (1973), *Bertolucci's Dream Loom: A Psychoanalytic Study of Cinema* (1987), *I film di Bertolucci* (1992), *Screening the Text: Intertexuality in New Wave French Film* (1992), *Bernardo Bertolucci Interviews*, co-edited with B. Sklarew and F. Gerard (2000), *Unraveling French Cinema* (2009), and numerous articles on the French novel, French theater, and European cinema.

Thomas Y. Levin is Professor of Cultural and Media History in the German Department at Princeton University. He is the author of the forthcoming *Resistance to Cinema: Reading German Film Theory*. He has edited and translated a number of books on the work of Siegfried Kracauer, including *The Mass Ornament: Weimar Essays* (1995). Levin has also co-edited *Walter Benjamin, The Work of Art in the Age of its Technological Reproducibility, and other Writings on Media* (2008), as well as *CTRL [Space]: Rhetorics of Surveillance from Bentham to Big Brother* (2002). The latter book is based on a major exhibition curated by Levin, which was on view at the Zentrum für Kunst und Medientechnologie (ZKM) in Karlsruhe through February 2002.

Alex Lykidis is Assistant Professor of Film Studies in the English Department at Montclair State University. His research interests include contemporary European cinema, immigrant and minority representation, and political filmmaking. Born in Athens, Greece, he now lives in Brooklyn, New York.

Jean Ma is an Assistant Professor in the Department of Art and Art History at Stanford University, where she teaches in the Film and Media Studies Program. She is co-editor of *Still Moving: Between Cinema and Photography* (2008). Her forthcoming publications include *Melancholy Drift: Marking Time in Chinese Cinema* and an essay on Tsai Ming-liang and the post-classical art film in the anthology *Global Art Cinema*, edited by Rosalind Galt and Karl Schoonover.

Jörg Metelmann received his PhD in media and cultural studies from the University of Tübingen in 2003. He is the author of *Zur Kritik der Kino-Gewalt: Die Filme von Michael Haneke* (2003) and co-author of *"Irgendwie Fühl' Ich mich wie Frodo": Eine Empirische Studie über gelebte Medienreligion* (2006). He has edited *Porno Pop: Sex in der Oberflächenwelt* (2005) and co-edited *Ästhetik und Religion* (2007) as well as *Bild – Raum – Kontrolle: Videoüberwachung als Zeichen gesellschaftlichen Wandels* (2005). He is currently a researcher in the area of public value management at the Center for Leadership and Values in Society at the University of St. Gallen, Switzerland.

Leland Monk teaches literature, film, and queer studies in the English Department at Boston University. He is the author of *Standard Deviations: Chance and the Modern British Novel* and essays about Jane Austen, Henry James, and E. M. Forster. He is currently at work on a book about Hollywood endings.

Tobias Nagl is Assistant Professor of Film Studies at the University of Western Ontario. He has also worked as a researcher for CineGraph and curator for the Oberhausen Film Festival. He is the author of *Die unheimliche Maschine: Rasse und Repräsentation im Weimarer Kino* (*The Uncanny Machine: Race and Representation in Weimar Cinema*) (2009) and has published numerous essays on German cinema, popular culture, and film theory.

Fatima Naqvi is an Associate Professor in the Department of German, Russian, and East European Languages and Literatures at Rutgers University, where she teaches Austrian and German literature and film. Her book, *The Literary and Cultural Rhetoric of Victimhood: Western Europe 1970–2005* (2007), analyzes the pervasive rhetoric of victimhood in European culture since 1968. She has also written on the Czech photographer Miroslav Tichý, Elfriede Jelinek's post-dramatic texts, film adaptation as melancholic translation, the aesthetics of violence in Michael Haneke's films, and pedagogy and dilettantism in Thomas Bernhard's works. Her next book on Michael Haneke's films appears with Synema Verlag in Vienna (2010).

Brigitte Peucker is Elias Leavenworth Professor of German and Professor of Film Studies at Yale. Among her books are *Incorporating Images: Film and the Rival Arts* (1985) and *The Material Image: Art and the Real in Film* (2007). She is currently editing Blackwell's *Companion to Rainer Werner Fassbinder*, and is working on a book about Fassbinder and performance. Forthcoming work includes essays on Hitchcock and on Werner Herzog.

Brian Price is Assistant Professor of Screen Studies at Oklahoma State University. He is author of *Neither God Nor Master: Robert Bresson and the Modalities of Revolt* (2010) and co-editor of *On Michael Haneke* and *Color, the Film Reader* (2006). He is also a founding editor of *World Picture*.

Peter J. Schwartz is Assistant Professor of German at Boston University. He is the author of *After Jena: Goethe's "Elective Affinities" and the End of the Old Regime* (2010), and is writing a book on Aby M. Warburg and the ethnology of superstition during World War I.

Georg Seeßlen studied painting, art history, and semiology in Munich. The author of over twenty film books, he is a freelance writer for *Die Zeit, Frankfurter Rundschau, taz, epd-Film, Freitag,* and other publications.

xii NOTES ON CONTRIBUTORS

Christopher Sharrett is Professor of Communication and Film Studies at Seton Hall University. He is author of *The Rifleman* (2005), and editor of *Mythologies of Violence in Postmodern Media* (1999) and *Crisis Cinema: The Apocalyptic Idea in Postmodern Narrative Film* (1993). He is co-editor of *Planks of Reason: Essays on the Horror Film* (2004). He has published in *Cineaste, Framework, Film International, Cinema Journal, Postscript, Kinoeye, Senses of Cinema*, and elsewhere.

Kevin L. Stoehr, PhD, is Associate Professor of Humanities in an interdisciplinary liberal arts program at Boston University. He has authored, co-authored, and edited numerous publications in the areas of film studies and the philosophy of film. His books and articles deal with various topics including the directors John Ford and Stanley Kubrick, the rise of the A-production Western movie, expressions of nihilism in works of cinema and television, Jungian psychology, film noir, and the film theories of Sergei Eisenstein and Siegfried Kracauer.

Gregor Thuswaldner is Associate Professor of German and Linguistics and Chair of the Department of Languages and Linguistics, as well as a Fellow in the Center for Christian Studies at Gordon College in Wenham, Massachusetts. He has written articles on German and Austrian literature, culture, politics, religion, literary theory, and linguistics. He is the co-editor of *Der untote Gott: Religion und Ästhetik in deutscher und österreichischer Literatur des 20. Jahrhunderts* (2007) and the editor of *Derrida und danach? Literaturtheoretische Diskurse der Gegenwart* (2008).

Evan Torner is a doctoral candidate in German studies and film studies at the University of Massachusetts, Amherst, where he served as the program assistant of the DEFA Film Library from 2006 to 2009. As part of the 2007 Michael Haneke Retrospective, he subtitled the majority of Haneke's television films into English. He is currently studying at the Academy for Film and Television in Potsdam-Babelsberg on a Fulbright Fellowship for the 2009–10 academic year. His academic interests include German and Austrian science fiction, Cold War genre cinema, electronic music, and race theory.

Charles Warren teaches film studies at Boston University and in the Harvard Extension School. He is the editor of *Beyond Document: Essays on Nonfiction Film* and, with Maryel Locke, of *Jean-Luc Godard's Hail Mary: Women and the Sacred in Film*. He writes frequently on film of all kinds for books and journals, and has lately worked with filmmaker Robert Gardner to produce the DVD series *Screening Room* and the volumes *Making Dead Birds: Chronicle of a Film* and *Human Documents: Eight Photographers*.

Preface to the Paperback Edition

In 2009, when writing the introduction to the hardcover of the present volume, I described Michael Haneke as an anachronism, a belated representative of the great tradition of European art cinema that, ironically, had all but come to an end by the time Haneke's career as a director of theatrical features got under way in the 1980s. If Haneke's films constitute carefully wrought formal and narrative updates of the classic concerns of European art cinema, it is not by virtue of radical innovation. In place of stylistic iconoclasm, Haneke has created a cinema of aesthetic and discursive meticulousness. While his persona at times seems to mimic that of a schoolmaster who feels compelled to expound on what is good and what is bad for us as viewers, his films speak their own language, allowing us, by virtue of their unique tension between precision and openness, to make discoveries great and small.

The diverse, at times disparate qualities that have constituted both Haneke's work and his position as an artist seemed never more clearly in evidence than with *The White Ribbon* (2009). The film's black-and-white imagery conjures classical cinema's appeal to indexicality, but the digital cinematography's exaggerated crispness points to its status as a consummate artifact. The voice-over evokes the atmosphere of a literary adaptation, but there is no single corresponding source text. And while the story and treatment triggered speculation about the origins of fascism, the film's merits lie not in its teasing ambiguity towards the seductiveness of historical master narratives, but in the sprawling canvas it unfolds of unique faces, gazes, bodies, spaces, and sounds. As long as one keeps in mind that it is these qualities that have kept Haneke's output current, it may not be all that surprising that Haneke managed to push his success to yet another level with his follow-up film, *Amour* (2012), which trumped *The White Ribbon* in critical acclaim and audience popularity.

Since its main characters are lovable and its story personable and seemingly free from grand historical and philosophical issues, *Amour*'s release unfolded without the bouts of didacticism that traditionally accompany the critical reception of Haneke's films. With little perceived need for clearing up misperceptions about the narrative and its characters, Haneke was free to divulge on his personal connection to the story – a move that, no doubt, helped humanize him. Cannes, in addition to giving him a second *Palme d'or*, offered a standing ovation, and even American critics, relieved to have escaped another browbeating, enthusiastically embraced the film. In a 40-year history fraught with misunderstandings and mutual snubbings, *Amour*'s release became the first love fest between the director and his worldwide audiences. If less conceptually highbrow and more plainly humanist than his previous films, *Amour* still deals with classic Haneke territory in its exploration of questions of guilt and responsibility. It examines how to preserve human dignity in a technocratic world and what function art can play when faced with this challenge. In the way it treats these questions, *Amour* may turn out to be Haneke's most radical film yet.

In *Amour*, Haneke gives us another story about Georges and Anne, the bourgeois couple that, in various incarnations, has populated his films since the 1980s.* Here they are dignified elderly Parisians who act as patrons of the piano arts. Rather than being "glaciated," their relationship is characterized by warmth, intimacy, and honesty. Not long into the film Anne suffers an illness that leaves her lastingly incapacitated. Unable to provide her relief, Georges (Jean-Louis Trintignant) eventually suffocates Anne (Emanuelle Riva) with a pillow. But more interesting than its sympathetic portrayal of euthanasia is the film's depiction of Georges's and Anne's love, which undergoes a radical mutation. One way of appreciating this mutation is to relate *Amour* to the moral tales of French New Wave filmmaker Eric Rohmer. In Rohmer's films speculation is the daily bread of lovers, whose deliberations about their loved ones consistently outpace their actions. Haneke's way of paying homage to Rohmer is to subvert this formula by showing Georges change from romantic courtier to overwhelmed caregiver. As Anne's catatonic state makes it difficult for her to reciprocate his affection, the concept of the embrace – courtly love's main signifier of the desire for consummation – is perfidiously degraded to the harrowing routine of nursing a severely ill person, before it culminates, in a bitterly ironic repurposing, in the act of suffocation. Georges's brutal act may stand in contrast to the passivity of Rohmer's Moral Tales. But it follows a similar logic of romantic projection, while, at the same time, offering a radically new perspective on the implications of the concept of love.

Georges's killing of Anne startlingly foregrounds that love, even when it is at its most intimately transitive, is an utterly solitary affair. It may be shaped far less than commonly assumed by mutuality and shared experience, which are often coincidental. Instead, we may be forced to characterize it as nothing more than a private sensation sparked by an attitude towards the other – an attitude that

---

* For a detailed discussion of this film, see Roy Grundmann, "Love, Death, Truth – *Amour*," *Senses of Cinema*, Issue 65, December 2012.

ultimately eludes verification and lasting confirmation. The more Georges is separated from Anne by her advancing lifelessness, the more intimate grows his love
to her – and also the more speculative. This is precisely what interests Haneke.
The question is not whether the romantic couple's threat of separation can somehow be averted – clearly, it cannot – but how the concept of love may be
rethought through new forms of affect and togetherness, forms explored by
Amour through the ironic overlap between communion and separation, desire and
jouissance.

Key to the story's progression is Georges's transition back from caregiver to
lover, which is how Anne sees him and how she sees herself. This process is initiated by Anne's rejection of her status as a patient (by spitting out water Georges
forced into her mouth); it is reinforced by George's termination of Anne's miserable life through a "crime of passion;" and it becomes fully realized when, after
the killing, the film shows Anne reappearing in George's world in a radically
new way. Neither a ghost nor a mere figment of George's imagination, Anne's
existence suggests an aporetic continuity of irreconcilable orders of ontology.
In aesthetic terms, this unique representation of coupledom is not intended as
a simple trumping of reality by a reified form of cinematic fantasy – which, for
Haneke, would be a fake freedom. Following Frankfurt School thought, Haneke
attempts to replace the sheen of freedom with a more complex aesthetic concept
best articulated through a double negative – the negation of unfreedom – for
which he has devised this kind of aesthetic aporia. As the lovers cannot possibly
belong to the same ontological realm but are nonetheless shown together, their
status can best be characterized as the result of a radical enactment of their love.
We may dismiss this depiction as a mere whim or gimmick. Or we may regard
it as signifying a crisis of belonging that also involves us spectators.

Amour's subtle subversion of the ways the cinema handles realism, fantasy, and
character psychology constitutes one more instance of Haneke attempting to push
the artistic potentials of film as a popular medium. This impulse has marked every
phase of his career. His large and variegated body of work has offered us intriguing opportunities for assessing film's capabilities against the changing horizon
of its artistic and material possibilities. Originally published in 2010, the present
volume of essays was the first to address Haneke's oeuvre in a comprehensive
manner. If it has since been joined by a growing number of books and essays, the
fact that many of the more recent publications reference the contributions to this
collection testifies to its pioneering status. We are pleased to see it taking its place
in the widening discourse on Haneke that it helped initiate.

Roy Grundmann
Boston, July 2013

Acknowledgments

The present volume of essays is based in part on the international, interdisciplinary conference, "Michael Haneke: A Cinema of Provocation," organized at Boston University in October, 2007, in conjunction with the first comprehensive retrospective of Haneke's films in the U.S. and with a masterclass taught by Michael Haneke at Boston University during his visit the same month. Because the conference, the masterclass, and the retrospective brought together many people who provided a unique, stimulating environment from which the scholarship featured in this book could emerge, my list of individuals and organizations whom I wish to thank as chief curator, conference director, and editor of this volume is long. However, having the opportunity to express my gratitude fills me with excitement, pride, and many fond memories.

This book would not have been published had it not been for the original initiative of Boston University, the Goethe-Institut, Boston, and the Cultural Services of the French Consulate, Boston, to make a significant number of Michael Haneke's films available for English language audiences, critics, and scholars. My thanks go to Claudia Hahn-Raabe, former Director of the Goethe-Institut, Boston, and to Brigitte Bouvier, former Cultural Attaché at the French Consulate, Boston, for sharing the initiative to subtitle Haneke's television films with the help of a foundation grant from the Elysée Treaty Fund for Franco-German Relations in Third Countries. I would also like to thank former Dean John Schulz at Boston University's College of Communication for providing funding to supplement the grant. My gratitude also goes to Robert Gardner for his financial contribution. My very special thanks go to Karin Oehlenschläger, Programming Director at the Goethe-Institut, Boston, for her invaluable logistic assistance in coordinating many of the details of the retrospective. Heartfelt thanks also go to Hiltrud Schulz at the DEFA Film Library, University of Massachusetts at Amherst, for overseeing the subtitling of the films, which was performed by Evan Torner and Timothy Dail in Amherst and Silvia Beier in Boston. I would also like to thank the curators at our partner venues for their critical input in presenting Haneke's work, particularly Haden Guest, Director of the Harvard Film Archive, Ted Barron, former Programmer at the Harvard Film Archive, Bo Smith, former Film Curator at the Museum of Fine Arts, Boston, and Josh Siegel, Assistant Curator of Film and Media at the Museum of Modern Art, New York. I would further like to thank Laura Kim and Craig Platt at Warner Independent Pictures for their logistic and financial support with the retrospective and for making Michael Haneke's attendance of the retrospective and the masterclass possible. My special thanks go to Ulrike Lässer at Wega Film Productions, Vienna, for providing me with curatorial information about the films and with additional materials for this volume of essays.

I would further like to thank the various individuals and organizations who have made the conference at Boston University possible. As it provided a significant foundation for much of the scholarship featured in this collection, their financial, logistical, and intellectual support has also indirectly contributed to the publication of this volume. In particular I would like to thank Andreas Stadler, Director of the Austrian Cultural Forum, New York, and Martin Rauchbauer, Deputy Director, as well as Ulrich Grothus, former Director of the German Academic Exchange Service (DAAD), New York, and his team for their generous financial contributions and their overall enthusiasm for the project. My thanks also go to Irena Grudzinska Gross and Elizabeth Amrien at Boston University's Institute of Human Sciences, to the Max Kade Foundation, New York, the Boston University Humanities Foundation, the Boston University Department of Modern Languages and Comparative Literature, and the Boston University Distinguished Professorship in the Core Curriculum. I am grateful to David Eckel at the Boston University Institute for Philosophy and Religion, for helping organize part of the conference, and to Uwe Mohr, former Director of the Goethe-Institut, Boston, who provided vital logistic support and turned the Goethe-Institut into a splendid host venue for the first day of the conference. My very special thanks go to the conference manager, Colin Root, whose organizational skills and immeasurable patience vitally contributed to the success of this event. Additional logistic help with the conference and the retrospective were provided by Aviv Rubinstein, Allison Miracco, Alan Wong, Maureen Clark, Nat Taylor, Ken Holmes, and Jamie Companeschi at the Boston University College of Communication. Most importantly, I would like to thank former Dean ad interim, Tobe Berkovitz, and Charles Merzbacher, former Chair of the Department of Film and Television, for lending financial and logistic help to the conference and for dispensing me from teaching duties during the academic year 2008/2009 to edit this volume of essays.

I would like to thank the following individuals for their stimulating contributions to the conference that, in turn, also helped shape many of the essays in this volume: Silvia Beier, Odile Cazenave, Patton Dodd, David Eckel, Mattias Frey, Fatima Naqvi, Abigail Gillman, Bradley Herling, and Karen Ritzenhoff. A special thanks also goes to the students of the Michael Haneke seminar that I taught in conjunction with the retrospective and the conference in the fall, 2007, as well as to Charles Merzbacher and John Bernstein for contributing to the masterclass taught by Michael Haneke during his visit to Boston University. Additional research assistance and logistic support for the conference and for this volume has come from Alexander Horwath, Director of the Austrian Film Museum, and from his team, particularly Richard Hartenberger and Roland Fischer-Briand. I am grateful to T. Jefferson Kline, Julia Kostova, Peter Schwartz, and Brigitte Bouvier for lending their translation skills to various parts of the project. At Boston University I am particularly grateful to Robert Ribera, whose intelligence and skills have been indispensable in preparing the manuscript for publication, as well as to Colin Root for his careful compilation of the filmography.

At Wiley-Blackwell, my special thanks go to Jayne Fargnoli, Executive Editor, for her initiative and her vision in taking on this project, to Margot Morse, Senior Editorial Assistant, for skillfully steering the volume through the many details of the editorial process, and to Annie Jackson and Brigitte Lee Messenger for the patience and skill with which they have overseen the copy-editing.

If there is a single person whose vital support has counted for every part of this project, it is my partner, Mark Hennessey, who, in addition to lending various kinds of assistance and advice, has been a source of tremendous patience and personal support.

Finally, I would like to thank Michael Haneke for his accessibility, his cooperation, and his generosity in sharing comments about his work.

Text credits

The editor and publisher gratefully acknowledge the permission granted to reproduce the copyright material in this book:

Fatima Naqvi's essay "A Melancholy Labor of Love, or Film Adaptation as Translation: *Three Paths to the Lake*" was initially published as "A Melancholy Labor of Love, or Film Adaptation as Translation: Michael Haneke's *Drei Wege zum See*" by *The Germanic Review* (2007), pp. 291–315.

Jean Ma's essay, "Discordant Desires, Violent Refrains: *Le Pianiste (The Piano Teacher)*" was initially published in *Grey Room* 28, Summer 2007, pp. 6–29, and appears with kind permission of MIT Press's Journals Division.

Georg Seeßlen's essay "Structures of Glaciation" is a translated version of the author's essay "Strukturen der Vereisung" originally published in German in *Michael Haneke und seine Filme: Eine Pathologie der Konsumgesellschaft*. Franz Grabner, Gerhard Larcher, and Christian Wessely eds. (Marburg: Schüren, 2008), pp. 25–44, and appears here with kind permission of Schüren.

Michael Haneke's "Terror and Utopia of Form" is a translated version of the author's "Schrecken und Utopie der Form – Bressons *Au hasard Balthazar*" and appears here with kind permission of Michael Haneke.

Michael Haneke's "Violence and Media" is a translated version of the author's "Gewalt und Medien" and appears here with kind permission of Michael Haneke.

Every effort has been made to trace copyright holders and to obtain their permission for the use of copyright material. The publisher apologizes for any errors or omissions in the above list and would be grateful if notified of any corrections that should be incorporated in future reprints or editions of this book.

Introduction

Haneke's Anachronism

Roy Grundmann

If there is a dominant characteristic that can be said to mark Michael Haneke's path as a filmmaker, it is that of anachronism. But in contrast to what the term's comparative logic implies, Haneke's anachronism did not develop gradually over the course of his by now four decades-long career. It seems to be one of its long-standing attributes, having been inscribed into his formative years as a critic, screen-writer, and script editor, and having accompanied the evolution of his filmmaking through numerous phases. In 1989, in the first important critical essay on Haneke as a filmmaker, Alexander Horwath singles out anachronism as the very quality that characterizes Haneke's late transition into theatrical feature filmmaking and that distinguishes his artistic status across this transition. Citing examples from Haneke's TV films and his 1989 theatrical feature film debut, *The Seventh Continent*, Horwath places Haneke among a dwindling group of filmmakers who continue to occupy a middle ground between mass commercial entertainment and the marginal avant-garde and experimental scene (1991: 39). Thematically, Haneke's films remain concerned with central problematics of modernity; aes-thetically, they do not constitute radically new territory, but they do pervasively redeploy and combine stylistic idioms of four decades of European art cinema. Since *The Seventh Continent* premiered at Cannes, Haneke's image of being a hold-out from another period has also been cultivated by the director himself. When the same festival, twenty years later, awarded its *Palme d'or* to *The White Ribbon* – an austere, two and a half hours-long, black-and-white film about a German village on the eve of World War I – it reconfirmed this image.

But if the 2009 Cannes trophy has ensured that Haneke's image as a represen-tative of a past era remains current, adding to his cultural capital and public esteem even as it triggers a certain amount of critical ambivalence, Haneke's anachro-nism also adds to the factors that make him a rewarding subject of academic study. His body of work invites the full spectrum of approaches the field of cinema studies has brought to the analysis of narrative film. Consisting of twenty-one feature films[1] that were made over four decades in two media, in several countries, different languages, and divergent production contexts, Haneke's career is marked by detours and deferrals, belated debuts, and retroactively bestowed memberships. It constitutes a fertile case study for film historians and theorists alike. For historians Haneke's films exemplify the intertwined relations between television and national cinema on the one hand and transnational auteurism and art cinema on the other. For theorists, they raise intriguing questions regarding narrative structure, genre, spectatorship, and the ontology of the image, while also proving of interest to broader debates on the relationship between aesthetics, philosophy, and history, and presenting an intriguing challenge to aesthetic and philosophical periodization. While evincing strong affinities with philosophical and cinematic modernism, Haneke's films also address phenomena associated with postmodernism. Notwithstanding Haneke's own modernist posturing and postmodern critics' eagerness to take him by his word, it may be his films' dual referencing of the modern and the postmodern that merits further interest in them.

Born in 1942, Haneke is too young for his modernism to be based on generational membership. Instead, he has assimilated modernism through academic exposure to a broad literary and artistic canon. He has been influenced by a range of authors that include Stéphane Mallarmé, Jean Améry, Joseph Roth, Thomas Mann, Franz Kafka, and Ingeborg Bachmann; by composers Franz Schubert, Alban Berg, and Arnold Schönberg; by philosophers Theodor W. Adorno, Lucien Goldman, and Albert Camus; and, of course, by the filmmakers of the high modernist generation, specifically Robert Bresson, Ingmar Bergman, Michelangelo Antonioni, and Andrei Tarkovsky. Haneke's age sets him two generations apart from these directors, and still one full generation from most proponents of the various European new waves, whose more playful and irreverent films, together with those of the high modernists, formed the apogee of European art cinema, a period that lasted approximately from the mid-1950s to the early 1970s.

This period constitutes Haneke's formative years as an intellectual and his early phase as a director, which is accounted for in detail in Horwath's essay. In the early 1960s, after abandoning a career as a concert pianist, Haneke studied philosophy and literature at the University in Vienna. He worked as a feuilleton critic and, from 1967 to the early 1970s, as a script editor for television. But this job did not lead to any opportunities for directing films. He wrote his own screenplay, which garnered a major film subsidy award but went unproduced, which caused him to leave television and find work in theater. His growing reputation as a stage director finally earned him a directing commission from his erstwhile employer, the regional southwest German network SWF (Horwath 1991: 15). His first film, *After Liverpool* (1974), was a low-budget two-person drama based on James Saunders's play about the oppressive dynamics and entropic patterns of relationships, paying particular attention to the onset of routine, non-communication, alienation, and malaise. These issues would become standard Haneke themes.

Haneke's choice of source material suggests his critical interest in the bourgeoisie.[2] But in contrast to, say, Rainer Werner Fassbinder or Jean-Luc Godard, who also came from a bourgeois background, Haneke did not become politically radicalized during the 1960s. Instead of understanding contemporary politics through Marxist models of thought, as was highly common during this period, he was interested in more traditional humanist issues, in metaphysical themes and what he perceived as Western civilization's pervasive spiritual crisis. Thus, he remained closer to Sartre and Camus than to Mao and Marx and he took a particular interest in the religious philosopher Blaise Pascal. Though he developed a keen eye for the problems of his own class, his work did not focus on class struggle, imperialism, or the oppression of third world countries. While eager to work creatively in film and theater, he neither founded a political cinema collective (as Godard did with the Dziga Vertov Group), nor did he join any radical experimental theater group (such as Fassbinder's Antitheater). Instead of fighting the state, whether on the streets or in front of the Cinémathèque Française, he went to work for it, reading scripts for state-funded television. In the early 1970s Haneke quit his full-time job at the network, but his relationship to television would have a lasting impact on his career. Not only would TV remain a central source of film funding for decades to come, but it also in complex ways defined Haneke's status as a national and transnational filmmaker.

Television, Auteurism, and National Cinema

Although the heyday of the new waves was over by the time Haneke got to make his first film, their German variant had produced a second generation of filmmakers who were Haneke's age or slightly younger. By the mid-1970s, these directors, most notably Fassbinder, Werner Herzog, and Wim Wenders, were becoming international art house directors, making what was called the New German Cinema the decade's dominant European art cinema and, in fact, one of the last national cinemas in Europe to stand in this tradition. However, while the New German Cinema relied heavily on television for the financing and exhibition of many of its films and while most of Haneke's TV films of the 1970s and 1980s were made either exclusively by or with coproduction monies from various German television stations, Haneke did not become part of Germany's national film culture. Of course, we need to acknowledge that Haneke, while born in Germany, grew up in Austria and has lived there most of his life. But this statement does not, in and of itself, constitute an argument about the nationally specific aspects of Haneke's filmmaking. The question of national identification (in which citizenship is, in any case, only one aspect) is rather complex, because it tends to raise more questions than it answers about the national as a discursive category and about the cultural, institutional, and historical registers in which it gets debated and defined.[3] Raising these questions is partially the purpose of this introduction, and, as we have just started to see, looking at European cinema from the 1960s on means taking into consideration the institution of state-sponsored television.

The significance of television for Haneke's pre-theatrical feature career is twofold: it provided relatively steady employment for him as a filmmaker and it kept his films from being defined in terms of national cinema. Instead of becoming a nationally identified filmmaker (in either country) with the consequent effect of gaining international auteur status, Haneke during the 1970s and 1980s remained a sought-after theater director (more on this shortly) and a moderately well-recognized television director in both countries. Given the institutional nature of his TV films, they were treated as in-house commissions, holding the same for-broadcast-only status as most made-for-TV films.[4] Foreclosing theatrical distribution and also, at least until the mid-1980s, any opportunities for film festival participation, the modality of the in-house commission also made subsidy monies less visible, so that these funds, in Haneke's case, never acquired the status of distinct and publicly acknowledged awards. In Haneke's career, film subsidy did not become a factor of publicly bestowed prestige or publicly debated merit – his films never became politicized as art funded with taxpayers' money.[5] And while a small number of negative reviews vaguely echoed the populist attacks on state-funded art that were regularly leveled against the New German Cinema, Haneke's TV films never reached the level of attention accorded the New German Cinema's star directors, nor did the press associate him with this cinema even in general terms or in passing. This does not mean that Haneke did not share some of this cinema's proclivities, such as the construction of a self-conscious *mise-en-scène* that probed film's capabilities for producing both truth and illusion, as well as a preoccupation with such topics as postwar historical amnesia and the postwar generation's historical isolation and psychological alienation. Haneke also shares the New German Cinema's acute awareness of the profound impact of American movies and pop culture on postwar Europe – but in contrast to Wenders's and Fassbinder's complicated love–hate relationship to Hollywood, Haneke has been considerably more critical, to the point of categorically rejecting Hollywood's function as provider of entertainment.

Most of Haneke's TV films have been coproductions between Austrian and German television stations. In briefly outlining their characteristics in terms of nationally related themes and contexts, it should be noted that their status as coproductions in and of itself ensured a binational cultural legibility and an overlap of themes related to both national contexts. If Haneke, despite this dual legibility, can ultimately be read more or less clearly as an Austrian filmmaker, this argument, too, requires the kind of detail I want to provide below. By way of initial overview, we note that Haneke's career as a TV director veered from predominantly Austrian concerns in the 1970s to more German or international concerns in the 1980s and back to a more Austrian frame of reference in the 1990s. *Three Paths to the Lake* (1976), which the director himself has characterized as his first "real" film, adapts Austrian author Ingeborg Bachmann's story about an Austrian professional woman's melancholic return to her hometown in Carinthia, in the course of which the film develops a dense system of references to twentieth-century Austrian history.

His next film, the two-part drama *Lemmings* (1979), is a portrait of Haneke's own generation of Austrians, who came of age during the postwar decades. He depicts them at two historical moments, the late 1950s and the late 1970s, at which point the unacknowledged shortcomings of their youth, partially caused by Austria's inability to deal with the mid-century tension between tradition and modernity, have evolved into more pervasive dysfunctions. While *Three Paths to the Lake* and *Lemmings* were Austrian–German coproductions, two of the three television films Haneke made during the 1980s were exclusively produced in Germany and all three are explicitly related to German settings, topics, and cultural attitudes. *Variation* (1983), produced by a Berlin TV station (SFB), is a semi-comic story about a man and a woman's illicit love affair that is set in Berlin. It takes Goethe's drama *Stella* (about a triangular relationship) as its point of departure and its spectatorial address probes questions of the public sphere and TV's role as a consensus-building artistic medium. The Austrian–German coproduction *Who Was Edgar Allan?* (1984), though set in Venice and based on the book of Austrian novelist Peter Rosei, had the thematic and stylistic hallmarks of an "American Friend"-type story, replete with the kinds of nationally inflected Oedipal overtones, identification patterns, and meta-cinematic phantasmagorias that the New German Cinema became famous for. *Fraulein* (1986), an exclusively German production, is the story of a woman who runs a movie theater in a small town in post-World War II West Germany and who has to deal with her husband's release from a Russian POW camp ten years after the war. It was intended as a response to Fassbinder's *The Marriage of Maria Braun* (1979). Haneke's three TV films of the 1990s are once again related to a more specific Austrian context: the Austrian production *Obituary for a Murderer* (1991) is an experimental collage of an episode of a well-known Austrian talk show that dealt with a horrific killing that had shocked Austria the previous year. *The Rebellion* (1992), another exclusively Austrian production, is an adaptation of Joseph Roth's novel about a war veteran's failed integration in post-World War I Vienna. *The Castle* (1997), which was coproduced by Austrian Television, Bavarian Broadcasting, and the Franco-German network ARTE, is an adaptation of Franz Kafka's unfinished novel about a land surveyor's paralyzing social and professional entanglements in the fabric of a rural town. It has a specific Austrian frame of reference below its pan-national relevance.

Before discussing the specifically Austrian dimension of Haneke's work, we ought to understand the broader impact that television had on Haneke's evolution as a filmmaker and his status as an auteur. Haneke perceived television's emphasis of its communicative function and educational mission as a confinement of artistic possibilities. That his television films regularly constituted departures from, in some cases overt violations of, the medium's mandatory embrace of realism is self-evident. But their proto-cinematic aesthetics notwithstanding, these films, at the time of their broadcast, garnered neither the institutional definition nor the cultural trappings of cinema. This also affected Haneke's auteur persona: while his *de facto* creative efforts and his staging of authorship may have been no less defined by gestures of heroism, self-sacrifice, and rebellion against his main sponsor than were common for the directors of the New German Cinema, these gestures went unnoticed. When *Who Was Edgar Allan?*, which has a distinctive art cinema look, was invited to screen at the 1985 Berlin Film Festival,[6] the moment was marked by one of the ironies that have accompanied Haneke's artistic path and that constitute, as it were, his anachronism: just when he was poised to enter the institutional circles of art cinema, the kind of art cinema that he had been adulating and had found worthy of engaging was about to vanish. Its end was not merely metaphoric. Bergman officially retired in 1984 after making *Fanny and Alexander*; Antonioni had started to work for television, the medium Haneke was trying so hard to transcend; Fassbinder died in 1982, Truffaut in 1984, and Tarkovsky in 1986. But no matter the significance one might want to attribute to these individual markers of demise, just as important is the fact that, in terms of actual film output, modernist art cinema had already been superseded by a new, more adamantly postmodern European cinema that had little investment in upholding a divide between art and popular film. It was made by a new generation of filmmakers who were Haneke's juniors. They included Pedro Almodóvar (*Dark Habits*, 1982; *Labyrinth of Passion*, 1983; *What Have I Done to Deserve This?*, 1984), Stephen Frears (*My Beautiful Laundrette*, 1985), and Jean-Jacques Beineix (*Diva*, 1981; *The Moon in the Gutter*, 1983; *Betty Blue*, 1986).

But in what constitutes a further ironic twist, by the late 1980s it was arguably the very disappearance of the kind of art cinema with which Haneke had identified, but to which he stood at a historical remove, that created a vacuum for Haneke to step into, a need to which he could respond by more or less self-consciously assuming the persona of the last modernist. Its subtending attributes comprise the image of someone whose films resist pretty pictures and a slick commercial look; of someone whose films have controversial topics and idiosyncratic treatments, but eschew shock value for its own sake; of someone projecting a moral conscience that defines any assault on the spectator as an invitation to engage an argument – and, in this sense, of someone who proposes ethics not only as a topic of his films but as a central vector defining the filmgoing experience itself.[7] Thus, if Haneke's theatrical features since *The Seventh Continent* have incurred such labels as difficult, didactic, rarefied, abstruse, and excessively dark, I would argue – without detracting from Haneke's artistic project – that these adjectives say less about the films themselves than about art cinema as a cultural construct. Its nomenclature is eagerly taken up by distributors, particularly if the label in question helps generate controversy and aids the promotion of the film. And it tends to emerge in close interrelation with the persona of the filmmaker as auteur with whom the film forms a product package in the circuits of international art film exhibition.

When Haneke's auteur image fully emerged around the release of *The Seventh Continent*, which, in addition to screening at Cannes, received awards at the Flanders International Film Festival and the Locarno International Film Festival, it instantly threw into relief an auteur persona's requisite features, which are structured in terms of oppositions. On the one hand, the status of auteur, particularly if freshly bestowed, signals a sense of freshness, of being new, unused, and innovative, and it also implies provocation, perhaps even rebelliousness – all of which signify a break with the status quo. On the other hand, auteurs tend to project artistic, cultural, and, in some cases, political expertise, all of which also imply a certain authority that, in turn, already invites their alignment with tradition (if only at some point in the future, when they can be assimilated into lineages and are worthy of retrospectives). Haneke instantly fits the bill: *The Seventh Continent* was provocative, but not brattish. Its minimalism and its putatively nihilistic ending were controversial and confrontational, yet it projected gravitas – just like the artist himself, who was appealingly new and unknown, while also reassuringly middle-aged and "serious" about his work, so that authority itself could become a central part of his image. In this sense, Haneke's auteur persona is not simply the work of a self-fashioned self-promoter, but the result of a complex dialog between the auteur in question and film festival organizers and audiences, film and television producers, feuilleton critics, and "the public," to the extent that the latter pays attention to these discourses by following the arts pages in newspapers and their counterparts on late night television.

If Haneke in the decades after his first Cannes appearance would cultivate the persona of the serious artist, it was not the least in order to meet the public on the level it had designated for him. To this day, during audience Q&As and at press conferences, Haneke has no problem letting the audience know if he is dissatisfied with their questions. His answers can be teasingly short or elliptical, or they tend to take the form of counter-questions, or he answers a specific question with a more general, often parable-like story or by drawing on literary or philosophical references. By acting this way, however, Haneke is far from being uncooperative. "Difficulty" becomes a generic expectation. Add to this the inevitable observation that Haneke looks like a continental intellectual (full beard, gray hair, pensive expression), that he dresses like a continental intellectual (mostly in black), that he speaks like a continental intellectual (French and German; no English, please), and that he generally behaves like a continental intellectual (he is a careful listener; his demeanor ranges from the measured to the reticent; he tries to be polite and frequently smiles).

But the carefully fine-tuned anatomy of Haneke's auteur persona should not be seen exclusively against the background of the film world with its specific economic pressures, cultural protocols, discursive rituals, generic expectations, and psychological dynamics. What most commentators have thus far missed in assessing Haneke's persona and artistic development is the fact that he has, to a very significant extent, also been a theater director, and a rather prolific and prominent one at that. In contrast to Fassbinder, whose theater work quickly took the back seat to his filmmaking and was always firmly identified with bohemian radicality and considerable controversy, Haneke, with increasing success as a stage director, came to occupy a kind of middle position in German and Austrian theater similar to the one that would mark his status as a filmmaker. He situated himself between the radical experimental scene of urban subcultures and alternative spheres and the commercial orbits of musical theater, folk theater, and boulevard comedy. All through the 1970s and into the 1980s, he systematically pursued engagements at prestigious houses in the theater centers of Germany – Hamburg, Düsseldorf, Darmstadt, Berlin.[8] Building a reputation with his direction of bourgeois classics and the modern repertoire rather than authoring or staging experimental plays, he became appreciated among the educated bourgeoisie because he provoked audiences with intellectual arguments and with his solid professional skills (evident, most importantly, in his famously creative and precise direction of the actor) rather than through improvised performance pieces, absurdist scenarios, neo-dadaist shock experiments, or Marxist-inflected manifestos that were the domain of the politically radicalized avant-garde of the 1960s and 1970s.[9] Haneke's detour into theater ended up having a lasting impact on his career, as it significantly contributed to an intermedially defined persona and, indeed, an intermedially defined body of work. By this I do not mean that Haneke's films looked "stagey" or were structured like plays. Rather, his exposure to theater further broadened his already considerable and very precise understanding of the inherently textual nature of art and the literary possibilities of expression that can inform the medium of film. A further irony thus lies in the fact that, while Haneke's long years in the theater seem to underscore the anachronistic qualities of his emergence as a film director, it is this enforced sojourn outside of film that has made his films formally more advanced.

A final aspect should be considered with regard to the anachronism of Haneke's auteur persona, and it returns our discussion to the context of national cinema. Haneke's artistic identity never became determined by the same Oedipal dynamics that so heavily shaped the French New Wave and the New German Cinema. For filmmakers of both these cinemas, who had to overcome their own historical disconnectedness from earlier cultural and cinematic traditions, it became *de rigueur* to select in demonstrative, even ritualistic fashion a coterie of surrogate father figures either from Hollywood's studio era or from among the ranks of European modernist artists and intellectuals, whose work and influence had been disrupted by fascism and the war. New wave directors' adoption of such figures was widely perceived to be an act of historical bridging and, thus, a successful negotiation of burdensome historical legacies, which, in turn, made them and their work altogether contemporary and redemptive. It is not that Haneke's films and his artistic identity are free from Oedipal issues – a point I will discuss shortly. But in Haneke's case, these dynamics played out differently – and I believe there are two reasons for it.

First, because of the close association between auteurs and national cinemas, filmmakers' Oedipalized attempts to grapple with issues of generational succession and artistic legacy are intertwined with imaginary and actual negotiations of nationhood, national history, and national identity. But precisely to the extent that these dynamics are contingent on specific national histories and were played out among a particular generation of filmmakers, Haneke represents an uneasy fit. With Haneke being too young even to be a new wave filmmaker, and being neither fully German nor fully Austrian, let alone French, artistic identification with(in) specific national contexts was hampered by a lack of membership in any of the groups that constitute national cinema as a historical and socio-cultural formation. As became clear in the cases of the New German Cinema and the French New Wave, the dynamics of obtaining symbolic membership in a national project of reconstructing cultural lineages and realigning artistic traditions pivoted on highly publicized acts of transference that were the product of filmmakers' personal friendships, mentoring relations, elective affinities, and fate-wrought affiliations with past artistic and intellectual leaders and role models.[10] In Haneke's case, however, there was no attempt to compensate for his generational distance to European modernism by seeking out personal relations to figures such as Adorno or Bresson.

Certainly, Haneke's transnational status has not prevented his identification with both German and Austrian cultural traditions and legacies – which is most overt in Haneke's literary adaptations. But if one looks at the films themselves as an index of such national identification, and particularly at the way this identification is filtered through the director's imaginary relation to the paternal and the filial, we see the second reason why Oedipal issues in Haneke's films play themselves out differently from the new wave films. In contrast to Wenders, Herzog, and Truffaut, Haneke does not imagine himself on one level with his filial characters. With the exception of *Lemmings*, their purpose is not to become more or less direct stand-ins for the director himself, and, as it were, to invite the audience to empathize with him through them. If one wanted to look for biographical details about Haneke and his generation as inscribed in his films, one would have to note that Haneke, more than anything, seems to identify himself with the prominent postwar figure of the absent father. Here I don't even mean to refer to any actual depictions of initially absent but suddenly returning, inevitably dysfunctional, and ultimately failing fathers. While these certainly have a presence in Haneke's cinema, what I have in mind is the condition of paternal absence as such that Haneke has come to identify with.[11] This condition of absence – which is extendable to a range of experiences of loss that characterize modernity as the period of the decline of master narratives – structures Haneke's films on a very basic level. It determines their visual *dispositif*, their spectatorial address, and the fragmented state of their diegetic world.

Individually and as a body of work, the films function as an edifice, a house of sorts, that all protagonists get to live in as "children" – along with us, the audience, who become their siblings of sorts. When the kids become naughty – when they start wrecking the furniture, kill off a few guests, other home owners, random strangers, or even themselves, or, to cite an alternate scenario, when outsiders break into the house and pose a threat – the father remains aloof. He leaves it up to his audience to figure out why and how we, as puzzled and perturbed siblings and as menaced "co-tenants," should care about these goings-on. In this sense, Oedipal issues do assume a political-allegorical dimension in Haneke's cinema. But with the exception of *Lemmings*, they constitute a departure from, or even reversal of, the well-known filial dynamics of (self-)identification so common to other national cinemas and auteurs, for whom the part of fictional son and/or quasi-orphan became a place holder on whom they projected their own self-image as heirs to a disrupted history (Rentschler 1984: 103; Elsaesser 1989: 207; Kaes 1989).

However, the fact that the transnational nature of Haneke's personal and professional pedigree does not as easily fit the mold of a single nation's lost, exiled, or orphaned son did not mean his auteur persona became altogether lost to the discourse of national cinema and its twin projects of revising history and bridging historical discontinuities. In Haneke's case, however, his relative anonymity as a TV director for some time kept these twin projects from being officially attributed to the artistic labor of an auteur. When the auteur eventually emerged, this attribution, as is by no means unusual within the discourse of auteurism, had to proceed backwards. In fact, the construction of Haneke as an auteur was partially contingent on critics' appreciation of the construction of history in his films. Both were acts of reconstruction and, in their combined effort, led to a third axis of reconstruction: Critics and scholars who focused on reading Haneke's films as reflections on Austrian history also read these works as constitutive elements of Austrian film history. Haneke's belated and retroactive construction as an auteur thus went hand in hand with the overdue reconstruction of Austrian film history in terms of national cinema.

It is here that Haneke's anachronism generated another irony: Haneke's emerging auteur status became explicitly linked to the concept of Austrian national cinema at the moment when the very category of national cinema began to lose its significance, a process which was ushered in by the globalization of film financing structures and the rise of transnational cinemas, and which occurred more or less concurrently with the demise of art cinema and its great names. In this sense, even as this multilayered process of re/constructing the auteur and his national cinema was coming under way in the form of career overviews by critics such as Horwath, Haneke's emerging persona became heavily inflected by a new set of terms. These marked the era's shift away from expressing authorship through narratives of exile, return, and sacrificial heroism towards demonstrations of professionalism and a virtuoso command of film's artistic resources, capacities, and potentials (Elsaesser 2005: 51). In other words, the traditional figure of the auteur as a nation's prodigal son – a compendium of the divine bestowal of creative genius and the vicissitudes of biography – was left behind in favor of a self-conscious performance of the author as a globally recognizable craftsman, storyteller, and stylist.

The 1989 premiere of *The Seventh Continent* thus became a cumulative index of the anachronisms and ironies that mark Haneke's status as auteur and representative of a national cinema. One of three Austrian films in the Cannes program, it introduced Austria to the festival as a young filmmaking nation or, to cite the correlative rhetoric, a nation of young filmmakers (Horwath 1991: 12). Shot and produced in Austria with Austrian money and mostly Austrian actors, and made by a director who lived and had been raised in Austria, *The Seventh Continent*, on one level, seemed to tell the story of an average Austrian family living in an average Austrian town. It could thus be perceived as depicting contemporary Austrianness without the self-exoticizing markers of tourist iconography. Yet, most of these statements beg qualification: the film, based on a story about a family from Hamburg, Germany, whose suicide became publicized in a large German weekly, appealed to Haneke because the syndrome it depicted was symptomatic of most Western European societies and, thus, not specific to Austria. What was touted as Austrian cinema was initially planned for German television[12] and financed by an independent production company that, while based in Austria, sought financing on an international level.[13] In this sense, the film was only incidentally Austrian. Its director was not fully Austrian either, nor was he young. While none of these qualifications were strictly speaking unknown, no one seemed to object against the perceived necessity to recruit Haneke for what Horwath rightly calls a foundation myth of Austrian cinema.

To the extent that the retroactively constructed history of Austrian national cinema relied not just on Haneke's Cannes contribution but summoned his past body of work, it throws into relief the complex interrelation between film and television in constituting a national cinema. I have already outlined the reasons why Haneke's television films failed to enter the official orbit of national cinema during the period in which they were made, the 1970s and 1980s; I now want to consider the opposite reasoning: On what grounds were scholars and critics able to count these films *retroactively* as belonging to a national cinema? Because Haneke's films of the 1970s and 1980s were shown on German and Austrian national television – which, up until the mid-1980s, was without commercial competitors and, thus, had a captive national audience – they can be counted as being part of either nation's collective story reservoir. No matter how fleeting the appreciation for them and their director may have been at the time of their respective broadcast dates, they arguably contributed to some form of a collective unconscious. From this perspective, Haneke's television coproductions can legitimately be claimed by both Austria and Germany as part of their national film heritage, even if Haneke's selection of topics leaned at times more to an Austrian and at other times more to a German frame of reference. If the concept of a collective unconscious seems no less speculative today than it was when first applied to the study of national cinema by Siegfried Kracauer, there is one particular area of film culture in which the national does manifest itself in more tangible terms – the domain of filmed literature. But if, by virtue of this area, Haneke's national identification crystallizes more clearly as Austrian than as German, his literary adaptations' look at Austrian history immediately qualifies the notion of national unity and coherence at the same time that they place Austria in relation to its larger geopolitical environment – Europe.

Literary Adaptations: From Austria to Europe

In addition to their educational and entertainment functions, literary adaptations tend to be regarded as a means to showcase a country's literary heritage in the popular realm. If a book is adapted within its country of origin – that is, if the adaptation is a domestic production – the film, its filmmaker, and the production field that generates it (usually either an industry or a cottage industry) quickly acquire all the markers of the national. This holds true with regard to the image of the nation portrayed in the film, but also with regard to the (implied) image of the audience the film targets, particularly if the film is primarily intended for domestic release, as most TV-commissioned literary adaptations are. Yet, before we turn to the point of national specificity – by which I mean Haneke's identification as an Austrian filmmaker contributing to what may be perceived as Austrian film – we still have to consider those aspects of Haneke's literary adaptations that applied to both the German and the Austrian context.

On one level, Haneke's own view on the relationship between a literary adaptation and its implied national audience is rather pragmatic. It first and foremost reflects the realities and exigencies of Austro-German state-sponsored television's mandate for consensus building: filmed literature can help TV fulfill its mission to get viewers interested in reading the book on which the film is based. This pragmatism, guided by the goal of capturing and sustaining viewers' interest, indirectly confirms Haneke's status as a filmmaker situated between the avant-garde and outright commerce. Traditionally middle brow by nature, adaptations have been a staple of the film industry – their ubiquity reflects not so much a literary bias as an industrial need for product, as well as a (perceived) desire for politically "safe" prestige projects (Elsaesser 1989: 107). This was certainly the case in Germany, where the New German Cinema, by the mid-1970s, became a cinema of literary adaptations (Rentschler 1984: 129). But historically speaking, German cinema has always favored literary adaptations – the New German Cinema merely gave this favoritism a highbrow spin and adapted the favorites of the educated bourgeoisie and the new left (Elsaesser 1989: 107). Haneke's own choices of source materials are consistent with this pattern. They reflected his own modernist bias and, thus, made him more employable in both Germany and Austria.

The second observation about literary adaptations that transcends a specific national context is the widespread ambivalence towards filmed literature. Looking at the press responses to Haneke's television films, one can detect a dual response by critics: on the one hand, Haneke's literary adaptations consistently fared better with critics than films based on his own screenplays, such as *Lemmings* and *Variation. Three Paths to the Lake, Who Was Edgar Allan?*, and *The Rebellion* all earned praise for the intelligence, creativeness, and independence with which they had adapted their respective sources, whereby they implicitly revealed such categories as "faithfulness to the original" to be burdensome and outmoded.[14] But some of their reviews are also prefaced by expressions of skepticism towards the general project of adaptation, with critics being weary of the inflationary presence of adaptations on television and, given that the majority of these were considered mediocre or failed efforts, being wary of any new ones.[15]

If such responses are not necessarily nationally specific, Haneke's proclivity for filming Austrian authors has enabled film scholars and historians to assign Haneke's films retroactively to Austrian national cinema.[16] In this context, what emerges as important is the films' themes, their style, and the way they address the spectator. The thematic focus of Haneke's films is the dissolution of order and the process of falling apart, whether in concrete political and historical terms (as with the downfall of the Austro-Hungarian Empire in *Three Paths to the Lake* and *The Rebellion*), or in psychological and phenomenological terms (*Who Was Edgar Allan?*), or in a mixture of both (*The Castle*'s thematization of the individual in a bureaucratic maze). Their style consists of a fragmented aesthetic that comprises a broad spectrum of cinematic devices ranging from disjointed editing, the dialectical use of found footage, and the alternation of color and black-and-white film stock to the allegorical function of music and the self-reflexive use of voice-over narration. As such, these films' implied viewer is not only a *Bildungsbürger* (a member of the educated bourgeoisie, who may be interested in learning more about the subject portrayed and who, as a result of watching the film on television, may be prompted to (re)read the novel), but an Austrian one, with whom the films' historical frameworks are likely to resonate strongly.

Haneke's literary adaptations do not have the formal austerity of his theatrical features. They acknowledge the audience's appetite for the "culinary" aspects of cinema and of literary adaptations in particular. And, to a far greater extent than the theatrical features, they offer viewers opportunities for engaging the subjectivities of their protagonists. But Haneke's deployment of these dynamics is only partially motivated by the need to communicate with the television viewer. In fact, as I will make clear further below, the films' complication of the dynamics of identification reflects the influence of European art cinema. It also testifies to Haneke's acute understanding of Austria's literary history and its authors' respective literary projects. As Fatima Naqvi has shown, a prominent element in *Three Paths to the Lake* is the female protagonist Elisabeth's remembrance of her late ex-lover, Trotta, which allows the story to open a mnemonic discourse about the lost Austro-Hungarian Empire. To understand this mnemonic reference requires intertextual knowledge of the fact that Ingeborg Bachmann, the author of the story, had picked the name Trotta to allude to the late novels of Joseph Roth. It is Roth who invented the figure of Trotta for his own melancholic discourse of remembering the great empire, in which the Trotta dynasty plays a central part (Naqvi 2009: 169). However, in the late modernist Bachmann's continuation of the fiction of the early modernist Roth, Trotta is no longer a signifier for nostalgia for the lost empire (ibid.); the character's radical cosmopolitanism and spectral existence (he belonged to no nation and has no grave) allude to the utopian potential implied in Austro-Hungarian society's multi-ethnic structure, against which the commerce-driven post-World War II cosmopolitanism of Elisabeth (she is an international photographer) rings false and hollow. Naqvi further points out that the formal structure of *Three Paths to the Lake* honors Bachmann's mnemonically motivated citation of Roth's work: the film's fleeting, fragmented, and multiperspectival images of Trotta dislodge the figure from the suturing effect of Elisabeth's memory, which it thereby turns into a semantically open mnemonic stream (ibid.).

Three Paths to the Lake is exemplary of most of Haneke's television films in two ways: It uses the depiction of the protagonist's personal struggles of reconciling her past and present life as a means to comment on broader, and rather cataclysmic, historical changes of late modernity and postmodernity; and it critiques our culture's pervasive resistance to a historiographically radical, politically progressive, and ethically motivated response to these changes. The teenage protagonists of *Lemmings*, Part I, find themselves living in a post-World War II society that, for all its clinging to nineteenth-century religious and moral values, is no less part of the political realities and the mass cultural environment of the second half of the twentieth century. Their problems as alienated and suicidal bourgeois continentals may strike one as an instance of Haneke attempting at rehashing European art cinema's discourse of malaise. Nonetheless the film represents an early instance of the director's pervasive critique of continental culture's inertia about understanding its own relation to the past and of its society's resistance to reflecting on their positions as historical subjects. Anachronism is thus not simply Haneke's artistic seal of fate which, as it were, he tries to turn into a virtue by ostentatiously performing his auteur status; nor does it constitute a negative or limiting quality in his films. Instead, we need to understand it as a deconstructive hermeneutic device and, as such, one of the pivotal critical tropes of his artistic project.

We encounter it again in *The Rebellion*, which tells the story of Andreas Pum, whose failure to reintegrate into post-World War I society and whose criminalization by the state and subsequent social decline transform him into a fervent anti-nationalist. By the time Andreas returns from the war, the emperor has been dead for two years, his empire broken up, and Austria turned into a republic. That the film closely analogizes the personal and the historical, presenting both as a story of shattering, loss, and decline, should not be interpreted as a sign that Haneke shares Roth's yearning for a return to feudalist structures. As Naqvi argues, the film acknowledges what has been identified as the utopian strain in Roth's writing – a rebellious response against the country's reconstitution as a republic along the lines of "a limiting, exclusivist bourgeois model"[17] – which may be said to offset the novelist's reactionary side. The film features historical footage of Emperor Franz Joseph's 1916 funerary procession and of World War I trench battles, explosions, and crosses of unknown soldiers, but not for the mere purpose of historical illustration. The footage's fragmented nature, in addition to signifying the traumatic aspects of loss and cataclysmic upheaval, conveys the stark anachronism of the era's key events, suggesting that historical connections may be explored between the demise of outmoded political structures and the barbarities of the modern war (ibid.).

The aesthetics of *The Rebellion* and *Three Paths to the Lake* constitute a form of self-reflexive historiography in which the end of the empire and the foundation of the Austrian republic are explicitly thematized. What remains unthematized, but what, as Naqvi has pointed out, becomes a structuring absence particularly in *Three Paths to the Lake* is Nazi Germany's annexation of the First Republic and Hitler's cleansing efforts of the former empire's ethnic minorities.[18] This structuring absence within the text represents a variant of anachronism that has implications for questions of spectatorship. It may be regarded as an ironic comment on Austria's resistance to engaging with its past. Thus reconceptualized, anachronism prompts a meditation on the status of the nation as a precarious ideological construct, haunted as it is by the experience of loss, to which the formation of the nation and of nationalism must be regarded as reactions, but which they also seek to deny, as becomes evident through the revelation of the various structuring absences that tend to inform official national histories. As the textual modernism of Haneke's literary adaptations dialectically enlists spectators in the project of unearthing these structuring absences, these made-for-TV films potentially mitigate against the homogenizing impulses of their own production and exhibition context of state-funded, mass mediatized, consensus-oriented public education.[19] The second implication of the troping of anachronism is that it enables Haneke's adaptations of Bachmann and Roth to expand their historiographic purview via the connotative register, whereby the treatment of the Austrian theme furnishes implicit links to a wider political and historical terrain. In *Three Paths to the Lake*, the connotative register functions to link the First Republic and the Third Reich. In this as well as in some of Haneke's other films, the expansive dynamic of this register establishes analogies and comparisons with contemporary Europe. But before considering these in greater detail, we need to acknowledge that Haneke's TV films did not exclusively focus on Austria to illustrate the dynamics of historical amnesia. His film *Fraulein* also analyzed its German variant.

Fraulein's female protagonist, Johanna,[20] runs a movie theater in which she projects prewar Disney movies, as well as postwar rubble films starring Hans Albers, whose popularity with German audiences extended from the Weimar period into the 1950s. The screening of Albers's rubble film reminds *Fraulein*'s diegetic audience of a period that they think they have left behind by virtue of their successful reconstruction efforts and the postwar economic miracle; yet, Haneke makes clear that the rubble film's tracking shots featuring Albers walking through rows of women recycling bricks from the bombed ruins literally come to "re-present" this history in an ideologically and historically obfuscating light: underscored by a wistful song featuring the line "What has become of us?," which Albers intones rather than sings (though with the same melodramatic contralto with which the actor used to deliver all his lines), the shot of Albers walking through the rubble is meant to echo the feelings of those who survived the allied bombing campaigns.

What Albers's film does not lend itself to, which is why its consumption in 1955 is still possible, are questions that inquire into the causes for the catastrophes of World War II and the Holocaust – questions that show that it is necessary to assume responsibility for the critical retelling of history. Johanna's recycling of Albers's walk through the rubble thus falls short of having any disruptive effect on its 1950s viewers. Haneke contrasts this *mise-en-abyme* of amnesia to the return of Johanna's husband from a Soviet POW camp – a return so belated and incommensurate with what the character has gone through that it turns him into a real-life anachronism, a ghost from the past who wanders the present but who, unlike Albers, cannot be assimilated to this present. In this sense, the films that Johanna shows in her movie theater are identified with postwar amnesia, prosperity, and Americanization. Their ideologically and historiographically obfuscating effect can be read as Haneke's interpretation of Adorno's culture industry argument. At the same time, however, Haneke's own dialectical use of film and of cinema history in *Fraulein* – by juxtaposing its protagonist's jouissance to post-war broken masculinity (see Nagl, this volume) even when she is identified as an instrument in disseminating illusion),[21] by abruptly switching from black-and-white to color stock in order to mark this illusionism, and by ending with an excerpt from the Nazi spectacle *Münchhausen* (Josef von Báky, 1943, starring Albers and filmed in color) – indicates Haneke's conviction that film is a (however limited) tool for critical reflection.

While most of Haneke's TV films constitute critical commentaries on the concept of the nation and the writing of national history, his literary adaptations in particular also pursue another objective: they seize on Austria's multi-ethnic and supranational past in order to develop a broader European outlook – a perspective that Haneke would extend to his theatrical features. Supranationalism in Haneke's work is accorded a certain interest by virtue of the fact that it questions, qualifies, or potentially abrogates nationalism that, as a root cause of imperialism and warfare, has shaped European and world history since the eighteenth century. Nationalism, as Thomas Elsaesser has pointed out, must be regarded as a product of modernity – a response to the historical reality of a post-medieval Europe, whose history of distinct regions and different ethnicities and tribes tended to be eclipsed, first, by their consolidation into nation-states (which then went to war against each other), but, second, also by the seeming abatement of this historical phase after World War II. The prosperity, the peace-making efforts, and the bi- or multilateral initiatives of post-World War II Western European nation-states, which have transpired largely within the developing framework of the European Union (EU), have failed to abrogate the concept of the nation. If anything, the latter has mutated into different forms, constituting returns to the substate as well as the suprastate level that manifest a host of new challenging realities (Elsaesser 2005: 27). If placed against this background, it becomes clearer why Haneke's films, rather than simplistically endorsing supranationalism by pointing to contemporary Europe as its logical and legitimate historical culmination, uphold it as an abstract ideal – a utopia that emerges implicitly in constrast to the pitfalls and vicissitudes of the concrete supranational phenomena and formations that have manifested themselves in Europe since World War II.

Haneke's source novels already constitute critical commentaries on these pitfalls and vicissitudes – and Haneke, as Naqvi lucidly argues, seizes on them in order to express his own ambivalence towards the supranationalist project of the EU. The signifying power of the figure of Trotta in *Three Paths to the Lake* is constituted by the character's political and personal unavailability to the viewer. His sealed-off anachronism protects what he stands for from direct comparison to its present-day European manifestations, lest the compromised aspects of Europe's difficult march towards union threaten to assimilate and falsify Trotta's ideals. Instead, Elisabeth's memories of him initiate a certain dialectics.[22] Its oblique nature makes it a more cautionary and, thus, politically more responsible way of thinking supranationalism. The yearning of Andreas Pum, protagonist of *The Rebellion*, for the lost Austro-Hungarian double monarchy is, despite the latter's imperialist trappings, readable as an implicitly progressive sign, as it points to that empire's lost cultural and political potentials. At the same time, Pum's disenchantment with life in the newly founded Austrian republic can be read as constituting a critical commentary on the advanced bureaucratization of contemporary Europe, exacerbated rather than attenuated by the mushrooming supranational structures of the European Union (Naqvi 2009: 176). Made two years before Austria's scheduled and widely debated obtainment of membership in the EU, the film, as Naqvi argues, registers these debates also in its formal structure. One of the clearest indications is the sound montage of the hymns of several nations that succeed the anthem of the past empire and that, in connection with the footage of the emperor's funeral that is itself succeeded by battlefront coverage, provides a direct link to Pum's traumatic loss (ibid.).

The 1997 adaptation of Franz Kafka's *The Castle* may be regarded at once as the most general and most specific instance of Haneke's critical meditation on supranationalism. Kafka's novel is a stark parable about the dehumanizing dynamics of bureaucracy that are central to the modern condition – the text's broad applicability has led to it being referenced in numerous critiques against anonymous administrative systems and abstract forms of organization. But the picture Kafka paints of a village's eerie, disconcerting willingness to be governed by a higher administration, about which the villagers know very little but whose power and purview they righteously defend, gives uncanny expression to Austria's millennial anxieties about its relation to a centralized European authority. What is being expressed, however, is not a simple binary between legitimate claims to self-governance and the untrustworthy aloofness of a supranational governing body. Rather, collective dread about the loss of control and a lack of transparency and accountability closely overlap with their reactionary correlative – a parochial fear of the other and the outside, which, in millennial Austria, could be associated not simply with provincialism but, significantly, with the rising tide of a new nationalism. By seizing on the inherently aporetic nature of Kafka's modernism and its ascription of a double valence to each of the parable's components, Haneke can implicitly indict pro-nationalist sentiments (as voiced, for example, by Jörg Haider and Austria's new right) while, at the same time, keeping the material from lapsing into nostalgic longing for premodern forms of political organization. Almost completely filmed indoors and characterized by a highly disorienting absence of establishing shots and outdoor locations, the film creates a hermetically sealed yet highly fragmented space that forms a double allegory of self-determination: its negative version may be understood as a political reaction formation that wards off any authority from the outside but that is controlled from within by a powerful if intangible force; its positive variant is the idyll of an organically evolved mosaic of regional communities (and their defiance of national borders) that implicitly identify the nation as historically splintered, displaced, and, indeed, always already transnational.

Glaciation on the Big Screen: First World Malaise and European Anxiety

Haneke's first three theatrical features that constitute what has come to be known as his glaciation trilogy – *The Seventh Continent* (1989), *Benny's Video* (1992), and *71 Fragments of a Chronology of Chance* (1994) – were made in the years leading up to Austria's accession to the EU. In this light, it seems apposite to also read these films for the ways in which they reflect anxieties about Europe's political restructuring, as well as for their skepticism towards the terms on which this restructuring proceeded. Yet, the films articulate their critiques in ways that differ from many of the television films. Their depictions of contemporary Western Europe's middle class and its symptoms of decline – particularly the deterioration of familial and social bonds and the vanishing of spiritual values – are consistently readable beyond the concept of the national.[23] They may be considered system critiques of the dehumanizing regulation of everyday life through advancing bureaucratization.[24]

But this claim also begs qualification. The glaciation trilogy continues Haneke's critical exploration of the dynamics by which guilt and denial are passed from the parental generation to that of the children. Situated within the private sphere of the family, these dynamics no less constitute a form of historical amnesia. And while the focus on the family, on one level, transcends national specificity, on another level, the films imply relevance to a particular group of countries – Austria, Germany, and, in Haneke's more recent films, France. Their governments' commitments to fostering democracy and political consensus and their declared efforts to face up to their countries' historical legacies and educate their citizens into historical subjects stand in uneasy tension with the *de facto* erosion of state power, brought on by a pervasive redefinition of the body politic in terms of commercial consumption. As this contrast has been amplified rather than resolved by the EU's outward expansion and inward restructuring, Haneke's analysis of the intricate links between consumerism, the decline of the family, and historical amnesia is once again European in its outlook.

Horwath's early assessment of Haneke's work, though it was able to consider only the first of his feature films, would prove prescient. While the glaciation trilogy constitutes an expansion of Haneke's artistic scope and aesthetic means of expression, this expansion feels more like a specification. Rather than doing something completely new, the films' most notable qualities lie in their combination of old and new themes, and in the manner in which they place diverse formal components in synergy with one another. Existing elements thus find themselves reiterated and reapplied in innovative ways that reflexively comment on preexisting conventions and traditions. The most striking formal aspect of the films of the glaciation trilogy is the sparse, often downright impoverished quality of their images and the films' overt structural markers. David Bordwell has described this quality as characteristic of a high modernist variant of art cinema, parametric cinema. It suggests the immanence of structural laws in a work – the prominence of a perceptual order that coexists with or even trumps representational meaning (1985: 283).[25] Haneke's early theatrical features have strong similarities to what Bordwell calls the "ascetic" or "sparse" variant of this cinema, which he sees embodied by the films of Bresson and Ozu (1985: 285). In a relatively short time span, these films rotate through a limited number of settings and feature a likewise limited number of shot types and ways in which the characters and the camera move. Social dynamics and rituals have a high degree of recognizability. Some of them, in a further parallel to parametric cinema, may be said to cite serious social concerns *as* clichés. Their minimalist and overtly organized form (Haneke favors long fades to black over conventional cuts) underscores the effects of ellipsis through the omission of information and the sense of distended time.

Haneke varies and recombines these parametric aspects with each new film. *The Seventh Continent* and *71 Fragments of a Chronology of Chance* early on reveal their divisional structure in a manner that is typical of parametric cinema's announcement of a "recognizably pre-formed style" (ibid.). In *Benny's Video* the structuration occurs through the alternation of video footage and film footage, which makes the narrative more immediate and, at the same time, less reliable. In *Funny Games* (1997), structure is diegetically inscribed through the game format, but also identifies the film as an artifact (albeit through a very specific device – the breaking of the fourth wall). Haneke's later films also have parametric qualities. *Caché* (2005) combines *Funny Games'* utilization of diegetic ritual with *Benny's Video's* intermediality; and *Code Unknown* (2000) may be related to what Bordwell calls the twin to parametric cinema's "ascetic" variant – the "replete" model; still relying on the long take and the tracking shot, this film, to borrow Bordwell's phrase, "brings many disparate stylistic procedures to bear on the problem of representing character encounters" (ibid.). Events are imbued with similarity but become subject to stylistic deviation.

Notwithstanding their similarities to Bordwell's description of parametric cinema, I would argue that Haneke's films are hybrids between different kinds of styles. They also rely on some of the broader stylistic conventions of art cinema.[26] They have elliptical narration, they encourage symbolic readings, and they feature privileged moments of character subjectivity. In art cinema, the meanings generated by these devices remain ambiguous; they stand in uneasy tension with the films' commitment to surface realism and their overtly declared intention to be "about" modern life.[27] When spectators of art films experience difficulties reconciling the films' realism with the ambiguity of symbolism and point of view, they can, in classic art cinema fashion, mediate these contradictory elements by taking recourse to the fact that none of these are random because the auteur put them there. This is nowhere more the case than in Haneke's cinema. His presence behind the camera and at festivals has ensured that his films, notwithstanding their stylistic hybridity, are being received within the institution of art cinema, as were Bresson's and Godard's.

If some of the topics of the glaciation trilogy are well worn, they acquire a contemporary dimension. They may be based on actual events (as in the case of the family suicide in *The Seventh Continent*), which lends a disturbing actuality and contemporaneity to the film; or they combine some of art cinema's traditional concerns, such as the crisis of modern civilization and its impact on children, with a representation of more recent problems, such as the proliferation of media violence and its mindless consumption. The more traditional of these two topics, a civilizational critique coupled with a focus on children, has been a staple of art cinema since Italian neo-realism. It finds renewed focus through Haneke's inter-rogation of the ethics of parenting, which his films further link to an investigation of the decline of institutions of learning. Their failure, in turn, points to a crisis of pedagogy and signals deeper impoverishments on the level of the cultural im-aginary. What neo-realism depicted as a material crisis that could be attenuated through children's redemptive influence has mutated in Haneke's world into a pervasive absence of ethical visions and role models that impedes, jaundices, or obviates identification.[28] *The Seventh Continent*'s child protagonist, Evi, rebels against the world's indifference by claiming to have lost her ability to see, which prompts insensitivity and indignance from her teacher and triggers punishment from her mother. The film also indicts the parents for presuming their child is as devoid of spirituality as they are, whereby they justify their decision to include her in their suicide. *Benny's Video* presents Benny's parents' systematic neglect of parenting obligations and their cover-up of their son's killing of the girl as two aspects of the same phenomenon. Several of Haneke's films contain visual allusions to the crisis of institutions of learning. These consist of shots of the front entrances of high schools, whose names are displayed but with letters missing or crumbling. If *The Seventh Continent* depicts the institution's lack of understanding towards the child, *Benny's Video* shows how the inadequacy of its structures invite the child's abuse of them, as evident in Benny's bully behavior and his cynical repurposing of choir practice. *71 Fragments* effectively uses its depiction of foster care to trace the contrast between a society's aspiration to care for its young and the massive, irreversible damages caused by the limitations of this system of care. However, the film compares the stories of two children – the deeply damaged Austrian orphan girl, Anni, who is pursued by a bourgeois couple for adoption, and the Romanian refugee boy, Marian, whom the couple eventually favors over Anni – not only to explore the ethical dilemmas and pitfalls inherent in the system of foster parenting, but also to meditate on the inescapability of injustice as a philosophical conundrum.

The circumstances of Marian's adoption prompt us to consider a second area of interest that weaves through Haneke's films and that beg discussion in slightly more detail, as it further illuminates the European dimension of the glaciation trilogy: the role accorded to television as a mass medium. Within the glaciation trilogy, *71 Fragments* contains the most extensive discourse on television. Featuring numerous TV news casts, some of which are authentic, others fictional (such as Marian's story, as it is shown to become TV news), the film weaves the representation of the medium into its aesthetic structure. Its final, fictitious news sequence reports the shootings of several customers in a bank, a climactic act towards which the narrative moves, but which is already announced at the beginning in reference to the real-life event that inspired the film. Television's position in *71 Fragments* is thus supradiegetic: it functions as an external divider between some of the film's narrative fragments, but it also links several of the film's individual narrative strands by constituting their protagonists as television's public, whereby it assumes a diegetic presence within the frame. Fragmenting the whole and being internally fragmented, television still encompasses the world like a gigantic cloak. This duality also points to TV's social function. As sole companion for many, TV's role as a one-way communication tool is identified as both cause for and symptom of a monadic, stratified society. But being the most important source of information for the very public that it helps constitute, television not only keeps people apart but also brings them together. It is something inbetween a surrogate and a prosthetic device for human interaction. This is already perversely on display in *Benny's Video*, where Benny uses the TV news, attentively watched by his parents, as a kind of overture for the confessional replay of his recording of the killing of the girl. TV's ambiguous function as a force of social fragmentation as well as cohesion is demonstrated most effectively in the depiction of the impact of TV news on the adoption story in *71 Fragments*. Its darkly ironic twist is that the same medium that brought Marian new foster parents will later eclipse his reorphanization (after his new mother is among the victims in the bank). He is yesterday's news – the spotlight has already shifted from him to the assassin. Television, by highlighting the existence of one character, automatically renders invisible, and thus virtually non-existent, that of another.

While television's role in the adoption story in *71 Fragments* implicitly raises larger questions of ethics and philosophy, Haneke's showcasing of TV in the trilogy also reflects a historically and politically specific phenomenon: the shift the

medium had recently undergone from public service organ to commercial platform for advertisers. While this process was contingent on the specific national
histories of the medium,[29] it clearly came to assume a trans-European dynamic.
Some broader characteristics of this transition are glossed in exemplary form in
71 Fragments' depiction of the Brunners, the couple that adopt Marian. After watching Marian's Romanian refugee story on the news, they spring into action and
seek him out. Their decision thus appears to have a democratic, humanitarian,
and public sphere-oriented character. Their construction as viewers codifies
them as "socially responsible" citizens, except that the social is now no longer the
realm of the nation but of Europe. Yet, this codification is revealed as being mere
sheen. The ethical dilemmas raised by the story suggest that the position of the
Brunners in this scenario is rather closer to that of conventional, that is, private
and personally motivated, consumers, whose choice of the boy is influenced by
the same factors that would make them select a particular toy brand or a pet.
It is contingent on psychological impulses, individual responses to marketing
strategies (not the least those of Marian himself, who shrewdly understands that
"going on TV" will increase his chances of finding new parents), as well as on
their personal tastes, and the way the medium, which is now basically a commercial
medium, can deliver consumers to specific products, whereby it eclipses other
products in the process.

TV's shift away from being the architect of a national consensus and towards
becoming a transnational tool for the stratification of consumers is central to understanding Haneke's films of this period. It reveals something about the construction
of the trilogy's implied spectator. It has often been stated that Haneke became
rather disillusioned with television as an artistic medium – due to public television's increasing unwillingness to ignore the ratings factor and produce artistically
challenging films. But his first theatrical feature was still written for TV and with
TV viewers in mind. Not the kinds of viewers who became known as channel
surfers, but the TV viewers who considered themselves selective and demanding
viewers, and who had been "abandoned" by TV in the same way Haneke felt he
had been abandoned by TV as a demanding artist. The portmanteau aesthetics
of *The Seventh Continent* – the long takes and extreme long shots typical of art
cinema combined with the close-ups that are characteristic of television – enable
the film to convey humans at once starkly isolated from one another and fully
rendered through the language of consumer culture.[30] Close-ups are being
sequenced together, whereby the semantic field is drastically narrowed, which creates unbridgable gaps to the visual environment. This decontextualization of space
engenders a connotative surplus of potential structuring relations. We already noted
that a founding condition for the allusive power of Haneke's films is his creation
of structuring absences. They often manifest themselves in the form of a missing
middle element – whether encountered on the aesthetic level, as in the missing
mid-range shots that conventionally mediate between extreme close-ups and long
shots, or on the level of narrative, which Haneke habitually eviscerates by creating

gaps between the initial conflict and the films' often casually rendered or pre-stated outcome, or even on the level of historical referencing, which, as we have seen, is apt to suppress a crucial middle period. In each case, the ostentatiously withheld center points to anxieties about the periphery.

In the present context, these anxieties are directed towards what may be characterized as a looming Europeanization that affects the individual citizen, the state and society he/she lives in, and the media that traditionally used to mediate between these two planes. The narrow, partial, or compromised legibility of so many images in the films of the trilogy acutely foregrounds the existentialist situation of the individual caught in an ever more complex maze of political, cultural, and bureaucratic coordinates. In this regard, the task of fitting together the pieces of a puzzle, to which the act of reading Haneke's films tends to be compared, relates to the no less challenging task of internally restructuring Europe. The broader parameters are set, but the configuration of the internal components is difficult to figure out. This is because the evolving concept of a unified, centralized Europe has contributed to the erosion of the concept of the nation on two levels: on the political level – by voiding the state of decision-making powers that are shifted to the subnational plane (by increasing the autonomy of regional governments) and to the supranational plane (by centralizing bureaucracies with the EU) (Elsaesser 2005: 58); but also on the cultural level, registering what Elsaesser has termed the "increasing retribalization of European nation states" (ibid.). This dynamic also applies to the media, and it does so in two ways: The advent of cable and satellite TV has significantly eroded the sway of many a state-sponsored TV channel, whose national domain has found itself invaded by the programming of other nations, as well as by domestic and foreign regional networks[31] or the private channels of further splintered special interest communities. As this development happened concomitantly with the advent of, or was directly catalyzed and executed by, private and commercial broadcasters, the Europeanization of national television has been nearly synonymous with a commercialization of the medium.

The paradigmatic trailblazer in this regard was Radio Television Luxembourg (RTL). Its location had made its reach into France, Belgium, Holland, West Germany, and Switzerland feasible even before the advent of the new transmission technologies. Echoing Luxembourg's slightly *sub rosa* status as tax haven and gambling center, RTL from the beginning had an adamantly mercantile profile. It targeted viewers through dial-in responses and featured a generous array of game shows, music videos, and recent movie releases, frequently interrupted by commercials. In this sense, RTL, even before the advent of cable and satellite technologies, had put into practice one of the underlying teleologies of European unification: unlimited commerce and consumer freedom – notions that RTL attuned to Europe's evolving political integration by creating multilingual programming with a heavy emphasis on pop music and youth culture. The "RTL factor" is heavily alluded to in a scene in *The Seventh Continent* that shows the protagonists watching the annual Eurovision Song Contest on television, traditionally one of Europe's most widely broadcast events. Because of its international format, the competition requires a multilingual moderator who welcomes artists, explains the protocol, and reports the voting results in English, French, German, and Italian. The moderator of the show featured in this scene is a Luxembourg native and erstwhile RTL show hostess, whose laborious multilingual moderation is foregrounded to near-satirical effect.[32] Haneke places the communicative excess of the show's cumbersomely multiglot protocol in contrast to the film's diegetic viewers who, being reduced to consumers and glaciated (European) subjects, are unable to communicate with one another. At the same time, Haneke undermines the notion of plenitude (and, implicitly, the notion of Europeanness that sponsors it) by rendering it diminutive in visual terms, as it emanates from a small TV monitor that is contained by the larger cinematic shot of the living room with the family in it.

Haneke's critical assessment of the changes in television go hand in hand with his skepticism towards a continent that, while historically having no other option but to move towards integration, has done so in problematic political ways that have also dramatically changed the media landscape that Haneke himself has been part of for so long. Of course, as the history of RTL shows, it would be wrong to claim that European integration began to affect national television only with the advent of satellite TV and the fall of the Eastern bloc. However, by the time Haneke made *The Rebellion*, European integration had not only affected television as a specific medium, but was also already instrumentalizing it for intermedial purposes – such as for the definition of art and literature as one European cultural good. Haneke's adaptation of *The Rebellion* was very clearly defined under these auspices: it was commissioned by Austrian National Television (ORF) as Austria's contribution to a series of showcases of films that were based on novels from nine European countries, whose respective national networks commissioned the adaptation of the work of one of the nation's prominent authors.[33] This institutional confidence in film's intermedial power notwithstanding, for Haneke's filmmaking, from the mid-1980s on, the delicate balance between national (i.e., economically and artistically protected) and international enunciation began to devolve into a schism. By the early 1990s, there were two Hanekes – the Haneke of national television and the Haneke of European art cinema. The first Haneke, while still occasionally working in TV, increasingly saw himself as an ex-TV director, someone who had more or less abandoned the medium because the medium had abandoned him, which registered in the allegorically fraught address of the national TV viewer.

At the same time, the second Haneke, the director of European art films, had begun to consolidate his auteur persona and to expand and fine-tune his cinematic vocabulary. This vocabulary has been associated with various kinds of non-mainstream, art, avant-garde, and counter-cinemas. But it is important to note that Haneke did not just discover this broad range of non-mainstream devices with his move into theatrical feature film production. His TV films already used some of them – one recalls the highly elliptical editing in *Three Paths to the Lake*; the harrowing long take of the abortion attempt in *Lemmings*, Part One; the creative disjunction of image and sound in *Variation*, the use of color and black-and-white stock in *Fraulein*, and the plethora of anti-illusionist devices boasted by *Who Was Edgar Allan?*. The difference constituted by Haneke's move into theatrical features lies in a selective expansion of devices, their more consistent deployment, and their creative variation. One of the particularities of Haneke's cinema is that the individual and combined deployment of these tools lifts them out of the contexts of the various cinematic movements they are associated with and puts them to new use. The best examples are the long take and the static camera shot: Both are stylistic staples of Haneke's theatrical features. But while the long take is often associated with realism (and, thus, with art cinema and the documentary tradition), Haneke's use of it significantly marginalizes its realist function in favor of different aesthetic and philosophical interests. In contrast to narrative realism, Haneke combines the long take with the close-up, or he implants into it the *dispositif* of another medium, such as video. Or he combines it with the static camera shot. Both the static camera shot and another device prominent in the glaciation trilogy, the lengthy fade to black, are generally associated with the avant-garde and, more specifically, with counter-cinema and structural film. Haneke's use of thick framing, his partial blocking out of the image, and his refusal to render psychological motives are indebted to Brecht's theses on epic theater. To an extent, Haneke's deployment of these devices echoes their original contexts, in that he, too, uses them to build up intensity subversively, that is, not for the obtainment of conventional spectatorial pleasure. As Jörg Metelmann has argued, Haneke's glaciation trilogy and *Funny Games* partake in the Brechtian tradition, but also, importantly, go beyond it. Haneke understands that art's function as an aid to help spectators gain political consciousness through alienation and subsequent reintegration of their experience is insufficient. This dynamic needs to be supplemented with the self-reflexive manipulation of affect, so that the film lingers more lastingly with spectators (Metelmann 2003: 153–79). One of the ways to do so is by using sound. Sound hits the human sense apparatus at a more basic level, where the latter is more vulnerable, which greatly intensifies the production of affect. Because sound and image get processed by the brain differently, their use produces a cognitive frisson that the artist can exploit not only to manipulate semantics, but also to expand the cognitive and affective range.

However, Haneke consistently layers these counter-cinematic devices with more mainstream formal components, such as realist lighting and acting. His films have a narrative arc that, while fragmented and strategically deprived of key information, is nonetheless recognizable as an arc. His films tell stories. He shares the broad vocabulary of political modernism, but not for the purpose of destroying illusionism, as had been the concern of structural film and of the Brechtian avant-garde. As Catherine Wheatley has observed, Haneke's focus on sentiment and affect, and his concerns with questions of guilt, shame, and moral responsibility have traditionally not been the focus of political modernism, which is concerned with intellect, epistemology, and, as the name itself indicates, with politics. Wheatley argues that the ethical problems which Haneke's films thematize (as evident in protagonists' confrontations with or implications in other people's fates or deaths) are mirrored in the self-reflexive exploration of the ethical relation between the film and the viewer, where questions of the spectator's complicity with the cinematic apparatus become foregrounded. In this sense, Haneke's aesthetics produce not only an intellectual-epistemological reflexivity, but a moral one (Wheatley 2009: 4, 87).

Given the theoretical debates that Haneke's films have sparked in a relatively short period of time and given the insights these debates have already yielded, to characterize Haneke's films as merely repositing well-worn devices of fifty years of art cinema would thus obviously miss the point. Perhaps this reaction is understandable, however, if one considers that art cinema is still considered largely synonymous with European cinema – and, thus, with cultural elitism and snobbery. Haneke's films, particularly if encountered in the same context as his image as the last "grand" auteur of European art cinema, trigger this reaction.[34] A central role in the creation of Haneke's image falls to the international film festival as the premier platform where Haneke's Europeanness gets staged and the conjunction between his films and his persona gets forged. In this sense, the impression of the Europeanness of Haneke's films may itself be regarded as an effect of the waning of European art cinema and the subsequent nostalgic reification of its cultural signifiers for the festival circuit's postmodern, globalized era. In the late 1980s, as Thomas Elsaesser has pointed out, the global was becoming the new referent with regard to which the auteur performed – not only his/her own authorship, but the history and cultural specificities of his/her own nationhood, including the stylistic and thematic archaeology of his/her own national cinema (Elsaesser 2005: 57). That in Haneke's case this did not lead to a performance of Austrianness or Germanness or Frenchness, but to the projection of a more general Europeanness, testifies not only to the transnational pedigree of the filmmaker and his films, but also to the fact that Europe itself had lost its status as the geopolitical and cultural center of art cinema. Now forced to compete on a global scale with numerous cinemas from the Middle and Far East, as well as from revitalized cinemas of Latin America and a growing number of African filmmaking countries and, last but not least, with a tide of new films and filmmakers from Eastern Europe, European art cinema, long synonymous with French, Italian, German, British, and Scandinavian national cinemas, had become part of the past. But this also meant that it could be remembered – that is, it could be distilled into an attitude that became nostalgically codified as Europeanness.

During the 1990s and beyond, Haneke became one of the primary signifiers of this Europeanness, but it is important to understand that the image of the last auteur of European art cinema comprised only one half of his persona. The other had little to do with anachronism and even less with nostalgia. On the contrary, what guided the reception of Haneke's films and built his reputation were the shifting, highly contemporary, criteria that define the auteur for the age of globalization.

They constitute the filmmaker as post-new wave, post-national, post-metaphysical craftsman, whose auteurism manifests itself in film historical knowledge, in consummate professionalism, and in artistic bravado – by which is meant the ability to demonstrate virtuoso command of the medium and to deliver tour-de-force cinematic experiences (Elsaesser 2005: 51). In Haneke's case, it was particularly the Cannes International Film Festival that became a highly propitious forum for defining and promoting the auteur's evolving qualities, at the same time that it helped create his persona as one of the last greats.

In addition to profiting from a festival's vast promotional machine and the concentrated attention by critics and the public, Haneke's films at Cannes have often sparked what Elsaesser calls "irruptions" – walkouts, displays of audience dis/approval, or provocative remarks traded during a post-screening Q&A – that slice through the protocol but also become a desirable if unpredictable vector in a festival's psychological and cultural dynamics (ibid.). Or else, the films themselves would turn into events, either because expectations are pitched to a premium, or post-screening responses create the phenomenon of "critical buzz," as was the case with *The Seventh Continent* and *Benny's Video*. But the films and their maker are not the sole beneficiaries – these dynamics also add to a festival's own brand identity by sustaining the mythology a festival has created for itself.[35] In this regard, Haneke is but one among hundreds of artists to have enjoyed a symbiotic relationship with Cannes and other festivals that comprise the international circuit.

Yet, Haneke's films can be called festival films in an even more apposite way. Their main cognitive and affective markers (the production of anxiety, dread, shock, and the effects of violence) and the means of triggering these (by encouraging inference, raising suspicion, and prompting "cognitive switches"[36]) are structurally homologous to the dynamics operative in film festivals with their hieratic protocols and their performative rites of anticipation and response. Haneke's audiences are regularly made to watch characters watching other characters, or watch characters watching television. These dynamics replicate the festival's atmosphere of collective viewing and its dynamics of nervous-feverish evaluation, followed by anxiously anticipated, often shocking or scandalizing verdicts. Haneke's films' careful initiation of processes of inference, their prompting of hermeneutic second-guessing, and their stratified targeting of different viewers through coded information are highly allegorical – in fact, they often become more directly synecdochic – of festivals' dynamics of controlling their patrons. The films mirror what Elsaesser and Daniel Dayan have identified as festivals' hierarchized accreditation systems, their zones of exclusion, their kept secrets and carefully orchestrated release of information, all the way to the festivals' role in shaping the parameters of reception. Haneke's films make for great festival talk: they generate testy disputes about plot details and their implications, anxious comparisons of "readings" of certain scenes, and righteous pronouncements on having been manipulated or let down as a spectator or critic.

The structural similarities between the economy of Haneke's spectatorial address and the dynamics of the film festival suggest how certain neo-auteurist labels such as artistic virtuosity and tour-de-force experience came about in Haneke's case, and also how they came to constitute this highly contemporary side of Haneke's auteur persona. Making it converge with Haneke's other side, that of the grand European master, is a process in which the film festival has likewise played its part. It has frequently provided a public platform from which Haneke can proselytize his European values of film being a serious art and a tool for cultural and philo-sophical reflection. And because the festival's function as a marketplace, competitive avenue, and cultural showcase of world cinema defines it against American notions of film as mass-manufactured entertainment (Elsaesser 2005: 84), it becomes an effective forum for Haneke to stage his critique of film as mass culture. This polemic masks a *de facto* interdependency and reciprocity of European and American cinema on numerous levels ranging from international coproduction and distri-bution deals and the historically steady migration of artists in both directions to the more recent globalization of film style and narrative form. Yet, in the late 1990s – when the drastic increase and accessibility of information through the Internet was making these signs of interdependency more overtly visible, Haneke deliv-ered a film that seemed to reinvigorate the old binary between Europe and America with new polemical force.

Didacticism at the Box Office, or: Europe versus America

If one follows Haneke's own comments that, given the irredeemably jaundiced nature of genre cinema, European filmmakers can at best make parodies of genre films,[37] one is led to read *Funny Games* (1997) as the darkest of genre parodies. Drawing on the family-under-siege genre, Haneke at once mobilizes and subverts formulaic components, such as the transformation of the victims into (self-) liberating heroes. The film denies the genre's conventional plot resolution; the villain's direct audience address and the sustained, highly unpleasurable depiction of the effects of violence are intended to demonstrate to spectators their com-plicity in and indispensability for the existence of violence as a commercial enter-tainment spectacle. The funny games are being staged for the audience, which is placed in a double bind: taken out of its moral vacuum and brought into existential proximity with the characters, the audience wants to stay with the victims and bear witness to their suffering, but it is also told that its very specta-torship is the actual reason for this suffering. *Funny Games* became the most drastic example of Haneke's moral reflexivity, raising the question whether he may have raised the moral stakes too high. How effectively can any film sponsor aesthetic experience if it basically begs to be abandoned? Does Haneke shed the baby with the bathwater? Does his existentialist critique of commodification implicitly declare representation unimportant? Does his filmic attack on consumerism still see any purpose in reflecting on the film itself, other than in the most totalizing binary terms of take it or leave it?

These questions are of theoretical more than historical nature. It is not surprising, then, that they posed themselves almost identically and with renewed force on the occasion of the release of the remake of *Funny Games*. Haneke's rationale for remaking the film was that the original never had a chance to wield its subversive effect, as it never reached the kind of spectator he had in mind for it. Targeting an American entertainment mindset, the original actually never received US distribution. And because it was shot in German and thus required subtitling for foreign release, it automatically was removed from the multiplexes of English-language markets, giving it marginal and scattered exhibition in art houses. But art house spectators, if they saw the film at all, did not appreciate being this abrasively preached to. The 2007 remake, which was made in English with an international cast including Naomi Watts, Tim Roth, and Michael Pitt, was supposed to correct these erstwhile limitations and put Haneke's strategy to a new test. But while the remake's more commercial wrapping suggests an awareness of the mercantile makeup of mass culture, its failure at the US box office showed that this awareness begged supplementing by a deeper understanding of the concrete dynamics that actually drive consumption. No matter the conceptual integrity of its premise, the film still operates primarily via displeasure instead of pleasure, and it moralizes against its audience. But even these rationalizations of the film's failure with audiences seem specious, given that the very industry Haneke attempts to subvert with the remake of *Funny Games* often fares no better than Haneke in gauging the inclinations and predispositions of audiences. Left searching for reliable reasons for *Funny Games*' commercial failure, one is ultimately tempted to agree with consumer comments that criticized the film for being plain boring and, in fact, not (overtly) violent enough.

If *Funny Games* must be regarded as a failed experiment on one level, the remake remains of interest for our discussion of Haneke's relation to the binary between European and American cinema. While the film's rejection by American audiences seems to be the clearest proof of this binary, the film's production history ironically refracts such binary thinking. To begin with, the remake of *Funny Games* was born at the fortress of European art cinema – Cannes – where Haneke was approached by a British (not American) producer with a request to remake the film. American financing came into the picture only after the European monies had run out. *Funny Games* received completion funds and a distribution deal from Warner Independent, an art house subsidiary of Warner Brothers, established to diversify the studio's production line into art house fare and extend its profit reach to American independent, European, and global concepts and talent. If Haneke ever intended *Funny Games* to become part of a counter-hegemonic cinema (Lars von Trier's films would be a different but related instance), the film's low-risk American boutique treatment showed that the culture industry has sufficiently diversified to assimilate these types of subversive games. By financing its own subversives, Hollywood, in the case of *Funny Games*, proved perfectly capable of assimilating a European image of American culture and throw it right back at Europe. That the film was released in France and some other European countries under the title *Funny Games U.S.* stands in ironic relation to the tale, cherished in the circles of European cinema culture, of the European artist who comes to understand his Europeanness only when going into creative exile to America. One of the challenges of remaking *Funny Games*, according to its director, was to recreate an already existing work from scratch – a work, we might add, that not only constitutes a European product but a European fantasy of an American setting. Another challenge, according to Haneke, was presented by the shooting of the film in Long Island, New York, whose logistics were difficult because of labor regulations. The European artist working abroad thus encountered not only his own European self, but one of the most European institutions in history: a workers' union.

At the same time, one shouldn't ignore that the remake of *Funny Games* does evince subtle changes from the original and that these changes arguably constitute an Americanization of the treatment. One of the most prominent changes is the sexualization of the family's mother, played by Naomi Watts. As a voluptuous blonde, Watts strikes a slightly different tone in her performance than Susanne Lothar in the original. The film makes her strip to her underwear, which provides a tantalizing contrast to the torture she receives. While Haneke focuses on the commodification of violence, he exempts sexual representation from this critique and, rather problematically, downplays the fact that the representations of violence and of sex operate by the same logic and are intrinsically connected. The film punishes spectators for consuming violence but not for looking at Watts as a sexual object (although it does not reward them for doing so either).

Gender, War, and Social Conflict: Of Agonies and Agonisms

The treatment of gender and sexuality is obviously central to Haneke's 2001 adaptation of Elfriede Jelinek's 1983 novel, *The Piano Teacher*. While the film's portrait of piano teacher Erika Kohut's ill-fated and hazardous attempts to develop a BDSM relationship with one of her students points to the pervasive patriarchal system of interdictions that oppress women, the fact that the novel was adapted by a male director who also wrote the screenplay[38] raised questions about the preservation of the integrity of what has been canonized as a feminist literary work. Haneke's screenplay deletes any reference to Erika's memories of her father and her childhood, whereby her complicated sexual behavior is bereft of its psychological background. The film further privileges the relationship between Erika and her student suitor, Walter Klemmer, at the expense of an in-depth depiction of Erika's relationship to her mother. The history of this relationship is only alluded to, the mother's screen part is smaller than her part in the book, and she is played by a rather elderly Annie Girardot whose performance is eclipsed by the strong presence of Isabelle Huppert and Benoît Magimel. Most significantly, Haneke transforms Walter from a middling if manipulative character into an attractive charmer, exchanging the contempt reserved for him by the novel's author for a much more sympathetic portrayal. This makes it harder for audiences to see Walter's coldness and cruelty, but it also makes the contrast between his initial demeanor and his later treatment of Erika more drastic. Haneke's treatment at least implies that an effective analysis of patriarchy as a system does not benefit from a focus on stereotypes. Furthermore, the film shrewdly exploits Walter's comeliness through its specifically cinematic properties of casting and *mise-en-scène* to build up and then subvert the oblique dynamics of romance that further complicate their relationship.[39]

Haneke's casting of Huppert had a similar impact on the representation of Erika, who now comes across as more glamorous, including her suffering, than conceived by Jelinek in the novel.[40] The ending – in both the novel and the film – has Erika "respond" to Walter's rape of her by stabbing herself in the chest but, importantly, walking away with the injury to suggest she'll survive. But the film's depiction of this ending arguably has a different impact from the novel's rendition of it. The visuals allow spectators to empathize with Erika more strongly, adding emotional resonance to our understanding that her act of stabbing herself, no matter whether planned or impromptu, expropriates the discourse of violence from the male and returns it to the female enunciative realm. Superseding a male act of violence through a female one that testifies to the woman's authorship and showcases her imaginary constitutes, however perversely, Erika's reclaiming of power over herself. This power is coded as a destructive power, to be sure, but it is impossible to ascertain with definitiveness that it will lead to her complete self-destruction. Her stabbing herself in the upper chest, near the shoulder, but not in the heart (the novel spells this difference out explicitly) thus makes Erika's self-laceration differ only in gradation, not in nature, from her advancing BDSM practices.[41]

Haneke's casting, filming, and direction of Huppert counter some of the potentially limiting aspects of his adaptation. Huppert's performative prowess unfolds a vast signifying power that potentially transcends textual limitations. As Jelinek has noted, the actress uses her craft to convert her face into a text – indeed, into writing (2001: 120). Her rigidity makes her character uniquely individual, yet representative of women's broader dilemma: she is a character who is pushed into the position of object to be looked at, yet she also feels entitled to look (122). The considerable challenge to overcome this binary, to transgress against the prohibition for women to look, makes for the story's tense atmosphere of drama and its near-grotesque moments of comedy. Grotesque because language is inherently comic when it signifies violation of its own structures. The moment of irregularity tends to figure simultaneously as transgressive, as tragic, and as comic in being

at odds with the structural law, whose authority it at once disqualifies and recon-
firms. Haneke and Jelinek share a strong interest in these deeper dimensions of
language. Jelinek's intention is to depict individual fates as endlessly repetitive rebel-
lions against the elimination of human individuality in the post-bourgeois era (126).
In this agenda we sense strong echoes of the glaciation trilogy. In addition, both
artists share a concern about the jaundiced concept of national culture. Jelinek's
story contains an elaborate and nuanced critique of Austria's relationship to music,
which is considered the nation's premier cultural good, but which is largely contained on the level of middlebrow culture, where it receives systematic commercial
exploitation. The novel identifies this phenomenon in its theme of piano instruction, which is a large cottage industry and source of income for women in Austria,
who thus come to bear the brunt of the nation's self-denigrating impulse to its
musical heritage (131). It is not difficult to see how this aspect complements Haneke's
long-standing critique of mass culture. While Haneke's condescending attitude
towards popular music is well known, he feels similarly negatively about the fact
that much of nineteenth-century classical music has proven just as prone to commercialization. And he readily admits that high modernist styles of classical music
are extremely limited in their effectivity and sphere of impact. *The Piano Teacher*
thus combines concerns of Jelinek and Haneke into a far-reaching critique of Austria's
national culture industry that has commodified the country's cultural heritage.

Shot on location in Vienna but with a French-speaking cast, *The Piano Teacher*
constitutes a further stage in the evolution of the Europeanness of Haneke's
cinema. The film's settings are unmistakably Viennese (featuring some of the city's
representational buildings) and its characters are Austrian. Haneke's decision to
use French as the film's dialog language is partially determined by the fact that
the lead actress is French. More will be said shortly about the significance of French
actresses in Haneke's recent work, but we should add to our observation about
the film's use of French that it does, of course, create a distancing effect that, once
again, points to tensions between a coherent body and its underlying fractures
and self-contradictions. In *The Piano Teacher*, Vienna becomes Paris and vice versa,
but this is also, and obviously, not the case. The film paints the picture of a continental Europe that, while in the process of becoming more and more integrated,
will nonetheless reveal its subdividing boundaries (traditional and new ones) with
renewed force. The Europe it depicts is Janus-faced in another way, too – it is a
continental Europe of past but preserved royal splendor, of cultural refinement
and substantial artistic accomplishments and traditions; it is also a fortress that
excludes non-Europeans, especially ethnic immigrants. And when they succeed
in entering the fortress, they become its cultural others and economic bottom.
The film creates yet another contrast to its images of continental refinement with
its depiction of patriarchal violence coursing just beneath the surface and in the
shadow of official institutions such as sports.

While Haneke's earlier films from time to time featured well-known actors from
past periods of popular cinema, those appearances were mostly cameos or supporting

roles and they were meant to imbue the films with an additional level of reflexivity.[42] Haneke's use of Isabelle Huppert and Juliette Binoche in the French-language films are of a different nature. But Huppert's significance in the evolving construction of Haneke's Europeanness goes beyond her artistic influence on her screen parts. She is partially responsible for the fact that Haneke was able to make *Time of the Wolf* (2003). Haneke had written the screenplay in the early 1990s, during the time of the civil war that raged in the wake of the breakup of the former Yugoslavia (several of his films feature news casts about various instances and stages of this conflict). But he could not find funding for the film for the rest of the decade. Only after the success of *The Piano Teacher*, and with Huppert's name attached to the project, did the film find backers. His script did not contain any references to the conflict, but invented a dystopian science fiction scenario. Set in a time just after an unspecified disaster has occurred, it depicts bands of survivors roaming the countryside (among them Huppert, mother of two, whose husband has been killed by vagrants who, in their own need to survive, had occupied the family's weekend cabin). The film shows how bare survival needs clash with civilizational codes. But the depiction of the formation of fragile, tentative bonds among survivors and of their organization into alternative families, looting packs, and make-shift tribes is intended to go beyond the formulaic scenarios of post-apocalyptic genre films. It shows Haneke's skepticism towards society's capacity for ethical and political regeneration, whereby it inevitably alludes to the riven field of ethnic, religious, and cultural fiefdoms that were cast adrift and set into conflict after the breakup of the Eastern bloc.

In this sense, one can read *Time of the Wolf* as taking place not in France but somewhere "east." It suggests that Europe has an "other," a back door, a zone beyond the influence of the Geneva conventions. The sense of threat, despair, and hopelessness that is so palpable in its diegesis includes an allusion to unchecked military action which, at least implicitly, evokes the possibility of genocide. Yet, the film's allegorical nature precludes a rhetorical demarcation of East from West. Its final traveling shot, which is filmed from a moving train and has frequently sparked interpretations that Haneke may be providing a glimmer of hope here, could just as easily evoke a Nazi deportation shipment of Jews to Auschwitz – the mode of transportation and the isolated landscape through which the train moves certainly make such associations possible, as does the fact that the film holds us completely in the dark about the destination of the journey and what might follow its termination. It is Europe's long history of political and humanitarian catastrophes, of wars and genocides performed with increasing first world technological efficiency that the film alludes to as pertaining equally to West and East. On the other hand, the film's depiction of the struggle between different ethnic and political groups at the train station that is turned into a refugee camp also implies the possibility of a utopia – if these parties were able to create a new, more democratic, and genuinely pluralistic society. On this level, Haneke's film approximates the utopianist implications of Austrian authors

Roth and Bachmann. The train station is an allegory of the modern world that is consumed by hoping and waiting; whether it is allowed to move forward depends on its ability to redefine its approach to the governance of political, ethnic, religious, and cultural difference.

If Huppert's presence in the ensemble cast of *Time of the Wolf* is perhaps less important than her role behind the scenes, Haneke's relation to the actress throws into relief the importance he accords to his actors – to their pedigree, their range, and their usability for a particular project. This is even more true of Juliette Binoche. Already in his first French-language film, *Code Unknown* (2000), Haneke used Binoche for a prominent part in the film's ensemble cast. Like Huppert, though in a more melodramatic register, Binoche is able to embody the kind of ordinary characters that Haneke's films feature to tell individual stories with representative character. It is notable that in both *Code Unknown* and *Caché* Binoche's characters have to confront or are faced with diverse diegetic environments within the fiction of the film, leaving audiences at times confused as to the nature of each space and the interrelationship between them. In *Code Unknown*, Binoche plays an actress who is placed into several acting scenarios: She is placed in a scene that takes place in an enclosed chamber from which she may never be able to escape; another scene shows her auditioning on an empty stage for a Shakespeare play; in yet another scene, one of her characters is in carefree play with a man in a rooftop pool, while her fictional child is in danger of falling off the roof. Binoche's pledging eyes and melodramatic face have a distracting, perhaps fetishistic, effect. Initially, these scenarios are slightly confusing for us viewers. Their stylistic heterogeneity foregrounds the sense of emotional anxiety associated with the loss of one's bearings. Binoche's emotional realism provides a strong mimetic connection between these scenarios, but it also carries over into her characters' private, off-screen life. The actress thus becomes a great casting choice for Haneke – she can tie together films of great textual heterogeneity. This was of importance for Haneke's film projects in France, because these films are not only about post-apocalyptic civil war, but about the radical heterogeneity of contemporary Europe, particularly its cities. They are about the agonistic conflicts of a pluralist, multi-ethnic and multicultural society.

Code Unknown's spectacular opening long take lays out this fraught territory with great skill. Its tour-de-force tracking shot strategically includes Binoche's character, Anne, who gets embroiled in the confrontation of members of several ethnic and geopolitical territories. Her behavior registers familial protectionism (her partner has a teenage brother who is with her at the time and who causes a fight on the street with an African man over the boy's mistreatment of a Romanian beggar), but she also experiences moral conflict (it is her protégé's behavior that escalates the situation). A similarly complex connection between moral, ethical, and spatial dimensions can be found in the film's representation of a subway incident, in which Binoche's character is taunted and spat upon by a young Arab man. The scene throws into relief her dual situation as threatened female victim of male violence and as privileged first world citizen drawing the ire of the subaltern subject of French colonial history. We experience the scene through the forged perspectival hybrid of a long shot/long take that is, however, filmed in an extremely narrow frame of vision. The spectator senses acute claustrophobia and threat, as the scene provides no knowledge about the space and about the narrative outcome, all the while conveying the complex and contradictory ethical implications of the incident.

In Haneke's French films, a destabilization of the image never occurs for its own sake. Placing visual and spatial ontologies in question is Haneke's way of addressing the reality of war-torn geopolitical territories, riven topographies, and their symbolic and imaginary borders, whose histories of occupancy, shifting political allegiances, and complicated moral and ethical rules the films obliquely address.[43] In these often highly disorienting ontological games, the well-known French actress is a stand-in for the confused subject who is confronted with these hazardous borders. Through her, we experience the anxiety and confusion vicariously, but she also has the role, however complicated and compromised, of being the beneficiary of an education in ethics. In this sense, Binoche in particular expands the system of displaced spectatorial identifications that, as I noted earlier in this introduction, constitutes the structure of the house of Haneke's films. Her characters are among the children who live in this house, who must get along with the other inhabitants, and who must find their way through the maze of mysterious, doubly occupied, and anxiously defended rooms. As such, Binoche's characters are offered to us for identification. But a new element is introduced: these characters now also function as stand-ins for the director himself. Their hegemonic position is constituted by their dual membership in the dominant and the oppressed: they are members of a historically dominant group – Western Europeans – but as women they are also subject to male oppression. This second membership is something Haneke obviously does not share. But he replaces gender as the vector of subordination with a specific aspect of the first level of membership – Europeanness – which, in the larger binary between Europe and America, comes to function as the David to America's Goliath. What Binoche and Huppert as French actresses have in common is that, while their international success includes recognition in the US, their careers have not been tainted by their "selling out" in Hollywood-produced or financed films. Some sorties may not have been successful (one thinks of Huppert's ill-fated Hollywood thriller, *The Bedroom Window* [Curtis Hanson, 1987]), but unlike other European actresses (such as Maria Schell, Romy Schneider, Nastassja Kinski), neither Huppert nor Binoche ever tried to break into the American market with any lasting aspiration – neither one ever tried to become a bona fide Hollywood star. Instead, both have cast their English-language parts very successfully in the mode of an expanded notion of "guest appearance" and, like Catherine Deneuve, Simone Signoret, and Jeanne Moreau before them, have fared extremely well with this strategy. If one now considers this successful inhabitation of hegemony – to be a world-famous European star who is "recognized" more than used by the American industry – one sees Haneke's identification with Huppert and Binoche. He, too, has been recognized in America, particularly after *The Piano Teacher* became a considerable art house success and *Caché*'s even greater success prepared a certain public momentum for the arrival of the remake of *Funny Games*. This remake, while a critical and commercial failure in the US, still got Haneke considerable attention – and in identifying him as a highbrow subversive from Europe whose other films are acclaimed by American critics and coveted as potential sources for Hollywood remakes[44] – *Funny Games* made Haneke's public image in America more coherent and recognizable. While it was clear that *Funny Games*, for the time being, would be a one-off deal, Haneke has not, in principle, ruled out working in America again. In the meantime, it was under the auspices of one of his two French actresses, Isabelle Huppert, who presided over the 2009 Cannes jury, that Haneke was able to stage his triumphant return to the zenith of European auteur cinema with *The White Ribbon*.

But Haneke's position within the Europe-versus-Hollywood binary is trumped by another, even larger binary, in which he stands at the top of the pyramid. It is the binary between white male Western European privilege and the various male and female political subjects that make up Europe's colonial other, its history, and its present in the form of legal or illegal aliens and immigrants living at the margins of European society. Haneke's French films are about these subjects, but in being about them, they cannot avoid being about him as well – as the representative of the group that has historically oppressed these subjects. As Rosalind Galt has pointed out, *Caché* and *Code Unknown*'s classic left-liberal, multicultural portrait of ethnic diversity may not be what's most interesting about these films. Despite these films' merits, they also end up replicating the existing hegemonic structure of the society they aim to critique.[45]

This dilemma is epitomized in *Caché*. Its middle-aged white male protagonist, Georges (Daniel Auteuil), is confronted with his guilt over having caused the institutionalization of his childhood friend, Majid, in a foster home. George's paranoid reencounter with Majid leads to the latter's suicide, which triggers an alternating pattern of culpability and self-acquittal that presents the white male subject in a *mise-en-abyme* of nagging moral doubt (Shaviro). This *mise-en-abyme* has been characterized as one of the more sophisticated discursive structures in recent cinema. But it could not be so without the irreducible vector of Majid's recorded suicide – recorded, at the very least, for us, the film's spectators. The function Majid has for the education of *Caché*'s spectator is not the same as the function of the family in *Funny Games* – it is imbricated in a colonial past and postcolonial history, in which such instrumentalizations, whatever else they may accomplish, always already reflect – and, to a certain extent, reproduce – the historic and contemporary power imbalance between the former colonizers and their colonized. *Caché*'s morally reflexive game of the mind cannot extricate itself from some of the dynamics of colonization, even if it is deployed in the service of a postcolonial argument.

Would this type of scenario ever be staged the other way round, that is, with the white colonizer in a position of diminished speaking power? Haneke does not envision a radical inversion of the historical power imbalance; his vision is one of putative equality and balance between former colonizer and former colonized. At the end of *Caché*, we see Georges's and Majid's sons meet at the steps of a high school. We do not overhear their conversation; Haneke places their interaction in a radically open textual relation to the film. This scene might actually constitute the beginning of the film, in which both sons possibly plan the production of the anonymous tapes that unsettle the Laurent household and trigger Georges's crisis; or they might come together at the end of the film as a result of the conflict, and as a sign that the new generation wants to make peace and take their place in the course of history. What we do see, however, is that this is a conversation of two – one representing the white class of the colonizer, the other that of the colonized. The fact that they form the new alliance, the future, does give us a clear indication of Haneke's world view. For him, there cannot be – there must not be – a unilateral change constituted by "the Majids of this world," as Paul Gilroy has put it (2007: 234). It will have to be a force comprised of two equal halves, with the white force assuming half the power. But this fifty/fifty-type arrangement renders doubtful the possibility that the pervasive lack of equality between former colonizer and former colonized can be redressed effectively. It could be argued that, if such a proposal were ever to be made, it could only come from the former colonized, and only as a result of the latter's own historical and political meditation on the feasibility of such an arrangement for the process of healing and reparation. Haneke's identity as a white European, or so it may be argued, may in and of itself make it impossible for him to proffer such a proposal. At the same time, the undeclared content of the conversation and the fact that it takes place on the steps of an institution that bears the name Stéphane Mallarmé indicate that Haneke's political vision is, once again, informed by a fragile, oblique political utopianism. For Haneke, the only option in the negotiation of irresolvable social conflict is the hope that this conflict gets cast into a radically overarching, abstract, universal language. The casting of conflict into language, instead of leading to violence or deadlocks, is in itself not a solution, even if it has been cherished as a viable approach by modern as well as postmodern philosophers. But it might be a potential beginning, provided language is turned into a radically fluid poetry of the kind associated with the school's namesake. This proposition, which is not about multicultural politics but abstract linguistic and philosophical thought, is certainly a more comfortable territory for Haneke. It invites comparison to the utopianism that is embodied in Austrian literature by Bachmann's Trottas. If it is still a Eurocentric proposition, its radical linguistic potential bears the seed for the unmaking of Eurocentrism.

Haneke has thus revealed his limitations along with his sophistication. He has since returned to German history and Germanic culture. Filmed in Germany and financed with German subsidy money, *The White Ribbon* is a portrait of a generation of Germans who were children before and during World War I and who would be adults when Hitler came to power. The film is also a tense study of violent acts of discipline that occur in a small village. The historical dimension, like so often in Haneke, is kept at bay but also kept in reach through the investigation of the impact of powerful institutions, ideologies, and cultural norms, such as the combination of authoritarianism, nationalism, and Protestantism that the film depicts.

The present collection of essays reflects another ramification of Haneke's anachronism. Because his work remained in relative obscurity for so long, the English-language academy did not take note of Haneke until well into the first decade of the new millennium. The purpose of the international, interdisciplinary conference, "Michael Haneke: A Cinema of Provocation," held at Boston University in October 2007, in conjunction with the first Haneke retrospective in North America that also included most of the television films, was to catalyze critical discourse on Haneke's work in relation to recent debates in film and media studies as well as literary and cultural studies. While this conference serves as a foundation for the present volume, several essays have been added that reflect the interest that other fields, such as art history, religion, and architecture, have taken in Haneke's cinema. Because aesthetics and philosophy assume such a prominent position – and, in many instances, an overt presence – in Haneke's work, most of the essays in this book on various levels devote themselves to developing new theoretical approaches to the films. The first section, which focuses on critical and topical approaches to Haneke's cinema, begins with an essay by Thomas Elsaesser that is at once a recontextualization of Haneke's cinema within the landscape of contemporary film theory and a reappraisal of several key thematic and aesthetic aspects of the films in the context of European cinema. Titled "Performative Self-Contradictions: Michael Haneke's Mind Games," the essay argues that Haneke involves his viewers, and to a certain extent also himself, in a spiraling game of hypothesizing that simultaneously asserts and questions that the cinema can be a vehicle for making epistemological truth claims. While the essay's main focus is devoted to discussing the structuring of several of Haneke's recent films as mind games, Elsaesser shares with several other contributors to this volume an interest in Haneke's deployment of specific cinematic devices, such as the long take, the static camera, and framing and reframing of the image. Thomas Y. Levin discusses the interplay of the static camera and the intermedially informed aesthetic of *Caché* to trace Haneke's deconstruction of surveillance both as a theme and as a visual *dispositif* with political and ideological implications. Vinzenz Hediger reads the thematic and aesthetic position of video in *Benny's Video* as a sign of the ambiguous status of the medium in Haneke's work: It is an index of the cultural and psycho-social impoverishment of modern civilization, but it is also, potentially or provisionally, an antidote or, as Hediger calls it, a *pharmakon*, that intervenes in the atrophying of cognitive-epistemological processes. Tom Conley proffers a detailed analysis of the long take and its philosophical implications in Haneke's cinema. Conley analyzes the opening sequence of *Code Unknown* to argue that Haneke's *mise-en-scène*, in self-reflexive manner, connects the political and historical dimensions of conflict within French society via the use of mirroring dispositifs, verbal puns, and a strategic deployment of minor yet important visual elements.

A second group of essays in this first section theorizes recurrent cultural tropes and textual figures in Haneke's cinema: the concepts of disgust and of evil, the representation of violence, the status of religion and faith, the related notions of play and performance, and critiques of spectacle and of melodrama. Approaching Haneke's cinema from the perspective of architecture, Peter Eisenman sees Haneke's artistic approach as a corrective to the postmodern aesthetics of empty spectacle. Reading *Caché*, *Code Unknown*, and *Funny Games* via Guy Debord's figure of *détournement*, Eisenman argues that Haneke, rather than rejecting the aesthetics of mainstream cinema wholesale, engages them subversively. Brigitte Peucker's essay "Games Haneke Plays: Reality and Performance" focuses on another figure that has a dual – that is, thematic and conceptual – role in Haneke's cinema: the figure of play, which Peucker, pointing to the dual meaning of the German word *Spiel*, extends to the areas of performance and of games, both of which Haneke's films probe for their respective distinctions between chance and determinism (in the case of games) and reality and illusion (in the case of performance). Christa Blümlinger draws on Julia Kristeva's concept of the abject to discuss an aspect that has echoed through Haneke's work from the early television films to the present – the figure of disgust, which enables Haneke's cinema to link formal, diegetic, and allegorical elements in a paradoxical bind of rupture and conjunction that succeeds in addressing spectators on multiple levels. Michel Chion analyzes the far-reaching implications of the use of music in Haneke's cinema. His analysis of the implications of a complete absence of music in *Caché* can be related to the observation, made by other authors in this volume, that Haneke's cinema distinguishes itself through an extremely intentional and controlled use of music. Jörg Metelmann, drawing on Peter Brooks's seminal work, offers a comprehensive analysis of Haneke's critical use of melodrama. Metelmann argues that Haneke's evolving body of work has incorporated various approaches to Western culture's tendencies for mystification, fighting it via Enlightenment-based dramatic and narrative interventions, but also by engaging the concept of tragedy to deflect the hope for salvation. Both sets of strategies, as Metelmann claims, are not mutually exclusive but may be interpreted as constituents *and* as critiques of what may be called "melodrama." Going beyond questions of genre and dramaturgy, Metelmann reads melodrama as one of the prevalent emotional-cognitive schemes of Western culture. Finally, Gregor Thuswaldner analyzes the position of religion in Haneke's cinema. Paying particular attention to Haneke's interest in Pascal and Jansenism, Thuswaldner analyzes Haneke's attempts to thematize the crisis of faith and the disempowered, outmoded, or impotent status of organized religion without giving up on faith altogether.

Part II of this volume is devoted to a more specifically focused discussion of Haneke's television films. The first contribution is by Fatima Naqvi, whose extensive writings on Haneke I have already drawn on in this introduction. Her essay "A Melancholy Labor of Love, or Film Adaptation as Translation: *Three Paths to the Lake*" uses Walter Benjamin's essay, "The Task of the Translator," to develop a theory of adaptations that wrests the figure of melancholia from its implications of dysfunction and reads it as a vital component of the dialectical modernism of Haneke's adaptation of Bachmann's prose text. Peter Brunette discusses the central themes of *Lemmings* both in relation to Haneke's later theatrical features and with regard to the limitations imposed by television's aesthetics and its mode of production. Television as a mode of production is also a focus of analysis for Monica Filimon and Fatima Naqvi's essay, "Variation on Themes: Spheres and Space in Haneke's *Variation*." The authors analyze the film as Haneke's attempt to use television to create a public sphere for the viewer who is normally conceived of as an insulated, privatized consumer. Tobias Nagl's essay on *Fraulein* places Haneke's representation on gender in relation to the film's dual focus on German history and German film history. Nagl's discussion of *Fraulein*'s film historical reflexivity dovetails with Janelle Blankenship's discussion of Haneke's adaptation of Peter Rosei's novel *Wer war Edgar Allan?*. In addition to discussing the film's generally meta-cinematic qualities, Blankenship reads some of its key visual tropes, such as the moving image representation of a galloping horse, as Haneke's attempt to place the novel's treatment of deception and phantasmagoria in relation to an archaeology of the cinema. Brian Price's detailed analysis of the tracking shots of *The Castle* argues that these shots not only constitute the film's structural conjunctions, but that, as deconstructive allegories of bureaucracy and state power, they mine the philosophical potential of inbetweenness and provide an implicit corrective to teleologically informed political theories of the state.

Part III of the book, which focuses on Haneke's German-language theatrical features, begins with a translation of German film critic Georg Seeßlen's essay "Structures of Glaciation." Seeßlen was the first critic to proffer a comprehensive analysis of the formal and thematic components of Haneke's glaciation trilogy. The essay's great acumen and concise format make it one of the cornerstones of Haneke scholarship and an indispensable teaching tool for lecture classes and seminars on Haneke's films and on film aesthetics in general. With a particular focus on *The Seventh Continent* and *Benny's Video*, Peter J. Schwartz discusses the glaciation trilogy's focus on the bourgeois subject, whose precarious status was already acknowledged in the very moment of its construction in Renaissance painting and literature, and which he sees critically commented on by what he terms Haneke's hieroglyphs of identity. Situating Haneke's representation of violence within a critique of film theory's overreliance on Platonic philosophy, Eugenie Brinkema argues that violence in Haneke's work should not be approached in terms of representational content, but predominantly in terms of form. Drawing on the work of Jean-Luc Nancy, Brinkema analyzes *Benny's Video* as an exemplar of the "deployment" of violence that can be more productively read in relation to registers of affect rather than to representations of reality.

The last two essays in this section read the German-language features in relation to Haneke's evolving body of work. My own essay compares the final installment of the trilogy, *71 Fragments of a Chronology of Chance*, with Haneke's first French-language film, *Code Unknown*. I discuss these two multistrain narrative films in relation to two philosophers of the fragment, Theodor W. Adorno and Jean-François Lyotard. Appraising Haneke's complex position between modernism and postmodernism, I argue that Haneke's approach to *71 Fragments*, while broadly inspired by Adorno's *Aesthetic Theory*, more concretely engages his late writing on film. Haneke's engagement with Adorno then finds its intriguing companion piece in *Code Unknown*, which I discuss towards the end of the essay in relation to Lyotard's theory of agonistic linguistic struggle and the impossibility of social justice, put forth in *Le Différend*. Leland Monk's essay, "Hollywood Endgames," compares Haneke's post-glaciation trilogy film *Funny Games* with its American remake. Monk compares both films' deployment of iconographic signifiers of middle-class status (house, car, family dog), as well as their respective representations of the couple. He argues that, while the remake somehow attenuates the rhetorical force of the original's Brechtian devices (such as the breaking of the fourth wall), its deployment and subsequent violation of more conventional cinematic and generic codes are more successful.

Part IV of the book focuses on Haneke's French-language features. Barton Byg analyzes *Code Unknown* for the broader significance of one of the film's iconographic scenes – the assault scene in the Paris metro – which he juxtaposes with comparable examples in two other films that likewise single out mass transportation as a rich site for the clash of diverse existences in the modern urban space. Alex Lykidis widens a discussion of volatile scenarios of diversity in his analysis of the representation of multiculturalism in *Code Unknown*, *Time of the Wolf*, and *Caché*. Lykidis reads these films specifically against the history of French immigration laws since the early 1960s. He also argues that, while Haneke's identification of the gradually diminishing role of the state in the protection of white French citizenry constitutes an implicit critique of the universalist ideology of the white bourgeois subject, this critique does not abrogate universalism but is limited to the self-reflexive foregrounding of it. In contrast to this reasoning, Kevin L. Stoehr reads *Code Unknown* and *Caché* as evidence of Haneke's hermeneutic-minded perspectivism, which advocates a potentially open-ended discourse ethics that stresses dialog over teleological notions of the universal and of consensus. Two essays in this section are devoted to *The Piano Teacher*. Drawing on Stanley Cavell's critical trope of the unknown woman, Charles Warren reads the film as a fascinating intertextual web of references to the actresses of high modernist European art cinema and the characters they embodied in such films as *Cries and Whispers* (Ingmar

Bergman, 1972) and *The Silence* (Ingmar Bergman, 1963). Jean Ma's essay, "Discordant Desires, Violent Refrains: *La Pianiste* (*The Piano Teacher*)," originally published in *Grey Room*, lucidly combines a feminist discussion of the radical potential of the protagonist's sexual practices with an assessment of the film's deployment of high modernist classical music. Evan Torner discusses *Time of the Wolf* as a response to the genre of the post-apocalyptic film. Paying close attention to the film's refutation of heroism and its anti-teleological narrative, Torner joins the contributors in this volume who argue that Haneke, rather than totally rejecting generic conventions, engages them for his own purposes. The final essay in this section is devoted to *Caché*. T. Jefferson Kline analyzes the film's intertextual foregrounding of what he terms the discursive origins of terror. He reads the film's oblique referencing of the October 17, 1962 massacre of Algerians by the Parisian police in relation to discourses of violence and victimization in *The Song of Roland* and Camus's *The Stranger*.

The final section of this book, entitled "Michael Haneke Speaks," is comprised of four texts – two essays that have been authored by Haneke himself and that appear for the first time in unabridged English translation, as well as two interviews conducted with Haneke. Haneke's views on filmmaking, film aesthetics, and the representation of violence are articulated in his two essays, "Terror and Utopia of Form: Robert Bresson's *Au hasard Balthazar*" and "Violence and the Media." While these texts also reveal some of Haneke's lacunae and biases, their publication is meant to place these views in productive tension with the critical essays in the preceding sections. Christopher Sharrett's interview, "The World That Is Known," is one of the most extensive conversations conducted with Haneke in English and features the director's views on many of the topics that are explored in the scholarly essays of this book. My own interview with Haneke was conducted with a specific focus on *The White Ribbon*, but it also seeks to explore larger questions with regard to Haneke's body of work.

Notes

1   This list counts the two parts of *Lemmings* (1979), *Arcadia* and *Injuries*, as two separate films and also includes the non-narrative, but feature-length television collage, *Obituary for a Murderer* (1991). To this list may be added another work, Haneke's contribution to the omnibus film *Lumière and Company* (1995). Haneke also wrote two screenplays for films directed by Paulus Manker, *Schmutz* (Dirt) (1985) and *Der Kopf des Mohren* (The Moor's Head) (1995).

2   *After Liverpool* is one of two Haneke films I have not been able to see (the other one is *Sperrmüll* [Trash], 1975). However, Horwath's description indicates Haneke's sharp sense for analyzing the dynamics by which the radical aspirations of the 1960s turned into private dysfunctions when the radicals reverted back to their bourgeois identities in the 1970s. Many of Haneke's later films feature post-radical protagonists, such as the parents in *Benny's Video* (1992), whose liberalism masks their selfishness

and lack of interest in their son. With regard to *After Liverpool,* Horwath also points to the film's (and the play's) transposition of personal dysfunction onto the linguistic level. Characteristically, Haneke's later films would likewise seize on language usage to express broader structural problems.

3   For a good summary of the academic discourse on national cinema, see Elsaesser (2005: 64–7, 77). For a recent attempt to theorize national cinema, see the essays in Hjort and MacKenzie (2000) and in Vitali and Willemen (2006).

4   Of course, made-for-TV films, too, must be divided along a range of subcategories. Haneke, for example, never made anything that was less than feature-film length, nor was he involved in serial production. He did, however, write a treatment for an episode of the popular German crime serial *Tatort* (the term can be translated as "Crime Scene") in the early 1990s. The show has a hybrid character in that its episodes are feature-length and have the status of autonomous films with fairly high production values. Production of the show is divided up among Germany's regional networks, with each station putting a particular cultural stamp on its own episodes, including a regionally specific location, investigative team or detective-protagonist, and particular script writers and directors. Haneke wrote an elaborate story treatment involving the series' most popular protagonist, Inspector Schimanski. The treatment, which Haneke did not get to direct, but for which he received a writing credit, involved a criminal incident in a nuclear power plant and, thus, reflects Haneke's interest in apocalyptic aspects of modernity already evident in *Lemmings*, Part Two, where one of the characters, the army officer, attends training sessions involving a secret nuclear arms project. Haneke's interest in writing an episode for *Tatort* reflects his view that television, unlike film, is not a medium of art but of mass communication and entertainment. Hence, the status of popular genres such as the crime thriller and the *policier* should be used to raise social consciousness about such problems as nuclear energy and armaments. But the show had further appeal because of the character of the inspector. Schimanski is played by famous German stage actor Heinrich George's son, Goetz George, who became one of Germany's biggest domestic TV stars, and who started his career in German popular films of the 1960s. Haneke has thus always understood the popular appeal of stars, but by writing this part for George and by casting well-known older German filmmakers and actors such as Bernard Wicki in his other films, Haneke can be said to have emulated Fassbinder's effort to use his own films to construct a dialog with German film history.

5   The intricate system of film subsidies has been discussed by numerous scholars of the period. For detailed accounts, see Jan Dawson (1980/81), Thomas Elsaesser (1989), and Collins and Porter (1981).

6   At this point in his career, Haneke began to regard his TV productions more systematically as underappreciated and unacknowledged works of the cinema. In an unusual and ultimately unsuccessful move, Haneke sought post-broadcast theatrical exhibition for *Who Was Edgar Allan?*. See correspondence between distributor Hans Peter Hofmann, whose distribution company expressed interest in distributing the film, and August Schedl of Austrian Film Fund, April 20, 1984. Haneke Archive, Austrian Film Museum, Vienna.

7   For a discussion of the significance of ethics as a textual component and in the spectatorial address of Haneke's films, see Wheatley (2009).

8   Haneke's early 1970s engagements alone constitute an impressive array of directo-
    rial projects: he directed Marguerite Duras's *Whole Days in the Trees* in Baden-Baden
    (the seat of SWF, his TV employer); in Darmstadt he directed, among other works,
    Heinrich von Kleist's *The Broken Jug*; in Düsseldorf Friedrich Hebbel's *Maria Magdalena*
    and August Strindberg's *The Father*. Later, his career expanded to other German cities
    and theaters. In Berlin he directed Ferdinand Bruckner's *Krankheit der Jugend* (Illness
    of Youth), in Hamburg Per Olov Enquist's *The Night of the Tribades*, and in Vienna
    Johann Wolfgang von Goethe's *Stella* (Horwath 1991: 16). It becomes apparent that
    many of the themes of these plays find their way into Haneke's films.

9   At the same time, the status of star director, state-funded agent provocateur, or enfant
    terrible also eluded Haneke in the theater. To this we must add, however, that German
    theater was an even more specialized, secluded scene than the New German Cinema,
    boasting extremely few publicly and nationally recognized auteurs (one of the few
    exceptions is Peter Zadek).

10 Like Fassbinder, he would convey his admiration for a role model (in Fassbinder's
    case, Sirk; in Haneke's, Bresson) in an essay (reprinted in this volume). But unlike
    Wenders or Godard, he would not cast an internationally recognized cult director
    in his films; unlike Schlöndorff, he had no apprenticeship with one of the greats (Louis
    Malle); unlike Kluge, he did not have a personal friendship with Adorno.

11 However, as Fatima Naqvi has pointed out to me, it is because Haneke's films show
    the structuring effects of this paternal absence that they come across as ambivalently
    patriarchal.

12 The screenplay for *The Seventh Continent* was commissioned by Radio Bremen, a north
    German network. After Haneke submitted it, the network rejected it because it
    contained "too many deaths for television." Around the same time, the Austrian Film
    Institute encouraged Haneke to make a theatrical feature, which became *The Seventh
    Continent*. Correspondence with Ulrike Lässer of Wega Film, Thursday, August 6,
    2009, to whom Haneke has recounted the circumstances of the making of the film.

13 The production company with which Haneke has most frequently and closely col-
    laborated is Wega Film in Vienna. It was founded by Veit Heiduschka in 1980 and
    is a highly typical example of what Thomas Elsaesser has identified as the "post-Fordist"
    model of European cinema production, which is based on a small-scale production
    unit that is usually run by a director and a producer and that closely cooperates
    with television as well as commercial funding partners. These companies, of which
    Lars von Trier's Zentropa Films is another example, have a national base but seek
    global investors and European Union funding (2005: 69) in accordance with a film's
    production profile. The influence of Heiduschka on Haneke's films and, ultimately,
    on his development as an auteur of Austrian and trans-Austrian films cannot be
    overstated. Heiduschka has had one foot in the arts and one in commerce. He encour-
    aged Haneke to make the aesthetics of his first theatrical feature more severe and
    stringent and also, as a sales pitch more than out of artistic considerations, encour-
    aged him to develop his thematic area of glaciation into a trilogy. Heiduschka has
    for some time assumed a central role in Austrian cinema. He has been the President
    of the Austrian Film Commission, the Vice-President of the Association of Austrian
    Film and Video Producers, and Austria's official representative in the negotiations
    for the foundation of European funding and administrative structures for audiovisual

culture. For more detailed information, see Willy Riemer's highly informative interview with Heiduschka (Riemer 2000: 62).

14 For *Three Paths to the Lake*, see *Abendzeitung München*, n.d., *St. Pöltner Kirchenzeitung*, n.d., *Salzburger Nachrichten*, n.d., *Kurier*, n.d., and *Neues Volksblatt*, n.d. For *Who Was Edgar Allan?* see *Die Presse*, n.d., *Süddeutsche Zeitung*, 14.01.1986, *Die Welt*, 14.01.1986, *Abendzeitung München*, n.d. For *The Rebellion*, see *Süddeutsche Zeitung*, 13.01.1994, *Wiesbadener Kurier*, 13.01.1994, *Westfälische Rundschau*, 13.01.1994, *Abendzeitung München*, 13.01.1994. Please note that only reviews that have either at least an identifiable date or identifiable author appear in the bibliography. For a convenient compilation of these reviews, visit the Haneke Film Archive, Austrian Film Museum, Vienna.

15 In their German context, literary adaptations were considered a tedious playing-it-safe gesture on the part of filmmakers, a sign of their lack of imagination and creativity. In some corners, they were also considered a sign of an increasing political conservatism (Elsaesser 1989: 108) that was part of an anti-liberal groundswell in the Federal Republic of Germany, prompted by the failure of the state and state-funded cultural institutions, as well as of the political left in general, to proffer convincing responses to the challenges of the urban guerrilla movement.

16 However, this reasoning needs to apply a larger view to the retroactive scope that determines the project of claiming Haneke for Austrian national culture. At the time of Horwath's writing, *The Rebellion* had not yet been made, and *Who Was Edgar Allan?*, while arguably presenting its student protagonist as a critical-deconstructive allegory of the Austrian notion of nation-as-victim, also significantly transcends a specific Austrian national context, given its "American Friend"-type story. Yet, if one considers the critical project of retroactive construction as an ongoing one, Haneke's literary adaptations of the 1990s have, if anything, confirmed its purpose.

17 Piloui (2007), particularly 34–7. Cited in Naqvi (2009).

18 Fatima Naqvi characterizes this historiographic trope as "telescopage," based on Sigrid Weigel (1999).

19 Haneke has explicitly tried to subvert this context with *Variation* and *Obituary for a Murderer*. In each case, his experimentation on the level of form is conducted to address the spectator as part of a public whose mode of reception he assumes to be overdetermined by privatization, passivity, and consumerism. *Variation* seeks to redress this perceived problem by giving viewers the sense they may be in dialog with the film. On this, see Monica Filimon's and Fatima Naqvi's essay in this volume. *Obituary for a Murderer* is a dada-like collage (one may call it TV graffiti) of clips of entertainment and news shows that aims to make viewers realize their habits of media consumption and that, in its own way, attempts to reach into the private sphere of TV consumption through a neo-dadaist deployment of tactile attack.

20 The title of the film is doubly ironic. It references the German diminutive form of the female formal address, "Frau," which is now considered sexist but, up until the 1970s, was used for young women and for any unmarried woman. The film's title thus rhetorically negates Johanna's status as a married woman on multiple levels (prior to her husband's return, she might have been considered widowed, but the address also alludes to women's newly gained independence during and after the war). Second, the missing umlaut above the "a" mimics the pronunciation of the

word by American GIs and thus places Johanna's female discourse within the context of postwar American occupation, even if her lover in the film is a former French
prisoner of war.

21   While the film has been deemed a failure in its intended attack on Fassbinder's
The Marriage of Maria Braun (Fassbinder's film is as demystificatory of its female
protagonist and her era as Haneke's), Haneke's Johanna may in some respect
also be compared to the protagonist of Brecht's *St. Joan of the Slaughterhouses*.

22   Naqvi (2009: 170) characterizes the film's presentation of Trotta as the result of a
"multiperspektivischen Bilderpolitik," a multiperspectival politics of images.

23   In this comparison, *Lemmings* assumes a twin position: while the depiction of malaise
of Haneke's generation on an iconographic level transcends national boundaries (in
both parts, the setting is small-town Western Europe, the iconographic markers being
those of postwar prosperity, American pop culture, and bourgeois lifestyle), it is fair
to say that the first part moves within a frame of reference that is at least intended
as specifically Austrian – consider especially the foregrounding of the stark discrepancy between a stubborn adherence to rigid nineteenth-century religious values and
its disorientation amidst twentieth-century mass culture.

24   See, for example, Naqvi (2007), Metelmann (2003), and some of the essays in
Wessely et al. (2008).

25   Citing Noël Burch, Bordwell emphasizes that film, because it remains beholden to
representational content, cannot be organized as rigorously as music (1985: 278), but
that it can downplay content in favor of structure, while keeping the films cognitively manageable for the viewer (284).

26   Bordwell's summary of art cinema can likewise be found in *Narration in the Fiction
Film* (1985: 206–13).

27   Ironically, if one compares Haneke's television films to the pared-down formal
structure of the glaciation trilogy, the former are more overtly art films in theme and
style: *Three Paths to the Lake* features the classic art cinema event of the protagonist
facing a crisis of existential significance, conveyed by "flash frames of glimpes or
recalled events" (Bordwell 1985: 209); *Who Was Edgar Allan?* and *The Castle* take the
labyrinthine maze as a diegetic and formal trope; and *Lemmings* and *Variation*, while
more realist in style, are excessively concerned with the "discursive treatment of
characters' feelings" (ibid.). It is, of course, possible to see the shift from TV to
theatrical features in teleological terms. But apart from the fact that such a view
plays into dominant narratives of artistic advancement, it fails to account for how
the parametric format retains some of the aesthetic qualities of television, such as
the plain, "dirty" look of the images.

28   This theme is already implanted in the bitter irony of the subtitle of the first part of
Haneke's early TV drama, *Lemmings: Arcadia*. It refers to a region in Greece which
acquired the mythological connotation of a carefree natural idyll populated by
shepherds. This myth stands in ironic contrast to postwar Austrian society, which
Haneke depicts as repressed and deformed, and which commits an ethical betrayal
of its young. The irony is carried further by the film's plot, which includes a highly
illicit affair between a high school student and the wife of his teacher, whom he tenderly calls "shepherdess." When she becomes pregnant by him, society's oppressive
nature pushes her into an illegal and highly risky attempt to abort her child. In the

film's second part, *Injuries*, the sins of the parental generation have been fully visited on the children, who now are plagued by injuries, but also inflict these on one another.

29   The reasoning in this part of the discussion is indebted to Thomas Elsaesser's essay, "British Television in the 1980s: Through the Looking Glass," reprinted in Elsaesser (2005: 278–98), which was written in 1990 and first published as "TV Through the Looking Glass" in Browne (1993: 97–120). I am aware of the specificities Elsaesser outlines for British television's shift in the imaginary, but believe that part of his characterization of Channel 4 can be applied to the situation of German and Austrian television a few years after the publication of his essay in 1990.

30   This relation merits further discussion. For my initial observations, see Grundmann (2007: 9).

31   It might initially appear that the mosaic of regional networks in Germany has somewhat anticipated this development. But one needs to keep in mind that regional broadcasting in Germany is rooted in the federalist political philosophy of West Germany, whose internally diverse parts are nonetheless oriented towards the nation as the largest unifying body.

32   The moderator featured in the excerpt is identifiable as Désirée Nosbusch, who had appeared on RTL radio as a show hostess at a very young age, then became cultivated by German public television as a teenage show hostess, emcee, and quiz master, and, in the 1980s, became one of the best-known TV personalities on the continent. Widely admired for her multilingual talent, she became the prototype for the cosmopolitan teenage show host that was soon seized on by television stations in their efforts to remain attractive to young audiences. Nosbusch not only worked for state-funded TV in the 1980s but also became a popular freelancer. Her success epitomizes the commercialization of television and its turn to youth culture during the 1980s and 1990s. For detailed information, see de.wikipedia.org/wiki/Desiree_Nosbusch (accessed October 22, 2009).

33   The film was part of the EPG (European Production Community) and its series "The Europeans," which included as participating networks Austrian Television (ORF), ZDF (Second German Television), France 2, Channel 4 in Britain, RAI Uno of Italy, TVE of Spain, SSR of Switzerland, and Greek Television. See *Wiener Zeitung*, January 11, 1992.

34   For a critique of the nexus of Haneke's Europeanness, the tradition of art cinema, and cultural elitism, see Rosalind Galt (2010).

35   And, thus, sustaining what Daniel Dayan (1997) has characterized as a festival's sense of its own significance and self-importance, cited in Elsaesser (2005).

36   I am borrowing the term "cognitive switch" from Thomas Elsaesser's essay in this volume.

37   Haneke's statement appears in an interview with Scott Foundas, "Michael Haneke: The Bearded Prophet of *Code inconnu* and *The Piano Teacher*." Haneke's statement has been criticized by Rosalind Galt, who argues that Haneke's polemicizing against Hollywood distracts from his own hegemonic Eurocentric perspective.

38   Jelinek told Stefan Grissemann and Christiane Zintzen that she would certainly have had the opportunity to write the screenplay herself, but declined to do so. Haneke originally wrote the screenplay as a commission for another director, but then ended up directing the film himself. However, years before the new adaptation came to

pass, Jelinek had, in fact, collaborated on a screen adaptation together with Austrian avant-garde filmmaker and video artist Valie Export, whose project was then canceled by Austrian National Television (ORF), because an earlier Jelinek adaptation had been too controversial. In the same interview, Jelinek acknowledges that there are a thousand ways in which the novel can be adapted and that Export's version would have been very different from Haneke's. It would have been more artificial and, thus, more removed from the novel's autobiographical elements. Jelinek makes clear that she very much respects Haneke's film, but that watching it is a more personal experience for her (2001: 126).

39   As Stefan Grissemann puts it in his interview with Jelinek, Haneke almost seems to be in love with Klemmer. The director's defense of the character is an attempt to shape the relationship Erika / Walter into a dynamic that can be mined for the cinema (Jelinek 2001: 132).

40   Jelinek herself has stated that Erika and her suffering seem more glamorous in the film and that the film gives the character back her integrity, which she had forfeited. With regard to the autobiographical components of the material, Jelinek thus claims that the film has in some ways constituted a salvation of her own person (Jelinek 2001: 132).

41   It is at this point that a split can be perceived within feminism as to what strategies to adopt in response to patriarchy's multi-level oppression of women. While Erika's self-stabbing echoes an earlier feminism rooted in structuralism and abject art that is associated with Jelinek's generation, more recent feminists might want to invoke Audre Lorde's argument that the master's tools never dismantle the master's house and, instead, invest in postmodern-inflected responses. On the other hand, it might be possible to claim that the less-than-lethal nature of Erika's self-stabbing precisely constitutes this second kind of response, if one were to argue that the infliction of injury, if authored and controlled by the oppressed female subject herself, differs categorically from any use of violence inflicted by men.

42   Bernard Wicki played the father in Lemmings, Part One, and Trotta's cousin at the end of Three Paths to the Lake. Doris Kunstmann played a sailing guest during a fleeting visit of the family's jetty in Funny Games. Anne Bennent played the mother who seeks to adopt first Anni then Marian in 71 Fragments.

43   Galt's observation that Haneke's mise-en-scène points to the instability of Europe's political borders corresponds to Elsaesser's observation that much of contemporary European cinema is marked by depictions of multiple parties' physical, cultural, and spiritual claims onto one and the same space – a phenomenon he terms "double occupancy" (2005: 109).

44   Hollywood director Ron Howard has allegedly sought to option the rights to remake Caché.

45   Rosalind Galt (2010).

References and Further Reading

Assheuer, Thomas: *Michael Haneke: Gespräche mit Thomas Assheuer* (Berlin: Alexander Verlag, 2008).
Böbbis, Peter: "Das Fest der leisen Töne," *Die Welt*, January 14, 1986.

Bordwell, David: *Narration in the Fiction Film* (London: Methuen; Madison, WI: University of Wisconsin Press, 1985).

Browne, Nick, ed.: *American Television* (Langhorne, PA: Harwood, 1993).

Collins, Richard and Porter, Vincent: *WDR and the Arbeiterfilm* (London: British Film Institute, 1981).

Dargis, Manohla: "Violence Reaps Rewards at Cannes Film Festival," *The New York Times*, May 24, 2009.

Dawson, Jan: "A Labyrinth of Subsidies," *Sight and Sound* (Winter 1980/81): 14–20.

Dayan, Daniel: "In Quest of a Festival (Sundance Film Festival)," *National Forum*, September 22, 1997.

Elmerich, Ilse: "Der Kommentar: Spurensuche," *St. Pöltner Kirchenzeitung*, n.d.

Elsaesser, Thomas: *European Cinema: Face to Face with Hollywood* (Amsterdam: Amsterdam University Press, 2005).

Elsaesser, Thomas: *New German Cinema: A History* (New Brunswick, NJ: Rutgers University Press, 1989).

Foundas, Scott, with Haneke, Michael: "Michael Haneke: The Bearded Prophet of *Code inconnu* and *The Piano Teacher*," *Indiewire* (December 4, 2001), www.indiewire.com/ article/interview_michael_haneke_the_bearded_prophet_of_code_inconnu_and_the_ piano1/.

Galt, Rosalind: "The Functionary of Mankind: Michael Haneke and Europe," *On Michael Haneke*, ed. John David Rhodes and Brian Price (Detroit: Wayne State University Press, 2010).

Gilroy, Paul: "Shooting Crabs in a Barrel," *Screen* 48:2 (Summer 2007; special dossier on *Caché*): 233–5.

Görzel, Klaus: "TV Kritik: Mut zum Schweigen," *Westfälische Rundschau*, January 13, 1994.

Grissemann, Stefan: "In zwei, drei feinen Linien die Badewannenwand entlang: Kunst, Utopie und Selbstbeschmutzung: zu Michael Haneke's Jelinek-Adaption," *Haneke: Jelinek: Die Klavierspielerin: Drehbuch, Gespräche, Essays*, ed. Stefan Grissemann (Vienna: Sonderzahl, 2001), pp. 11–32.

Grundmann, Roy: "Auteur de Force: Michael Haneke's 'Cinema of Glaciation'," *Cineaste* 33:2 (Spring 2007): 6–14.

Hillgruber, Kathrin: "Schlafendes Herz: Die Rebellion (ZDF)," *Süddeutsche Zeitung*, January 13, 1994.

Hjort, Mette and MacKenzie, Scott, eds.: *Cinema and Nation* (London and New York: Routledge, 2000).

Horwath, Alexander: "Die Ungeheuerliche Kränkung, die das Leben ist: Zu den Filmen von Michael Haneke," *Der Siebente Kontinent: Michael Haneke und seine Filme*, ed. Alexander Horwath (Vienna: Europaverlag, 1991), pp. 11–39.

Jelinek, Elfriede: ". . . dass dieser Film auch eine Rettung meiner Person ist: Christiane Zintzen und Stefan Grissemann im Gespräch mit Elfriede Jelinek," *Haneke: Jelinek: Die Klavierspielerin: Drehbuch, Gespräche, Essays*, ed. Stefan Grissemann (Vienna: Sonderzahl, 2001), pp. 119–36.

Kaes, Anton: *From Hitler to Heimat: The Return of History as Film* (Cambridge, MA, and London: Harvard University Press, 1989).

Kathrein, Karin: "Kunst ist Beschreibung von Krise: Gespräch mit dem Theater- und Filmregisseur Michael Haneke," *Die Presse*, n.d.

Kramberg, K. H.: "Schwarze Romantik: *Wer War Edgar Allan?*," *Süddeutsche Zeitung*, January 14, 1986.

Lange, Hellmut A.: "Sternstunde des Programs," *Wiesbadener Kurier*, January 13, 1994.

Metelmann, Jörg: "Die Autonomie, das Tragische: Über die Kehre im Kinowerk von Michael Haneke," *Michael Haneke und seine Filme: Eine Pathologie der Konsumgesellschaft*, ed. Christian Wessely, Franz Grabner, and Gerhard Larcher (Marburg: Schüren, 2008), pp. 113–30.

Metelmann, Jörg: *Zur Kritik der Kino-Gewalt: Die Filme von Michael Haneke* (Munich: Wilhelm Fink Verlag, 2003).

n.a.: *"Die Rebellion,"* *Abendzeitung München*, January 13, 1994.

n.a.: "Michael Haneke verfilmt Joseph Roth: Ein 'naiver Jasager' rebelliert," *Wiener Zeitung*, January 11, 1992.

Naqvi, Fatima: "Postimperiale und postnationale Konstellationen in den Filmen Michael Hanekes," *Österreich 1918 und die Folgen: Geschichte, Literatur, Theater und Film*, ed. Karl Müller and Hans Wagener (Vienna: Böhlau, 2009), pp. 165–78.

Naqvi, Fatima: *The Literary and Cultural Rhetoric of Victimhood: Western Europe, 1970–2005* (New York: Palgrave Macmillan, 2007).

Piloui, Rares G.: "Joseph Roth and Austro-Marxism," *Modern Austrian Literature* 40:3 (2007): 21–42.

Ponkie: "Flucht vor der Stille," *Abendzeitung München*, n.d.

Rentschler, Eric: *West German Film in the Course of Time* (New York: Redgrave Publishing, 1984).

Riemer, Willy: "Producer's Challenge: Art and Commerce: Veit Heiduschka (Wega-Film)," *After Postmodernism: Austrian Literature and Film in Transition*, ed. Willy Riemer (Riverside, CA: Ariadne Press, 2000), pp. 62–7.

Shaviro, Steven: The Pinocchio Theory, *Caché*, www.shaviro.com/Blog/?p=476.

Vitali, Valentina and Willemen, Paul, eds.: *Theorising National Cinema* (London: BFI Publishing, 2006).

Weigel, Sigrid: "Telescopage im Unbewussten: Zum Verhältnis von Trauma, Geschichtsbegriff und Literatur," *Trauma. Zwischen Psychoanalyse und kulturellem Deutungsmuster*, ed. Elisabeth Bronfen and Sigrid Weigel (Vienna: Böhlau, 1999), pp. 51–76.

Wessely, Christian, Grabner, Franz, and Larcher, Gerhard, eds.: *Michael Haneke und seine Filme: Eine Pathologie der Konsumgesellschaft* (Marburg: Schüren, 2008).

Wheatley, Catherine: *Michael Haneke's Cinema: The Ethic of the Image* (Oxford and New York: Berghahn Books, 2009).

PART I

Critical and Topical Approaches to Haneke's Cinema

1

Performative Self-Contradictions
Michael Haneke's Mind Games

Thomas Elsaesser

Writing about Michael Haneke has been a learning curve, mostly about how to deal with the ambivalence his films invariably provoke. Far from having been able to resolve the sense of being divided, discomfited, and often on the verge of disgust, my mixed feelings about his films have deepened, though not without a twist: Haneke also took me into directions and places of the contemporary experience that were as much a discovery as they were unsettling. Before I began, my view was roughly as follows: shock and awe after seeing *Caché* (2005), intrigued and interested by *Code Unknown* (2000), uneasy and queasy about *The Piano Teacher* (2001), repelled and exasperated by *Funny Games* (1997) and *Benny's Video* (1992), and not a little bored by *71 Fragments* (1994) and *The Seventh Continent* (1989). After reseeing these (and a few other) films and letting them do their disturbing work, my ambivalences, initially targeting the director, started to shift to the world he depicts, and then to the filmic means he deploys. Now I feel I have come full circle, but emerged on the other side: Focused first on the messenger, and then on the message, my doubts ended up being directed at the recipient: me, the spectator. As Haneke might put it: case proved.

Haneke and Film Philosophy

Haneke's films, I want to argue, exhibit to the point of possible contradiction, but they also expose, to the point of celebrating the resulting deadlocks, the pitfalls of an epistemological conception of the cinema. At the same time, and unlike others who have also voiced doubts about the cinema's inherent realism, Haneke does not embrace a phenomenological perspective. His films play with, but do not endorse, the cinema's purported truth claims, usually made by pointing to photography as the basis of indexical evidence ("photographic realism"), or appealing to ocular verification and human observation ("scientific realism"): both would full under what I call the *epistemological* position. An *ontological* position – arguably attributable to Siegfried Kracauer, Gilles Deleuze, and Stanley Cavell – would contend that the cinema's unique strength is to rescue the every-day, by redeeming the mundane and recognizing a place for contingency in human affairs. But cinema can also restore to us our "belief in the world," by the paradoxical affirmation that the meaninglessness of things (as they appear to the mechanical eye which is the camera) may actually be our best hope: not for making sense of, but for giving sense *to* our lives. This, too, would be an unlikely position for Haneke to hold, considering his grim view on contingency and chance (of which more later). According to the *phenomenological* position, finally, the cinema provides the consciousness and knowledge of the world, but not by concentrating on the look, the gaze, the mirror-phase, or locking the subject into a panoptic prison of vision and visuality.[1] Instead, phenomenology espouses a more holistic approach, extending vision beyond the disembodied eye and conceiving of an "embodied" and active consciousness, at work in the filmic experience, which in turn gives new value to touch, contact, skin, and the material body of cinema: tactile sensations and haptic vision, the accent or grain of the voice and of the video signal, the interactive, immersive potential of digital images.

Little of this seems at first to apply to Haneke's work and yet, how can it not? Up until the critical success of *Caché*, the difficulty in placing his films in the current debates tended to polarize the film critical community. Those interested in the philosophical aspects of contemporary cinema have only begun to engage with his work, whether negatively or positively.[2] As a consequence, Haneke's reputation has tended to align his admirers, as well as steer the discussion about his films, along classically auteurist lines.[3] A little too conveniently, perhaps, a European, state-funded, high-culture director-as-artist pronounces himself – ex cathedra, via interviews, and ex opera, through the message extrapolated from his films – on the prevailing evils of the world, namely, lack of meaningful interpersonal com-munication, coldness between marital partners, neglect by parents of their children. In interviews, Haneke also tends to denounce media trivialization and Hollywood violence, often with the implication that the former (coldness and indifference of the world) is caused by the latter (Americanization and the mass media).[4]

Elsewhere, I have tried to argue that attributing such a representative function to the "author" risks doing a disservice to European cinema in a globalized film culture, besides joining prejudice with complacency vis-à-vis the American cin-ema and so-called "Americanization."[5] In other words, were I to judge by these criteria alone, I would be hard put to justify to myself why I should be writing about Haneke. And yet, his recent, notably the French-made, films seem to be on the cusp of something else that intrigues me sufficiently to revisit my prejudices. For instance, I detect an auto-critique of Haneke's so often confidently asserted moral high ground, and of his forthright – some might say misanthropic – positions as a European auteur. With a Protestant father and a Catholic mother, Haneke's private ethics of guilt does creative battle with a public imagination of shame. In the figure of the clumsy, alcoholic, faith-abandoned priest in *Lemmings* (1979) one senses the negative "Protestant" theology of Ingmar Bergman more strongly than the austere but redemptive Jansenism of Robert Bresson, with whom Haneke's moral universe has been compared.[6] I also read the film-within-the-film interrogation scene in *Code Unknown* ("show me your real face") as offering almost a pastiche of his early work, just as I see more of a self-portrait in the central character of *Caché* than his genealogy as yet another bourgeois "Georges" would at first seem to warrant. Indeed, there may be in *Caché* another auto-portrait of the director in the figure of the guest at the dinner party, telling a shaggy dog story about an old lady whom he reminded of her deceased dog: It not only foreshadows plot developments in *Caché* itself – the reference to a neck wound being the most obvious one – but it is also a moment of self-reference, in that it thematizes Haneke's own way with coincidence, predetermination, and their manipu-lation by a raconteur or storyteller, while harking back to a similarly spooky story in *Lemmings* about a dead canary, prompting the female lover listening to ask anxiously, "Is it true?," to which the man gives the revealingly ambiguous answer, "I think so." Finally, one senses in the French films that Haneke is perfectly aware of the possibility of paradox (or deadlock) in his position on "realism and truth," and that he has been exploring other strategies, notably those of the equally productive and equally contradictory notion of "game," which nonetheless might allow for a more properly philosophical grounding of his cinema (for the critics) and (for the filmmaker himself) might open his work up to a less dystopian view of a world irreversibly in the grip of media manipulation, and thus condemned to mendacity, deceit, and self-delusion.

The paradox I struggle with in Haneke's earlier work concerns above all his claim that one can "critique" violence through violence: In his interviews, the director suggests that by subjecting the spectator to witnessing, experiencing, or actively imagining acts of extreme violence, he can make him or her "aware" of the nefarious role that violence plays in our modern, media-saturated world. To me this is a dubious claim, and a contradictory one, on two grounds. Dubious, on what one might call didactic grounds: To "rape" an audience into enlighten-ment, or to educate someone by giving them "a slap in the face," seems to come from a rather peculiar corner of Germanic pedagogy that I thought we had no need to revive, either in schools or on the screen. Stanley Kubrick (and Anthony Burgess) called it the Ludovico Treatment – after Ludwig van Beethoven, whose Ninth Symphony is used as a Pavlovian aversion therapy – and in this respect at least, Haneke reminds me of Alex, not the young thug but the liberal writer in *A Clockwork Orange* (Stanley Kubrick, 1971), who, having been made to witness the rape and murder of his wife, retaliates by advocating this enlightened form of punishment, whose only flaw is to deprive the wrongdoer of his free will. It is an open question how serious Haneke is about his raping the audience, but to me his provocative formulations prove that he is very well aware of what a knot of contradictions he is potentially tying himself into. Yet even if he may be hoisting himself on his own petard, it still looks like he is determined to demonstrate both to his characters and to the audience that they are deprived of "free will." This is the second, more philosophical reason I have trouble with his position, but also find it fascinating. Haneke's stance on cinematic violence, no less than his views on chance and free will, involve what the discourse philosopher Karl Otto Apel would call a performative self-contradiction, a version of the conundrum better known as the liar's paradox: All Cretans are liars, says the Cretan.[7] Violence is bad for you, says the director who inflicts violence on me. But Haneke is also the control freak who likes to play games with chance and coincidence. Once formulated, the paradox becomes interesting, because it ties not only Haneke in knots, but also Haneke's critics, who risk putting themselves into a double bind, contradicting Haneke contradicting them.

In what follows I want to explore this idea of performative self-contradiction in Haneke, because I think his position – and not only his – relies on what I would call the "epistemological fallacy," that is, the often implicit assumption that the cinema is capable of making valid truth claims, while explicitly criticizing most films and filmmakers, notably mainstream directors, for failing to come up to these standards. The fallacy, in other words, puts the cinema on a pedestal, to better push its practitioners off theirs, compounded by the implication that the cinema is a virgin whom directors have turned into a whore, while audiences who love this whorish cinema are themselves depraved. Embedded in Haneke's negative judgment about today's cinema and its effects is an assumption beneath the assumption, constantly asserted but also constantly put in question: namely, that the cinema can be a vehicle for secure, grounded knowledge if only it is used in the "right" way. But even Bazin argued that the cinema's realism is real only to the extent that we believe in its reality. In fact, the epistemological fallacy is typical not so much of realist film theory, as it was proposed by advocates of neo-realism in the 1950s, as of the critiques of realist aesthetics as they have been voiced in ideological accounts and constructivist theories since the 1970s, when Bazin's theories, among others, were denounced as "naïve." Haneke, a filmmaker who came to artistic maturity in the 1970s, evidently shares this belief in "consciousness-raising": By forcing us to "see" something, he can make us "know" something, and by making us know something, we will be able to act accordingly, that is, for the betterment of ourselves and, by extension, of the world. But what if seeing does not lead to knowing, and knowing does not enable action? Sigmund Freud would have understood the problem, and Gilles Deleuze, in his analysis of the movement-image, provides historical as well as film-philosophical reasons why a cinema of consciousness-raising will remain a problematic proposition.[8]

One radical way of unraveling the double bind of self-contradiction in the epistemological fallacy would be to conceive of the cinema as something altogether different than a "realist" medium. Several philosophers, besides Deleuze, have tried to think this through: Jean-Luc Nancy, for instance, also chose to put the matter in the form of a contradiction: "the lie of the image is the truth of our world," elaborating around it a theory of "evidence," which for him is an ontological category rather than an epistemological one.[9] Or one might turn to another French philosopher, Alain Badiou, for whom "[i]t is the principle of the art of the cinema to show that it is only cinema, that its images only bear witness to the real insofar as they are manifestly images. It is not in turning away from appearance or in praising the virtual that you have a chance of attaining Ideas. It is in thinking appearance as appearance, and therefore as that, which from being, comes to appear, gives itself to thought as deception of vision."[10] In other words, Badiou, too, puts forward an "ontological" view of the cinema, where the inherent limits of vision, its dwelling in the realm of appearances, are the very grounds on which the cinema's realism can be justified.

Funny Games or Mind Games?

From an epistemological perspective, Haneke, it would seem, has painted himself into a corner, and nowhere more so than in *Funny Games*, which is said to confront us with our voyeurism, but does so by brutally exploiting it. However, in terms of the argument I am here advancing, *Funny Games* is disturbing mainly because of its own kind of performative self-contradiction, that is, the unusually wide gap between the subject of enunciation and the subject of the enunciated: a gap for which the concept of "lying" seems radically inadequate. Peter and Paul's jovially polite words, contrasted with their horrible acts, their constant invitation, bordering on reproachful admonition, to play along with the game and not be spoilsports, while clearly announcing the lethal stakes they intend to play for, instantiate such a purposeful discrepancy between words and actions, gesture and intent, that they constitute an extremely potent critique of the very model of consciousness-raising, with its chain of seeing, feeling, knowing, acting (what Deleuze would call the sensory-motor schema of the movement-image) that Haneke implicitly needs to appeal to in order to maintain his moral high ground. *Funny Games* in this respect is comparable to, but also the reverse of, *Pulp Fiction* (Quentin Tarantino, 1994), which operates a similar disjuncture, while retrieving it, making it bearable, thanks to the different function that chance and contingency play both within Tarantino's story-world and in the overall narrative trajectory, which famously jumbles chronology and causality, wrongfooting us in its own way into thinking that what we are seeing is actually a happy ending, when the opposite is the case (whatever "is the case" might mean). *Funny Games'* relentlessness and irreversibility – powerfully underscored by the impossible and impossibly ironic "rewind" – highlights the one-way contract that the film proposes to the viewer, rubbing it in that we wish for a happy ending but won't get one, not because that is the way life is, but because the director has decreed it so, letting chance in by the front door, as it were, only then to bolt all the doors and windows from the inside. On the other hand, because of these unresolved tensions between contingency and determinism, *Funny Games* seems to me interesting precisely insofar as it is symptomatic of a wider tendency in contemporary cinema – what I have elsewhere called "mind-game movies" – where a number of assumptions about how we understand what we see and hear in a film, as well as what comprises agency, are tested and renegotiated.[11]

My suggestion would be that besides *Funny Games*, *Code Unknown* and *Caché* also qualify as mind games, albeit in ways that would have to be further specified, for instance, with respect to agency and control. Their sado-masochistic under-tow of revenge and guilt calls for special comment, as does the manner in which the masters of the game in Haneke's films reveal themselves. Although *Funny Games* would seem to fit the mind-game mold almost too perfectly, *Code Unknown* and *Caché*, while intermittently playing their own sadistic games, also propose to us a more indeterminate or at least less deterministic way of thinking about the cinema's ontological and epistemological status, especially when Haneke reinvests in the notion of game and play, distinctly different from the games being played in *Funny Games*, and yet perhaps related nonetheless. If Haneke (mark I) comes across as an unreconstructed epistemological realist, Haneke (mark II) approximates an ontological realist, a position from which he both revises and rescues Haneke (mark I). Although I will not be able to fully substantiate these assertions about a possible "turn" in Haneke's work, I risk advancing this suggestion, not by rehearsing the classic themes of Haneke's work, but by using some of them to speculate on his cinema's ontological hesitations and cognitive switches, with their potential enfolding (or *Aufhebung*) in the idea of "frames" and "games."

Three Haneke Themes

There is widespread consensus about Haneke's principal themes, so I hope I will be forgiven for not speaking about "glaciation," "repression," Haneke's critique of middle-class coupledom, the bourgeois nuclear family, or his hatred of in-stitutional life, such as schools, offices, banks, or the Austrian army, police, and military academy.[12] However, I was intrigued by the extent to which certain of his themes have already been canonized, as can be gauged from Haneke's French Wikipedia entry, where one finds the following list:

- the introduction of a malevolent force into comfortable bourgeois existence, as seen in *Funny Games* and *Caché*;
- a critique directed towards mass media, especially television, as seen in *Funny Games*, where some of the characters are aware that they feature in a movie, and *Benny's Video*;

- the unwillingness to involve oneself in the actions and decisions of others, as seen in *Lemminge, Benny's Video, 71 Fragmente einer Chronologie des Zufalls* and *Code inconnu: Récit incomplet de divers voyages*;
- characters named Georges and Anna (or some alternate version of those names).[13]

Borrowing three of these themes – the "introduction of a malevolent force," the "media critique," and the "unwillingness to involve oneself in the actions of others," I shall briefly recontextualize them, also within film history, in order to facilitate the lead into my main argument.

The intruder as *deus ex machina*

The intruder or "home-invader" is a standard character/motivator of the horror film, of course, but he is also a relatively prominent feature of the European art film. On one level, he (and it is mostly a "he") acts as a catalyst or "trigger" for an internal crisis of self-deconstruction or auto-implosion, often of the nuclear family unit. An early example in Haneke is the homeless tramp who comes to knock on Evi's door in *Lemmings*, and whose hand she squashes (in a visual reference to *Un chien andalou* [Luis Buñuel, 1929]): an experience that subsequently serves as a telling index for the degree of affective breakdown in Evi's marriage.

Roman Polanski's films might be cited as classic precursors of this motif – from the young man in *Knife in the Water* (1962), to *Repulsion* (1965) and *Rosemary's Baby* (1968), via *Cul-de-sac* (1966), all the way to *Bitter Moon* (1992) and *Death and the Maiden* (1994). But the acts of intrusion in *Funny Games* and *Caché* are more comparable in their psychodynamics and social pathology to Joseph Losey's *The Servant* (1963), Sam Peckinpah's *Straw Dogs* (1971), or the already mentioned *A Clockwork Orange*, rather than to the films on the theme of intrusion that are contemporaneous with Haneke's work, such as *Bin Jip/Empty Houses/Three Irons* (2004) by Kim Ki-duk, which incidentally also features a lethal golf club, or *Die Fetten Jahre sind vorbei* (Hans Weingärtner, 2004). In *Caché* (as in David Lynch's *Mulholland Drive*, 2001) the "malevolent" force impinging is clearly as much inside as outside the central character; indeed, it might be identical with the family unit (if we follow the suggestion that perhaps Pierrot, Georges's and Anna's son, is in on the "game" with the tapes and drawings). In *The Seventh Continent* the malevolent force intruding is, so to speak, life itself, in its eternal recurrence of the Same.

From another perspective, however, the intruder is a positive figure: He can open new possibilities, create forks in the road, or even introduce orders of being that previously were not apparent. I wonder, for instance, if Haneke's didacticism in *Caché* about bourgeois *mauvaise foi* and his moralizing about France's repressed colonial past might not prevent the viewer from seeing something else in this constellation of the bourgeois household. Is there not also the hint that the permeability of inside and outside, of private and public, of classic individualist self-surveillance and the displacement or delegation of such self-monitoring to an external agency are part of broader cultural shifts? And that these shifts can actually be seen to have beneficial as well as nefarious effects, if not on the individual, then on the community? The model would be what Robert Pfaller and Slavoj Žižek have called "interpassivity," according to which belief, conscience, guilt, but also pleasure and enjoyment, are being "outsourced," as it were, and delegated to others, so that one can participate in "life" by proxy (a solution, if you like, to the problem alluded to earlier, of knowing too much and not being able to take responsibility and action).[14] Alternatively, it would be instructive to compare the intruder in Haneke to the intruder/outsider, say, in Pasolini's *Theorem* (1968), in Alejandro Amenabar's *The Others* (2001) (an especially intriguing example of belief and interpassivity), or, for that matter, in Lars von Trier's films, notably *Dogville* (2003). Haneke, it seems, leaves open the question of whether the intruder in his films is malevolent, benevolent, or both, and thus he joins other international directors in an ongoing reflection on one of the key issues of the new century: the difficult realignment of public and private sphere, of exclusion and inclusion, and – mostly subtly – exclusion *through* inclusion.[15]

Involving oneself in the actions and decisions of others

In addition, I want to argue that the third theme listed on Wikipedia – "the unwillingness to involve oneself in the actions and decisions of others" – should be seen as belonging to the theme of the intruder, as part of either a dialectical reversal or an instance of interpassivity. Several of the films just mentioned explore – precisely in the context of the classic "outsider" of the European cinema (in Godard, Wenders, Varda, Fassbinder, Angelopoulos) now having turned outsider-intruder (in Akin, Kaurismäki, Jeunet, and others) – the idea that such intrusion need not be intended to destroy or kill or wreak emotional havoc. The new type of "housebreaker" is more likely to bring about a small but crucial perceptual adjustment in "the lives of others": elsewhere, I have called this "double occupancy" and shown how it applies (besides *The Others*, *The Lives of Others* [Florian Henckel von Donnersmarck, 2006], *Bin-Jip*, *Vive l'amour* [Ming-liang Tsai, 1994]) even to comedies, such as the critically dismissed but symptomatic Euro-successes *Goodbye Lenin* (Wolfgang Becker, 2003) and *Le Fabuleux Destin d'Amélie Poulain* (Jean-Pierre Jeunet, 2001): films where the intruders have a more equivocal role in the commerce of intersubjectivity and interpersonal relationships.[16]

Critique of the media

Perhaps the most common of commonplaces about Haneke is his critique of the mass media. One Internet blogger has conducted an interview with himself about

Haneke. In response to the question "What about the role of the media?" his alter ego says: "Ah, yes. The media is a reliable Haneke bête noire. He worked in television for fifteen years and reserves for it his choicest vitriol."[17] By way of mitigating circumstance, one could argue that Haneke, like other filmmakers, is most eloquent in his critique – especially of the general mediatization of domestic life, colonized by the television set – when he speaks from the modernist high perch of the less tainted, because more self-reflexive, "art (of) cinema." His switch from television to feature films (motivated, he said, by the decision of the television broadcaster who had commissioned *The Seventh Continent* to shelve it unscreened) has left him, so the argument runs, more independent and free, uncompromised by commercial pressures or having to "sell out" to the ratings. But it seems that Haneke himself knew that any "setting oneself off from television by making cinema" (as had been the call of directors of the New German Cinema in the 1970s) was not an option (in countries like Germany, Austria, and to a large extent even in France, where film production is mostly underwritten by public service broadcasting, the taxpayer, and the occasional commercial television company). Similarly, his 2007 remake of *Funny Games* in the US is an acknowledgment that it is has become less credible to critique "bad" Hollywood cinema in the name of "good" European auteur cinema (another frequent argument in the 1970s). In fact, there are moments in *Funny Games U.S.* that could be seen not only as an attack on gratuitous violence in mainstream cinema, but also as Haneke's auto-critique of his earlier films, such as *Lemmings*, when Paul explains Peter's behavior by calling him "a spoiled child tormented by ennui and world weariness, weighed down by the void of existence" (an almost verbatim quote from the earlier film), while winking at the camera.

Framing, and Reframing

A more productive way of understanding how Haneke's films qualify for the label "mind-game movies" and how they are able to suggest different levels of reality or reference without playing one medium off against another – that is, cinema against television, or art cinema against Hollywood – is to focus on a feature that is arguably one of Haneke's most significant contributions to the cinema today, namely, his deployment of the cinematic frame. The choice of frame, the act of reframing, or the refusal to move the camera in order to reframe are not only distinctive traits of Haneke's visual style, they are also something like an entry-point or, indeed, a frame of reference for his moral universe and his struggle with the relation between contingency and determinism. Again, it might be useful to see his work at the cusp of several possibilities. On the one hand, with framing Haneke achieves the sort of distancing effects that have earned him the epithet "Brechtian" – with some justification, when one thinks of all the didactic framings that willfully withhold information that we, as spectators, are expected to expect. This is the case with the family members in *The Seventh Continent*, whose faces we do not see until some 10 or 15 minutes into the film, or the notorious kitchen scene in *Funny Games*. Other kinds of framing, such as the ones in the metro in *Code Unknown*, are not so readily described as Brechtian and might be called distantiation effects only insofar as they "create a distance which collapses distance," that is, they create an inner distance, for which there is no room or space – in other words, almost the opposite of distancing.

This is in contrast to earlier, and again more conventionally Brechtian ways of distancing the spectator, when Haneke is reminding us of the fact that we are watching a film. The fades to black in *The Seventh Continent*, the manipulation of the video footage in *Benny's Video*, the references to the cinema and the moments of direct address in *Funny Games*, the film-within-a-film in *Code Unknown* are some of the better-known instances, but as *Code Unknown*'s interrogation scene shows, the more effective effect is to deprive the spectator of distance, which is to say, of a "reality-versus-fiction" frame: The effect is not to make us aware of being voyeurs and in the cinema, but to undermine even the voyeuristic ground on which we normally arrange ourselves as cinemagoers. If until that point in the film we thought ourselves safe and "outside," we now realize how generally unsafe we are and how we may be caught "inside" whenever we are in the cinema: If classical narrative cinema's spectator felt safe at any distance, however close he or she got, the spectator of Haneke's films might be said to be unsafe at any distance, however far that person thinks he or she is. This would be a prime instance of an ontological hesitation, requiring a cognitive switch, to which I referred earlier, and such moments are the hallmarks of the mind-game genre.

To mind-game films also apply what Henri Bergson has said about the image in general: "An image – situated between representation and the thing – is forever vacillating between definitions that are incapable of framing it."[18] In other words, mind-game films propose to us images that are at once overframed and unframed, and they thereby differ from films thematizing character subjectivity or mediated consciousness. Whereas the latter – the films of, say, Atom Egoyan, Wim Wenders, or early Haneke – use the different media technologies of 16 and 35 mm celluloid, of camcorder home movies, grainy photographs, or of video footage as auto-referential materials, signifying different levels of consciousness by which to "layer," combine, and contrast past and present, memory and history, private and public as so many distinct "frames of reference," mind-game films tend to go the other way. Rather than ratcheting up the degrees of reflexivity and self-reference, they do their utmost to remove many of these kinds of frames, and to make their embedded frames "invisible." It is with this distinction in mind that one might want to reexamine Haneke's use of framing, and in particular his use of the plan fixe/static shot and the plan-séquence/long take.

The plan fixe/static shot

Despite his reputation as Brechtian, Haneke seems to have gone to some lengths to identify himself also by a "realism" that film scholars associate with the Bazinian tradition of realism and neo-realism. Examples often invoked are the long takes in *Code Unknown*, the deep focus in the many shots through passageways, corridors, or, most often, through open or half-open doors.[19]

By contrast, the scene in the metro in *Code Unknown* depends for its extraordinarily complex effects on the unusual combination of a restricted frame executed as a plan fixe, positioned below eye level, and coupled with deep focus. This not only makes us uncomfortably aware of our position in space, it also puts us initially at a considerable distance from Juliette Binoche and her verbal assailant. In the second half of the scene this line-up is inverted, insofar as we are now too close, at once face to face and yet included through exclusion, while still aware of the other onlookers, once more in deep focus and thus acting as the deferred surrogates or mirror-images of our own position in the first half of the sequence.

Haneke is similarly purposive in his use of off-screen space, a dimension of the cinematic image that does indeed distinguish it from television, where one rarely if ever encounters off-screen space, at least not one that is not immediately retrieved as on-screen space through camera movement or the reaction shot.[20] More directly conducive to the experience of an ontological switch are the scenes where *on-screen space is reframed by sound-over*, for instance when in *Benny's Video* we see and hear for the second time Benny's parents discuss how to dispose of the girl's body, only to be startled into realizing that this time it is Benny and the policemen who are watching the footage, now as evidence for an indictment. This scene thus prepares the ground – or, more precisely, it prepares the groundless ground – for the opening scene in *Caché*, of which more below.

The typical effect of Haneke's manner of framing is thus to make us aware of a gap, to force us into a double take, or occasion a retrospective revision of our most basic assumptions.[21] The different ways of framing that I have just enumerated far too sketchily nonetheless make explicit the perceptual structure that holds us in place, palpably inscribing the viewer at the same time as it can mark his or her place as a non-space and a void, in contrast to the genre film (or television), which thanks to editing and camera movement covers over the fact that what we see is not "out there" (and we are invited to share it), but only exists because we are "in here" (and willing to pay for it – with our attention, our fascination, our guilt-relieving empathy). This covering over, or stitching of the spectator into the fiction, used to be known as suture theory, and thus Haneke might be a good case to amplify the argument most recently made by Slavoj Žižek, à propos Krzysztof Kieslowski, about the importance of the unsutured shot as a way of obliging us to rethink the "ontology" of the cinema.[22] Going back into film history, one could argue that the famous misunderstandings between Bertolt Brecht and Fritz Lang when they worked together on *Hangmen Also Die!* (1943) revolved precisely around this point: Where Brecht sought to introduce distantiation effect of from the theater into Hollywood, the Hollywood veteran Lang wanted to work with reframing and retrospective revision, with the unsutured moment or the doubly sutured shot, in order to produce the even more unsettling effect of a world of move and counter-move, in which the overtly sadistic deceits of the Nazi regime could only be matched by the Czech Resistance with an even more skillful deployment of unframed or doubled illusionism: indeed, such ontological switches were the German director's acts of anti-Nazi the resistance.[23]

The Opening of *Caché*

An altogether extraordinary and exemplary moment of reframing in Haneke's work is the opening of *Caché*, which is worthy of precisely the grand master of the *mise-en-scène* of ontological voids and of wrongfooting the spectator that I have just introduced, namely, Fritz Lang. Haneke is able to accomplish this reframing without moving the camera, a particular feat, reframing first through off-screen sound and then by simultaneously reframing our perception of time, of space, and of medium, thanks first to the credits, mimicking the computer monitor, and then to the famous video scan-lines suddenly appearing in the image as it is fast-forwarded.

The opening of *Caché* is already in line to become one of the most commented-upon scenes in movie history, likely to take its place alongside the shower scene in *Psycho* (Alfred Hitchcock, 1960) and the extended tracking shot from *Touch of Evil* (Orson Welles, 1958) as the very epitome of what cinema can do like no other art. And for similar reasons: By means that are specific, if not unique, to film – editing, camera movement, framing – each of these scenes induces a particular kind of vertigo which I have here called the *ontological switch*, typical of the mind-game film. With these references, one is not only able to give Haneke an impressive cinematic pedigree, but one also comes to regard him as one of those directors who helps us understand if not the true condition of cinema as a negative ontology, then certainly as one who pinpoints a significant development of the cinema in the new century, whether one thinks of it as "post-photographic" or not.

Among the literally hundreds of reviews of *Caché* on the Internet, all discuss the opening scene. Surprisingly many of them grasp one of the essential points of Haneke's reframing, namely, that it functions first on the temporal axis, by radically disturbing our sense of chronology and temporal hierarchies of past,

present, future, and even future anterior. Already in his earlier films, the articulation of time, and with it the different temporal registers inherent in the cinematic flow, was an important resource for Haneke. It generally took the form of
proleptic or metaleptic shifts (that is, foreshadowing later or recalling earlier
moments), rather than employing the more conventional tropes of flashbacks,
interior monologue, or subjective time. As an example: The enigmatic final scene
of *Caché* is made even more so by the possibility that it might be proleptic
insofar as it might form a loop or Moebius strip with the film's opening, such
that the ending of the film is in fact the beginning of the plot, in the sense of
being chronologically prior to the beginning, even though shown at the end. In
other words, Haneke leaves open the possibility that the scene between Pierrot
and Majid's son may precede rather than follow the suicide and the dénouement.
On the other hand, as we saw, metalepsis, that is, retrospective revision, is much
more frequent, with just about every one of Haneke's films having a moment
where framing and reframing wrongfoots us as to the time or place of what
we thought we saw or recognized. Indeed, it is these moments of metalepsis that
give his films their seeming power – appreciated as "uncanny" by some, rejected
as manipulation or "cheating" by others – to invade the spectator's psychic
and emotional life, in much the same way as his intruders invade the self-
contented "happy families" of his films. In fact, the playing off of one medium
against the other, or of "live" versus "recorded" action, discussed earlier as a
kind of residual Brechtianism, can itself be reframed as significant mainly in
respect of the almost imperceptible time shifts thereby effected. Their payoff
is invariably small ontological shocks, as from a low-voltage cattle prod, achieved
by what I now want to call Haneke's particular *metaleptic indexicality*, that is,
the way he obliges the viewer to enter into a series of retrospective revisions
that leave him or her suspended, unsettled, and ungrounded, yet powerfully
aware of his or her physical presence in the here-and-now of the moment of
viewing.

By refusing the reverse-shot in *Caché*'s opening, Haneke not only inhibits "suture,"
or the binding of the spectator into the diegesis, he also introduces as part of
his narrative space that ontological no-go area, namely, the space *in front*, first
theorized by Noël Burch in the 1970s and occasionally exploited by avant-garde
filmmakers.[24] This space in front is not what is in front of the camera, the pro-
filmic space, but rather the space in front of the screen, the space in front of the
image, but also part of the image – if such a space is conceivable. It is usually
elided in feature films (at least those of the classical period: in Griffith and early
cinema it is very much present, and fully signifying, for instance in the famous
"breadline" scene in *A Corner in Wheat* [1909] or in *An Unseen Enemy* [1912]). Said
to undermine or suspend the status of external referentiality, this space in front
becomes crucial whenever a director (Lang, Hitchcock, Welles, Buñuel, or Polanski
are obvious examples) puts the world of reference under erasure in order to either

make the spectator fall into the ontological void, or to direct our attention else-where, usually at ourselves.[25]

Gaming: The Loop of Necessity

The attention that Haneke directs elsewhere is, as just argued, in the first instance to us, the spectators, making us hyperconscious not only of our physical here-and-now, but (in Hitchcock–Lang fashion) also of our position as watchers being watched, watching: watched by the very same instance, in *Caché*, that stalks the protagonists in the film and delivers the tapes. That such a tightening spiral of spectatorial self-reference has ethical repercussions as well as ontological impli-cations is demonstrated by a perspicacious comment from Steven Shaviro:

> What's most powerful about *Caché* is that it not only decrees guilt, but cranks the guilt up to a self-reflexive level: the guilt is reduced or managed by the flattery and privilege that we retain while observing all this; but such a meta-understanding itself creates a new, higher-order sense of guilt, which in turn is cushioned by a new, higher-order sense of self-congratulation as to our superior insight, which in turn is an unquestioned privilege that, when comprehended, leads to a yet-higher-level meta-sense of guilt, and so on ad infinitum. There's complete blockage, no escape from this unending cycle. The experience of the film is one both of self-disgust and of a liberation, through aestheticization, from this self-disgust.[26]

In Shaviro's description, a closed loop of guilt and insight into the guilt opens up, with neither producing the kind of understanding that might lead to action. It is similar to the loop I have characterized as "ontological," where each time a possible ground for reference appears, it is pulled from under us, to open up another gap, and to reveal the groundlessness of cinema's mode of viewing the world. *Caché* would thus also instantiate what I have argued is Haneke's first level of performa-tive self-contradiction, namely, the fallacy that seeing can lead to knowing and knowing to action. *Caché*, in other words, continues the auto-critique I claimed was present in *Code Unknown*, making self-contradiction the very resource of Haneke's film philosophy, as it were, and yet another sign that Haneke is aware of the pro-ductive double bind at the heart of his work. Corresponding to what Shaviro calls the oscillation between self-disgust and liberation on the part of the spectator are, perhaps, on the part of the director not so much his well-known sadism, but instead a tragic insight that helps renew his intellectual and creative energies. It may even give us a glimpse of the ecstatic side – the moments of *jouissance* – sustaining Haneke's apparently irredeemably gloomy world view. Put differently: God is near-est when all exits are blocked, when the trap is sprung and shut tight, and only a Pascalian wager or leap of faith can rescue the fallen soul.

Game Control, Remote Control

The idea of a wager, but also the mention of God, brings me to the other aspect of what I have called Haneke's performative self-contradiction, namely, the sense I have in his films of a control freak playing games with contingency and chance. The question that all his films raise, implicitly in some, but most often quite explicitly, is: Who plays with whom, by what means, and who is in control?

Put in a nutshell, one could say that those entities playing God in Haneke tend to extend the scope of their control the further they remove themselves from the scene. In *Benny's Video*, it is Benny who wants to be master over life and death but who in the end hands himself and his parents over to another authority; in *Funny Games*, the young men may be playing God, but they claim to be controlled, or rather, remote-controlled, by us as spectators, creating the diabolical loop of agency that is meant to produce in us the spiral of voyeurism and guilt, desire and its disavowal, which Shaviro has pinpointed in *Caché*. In *Code Unknown*, it is the invisible but audible director of the film-within-the film who so uncomfortably morphs in and out of the film we are watching, while in *Caché* there is not even a voice: the ubiquitous, omniscient, omnipresent God of the tapes – at once remote and "outside," yet totally "inside" as well.

Furthermore, in *Caché*, the kind of zero-degree of "groundlessness," the sort of void in the cinematic system of representation that yawns before us, is such that, once we have recovered from the shock, we are invited to try and "fill in," mainly thanks to the thriller narrative, providing us with an epistemic bait, the identity of the stalker and his motives. However, by the same token, it makes the historical referent, namely, the colonial legacy, and its purported ideological referent, latent racism, or bourgeois guilt and complacency, no more than that: also a bait, and thus, quite logically, something that can turn out to be merely a hook. On the other hand, there may also be another, equally specific historical inscription, which relates not to France but to Germany, and to Haneke's generation, preoccupied as it was – and still is – with *Vergangenheitsbewältigung*. For proof of such a link, one needs not only to look more closely at the notion of the director as God, but also to ask oneself in what sense this God is obsessively playing games with contingency and chance, and why.

Chronology of Contingencies: A Historical Trauma

One of the most remarkable things about *71 Fragmente einer Chronologie des Zufalls* (*71 Fragments of a Chronology of Chance*) is surely its title – which seems not so much a title as a program, a motto, albeit one to which Haneke is dedicating his creative life. *Eine Chronologie des Zufalls* – a chronology of chance – seems a fitting oxymoron by which to advertise another layer of the performative self-contradiction I have been trying to track, because how can chronology – the ordered sequence of temporal succession – be reconciled or made compatible with *Zufall*, signifying accident, collision, or chance encounter – the very epitome of randomness and contingency?

In the film of this title, for instance, the fixed camera positions in the "fragments" have nothing accidental/coincidental about them. Their selection and angles, as well as the length of the scenes, are all (pre)determined by the director, as is the predetermined outcome of all these mosaic pieces, which we learn from the first intertitles. The film may purport to be about chance, but it is the chance of a jigsaw puzzle, which can be laid out and assembled in only one way if it is to yield one particular "image."

On the other hand, one can easily see the chronology of contingency as offering a modality of both "control" and "chance," a way out of random senselessness and predestination, a condition of freedom, if you like, and with it the possibility that it might also be otherwise. A small scene in *71 Fragments* beautifully indicates this point in time and space of forking paths, of the moment when things could have gone the other way. This is the game of pick-up sticks between the ping pong-practicing student and his computer software friend. They are just taking time out after having successfully programmed the solution to a Rubic cube-type puzzle that has been played at various points earlier, and which necessitated a kind of "Gestalt-switch" in order to be correctly solved. The unstated implication is that at this "game" (of pick-up sticks), the student might have lost the newly acquired gun to his friend, and would thus have been prevented from using it when his nerves snapped in the bank.

Fig. 1.1   The pick-up sticks game. *71 Fragments of a Chronology of Chance* (1994), dir. Michael Haneke, prod. Veit Heiduschka.

A more directly historical reference comes into view, however, if one compares Haneke's chronology of contingency with a famous saying by another German director, Alexander Kluge: "Tausend Zufälle, die im Nachhinein Schicksal heissen" ("a thousand coincidences that afterwards, in retrospect, are called 'fate' "),[27] a phrase which in Kluge functions as an answer to the always present, if implicitly stated, question, "How could it have come to this?," where "this" invariably stands for the German disaster of the Nazi regime, World War II, and the Holocaust. *71 Fragments* purports to be about a different "this," but it, too, poses the same question.

The question posed to us, the (re)viewers, must be something like this: If it is possible, indeed inevitable, to read Haneke's early films also against this obsessional foil of German political and cultural debates of the 1960s and 1970s, then the so-called glaciation films must also be seen as answers to this key generational question. They would be the sort of retroactive effect – that is, in a series of metaleptic slippages – of the hypothetical cause: How small steps of frustration, anger, envy, and humiliation can bring people – a people – to give themselves (to "outsource" themselves to) a fascist *Ubervater* and malevolent God. *71 Fragments* can be read within such a set of presuppositions, as can *Benny's Video*. Performative self-contradiction would then be Haneke's very personal way of bearing the burden of his generation, as well as of his country of birth, to which he belongs, no matter how far he has moved, whether geographically or in his films' subject matter.

This line of interpretation would also help place in a more layered, but also more historically determinate context another recurring feature of Haneke's films: the tendency to play with the possibility of rewinding the film of the characters' lives. While these scenes, for example in *Benny's Video* and *Funny Games*, are usually interpreted as yet more instances of meta-cinematic reflexivity, they could be read, when seen against the backdrop of what I have elsewhere called the temporality of regret typical of the New German Cinema, also as attempts, however doomed or derided, to undo what we know cannot be reversed, even if this had been the result of a concatenation of circumstances and accidents. Brigitte Peucker hints at such a possibility when commenting on Benny's obsessive replay of his video: "Necrophilic fascination may be one explanation for his behavior, but another aim is the control of narrative flow and time: he manipulates this footage in order – half-seriously – to interfere with the inevitability of its narrative and to reverse 'reality.' "[28] In light of such an impossible, but also impossibly fraught, desire, punished in *Funny Games*, obliquely endorsed in *Benny's Video*, the fast-forward in *Caché* also assumes a further layer, giving what I have called Haneke's metaleptic moments their special ethical charge.

Gaming: Play

How does any of this relate to that other idea of game, also present in Haneke, and which I argued might provide a way out of the epistemological fallacy, as well as untying the performative self-contradictions, however much they might provide moments of *jouissance* to the director and moments of frisson and thrill to his audiences?

Here, I need to appeal to the special status of games, namely, that they constitute a contract between two or more parties, freely entered into of one's own accord, but, once agreed to, rules apply that cannot be renegotiated or arbitrarily changed. A game is also open-ended – otherwise it is rigged – but nonetheless obliges one to stick to the rules, and these are predetermined. Games in this sense are thus parables of the intertwining of free will and determinism, and at the limit performative – indeed addictive – double binds or self-contradictions.

This is one level at which the game metaphor is operative and instantiated in Haneke's work, and where, as we saw, the frame sets the rules, regulating distance and proximity, and thus conceiving of the world in terms of subject–object relations, so that to enter is to hand over one's freedom to someone determined to exercise control, to the point of turning the viewing subject into the object. Yet there is another level, where gaming introduces a different set of terms, and may indeed propose a different paradigm altogether. In a discussion of *Funny Games*, Roy Grundmann details several levels of the game that the boys are playing with the family. It is the last one that concerns me here: "Their ultimate rationale is found on the third level of the game, the film's explicit, perversely playful acknowledgment that these 'funny games' are enacted only because there's an audience for them – us viewers."[29]

Again, my suggestion would be to see this not only as proof of reflexivity and a meta-level self-reference, but also as an indication that the idea of play here involves a particular kind of contract: If, as Grundmann's third level suggests, the relevant level of referentiality is the film performance, the film experience, the film fact, then each film must propose to the spectator the set of rules by which it wants to be "played". This pragmatic – or semio-pragmatic – perspective is implicitly present in every Hollywood film, which in its opening scenes, and often already in its credits, provides the viewer with a kind of instruction manual, a sometimes more, sometimes less easily decodable set of clues as to the type of contract it intends to honor. European cinema is less overt about this, insofar as it is usually a matter of the director speaking to the audience across his or her characters. In the case of Haneke, as indeed with other directors of what I have called "mind-game films," this direct voice has increasingly taken the form of a game between the director and the audience. Haneke's acknowledged mastery lies in the way he manages to combine stern control over his mind games, while only indirectly revealing himself to either his characters or the audience. Yet there are glimpses and moments – at the margins of these parables – also of another form of game, one more in line with what I have called a pragmatic view, but which also brings me back to the "ontological" view of the cinema, as outlined by Alain Badiou in an earlier passage. This would imply that the director does not so much play the sadistic God as one who is as concerned as we, the spectators, are with "that, which from being, gives itself to thought as deception of vision" (Badiou), or who can come to terms with the paradox that "the lie of the image is the truth of our world" (Jean-Luc Nancy). It would mean attempting to engage with the world, via the cinema, and thus to enter into a different kind of wager or "game," now, as it were, on the far side of predetermined rules or control.

I have found at least three moments in Haneke's films that intimate what such a different game might signify. One refers to a diegetic moment, in *Benny's Video*, which Brigitte Peucker describes in terms of a kind of epiphany, and which precedes Benny's handing over of the tape to the police. Benny and his mother are on holiday in Egypt, without the father, who meanwhile has to dispose of the murdered girl's body. At a time of utter tragedy, guilt, moral squalor, and impending disaster, the two of them, each armed with a video camera, seem to be experiencing a time out of time, a deeply resonant moment of freedom, at once a pre-Oedipal fusion of the mother–child dyad and the utopian moment of art and creativity – made possible because of the cameras, rather than (as one would expect) in spite of them. It is as if the very instrument of Benny's alienation – the video camera – is here enlisted to exorcise the damage it has done.

My second example is the school entrance scene at the end of *Caché*. Whether we decide to place it chronologically at the end or at the beginning of the plot, or whatever we think its significance might be, the scene – filmed as a static long shot and held for what seems like an eternity – requires us to enter into a game of open-ended surmise. Given that we are too remote to hear what is being said and the composition is too flat and distributive for us to know exactly where to focus our attention, this lack of focus becomes the very point of the scene: It functions as a form of invitation to change our mode of perception, to begin to "read" flatness, instead of depth, and thus to rely not solely on the ocular-centric perspectivism of classical representation.

My final example is one that is both diegetically relevant and requires our active inclusion as the audience: I am referring to the framing scenes of *Code Unknown*, where at the end the mute children still play their game, and they persist in playing, offering "a pre-verbal state of pure, ecstatic communion/communication using the sound and rhythms of tribalistic drums." In a code that remains "unknown" to most of us, they thus extend an invitation, an opening up, whereas Anne, changing the code on her front door to stop Georges from gaining entry, seems to shut herself in. The next generation, whatever their handicap, the film seems to say, is still capable of playing the game of communication, however fraught it is with misunderstanding or plain incomprehension. And because no subtitles are provided, we too have to enter into the game in order to be present and to participate. As one commentator put it: "These bookend deaf children frame the film and seem to say that the consequences of Babel are artistry and ingenuity, not silence and despair."[30]

Playing the game before knowing the rules is no doubt a risky undertaking, but in certain circumstances this might be the necessity that gives us a measure of freedom. If Haneke's films have, from the beginning, proclaimed that there is no outside to the inside of the mediatized world, then "the lie of the image" and "deceptive vision" can only be redeemed once we can also understand "the truth of our world" as the game we all are obliged to play, even if none yet knows the code. Beyond performative self-contradiction, this ontological choice is our challenge, but also our chance – now in both senses of the word, and I trust this is also the way Haneke understands it to be understood.

Notes

1   Haneke's ambivalences of the ocular-centric view of cinema are touched upon in Karl Suppan (1996).
2   See, for instance, Mattias Frey (2003).
3   The first collection of auteurist essays on Haneke was *Michael Haneke und seine Filme*, edited by Alexander Horwath (Vienna: Europaverlag, 1991).
4   For a sample of the director's blend of Aristotelian aesthetics and Brechtian politics, see Michael Haneke (1992).
5   Thomas Elsaesser (2005).
6   Other European directors who are brought up in one Christian religion but tend to the values of other ones are Krzysztof Kieslowski, Jacques Rivette, Lars von Trier, and Tom Tykwer.
7   On K. O. Apel's performative self-contradictions, see Matthias Kettner (1993).
8   For an attempt at a Deleuzian reading of Haneke, see Mattias Frey (2002).
9   Georges Didi-Huberman, paraphrasing Jean-Luc Nancy, in a lecture in Amsterdam, March 10, 2005. Didi-Huberman was referring to a passage from *The Ground of the Image*, where Nancy notes: "If truth is what lends itself to verification, then the image is unverifiable unless it is compared with an original, which one assumes it must resemble. But this assumption is a discourse that you will have introduced, to which the image gives no legitimacy. If truth is what is revealed or manifested from itself, it is not only the image that is always true, it is truth that is, of itself, always image (being in addition and simultaneously image of itself)." Jean-Luc Nancy, "Distinct Oscillation," *The Ground of the Image* (2005: 76–7).
10   Alain Badiou (2005: 129).
11   Thomas Elsaesser (2009).
12   For a good summary of Haneke's themes, see Christopher Sharrett (2004). (This interview is reprinted in this volume.)
13   See fr.wikipedia.org/wiki/Michael_Haneke (accessed June 2007).
14   Robert Pfaller (2003) and Slavoj Žižek, "The Interpassive Subject."
15   Haneke often supplements the inner framing by an unexpected outer framing, to draw attention to this dynamic of exclusion and inclusion – via editing and the multiple boundaries and enframings it makes possible. An intriguing example of "exclusion through inclusion" occurs at one of the dinner parties in *Caché*, when the black woman guest is absent in her very un(re)marked presence and, as I recall, is almost as decoratively silent as a cigar store Indian.
16   See Thomas Elsaesser (2006).

17 "Code Unknown: An Auto-Dialogue."
18 Henri Bergson, *Matière et mémoire*, quoted in Gilles Deleuze (1992: 61).
19 Brigitte Peucker (2004) calls these compositions "Haneke's signature shots," although she associates them more with a meta-cinematic level of self-reference to the cinematic apparatus than with neo-realist deep-staging. I would argue that the reference to both neo-realism and the cinematic apparatus is apposite, however much this seems at first glance contradictory.
20 Examples of off-screen space not retrieved or sutured by a reverse shot occur famously in *Benny's Video*, when the girl is dying off-frame; in *Funny Games*, when the son is killed off-frame; and in *Code Unknown*, when the neighbors' child is physically abused and presumably killed.
21 This contrasts with, but is also complemented by, a *mise-en-scène* that – as in many horror films – maintains another kind of division, namely, that whereby the viewer is affectively sharing the emotional point of view of the victim, while the framing obliges him or her to share the point of view of the perpetrator, in short, the author of the misery or torment inflicted on the characters.
22 Slavoj Žižek (2001).
23 See Gerd Gemünden (1999).
24 Noël Burch (1981).
25 Evidently, such a scene, coming at the very opening, puts us on red alert as well as on our guard, drawing attention to the conditions of spectatorship, specifically in the cinema, but also perhaps more generally in the world itself – the world viewed, as we might paraphrase Cavell, who understood this as an ontological rather than an epistemological issue.
26 The Pinocchio Theory (Steven Shaviro), www.shaviro.com/Blog/?p=476.
27 Alexander Kluge and Oskar Negt (1981: 47).
28 Brigitte Peucker (2004).
29 Roy Grundmann (2007).
30 See theeveningclass.blogspot.com/2006/02/blogathon-no-2-michael-hanekes-code.html (accessed June 4, 2007).

References and Further Reading

Badiou, Alain: *Handbook of Inaesthetics*, trans. Alberto Toscano (Stanford, CA: Stanford University Press, 2005).
Burch, Noël: "Nana or Two Kinds of Space," *Theory of Film Practice* (Princeton, NJ: Princeton University Press, 1981), pp. 7–21.
"Code Unknown: An Auto-Dialogue," www.girishshambu.com/blog/2006_02_01_archive.html.
Deleuze, Gilles: *Cinema 1: The Movement-Image*, trans. Hugh Tomlinson (London: Athlone Press, 1992).
Elsaesser, Thomas: "Double Occupancy: Space, Place and Identity in European Cinema," *Third Text* 83, 20:6 (November 2006): 647–58.
Elsaesser, Thomas: *European Cinema: Face to Face with Hollywood* (Amsterdam: University of Amsterdam Press, 2005).

Elsaesser, Thomas: "The Mind-Game Film: A New Genre, or an Old Ontological Doubt?," *Puzzle Films: Complex Storytelling in Contemporary Film*, ed. W. Buckland (Oxford: Blackwell, 2009), pp. 13–41.

Frey, Mattias: "A Cinema of Disturbance: The Films of Michael Haneke in Context," *Senses of Cinema* (September–October 2003).

Frey, Mattias: "Supermodernity, Capital, and Narcissus: The French Connection to Michael Haneke's *Benny's Video*," *cinetext* (October 2002), cinetext.philo.at/magazine/frey/bennysvideo.html.

Gemünden, Gerd: "Brecht in Hollywood: Hangmen Also Die and the Anti-Nazi Film," *TDR: The Drama Review* 43:4 (164) (Winter 1999): 65–76.

Grundmann, Roy: "Auteur de Force: Michael Haneke's 'Cinema of Glaciation'," *Cineaste* 33:2 (Spring 2007): 6–14.

Haneke, Michael: "Film als Katharsis," *Austria (in)felix: zum österreichischem Film der 80er Jahre*, ed. Francesco Bono (Graz: Blimp, 1992), p. 89.

Kettner, Matthias: "Ansatz zu einer Taxonomie performativer Selbstwidersprüche," *Transzendentalpragmatik*, ed. Marcel Niquet et al. (Frankfurt: Suhrkamp, 1993), pp. 187–211.

Kluge, Alexander and Negt, Oskar: *Geschichte und Eigensinn* (Frankfurt: Zweitausendeins, 1981).

Nancy, Jean-Luc: *The Ground of the Image* (New York: Fordham University Press, 2005).

Peucker, Brigitte: "Effects of the Real," *Kinoeye* 4:1 (2004), www.kinoeye.org/04/01/peucker01.php.

Pfaller, Robert: "Little Gestures of Disappearance: Interpassivity and the Theory of Ritual," *Journal of European Psychoanalysis: Humanities, Philosophy, Psychotherapies* 16 (Winter–Spring 2003).

Sharrett, Christopher: "The World That is Known: An Interview with Michael Haneke," *Kino-Eye: New Perspectives on Austrian Film* 4:1 (March 8, 2004), www.kinoeye.org/04/01/interview01.php. [Interview reprinted in this volume.]

Shaviro, Steven: The Pinocchio Theory, *Caché*, www.shaviro.com/Blog/?p=476.

Suppan, Karl: "Der wahre Horror liegt im Blick: Michael Hanekes Ästhetik der Gewalt," *Utopie und Fragment: Michael Hanekes Filmwerk*, ed. Franz Grabner, Gerhard Larcher, and Christian Wessely (Thaur: Kulturverlag, 1996), pp. 81–98.

Žižek, Slavoj: "Back to the Suture," *The Fright of Real Tears* (London: BFI Publishing, 2001), pp. 31–69.

Žižek, Slavoj: "The Interpassive Subject," www.egs.edu/faculty/zizek/zizek-the-interpassive-subject.html.

2

Five Tapes, Four Halls, Two Dreams

Vicissitudes of Surveillant Narration in Michael Haneke's Caché

Thomas Y. Levin

While most of the critical response to Michael Haneke's 2005 feature *Caché* ("Hidden") has noted its unusual and foregrounded appropriation of surveillance, the film's particular mobilization of surveillant audiovisuality and temporality (e.g., unusually long and static shots seemingly lacking in any diegetically attributable point of view) is almost never subjected to critical reading as a *narrative* practice. The perceived centrality of political allegory in *Caché* seems to have licensed a tsunami of *thematic* interpretations of the film.[1] What this essay will explore, instead, is the *aesthetic politics of the film's mise-en-scène of the surveillant*.[2] *Caché*'s intriguing narrative mobilization of surveillance effectively undergoes a fundamental transformation over the course of the film – so it will be argued here – such that by the time we get to the last shot, the concluding long take on the steps of the Lycée Stéphane Mallarmé, the nervous and unsettling quality of what could be described as a *panoptic undecidability* – which is the intriguing stylistic signature of much of the *first half* of the film – is now strikingly *absent*. Indeed, having operated as the motor of the film's diegetic call to ethical conscience, what I will call the film's surveillant narration has, by the end of the film, produced a spectatorial position that is, in fact, *fully identified with the panoptic*. As a result, irrespective of what the film may be doing at the thematic level, the aesthetic politics of *Caché*'s narrational economy is utterly at odds with its ostensible media-critical stance.

Some readers have suggested that the final scene in *Caché* – the very long immobile take of the children leaving the school – is so narratively unmarked that it could easily be placed at the beginning of the film (in the fashion of the brief shot of the cowboy aiming and firing his gun directly at the camera/audience which usually appears at the end of *The Great Train Robbery* [Edwin S. Porter, 1903] but was sometimes also placed at the beginning). This claim, I believe, is deeply mistaken, for it fails to recognize the degree to which this final shot has a very specific narrative function carefully constructed by the film's complex internal economy of surveillant narration. It is only once this economy has been grasped that one can understand not only why the final shot *must* come at the end, but also how it plays a very specific role in the logic of the film's moralist invocation of surveillance. I will attempt to sketch that logic through the following close analysis of a series of key moments in *Caché*; specifically, five tapes, four halls, and two dreams.

From the very start of the film, the fascinatingly long, static, and ultimately complex opening shot that establishes the film's first, and crucial, internal norm, there is a curious tension. In many ways, of course, this sequence bears *none* of the classic hallmarks of ciné-surveillance: The patina of the image is high-definition and color (not the grainy black and white of classic surveillance videotape), the camera angle is straight-on (eschewing both the fish-eye perspective of a wide-angle lens and the classic high-angle surveillance point of view), and the shot is completely static (employing neither the mechanical back-and-forth pan of CCTV fame, nor the multiple screens of *Time Code* [Mike Figgis, 2000]). It is nevertheless a very specific *temporal* feature of this opening sequence – its extended duration and the concomitant recalibration of eventhood – that gives it its surveillant signature. This is only exacerbated by the credits themselves, which – expanding the on-image writing characteristic of the surveillant feed (which usually consists only in a date and time stamp, camera number and placement, etc.) – unfold interminably in data-entry fashion and ultimately form a rectangular shape (a screen perhaps?), the title of the film "hidden" within the textual mass (Fig. 2.1). Why are these credits so small? Could it be that the strikingly minuscule font size which requires the spectators to really work to make out what's there puts these viewers in a scrutinizing position which, as we will discover in a moment, is rather analogous to Georges's hermeneutic puzzlement (when viewing the first videotape) at the strange trace of the daily life outside his house that has burst into his domestic space? What might be at stake in this isomorphism of the spectatorial position of the film audience and that of the various forms of spectatorship staged within the film?

The long opening take is marked not only by its duration but also by a complex series of reframings on the part of the spectators as they attempt to establish the semiotic status of the shot. We first take it to be a still photograph and then recognize certain cues (sound, minimal movement within the frame) that reveal it to be a time-based image. We then assume that this footage is in the present tense but subsequently recognize that what it captures belongs to a (soon to be specified) time past while what is present is its status (revealed by the soundtrack) as a trace being re-viewed, a recognition subsequently confirmed and foregrounded by the fast-forwarding of the image *as videotape*. In other words, despite its surveillant signature, what the tape indexes is not simply what it depicts but rather the fact of its status as *something being viewed*. Indeed, one could say that what we see in the first scene of *Caché* is somebody discovering by watching the

Fig. 2.1   Opening credits. *Caché* (2005), dir. Michael Haneke, prod. Andrew Colton and Veit Heiduschka.

fact that they are being watched. The narrative deployment of surveillant video-tape in cinema seems to have an elective affinity for such metaleptic indexicality, to use Thomas Elsaesser's felicitous coinage,[3] which enables this sort of footage to serve a wide range of narrational functions.[4] It is of course tempting to read the very similar retrospective recasting that we undertake as spectators of the opening of *Caché* as the performance of what we will eventually recognize as the film's central gesture, to the extent that here we enact spectatorially what the film posits as the ethical imperative for its main character Georges: a retrospective re-vision, a rereading of a past that is (in his case) repressed and/or traumatic. In any event, one can certainly read the fast-forwarding of the tape – marked here by the rippling in the image (Fig. 2.2) – as the moment when the metalepsis (heretofore entirely acoustic) becomes inscribed *visually* in the readable trace of the image as a videotape-being-viewed. Indeed, the fast-forward could also be read as revealing the *character* of that viewing (both Georges's and ours) as a search for event-hood, the ripple marking visually the desire – schooled by a certain economy of narrative cinema – for a specific pace of events (sometimes called "action") largely absent in surveillant temporality. The tape, Anne tells us in the voice-over, runs for over two hours without much of anything happening. What they are searching for is in fact nothing other than an event, in this case something that indexes the duration temporally, a time code or other form of temporal marker that might reveal when (and in turn by whom) this sequence was shot (in this case it is the moment Georges leaves the house).

As if to foreground the specifically surveillant signature of the temporality of the film's opening sequence, the two subsequent scenes are effectively *variations on a durational theme*, each of which iterate in formally very different ways the

Fig. 2.2   Ripples in the image. *Caché* (2005), dir. Michael Haneke, prod. Andrew Colton and Veit Heiduschka.

durational character – and concomitant anxiety – characteristic of the panoptic narration in what we will soon learn is only the first of a series of surveillant video-tapes. The first of these durational variants is a complex three-minute-sequence shot that relentlessly tracks into the kitchen and then back out to the dining room.[5] The next scene in the pool is also a long, continuous shot which is marked by a more insistent (parental?) observational formalism in the relentlessness of its up and down tilt. The signifying rift between the audio and visual components of the opening scene is here rehearsed in the subtle disconnect between the *sonic* trace of the attention of the acousmatic coach (who comments on the swimming technique of *each* of the three boys' "turns") and the *visual* focus of the camera, which relentlessly follows Pierrot and only Pierrot. What these two scenes already manifest, albeit in ways that only become legible retrospectively (and which will hopefully become clearer through what follows), is the surveillant dimension of the film's narration *even when and where it is not thematically motivated.*

Against the background of this newly established internal *temporal* norm – all scenes in the film so far having been of extended, indeed excessive and foregrounded duration – the pool scene cuts abruptly to yet another, this one seemingly a noc-turnal iteration of the opening surveillant shot with nearly identical framing and stasis (Fig. 2.3). Based on our experience with the previous instance of this sort of largely still panoptic temporality, we anticipate (according to another of the film's internal norms) the moment when this shot will also in turn be *reframed*, its indexicality metaleptically recast by a voice-over or by some work on the image as the object of a diegetic gaze. But this time the only sound from the image is local and there is not a ripple or any other indication that it too is a taped sequence. Our search for a cue that will also reveal this image as one that is being watched

Fig. 2.3   The house at night. *Caché* (2005), dir. Michael Haneke, prod. Andrew Colton and Veit Heiduschka.

within the diegesis is in vain. So how do we read this scene? Is it not just as "unmarked" as the final scene, if taken on its own? But that is just the point – it cannot be taken on its own but must be read, indeed can *only* be read, in relation to what has preceded it and what follows. And this will turn out to be crucial. While the status of this sequence at this point is strictly *undecidable* within *Caché's* narrative economy, the lack of alternative options to account for it opens up an intriguing possibility which (for reasons I hope will become clear) is *not* available for the final scene: One could say that here the *narration itself is functioning in a surveillant manner*, that is, that the diegetic issue of the surveillant observation of tape #1 has here become the very condition of the film's narration as such.

To get a sense of what this might mean, consider what I would insist is the paradigmatic instance of this migration of surveillance from the thematic and diegetic to the very condition of the narration itself, the final scene in Francis Ford Coppola's magisterial *The Conversation* (Fig. 2.4). In this closing sequence we find the film's paranoid hero Harry Caul suddenly confronted with the terrifying fact that now *he* is being listened to in his own home. Determined to uncover the condition of possibility of this invasive violation, he systematically takes apart his living quarters to find the bug – but to no avail. In the film's final shot we are shown Caul, sitting in the ruins of his deconstructed domesticity, from a high-angle camera that pans back and forth and back and forth, its foregrounded mechanical regularity formally invoking the movement of a surveillance camera. But, as I have argued at greater length elsewhere,[6] this panoptic device is not *in* Harry's space (since otherwise this surveillance expert would certainly have found it). Harry cannot locate this CCTV device because it is in a space that is epistemologically unavailable to him; the camera here is no longer part of but instead *the very*

Fig. 2.4   Harry Caul (Gene Hackman) in the ruins of his apartment. *The Conversation* (1974), dir. and prod. Francis Ford Coppola.

condition of possibility of the narrative space he inhabits. In short, the narration of the film as such has itself become surveillant, the explicit focus of the diegesis has begun to contaminate the extra-diegetic as well.[7] Returning now to the curious nocturnal surveillance scene in *Caché*, its very *lack* of any clear reframing cues (which would provide a diegetic source for its gaze) puts the viewer into a sort of hermeneutic overdrive, with his or her attention recalibrated to attend to the smallest detail, be it a passing car or the wind rustling the leaves. Exactly halfway through the scene a car arrives and as it parallel parks it exposes with its head-lights a shadow of something that one is tempted to say looks like a movie camera. Is this a cue, a blooper, a Rorschach-like test of our hermeneutic projection – or perhaps what one might call a MacGuffin of surveillant narration? In any case, Georges eventually appears in the shot and walks towards and enters his house; a light is turned on – and that's it. Nothing else. The scene simply provides narrative information (Georges has returned home at night), but now does so using the vocabulary – static camera, surveillant duration, and identical framing – of the earlier diegeticized surveillant scene. As in the final scene of *The Conversation*, a surveillant activity that was previously the explicit object of attention within the narrative here seemingly has *become* the signature of the film's narrative activity itself.

The reframing we expected but were denied in this scene is then immediately provided *literally and figuratively* in the next scene in which, having cut to Georges speaking directly to the camera on the set of his literary TV talk show, as the shot pulls away (reframing him to include the guests on his program), we have an erup-tion of an acousmatic voice which instructs everyone not to get up during the credits – *which we do not see.*[8] As Georges leaves the set to take a phone call we cut to a close-up of a crude child's drawing and two remote controls (Fig. 2.5)

Fig. 2.5 Two remote controls. *Caché* (2005), dir. Michael Haneke, prod. Andrew Colton and Veit Heiduschka.

with Anne explaining in voice-over that yet another surveillant *envoi* (tape #2) was wrapped in it. The film then cuts to the *same* nocturnal shot of the house which was just shown, except now marked *from the start* by what we recognize (and were cued by the presence of the remote controls to read) as the ripples of the VCR *rewind*. This is significant, for Georges is here rewinding within the diegesis what *we* as spectators have already seen; the narration could thus be said to be effectively implicating *us* in the surveillant intrusion into Georges's life. Moreover, the reason Georges cannot find out who is "behind" the surveillance tapes is thus similar to the reason Harry Caul could not find the surveillant device in his apartment: The "sources" of the surveillance are epistemologically unavailable to both because in each case *it is the narration itself that is watching*.

The temptation here to *read* the rewind direction marked by the ripples in the image *figurally* – "going backward" as the *mise-en-scène* of recollection? – is then encouraged by a most curious montage immediately following the iteration of what my own hermeneutic overdrive (perhaps the *déformation professionnelle* of people who work on surveillance?) wants to read as a silhouetted camera: the shot of a bloody-mouthed North African child (Fig. 2.6), himself an invocation of the child's drawing of a bloody-mouthed stick figure that opened the scene, looking up as if startled and wiping his mouth. We now begin to read the surveillant image no longer simply as the object of a *diegetic* viewing by Georges and Anne (as before), but increasingly as a *psychologized* point of view belonging solely to Georges. This subjective cast of the surveillant image is emphasized by Georges's distracted non-response to the repeated voice-over questions by his wife: "Qu'est-ce qu'il y a?" ("What is it?") and then a few seconds later, "Qu'est-ce qui s'est passé?" (What happened?"), and then again, after a few moments, "Georges!" – to which he responds, "Quoi?" ("What?") and then, "Rien, rien. Je . . . Je suis fatigué" ("Nothing, nothing.

Fig. 2.6   The bloody-mouthed boy. *Caché* (2005), dir. Michael Haneke, prod.
Andrew Colton and Veit Heiduschka.

I . . . I'm just tired"). Might this explain why, when we cut back to the drawing
at the end of the scene we no longer see *two* remotes (figures of diegetic VCR
watching) but only one: Not only is Georges's relation to these images no longer
simply televisual or spectatorial (it is in the process of becoming something else),
but also he is no longer "in control" of the remote (i.e., of the [repressed] past),
which is here returning with a vengeance.

   The last of the film's (hermeneutic) internal norms established here – read scenes
marked by surveillant features as somehow a psychological manifestation or
externalization of Georges's subjectivity – is confirmed by the next surveillant *envoi*
(tape #3), which arrives (wrapped in the now *de rigueur* drawing) during the dinner
party. This tape first violates at least two other internal norms: (1) surveillance
tapes are always images of the outside of Anne and Georges's house; and (2) such
tapes will always be marked by the ripples of a "fast-forward" and/or "rewind"
that themselves betray the full-screen image of the tapes as images being watched
(a violation whose frequency here risks making violation and its concomitant unsettling a new internal norm). Tape #3 is a video shot from inside a car (a fact emphasized by the windshield wipers; Fig. 2.7). This clearly readable framing has the
effect of *foregrounding the agency* at work in the surveillance video, which was much
more "unmarked" (even if no less of an issue) in the stasis and extended duration
of the previous tapes. Indeed, this inscription of a foregrounded surveillant
agency is rendered even more pronounced by the sudden 90-degree pan that reveals
a country house which – as Georges explains in voice-over to the astonished (silent)
dinner guests and fellow diegetic spectators of the surveillant *envoi* – was his childhood home. At this moment, the now full-screen image of the house is *exclusively*
Georges's point of view since he alone is standing next to the large-screen TV
while everyone else has remained seated at the dining table. What is this image

Fig. 2.7   Video shot from inside a car. *Caché* (2005), dir. Michael Haneke, prod.
Andrew Colton and Veit Heiduschka.

if not the externalization of Georges's creeping – and as yet completely unarticu-
lated – anxiety that whatever it is that these tapes represent has something to do
with the complicated past of his childhood?

In a further confirmation of this new internal norm of surveillance-as-
materialization-of-personal-psychology we now cut to tape #4 abruptly, without
any prior notice or diegetic preparation, and directly after Georges has woken up
from a bad dream in – and about – his childhood home. Like the initial "tape" of
the film's opening scene, no drawing accompanies this one, whose first section is
(again) shot from inside a car, this time driving down a street in a Parisian sub-
urb before it cuts, again with local sound, to a hand-held track down the featureless
hallway of a high-rise housing project until the camera stops in front of an apartment and pans to reveal the apartment number. At this point the image freezes
and, in the by-now familiar gesture of metaleptic reframing, starts to rewind
(Fig. 2.8), the ripples revealing once again that we are (indeed, have been from
the start) watching watching, i.e., that we are/have been seeing what – as we (once
again) quickly learn from the soundtrack – Anne and Georges are/have been
seeing, a fact confirmed by the subsequent close analysis of the tape that the two
of them undertake in order to decrypt the street sign (Avenue Lénine).[9]

The change of direction in mid-tape here (from "play" to "rewind") marks the
film's *peripeteia*, a subtle but important shift clearly indicated shortly thereafter
when Georges goes to visit the building seen on the tape. As he waits in a snack
bar across the street (perhaps to get up the courage to actually undertake the
pilgrimage to the scary site of surveillant reference), we see a long static shot of
the building which has all the hallmarks of the surveillant aesthetic we have come
to recognize. Like previous panoptic takes, this one is also subjected to a reframing,

Fig. 2.8   Hallway (1), ripples. *Caché* (2005), dir. Michael Haneke, prod. Andrew
Colton and Veit Heiduschka.

but of a wholly different sort. While once again the image is revealed as one that
Georges is watching, in this case he is no longer watching an "other" watching
(i.e., a videotape): This is now *his own point of view as a surveillant point of view*.
As such this scene performs a dramatic modification, an almost complete evacuation
of the anxiety from the surveillant point of view as that gaze increasingly becomes
Georges's own – the unknown "agency" of the early tapes now recast as the externalized workings of Georges's bad conscience (think: return of the repressed).

The psychologized subjectivization of the only apparently panoptic sequences
suddenly allows one to make sense of the striking difference in character of the
fifth and last "surveillance" tape, which we cut into directly from a triumphant
parental moment at a swimming match. As if signaled by the lack of any ominous arrival narrative or the concomitant menacing drawing, the question of who
made this tape is no longer an issue as it was before. It is, rather, first and foremost about *what we see* after Georges leaves (i.e., the sobbing Majid) as a compelling performance of the truth of Majid's claim, reiterated here, that he had nothing
to do with any of the tapes, drawings, etc. If the metaleptic reframing via the soundtrack (which reveals once again that we are watching Georges and Anne *watching* this tape) produces unease, it is now *not* due to the frustration of our desire
to know who made this recording. Rather, the discomfort stems entirely from the
deception on Georges's part that this tape reveals: He has lied to his wife and *that*
is the issue here. The question as to *who* shot the footage has given way entirely
to the issue of *what the tapes reveal* and, more specifically, what they reveal *about
Georges*. Moreover, to the extent that the tape here seems to have taken on a truth
function *qua surveillance*, we can begin to see a decisive shift in the viewer's
relation to that surveillant position: Instead of being a source of anxiety, it now
increasingly functions as a welcome locus of disambiguating omniscience.

We can track the very same shift from a disconcerting surveillant undecidability (with respect to the source of the image) to a completely decidable and no longer surveillant point of view by examining the four iterations of the scene in the hallway in Majid's building. The first time we see this space it is through a shot marked very clearly as a subjective camera while remaining entirely unascribed – and as such raising the by-now familiar yet still disturbing question, "Whose point of view is this?" When we return to the hall with Georges following the panoptic shot of the housing project that is then "revealed" as his point of view, we immediately perceive a marked difference: If Georges's relation to this hallway the first time we see it is as spectator (he is the person watching the surveillance tape), here the same shot has become his *actual* point of view, an "ownership" of the image that is complicated when, at the very moment in the previous iteration where the image rewound, this time Georges himself *enters* the shot to knock at the door (Fig. 2.9)! The third time we encounter the hallway it is almost a cut-on-action of Georges walking across the street towards the housing project and then down the hall *within the shot* (Fig. 2.10); there is no hint of ascriptive ambiguity here. By the time we see this same space a fourth time, when Georges returns for the rendezvous when Majid will commit suicide, Georges is now shot walking down the hall *towards* the camera (Fig. 2.11). While there surely are many ways to read this progression (from denial to acknowledgment, a formalism of a "working through"), it clearly marks a shift in the film's internal narrative economy – from a surveillant to a classical (i.e., unmarked) omniscience – which is anything but *caché*.

What is suggested by the comparison of the film's four different treatments of the hallway becomes equally manifest through the juxtaposition of the structural logics of Georges's two dreams. In the first, we cut from Georges at his mother's

Fig. 2.9 Hallway (2), Georges (Daniel Auteuil) enters. *Caché* (2005), dir. Michael Haneke, prod. Andrew Colton and Veit Heiduschka.

Fig. 2.10　Hallway (3). *Caché* (2005), dir. Michael Haneke, prod. Andrew Colton and Veit Heiduschka.

Fig. 2.11　Hallway (4). *Caché* (2005), dir. Michael Haneke, prod. Andrew Colton and Veit Heiduschka.

house to Anne at a book party and from there to the chicken being decapitated by the child Majid as seen from the point of view of Georges as a young boy. Only at the end of the sequence, as the axe-wielding Majid is about to envelop Georges, do we hear heavy breathing on the soundtrack – metaleptic reframing! – and then cut to an image of a sweat-drenched Georges in bed, awakening from the nightmare we have just seen. The recoding of the scene as the psychological point of view of a diegetic dreamer is here, obviously, *post factum*. By contrast, the *next* dream sequence not only establishes the fact that we are *about to see* a dream (by showing Georges taking a sleeping pill and getting into bed), but stays with the sleeping Georges *a full twenty seconds* before cutting to the dream sequence of young Majid being taken away by force from Georges's childhood home. The scene is shot from an immobile point of view in the shadows (the same point of view that Georges had in the last dream) and the sync sound has bird sounds exactly like (if not identical to) the film's opening scene. Having thus gone from a dream only readable as such after a *post factum* reframing to a dream of the repressed *ur*-trauma, which the film goes to great lengths to present to us as such, it is not surprising that the shot that *precedes* the second dream sequence is one which revisits the film's very first image (Fig. 2.12). Here we see the same static surveillant framing of the film's opening moments, with a minutes-long duration that would otherwise mark it as surveillant, but now suddenly and strangely *evacuated* of all the anxiety associated with its prior iteration. It is just a scene of Georges arriving at, and parking his car in front of, his house. Period. The formal characteristics of what was previously read as surveillance are still present here, but are now no longer perceived as such: The stylistic signature of anxious omniscience *devoid of any unease* has here become the mode of the film's narrative omniscience.

The same holds for the final scene in *Caché* – the four-minute static shot of the kids leaving the (aptly named, given the film's formalist dynamics) Lycée Stéphane Mallarmé (Fig. 2.13). We could argue that this sequence effectively demands a surveillant attention to decipher what is going on in the busy comings and goings of the image field. However, the very fact of the huge amount of (ultimately futile) hermeneutic speculation about what is or is not happening in this shot – are Majid's son and Pierrot in fact *friends*? And if so, were the tapes their doing? etc. – is itself

Fig. 2.12   Georges arrives at his house. *Caché* (2005), dir. Michael Haneke, prod. Andrew Colton and Veit Heiduschka.

Fig. 2.13   The school entrance. *Caché* (2005), dir. Michael Haneke, prod. Andrew Colton and Veit Heiduschka.

indicative of the fact that, *despite the duration and the stasis of the scene*, it no longer provokes us to ask "Who is watching here?" but rather, "What is going on here?" This question, however, can only be asked from a spectatorial position that is itself fully identified with, rather than critically aware of, the surveillant point of view. If, as I have tried to show, this shift, this evacuation of the anxiety associated with the undecidability of a surveillant narration, is one that the entire film has worked very hard to prepare, then this would also mean that this scene can only be read in the polysemous manner in which it has been read *because* it occurs where it does, as the film's final scene. And this, in turn, is important because it reveals the absurdity of the claims of readers who, possibly following Haneke's lead,[10] have lauded *Caché* as an "open" film (in Umberto Eco's sense of the term[11]), that is, as a work whose ostensible lack of closure and seeming polyvalence allow for a multiplicity of readings. Indeed, unlike the irreducible polysemy of David Lynch's remarkable and deliciously baffling *Lost Highway* (1997) – whose three video-cassettes of domestic surveillance mysteriously left at the front door have numerous intertextual resonances with *Caché* – Haneke's film is quite the opposite: a meticulously crafted, but ultimately very "closed" work which subtly mobilizes a narrative rhetoric of surveillance to tell – once again for those familiar with Haneke's other films – a media-critical *conte moral* about the bad faith (both personal and political) of a televisual star. In doing so, however, it ends up, literally and figuratively, with a narrative enunciation whose aesthetic politics is oddly complicit with the very surveillance so pejoratively connoted, at least ostensibly, by the film's thematic concerns.

Notes

1   Indeed, even where such politico-historical readings acknowledge the issue of surveillance, it is invariably reduced to a simple figure of power. In Ranjana Khanna's reading of *Caché* as "a film about anxiety in relation to a history of colonial violence and the technology associated with it," for example, she suggests that the film's invocation of surveillance "this time attributed to Algerians in spite of the surveillance mechanisms used against the Algerians by the French, unfolds a narrative of revenge in which a camera gaze is returned in an oppositional structure." See Ranjana Khanna (2007).

2   One can perhaps get a sense of what I mean by thinking of a film like *Enemy of the State* – Tony Scott's 1998 "remake" of the *ur*-surveillance classic *The Conversation* (Francis Ford Coppola, 1974). In the later Will Smith vehicle which also features Gene Hackman as (once again) the seasoned and rightly paranoid surveillance expert, the explicit focus on the threats of identity theft and the abuses of dataveillance on the part of a legislatively unrestrained government security agency seems at first glance to be thoroughly progressive and critical. Yet despite its extensive pedagogical catalog of the modalities and capacities of state-of-the-art invasive surveillance, and despite its articulation of important positions in the debate on the politics of security ("But who is watching the watchers?," Carla Dean asks her husband at one point), as the film unfolds the viewer finds him/herself increasingly placed in a narrative position where what *we* want to know – where is Robert Dean? – is exactly what the evil NSA operatives want to know. Thus despite its critical thematic proclivities, the film's narrative logic effectively produces a structural *identification* with surveillance which complicates, indeed compromises, the aesthetic politics of its enlightenment project.

3   In his plenary lecture at the interdisciplinary international conference "Michael Haneke: A Cinema of Provocation," which took place at Boston University, October 25–7, 2007. See also Elsaesser's chapter in this volume.

4   A marvelous example can be found in the complex narrative inflections performed by the surveillance camera footage in *Thelma and Louise* (Ridley Scott, 1991) following Thelma's robbery of the rural convenience store. In response to Louise's demand to know what happened, Thelma explains, "Well, I just walked on in there and . . . ," at which point the sequence cuts to an *enacted flashback* in the form of what is immediately readable as a black-and-white surveillance tape from the store's security camera. By means of a brief cut to a group of men focused on an off-screen monitor, this footage quickly changes its status to a *flash-forward* in which the same tape is being viewed by the police at an unspecified later date, before shifting back to the (immediate) past tense of the initial enacted flashback.

5   It is also worth noting how two future scenes are proleptically invoked here, the first by Georges' question "Where's Pierrot?," prefiguring his worrisome disappearance later in the film, and the second by the phrase "Was there a note with the tape?," which prepares us to expect the iconic supplements that will accompany the subsequent surveillance missives.

6   Levin (2002).

7   Were one tempted to give this formal dynamic a thematic reading, it could certainly be argued that it effectively performs the paranoid fear of a completely pervasive panopticism in the post-Watergate mid-1970s.

8   It is clear that *Caché* accords great significance to the question of credits both *seen* –
    as in the first and last shots – and *unseen* – as here and in the later scene where Majid
    explains that it was the credits at the end of Georges's TV show that allowed him
    (retrospectively of course) to realize that he was watching the terrible boy he knew
    from his childhood. Might it be because the anxiety posed by the so-called surveil-
    lance tapes is effectively nothing but the disturbance provoked by *images without
    credits*, by the absence of the desperately sought-after information as to who shot
    these scenes (and why)?

9   And since this is surveillance footage, this street of course really does exist, in a
    commune named Romainville in the eastern suburbs about 5 miles from the center
    of Paris. Appropriately for the context of the film, there is no way to get to this
    working-class neighborhood from Paris using public transportation as neither the
    subway nor the RER regional commuter lines go anywhere near what one can only
    call this non-place.

10 Consider, for example, the following, astonishingly neo-Bazinian statement that one
    finds in Haneke's interview with Serge Toubiana on the Sony Pictures Classics *Caché*
    DVD (#13875): "I always try to find an aesthetic that is open, that is readable, that
    is transparent for the viewer." Thus his preference for long takes which are sup-
    posedly easy to decipher and in which (unlike television, so the obvious implication)
    "there is no manipulation of the viewer [*sic!*]."

11 Umberto Eco, "The Poetics of the Open Work," *The Role of the Reader* (1984: 47–66).

References and Further Reading

Eco, Umberto: *The Role of the Reader* (Bloomington: Indiana University Press, 1984).

Khanna, Ranjana: "From Rue Morgue to Rue Iris," *Screen* 48:2 (Summer 2007): 243.

Levin, Thomas Y.: "Rhetoric of the Temporal Index: Surveillant Narration and the Cinema
    of 'Real Time,'" *CTRL (Space): Rhetorics of Surveillance from Bentham to Big Brother*,
    ed. Thomas Y. Levin, Ursula Frohne, and Peter Weibel (Cambridge, MA: MIT Press,
    2002), pp. 578–93.

3

Infectious Images

Haneke, Cameron, Egoyan, and the Dueling Epistemologies of Video and Film

Vinzenz Hediger

Benny (Arno Frisch), the eponymous protagonist of *Benny's Video* (1992), likes to shoot and watch videos. He meets his victim, a young girl (Ingrid Straßner), in a video store, and he uses a video camera to record her murder. While his parents (Ulrich Mühe and Angela Winkler) react to the video with shock when he shows it to them, Benny himself seems to be unable to develop any other emotion than bemused curiosity in response to both his deed and the video that records it. We don't know whether his obsession with video images caused this pathological emotional detachment, or whether the ubiquity of video images and other, comparable images such as comic books – there is a long take showing Benny reading comics at the family dining table in all tranquility immediately after the murder – simply fuel and prolong a pathology that has other sources. There can be little doubt, however, that in Haneke's film, video is a pathogenic medium.

One way of approaching *Benny's Video* is to read it as a piece of *Kulturkritik* in the guise of media critique. Every new medium provokes a wave of scientific angst which comes to the fore in empirical research that reveals the pernicious effect of that new medium.[1] One could argue that Haneke's film subscribes to this line of argument and proposes a reading of video as a harmful influence on our youth, a medium that creates a generation of moral zombies who, despite the loving care of their families, turn into cold-blooded murderers who like to kill just for the fun of it. If the rapid obsolescence of VHS video makes the argument seem somewhat trite today, it is quite possible to imagine a contemporary remake of the film, with DVD taking the place of video and advanced computer games and the Internet replacing comic books. The film's title would have to be modified to *Benny's Online Multiple User Dungeon Game*, but the argument would still remain: namely, that new media and entertainment technologies generate social pathologies by subverting the individual user's capacity to act morally and responsibly.[2]

Yet *Benny's Video* is not a moral tract nor a scientific study, but a film. If we are to understand what Haneke has to say about video, or rather what his film does with video, we need to do so in aesthetic terms. What we need to come to terms with is the film's *entre-images*, to use Raymond Bellour's concept, the way the film unfolds the in-between of two images of a different origin, in this case video and film.[3]

But why should we care?

One possible answer is that, as much as I was ready initially to dismiss Haneke's treatment of video as the kind of facile *Kulturkritik* I attempted to paraphrase above, I now think that the director's engagement with video is part and parcel of his very conception of film. Haneke has taken up the question again in his later work, particularly *Funny Games* (1997) and *Caché* (2005). If we are to engage in the time-tested game of auteur studies, which this volume does, we can trace Haneke's thinking on cinema by studying how his take on video has evolved over time.

But I believe that there is more at stake. Clearly, Haneke chose to integrate video images into his film not because they look good (they don't). They raise other questions. In fact, as I would like to show, Haneke posits a fundamental difference between film and video in terms of their epistemic value. What is at stake in Haneke's *entre-images* is film's very ability to project a world.[4] Film images afford the viewer a firm grasp on the world and the time and space to reflect upon what he or she sees. Video images undermine that grasp and infringe upon the viewer's temporal and spatial integrity. Video, in other words, threatens film's epistemic privilege. But at the same time, video is contained within film. In Haneke's films video figures as a sort of image virus, a *pharmakon* that infects film but also provides film with an antidote.[5] Rather than being merely a question of personal style, video in Haneke's films addresses a fundamental problem of film theory. *Benny's Video* really is a filmic *conte philosophique*, a film that lays out a theoretical argument in narrative form.

Ultimately, however, Haneke's *conte philosophique* touches upon a problem of media history. As I suggested above, we could argue that Haneke's film belongs to a history of media pathologies and contributes a chapter on video to that history. But it also belongs to a history of film as a medium that distinguishes itself from other media and evolves alongside, but also in competition with, other media. Ever since the early days of the medium, films have incorporated other media, from writing to the telephone, the telegraph to radio, and later television, video, and the computer. Films often use other media as narrative devices. In early train films, the telegraph allows the good guys to coordinate their actions against train robbers and other assorted bad guys. But it is quite possible to go beyond the horizon of auteur studies and read any random example of a film that frames other media as a *conte philosophique* that raises basic problems of film theory. What emerges from these countless *contes* is a media history of film as written by film itself, a history of film's various attempts to define itself by and through the representation of other media and their relative merits, particularly in terms of epistemology: *Histoire(s) du cinéma* as *Histoire(s) des médias*, if you will.[6]

The question of video in Haneke's films as I will address it in this essay, then, is one of personal style nested in a problem of film theory nested in a question of media history as written by and through film. In order to unfold these various questions nested into one another, I will start at the outer confines and turn to mainstream cinema to show that claims of an epistemic privilege of film such as that put forward in and through Haneke's film are actually generic and commonplace. I will then turn my attention to the very heart of the matter and discuss how Haneke dramatizes the image virus in *Benny's Video*, with a particular eye on how his take on the epistemic privilege of film relates to that proposed by the previous examples. Next, I will shift my focus to the middle ground of film theory and contrast Haneke with two other directors whose work deals with video images: James Cameron, a mainstream auteur if ever there was one, and another Canadian, Atom Egoyan. Much as in Haneke's case, the work of both Cameron and Egoyan dramatizes a conflict of dueling epistemologies of video and film. Rather like in Haneke, video images in both *Terminator 2: Judgment Day* (1991) and *Titanic* (1997) suffer from an inability to tell the truth when left to their own devices. But where, for Haneke, video is a pathogenic medium that creates a void within the world of the film, Atom Egoyan's *Family Viewing* (1987) frames video as a medium that transcends the world of the film and provides a conduit for love both in the sense of *eros* and *agape* for the film's characters. Having thus compiled three chapters towards a media history of film in relation to video, I will turn to Haneke's later films in my concluding remarks and combine history and theory to ask how the video virus has evolved over time, whether film continues to be immune to the virus that it carries within itself, and how the virus may actually have adapted to its host. For viruses do adapt, and quickly.

Before I start, a few clarifications seem to be in order. They concern the concepts of "medium" and "art," as well as the question of knowledge, which is implicitly raised in any discussion of a medium's epistemology. Let me first map the territory upon which I intend to argue.

Prologue

"Medium" has so far been used in a way that suggests a techno-essentialist reading of the term, that is, an understanding of each medium as a distinct *dispositif* of communication technology, as in "film," "television," "radio," "newspaper," "video."[7] First, it is important that "medium" is different from "media," a term that foregrounds the institutional structures and practices of modern mass communication (as in "blame the media"). The term "medium" emerges in its modern sense as a synonym of "milieu" in the biological writings of Lamarck around 1800.[8] In the twentieth century and through the writings of such authors as Austrian psychologist Fritz Heider, "medium" emerges as a general term for all that which enables perception and communication (e.g., air and the voice).[9] It is the techno-essentialist understanding of the term, however, that has become current since the 1960s in both media and communication studies, as well as in everyday usage, thanks at least in part to the writings of Marshall McLuhan.[10]

But how does a medium become an art? And what does it mean that an artist in his or her work relies on, and reinforces, the epistemological claims of a given medium? According to theorists such as Rudolf Arnheim, a medium can be an art, as in the case of film and radio, for both of which Arnheim proposed aesthetic theories. In other cases a medium fails to become an art, as in the case of television, which Arnheim suggested would end up destroying both the art of film and the art of radio.[11] The emergence of video art, however, seems to suggest that even television can be subjected to formal strategies that transcend immediate communicative purposes. Depending on context and formal strategy, every medium can be an art, and most art forms can be said to rely on some sort of technological setup that could be characterized as that art's medium.

As for the question of knowledge and epistemology, the connection of art and knowledge dates back to Aristotle, who related aesthetic objects to an experience of learning in his *Poetics*.[12] Furthermore, one could argue that modern aesthetic theory emerges from an epistemological problem, that is, from the question of intersubjectivity of taste, which is the key issue in both Burke's *Inquiry into the Origin of Our Ideas of the Sublime and Beautiful* from 1757 and Kant's *Critique of Judgment*, first published in 1790.[13] Disappointed by the violent turn of the French Revolution, Friedrich Schiller proposed in his letters on the *Aesthetic Education of Man* that aesthetic experience, rather than reason alone, was the key to a better future for mankind.[14] Whether we are able to trace the idea back to Schiller or not, part of what makes us modern is that we somehow believe that art has a formative value. Particularly in the twentieth century, aesthetic theories have discussed "true" art in terms of an intellectual challenge posed by works of art. Art is thus understood in contradistinction to mere entertainment, which has long-term detrimental effects on our cognitive abilities.[15] In fact, we have become so accustomed to assuming that art poses difficulties of understanding that we accept the degree of difficulty an artwork presents as a standard according to which we may measure the aesthetic value of that object. Kitsch, in turn, is usually defined as art that lacks complexity and is not felt to be sufficiently difficult. But while many theorists equate difficulty in art with twentieth-century high modernism,[16] Jacques Rancière argues that the decisive shift occurs much earlier, around 1800, when art acquires what he calls an "aesthetic unconscious." Ever since the early nineteenth century, the experience of art carries with it both an element of opacity, of non-understanding, and a learning experience, a hermeneutic effort.[17] Modern art criticism is essentially the enterprise of explaining to the audience works of art that do not explain themselves. No matter how you look at it, art in modernity entertains a privileged relationship with problems of knowledge.

Some will tend to deny that this pertains to cinema as well. As I will show, Haneke himself seems to agree with the Frankfurt School argument that Hollywood cinema is the very antithesis of modern art, a machinery for dumbing down rather than challenging and educating the audience. It is hard to deny that most films, content to merely entertain and address as large an audience as possible, strategically forego the complexity and opacity of the "aesthetic unconscious" in favor of transparency and redundancy. Still, one can argue that even in cases where one would least expect it, Hollywood cinema wholeheartedly subscribes to a modernist understanding of the aesthetic, that is, to the assumption that art, and in this case cinema, produces some kind of epistemic surplus. Thus, Hollywood films tend to claim that they know more, and make you see and know more, than other media. Or so at least we can conclude from the way Hollywood narration frames other media: by systematically contrasting cinema's capacity to produce and convey knowledge with that of other technical media. In order to illustrate this point, let me turn to a film by a director who figures liminally at best in the canons of auteur cinema.[18]

Opening Sequence

The opening sequence of *All the President's Men* (Alan J. Pakula, 1976) consists of the following shots: First, the Warner Bros. logo, then a grayish-white screen for about twenty seconds. This is followed by an extreme close-up shot of a piece of paper and a typewriter head hammering the date of June 1, 1972, onto the paper. The close-up is so extreme, in fact, that you can see the structure of the paper. Individual threads of the whitened wood pulp that make up the paper's body are discernible through and below the surface. Segue into television footage of Marine One, the president's helicopter, landing outside the Capitol. The president has returned from a trip to Europe, just in time to address the full Congress, a voice-over informs us. The voice is almost a whisper, with a tinge of awe and breathlessness. Another archival TV footage shot shows Nixon entering the hall to the applause of senators and representatives, then taking the podium, all smiles. This is followed by black film. The names of the producers and the title of the film appear in white type. On the soundtrack, we hear a kind of metallic rustling. It is the sound of a key lock being manipulated. The black screen lights up: A door opens at the end of a hallway, a field of light and silhouettes of men entering the hallway in the middle of the screen. This is the Watergate burglary, and the camera is already there at the moment of the break-in.

In cinematic reconstruction, French critic Antoine DeBaecque once suggested, History (with a capital H) gets a second chance. Something of this kind is at play in this sequence. By featuring the celebratory television sequence at a moment when everybody already knows that Nixon is a crook rather than a president

worthy of adulation, the film's opening sequence contrasts an obsolete perception of a historical figure with what, for the sake of convenience, we may call the
truth. And by being present at the burglary the very moment that it happens, the
film makes sure that this time around nothing will remain hidden in the dark.
Opening sequences are strategic areas of cinematic narration: They present not
only the film's topic, but also its stylistic and narrative strategy. However implicitly, a film's opening declares what the film wants to accomplish and how. The
sequence of shots that I have just described, then, is programmatic in nature. By
juxtaposing Nixon addressing Congress with the reconstruction of the burglary,
and by being present at both events, the opening sequence makes the claim that
this film is the repository of the historical truth about the biggest scandal in American
politics (prior to George W. Bush's bungled rise to the presidency and subsequent
events, of course).

But the claim that the film represents the truth about a historical event is anchored
in another claim that goes even deeper. This second, and literally more fundamental, claim concerns film's ability not only to project the world as it is, but to
do so better than other media. In the first two shots, the film makes the typewriter and paper emerge out of what may best be termed a shot framing an
amorphous gray substance. This film claims to be about information in a literal
sense: about framing an amorphous matter and imprinting it with a form, about
informing and information in an Aristotelian sense, if you will. The cut from the
gray frame to the paper shows film's power to do so in the most general sense:
First there is only matter, then there is form, imprinted on the matter through
the editing process. The second shot frames the medium of writing, but in a particular manner. What we see is on the one hand highly conventional. Showing a
close-up of a piece of paper in a typewriter in order to convey plot information,
particularly information about time and space, is a technique that is at least as
old as 1912 and the Edison serial *What Happened to Mary?*. The typewriter sequence
at the beginning of *All the President's Men* transcends the convention, however. The
camera is close enough to reveal the structure of the paper, and the hammer of
the typewriter fills the entire frame, not once, but repeatedly. The sound underscores the sense of the process of writing as an outsize spectacle. What this sequence
of shots does is open up the conventional shot of a typewriter conveying story
information to what Benjamin calls the "optical unconscious." As Hannah
Landecker has shown in her discussion of microcinematography, the notion of
"optical unconscious" refers to the exploration of a realm of visibility that is just
below the threshold of perception, rather than to the unveiling of a realm of repressed
realities.[19] This is exactly the operation that the film is performing at this point.
The sequence of shots of the typewriter shows the process of writing and
enlarges and thereby transcends it at the same time. The cinematic *mise-en-scène*
produces an epistemic surplus. This holds true in the same way for the framing
of the television footage. The film does not only show the television footage. By
showing it as part of a film that is about what people did not know about Nixon

at the time, the cinematic narration proposes that the television footage hides the truth as much as it shows anything, and that it is only through film and the reframing of the TV footage in the film that we fully understand what is at play in this scene. Cinematic narration assures the readability of the footage, and the archival video footage depends on the film to reveal what it really shows: namely, a president who is also a crook and who does not deserve to receive the adulation that Congress offers him.

All the President's Men is a historical reconstruction, a film based on a true story, as the formula goes. It is a film based on a book which in turn was based on a series of newspaper articles. The film, then, comes last in line in a series of versions of the same story. This is part of what the opening sequence shows: that the story of the film was first told via typewriter and television. But in coming last in a temporal sequence of retellings of the same historical facts, the film also comes first in terms of the hierarchy of media that the title sequence implies. Film simultaneously represents and performs the other media, and through its performance both comprehends and transcends them. In that sense, the opening sequence of *All the President's Men* anchors the film's claim for historical truth-telling in a performance of an epistemic privilege that film holds, or claims to hold, over (all) other media. This claim is further underscored by the film's extensive use of extreme deep-focus long takes and slow, almost imperceptible forward tracking shots, particularly of the newspaper offices, as the story unfolds. The long takes and slow tracking shots suggest a comprehensive grasp of narrative space, particularly in conjunction with the extreme close-up that emerges out of indistinct grayish-white matter at the very beginning of the film. Consider, by comparison, the flatness of the television image at the film's beginning, particularly in the shot of the hall of Congress. Film's grasp on the reality of the projected world is complete, both temporally and spatially.

As memorable a film as *All the President's Men* might be, however, this is not an isolated case. Rather, the claims of spatio-temporal grasp and epistemic privilege that the film makes surface in Hollywood films from all periods. *The Big Broadcast of 1938* (1938), a Paramount musical comedy featuring Bob Hope and W. C. Fields and directed by Mitchell Leisen, tells a story of a steamship competition that pits a streamlined super-cruiser against a more traditional boat as they cross the Atlantic from New York to London. On-board entertainment is provided by famous entertainers like Bob Hope, and all entertainment broadcasts, as well as other events in relation to the boat race, are broadcast live on national radio. The boat race is a metaphor, if you will, for the competition between national network radio and film in the 1930s, a competition that is turned into an alliance in the Paramount film in the sense that the film features a number of radio personalities in film roles. Paramount, we should not forget, was also a major shareholder in the Dupont network.[20] According to the film, however, the race between film and radio is one that film always wins. In one scene, a radio broadcast announcer standing before a curtain announces an orchestra performance. The curtain opens, the music starts, and suddenly, the painted background merges with the foreground. An animation sequence begins. In a manner later repeated in *Who Framed Roger Rabbitt* (Robert Zemeckis, 1988), a small animated figure, a water spirit of sorts, exits the painted area of the screen and starts to interact with the musicians. It is a splendid trick sequence that very self-consciously puts on display all that cinema is capable of, particularly, of course, combining real-life images with animated footage and music.[21] Musicals usually address a double audience, as Jane Feuer points out: the diegetic audience of the show, and the film's audience in the cinema.[22] This scene, however, addresses a triple audience: On top of the two standard musical audiences there is also the diegetic radio audience, which by any measurement would be by far the largest of the three. The size of the cinema and the size of the in-ship theater are roughly comparable, but the radio audience numbers in the tens of thousands, if not millions. The setup of the scene, however, puts the radio audience at a serious disadvantage. They may hear the music, but they do not see any part of the visual spectacle. The scene, then, is more than just a musical number: It shows cinema's triumph over radio and provides a performative proof of cinema's superiority to the competing medium. After all, it is clearly better to watch a film than to listen to the radio, since the film gives you both the sound and the music.

Examples of this type abound. To cite just one more: In *The Phantom Broadcast* (Phil Rosen, 1933), a radio-days take on Edmond Rostand's *Cyrano de Bergerac*, with a dose of Hugo's *Hunchback of Notre Dame* and Leroux's *Phantom of the Opera* thrown in for good measure, a radio singer owes his success to a hunchbacked piano player who also lends him his voice. When they both fall in love with the same woman, murder and mayhem break loose. While the diegetic radio audience is left in the dark, the film's audience obviously knows from the outset what the problem is, because they get to see the hunchback.

Whether the *mise-en-scène* strategically claims an epistemic advantage for film, as in the case of *All the President's Men*, or just plays on film's properties as an audio-visual rather than simply an audio medium, as in the radio film examples, there seems to be what might be called an inherent and systemic tendency in films to foreground the epistemic privilege of film.

But if so, why do such claims work, at least to the extent that we do not feel the need to reject them outright? Why do they not appear to be obviously false but rather intuitively right? In the case of the radio films, the argument is simple: Because film appeals to two senses and not just to one. There is what you might call a quantitative sensualism at play here. The films I cited ask us to believe, and we apparently tend to agree, that an experience is fuller, more comprehensive, and eventually more truthful the more senses it involves.[23] The epistemic advantage of film is first a sensual advantage that then translates into an epistemic advantage. With *All the President's Men*, things appear to be more complicated. The sequences I described connect film to other technical media and highlight their respective technical properties. The extreme close-up that reveals the paper's structure certainly claims an advantage of the visual medium of film over the typewriter in that the film image includes writing but offers something more. For the film theorist, the obvious answer would be that the truth claims made by this opening sequence are ultimately anchored in the film image's indexicality. The film image, as a photographic image, has the property of being both icon and index, to use Charles Sanders Peirce's terminology: It is both a likeness and a physical trace of the object it shows.[24] Moreover, the film camera is a machine that produces images "automatically," as André Bazin suggests: The object imprints itself onto the photographic support unencumbered by human interference or an artist's subjectivity.[25] Every time cinema compares itself to another technical medium, indexicality comes into play. Cinema always has the advantage of what Bazin proposes to call a "transfer of reality" from the object onto the image: Film, as a photographic medium, partakes in the very being of the object it depicts in ways not open to any other medium.[26] But whether films rely on quantitative sensualism or the ontological realism of "reality transfer," it would seem that cinema, and particularly Hollywood cinema, has indeed a habit of claiming a privileged take on, and of providing privileged access to, the world.

Cut to Haneke

All my examples so far have been from American films. If we were to ask Haneke himself, he would probably respond that none of what I have just discussed is pertinent to his own work.

> My films are polemical statements against the American "taking-by-surprise-before-one-can-think" cinema and its disempowerment of the spectator. It is an appeal for a cinema of insistent questioning in place of false because too quick answers, for clarifying distance in place of violating nearness. I want the spectator to think.[27]

A programmatic statement if ever there was one: Haneke wants his films to empower the spectator to think, and he intends to do this by assuring the integrity of his viewing position, by maintaining a "clarifying distance in place of violating nearness." For one, Haneke, too, is a subscriber to the modernist theory of art that suggests that true art should produce an epistemic surplus by inducing the spectator, or reader, or listener, to think and thus to learn. His alien other, that against which he stakes his artistic claim, is an American cinema that supposedly disempowers the spectator by intruding upon his or her physical and intellectual integrity in both temporal and spatial terms: a cinema that goes too fast and comes too close for epistemic comfort.[28] Obviously, *All the President's Men* does not fit that description. Quite to the contrary, which raises the question whether (1) it is not an American film (as somebody like David Bordwell would probably suggest, potentially labeling Pakula's film a misbegotten example of "European art cinema narration"), or (2) Haneke's understanding of American cinema is some-what deficient. What I am interested in here, however, is something else, namely, how video partakes in Haneke's project of liberating the spectator through polemical art.

As it turns out, Haneke is a master of "taking-by-surprise-before-one-can-think" cinema. *Benny's Video* opens with a shot of a pig being killed with an air gun (Fig. 3.1). This is footage, we later learn, that Benny shot on his grandparents' farm, and it documents what is, of course, a fairly regular occurrence on a farm that raises pigs for meat production. No forewarning prepares the viewer. As such, this first shot has an intrusive quality. Edison could advertise the advantages of direct current over Nikolas Tesla's alternative current by electrocuting an elephant in front of the camera in 1903, doubtless to the astonishment of the film's audi-ence.[29] But while animals continue to die on camera,[30] it has now become imper-ative to add a disclaimer at the end of the film stating that "no animals were harmed during the making of this movie." The animal rights movement and the unfold-ing of ecological consciousness in the twentieth century have made certain that an image of an animal actually dying in a film now constitutes a scandal. There is little doubt that the image of the dying pig in *Benny's Video* provides a shock. It comes as a surprise, and it implies a loss of distance. We are exposed to this image without the benefit of any discursive framework to fall back on. The footage of the dying pig produces precisely the effect of collapsing distance and shocking surprise that Haneke attributes to the "American cinema" that he claims to crit-icize in and through his films. Video stands for, or appears to stand for, that against which film is a true art, one dedicated to the intellectual freedom of the specta-tor, that has to be defended, and against which film has to protect its spectator.

If the opening of *Benny's Video* exposes the viewer to a troubling experience of video as a medium that provokes a loss of moral and intellectual perspective, the

Fig. 3.1   Opening shot of the dying pig. *Benny's Video* (1992), dir. Michael Haneke, prod. Veit Heiduschka and Bernard Lang.

film reiterates this point at every step of the way. Benny not only watches video footage, he also produces it. He has a full set of equipment, camera, editing console, and monitors in his bedroom, and the opening shot, we later learn when he shows it to his victim, is his material. For Benny, being alone in his parents' apartment with the young woman presents merely an opportunity to restage the experience of videotaping the killing of the pig with a human victim. He is a zombie, of sorts, one of the living dead infected with the video virus. In this respect, however, he is not different from his victim. The girl comes from a working-class family and lives in a less reputable part of Vienna. The apartment that Benny lives in suggests that his family belongs to the educated upper middle class. The narration, however, characterizes both as equally deprived of moral and emotional perspective in the face of video images. Benny meets the girl in a video store. They both share a passion for video films, particularly cheap, violent genre films, and her reaction reflects his when he shows her the pig footage. But the difference between the opening and the latter parts of the film is that the opening subjects the viewer to the same kind of loss of perspective that it later attributes to Benny and his victim. Haneke's artistic antidote to "taking-by-surprise-before-one-can-think" cinema is a "taking-by-surprise-before-one-can-think" opening that implicates the viewer in the very same epistemic vertigo that supposedly ails the film's video-infected characters.

Interlude

Compare this to James Cameron's take on video. Haneke would probably list the Canadian director among the main perpetrators of the kind of American cinema he seeks to supplant and subvert. Still, like few other Hollywood directors, but much like Haneke, Cameron has been preoccupied, if not obsessed, with video. In *Titanic*, a group of bounty hunters pilfers the wreckage of the ship with a remote control submarine that operates using video cameras. The film marks the transition from the present to the past and the wreckage of the *Titanic* to the story of the ship's maiden voyage with a passage from a colorless video image to a white screen. The white screen in turn gives way to a cinematic reconstruction of the *Titanic* and life on board ship. Video barely grasps the wreckage of the ship, while film projects the world of the *Titanic* in its full glory. If 1930s radio films relied on quantitative sensualism to demonstrate film's superiority over radio, *Titanic* uses qualitative sensualism to demonstrate the epistemic advantage of film over video: The better, fuller, more detailed image wins. In fact, one of the purposes of the video image in this scene is to underscore, by contrast, the production values of the film. But there is a moral aspect to the denigration of video as well. Video is the medium of the morally dubious bounty hunter. Film is the medium of the storyteller: The flashback is really that of the female protagonist who comes aboard the research ship to authenticate some of the findings of the bounty hunters and then tells us her story, serving as a conduit for cinematic narration to supplant the deficient video image with the infinitely more detailed and vivid film image.

Similarly, in *Terminator 2*, it is cinematic narration as an institution that trumps video. In this sequel, produced one year before *Benny's Video*, we find Sarah Connor (Linda Hamilton), the mother of the future leader of the human resistance to robots and computers, in a psychiatric ward. She has a hearing with the director of the clinic about whether she should be released from solitary confinement. The psychiatrist confronts Sarah with a video recording of her first interrogation. The footage shows Sarah trying to convince her interlocutors of the danger of an impending nuclear holocaust. When she realizes that they do not believe her she goes into a fit of rage. The psychiatrist confronts Sarah with the recorded video image and asks her if she still holds on to those views. She now denies ever having encountered the Terminator and admits that since there were no traces left whatsoever of the cyborg fighting machine, the whole story had obviously been a figment of her imagination. We know that this is not true if we have seen the first film, but even if we have not, we now learn that Sarah is not telling the truth. The film cuts to the computer lab Sarah tried to bomb, Cyberdyne Systems, where engineer Miles Dyson (Joe Morton) works on a reconstruction of the original Terminator, using the remaining fragments of the old machine as his material. Cut back to the psychiatric ward where the interrogation continues, while a team of assistants to the psychiatrist videotape the proceedings behind a two-way mirror. The psychiatrist tells Sarah that he will deny her request and still considers her as dangerous. Once again Sarah goes into a fit of rage, and once again, the video camera records her outbreak. The scene ends with a video image of the psychiatrist turning to the camera, sarcastically uttering the phrase "A model citizen!" (Fig. 3.2).

Fig. 3.2　A psychiatrist watches videotapes but fails to see the truth. *Terminator 2* (1991), dir. and prod. James Cameron.

This scene not only pits film against video, it also pits one image-producing institution against another: the institution of (narrative) cinema against that of psychiatry. It is a case of one Foucauldian *dispositif* framed by another.[31] We must assume that the psychiatrist tapes all interrogations, and he does so for the purposes of argument. The video images provide proof of his written assessments of his patients. They are part and parcel of the psychiatric *dispositif* of truth-telling: They show, and thereby prove, the madness of the patient. They prove it to the psychiatrist, to the other doctors, but also, supposedly, to the patient herself. The problem with video in this case is not that it is inherently untruthful. Rather, the video image is in and of itself impotent to show, or tell, the truth. As viewers of the film we know that Sarah Connor's rage is justified, and that she does indeed tell the truth. The psychiatric institution, however, systematically misreads the evidence of the video image and arrives at a contrary conclusion: Connor is not telling the truth, but is simply trying to rationalize her random criminal act by appealing to the greater good of mankind. Holding sway over her, the psychiatrist forces Sarah Connor to acknowledge this misreading as the actual truth. By denying her request for partial release, the psychiatrist provokes another fit of rage, and the institution produces more video footage that apparently proves the madness of the patient. The inability of the psychiatrist and his team to read the images that they produce correctly stands in stark contrast to the truth-telling of the framing institution, the cinematic narration. The film knows, and lets us know, that Sarah is telling the truth. The video image can be misread, the film image cannot. Video is ontologically unreliable, film is not. The video image has no stable truth value, the film image, by comparison, is the repository of truth in the realm of the moving image. Or, to put it in Foucauldian terms: Video-producing *dispositifs* simultaneously produce truth and falsehood, film-producing *dispositifs* can always be relied on to tell the truth.

But while video may be inherently unreliable and unable to tell the truth without the support of film, video, according to Cameron, is not inherently pernicious. It is a weak medium, not a force unto itself.

Cut Back to Haneke

Benny's Video has echoes of Ödön von Horváth's 1937 novel *Jugend ohne Gott* (Godless Youth), which is about the random killing of a youth by other youths, and of two somewhat notorious films: Hitchcock's *Rope* (1948), in which two young students kill one of their colleagues because they want to know how it feels, and Michael Powell's 1960 film *Peeping Tom*, featuring Karl-Heinz Böhm as an amateur filmmaker-cum-serial killer who eviscerates his female victims with a knife attached to the tripod of his camera. Horváth decries the moral emptiness of 1930s Austrian society and traces the reason for the killer's behavior to a loss of faith and, by implication, a loss of respect for life. Hitchcock's protagonists suffer from an overdose of badly digested Nietzsche. The title character of *Peeping Tom* acts out a childhood trauma brought about by his scientist father's use of him as a childhood guinea pig in his experiments on fear. The decline of religion, the rise of dangerous philosophical doctrines, and psychological trauma respectively serve as explanatory templates for the behavior of the protagonists. *Benny's Video*, even though set in Vienna, has no place for psychoanalysis and even less for religion and its loss. Rather, as in Hitchcock's film, Benny's behavior is due to the emergence of a disturbing new outside force. While in *Rope* Nietzsche's philosophy (or whatever the students and their professor take it to be) provokes a loss of moral perspective and disconnects the students from their peers, in *Benny's Video* it is video that takes the place of the *Übermensch* doctrine. Rather than being the result of any social or historical circumstance, the moral emptiness of the title character is an effect of technology, the technology of the video image.

One might call this a techno-Hegelian explanation of moral decline. In his artwork essay, Benjamin argues that film raises a specific problem with regard to art. The question, Benjamin argues, is not whether and how film can be an art. Rather, it is what art is after film. The emergence of film and other technical media like it fundamentally alters the nature of art. We may call this techno-Hegelianism in the sense that Benjamin argues that media technology, rather than the Hegelian *Geist*, drives the development of art and our philosophical conceptions of art. In a strikingly analogous fashion, *Benny's Video* offers an argument from media technology to explain the moral decline of society. Video technology brings about a change in the moral constitution of the individual and, by implication, in the moral fabric of society. But the argument is more sophisticated than the usual diagnoses of the pernicious effects of media use. Video apparently produces not just higher levels of aggression in the behavior of adolescents, but effects a fundamental change in the structure of subjectivity. In Cameron's films, the threat of video comes from the people who use it rather than from the medium itself. In Haneke, the threat comes from people who use video *because* they use it, not because of *how* they use it. In fact, one could argue that Haneke's film subscribes not only to a techno-essentialist rather than social constructivist view of media, but also to the view that subjectivity is a mere afterthought to media technology.[32] Whether by coincidence or elective affinity, Haneke's film, released in 1992, nicely captures the *Zeitgeist* of media theory in the 1990s, as expressed in the writings of Friedrich Kittler and others.[33] The medium clearly still is the message. But it is no longer an extension of man. Man is now an extension of the medium.

It is important to note, however, that *Benny's Video* is making a point not just about video, but about film in relation to video. So how does film, as film, come into play in the film's representation and performance of video? Branching out into the vocabulary of theology, one could argue that film in *Benny's Video* is a *kat'echon*, a countervailing power that holds up evil, in that film not only documents and dramatizes, but also counters the detrimental effects of video. Rather than just lament the moral decline of youth from the point of view of a concerned but unaffected observer, *Benny's Video* exposes the viewer to the shock, surprise, and loss of distance induced by the video image in the very first shot of the film. As much as an aesthetic experience this resembles a scientific experiment: Let's expose viewers to the footage and see how they deal with it.[34] Film thus integrates video into an experimental setup and turns the cinema into a laboratory. This implies mastery of one medium by another. Film frames, and controls, video. Film provides a framework that makes it possible to unleash, but also to contain, the effects of video. As the film's narration progresses, the experimental setup of the first shot morphs into what one might call a setup of mastery through style. Wherever possible, the film uses carefully composed long shots and plan-séquences, i.e., long, uninterrupted takes. The spatial depth and the temporal integrity of the takes create a stark contrast with the flatness and the lack of perspective of the video images, and with the nervous editing of the television programs. The experimental, or scientific, attitude remains in play, however. There is a long take of Benny sitting at the dining table and reading comic books right after the murder. This is a textbook example of what Haneke refers to when he claims that his films preserve the liberty of the spectator and let him or her think. Deliberately slow in pacing, the scene dedramatizes the event and creates the space and time to reflect on what has just happened. But the scene also creates an observational setup. We watch Benny, and the spectacle of what we see is his apparent lack of reaction. He does not seem to display any kind of reaction to what he has just done and lived through. He just goes on with his life as if nothing has happened, supplanting one set of images, the video images, with another set of (supposedly harmful) pictures, the comic book. The sheer length of the take gives us the measure of how detached from his own actions this character has become. The long take, then, is not just an antidote to the video image but is also a device for laying bare and studying the effects of the video medium on the moral universe of the film's protagonist. The film may open with a "taking-by-surprise-before-one-can-think" segment, but luckily for the viewer there is the rampart of the long take that protects her from further damage and affords her all the time she needs to think about the surprise that she experienced in the opening sections of the film. Rather like in *All the President's Men*, then, the very process of cinematic narration protects, and elucidates, the epistemic privilege of film over other media.

Perhaps nowhere is this more apparent than towards the end of the film. When Benny's parents learn about his crime they help him get rid of the body. Finally, in order to take him away from everything, Benny's mother accompanies her son on a long trip to a country in the desert. The film tells the story almost entirely through reframed video footage and relegates the characters to the status of video personalities. By covering up the murder rather than handing over their son to the authorities, the parents subscribe to and pass into the moral, or rather amoral, universe of their videographer son. What the final sequences of the film show us, then, is a video universe from which there is no escape for the characters of the film, or rather, for the former characters of what, for them, is no longer a film. Film still controls the video universe, but the cinematic world has been entirely submerged by video. Where McLuhan claims that the content of a new medium is an old medium, in the case of Haneke, the new medium ends up as the content of the old medium, and the old medium contains the new also in a moral and eschatological sense, that is, in the sense of containing the danger that it represents. Rather than straight techno-Hegelianism, Haneke proposes an eschatological view of a struggle of quasi-mythical proportions between an older technology of the moving image and a new one, in which the old eventually defeats the new.

At least for the time being.

Pan to Egoyan

While video images feature prominently in many films by Atom Egoyan, another Canadian director, *Family Viewing*, the film that first brought Egoyan to international attention, is probably the key to a discussion of the issues at stake in this essay. In *Family Viewing* a young man about to finish high school is tending to his ailing Armenian grandmother who was sent by his father to a home. His parents are divorced, and his father tapes his sexual encounters with various lovers on old videotapes that contain footage of the young man's childhood. The young man finds this out when he takes some of the old tapes to the home where his grandmother lives in order to show her his childhood films. The grandmother first reacts with mute bliss to the images of her grandson on the television screen. As we look at her from the point of view of the video screen, the expression on her face turns into one of abhorrence, and she turns away in her wheelchair. Her grandson steps up, and we see what he sees: footage that his father shot over the footage of his childhood days, an image of his mother being forced into submissive sadomasochistic sex games. The scene ends with a close-up freeze frame of the young man's mother's face in pain. His father's perverse sexual appetites destroyed the family, and this iconic image of suffering furnishes the visual proof (Fig. 3.3). Video creates a moral and epistemic void in Haneke's film and cannot speak the truth in Cameron's film. In this scene, it could be argued, video figures as a medium that adds another dimension to the world of the film. Video opens up a conduit for love both in the sense of *agape* and *eros*, of compassion and desire. Showing the childhood videos to the grandmother is an act of compassion, of *agape*. The young man provides the joy of reliving his youth to himself and the grandmother, a shared emotion that transcends her ailment, and his. At the same time, video also figures as the medium of the sexual desire of the father. Nonetheless, the screening of the tapes reveals the truth about his father to the young man (and the grandmother). Following this scene, the son decides to break off contact with his father and build a new life for himself and his grandmother with the aid of a telephone

Fig. 3.3   Video as transgressive icon. *Family Viewing* (1987), dir. and prod. Atom Egoyan.

sex worker he had encountered earlier. Video, then, offers a conduit for both com-passion and sexual desire that transcends the immediate world of the characters to open up a realm of memory as well as fantasy.

But there is a spiritual dimension to the video image in Egoyan's film, too. In *Terminator 2*, cinema frames video as part of the truth-telling *dispositif* of psych-iatry. In *Family Viewing*, the framing of video brings to mind an entirely different *dispositif*: the religious *dispositif* of iconostasis, the wall of religious images that grace the interior of every Orthodox church. Egoyan, it is useful to remember, was born to Armenian parents in Egypt. The images, or "icons," of the iconostasis are more than just images: They are likeness and presence at the same time. According to religious doctrine, rather than simply representing religious motifs and saints the icon is a medium that creates a presence of the object.[35] In that sense, they add a presence to the space in which they are shown, and they transcend that space by opening it up to a spiritual dimension. The image logic of video in the *Family Viewing* sequence may be described in similar terms. The childhood videos open up the diegetic space to the realm of memory and create a presence of the life lived. The image of the mother's suffering, on the other hand, is doubly transgressive. In Orthodox religious painting suffering may not be shown. The true extent of the father's transgression, then, becomes apparent in the suffering the video image shows. Rather than creating a void in the character's world, the video image in Egoyan is a revelation, a revelation of the truth of both memory and fantasy.

Despite the intellectual temptations of techno-essentialism which Haneke so wholeheartedly succumbs to in *Benny's Video*, then, it appears that video as a medium has no essence other than what the respective framings of video in film ascribe to it. And that essence may even be, as in Egoyan's case, that video, rather than film, is the true repository of memory and fantasy.

Cut Back to Haneke; End

With regard to *Benny's Video* we could say that film contains video, and the dangers of video, for the time being. Two more recent examples seem to indicate that Haneke is no longer sure that film is safe from an infection by video images.[36] In a famous scene from *Funny Games*, one of the young tormentors of the bourgeois family in the film is shot and fatally wounded. His companion, unwilling to accept this outcome, grasps the television remote control and rewinds the scene in order to interfere and prevent the shot from being fired. All of a sudden, film appears to be subjected to the same technological conditions as video. Rewind is possible. While this remains an isolated incident in *Funny Games*, the subversion of film becomes endemic in *Caché*, Haneke's film about colonial guilt in France. His betrayal of an Algerian boy in his childhood comes back to haunt the main character, Georges, played by Daniel Auteuil. In a similar fashion, video haunts film throughout *Caché*. The opening shot shows the Paris residence of Georges and his wife. It is a long shot, exactly one of the kind that assured the primacy of film over video in the *mise-en-scène* of *Benny's Video*. As it turns out when the shot suddenly freezes and a rewind sets in, this is really a video image. Georges keeps receiving videotapes, but we never find out who shot them, not even at the end of the film. Video is still very present in Haneke's film, but it seems that it has now insinuated itself into the very fabric of film. While *Benny's Video* could still safely rely on the superior quality and the indexicality of the photographic image to provide the foundations of film's epistemic privilege over video, video now has reached a quality of image that makes it indistinguishable from film, as in the opening of *Caché*. Video appears to be shaking up the very epistemological foundations of film. What is more, we cannot count on cinematic narration to resolve the issue, either – after all, we never learn who makes the videos in *Caché*. Rather than a *pharmakon* that eventually strengthens the old medium, video has now become a resident virus permanently nested inside film. It remains to be seen whether this is simply yet another in the long list of deaths that the cinema has so far survived in the course of its history, or whether the video virus is actually a kind of germ that ends up creating a new form of cinema. As indeed it may.

Notes

1   Sometimes these studies lump in old media with new to underscore their point. German neurologist Manfred Spitzer is a case in point. After publishing a book extolling the

virtues of aural culture and the beneficial impact of listening to music on the development of the brain, he went on to publish a scathing critique of *Bildschirmmedien*, i.e., screen media, from television to the computer screen, claiming that exposure of the human perceptual system to audiovisual media would of necessity damage our intellectual capacities and the moral fabric of society. It is a critique that calls for a meta-critique and, among other things, brings to mind Marshall McLuhan's observation that democratic societies are inherently visual while atavistic non-democratic societies favor the aural. See Manfred Spitzer (2005, 2006).

2   On the history, and hastened historicization, of video see Ralf Adelmann, Hilde Hoffmann, and Rolf Nohr (2002). On the art history and aesthetic theory of video and video installations see Juliane Rebentisch (2003) and Yvonne Spielmann (2008). Some authors suggest a gendered view of video and its demise, elaborating on both Laura Mulvey's hypothesis of the male gaze in cinema and the 1980s television studies assumption that TV, as the domestic medium *par excellence*, is a female medium. Thus, for instance, Caetlin Benson-Allott (2007) suggests that video is neither male nor female, but a hermaphrodite technology, which may be part of the reason for the technology's relatively rapid obsolescence.

3   Raymond Bellour (1990). For an analysis of one of the key films of modern cinema that deals with the relationship of photography and film in a manner similar to the argument put forward in this essay, see Roger Odin (1981).

4   See Stanley Cavell (1979).

5   For the concept of *pharmakon*, see Jacques Derrida (1981).

6   For a different approach to the same field, focusing on how the advent of new media led to imaginary constructions of other media technologies and in turn reshaped Hollywood film narrative, see Paul Young (2006).

7   *Dispositif* here designates a hybrid ensemble of technological devices and discourse rules. For a comprehensive survey of the notion of *dispositif* see Frank Kessler, "Notes on *Dispositif*," and Joachim Paech (1997).

8   Georges Canguilhem (1952: 160–93); here p. 180.

9   Fritz Heider (2005).

10   Marshall McLuhan (1994).

11   Rudolf Arnheim (1956, 1971).

12   "Objects which in themselves we view with pain, we delight to contemplate when reproduced with minute fidelity: such as the forms of the most ignoble animals and of dead bodies. The cause of this again is, that to learn gives the liveliest pleasure, not only to philosophers but to men in general; whose capacity, however, of learning is more limited. Thus the reason why men enjoy seeing a likeness is, that in contemplating it they find themselves learning or inferring, and saying perhaps, 'Ah, that is he'" (Aristotle 1997: 6).

13   Drawing on Burke, who opens his *Inquiry* with a chapter on taste, Kant's *Critique of Judgment* attempts to establish precisely the foundations of the intersubjectivity of aesthetic judgments and thus of aesthetic experience as an experience conducive to knowledge.

14   Friedrich Schiller (2000).

15   One of the classic authors to defend this position is Theodor Adorno, who couples a ferocious critique of the culture industry with an aesthetic theory that extolls the virtues of high modernism.

16   For an influential example see Rosalind Krauß (1986).

17   Jacques Rancière (2001).

18   The only monograph on Pakula that I know of is Jared Brown's biography. Other than that, Pakula's films seem to be more likely to be discussed in law journals than in film studies journals. See Brown (2006) and Christine Alice Corcos (1997).

19   Hannah Landecker (2005).

20   On the relationship of the radio and film industries in the 1930s see Michele Hilmes (1990, 1997).

21   Since I have quoted Stanley Cavell above it is important to note that Cavell suggests, in *The World Viewed*, that animation is not cinema because animated images are not properly photographic in nature. Kracauer holds a different view, allowing animation to redeem physical reality as much as the photographic image does.

22   Jane Feuer (1993: 23).

23   One argument detractors of film like to use against the film medium is that literature liberates the human imagination whereas film enslaves it by flooding the mind with images that the reader is free to produce on his or her own. Christine Noll Brinckmann proposes turning this argument on its head by suggesting that literature actually enslaves the human imagination by putting it to work, whereas film liberates the imagination by providing the images and setting the mind free to imagine other things. Noll Brinckmann's argument is, of course, debatable, but it has the advantage of pointing out the shallowness of the received notion that she criticizes. (Personal communication with Christine Noll Brinckmann.)

24   On Peirce and photography see François Brunet (1996). For the *locus classicus* of the application of Peircean terminology to film see Peter Wollen (1969: 116–54).

25   Cf. André Bazin (1960).

26   The problem with the argument about the indexicality of the photographic image is that it derives an aesthetic, experiential property from the technical process of the image's production, i.e., it combines an aesthetic and epistemological argument with a genealogical argument in a somewhat awkward manner. Nonetheless, the argument has the advantage of seeming intuitively pertinent and correct, which is probably why film theory has subscribed to the idea of indexicality for so long, and continues to do so, in order to determine the aesthetic specificity of the film image. I have set out this critique in more detail in Vinzenz Hediger (2006).

27   Amos Vogel (1996).

28   It is tempting to suggest that at the heart of this critique is a strong concern for the privacy of the bourgeois subject. However that may be, Haneke's critique has strong echoes of Adorno, particularly in its defense of subjectivity and the individuality of the individual. Ironically, Adorno's theory of subjectivity, and by extension his critique of the culture industry, is anchored as much in Emerson and Transcendentalism as it draws on nineteenth-century German philosophy. Cf. Dieter Thomä (2007).

29   Tom Gunning (1989).

30   Akira Mizuta Lippit (2003).

31   "What I'm trying to pick out with this term is, firstly, a thoroughly heterogenous ensemble consisting of discourses, institutions, architectural forms, regulatory decisions, laws, administrative measures, scientific statements, philosophical, moral and philanthropic propositions – in short, the said as much as the unsaid. Such are the elements of the apparatus" (Foucault 1980).

32 Jörg Metelmann makes an apparently similar point in his analysis of the film, which he later expanded into a book from his doctoral dissertation. He writes about a *"system Benny-video"* which slowly but steadily infects all of society. I would argue that this is a variation on the cyborg trope, also very current in 1990s media theory and proposed, most prominently, by Donna Haraway, as well as in James Cameron's *Terminator* films (of which more below). Cf. Jörg Metelmann (2001, 2003).

33 Friedrich Kittler (1985, 1998).

34 Critics like to point out Haneke's indebtedness to the epic theater of Brecht when discussing his films. The text of reference for this line of analysis is Metelmann's book, *Zur Kritik der Kino-Gewalt* (2003).

35 For a comprehensive discussion of these issues see Hans Belting (1993).

36 For a similar argument see also Mattias Frey (2006).

References and Further Reading

Adelmann, Ralf, Hoffmann, Hilde, and Nohr, Rolf, eds.: *REC – Video als mediales Phänomen* (Weimar: VDG, 2002).

Aristotle: *Poetics*, trans. S. H. Butcher (New York: Dover, 1997).

Arnheim, Rudolf: *Film as Art* (Berkeley: University of California Press, 1956).

Arnheim, Rudolf: *Radio* (New York: Arno Press, 1971).

Bazin, André: *The Ontology of the Photographic Image*, trans. Hugh Gray. *Film Quarterly* 13:4 (Summer 1960): 4–9.

Bellour, Raymond: *L'Entre-image* (Paris: POL, 1990).

Belting, Hans: *Likeness and Presence: A History of the Image before Art* (Chicago: University of Chicago Press, 1993).

Benson-Allott, Caetlin: "VCR Autopsy," *Journal of Visual Culture* 6:2 (August 2007): 175–81.

Brown, Jared: *Alan J. Pakula: His Films and His Life* (New York: Back Stage Books, 2006).

Brunet, François: "Visual Semiotics versus Pragmatism: Peirce and Photography," *Peirce's Doctrine of Signs*, ed. Vincent Michael Colapietro and Thomas M. Olshewsky (New York: Walter de Gruyter, 1996), pp. 295–314.

Canguilhem, Georges: *La Connaissance de la vie* (Paris: Hachette, 1952).

Cavell, Stanley: *The World Viewed: Reflections on Photography and Film*, enlarged edition (Cambridge, MA: Harvard University Press, 1979).

Corcos, Christine Alice: "Presuming Innocence: Alan Pakula and Scott Turow Take on the Great American Legal Fiction," *Oklahoma City University Law Review* 22 (1997).

Derrida, Jacques: "Plato's Pharmacy," *Dissemination*, trans. Barbara Johnson (London: Athlone Press, 1981).

Feuer, Jane: *The Hollywood Musical*, second edition (Bloomington: Indiana University Press, 1993).

Foucault, Michel: "The Confession of the Flesh" (1977), *Power/Knowledge: Selected Interviews and Other Writings*, ed. Colin Gordon (New York: Pantheon, 1980), pp. 194–228.

Frey, Mattias: "Benny's Video, Caché, and the Desubstantiated Image," *Framework: The Journal of Cinema and Media* 47:2 (2006): 30–6.

Gunning, Tom: "An Aesthetic of Astonishment," *Art and Text* 34 (1989).

Hediger, Vinzenz: "Illusion und Indexikalität," *Deutsche Zeitschrift für Philosophie* 54:1 (2006): 101–10.

Heider, Fritz: *Ding und Medium* (Berlin: Kadmos, 2005).

Hilmes, Michele: *Hollywood and Broadcasting: From Radio to Cable* (Urbana: Illinois University Press, 1990).

Hilmes, Michele: *Radio Voices: American Broadcasting, 1922–1952* (Minneapolis: University of Minnesota Press, 1997).

Kessler, Frank: "Notes on *Dispositif*," www.let.uu.nl/~Frank.Kessler/personal/notes%20on%20dispositif.PDF.

Kittler, Friedrich: "Hardware, das unbekannte Wesen," *Medien Computer Realität*, ed. Sybille Krämer (Frankfurt am Main: Suhrkamp, 1998), pp. 119–32.

Kittler, Friedrich: *Aufschreibsysteme 1800/1900* (Munich: Wilhelm Fink, 1985).

Krauß, Rosalind: *The Originality of the Avant-Garde and Other Modernist Myths* (Cambridge, MA: MIT Press, 1986).

Landecker, Hannah: "Cellular Features: Microcinematography and Film Theory," *Critical Inquiry* 31:4 (Summer 2005): 903–37.

Lippit, Akira Mizuta: "The Death of an Animal," *Film Quarterly* 56:1 (2003): 9–22.

McLuhan, Marshall: *Understanding Media: The Extensions of Man* (Cambridge, MA: MIT Press, 1994).

Metelmann, Jörg: "Living Video. Mediale Kontrolle und humanistischer Kontrollverlust: Eine Relektüre von Michael Hanekes *Benny's Video*," *nachemfilm* 10 (2001), www.nachdemfilm.de/no3/met01dts.html.

Metelmann, Jörg: *Zur Kritik der Kino-Gewalt. Die Filme von Michael Haneke* (Munich: Wilhelm Fink, 2003).

Odin, Roger: "Le Film de fiction menacé par la photographie et sauvé par la bande-son (à propos de *La Jetée* de Chris Marker)," *Cinémas de la modernité: Films, théories*, ed. Dominique Château, André Gardies, and François Jost (Paris: Publications du Centre Culturel International de Cerisy-la-Salle, 1981).

Paech, Joachim: "An-Ordnungen (Dispositive) des Sehens," *Literatur im multimedialen Zeitalter* (Asiatische Germanistentagung), 1 (1997): 126–40.

Rancière, Jacques: *L'Inconscient esthétique* (Paris: Galilée, 2001).

Rebentisch, Juliane: *Ästhetik der Installation* (Frankfurt am Main: Suhrkamp, 2003).

Schiller, Friedrich: *Über die ästhetische Erzierhung des Menschen in einer Reihe von Briefen* (Stuttgart: Reclam, 2000).

Spielmann, Yvonne: *Video: The Reflexive Medium* (Cambridge, MA: MIT Press, 2008).

Spitzer, Manfred: *Musik im Kopf: Hören, Musizieren, Verstehen und Erleben im neuronalen Netzwerk* (Stuttgart: Schattauer, 2005).

Spitzer, Manfred: *Vorsicht Bildschirm! Elektronische Medien, Gehirnentwicklung, Gesundheit und Gesellschaft* (Stuttgart: Klett, 2006).

Thomä, Dieter: "Verlorene Passion, wiedergefundene Passion. Arendts Anthropologie und Adornos Theorie des Subjekts," *Deutsche Zeitschrift für Philosophie* 55:4 (2007): 627–47.

Vogel, Amos: "Of Non-Existing Continents: The Cinema of Michael Haneke," *Film Comment* 32:4 (1996): 73.

Wollen, Peter: *Signs and Meaning in the Cinema* (Bloomington: Indiana University Press, 1969).

Young, Paul: *The Cinema Dreams Its Rivals: Media Fantasy Films from Radio to the Internet* (Minneapolis: University of Minnesota Press, 2006).

4

Tracking *Code Unknown*

Tom Conley

In *Casablanca*, an autobiography in which he jogs his early wartime memories through those of Michael Curtiz's film of the same name, Marc Augé recalls how the Liberation of Paris was pocked with strife. He saw survivors of the camps gingerly climb down from trucks that had brought them to the Hôtel Lutetia, only a few months after he had witnessed, from the Place Maubert, free French soldiers immolate two German motorcyclists at the corner of the Montagne Sainte-Geneviève. It was just before Tiger tanks, dispatched to the summit of the rue Cardinal-Lemoine, in reprisal, fired onto the rue Monge. As soon as the violence subsided Augé scurried with his parents to the square in front of Notre-Dame to welcome the return of Charles de Gaulle. All of a sudden snipers opened fire on the crowd. His father thrust Augé onto his shoulders and carried him home.

> The streets along which we went back, running as we did from one doorway to the next (there were no codes and so shelter could be sought everywhere), have today become luxurious thoroughfares where, at every floor, exposed wooden beams are on the ceilings above antique furnishings. But at that time these were simply poor and dirty streets. We prudently were initiating ourselves to what was not yet called urban guerrilla warfare.[1]

Augé, an ethnologist of autobiography, takes what seems to be a black-and-white snapshot of the past. In 1944, a time when electronic entries were unknown, he and his father found sanctuary in a courtyard behind a *porte cochère* (overhang). Had the protective device not existed the boy and his elder might have lost their lives. Augé's passing thoughts about door codes in the midst of a chilling flashback to the war suggest that Paris, then an open city, has since become closed. Now the metropolis has become a bourgeois citadel, a mass of upscale buildings displaying *poutres apparentes* (exposed beams) behind ample windows that give onto the streets below. Paris is no longer a place where shelter is available for anyone. The new system of door codes assures safety only for those who can afford to live in spaces of confined splendor.

The slight but telling mention of the "door codes" to refurbished Parisian apartments can serve as an epigraph to this brief reflection on a tracking shot at the
outset of Michael Haneke's *Code Unknown* (*Code inconnu*, 2000). The film is set in
motion at the point where the "code" of the title matches the sight of the device.
Glimpsed fleetingly, following the credits and a silent sequence in which children
are shown using sign language, the mechanism designates a point of departure
(and, as will later occur, a point of closure). When the "door code" is seen the
film makes clear a relation between what is known and what is not in both a
spatial and somatic sense. The film brings the unknown into the fleeting tenor
of everyday life.

It suffices, for what might serve as a second epigraph, to recall that for the
psychoanalyst Guy Rosolato the unknown is tied to what he calls the *objet de
perspective* (object of perspective) that can signify the unknown, "what moves desire
in all ideals."[2] The object is what is visibly or mentally glimpsed, yet never quite
known, that drives us to wonder about how we are in the world and why at the
same time we sense ourselves detached from it while we gain experience within
it. A hinge on what we see and on our phantasms at work in the visual field before
our eyes, it begs us to locate ourselves in respect to where we are and what might
be our geography of subjectivity. The object of perspective is located at a juncture (which is also a point of rupture) between the aural field – marked by a shard
of speech, a note of music, or an unsettling sound – and the world seen. It is a
visible fragment that floats before our eyes and baffles or annoys enough to prod
us to want to "know" why, unknown, it is as it is.[3] For the analyst who listens to
his or her patient, the object of perspective might be a fragment, *seen when heard*,
that brings forward unconscious demands or desires. It entails "discovering something beyond, a surge aiming at something unknown, distant from our acquired
bearings and surpassing them, but nonetheless *in a narrow relation with repressed
phantasms* that need to be discerned [*repérés*]" (Rosolato 1996: 152, stress his). The
analyst, he concludes, must disengage in the other's desire – the other can be
an analysand, an interlocutor, or a film – the perspectival objects, that is, "these
ideals activating desires toward an unknown so that transformations or discoveries
can be reached" (ibid.). He notes that the discovery is a matter of one's own and
first step toward a "cure" – even if the latter might yield a sense of horror and a
realization of the defensive mechanisms a person has mantled in order not to recognize the unknown. Or, too, it might be a point of departure for illumination
and delight, either a "taste for life" in the poetry of everyday things, in metaphors
that bear (*portent*) the unknown, or a desire for and acquisition of knowledge. In
all events it must be known that the unknown is a vital part of the very experience of life *tout court* (167).

The title and execution of Haneke's film seem to build on these reflections and
to cause the unknown to resemble, too, what Roland Barthes had noted about
the enigmatic nature of the photograph insofar as it is a "message without a code."
The unknown inhabited what, long before the advent of digital photography, he

had called the "photographic paradox." The message that a still photograph conveys is nothing but itself, and not a transformation of what it registers:

> [E]very sign presupposes a code, and this code (of connotation) is what needs to be established. The photographic paradox would thus be the coexistence of two messages, the one without a code (which would be the photographic analogue) and the other with a code (this would be either "art," treatment, or *écriture*, or the rhetoric of photography); structurally, the paradox is obviously not the collusion of a denoted message and a connoted message: such is the probably fatal status of all mass communication; here it is because a connoted (or coded) message is developed from a message *without a code*.[4]

For Barthes, much as the unknown happens to be for Rosolato, the photographic message is read according to a *code inconnu*. It opens onto the unknown and ultimately cues interrogation about who and where one is in a welter of spatial and symbolic relations. The continuousness of the photograph assures the fact and discovery of the code that is nothing other than the unknown itself. Its own quiddity or haeccity (the term belongs to Gilles Deleuze), in other words its matte presence before our eyes that register its strangeness, is cause for the unknown to be the absence of an analogy that would otherwise explain or mediate what we see.

Such is what the opening tracking shot of Haneke's *Code Unknown* brings forward. Lasting eight minutes and ten seconds, it rivals with the many sequences that Jean-Luc Godard has invested with a "moral" or critical dimension. For the filmmaker of the traffic jam in *Week-end* (1967) or of the expanse of checkout aisles in the hypermarket at the end of *Tout va bien* (1972), the tracking shot elicits both identification with the subjects shown and simultaneous distancing. The tracking shot "identifies" with what it records because it literally *conveys* the scene, yet it remains detached since it never closes in upon what is shown. It offers a perspective of critical appreciation as it draws attention to the mode of perception it elicits. For Godard the shot bears a political virtue inasmuch as it primes our desire to identify or make known the relation of the subject to the construction of the shot itself. If Godard's reflections of the 1960s are held in view today, a broader history of its politics comes forward. The front-credits and inaugural sequence of *The Player* (Robert Altman, 1992) include in their duration ample reflection on film form. A crane and tracking shot of about eight minutes' length includes two personages, one walking with his bicycle, who stroll along a pathway in a studio lot. One of them offers a thumbnail history of tracking shots to his interlocutor: "All they do now is cut, cut, cut. Remember the two-minute tracking shot of *Touch of Evil*," he quips, just as the camera appears to be rehearsing the same *tour de force*. The bicycle refers immediately – which a moderately informed viewer immediately notes – to *Bicycle Thieves* ([Vittorio de Sica, 1948], the end of which is later seen in *The Player*) in which the tracking shot, always close to the protagonist and his son, but always held at a distance, brings social contradiction into the style of presentation.

Haneke's sequence figures in the pantheon in which these shots are found. As the black title card, *écrit et realisé par Michael Haneke* (in white characters in sans-serif typeface on a black background), fades out, the shot of a refashioned entrance to an apartment begins. It is registered at eyeline level from the side of the boulevard that the greater building is facing. Two frosted-glass doors, one large (to the left), the other small (to the right), display a smaller electronic device (shown as a white rectangle in a black frame) on the polished stone façade. Street noise is audible as two men pace by, from left to right, in the foreground when suddenly a woman in a tan raincoat, wearing gym shoes, hurriedly exits the larger door. She anxiously checks her bag whose strap is slung over her right shoulder. The track begins as the woman emerges into view and passes between three pedestrians standing in the street. For a moderately seasoned spectator it is glaringly clear that her departure from the apartment is coded to recall a "primal scene" of cinematography, notably that of the Lumière Brothers' "La Sortie des usines Lumière" (1895), in which the opening of a door, and the exit and the diffusion of a mass of workers into a street, is taken to be the inaugural moment of the seventh art. If cinema typically rehearses its own "primitive" or primal scenes here it can be affirmed that from its very onset the shot recoups the invention of cinema.

The woman hurries along her way. The alternation of doors and walls in the background draws attention to the motion of the shot when suddenly the woman – now, no longer *inconnue*, is recognizably Juliette Binoche, a French *bourgeoise par excellence*. She looks back in response to an interpellation out the frame: *Anne!* She stops just as a pedestrian carrying a packsack continues his way to the right. Suddenly a youth dressed in a light green jacket appears when, reaching toward and then embracing him, the woman calls his name – *Jean!* – and immediately asks him why he (Alexandre Hamidi) is where he is. The camera has lightly retraced its course by moving backward, ostensibly to hold in view, in the background, the "code" of entry to the door that has just opened. The camera has stopped so that in a two-shot (within the frame of the track) the boy and the woman exchange words about the unknown location of his brother "Georges" (appearing later and played by Thierry Neuvio). She remarks that having been gone for three weeks, he is in Kosovo (which, at the time of the making of the film, was in unprecedented conflict and turmoil). Perturbed because Georges is gone (and clearly not because he is in a region of conflict), the boy pirouettes and mimes an expression of frustration by looking away so as to *beg* the woman's concern for him. His gesture succeeds. As it does his hand is shown poised before the door code that seems to be a miniature title-card. No sooner has he done so than, responding to her solicitude, he turns away as if to hold the code in view. Two businessmen speak in the background while the boy asserts that he won't "go back home."

The camera begins to move again when the woman admits that she's pressed and can hear him out as they walk. They pass by walls and upscale windows of a bank before they cross a street. As the camera continues its career he grouses about having waited for an hour and been unable to gain access to the apartment.

Fig. 4.1 Anne (Juliette Binoche) and Jean (Alexandre Hamidi). *Code Unknown* (2000), dir. Michael Haneke, prod. Marin Karmitz and Alain Sarde.

"Ton putain de code, il a changé" (subtitle: "your fucking door code's changed"). She responds, facing him (as a red car moves toward the intersection behind the camera, setting the boy's green jacket in high contrast to the gray character of the street), asking him why he didn't call from a telephone booth said (and later shown) to be standing just in front of the apartment and the door code. He answers that indeed he had called and left a message. In getting back to the sidewalk and passing by an outdoor flower shop the misunderstanding is resolved until, passing by the rows of red, yellow, and blue bouquets, the boy claims that he needs a place to stay, "here in Paris." She again turns backward while advancing, then stops, poising herself in a medium two-shot in which she learns, in his words, that he has "fucked off" ("je me suis tiré"). Looking as him, she smiles as if to prompt the shot to begin moving again, that "life goes on." It goes on – like the tracking shot – despite the fact that the boy "can't stand" ("je ne supporte pas") his father, a bumpkin who is said to be redoing "an old barn."

The camera has just passed the flower stand and stops again when the woman intercedes, asking him if he is as hungry as she is. She turns to enter the doorway of a pastry shop from which one woman has exited and another is shown in the background inside. The store window on which are printed, in an arched shape, the upper-case letters that spell VIENNOISERIE displays three racks of cakes. The word on the window, reflected in reverse on the glass box containing the pastries, seems to be an implicit subtitle that links the heads of the two characters. Would this sign, like the door code at the beginning of the shot, be of something strange or of another familiar place? The camera holds long enough to identify a "code" for the name that links the two conflicting characters to a common place. The sound of a singer crooning and strumming a guitar is heard *off* before the camera follows the boy, walking to the right, who investigates where the performer might be. In moving along with the boy the camera opens onto a passageway filled with people who have stopped to listen to the singer in the background. The song stops and people clap. Noticeable are two posts (erected to keep traffic from entering the space) on which are painted long green arrows, matching the color of the boy's jacket, which indicate the way to a *supermarché*.[5] The camera continues its course, and its slight focus pull draws attention to the boy, now alone, who seems lost in thought. He continues his path by the window of a real estate office and then another bank (whose façade is painted in blue) at the corner of the next intersection when, all of a sudden, the woman catches up with him, chomping on a *pain au chocolat*. Speaking with her mouth full, she tells him that when she is in the bathroom she can't hear the telephone: thus, the possible misunderstanding and the failure to establish previous contact.

In a casual and seemingly meaningless gesture, as if in a friendly way and in curt response to the boy's failure to acknowledge her explanation, she hands him a piece of pastry just as she looks away to see if traffic is coming as they cross the street. She moves across the dashed median (perpendicular to the axis of the shot) in asking – hurriedly, casually – if something is wrong ("ça va pas?"). He opens the bag while in deep focus the shot reveals that the trailer of a large moving van in the background carries the name DETROIT. Their pace accelerates with that of the camera. She eats while he stuffs his hand in the bag that crinkles in the midst of the street noise. They reach the curb again and seem once more to reconcile their differences. As he begins to munch the pastry she resumes conversation ("alors, où en étions-nous?"), just after their passage their bodies have scanned the letters printed on the moving van.

Their conflict seems greater when they are in the street than on the sidewalk. Or at least until the name of another real estate agency emerges into view obliquely, at the corner, in red neon: JEAN FEUILLADE IMMOBILIER. At that moment the plot thickens. The woman inquires of his father, whom he reports, again, is fixing up a barn that would eventually become a "place to live" for him when he is older. The irony is that the real estate agency, highly visible in the background, displays behind its windows rectangular small pictures of domiciles that are visually analogous to the door code seen on the wall at the beginning of the shot, and, furthermore, that the conversation has to do with habitus: where to be, how to live, in what milieu, whether urban or rural, and under whose aegis. As workers pass by or ogle at the images in the window the boy remarks that he would never live in the manner that his father proposes ("jamais de ma vie!"). The milieu is at once that of a familial conflict, another of places *in* and *off* or urban and rural, and of what is being shown and, behind that, as the name Feuillade cannot fail to indicate, the history of cinema.

Just after having passed by the real estate agency the camera moves into a space in deep perspective (for the fourth time, if the passageway to the supermarket and the two streets are counted), in front of an open entry into a mall of shops in a contemporary arcade. Standing on opposite sides of the corners to the entry in which some well-to-do shoppers are visible, the two characters seem to face off and be at odds with each other. The camera underscores the deep focus when the woman mutters a banality in the shape of a regressive double bind: You are no longer a minor, she asserts, staring coldly, because now it is urgent that you do as your father says. At the utterance of the mixed command the tracking shot comes again to a stop, exactly at the point where the couple separates. Not having slept, late and in a hurry, the woman must get to work. She fumbles in her bag to search for the keys to the apartment that she gives to him along with mention of the code. "The code is 48B13." When they both hold the keychain she insists that there are "no more misunderstandings." He can stretch out on the couch before she returns at noon, and he must be sure to know, she reminds him, that there is no room "for three." After asking, "Do you remember the code?," she kisses him on the cheek and departs at the point where the tracking shot now begins its reverse career, retracing the path it had just followed.

The boy walks back by the Feuillade agency (a man strolling with a dog now looks at the images behind the window). In voice-off Anne intervenes (her interpellation matches Jean's which began the shot) to tell him not to answer the phone because the action will not engage the message-machine. The camera catches up and keeps pace with the youth, as he crosses the street, such that the name DETROIT on the van (whose workers attend to the emptying or filling of an apartment) inflects the issue of location and disruption while also signaling, in the fleetingly deep perspective of the street, the idea of a narrow passage for the boy lost in thought.[6] He thus walks across the intersection and toward the arcade where music is now heard, *off*, as he glides by the first of the two real estate agencies. When he turns to his right to observe the musician and his half-dozen spectators the camera stops, repeating again a view in deep focus in which the two posts printed with arrows indicating the location of the supermarket in the field of view are framing the boy in the middle. Four or five pedestrians cross by before it becomes clear that now – two minutes and forty seconds later – a beggar woman (who will be known as Maria, played by Luminita Gheorghiu) sits cross-legged on the pavement at the left-hand corner of the passageway. Having held its position for about fifteen seconds, the camera moves as the boy exits and passes by the beggar, at once advertently and inadvertently tossing – slam-dunk – the wrapper into the beggar's hands as he looks away. He passes again by the Viennese bakery. Wiping his hands while its storefront is still in view (just as the rows of flowers appear again) another interpellation follows. A husky black youth (later identified as "Amadou," played by Ona Lu Yenke) enters from the right, putting his right hand on the boy's shoulder before he stops him – and the camera movement – to frame, *exactly in the same position that the boy and the woman had occupied earlier in the shot*, the two youths, black and white, standing at either side of the arc of VIENNOISERIE on the store window. "Tu trouves ton comportement correct?" ("do you think you're behaving correctly?"), the black youth asks the boy (who immediately tells him to go to hell) before the camera continues its itinerary to the left.

Fig. 4.2   Jean and Amadou (Ona Lu Yenke). *Code Unknown* (2000), dir. Michael
Haneke, prod. Marin Karmitz and Alain Sarde.

The camera stops to catch the boys tussling. It then returns to the entry of the
arcade to frame the two adversaries facing each other on either side of the
beggar. The commotion brings a storekeeper into the fray before, all of a sudden,
the woman returns. As the beggar woman leaves (off-screen) the black youth
follows. The tracking shot resumes, following and then keeping pace with the white
youth (in medium close-up) as he walks by the racks of flowers. The African youth
enters from the right, engaging in fisticuffs before the woman returns, again,
begging him to let go. The camera laterally reframes the field of view before
two policemen enter (from the right) to impose law and order.

The tracking shot seems to have come to an end when the camera stops to
frame an apparent two-shot. The angry black, facing the police, explains what
prompted him to correct the youth's (or, as he corrects his own words, the "young
man's") humiliation of the beggar. As soon as the police seek the beggar the camera resumes its track, moving to the right, then back to the left, across the arcade
and back to the point where the camera had shown the black youth informing
the police of the boy's infraction. He cedes his identity papers to the police. Refusing
to let them touch him, he tussles with the two officers.

After eleven minutes and thirty seconds the shot cuts to black before the next
sequence begins. At the end of its itinerary the tracking shot has staged a plethora
of "codes" in multifarious conflict. A thematic reading invites reflection on how
civil conduct can be respected in situations inviting or inciting violence. The white
youth has made a gesture, possibly unbeknownst to himself, that in the eyes of a
black bystander is flagrantly demeaning to a woman shown to be derelict for no
cause of her own making. A self-involved adolescent tosses a ball of crumpled paper
into the hands of a *sans-papiers*. A black youth feels impelled to make the young
man apologize to the beggar and to honor a code of decency for which he shows

that he is a dubious representative when he projects his own frustrations onto both the youth and the police. His own violence betrays a conflict of class or struggle between haves and have-nots which no sooner gives way to another of gender and social geography. The black man is clearly an outsider in an elegant area of Paris, but so also is the white youth, who does not quite have a place of his own in the space shown in deep focus. The bourgeois woman is so hassled that she has no idea about the contradiction in the street she inhabits when she goes to and from work.

Some of the codes unknown to the participants are cinematic, and herein Haneke's rewriting of Godard's "moral drama of the tracking shot" at once identifies, identifies with, and draws a distance from the conflicts it records. At its very beginning the shot inscribes an icon of a "code" into the play of rectangular shapes that comprise the wall of the building and the entry out of which the woman emerges. It immediately becomes a point of reference because the adolescent had no idea that the "putain de code" had been changed; at the axis of the tracking shot the subtitle records the number ("48B13") that the woman conveys to the adolescent and then reminds him to remember. The Viennese pastry shop where Anne buys the snack in wrapping paper (the lure or "floating signifier" that prompts the violence of the scene) twice serves as a background to two dialogues of conflict. In the first half of the shot its name, much like an implicit intertitle in a silent film, both links and separates Anne and Jean; in the second, the youth and his black (and third world) counterpart are shown in almost identical poses. *Viennoiserie*: Because the film has inscribed its title in the field of the image at the very beginning of the shot, the camera signals that the image-field itself is layered or even rife with conflicting codes of visual and aural form. Like a cartographer's signature associated with a toponym on a map, the name of the bakery would possibly refer to the director's Austrian origins shown "displaced" into Paris. It would affirm that the film is not entirely of the "French" style of the tracking shot and is of a mixed and perhaps conflicted origin.

Closely analyzed, say, in the manner by which Michel Foucault and Gilles Deleuze ask their readers to "break open," "split," or "crack apart" visible and discursive forms that convey the signs of everyday life, "viennoiserie" is a visual symptom of the broader conflicts of code that Haneke stages in this film.[7] *Vienne . . . noiserie*: "let there be noise" or a staging of violence, if indeed *noise* is understood as din and shuffle that mediate discord and conflict of one kind or another. *Noise* remains one of the most charged substantives of the French literary idiolect, and in Haneke's film, spelled out at two key points adjacent to the major players in the tracking shot, it encodes much of the conflict seen here and elsewhere in the film.[8] The disruptions calling attention to rules as they ought to be observed – or transgressed in order to be made visible – make clear the contradictions defining the given social space. The history of cinema, however, bears on Haneke's implicit anthropology of well-to-do Paris. The tracking shot allows the ritual conflict to be seen as a telling event because of the nature of the shot and the allusions to cinema that it makes along the way. Thus through its self-consciousness or "coded" aspect the film at once exacerbates and mediates the very violence it displays.

Its effect spills onto other films and thus becomes a trait of the signature of Haneke the auteur. In *Caché* (2005) the harried protagonist (Daniel Auteuil), seen in his office making a telephone call to his wife while he plies a postcard on which a child's drawing of a boy vomiting blood (much as the protagonist in Altman's *The Player* does with a similarly threatening card), reflects on what he sees. In the space of the office seen in extreme depth of field the ceiling lights offer converging dashed lines. The camera holds in the extreme foreground a shelf of books adjacent to the protagonist's head that include, among others (and suitably bringing forward the conflicts of the feature in general), Georges Perec's *Les Choses* and *La Grande Histoire des Français sous l'Occupation*. Each is an object of ideological and historical perspective. Perec's classic applies to the uninformed and otherwise self-satiated condition of the couple mysteriously threatened by an anonymous party while the study of France during the Occupation is an analogue to the situation that is cause for the dilemma in the film and its effects as the couple experience them. The titles on the spines of the books "code" the unknown that menaces the couple.

A straight cut to a medium long shot of the couple exiting the doors of a police precinct draws attention to the street, which they cross in moving between a parked police van and squad car. The blur of a man on a bicycle crosses the protagonist's path. The film cuts to the street where the cyclist, a black man, pirouettes when the husband interpellates, voice-off, "Ça va pas, connard!" ("What's wrong with you, fuckface!"). The black man comes forward to hear him cry, "Why, idiot, can't you see where you're going!": to which the black man responds, as the wife (Juliette Binoche) tells him to forget what has happened, inviting – goading – him to repeat his insults. Although the black man (of African origin) has sped the wrong way down a one-way street (which in the depth of field is indicated by two circular red signs crossed with a white bar, the colors rhyming with those of the threatening postcards), having broken one code, he demands that the white man respect exactly that which the black youth of *Code Unknown* had summoned from his white counterpart. The camera pans and tracks to follow the couple who take refuge in their parked car before the film cuts to the long shot, anticipating the finale of *Caché*, of the front steps, seen from a street on which cars are parked, of a school from which students are exiting in the afternoon.

The conflict staged in the tracking shot of *Code Unknown* is rehearsed five years later in *Caché* in order, it seems, to imply that in their complacent isolation a couple cannot yet fathom the greater history informing the dilemma in which they find themselves. The tracking shot cues, too, on the director's penchant to execute each sequence in a single take, and thus to be aligned with André Bazin, who had been the champion of "reality" in the long take, while also, elsewhere in the same film, its connection with similar shots underscores the constructed nature of that reality. It clearly affiliates with Godard by bringing the style of the film into the political and moral dilemmas it explores. The visual "code" at the doorway invites comparison to Marc Augé's mention of entry devices in *Casablanca*, in which the anthropologist reads his own history in the context of that of his nation at the time of the Occupation, a moment that is also present in Haneke's film. And much like Guy Rosolato's therapist and patient who seek discovery in the attraction and menace of the unknown, and even Roland Barthes's view of the unforgiving effect of photographic messages that would be without relay, Haneke's characters find themselves encoded *unknown*, in an arena in which our relations with the world are set in play. Within the context of what the director calls "an incomplete story of various journeys," the great tracking shot that begins *Code Unknown* brings us close to the vital force and consequence of the unknown.

Notes

1 Marc Augé (2009: 71).
2 Guy Rosolato (1996: 153). (Here and elsewhere all translations from the French are by the author.)
3 Tom Conley (1991/2006: xxvii–xviii); Conley (1996: 13–17); à propos René Clair, Conley (2007: 38).
4 Roland Barthes (1982: 13).
5 Which becomes the site of a later sequence, comparable to the tracking shot in this instance, that follows Anne and her companion in conflict.
6 In the narrative he is later last seen driving away from the farm on a moped. In the penultimate sequence of the film, when she returns to the apartment, a boy on a moped passes by, as if to remind the viewer of his absent presence.
7 Gilles Deleuze (1986: 124ff.).
8 In *Mythologiques 1: Le cru et le cuit* (Paris: Plon, 1962), Claude Lévi-Strauss notes saliently that ritual noise belongs to the tradition of the *charivari* in which the din had signified "the breakage of a chain, the appearance of a social discontinuity" which "the compensatory continuity of noise" sought to obviate through "a different code" (343–4, translation mine), which in Haneke's film would be the very sequence as it is shown in theaters in France.

References and Further Reading

Augé, Marc: *Casablanca* (Paris: Editions du Seuil, 2007); *Casablanca: Movies and Memory*, trans. Tom Conley (Minneapolis: University of Minnesota Press, 2009).
Barthes, Roland: "Le Message photographique," in Barthes, *L'Obvie et l'obtus: Essais critiques III* (Paris: Editions du Seuil, 1982).
Conley, Tom: *Cartographic Cinema* (Minneapolis: University of Minnesota Press, 2007).
Conley, Tom: *Film Hieroglyphs: Ruptures in Classical Cinema* (Minneapolis: University of Minnesota Press, 1991/2006).
Conley, Tom: *The Self-Made Map* (Minneapolis: University of Minnesota Press, 1996).
Deleuze, Gilles: *Foucault* (Paris: Editions de Minuit, 1986).
Rosolato, Guy: *La Portée du désir, ou la psychanalyse même* (Paris: PUF, 1996).

5

Michael Haneke and the New Subjectivity

Architecture and Film

Peter Eisenman

Unlike other contributors to this anthology I have no relationship to the film community. I am by profession an architect and a teacher: My remarks below, while they may reflect a naïveté with regard to their subject, are intended to interest those who think about architecture, architecture critics, and students. However, I believe there are important correlations between film and architecture. The ideas outlined here originated, for the most part, with a lecture given at Cornell, where I screened the three Michael Haneke films under discussion while visiting as a guest professor. My remarks also come out of an interview between Haneke and myself published in 2008 in the British magazine *Icon*. I am confining myself here to what I determine as *critical* concerns in Haneke's films. These concerns might operate across disciplines, or relate to analogous concerns in architecture. In one sense Haneke is a sublimation, in Freudian terms, to perhaps free my own thinking from the current nihilistic state of architecture, to what seems to be a more provocative state of film. For my critical thinking, Haneke's work serves as a site of displacement (in a Freudian sense) for architectural questions. The current nihilistic state of architecture inhibits those provocations that I find with much less effort in film. These provocations are nowhere more clear than in the three Haneke films, *Caché* (2005), *Code Unknown* (2000), and *Funny Games* (1997), scrutinized in this essay. Through the deflection of conventions, something akin to what Guy Debord has called *détournement*, these films reconceptualize the spectator's relationship to vision, meaning, and time.

If there is one subject that today might relate architecture and film it is the idea of the spectacle. In Debord's 1967 *The Society of the Spectacle*, the spectacle is articulated as an agent of contemporary society's passivity. The spectacle deceptively smoothes out and unifies the fragmentation, the breaks and pauses, that define the world of mediated appearances. Revealing this fragmentation is the role of an authentic art. Debord's description of a subject sedated by the mediated image seems ahead of its time. This predominance of image-driven media has produced a society increasingly immune to any confrontation with the arts. Debord states: "The spectacle . . . is the sun that never sets on the empire of modern passivity." Media, which stages the appearance of the image as a new reality, is one of the causes of such passivity. It can be argued that passivity is the dominant state of today's subject who, conditioned to consume images, confuses them with reality. The material relation between image and reality is particularly evident in architecture: Buildings have become increasingly more spectacular. As these buildings become more abrasive visually, they become less confrontational conceptually and critically. Much of this is due to the influence of media, of branding and quick imagery that has co-opted even our most resilient critics. Architecture and film are two of the most pervasive forms of image-driven media.

While architecture is a weak medium, in that it cannot express the range of emotion and feeling that imagery from painting, sculpture, or even film can, its imagery is the dominant mode of understanding the urban environment. Film, although it competes with television, remains a credible repository of public imagery. But in one way or another, both architecture and film today have fallen prey to the spectacle.

Debord describes the spectacle as the victory of appearances over reality. He writes: "All that once was directly lived has become mere representation." But Debord also claims that these representations constitute a new reality. The spectacle, which relies on images to mediate social relationships, becomes "a concrete inversion of life." Debord suggests that the more spectacular the object – the more active, dynamic, and explicit the image – the more dependent the subject becomes on seeing as the dominant mode of understanding: The spectacle evidences the privileging of vision as the basis of a Western philosophical project. And yet, Debord writes, "The spectacle does not realize philosophy, it philosophises reality."

If in 1967 it was possible for Debord to say that the real world had become real images, today one might equally argue that the reality of images produced by media has largely overtaken material reality. This suggests that the spectacle may have become so wholly integrated in everyday existence its effect on the reality of the physical world is no longer noticed.

But Debord suggests it is possible that the very idea of spectacle contains its own possibility of redemption. Instead of seeing the spectacle or passivity in dialectical terms, each can be seen as potentially positive through a form of reversal that Debord called *détournement*. *Détournement* differs from the clichéd terms of collage or quotation in that it turns what is negative in any context back onto itself and into its own negativity. In reactivating the "subversive qualities" of the original, *détournement* embodies a critique. Debord says that *détournement* within communication makes visible the impossibility of inherent certainties or truths. *Détournement* mobilizes the internal coherence of the original against its own order. It is in this sense that *détournement* turns the dialectics of the spectacle inside out.

With the concept of the spectacle in mind, it is possible to turn to three Michael Haneke films, each of which uses a process of turning inward to question filmic conventions of vision, meaning, and time, conventions that are also central to the discourse of architecture.

It is the question of vision that is central to the first film under discussion, *Caché*. But the question of vision in Haneke must begin, first, with the questioning of vision and spectatorship in an earlier auteur period. In the early 1960s, Robert Bresson anticipated some of the issues of sight and vision raised by Haneke, in that Bresson often presented a deflected use of image in relationship to narrative which required a different form of participation from the audience. In refraining from producing the equivalent of literal, narrative imagery, Bresson's *Pickpocket* (1959) is clearly anti-visual, arguably even anti-cinematic. The film challenges the viewer's passivity by excluding narrative action. The film is a narrative of action but without images of action. Early in the film, the viewer observes the pickpocket going to the racetrack for the first time, ostensibly to practice his craft. The audience is set up, expectant, waiting to see what will happen. We see the pickpocket entering the racetrack and mingling with the spectators. Suddenly, we see him handcuffed and seated in the back of a police car. While jump cuts were a staple of the films of the 1960s, the jump cuts never eclipsed the action. Everything that could be considered important to the action – the pickpocket's attempted crime, his discovery, the assumed chase, and his apprehension – Bresson omits, countering the audience's expectations of a conventional cinematic experience. Bresson sets up cinematic mechanisms that frustrate the audience yet provoke them to participate. The audience must confront such gaps in the narrative. This gap – unlike the jump cut which functions, in fact, as a kind of narrative stitch – calls into question the very possibility of a coherent and unified narrative.

Bresson's work presented a different use of the image in relationship to narrative to transgress the filmic norms of both high-modern Hollywood and Italian neo-realism. Another scene in *Pickpocket* emblematizes this changed sense of the image. This is the banal shot of a closing door. The editor conventionally cuts quickly away from such anti-climactic – and, here, predictable – action to the next scene, rather than watch the door close, a detail irrelevant to the action and of a different temporal order than cinematic narrative. In *Pickpocket*, not only does the camera watch the door close, but it lingers on the closed door for four or five seconds, introducing a pause and a change of pace. This slowed pace again counters the audience's expectations and requires them to engage the film differently to understand these pauses, their slowness, silence, and nuance. The film requires that its audience begin to read the film differently than the traditional close reading of the modernist crime mystery. In deflecting the audience's passivity, Bresson's method of filmmaking clearly sets up Haneke's critique of image-based filmmaking.

But Haneke moves beyond Bresson's critique of cinematic narrative. Using a process akin to *détournement*, Haneke questions the internal relationship of different, overlaid sets of images. In *Caché*, Haneke undermines the assumption that any meaning is harbored in the image, or that a close reading of the image can yield meaning. The film initially appears to take the form of a classic mystery – an archetypal modernist genre – with all of the requisite ingredients: surveillance, anonymous packages, a violent death caught on videotape. The film, however, is anything but archetypal. The initial scene is a still shot – a trope. We see a house, which is being filmed. But, also, someone is making this film. The two cameras set up the idea of a film within a film. But when the initial still shot is revealed to belong to a tape that had been sent to the protagonists of the film, a couple, which shows that it is their house that is under surveillance, all of the traditional modernist mystery tropes come into play. Who sent the tape and why? What is the cameraman's relation to this couple? The film's premise suggests that the identity of the voyeur/cameraman will be resolved. But the film never answers this question. While the film continually suggests that a solution can be found through a close reading – forcing the viewer to search for clues – this film reveals nothing. The film can only be properly understood on a second viewing, after the assumed goal of solving a mystery has been discarded. This produces an entirely different reading of the film. A second viewing of *Caché* enables a closer analysis of the internal languages of the different cameras: the filmmaker's pan versus the stillness of the voyeur's surveillance camera. When the viewer realizes that *Caché* is not organized around the close reading of images, the viewer must shift toward a new engagement with the image. Rather than a narrative in which "truth" – the identity of the voyeur – is revealed, the film remains unresolved – positing what Jacques Derrida has termed an "undecidability." The film refuses to acknowledge a dominant camera or view, undermining or denaturalizing the spectator's relationship to the images onscreen. This undecidability frustrates the demands of both an active and a passive viewer, and suggests instead a different type of consciousness and subjectivity, what can be called a radical passivity, or a non-passive passivity.

For Debord, the language of the spectacle is composed of signs of the dominant organization of production. *Caché* appropriates this mode of the spectacle – presenting a pseudo-world apart – through its use of the surveillance camera. Haneke turns the techniques of surveillance against themselves, offering the camera as an autonomous agent. (A cameraman is never seen.) This camera conforms to the notion of the spectacle as a negative vision containing its potential critique. Surveillance, which has negative connotations in reality, is used productively to make a film within a film. But the result, a film without conclusion or resolution, turns film back on itself, leaving the viewer in doubt.

Haneke's *Code Unknown* engages a similar idea of undecidability, providing a set of clues or codes whose meaning is never revealed. The title itself already asks the audience to suspend their expectations for knowledge. The film begins by offering a metaphor for the impossibility of communication – a scene of deaf children playing charades. While Haneke claims that sound is more important than sight in his films, by presenting images of non-aural communication he questions the very relationship between sound and meaning on which he stakes his own practice.

The film presents a set of disparate protagonists who meet in a chance incident on a street, only to be dispersed throughout the film in five self-contained episodes. This dispersal is made up of fragments that sometimes suggest scenes within scenes and sometimes deny implied connections that may or may not be seen. These episodes are, in a sense, parts which need to be rearranged. Whatever narrative structure of *Code Unknown* that exists after the first encounter is interspersed with scenes of deaf children drumming, a reminder of Haneke's ongoing attempt to undermine his own understanding of the aural basis of his film. Haneke's attacks on the medium also take aim at the temporal dimension of film. Long, unedited takes are shifted out of real time, forcing the viewer to acknowledge this unexpected juxtaposition of "the real" – and its own unreality. Scenes change without interruption; these are not jump cuts, but rather an enfolding of one scene into the next.

Another important issue implicated in the spectacle is what Debord calls irreversible time. This is a form of historicism in which history propels the past forward into the present and the future. It is also a manifestation of linear narrative. *Détournement* is an attempt to question such linear time. The questioning of linear time is posed, literally as a kind of question, in an important moment in Haneke's *Funny Games*. In the scene where the wife appears to have wrested a gun away from one of her captors and shot him, the audience expects – perhaps – a resolution. At the film's Cannes premiere, the collective sigh of relief was not only audible, but palpable. Would there be a happy ending? Unexpectedly, the other psychotic captor takes control of an, until now, unseen filmic mechanism: He rewinds the film to the moment before his accomplice is shot and inserts a different narrative. If nothing else, this moment makes us aware of the irreversibility of time.

This question of time, so important in Haneke's work, suggests again to the relationship between film and architecture. While time is more pliable and fluid for the subjective reaction to film, it is less so in architecture. While the subject in architecture is in motion and the object static, the experience of architecture may be one of a series of stills conceptualized in our somatic memory. How those stills are organized and read in real space and time occurs much as in film, in a conceptual space and time. In both film and architecture, what is analogous is the attempted suspension of a reading of real time.

Architecture, like film, faces the question of real time as the time of experience. Since the Renaissance, the time of the experience of the subject has been linked to the time of the object, the reading of its narrativity and conception. There is no question that the unhooking of narrative from the image in recent film has influenced architectural production. Haneke adds to that knowledge.

The difference between Bresson and Haneke is also instructive for architecture. If Haneke's films suggest that there is no longer an interest in close reading, is it possible that there could be another mode of reading? In other words, does the mode of reading provoked by films such as *Caché* and *Code Unknown* – a reading that is not looking for clues, indices, or narrative – suggest the possibility of another mode of reading architecture?

To see Haneke's probing of filmic conventions triggers, perhaps more than any other visual medium, new possibilities for architecture. Such issues as speed, scale, materials, texture, and light are components both media share. For both architecture and film, overcoming what is perceived as their respective realities (whether it is comfort in architecture or entertainment in film) is what makes each art so difficult to achieve. It is this overcoming, a possible turning inward, that is a challenge for both media. It remains for architecture to again question, as it did in the early days of the twentieth century, its own conceptual tropes. Haneke poses a few of these important questions.

Reference

Debord, Guy: *Society of the Spectacle* (Oakland, CA: AK Press, 2006).

6

Games Haneke Plays

Reality and Performance

Brigitte Peucker

Breaking the Code?

Code Unknown (*Code inconnu*, 2000) repeatedly subsumes an impulse towards realism within modernist concerns, substituting a perceptual realism situated in the spectator for the Bazinian realism of the image that it calls into question. Games with reality and illusion are its dominant strategy for achieving this end, and sometimes they are emblematized by actual game structures. In *Code Unknown*, the moments of undecidability that punctuate Haneke's films tend to be located in performances; in German, the word for playing – *spielen* – is identical to that for acting. Charades of a special kind bracket the film: Its pre-title sequence records a frightened little girl who moves awkwardly towards an empty backdrop as a shadow falls over her cowering form. She does not speak or cry out. It is only when she reaches the wall that the shadow is revealed to be her own, only then that this austere white wall proves to mark the boundary of a performance space. The little girl's cowering movements constitute a performance, as it turns out, and it is witnessed by a diegetic audience. While we're relieved that the child's pain is mimed, our discovery that deaf and dumb children are her audience renews our discomfort. As the children guess at the import of her charade, they pose their questions in Sign; after each question, the little girl shakes her head "no." The game that is being played is didactic – part of a school curriculum, we surmise – its goal to teach the deaf and dumb to speak through and read the body. But while Sign is a language that relies on images, on a combination of gestures and letters that, in other words, has a code, this game of charades resorts to pantomimed actions that serve as clues to a word that "solves" the puzzle. Such actions aren't signs in an established code; they suggest a wide range of significations. As we, the film's audience, come to understand, the word that provides the key to the child's performance will remain unavailable to her diegetic audience – and to us. Need we add that the words of the film's title are over-determined?

For the spectator two sets of questions are generated by this sequence, and they are at the crux of *Code Unknown*. One of these is how images can be understood without the benefit of language, a question central to writing on the ontology of the photograph, evoking especially Roland Barthes's analysis of its uncoded and coded aspects in "The Photographic Message" (1961) and "Rhetoric of the Image" (1964). The other question is this: What is the boundary between real emotion and mimed emotion, between life and performance, between reality and illusion? The film's movement from what appears to be "reality" – in this case, a frightened little girl – to its acknowledgment as a diegetic performance is a strategy central to Haneke's film. Time and again *Code Unknown* presents us with sequences that promote confusion between the diegetic reality of the film and a performance within it, sequences that promote the spectator's uncertainty about the status of the image. Since the action of such sequences always involves emotional pain, they promote strong affects in the film's audience, feelings followed by relief that such actions are doubly distanced from the diegetic real, that even in the fictional reality of the film the sequence is "only a performance." Clearly, the spectators' relief is not unqualified; it is tempered, rather, by the knowledge of having been manipulated. For the moment, we are wary, distanced, wondering whether the scenes that unfold before us will stand revealed as diegetically "real" or "performed." How should we read this undecidability, other than as a spectator trap?

Code Unknown's ludic strategy recalls D. W. Winnicott's claim in *Playing and Reality* (1971) that the "inherently exciting" nature of play derives from "the precariousness that belongs to the interplay in the child's mind of that which is subjective (near-hallucination) and that which is objectively perceived (actual, or shared reality)" (52). While the function of play for the child will ultimately be to delineate these areas clearly, Winnicott contends, for the adult their confusion finds a place in art (3). In moving between illusion and diegetic truth, *Code Unknown* provokes in its spectator an uncertainty that is decidedly disturbing: Its ludic dimension crosses over into sadistic tricking. But then the film's compelling images catch us up again – at least until we play the spectator game of assembling its narrative fragments, until we try to decipher the film's governing code. This code, too, remains unknowable.

Tellingly, the subtitle of *Code Unknown* is "incomplete tales of several journeys," and its structure – one that interlards several tangentially and randomly connected narratives – takes us back to another earlier film of Haneke's, *71 Fragments of a Chronology of Chance* (1994).[1] Although the attenuated narratives of *71 Fragments* eventually merge in a horrific act of violence in which four people die, our desire to read this earlier film as a whole is consistently thwarted as well. In *71 Fragments* games have a central role to play – indeed, games in this film are the very figure for undecidability. Two games are centrally featured – a set of puzzle pieces and a game of pick-up sticks – and they purport to shape our act of reading. Repeatedly in this film puzzle pieces are manipulated into the shape of a cross, but the question of how this over-determined image signifies is left open. Two students vie with one another to create figures out of these pieces. After the actual game is transposed into a computer game, reality becomes virtual – but the point of the game remains unchanged. Whereas the goal of the puzzle is to create a whole out of fragments – 71, perhaps – the game of pick-up sticks aims at the dismantling of random arrangements – the figures created when the sticks are dropped. While the opposition set up between the games is rather pat, no answer is provided to the question of which activity – the construction of forms or the deconstruction of random arrangements – is more relevant to Haneke's film. The modernist interest in the relation of the fragment to the whole and its implied connection to Bresson (Haneke's self-acknowledged mentor) via the image of the cross (the final image of *Diary of a Country Priest*, 1951) is couched in a world view predicated on design, not randomness. But the pick-up sticks focus chance as determining their arrangements. Does the significance of the one game cancel the other out? At the end of the film, its stories come together in an act of violence that ironizes this question.

In *Code Unknown*, made six years later, the "tales of incomplete journeys" do not culminate in an act of violence, but they do emerge from a random act of hostility. In keeping with the multi-ethnic identity of contemporary Paris – the film's setting – three stories are told: a French New Wave-style romance, a Romanian story, and an African story, their multiple fragments separated by abrupt cuts, as in *71 Fragments*. The film is a social collage that emphasizes its acts of cutting, illustrating the experiences of a spectrum of characters, with each tale presided over by a modernist belief in selfhood. Like *71 Fragments*, *Code Unknown* is a "chronology of chance": a French actress meets her boyfriend's teenaged brother on the street and buys him a pastry – a seemingly insignificant act. But when he throws the pastry wrapper into the lap of a Romanian beggar, the teenager captures the outraged attention of a young African who defends the honor of the Romanian woman, demanding an apology from the teenager. When the teenager refuses, the African's irate shouting comes to the attention of the police, who predictably take him to the police station and – as we later discover – deport the Romanian woman. One of these stories ends in Africa, with the father of the young African – having abandoned his family, either temporarily or permanently – driving through a marketplace. Only the man's family is hurt by his return to his homeland; the people in the marketplace are not his target, although it's a clear indication of his distance from his culture that he negotiates this space by car. The Romanian story is equally unresolved, since the woman, Maria – urged on by her daughter – returns to Paris to beg, only to find herself displaced from her street corner by two Arabs. The film leaves her seeking another space, confirming her narrative entrapment in circularity and repetition. The French story, with its overtones of New Wave relationships and malaise, is resolved when the actress's lover is prevented from entering her apartment building because she's changed the door's security code, an ironic and deflating comment on the film's title. As a conclusion to their love affair, the woman's move is deflating as well. Her lover commits no acts of violence after having been locked out – he merely looks for a cab to take him away. The seemingly failed emigration and return to one's place of origin; the cyclical narrative of expulsion and return; the abrupt dénouement of the love story – these divergent ways of structuring narrative supplement one another. But insofar as these stories are susceptible to interpretation, it is grounded in the family dynamics that shape these melodramas. The family as cornerstone of the bourgeois social order remains the center of Haneke's attention in all of his films.[2]

While a modernist self-consciousness characterizes *Code Unknown* at the level of style, Haneke's interest in the bourgeois family is suggestive of a lingering realism in his filmmaking. Interestingly, another kind of code comes into play here. On one level, *Code Unknown* supports Fredric Jameson's contention concerning a different code – his contention that realism is "the restricted code of the bourgeoisie," and that its "peculiar object" is "the historically specific mode of capitalist production."[3] If, *qua* Jameson, bourgeois realism is currently being undermined by the "small group codes in contemporary film" (ibid.), this possibility is merely gestured towards in the case of the marginalized groups represented in Haneke's film; the Romanian and the African tale are shaped primarily by the family relations within a capitalist order that – in Jameson's understanding – structure realism. The Romanian woman's family is building a fine new house in Romania and chooses to believe that she holds a job in Paris, while the African man who seeks relief from family troubles owns his own taxi. Both of these families operate within realism's "restricted code," then, a code centered in and determining the bourgeoisie, a code that structures a world governed by the marketplace (169). Although neither the Romanian nor the African narrative is brought to closure, neither of them breaks out of a familiar pattern into a new kind of narrative. The circularity that structures the Romanian tale undermines hope, and the return to the African homeland isn't a happy one – there is no doubt that a politics obtains in these stories. But while its political text points to the mutually reinforcing entrapments of family, consumerism, and racism, Haneke's film makes no effort to suggest a "solution" to these conundrums of contemporary life. (Insofar as the film does so, it seems to suggest that immigrants are better off at home.) Further, the fragmentation that structures *Code Unknown* undermines the political impact it might otherwise make by also situating the film within the tradition of modernism, with its pronounced interest in form.

Games with Illusion

It is the French New Wave-style story that enables the film's meditation on the boundaries of the performed and the real by way of its main characters: a film and stage actress, Anne, and her live-in partner, Georges, a photojournalist.

Proceeding from and elaborating the situation of the film's opening scene with the cowering child engaged in a game of charades, performance *of* and *as* torture appears in a variety of guises in the film's French story. The first such scene shows Anne in a blood red, empty room in which a disembodied voice announces that she's been locked in and that she'll "never get out." Fritz Lang's *The Testament of Dr. Mabuse* (1933) looms large in this citation of a disembodied, commanding voice reverberating within a closed room.[4] But to what end, other than to serve as an example of the elision of Fritz Lang's directorial identity with that of the notoriously controlling, destructive character of Dr. Mabuse? Although this male voice has asked Anne whether it should read the "other part," almost from the first the boundary between performance and diegetic reality here is murky. The spectator soon takes Anne's terrified and frantic questions for filmic "reality," since the camerawork in this sequence is uncharacteristically dominated by the handheld effects of the horror genre. (In some sense, too, the red room literalizes a word in Kubrick's *The Shining* [1980] – where the inscription "redrum" is the mirror image of "murder.") The disembodied male voice claims to like Anne, claims that she has simply fallen into his trap. What the voice demands of her is to show "her true face," to show him "a true expression." Whose voice is this? Is it that of a psychopath? Is it the diegetic director's voice, reading a role for the sake of an audition? Or is this the director of *Code Unknown* – speaking, perhaps, in his own voice? Although it's suggested that the scene represents a screen test for a movie role – not Anne's imprisonment by a maniac – this is only confirmed retrospectively, in the manner of Hitchcock. In the meantime, the scene's ambiguities are sustained, and our desire to know frustrated. How and why the film camera is co-opted by the conventions of horror is never explained, although I'll offer an explanation later.

After it is established that Anne has a role in a film about a serial killer, *Code Unknown* includes two takes of a scene in which her character is terrorized, but each is obviously a movie shoot, with the actors surrounded by lighting equipment and subjected to the gaze of the camera. Bits and pieces of information about this thriller in the making emerge later: During dinner at a restaurant, Anne will remark that, in the plot of this film, the inspector can solve the crime because his personality resembles that of the murderer – a convention of some detective stories. Minutes later in this very Parisian restaurant scene – and very briefly – we catch a glimpse of Haneke himself, barely in frame, his surprising presence left uncommented upon. Is there a connection? While Haneke's appearance is not a cameo in the usual sense, it evokes Hitchcock's insertion of a costumed self into his films. Like the reference to Lang, the oblique reference to Hitchcock is to a controlling director, one noted for his cruelty to actors. Another sequence features Anne at an audition, this time for a role in *Twelfth Night*. In this scene Anne is on stage alone, uncostumed, a spotlight blinds her, while the rest of the theater is in semi-darkness. At the end of her monologue, Anne awaits a reaction from figures we only dimly perceive, whose whispers we barely hear. Anne stops speaking – hesitates, then asks: "Is there anyone there, perhaps?" Yet another unseen director has generated fear in a performer.

Two additional sequences center on Anne's performances, this time in a film-within-the film, where she plays one member of a self-involved couple who discovers that their child is about to fall from their balcony to the street below. Once again there are images of cruelty to children: Terrified by the threat of their son's death, his parents use physical violence against him and banish him from their presence. Again it is only retrospectively clear that what we're watching is footage from an interior film, this time when the two stars record the soundtrack for the film as they watch its images. While the actors try to recapture the intense emotions they acted in the film, the temporal gap between shooting and dubbing problematizes the affects generated for and by the images they – and we – are viewing. The film asks whether the images of a traumatic scene can evoke in its actors the intense emotions they once played. At first, the only sounds the images generate are their embarrassed giggles.

What is at stake in this sequence, a sequence that exposes the actors' performance as performance? Is it merely the question of whether the emotions evoked by the film images they watch are real or simulated? Or does this scene serve another purpose? Perhaps it asks questions about the screen presence of the actor – especially about Juliette Binoche's presence – in this film.[5] Does Binoche's centrality to Haneke's film – her appearance both in sequences coded as diegetic "reality" and those exposed as performance – serve as an anchor for the film's several layers of fictionality? One significant boundary crossing between reality and performance in *Code Unknown* is surely Juliette Binoche's pregnancy during the shooting of this film,[6] mostly camouflaged by clothing, but incorporated into the narrative when Anne taunts Georges about whether or not she is pregnant, whether or not she has had an abortion. Georges – like the spectator – remains unsure of the "truth." Does the actor's ontologically identical presence in scenes of performance and in scenes of diegetic reality make sequences coded as diegetic reality more "real-seeming" or less "real-seeming" in comparison? The stable presence of the actor's body in the oscillation between diegetic "reality" and performance would seem to diminish their difference, to muddy the epistemological waters.

In conversation, Anne mentions that the thriller in which she's acting is tentatively to be called "The Collector." But it's not the 1956 William Wyler film of that title from which the interior film – and *Code Unknown* – essentially borrow. That film, rather, is Michael Powell's *Peeping Tom* (1960). In Powell's film the central character's sado-masochistic project is to capture on film the quintessential image of (female) fear, "the true expression" of fear – as you'll recall, this is what the psychopath – or director – wants from Anne. *Peeping Tom* is a famously self-reflexive film that – like *Code Unknown* – blurs the boundary between "reality," "performance," and their filmic images several times over. Its central character, Mark, turns his film camera into a murder weapon whose assaultive eye projects outward literally in the form of a phallic dagger that kills the women who are the object of its gaze.[7] As the dagger approaches them, the women's faces are distorted by a convex mirror in which they view themselves, and by the terror Mark seeks to capture on film. Their fear in turn terrifies Mark. The relation between perpetrator and victim is a reciprocal one that plays out a dynamic Powell's film anchors in childhood experience.

As the story goes, Mark's father, a behaviorist who studies the reactions of the nervous system to fear, filmed his son's every move – especially the child's expressions of terror when awakened at night. From an early age, Mark's life is continuous with its representation. As cameraman and murderer, Mark reenacts the role of his sadistic father; as the one who is terrified by the face of fear, Mark masochistically identifies with the position of his female victim. At the end of the film Mark commits suicide by means of his own camera, producing what he calls the "end of a documentary," the film of his life begun by his father. Here, too, the epistemological waters are muddied, and the confusion between life and art in the diegesis of the film – and in the psychotic mind of its protagonist – encompasses the life of its director, Michael Powell, as well. What the film may have meant to Powell can only be conjectured, but since he cast his son Columba in the role of Mark as a child, and himself in the role of Mark's father, *Peeping Tom* must have held autobiographical significance for him. Powell remarks in his autobiography that "art is merciless observation, sympathy, imagination, and a sense of detachment that is almost cruelty" (24). But our impression that the detached, cold tone of Powell's film is not merely the result of objectivity is reinforced by the appearance of the Powells – father and son – in a film about a sadomasochistic bond between father and son played out by way of a film camera. Like Powell's, Haneke's film art seems detached and cruel.[8] Might there be other correspondences, as well?

Performance, cruelty, and game playing – imbricated in the little girl's charade mentioned at the beginning of this essay – are harnassed together in other Haneke films, as well. An attitude of game playing and theatricality is imposed upon acts of violence most centrally in *Funny Games* (1997). (Haneke's films share this attitude with two great landmarks of filmic modernism – Kubrick's *A Clockwork Orange* [1971] and Antonioni's *Blow-Up* [1966].) In *Funny Games*, the late-adolescent murderers, Peter and Paul, base their acts of torture on children's games – "hot and cold," "cat in the sack," and a version of "eenie-meenie-minie-mo." The murderers' adoption of game structures for their acts of torture is partly cued by one of their victims, Anna, who resorts to a commonplace regarding her German shepherd dog's wild barking: "he just wants to play. "Funny game," says one of the torturers in response. The acts of torture prepared by Peter and Paul theatricalize violence as they adapt a variety of plots and structures including clowning or mime (the egg game) and the imitation of pulp fiction plots (Anna is to act the "loving wife" while she watches her husband's brutal murder).[9] In *Funny Games*, games and performances provide the structure for acts of torture from which the spectator is not excluded. As I've said, the German for playing – *spielen* – is the same as the word for acting, and they are closely related in Haneke's film. Peter and Paul construct scenarios of inexplicable violence, scenarios they observe with detached – and aesthetic – pleasure. "Here are the Rules of the Game," they tell their victims in a barely veiled allusion to Jean Renoir.

The director has a game to play, as well, and it is cat-and-mouse. Recalling the many references to self-reflexivity in Haneke's interviews and to the mobilization of spectatorial response, we may wonder whether it is in this light that we are to read the efforts at distantiation in *Funny Games*. Media consciousness permeates this film: We find it in the aliases adopted by the murderers – Tom and Jerry, Beavis and Butthead – and we find it distressingly present at the moment in which it seems that one of Haneke's characters at least, Anna, is able to break through the "no exit" structure of the deadly games to which she has fallen prey. Seizing a rifle, Anna shoots and hits Peter, presumably killing him. But if the spectator feels relief at her action, it is momentary only, for Paul simply picks up the remote and rewinds the action, which then continues on its deadly and predictable course. Games of violence, Haneke would have us know, may be played by the director as well. Manipulating the narrative as if the film were a video and he its spectator, Haneke makes it abundantly clear that he is in control.

Uncoded Images

True to its centrality for Bazinian realism, it is photography that struggles against the duplicity of performance in Haneke's film. (Antonioni's *Blow-Up* comes to mind with respect to this issue, as well.) The photographic impulse is narratively embodied in the figure of the photojournalist Georges, who seeks to convey the "truth" of political events in Kosovo and Drenica in his photographs of wartime atrocities. Unable to remain long in Paris – where he's required to interact with others – Georges repeatedly plunges himself into dangerous settings where he can relate to people indirectly, as observer and camera eye. Haneke's film displays Georges's wartime photos in full screen in conjunction with a letter read by this character in voice-over. But Georges's aural letter is not "illustrated" by the photographs on screen; rather, it moves evasively from political events to Georges's difficulties in the personal realm. Is the point here that the mute photographic images cannot fully communicate – or that they communicate something incomprehensible? The static images depict the bodies of the dead and the moments they record remain enigmatic, illegible. The paradox of the photograph is that what it connotes must be "developed on the basis of a message without a code" – the denoted message based on the photographic analog suggests Barthes in "The Photographic Message" (19). Insofar as we read photographs, however, we also derive from them a second-order, connoted, message based on a linguistic code. A purely denotative meaning is possible only in the rare instances of traumatic images, those that record moments for which no connotative message is possible – moments when language is blocked, suspended. Their code remains unknown. Georges's images of the dead are traumatic images, images of the Real, of that which is insusceptible to meaning, bereft even of "analogical plenitude" (18).[10] As Georges admits in conversation, these photographs do not represent a "reality" even for him.

Defeated by his subject and scarred by his experiences, Georges opts for another kind of photography, and takes candid portraits of random strangers in the Paris metro. This turn represents a retreat into aestheticism. Haneke's film marks this set of images even more clearly as photographic: They are not shown in full screen, as the wartime photographs are, and they are not in color. The black-and-white images appear as portraits against a black background that suggests unexposed film stock: Against this background, they are doubly coded as art. There is a romantic residue in Georges's attempt to record the human face – even the multi-ethnic faces of today's Parisians – and it dominates over whatever aspirations to documentary are still latent in his project. Even the photographic act of registration – Georges displays his camera, but hides the cord that operates it – is problematic, voyeuristic, manipulative. These photographs neither reveal Atget's urban spaces nor exhibit the cataloguing intention of August Sander. The topography of the faces Georges records remains as enigmatic as the landscapes with their dead in the wartime photos. Interpretive access is not provided by the images themselves, nor is it provided by the voice-over of yet another letter spoken by Georges. Indeed, the Bressonian separation of the narrative of Georges's capture by the Taliban from his portrait shots of the face is designed to shock. If Georges was incapable of narrativizing his photographs of wartime atrocities – and if, as traumatic images, they are not susceptible to language – he now narrates his experience of capture and terror against images whose connection to his story remains oblique at best. What do these dissonances, these chasms between word and image have to say about film? While *Code Unknown* asserts its interest in the photographic imaginary of film, it's unclear whether it undermines or supports Georges's assertion that talk about the "value of the non-transmitted image" comes cheap, his claim that "what matters in the end is the result."

But Haneke's film does not read Georges's photos "without a message" as " 'flat' anthropological fact," as Barthes puts it in "Rhetoric of the Image" (45). In the later *Camera Lucida* (1981) Barthes takes a different stance towards the nature of the photograph's impact: In response to a photograph by Kertész, he waxes lyrical about the image of a dirt road whose "texture gives me the certainty of being in Central Europe; . . . I recognize with my whole body the straggling villages I passed through in my long-ago trips to Hungary and Rumania" (45). Thus, even denotation ultimately bears connotation within. Is it possible that the scene captured by Kertész – a blind, old violinist led over a dirt road by a child – is conjured up in Haneke's film by the Romanian woman and her grandson, walking along a dirt road enveloped in dust? Haneke's film also seems to revel in the affective charge of the photographic – the filmic – image, indeed, in any kind of image at all, the digital included. Thus, even if the filmic image is without explanatory power, it nevertheless has the power to move us. Like Barthes, Haneke's films ensure that the spectator will experience the image "with his whole body." It is by means of spectatorial affect that the real of the body is reintroduced into the experience of film. And here is where another aspect of the connection to Powell comes in: Haneke's films are linked to *Peeping Tom* not only by the questions they ask about the possibility of reading the face and body, not only by an appearance of the director that at least figures his involvement in the diegesis, not only by the violence that occurs in performance spaces, but also by their questions about the relation of the film image to the real of affect.

Playground Realities

Affect perforates the formalist surface of Haneke's films, and it often arises from the sight of pain. As I've suggested elsewhere, in all of Haneke's films there is a recurrent interest in the pain of children. Middle-class parents induce their daughter to join them in suicide in *The Seventh Continent* (1989); a young girl is cruelly murdered in *Benny's Video* (1992); a little girl who has been promised adoption is passed over for another in *71 Fragments of a Chronology of Chance*; a young boy is tortured and killed in *Funny Games*, and so on. As we've noted, the camera's direct gaze at deaf-mute children opens and closes *Code Unknown*, but that is just the beginning: Since Anne could not bring herself to intervene, the abused daughter of Anne's neighbors is killed by her parents; the little boy in one of the films-within-the film nearly falls twenty stories to his death, then is punished by his parents for frightening them; Amadou's younger brother Demba is the victim of playground racism and extortion; and finally, there is the child with which Anne may or may not be pregnant, which she may or may not have aborted. But pain is not only inflicted on those least able to defend themselves. As I've argued, there's also a pervasive interest in forms of emotional manipulation that especially dominate the space of performance.[11] Ironically, the message of Anne's audition for *Twelfth Night* may reside in two lines she speaks from the maid's monologue: "I know my lady will strike him – if she do, I know he'll take it as a great favor." Rendered innocuous by comedy, the dynamic these lines describe is that of sado-masochism, suggesting that the metaphor of the puppet master and his puppet mentioned by Haneke with reference to *Code Unknown* has something significant to say.[12] And it may also have something to say about a dynamic in his films that *isn't* confined to performance spaces.

Once again *Peeping Tom* looms large. Powell's film is more than a gloss on Haneke's films, serving as a possible source both for their mini-narratives of child abuse and for a modernist fascination with self-reflexivity and form. As mentioned earlier, the narrative of Powell's film is notable for its realist impulse to see and record the "true expression," as well as for the sadistic filmmaker whose films stage real violence. Does it also serve to model the masochistic child who resides in that director and who equates punishment with love, as in *Peeping Tom*? Watching the films of his aestheticized murders, *Peeping Tom*'s Mark commits suicide by means of the same camera with spike he used to murder his victims. But his suicide also marks the fulfillment of his desire for his father. Perhaps the dynamic most central to Haneke's film work lies in the simultaneous "acting out" of his "mastery" over "puppets" *and* the inclusion of scenarios of abuse and pain in which a vulnerable childhood self is figured as puppet, too.

This is certainly the case in *Time of the Wolf* (2003) in which the director as puppet master deploys his puppets at will. *Time of the Wolf* resembles Haneke's version of Kafka's *The Castle* (1997) in representing the victims of a powerful force that is unnamed, disembodied, and whose agenda is not understood. Suffering is simply endured, again with children among its most poignant victims. It begins with the murder of a father, a murder that empties the paternal space as though to occupy it with a more abstract power. The victims of the generalized suffering represented in this film do not know the reason for their pain, nor do they know its source, but they grow to accept their condition, struggling to survive within the framework of possibilities left to them. Like Haneke's characters, we spectators are aware that the rivers and lakes of this landscape are polluted, and that animals are dying of thirst. Is there a widespread drought? Has there been an ecological disaster? Is this the scene of some biblical plague? Is some malevolent deity visiting an obscure punishment upon all? An aged grandmother selfishly drinks the milk needed by a dying child. The young child dies of fever and dehydration. A young woman commits suicide. *Time of the Wolf* has a ship-of-fools, Noah's Ark structure, with multi-ethnic families gathering at the railroad station of some unknown town, waiting for a train – for Godot? – to release them from their suffering. Whether the unspecified malevolent power is an invisible divinity, the paternal function as penetrating camera (as in Powell), or embodied in a hostile state (as in Kafka), the source of human suffering is never specified by the film. Its spare landscape suggests an undisclosed allegory; the source of its devastation remains unknowable. Once again an act of violence involving a child is central to understanding a Haneke film: When the boy Benny hears talk of "the Just" – an elect whose acts of self-sacrifice guarantee that God will watch over the rest of mankind – he threatens to throw himself onto a self-styled funeral pyre.

Fortunately Benny is saved, not sacrificed. But as the film comes to a close there is a long traveling shot of a lush, green landscape – or so the soundtrack suggests – from the window of a moving train. It is a paradigmatic moment of modernist cinematic self-reflexivity, for the long take of the (seemingly) moving landscape through the train window engages film history in a way that makes such scenes stand in for cinema itself. Redemption would seem to be at hand. "It's enough that you were ready to do it," says the man who saves him to Benny. The uncannily disembodied view from the train suggests that it is cinema itself – or some god of cinema, a director – who, moved by Benny's intention, has released the land-scape from barrenness and stasis into fertility and motion. In the final scene of this film it is the camera eye – read as the director's eye? – that embodies the film's unspecified "power," a power that is moved to benevolence by a child's intention to harm himself.

In *Caché* (2005), the return of the abused child takes its vengeance on the adult – another Georges involved in the culture industry. It is a child who might have been his brother, had Georges not lied to prevent his adoption. Although *Caché* incorporates racial and political issues into its plot – the would-be adoptee is Algerian – the young Georges's motive for excluding the boy from his family is relentlessly Oedipal. This Haneke film glances back to the much earlier *71 Fragments*, set in Vienna, in which adoption is already the important political metaphor, and to *Benny's Video*, where both violence and love are enacted through videotapes.[13] While the failed adoption of the Algerian orphan in *Caché* reflects the political realities of France, it is grounded in the Freudian scenario operative in all of Haneke's films. The bourgeois family remains at the center of his filmmaking: *Caché* returns to its French origins Diderot's eighteenth-century insight that the wholeness of society is founded on the wholeness of the family. This seems a regressive posi-tion to take in the twenty-first century, but we should recall that metaphorical adoption allows for the possibility of a more liberal politics, as in Lessing's bour-geois drama, *Nathan the Wise* (1779), inspired by Diderot.

In *Caché*, as in *Time of the Wolf*, the camera is all-powerful. From its static position opposite the protagonist's residence, a video camera produces tapes of slice-of-life realism – the occasional passing car, a lone cyclist, people coming and going. While the film seems to begin in a still image, in imitation of Hitchcock's *Rear Window* (1954), master text of surveillance films, faint bird sounds indicate its status as film or video. When the camera holds on the scene for an unnatur-ally long period of time, it becomes clear that the recording function of the medium is at issue. Unlike *Code Unknown* – and Hitchcock's film – *Caché* relegates theatri-cality and performance to its periphery. As in *Benny's Video*, however, the spectators of *Caché* are repeatedly taken in as we are confronted with images we only retrospectively learn are being watched by diegetic viewers. Once again a Haneke film obscures the boundary between a diegetically "real" event and a performance when a dinner party guest narrates a "true" story that turns out to be a joke. And again a Haneke film has a fragmented narrative, with one small set of related fragments – the son Pierrot's participation in a swim team – proving to be a red herring, while an equally small set of narrative fragments is centrally significant. The latter begins with an insert shot of a boy standing at a window, bleeding at the mouth. We will see a shot of the boy again, ever so briefly – coughing blood – just before the dinner party sequence in which the guest tells his story. What is the nature of these images? Is the guest's story a key to these images, perhaps insofar as they, too, defy categorization as diegetic reality or illusion?

It's only much later in the film, when we are privy to a scene in which a chicken's head is being cut off and blood spurts into a boy's eye – images from a dream of Georges's – that we understand the link. Now coded as memory or daydream, these flashes of images relate to both of Georges's childhood lies: That Majid, the Algerian boy his parents wanted to adopt, was spitting blood (that is, had tuberculosis), and that Majid cut off a chicken's head in a random act of violence, rather than at Georges's instigation. Once again it is the child's relation to the family that is pivotal. Once again the family provides the key to a political scenario – to a different relation between the French and the Algerians that might have been. While the film is reticent about who is responsible for the surveillance tapes, it suggests that they are the collaborative effort of Majid's and Georges's sons.[14] But the surveillance tapes taken from the rue des Iris are technically continuous with the other images of the film, likewise shot in high definition format, suggesting – as in *Time of the Wolf* – that the disembodied eye (Iris) of the camera is none other than the director's.

The surveillance tapes are linked to the insert shots of the bleeding boy by the drawings in which the tapes are wrapped. There are two childish black line drawings, the first – in crayon – of a boy with mouth open, the second – in marker – of a rooster with its head cut off: Both of these images are marked by a prominent stripe of painted blood. Towards the end of the film, a tape is wrapped in a photo of Georges clipped from a newspaper, also adorned with a stripe of red. The jarring presence of painted blood on the line drawings and on the photograph, with blood represented by the fluid, viscous medium of poster paint, produces a hybrid image of sorts. In some sense, it marks the blood on the drawings – always denotative, according to "Rhetoric of the Image" (43) – *and* the photograph (with its paradoxical message) both as "real" and as *the* Real. Even *images* of blood serve as a reminder that, in an earlier time, blood was the substance that rendered visual representation authentic – even painted blood, for instance, served to authenticate the statues of Christian martyrs. Since the broad brushstrokes with which the blood is painted in *Caché* suggest that it was done by the hand of a child, the painted blood is figured as doubly authentic. But in what sense does it relate to the filmic images it resembles – to the bleeding boy in the insert shots or to Georges's dream images of the slaughtered rooster? Blood in or on the image – even if represented, indeed, even if represented by the video image, *Caché* suggests – brings the real into representation, introduces a "truth" into what is staged. Is the film's unexpected, bloody violence – the slitting of the chicken's throat, the suicide of Majid – designed to approximate the traumatic effect of the images of the dead for Georges the *photographer*? Are these images traumatic? It is their code that Georges the talk show host struggles to know, struggles to put into words.

Coda

Sado-masochism is centrally present in most of Haneke's films – beginning with his first feature film, *The Seventh Continent*, moving through *Benny's Video*, *71 Fragments*, *The Castle*, *Funny Games*, *Time of the Wolf* as well as *Caché*, and it is the center of attention in *The Piano Teacher* (2001), a virtual case study of this emotional double bind. Sado-masochism, of course, is the mindset described in Powell's *Peeping Tom*, as well. The adult Mark is the deadly filmmaker in whom his father – connected with the camera – and Mark himself as child are finally fused at the moment of his suicide. The camera is a deadly weapon in this film, complete with phallic spear. When Mark trains it upon himself and "shoots" himself, the sadistic aggression of the father (allied with the camera) and the sexual fulfillment of the child-victim (in the female position) collapse into one. There is a striking parallel between this collapse in Powell's film and a similar moment in Haneke's *Caché*. This moment occurs in the farmyard sequence we see after Georges has for the last time retreated to his bed; it is the final visualization of the childhood scenario produced when Georges's lies evict his rival Majid from Georges's parental home. Structurally, this is a signature shot of Haneke's – the shot from a dark space into a light space – and it reveals its human actors in long shot, across the expanse of the courtyard. Taken from a dark space – no doubt the barn – the location of the shot *suggests* that its point of view belongs to the six-year-old Georges, who is hiding in the shadows. However, since the sequence fails to establish who is the owner of this gaze, its point of view remains unclaimed, simply the look of the camera. This key sequence again brings *Benny's Video* to mind, where a similar camera setup is retrospectively shown to be from the point of view of Benny in his darkened room, videotaping his parents. In a stunning act of aggression, Benny will use the videotape that he shoots to implicate his parents in the murder that he himself has committed.

What I am suggesting is that the point of view of the farmyard sequence is deliberately double. As in Powell's film, child and father collapse into one: Georges's point of view as sequestered child and the eye of Haneke's camera – and, by implication, the surveillance camera – are aligned in this shot. In the diegesis of Haneke's film, of course, there are several couples across whom sado-masochistic drives play themselves out. When Majid – Georges's victim – commits suicide, he forces the adult Georges to assume the role of spectator: By means of his masochistic act, he enacts sadistic revenge upon Georges. Further, with Benny in mind, we might read Georges's son Pierrot and Majid's son as wreaking vengeance upon their fathers – one need not see their collaboration, insofar as there is one, as a utopian allegory. But why are the videotapes – products of the paternal gaze of surveillance no matter who produces them – tightly wrapped in images that suggest the hand of a child, if not to represent their interconnectedness? My point here is that the relation of victim to aggressor – represented in this film by several pairs of fathers and sons – plays itself out multiply, in different constellations, as functions distributed across the text, hence no longer necessarily embodied in its characters. Note the way in which the shot from the barn into the farmyard articulates these relations almost abstractly. The abstractly rendered paternal/directorial function – familiar from *Peeping Tom* – suggests that the obscure source of human suffering in *Time of the Wolf*, ultimately given a cinematic context, as well as the disembodied director in the theatrical scene of *Code Unknown*, merely acousmatic, a voice, *and*, finally, the surveillance camera of *Caché* share a common provenance.

   In recalling to mind Haneke's metaphor of the puppet master, it should be noted that the masochistic scenario described by psychoanalysis is a theatrical one. "The actual scene [of masochism] corresponds to the staging of a drama," writes Theodor Reik, "and is related to the phantasies, as is the performance of the dramatist's conception" (1941: 49). Masochism involves control over time, and it is a performance. Entailing a ritual that plays itself out in the flesh, it is a game with reality intimately connected with representation. Just like games and plots – and just like masochists – filmmakers impose control over performance. "It's a game, is it?" Georges asks Majid in *Caché*, initially claiming that he doesn't want to play, only to agree later that "I'll play along." Like games, masochistic scenarios are governed by strict and complex rules – and by relentless repetition. Only in the case of the endgame is repetition no longer possible: When Majid invites Georges to visit, it is to ensure that Georges will be present as he slits his throat. The constant in *Caché*'s abbreviated history of repeated remediation, the image of the bloody throat in the childish drawings migrates first to the newspaper photograph of Georges, then to the body of the film itself. Finally, we're shown Majid's bloody performance on videotape, where it can be replayed repeatedly after all. The constant through multiple mediatic transformations, blood produces authenticity for representation by way of its strong impact on spectator affect. Perhaps it is for this reason that the "drawing" of blood – represented or metaphorical, imaged as well as elicited – seems the goal of Haneke's cinema.

Notes

1   This narrative structure has become popular: Alejandro Gonzalez Innaritu uses the device of accidentally connected narratives in *Amores Perros* (2000) and *Babel* (2006); Steven Soderbergh makes use of it in a film he directed, *Traffic* (2000), and – as producer – in *Syriana* (2005).
2   While critics such as D. I. Grossvogel distinguish Haneke's Austrian films from his French films, there is, in fact, a pronounced continuity of concern.
3   Fredric Jameson (1992: 169, 162).
4   My thanks to Ryan Cook for this suggestion.
5   Stanley Cavell's important work on the screen presence of the actor triggered these questions, as did Haneke's assertion that he needed to find just the right actors for

the remake of his own film, *Funny Games*, and that he would not have made the film if Naomi Watts had not agreed to be in it.

6   Binoche gave birth to her daughter Hannah in 2000.
7   Carol Clover famously distinguishes between the assaultive and the projective eye (1992: 199).
8   I have written elsewhere about the cruelty of Haneke's films (Peucker 2007).
9   As characters, Peter and Paul would seem to derive from the two helpers in Kafka's *The Castle*. Indeed, Frank Giering plays both Artur in Haneke's Kafka adaptation and Paul in *Funny Games*. Peter and Paul do not only play sadistic games with the family they murder, they have a sado-masochistic routine worked out between the two of them, as well.
10 Here I am referring – indeed, Barthes is referring – to the Real as that which cannot be adequately represented – as is the case with death. The term is taken from the writings of Jacques Lacan, and famously deployed for film by Slavoj Žižek in *Looking Awry* (1998).
11 *Peeping Tom* also links cruelty to performance spaces: Two of Mark's murders occur in such spaces.
12 See Haneke's letter of March 2000 to his producer, Marin Karmitz, reproduced for the Kino Video DVD of *Code Unknown*. Haneke's reference here is no doubt to Fritz Lang, who stylized his character Dr. Mabuse – and, by implication, himself – as the great puppet master. As quoted by Lucy Fischer, Lang refers to Mabuse as the "great showman of the marionettes, the one who organizes the perfect crime" (1979: 26). Some of the unanswered questions that linger in Georges's story – as well as in Anne's – are formulated in this letter, which presents itself as a supplement to – perhaps even as a means of deciphering – the film's unknowable code. In this letter, Haneke interrogates the boundaries of reality and illusion.
13 In the sequence set in Egypt, Benny's mother and her son interact by way of their mutual videotaping.
14 Here is another echo of *Benny's Video*, where the son's taping implicates his parents as accessories to his crime.

References and Further Reading

Barthes, Roland: *La Chambre claire: Note sur la photographie* (Paris: 1980); *Camera Lucida: Reflections on Photography*, trans. Richard Howard (New York: Hill and Wang, 1981).
Barthes, Roland: "The Photographic Message," *Image-Music-Text*, ed. and trans. Stephen Heath (New York: Hill and Wang, 1977), pp. 15–31.
Barthes, Roland: "Rhetoric of the Image," *Image-Music-Text*, ed. and trans. Stephen Heath (New York: Hill and Wang, 1977), pp. 32–51.
Bazin, André: *Le Cinéma de la cruauté* (Paris: 1975); *The Cinema of Cruelty from Buñuel to Hitchcock*, ed. François Truffaut, trans. Sabine d'Estrée (New York: Seaver Books, 1982).
Bial, H., ed.: *The Performance Studies Reader* (New York: Routledge, 2004).
Clover, Carol: *Men, Women, and Chainsaws: Gender in the Modern Horror Film* (Princeton, NJ: Princeton University Press, 1992).
Deleuze, Gilles: *Masochism: Coldness and Cruelty* (New York: Zone Books, 1991).

Finke, M. C. and Finke, Carl N., eds.: *One Hundred Years of Masochism: Literary Texts, Social and Cultural Contexts* (Amsterdam: Rodopi, 2000).

Fischer, Lucy: "Dr. Mabuse and Mr. Lang," *Wide Angle* 3:3 (1979): 18–26.

Grabner, Franz, Larcher, Gerhard, and Wesseley, Christian, eds.: *Utopie und Fragment: Michael Hanekes Filmwerk* (Thaur, Austria: Kulturverlag, 1996).

Grossvogel, D. I.: "Haneke: The Coercing of Vision," *Film Quarterly* 60:4 (Summer 2007): 36–43.

Haneke, Michael: "*71 Fragments of a Chronology of Chance*: Notes to the Film," *After Postmodernism: Austrian Literature and Film in Transition*, ed. Willy Riemer (Riverside, CA: Ariadne Press, 2000), pp. 171–5.

Haneke, Michael: Letter of March 2000 to Marin Karmitz, booklet, *Code Unknown*, Kino Video DVD.

Hanly, Margaret and Fitzpatrick, Ann, eds.: *Essential Papers on Masochism* (New York: New York University Press, 1995).

Jameson, Fredric: "The Existence of Italy," *Signatures of the Visible* (New York: Routledge, 1992), pp. 155–229.

Noyes, John K.: *The Mastery of Submission: Inventions of Masochism* (Ithaca, NY: Cornell University Press, 1997).

Peucker, Brigitte: "Fragmentation and the Real: Michael Haneke's Family Trilogy," *After Postmodernism: Austrian Literature and Film in Transition*, ed. Willy Riemer (Riverside, CA: Ariadne Press, 2000), pp. 176–88.

Peucker, Brigitte: "Violence and Affect: Haneke's Modernist Melodramas," *The Material Image: Art and the Real in Film* (Stanford, CA: Stanford University Press, 2007), pp. 129–58.

Powell, Michael: *A Life In Movies: An Autobiography* (London: Heinemann, 1986).

Reik, T.: *Masochism in Modern Man*, trans. Margaret H. Beigel and Gertrud M. Kurth (New York: Farrar, Strauss, and Co., 1941).

Riemer, Willy: "Beyond Mainstream Film: An Interview with Michael Haneke," *After Postmodernism: Austrian Literature and Film in Transition*, ed. Willy Riemer (Riverside, CA: Ariadne Press, 2000), pp. 160–75.

Winnicott, D. W.: *Playing and Reality* (New York: Basic Books, 1971).

Žižek, Slavoj: *Looking Awry: An Introduction to Jacques Lacan through Popular Culture* (Cambridge, MA: MIT Press, 1998).

7

Figures of Disgust

Christa Blümlinger

Ethical and moral questions have often been discussed in connection with the representation of elementary bodily acts in critical writing on Haneke's films, while the motif of disgust has received little attention to date. As an aesthetic phenomenon it is difficult to grasp. As Winfried Menninghaus[1] has shown, the indestructibility of what Freud called the cultural thresholds of disgust is just as fundamental to the works of Rabelais as it is to the provocations of the Viennese Actionists or, most recently, to abject art. Taboos of disgust are a necessary precondition to the functioning of a kind of art that takes transgression as its goal, but they hinder purely internal aesthetic reflection. The phenomenon of disgust may be understood as a combination of judgment and affect and as a field of tension between repulsion and attraction. As Menninghaus notes, when the field of aesthetics began to establish itself in the eighteenth century, disgust fulfilled a double function: As the "downright other" of the Beautiful, it represented a kind of liminal value; as a feeling of disgust relating to satiation (*Sättigungsekel*), it could also represent the danger of beauty's turning into its opposite. In order to grasp disgust in terms of cultural theory, Menninghaus names three elementary characteristics of the phenomenon: "(1) violent repulsion vis-à-vis (2) a physical presence or some other phenomenon in our proximity (3) which at the same time, in various degrees, can also exert a subconscious attraction or even an open fascination" (Menninghaus 2003: 6). The effect, according to Menninghaus, is very often an ambivalence connected as much with the control of affects as with the intensification of feeling.

In this essay I shall not undertake to clarify the extent to which film as an art or a medium may generate an affective logic of disgust that differs from that of, say, literature or sculpture. Rather, I mean to identify apposite figurations in Haneke's work, analyzing their cinematic aspects and commenting on them in terms of cultural theory. If one investigates Michael Haneke's use of figures of disgust, it soon becomes clear that the apparently distantiating style of his feature and television films is shot through with figurations of bodily matters and bodily acts. These figurations play an essential role in the films; their importance is anchored not merely in the construction of the narrative, but also in their contribution to its undermining. They are symptomatic within epistemological configurations of the film, particularly with regard to questions of truth and reality.

In *Three Paths to the Lake*, a film made for television in 1976, Haneke adapts a story by Ingeborg Bachmann so as to develop a space for the sensation of a specific kind of *ennui* or disgust, which becomes the only authentic experience of existence. Franz Joseph Trotta – who says of himself that he does not live – becomes, after his death, a moral authority for the photojournalist Elisabeth. Trotta, a being from a different time, the time of old Austria, makes Elisabeth, as an exile in Paris, "unsure" of her work on the war in Algeria. In a complex play with time frames, the film draws attention to a line spoken by Trotta, and it does so by featuring this line twice. This line is uttered in different narrative configurations and settings, but each time it occurs in a dialog between Trotta and Elisabeth. The sentence first appears in an objective narrative configuration, like a short citation: "Do you think you have to photograph these destroyed villages and corpses for me to imagine war, or these Indian children so that I know what hunger is?"[2] The second time, this same dialog passage is marked as a flashback from Elisabeth's point of view, and is linked to a present moment of recollection that takes place during one of her walks to the lake. In a complex way, Trotta's statement thus comes to be a motto. The difference between the first statement and the repetition makes it a kind of hermeneutical riddle.

Haneke uses Bachmann's text to connect the experience of disgust with the achievement of knowledge (an analogy appearing in Nietzsche and later in Sartre). Advances in consciousness are accompanied by a sensation of nausea (*la nausée*). In his *Disgust: Theory and History of a Strong Sensation* (2003), Menninghaus describes such existential disgust as a "violent crisis of ordinary self- and world-perception, which suddenly experiences its very fundament as either absent or actively taken away."[3] In Bachmann's story, this crisis is transferred from one character to another; in Haneke's film, it is related to the form of the utterance as a typically modernist crisis affecting the linear temporal order characteristic of the classical mode of storytelling.

Bachmann's story sets its several temporal layers into relation with the position Elisabeth occupies at any given moment, switching between her walks to the lake and her recollections of Trotta and of moments in which she achieves a gaining of consciousness through Trotta and through his influence, which lasts even beyond his death. Haneke's film shapes these perspectives and temporal layers in a more ambiguous way than the written text does. Elisabeth's musings are filmed as flashbacks, most often introduced by a male voice (Axel Corti), which relativizes the internal focalization.[4] The use of an extradiegetic offscreen voice brings an objective authorial instance into play, one especially strong in one place. When this sonorous voice describes Elisabeth's career as a polyglot photographer, on the visual level we are shown a series of private photographs from her youth. The look back begins with a zoom into a large print of Elisabeth as a girl with pigtails; later, the camera travels to a painted portrait of an ancestor from the nine-teenth century. Here the camera accentuates the temporal aura of the family portrait: Like Elisabeth's youth, the world of the Austro-Hungarian monarchy is irretrievably lost.

If this "objective" flashback is introduced by a traveling shot to a picture of a girl, belatedly and paradoxically it makes Elisabeth an object of the gaze. The film's introduction here of photography does not introduce the narrative's complex temporal structure, which will later (via repetitions, complex bracketing, and abrupt cuts) become the sign of Elisabeth's existential crisis. Rather, what this flashback addresses – relatively conventionally – is the question of the power of the gaze: The object of the gaze is ultimately not the world as Elisabeth sees it, but Elisabeth herself, as shown to us by an invisible narrator. The private pictures from Elisabeth's childhood or the snapshots of her brother's wedding[5] may still exercise a (some-times deceptive) memorial function, but Elisabeth's own professional photographs of theaters of war are kept offscreen. They may be the object of Trotta's cultural critiques, but as reprehensible images they are elided. Here Haneke takes on Bachmann's cultural pessimism regarding the medial function of photography, except-ing family photos.

Trotta's disgust with the world of media is shown not only in flashbacks, but also in ghostly sentences that haunt Elisabeth from the beyond – from offscreen. The narrator's voice, like Trotta's, occupies a position of omniscience and omnipresence – unlike Elisabeth's gaze, which seems always to seek or flee some-thing. The central flashback represents a discussion between Elisabeth and Trotta of questions of disgust and shame. In a single long take, we see Trotta bearing down on Elisabeth, who meanwhile continuously changes her position, until the opposition between the two is resolved into a short shot–countershot sequence. Finally, Elisabeth looks out the window behind her, towards her uncertain future as a photographer, while Trotta looks forward left into offscreen space, indicat-ing his retreat, but also the end that he will set to his life. Trotta knows where he is looking; Elisabeth's gaze is blind.

This blindness is connected with Elisabeth's activity as a photographer, but it is not clear which wars she is documenting, or how. The film does not take a political position with regard to a specific set of intolerable present circum-stances, as do, for example, the essay-films of Jean-Marie Straub and Danièle Huillet, whose work Haneke has declared formative for his own. In their *Introduction à la "Musique d'accompagnement pour une scène de film" de Arnold Schoenberg* (1972), Straub and Huillet present shots of American B-52 bombers in such a way that (as Serge Daney writes) they are purged of any sense of *déjà vu*, which per-mits the power that produced them "to become clearly apparent".[6] Haneke's approach is here – in contrast with Straubian "pedagogy" (Daney) – neither his-torical, nor anchored in the present. Rather, it takes its cues from an existential negativity and general cultural pessimism characterized by a deep mistrust of the visual media.

Three Paths to the Lake ascribes existential nausea above all to Trotta, a figure whom the protagonist, Elisabeth, remembers and who, in his very lostness, facilitated her gaining of consciousness. For Elisabeth, recollection, just like the process by which she becomes aware of the implications of her work and her position in the world, is associated with physical pain. A loss of balance caused by an injury to her ankle during a walk through her native landscape leads, in an abrupt cut, to the memory of a similar injury sustained by her earlier in reaction to the news of Trotta's death, reported as gossip by a Viennese journalist. If for Elisabeth nausea emerges as a somatic symptom, this occurs after the fact, belatedly. The film does not show or produce affect in the form of disgust or *dégoût*, that is, as a negative attribute of *nausée*. However, Trotta does address such images in moral terms, as when he comments on "the war you photograph for other people's breakfasts."[7]

Disgust recurs as a symptom affecting the body in Haneke's later films, but there within a constellation of affect-images, which are presented both as invasive and too close, not as a loss of solid ground or as a crisis in the perception of the world. In the films belonging to the glaciation trilogy, such as for example *Benny's Video* (1992), the gaining of consciousness is no longer ascribed to a character, as it is in *Three Paths to the Lake*; instead, it is addressed directly to the spectator. It is well known that *Benny's Video* constructs a layered system of sounds and images, the origins of which are ambiguous and which sometimes turn out to be always already mediated. The video surveillance set that Benny has installed in his room is an example of this. Haneke's insistent framing of the monitor, first full-screen, then as a screen-within-the-screen, accentuates the confusion of inner with outer space, of observer and observed, of direct recording with repetition. In this way the question of where the gaze is located is staged as a question of power.

The plot of the film has often been described as a chain reaction of private videos that have a retroactive effect on the life of the protagonist: Benny films the slaughter of a pig and shows the video to a girl, who, like him, is a fan of splatter films; afterwards, he kills her with the same bolt pistol that the farmer in the film had used to kill the pig. He then shows the film to his mother, whose voice he later records while she is discussing the crisis with his father; at the end of the film he turns over this recording – the only remaining evidence – to the police. If (as Jörg Metelmann writes) this narrative serves less to present Benny as the controller of the video (as the title of the film suggests) than to present an all-encompassing system that finally transcends its own diegesis, then the character of Benny (as Roy Grundmann argues) may represent not so much the indistinguishability of video from reality as the wish to transform the world into a video.[8]

Benny's favorite film genre is the splatter film,[9] whose omnipresence in Haneke's films, like TV news and heavy metal, is marked as loud, obscene, and invasive, and thus as a symptom of disturbance. The counterpart to Benny's medial sound world is the desublimation of sacred choral music through the drug dealing of the choir boys. With regard to the figuration of disgust, an obvious opposition between a youth culture (obsessed as it is with violence and horror) and the sphere of high culture, or between disrespectful, anti-social drives and the sphere of culture, respect, and morality, is less relevant than the film's strategy of continuously interrupting the mode of narration and its temporal structures.[10]

Here, as in *Three Paths to the Lake*, Haneke employs a complex structure of repetition. He repeats the same sentence in different contexts, thus carrying to the extreme his play with the origin of the utterance. During a long shot–reverse-shot sequence set in their bedroom, Benny's parents discuss different techniques for disposing of the dead body and other pieces of incriminating evidence. The father asks the mother: "Will you be able to stand the disgust?" This very dialog returns half an hour later in the film (after a solemn church concert scene), this time shown not from the father's perpective, nor from the mother's, but from a third perspective: that of Benny's eavesdropping spot. This time, the father's sentences are recorded in a single, motionless shot, with Benny's partly open door framed from within his darkened bedroom. No sooner is Benny's point of view marked than the soundtrack adds yet another framing to this view. We suddenly hear a police interrogator, who asks questions from offscreen concerning the course of Benny's actions. This shot thus turns out to be not a flashback but a frontal view of a video monitor from an elevated perspective that changes the parents' cover-up project into a confession of guilt, for together with Benny's verbal witness it is the only remaining trace of the crime. With the acousmatic presence[11] of a police officer, who remains invisible, the ultimate position of enunciation is finally marked as virtual: It is not *in* the image, but rather *in front of* the image.

It is no coincidence that the sentences that thus become evidence at the end of *Benny's Video* are about the conventional disgust that is connected with the revolting manipulation of the corpse. It is, after all, as the "experience of an unwilled proximity" that Winfried Menninghaus (2003: 7) defines the basic character of the phenomenon of disgust. Haneke is concerned not simply to attribute to his characters the same three aspects of attraction, repulsion, and fascination that Menninghaus names as the basic characteristics of the phenomenon of disgust, as noted at the beginning of this essay; he also inscribes them directly into the cinematic image, beyond the dialog, removing them to another plane and thus marking them as inexpressible affects.

The *mise-en-abyme* of points of view and points of hearing instantiated by such repetition of dialog has usually been read, from the perspective of media theory, as a relativization of the relations between world and video.[12] In *Benny's Video*, as we know, this is achieved through the discursive fusion of diegetic image-recording (Benny's videos) and frame narrative (Benny's story). Yet what is symptomatic about the repeated scene is not only the reiterated displacement of the points of view from which the story is told (from the father, to Benny, to the police officer), but also the fact that precisely at the place where anticipation, recollection, and imagination converge, the object of revulsion is described only *verbally*. Benny – and along with him the viewer – is an earwitness to his parents' intention of dismembering and disposing of the body, but not an eyewitness to its execution. All that Benny has finally to show in the way of evidence is a recording of a speech act, for the visual images of his deeds have been erased by the father. Within the film's narrative logic, there is a plausible reason for this: An act that arose from fantasy is now subjected to instrumental reason. In addition, from a legal/forensic perspective, Benny's *passage à l'acte* can be shown more explicitly through sound documents (the parents' verbal response to the killing) than through visual documents (the recording). The difference of this last repetition is more than a screenplay gimmick. The acoustic replay of the discussion scene also marks the scenic omission of the father's actions. The question "Will you be able to bear the disgust?" is thus ultimately directed at the film viewer, whose anticipation, recollection, and imagination essentially compose the genre of which this film represents an exaggerated, excessive example.

The film's *mise-en-scène* of visible moments of disgust must also be seen against this background. In this context, it is significant that the film makes a figurative connection between Benny's acting-out of sadistic fantasies and the speech act of the father, between literal showing and mental projection. Connections are established between the confession scene and the visual configurations of disgust not only through the film's thematization of the reprehensible (the calculated complicity of the father, the crime of the son) and through the repetition compulsion transferred from the characters to the narrative structure itself, but also through frontal framing. The video that survives to become evidence, a last trace on taciturn Benny's Mystic writing pad, is structurally connected with the erased scenes of violence that we have seen repeated on other monitors, and repeatedly renarrated. If the videographic apparatus serves at first to prove the visual representability of elementary bodily acts, in the end it marks the significance of the Symbolic through the repetition of a speech act. This move from showing to not-showing, from the image to verbal language, once again underlines the ambiguity of filmic figuration. This ambiguity is more readily approached through analysis of the way in which disgust – conceived as an unwanted closeness – becomes image than if one simply analyzed the images, in terms of narratological or media theory, with regard to their system of reference.

The murder scene, too, is suggested above all by sound. As soon as the girl's body becomes a corpse, however, images that produce strong affect begin. At first, the details of the homicidal gesture itself either remain offscreen or are visible only at the edges of the screen. Then the automatic gaze of Benny's camera becomes systematically linked to Benny's subjective point of view. What follows Benny's stone-faced expression after the pistol shot is thus not *his* point of view, but the perspective of the live camera: We literally see the girl fall out of the frame of the control monitor. In later shots that are just as static and also closely framed, we see Benny's strained efforts to drag the corpse out of the room and then to clean up the blood spots that are left behind. The camera finally becomes mobile in a third phase, as Benny, standing before an invisible mirror, smears the murdered girl's blood on his naked belly. Suddenly we see electronic snow; the mirror is Benny's camcorder, the scene is a recording. It becomes clear only afterward that Benny, here, has been filming himself. However unrealistic this video "self-portrait" may seem to the "analytical" eye, its emotional effect as a vehicle for empathy is strong: The hand behind the camera echoes Benny's circling motions before the camera. This mimetic transfer of a touching movement lends the image a haptic quality. After the sensual hand-camera filming of the belly there follows a similar filming of the corpse. Benny's one-handed gestures loom from offscreen into the frame: He turns the dead girl around, so that a giant bloodstain becomes visible on her face.

Finally we see Benny replaying these images in his editing room – this time quickly and on rewind. The amateur video here embodies the repetition compulsion of its observer. As a fan of splatter films (and therefore of remakes and sequels), Benny is disposed to rituals and repetitions. Such reflexive interpolations are native to splatter films themselves, as Carol J. Clover has demonstrated with the example of *Texas Chainsaw Massacre II* (Tobe Hooper, 1986).[13] The figure of the assaultive gaze relayed by the camera has also been established within the modern horror film since Michael Powell's *Peeping Tom* (1960) (see Brigitte Peucker's essay in this volume); in post-classical cinema, offscreen space is often established as the starting point of visual pleasure. Whereas in classical cinema that which is absent from the image-field disappears into the seam between shot and countershot to disappear from consciousness, modern post-classical cinema turns its attention upon itself, in order (as Pascal Bonitzer writes) "to try to find the object at the origin of its desire, the gaze that one imagines in the offscreen space."[14] This mode of reference to the location and gaze of that which is absent may be understood as the motor of Haneke's editing, but it does not explain the form of representation. To what do the configurations of "unclean" bodies lead in *Benny's Video*, a film that desires to be an auteur film – one that is removed from the thriller genre by several degrees?

As I have noted, Haneke shows elementary acts of the body in a way that does not distance us from them in advance. Instead, he produces a kind of haptic empathy through narrow framing and small movements, in order to question how the gaze is affected through hindsight shifts in perspective. In this process, the materiality of blood is given a special status: As a viscous fluid, it has the capacity to stick and spread and deform the figurations. The blots of blood on the floor, on Benny's body, and on the face of the dead girl function as figural significations of an affect that lies between attraction and repulsion. If, as a character, Benny initially embodies the overcoming of disgust or the suspension of cultural thresholds of disgust, then here this suspension becomes the object of a higher level of reflection, of a disgust in the second degree, which elevates itself to the level of a capacity for judgment. We see Benny as a compulsive observer of obscene images – images aimed, just a moment before, at our own direct sensual perception.

At first it would seem that, in the above-mentioned scene, Benny's affirmative relationship to death in its material presence represents violence as the core of the erotic, in Georges Bataille's sense of a "fascination" with the disgusting or the depressing.[15] On further reflection, however, the medial setting within the filmic narration seems to interrupt this form of transgression. Here the imagination of "low, debased matter" and the figural work of decomposition do not quite lead to a complex mode of image production, such as the one described by Menninghaus with a tripartite model that relates such decomposition to Bataille's category of the *informe*, the formless: as the desublimation of beautiful forms, as the "liberation" of violent sexuality, or as the reestablishment of a connection with archaic practices of production of social life in feelings of repulsion or in acts of sacrifice.[16] This configuration of disgust in Haneke can be explained neither with Bataille nor with the Freudian conception of defense mechanism in which, due to an "unclean" body, a transference into an intellectual judgment (of negation) takes place, and which thus belongs to the field of cultural repression.[17] So what does this configuration amount to? Where does it lead us?

Approximately twenty film minutes after the blood scene and before Benny plays the electronic record of his horrible deed for the third time – this time with his mother watching – the image of the blot as a moment of defiguration recurs. Benny comes home and takes milk from the fridge that his mother had filled. He pours the milk so greedily that he spills it. After he drinks the milk, the camera jumps from a medium shot to a close-up. The shining white blot now completely fills the angular shot. Benny's hand is then introduced from offscreen into the frame and, with circular movements, he towels up the spilled milk. This repetition of a formal constellation not only establishes a structural reference to the blood of the girl he has killed, it also prefigures the taped return of the murder scene. Yet the close-up of the milk blot, as a figural rupture (one could also say, with Roland Barthes, as a *punctum*[18]), also alludes to the unstable position of the spectator. This close-up reveals an alluring detail while simultaneously strengthening its affective dimension by means of the enigmatic figuration.

It seems important in this connection that the materials in question are liquids – liquids possibly representative of a pre-Oedipal maternal essence. This has less to do with narrative relations or with the functions of the film's characters (Benny, his mother); rather, it calls attention to the affective status of the scene's *punctum*. This indicates a sphere called by Julia Kristeva, in her psychoanalytic-linguistic theory, the "semiotic," a sphere which, according to Kristeva, serves as the origin of a specific defensive position – namely, "abjection" – whose strongest physical indicator is the affect of disgust. The skin on the surface of milk or corpses becomes for Kristeva the embodiment of this defensive position because such skins decay or are secreted – thrown off – by the body; yet they are also things from which one cannot part, and "from which one does not protect oneself, as from an object."[19] The becoming of the speaking being, conceived as an entry into the symbolic order, demands – and this is where Kristeva distinguishes herself from

Freud and Lacan – the rejection of the maternal body, with its undifferentiated economy of fluids and rhythmic drives.[20] The abject confronts us therefore with the oldest attempts at delimitation, "with the constant risk of falling back under the sway of a power as securing as it is stifling."[21] The maternal body is repulsed and rejected as unclean and threatening to one's own boundaries, or, to quote Menninghaus's summary of Kristeva: "The body must bear no trace of its debt to nature: it must be clean and proper in order to be fully symbolic."[22] The dirtying of the body thus represents the part of a ritual whose goal is rejection. Such figurative or figural play with blood can also be found in other Haneke films.[23] In *Caché* (2005), for example, the slaughter of a rooster as an enigmatic pulsing blot, as something too close and disgusting, prefigures the later suicide of the character Majid. In *The Piano Teacher* (2001) the rape scene is crystallized in the bloody fouling of Erika's (Isabelle Huppert's) shirt.

Abjection is conceived by Kristeva as a "composite of judgment and affect, of condemnation and yearning, of signs and drives."[24] This term seems appropriate especially in cases when it is brought into relation with filmic narratives in which disgust is not only a theme, but where the narrative position itself is also structured so as to traverse a trajectory of abjection, a process that registers as pain to the inside and terror to the outside.[25] The texture of such a narration can be understood, with Kristeva, as a thin film, one constantly in danger of breakage, which would produce fissures, enigmas, interweavings and elisions. Precisely because of this, Haneke's language of disgust is sometimes able to achieve an intensity closer to poetic exclamation than to narration.

A corresponding aesthetic of the fragment and of suddenness characterizes the film *71 Fragments of a Chronology of Chance* (1994), as well as the structurally related *Code Unknown* (2000). Yet examples of this style of ellipsis and narrative interlock may already be found in Haneke's early television films. Thus, for example, there emerges at the end of the two-part television film *Lemmings* (1979) a form of fissure that strengthens the bodily dimension of the repulsion. From an unexplicit and ambiguous image of a mortally injured, bloody body, the film cuts to a piece of medical equipment, a shot that is immediately linked to an offscreen scream. Only when the camera tracks back is the source of the tortured voice evident: We see not Eva, who has suffered the accident, but Sigi in the midst of convulsions, overtaken by the elementary act of giving birth. A last scene of discharge serves as a coda for the film: In the end Eva's husband Beranek, having just survived a self-destructive car accident and lost both his military power and his wife, stiffens in a screaming fit which Haneke ends with a freeze frame.[26]

In *Lemmings*, Part Two: *Injuries*, Beranek is the only male character to whom the registers of somatic reactions and bodily eliminations are allotted: He has a stomach illness and frequently has to vomit, an act which Haneke represents in detail as a consequence of medial transmissions of violence, as seen, for instance, in the comparison, in a military school film, between the atom bomb and the neutron bomb. The other bomb discussed in *Lemmings*, namely in part one, is a

Russian bomb that hit Sigi's family at the end of the war. Her father lost a leg, her mother was paralyzed, and her brother,[27] years later, commits suicide by plunging to his death. Fatefully injured bodies seem here to convey a process of defense whose root cause cannot be narrated, whose signs, however, announce themselves figurally in an image or rupture: In the room of the bedridden mother a red light blinks constantly; the disabled father is overcome by a lonely destructive rage, which suddenly erupts while he is sitting at the table.[28]

This specific mixture of judgment and affect can finally be established as a figure of disgust through the analysis of other formal constellations in Haneke's work, which are equally connected to materials and acts of the body. In Haneke's made-for-TV film *Fraulein* (1986), the expressive framings and unusual perspectives of camera axes reiterate the estrangement of two bodies physically interlaced with each other. The figure of the husband in agony is shown from a high angle; the final seductive gesture of the wife is filmed in such a way as to draw attention to the opening of the legs, while the head disappears behind the body. In Haneke's adaptation of Joseph Roth's novel *The Rebellion* (1992), a story of the travails of an injured war veteran in the wake of the dissolution of the Austro-Hungarian Empire (portrayed as a matter of what Freud called *Schicksalszwang*, the compulsion of fate),[29] the spectator is put into the position of frontal witness to a ravenous sexuality. In this case, the perspective of the shot presents neither a neutral nor a subjective point of view; rather, it is established as a kind of neutral or impersonal master frame, one addressed explicitly to the spectator. One can describe such a configuration, with Francesco Casetti,[30] as "objectively unreal"; the underlining of the omnipotence of the camera strengthens the power of the author-enunciator. Such insistent compositions and framings not only "let the camera feel," they also produce a "free indirect speech"[31] through their own autonomous camera-consciousness – as one could extrapolate from the conception of modern cinema developed by Pasolini and Deleuze. Here the filmic author asserts himself indirectly via his characters by distinguishing himself from them. Conceived in terms of a theory of disgust, this permits the completion of the transition from disgust in the first degree (as a matter of affect) to disgust in the second degree (as a matter of judgment). The "objective configuration" of shots corresponds to the function of Trotta's voice recurring from the "beyond" in *Three Paths to the Lake*, in which the figure of *ennui* discussed above already belongs to the category of disgust in the second degree.

Thus, the ambivalent figuration of body boundaries and openings in Haneke's films can be shown to be a reiteration of epistemological configurations of disgust, reality, and truth. In these films the conflict between claims of the symbolic order and the insistence of abject lust, as described by Julia Kristeva, becomes manifest not only at the thematic level, as the other side of (post-)religious and moral codes, it is also transmitted through formal configurations and abrupt connections between the shots. The systematic repetition of these configurations of disgust can be read as a pattern reproduced not only within individual films, but also as a kind of transposition, from film to film, of a "demonic" symptom. Following Freud, one could call this symptom – a symptom culturally and historically anchored in Austria – *Schicksalsneurose*: a neurosis of fate. Therefore, if the notable traversal of abjection in Haneke's films assumes so prominently the character of a repetition, it ultimately also indicates a collective cultural symptom of this authoritarian society, initially formed under Catholicism. The declination of an art of repetition in Haneke is in this regard similar to the Vienna Actionists, whose art likewise aimed at achieving transgression. Thus, Haneke's civilized disgust is an ordering principle that refers to nothing less than a secular kind of apocalypse.

Translated by Peter J. Schwartz

Notes

1 Winfried Menninghaus (2003: 346–72).
2 See DVD subtitles of Michael Haneke (dir.), *Three Paths to the Lake* (1976).
3 Menninghaus (2003: 356). The awareness of contingency and the perception that existence is senseless and that time passes emptily have led in literature since the seventeenth century to treatments of boredom (*ennui*) and of melancholy. *La nausée*, on the other hand, revalues melancholy as a richness of experience, one that permits a break with false senses of senslessness. Nonetheless, as Menninghaus shows, in Sartre *la nausée* also reveals itself "in the medium of ordinary 'dégoût' (disgust)," that is to say, via negative attributes.
4 On the concept of "internal focalization" see Gérard Genette (1972); see also André Gaudreault and François Jost (1990: 128, 138). Bachmann's story is essentially one told in the third person that proceeds for the most part homodiegetically and is concentrated on the person of Elisabeth. With his male voice-over Haneke introduces an extradiegetic narrator and thus relativizes the focalization of the flashbacks. During her walk Elisabeth is shown as a figure looking off into the distance and sunk in memories, but with this voice the soundtrack adds another, more authoritative narrating agent.
5 According to the dialogs, the photographs that Elisabeth shows to her father were taken by her. However, Elisabeth herself appears on all the photos presented in the filmic shot from their subjective points of view. There are two gazes: The filmic point of view (Elisabeth and her father looking at the photos), and the point of view of the photo itself. Elisabeth's position as originary witness and observer is thus relativized.
6 See Serge Daney (1983: 85).
7 This is taken directly from Bachmann's story: "The war you photograph for other people's breakfasts hasn't spared you either in the end." See Bachmann (1989: 140).
8 See Jörg Metelmann (2003: 94–5) and Roy Grundmann (2007: 10).
9 The genre of splatter or slasher films can be described, with Carol J. Clover, as follows: "The immensely generative story of a psychokiller who slashes to death a string of mostly female victims, one by one, until he is subdued or killed, usually by the one girl who has survived" (Clover 1992: 21).

158   CHRISTA BLÜMLINGER

10   I mean here to distinguish, with Gérard Genette, between the *histoire* (story) of denoted events, the *récit* (narrative) as the syntactic and semantic product of the act of storytelling, and the narration as the utterance of the story. This permits analysis of the temporal relations between the told story and the time of telling, on the one hand, and of the modalities of regulation of narrative information (the perspectivization of the narrative) on the other. See Genette (1972); also Oswald Ducrot and Jean-Marie Schaeffer (1995: 588–9).

11   On the concept of the acousmatic voice, which remains endowed with omnipresence and the power of the gaze so long as its source remains invisible, see Michel Chion (1982).

12   Andreas Kilb describes Benny's room as a "Platonic cave of the video age." See Andreas Kilb (2005: 71).

13   There is in this film too the figure of a (horror) film-within-the-film. Clover calls this constellation a "metacinematic declaration of our common spectatorial plight" (Clover 1992: 200).

14   See Pascal Bonitzer (1982: 106).

15   Bataille exemplifies this fascination with the disgusting with menstrual blood and the decomposition of corpses and calls it the core of social life. See Georges Bataille (1972: 316); also Menninghaus (2003: 492).

16   See Menninghaus (2003); see also Georges Didi-Huberman (1995).

17   Freud derives the concepts of repression and rejection from the elementary codes of the pleasure-ego and constructs disgust as well as negation as aspects of the movement to neurosis that characterizes the process of civilization. See Sigmund Freud, "Negation"; see also Menninghaus (2003).

18   Roland Barthes (1981: 42–3) describes the *punctum* of the photograph as "that which attracts me," for example a detail (the *punctum* "should be revealed only after the fact" [53]; it does not reveal itself through study, but rather after a certain latency; a "blind field is created" [57], it is "a kind of subtle beyond" [59]).

19   They indicate what the subject needs constantly to reject in order to live, the loss at the root of every being: the non-objectal, pre-Oedipal rejection of the mother. Julia Kristeva (1982: 4).

20   Kristeva seizes on the development of a conception of self in the sense of Freud's primary narcissism or Lacan's mirror-stage, but specifically connects it to her own notion of the rejection of the *corps à corps* (body-to-body) with the mother in favor of establishing clear subject and body boundaries. Abjection is thus, for Kristeva, a precondition of narcissism. See Kristeva (1982: 13).

21   Kristeva (1982: 13).

22   Kristeva (1982: 102).

23   I use the term "figurative" as belonging to representation and form (including narration), whereas the term "figural" corresponds to the *informe* and the fissure in the narration. In the scenes under discussion both functions are at issue – the transformation of form into the *informe*; the formation of a fissure within representation.

24   Kristeva (1982: 10).

25   On Céline as a representative of the abject literature of the twentieth century Kristeva says that his "whole narrative structure seems controled by the necessity of going through abjection, whose intimate site is suffering and horror its public feature" (1982: 140).

26 This freeze frame represents, in a relatively conventionalized, late modern form, the end of the story and simultaneously its virtual continuation.

27 Here Paulus Manker plays a youth in the postwar period whose latent feeling of self-abasement expresses itself in his consorting with a servant girl he abuses as a sexual object.

28 There is a similar scene in *71 Fragments of a Chronology of Chance*. Here, too, a sudden, delayed reaction – a slap in the face – is represented in connection with the ritual of eating.

29 In *Beyond the Pleasure Principle* (1920), Freud develops the theory of a *Schicksalszwang* (fatal compulsion) experienced as negative or demonic, which he will later call *Schicksalsneurose* (neurosis of fate). See Sigmund Freud, "Beyond the Pleasure Principle," pp. 21–2. Freud's text may certainly be understood, from the perspective of cultural theory, as a postwar text (as he himself has underlined).

30 The omnipotence that Casetti relates to this "impossible objective configuration" has to do with seeing, with meta-discursive knowledge, but also with the level of belief, while the "subjective configuration" remains intradiegetic, transitory and limited. Francesco Casetti (1998: 50, 70–1).

31 Gilles Deleuze (1986: 74).

References and Further Reading

Bachmann, Ingeborg: *Three Paths to the Lake*, trans. Mary Fran Gilbert (New York: Holmes and Meier, 1989).

Barthes, Roland: *Camera Lucida: Reflections on Photography* (New York: Hill and Wang, 1981).

Bataille, Georges: *Œuvres Complètes*, Vol. 2 (Paris: Gallimard, 1972).

Bonitzer, Pascal: *Le Champ aveugle: Essais sur le cinéma* (Paris: Gallimard, 1982).

Casetti, Francesco: *Inside the Gaze: The Fiction Film and Its Spectator*, trans. Nell Andrew and Charles O'Brien (Bloomington: Indiana University Press, 1998).

Chion, Michel: *La Voix au cinéma* (Paris: Editions de l'Etoile, 1982).

Clover, Carol: *Men, Women and Chainsaws: Gender in the Modern Horror Film* (Princeton, NJ: Princeton University Press, 1992).

Daney, Serge: "Un tombeau pour l'œil (pédagogie Straubienne)," *La Rampe* (Paris: Gallimard, 1983), pp. 78–85.

Deleuze, Gilles: *Cinema 1: The Movement-Image*, trans. Hugh Tomlinson and Barbara Habberjam (Minneapolis: University of Minnesota Press, 1986).

Didi-Huberman, Georges: *La Ressemblance informe ou le gai savoir visuel selon Bataille* (Paris: Macula, 1995).

Ducrot, Oswald and Schaeffer, Jean-Marie: *Nouveau Dictionnaire encyclopédique des sciences du langage* (Paris: Seuil, 1995).

Freud, Sigmund: "Beyond the Pleasure Principle" (1920), *Standard Edition of the Complete Psychological Works of Sigmund Freud*, trans. and ed. J. Strachey (London: Hogarth Press, 1955), Vol. 18, pp. 1–64.

Freud, Sigmund: "Negation" (1925), *Standard Edition of the Complete Psychological Works of Sigmund Freud*, trans. and ed. J. Strachey (London: Hogarth Press, 1961), pp. 233–9.

Gaudreault, André and Jost, François: *Le Récit cinématographique* (Paris: Nathan, 1990).

Genette, Gerard: *Figures III* (Paris: Seuil, 1972).

Grundmann, Roy: "Auteur de Force: Michael Haneke's 'Cinema of Glaciation'," *Cineaste* 33:2 (Spring 2007): 6–14.

Kilb, Andreas: "Fragmente der Gewalt: Bildfetisch und Apparatur in *Bennys Video*," *Michael Haneke und seine Filme: Eine Pathologie der Konsumgesellschaft*, ed. Christian Wessely, Gernard Larcher, and Franz Grabner (Marburg: Schüren, 2005), pp. 67–77.

Kristeva, Julia: *Powers of Horror: An Essay on Abjection*, trans. Leon S. Roudiez (New York: Columbia University Press, 1982).

Menninghaus, Winfried: *Disgust: Theory and History of a Strong Sensation*, trans. Howard Eiland and Joel Golb (Albany: State University of New York Press, 2003).

Metelmann, Jörg: *Zur Kritik der Kino-Gewalt: Die Filme von Michael Haneke* (Munich: Fink, 2003).

8

Without Music

On Caché

Michel Chion

For the most part, *Caché* (2005) takes place in Paris in 2005. There are several signs of this, such as the design of mobile phones, or the content of the news on television (an item on the Palestinians in the Gaza Strip). The action takes place in several locations, such as the apartment of Georges (Daniel Auteuil) and Anne (Juliette Binoche), the streets near this apartment, their son's school, a municipal pool, streets, cars, a café, a low-rent housing complex, a farm, and so on. In other words, it takes place in extremely varied real public and private spaces. Yet, all of these different places in the film have one common element that makes each of them subtly unreal: the absence of any music whatsoever. I am not talking only about the absence of non-diegetic music, but the absence also of the kind of music, bits of which might be heard on television, in a café, or music one might listen to in a car or that might be playing in their son's room (decorated with a poster of Eminem), that we would likely hear in a world such as the one where the action takes place. Here, there is no music, none at all.

In this sense, the world of *Caché* is not our world; or rather, it is our world except that one crucial aspect has been voluntarily removed from it.

Of course one could argue that this absence has no precise meaning. In the majority of films, characters don't go to the bathroom either, nor do they usually wait for change when paying, and this does not mean that the omission of such scenes is meaningful for the film. But music, diegetic or not, is such an important element in the majority of films, as well as in the sonorous tissue of today's private moments, that films that do not offer such sounds "sound" different to us.

We might even say that we go to certain movies in search of a world that no longer exists elsewhere for us, especially in the city: a world stripped of music, and because of this absence, a world both fascinating and troubling. A little like what the noiseless world of silent cinema might have been like.

The question of the absence of music from the core of the film, and the fact that, at times, it is never so present in certain films as when it is completely absent, is particularly acute in several other films by Michael Haneke, such as the two versions of *Funny Games* (1997, 2007), *Benny's Video* (1992), and *The Seventh Continent* (1989).

This leads me to reopen the question of what is currently called music and to examine the way in which music is inscribed in, or is separate from, the sonorous fabric of our world.

There is a profound difference in the way in which the traditional visual arts (easel painting, frescoes, icons, and photography, which grew out of them) and traditional sound arts (grouped together in the term "music") are (or are not) situated in the real world. Traditional visual arts can imitate reality, its matter, its look, its forms, and they can try to create illusory effects, but the objects they create (aside from some well-known exceptions, such as the visual illusions in the villas of Palladio close to Venice) do not attempt to pass themselves off as reality. Even if they imitate these illusionistic figures, they are still distinct from them because they are inscribed on a tangible material surface, distinct from the real world, and are enclosed in a visual frame of the visible. A photograph hung on a wall in a well-lit room will not be confused as part of its environment.

Music, on the other hand, does not have a tangible support: The score alone is not enough to usher the work into existence (with very few exceptions, such as *The Art of Fugue*), neither are the instrument, the speakers, and so on. Furthermore, the sounds of music are not limited within any frame but blend with the sounds of reality, because sound does not emanate in a straight line, like a ray, but moves in a circular manner, like a wave. In order not to be confused with concrete material sounds, the sounds of music most often differentiate themselves through their own character.

In order to illustrate how music occupies space, I often use the comparison with odors. One can sense a very subtle perfume sprayed in a kitchen where fish is being grilled because it will simply blend with the other odors in the kitchen. Similarly, music in a noisy place blends with ambient sounds. It blends less well when it appears to be made of a different fabric – of instrumental musical sounds, and even more so when it is made of successive notes because such sequences rarely exist in the "natural" sound world.

There is a profound difference between the olfactory and the auditory fields. The auditory field displays the very singular property that certain notes of a precise pitch are easier to hear, not because they are more beautiful than other notes or more pleasing in and of themselves (an oft-repeated claim about music), but simply because of their particular pitch.

In my essay *Sound (Le Son)*, I write:

A note – the inscription of the sound in a musical phrase – is sometimes . . . the only means for a sound to be framed in relation to others. Even if the texture of a picture resembles the texture of a plant in the painter's studio or in the painting's owner's house, this presents no problem since the frame of the painting encloses the forms and allows them to be differentiated from the real. However, the same is not true for sound, because there is no sonorous frame for sounds. Thus, the fact that a musical sound takes a specific form, distinct from the sounds of the ordinary world, and is organized, together with other notes, according to a very precise law – and especially because it is produced by an instrument reserved for the production of musical sounds – the effect can be said to be the equivalent of framing: We know that this sound belongs to a work of art and not to the real, because, spatially, it is totally blended with the sounds of life.[1]

Thus, as soon as a film offers us music, be it diegetic or extra-diegetic, it will sound more or less like an "overture" to another world.

Silent cinema (excluding the projections of silent films accompanied by sound effects) presented us with the possibility of a world fully accompanied by music and notes – the equivalent of a ballet with pantomime, even if the characters spoke. Films with no music whatsoever, or with very little music, that appeared during the history of sound cinema tend in a way to invert this formula. The "silence" of real noises and voices, characteristic of silent cinema, has been replaced by another silence – that of an element created by humans.

Let us leave aside films with little or no extra-diegetic music: They are numerous, particularly in the early years of sound cinema (Hawks's *Scarface*, 1932; Wellman's *The Public Enemy*, 1931; Lang's *M*, 1931; Duvivier's *A Man's Neck*, 1933; Renoir's *The Bitch*, 1931), but they nevertheless give us a lot of diegetic music, because at that time, and all the more so today, nothing was easier than placing characters in situations and places featuring music: cafés, fairgrounds, banquets, concerts, street musicians, and so on. Let us limit ourselves to films that contain very little or no diegetic or extra-diegetic music. Such films are often linked to the idea of the end of the world or of some catastrophe, or at least to a *fatum*, such as Sidney Lumet's *Fail-Safe* (1964) (an excellent film on a subject very close to Stanley Kubrick's *Dr. Strangelove* [1964] but treated in a more somber register), or Bergman's *Shame* (1968) (about a couple plunged into disarray and degradation at the outbreak of a war), Lumet's *Dog Day Afternoon* (1975) (a hostage crisis that ends tragically), and, much more recently, Joel and Ethan Coen's *No Country for Old Men* (2007) (about a frightening mad killer) and Bruno Dumont's *Flanders* (2006) (about young men in the midst of war).

Notably, in Bergman's *Shame*, the main characters are two orchestra musicians. In the beginning of the film, Jan (Max von Sydow) sits on his bed, having just woken up, and recounts a dream he's just had in which he played Bach's Brandenburg concerto. (The similarity with Renoir's *The Rules of the Game* [1939], where the principal female character is the daughter of the maestro of an orchestra, is noteworthy: There, too, Octave talks of a concert to which we are not privy.) Jan's narrative is the only form in which music exists in *Shame* because the war, as it rips the characters out of their insulated musical world and throws them on the road, stops music from resounding, from chiming, from singing, from making us dream – in short, it interrupts everything that might allow us to escape from a difficult reality with no other way out.

There was a similar effect in Robert Bresson's late films, and most notably in his last film, *L'Argent* (*Money*, 1983), which features only briefly a chromatic prélude by Bach on a second-rate piano. Even this piece, which resonates with equal force throughout every room in the house, is brutally cut short by the breaking of a glass of white wine that the piano player – a failed former piano professor, destroyed by alcoholism – had carelessly placed on the edge of the piano. This film, inspired by Tolstoy's novella *The Forged Coupon*, transposed to modern France, ends shortly after in a terrible massacre, in which the hero assassinates an entire family.

In *The Seventh Continent*, Haneke seems to draw inspiration from Bresson, in the scene where little Evi waits for her father in a parking lot: We hear, "in the air," a precise passage from Alban Berg's violin concerto "in memory of an angel" (the famous chorale that evokes Bach) without being able to identify its source, then, as often happens, we realize only retroactively that the music was diegetic, ending suddenly and brutally when a car owner starts his car. Of course, we do not know if the young girl heard this music, nor, *a fortiori*, if the music left any impression on her. The brutality of the music's interruption by a character is a cinematographic effect, which consists of imitating, within the diegesis, a process available to cinema itself with regard to the reality it describes or reconstructs: the power to cut and to eliminate.

Cinema is in fact an art that brutally appropriates beautiful music and can then cut it (through editing), or drown it out (through sound mixing). In the case of Bresson's and Haneke's films, it is the very action – or clumsiness – of a character that interrupts the music, whereas in Godard's films this effect is achieved through editing.

If *Benny's Video*, *The Seventh Continent*, and the first version of *Funny Games* still contain "diegetic" music, *Caché* does not contain any at all; the absence of music seems to reinforce the feeling of a world "in prose," of a dry and lucid world, in which it is forbidden to dream. As if all music, even diegetic music, whether predominantly melodic, harmonic, or rhythmic, represented (for reasons discussed above) a sort of window that opens in the walls surrounding us, connecting our world to others. Perhaps also because music, in the classical sense, is perceived as a principle of association of sounds, which unfixes them from their origin, on the one hand (a sound is no longer just "a sound of," the sound of a piano, a voice, etc.), and, on the other, liberates them from language in the functional and everyday sense, from the "chains" of language, as Valéry put it.

This comes down to the difference between "prose" and "poetry." I often say, only half-jokingly, that if film characters spoke in verse, as in Shakespeare's *The Tempest* or in Racine's and Schiller's tragedies, and of course in Homer, the question of music would be completely different in cinema, and we wouldn't feel obliged to include so much music in films – because one of the characteristics of the sonorous and prosodic rules of poetry, as they have existed for a very long time in various languages, from Japanese to French, through English and Icelandic, is that they allow the written or the spoken word to partially escape from the necessity of making sense, from the rules of pure communication. The poetic rules of rhythm and sound make speech dance.

Caché's world is entirely "in prose," and we can glimpse nothing that would allow us to flee from its inescapable reality, where all actions have consequences.

The discreetness of the ambiance is a second important aspect of the sound in this film that reinforces the entrapment of Georges: His "bourgeois" apartment is calm, but so is the modest low-rent studio in the projects where his childhood friend, Majid (Maurice Bénichou), lives. In most films, and for good reasons, different places have different sound "atmospheres": The apartment in the housing project would feature noises from the courtyard, from the staircase, from neighboring televisions, while the bourgeois apartment would be calm, soundproofed, and so on. Here, by contrast, every space in the film enjoys the same silence, and this silence, far from being comforting, evokes a sense of danger, of a possible disruption: The more silence there is, the more we are on the lookout for a possible sound intrusion, a cry, a blow.

In *Caché*, there are several different types of images:

- images that are presented as the diegesis of the film;
- images we discover only afterwards are being watched by the characters on a videotape (Haneke purposely does not seek "technical" verisimilitude – the video images do not at all resemble those of a VHS tape from the 1990s but are much more defined, sharper, closer to professional images);
- images that we discover, again only afterwards, to be part of a television news broadcast (on the cable channel Euronews or on the literary program hosted by Georges);
- images of memories or dreams of the main character.

All these images are equally clear and sharp, and appear to derive from the same material. Nothing distinguishes them *a priori* – it is through editing, through content, through abstract deduction that they appear after the event as real, imaginary, dreamed, retransmitted, projected. The images of the dream sequences are as precise as those in the "real" sequence; the mediatized images (TV, video) are just as clear as those seen directly, with the naked eye.

The absence of music from all of these images helps to unify them: They all belong to a single world. The decapitated rooster beating its wings in Georges's dream is just as present and precise – not a bit less – as it might have been in the scene experienced by Georges. It is as if all places and all times were one, which is terrifying.

Compare the sound effects that accompany the death of the pig that the young boy in *Benny's Video* films – the sound of the axe blow on the animal, once recorded, is replayed, slowed down, and thus dramatized and transformed into a nightmarish sound. *Caché*, unlike *Benny's Video*, eliminates visual and sonorous differences between what we see "in the present" and what the characters film and watch on their video players.

The Seventh Continent, which precedes both *Caché* and *Benny's Video*, is, as we know, punctuated by simultaneous interruptions of sound (silence) and image (black screen), without fades to black or lap sound dissolves, which have multiple functions. This technique has the effect on images and sounds that are preceded or followed by interruptions of "temporal framing," which seems to isolate the sequences one from another and to structure them. This effect reinforces the implacable and fatal aspect of what we see and hear, but at the same time it evokes the possibility of another time and another space, which might occupy the place of this black emptiness, of this silence. Nothing like this happens in *Caché*.

Moreover, the culminating scene of *The Seventh Continent* is one of noisy destruction in which the Schober family meticulously destroys its house, not even sparing their daughter's treasured aquarium and its wriggling fish.

Children often derive pleasure from destruction. There are several reasons for and aspects to this. Notably, but not exclusively, we can observe their curiosity about the sound such destruction might make. Many gestures children make in these situations appear to be produced or guided by a curiosity to know what sound might emanate from the object or creature they're handling. They really hope, in these acts of destruction, to hear a different sound, a moan, or maybe a note, from these objects, from these living beings. Such children are conducting rapid experiments to see whether the same action will produce different sound reactions depending on the object, or on the surface. The same causes do not produce the same effects.

Similarly, in *Benny's Video*, one can always imagine that when young Benny hits the girl, it is in order to hear if his action might somehow produce a special and different sound. But instead of hearing a particular sound we hear the horrible cries of suffering; the murder itself does not produce any striking sound.

In the same way, the spectacular destruction of the house in *The Seventh Continent* may also appear to be a sort of experiment with the sounds made by everyday objects: Will they respond or not? This meticulous outburst is like a noisy venting of the tension created by the absence of music, on the one hand, and by the principle of "temporal framing," on the other.

In *Caché* there is no music, no outburst of sound, no "temporal framing" through fadeouts to black or to silence. The result is that we are on the lookout, and every sound constitutes a warning. For instance, in the scene of Georges's first visit to Majid in his modest apartment a strange silence reigns; then, in the middle of their dialog, the refrigerator starts a familiar humming sound, as Majid says: "How could I possibly blackmail you?"

This unease grows because in French – the language of the original dialog in the film – the word for "blackmail" is *chantage*. *Faire chanter* means both to have someone make music and to blackmail. Further, the term for "blackmailers" in French is *maîtres-chanteurs* (master-singers), in a word, *Meistersinger*.

We recall that at the beginning of the film, Haneke leads us to believe that we are watching his own images when in fact it is a scene that his characters are watching – the image of their apartment building, with the voices of Georges and Anne superimposed. Similarly, in various scenes we hear a voice-off, either in the present tense of the scene, or in the moment following our viewing of these images. At the pool, the swimming instructor calls Pierrot from offscreen; the voice-off of the producer of Georges's literary program speaks to the guests, and so on. Every image we see could be addressed, one might even say "accused," by a voice-off. At one point in the dialog someone uses the difficult to translate but typical French expression *gueuler dessus*, meaning to hurl accusations at someone aggressively. In several instances, an image of *Caché* will do exactly that – invite yelling, aggression, accusation.

There are, moreover, no instances of sound overlapping: If I'm not mistaken, a sound never precedes its image; as we move from one scene to another the cut is as sudden for the ear as it is for the eye.

In this regard, there is a difference between sight and hearing in our everyday experience. As Walter Murch argued convincingly, our gaze already does something similar to the cuts of visual montage when we blink. The soundtrack offers nothing comparable to the ear. The instantaneous bursts of sound that Haneke produces through sound editing remain a perceptive shock specific to the cinema.

The two sequences that show Pierrot, the son, swimming in the pool both begin abruptly, especially the first one, with a splitting sound cut, which transforms a normally pleasant sound into a sound that feels like a knife blade.

At the beginning and end of the film, we hear Parisian birds superimposed on exterior images: the chirping of sparrows and, towards the end, a flock of martins or swallows passing. This fleetingly evokes the idea of another time, of another reality that might welcome us, a livable and earthly time where we would not be like the main character, terrorized and defensive, feeling like a guilty man, awaiting and provoking condemnation, but instead one where we could just be happy to be there and to be alive.

Translated by T. Jefferson Kline

Note

1   Michel Chion (1998: 182, my translation).

Reference

Chion, Michel: *Le Son* (Paris: Armand Colin, 1998).

9

Fighting the Melodramatic Condition

Haneke's Polemics

Jörg Metelmann

Introduction

In recent discussions on the films of Michael Haneke, I have suggested two paradigms to describe his cinematic works: autonomy and the tragic (Metelmann 2003, 2005). In the Austrian films – *The Seventh Continent* (1989), *Benny's Video* (1992), *71 Fragments of a Chronology of Chance* (1994), and *Funny Games* (1997) – Haneke locates his subject matter, the horror of the middle-class nuclear family, in a setting that does not presume to represent "reality," but rather constructs it as a model in order to open the already known to new cognitions. Artistic devices such as long fades to black, long takes, emphasis on sound, and, most of all, the non-psychological, structural handling of characters are Haneke's means of creating an anti-mainstream aesthetic that nonetheless engages hegemonic narrative and visual codes. As I have argued in my book on the critique of cinema violence, these strategies make Haneke a successor to Bertolt Brecht's approach to theater: His films actualize Brecht's opposition of dramatic and epic form (Metelmann 2003: 153ff.). Haneke's opposition to Hollywood's cinema of manipulation can thus be seen as a call for alienation in the Brechtian sense of *Verfremdung*: as an attempt to tear the realities shown on the screen from the shadow of their "being-so" into the light of their "having-been-*made*-so." As with Brecht, this shift from individual psychology to the *Gestus* of the person (a central concept in Brecht's aesthetics) means to denaturalize, and thus make visible as social artifact, the habitus and economic modes of late capitalism. The goal (again as with Brecht) is to guarantee the autonomy of the critical, enlightened subject by empowering him or her as a spectator and enlarging his or her knowledge and options in dealing with the world. Against all Adornian readings of Haneke's early works (e.g., Meindl 1996) and their stress on the autonomy of art, its artwork-character, and the bulky semantics of the artifact, I submit that there was no other cinema auteur during the 1990s who insisted as rigorously as Haneke on this kind of spectatorial address and on influencing spectatorial cognitions and attitudes. It has been precisely this focus on reception, on disturbing entrenched habits of viewing, that aligns Haneke more with Brecht than with Adorno.

Brecht's essentially modernist aim was to activate critical judgment based on class consciousness and to overcome two confining notions of art – first, the bourgeois notion of "art for art's sake" (*Kunst als Selbstzweck*) and, second, art as a mere tool for consciousness-raising. In a socialist society in which freedom and creativity beyond economic constraints had been realized, art as conceived in these narrow terms would cease to exist altogether, because there would be no use for it. Haneke, in contrast, is worried about the loss of the capacity for judgment *as such* in the anything-goes mindset of postmodern plurality. His famous statement regarding the intent of his films, "to rape the spectator into autonomy,"[1] points to Brecht's method, but also beyond it. Differentiation and judgment, as basic modes of engaging with the social, should not be relinquished to the stereotyping and apathy that Haneke sees as characteristic of an amnesic mass-mediatized society. His central aesthetic intent, dramatically realized in the extreme acts of violence in the Austrian films, is to push alienation to an unprecedented degree of otherness. Whereas Brecht could suggest a return of reason from alienation to clear perspectives on (class) action, Haneke refuses to dissolve the tensions his films create. Instead, he irritates the spectator's moral and aesthetic judgment without offering any answers. Because of how he remodels Brecht's modernist concept of the potential of art, I have called Haneke the last avant-gardist, an artist who claims a *restitutio ad integrum* of a condition preceding the postmodern blurring of the frontiers between real life and fiction (Metelmann 2003: 220). His (ideal) viewer is a recipient conceived as a rational being who, in principle, is able to think independently, to order the heteronomies of everyday life – and, thus, to undergo genuine transformation.

In this emancipatory world view, errors are no stain, and guilt is not an inescapable destiny: Thanks to the force of reason, nothing is so tragic, i.e., hopelessly mired in guilt, that it could not be changed for the better. Yet Haneke's French films, from *Code Unknown* (2000) to *The Piano Teacher* (2001), *Time of the Wolf* (2003), and *Caché* (2005), do seem to be imbued with a tragic feeling. They outline constellations of guiltless (and hence tragic) guilt (Metelmann 2005: 291–9), exploring the feeling that something is wrong, that responsibility for the West's problems is somehow personal, yet that the individual invariably fails at something that is commonly characterized by the term "making a difference" (either by effecting concrete change for him/herself and for others, or by succeeding in receiving what he or she believes to deserve or merit). In these films, life in the West is regarded as neither exclusively right nor exclusively wrong; neither all good nor all bad, but as both right *and* wrong, good *and* bad, conspicuously lacking any position from where solutions might be developed. The characters in the films after 2001 go nowhere. They may undergo an arc of development (as does Georges in *Code Unknown*), but such developments don't seem to make any difference; there is no narrative point of escape, no act of violence to order or give sense to dramatic events. The stories simply go on, including the agony, the guilt, the pain of others that seems neither to implicate nor to affect us, although we perceive it and sense it, like phantom-limb pain. But there is no rescue, no remedy, no conceivable horizon from which to organize thought and feeling. In the French films, there is no glaciation, no resignation, only uncomfortable ambivalence. Even the negative utopias of the Austrian period have disappeared. Here utopia is not only nowhere – it will not come.

Haneke addresses the aporias of Western industrial culture by inscribing them in narrative structure, sometimes challenging viewers with new aesthetic approaches and sometimes using conventional means; sometimes rebelling in the name of the heritage of the Enlightenment, sometimes working to deflect (which is not the same as to overcome) the hope of salvation through a tragic constellation of guiltless guilt in the so-called first world. While these observations seem to point to marked differences between Haneke's Austrian and French phases, they are in fact two sides of the same coin and can thus be included in a single diagnosis, which is the subject of this essay. Both sets of strategies may be interpreted both as constituents and as critiques of what may be called "melodrama" and what can be characterized, beyond questions of genre and dramaturgy, as a prevalent emotional-cognitive scheme in the West.

Melodrama as a Cultural Mode

This relation first occurred to me when I heard of Haneke's plan to shoot *Funny Games U.S.* (2007) as an exact replication of his masterpiece of 1997. To me this seemed less a gesture of strength (as in "Now I'll finally confront my intended audience!") than a possible admission of the failure of his artistic ambitions. Didn't he understand that the plan to craft a close remake of *Funny Games* reflected an assumption on his part that the world hadn't changed in the previous ten years? Didn't he realize that such an assumption simply seemed too absurd? Now, however, it seems to me that there was also some truth in this unperturbedness, which I was not able to see at first. The quasi-symbiotic engagement of Haneke's aesthetics with the cinematic mainstream (which was the basis of my interpretations of Haneke's films through Brecht) can be reread as narratively and semantically synonymous with "melodrama as cultural mode." It is the crystallization of this mode in relation to Haneke's films that now merits attention.

The critical concept "melodrama" includes several features that vary in their interpretive usefulness and validity. The scholarship of the last forty years on the subject is characterized by a shift from seeing melodrama as a genre category to conceiving it as a cultural mode.[2] Linda Williams (1998, 2001) has argued that melo-drama, as an overwhelmingly popular form, exceeds any single generic category. Following this argument, Elisabeth Anker has recently provided a definition:

> Although melodrama is fluid and expansive enough to encompass international cul-tural products from Balzac's *Lost Illusions* to *telenovelas* to *Titanic*, I want to propose that the cultural mode of melodrama can be defined by five primary qualities: a) a locus of moral virtue that is signified throughout the narrative by pathos and suf-fering and can be increased through heroic action; b) the three characters of a ruth-less villain, a suffering victim, and a heroic savior who can redeem the victim's virtue through an act of retribution (though the latter two characters can be inhabited in the same person: the virtuous victim/hero); c) dramatic polarizations of good and evil, which echo in the depictions of individuals and events; d) a cyclical interaction of emotion and action meant to create suspense and resolve conflict; and e) the use of images, sounds, gestures, and nonverbal communication to illuminate moral legibility as well as to encourage empathy for the victim and anger toward the villain.[3]

Anker adds two further features to this good/evil action scheme. First, she cites Williams's argument that melodrama's dialectic of pathos and action (see point (c)) reveals moral and emotional truths. Second, taking up Peter Brooks's thoughts on the "melodramatic imagination," Anker claims that the underlying aim of melo-drama is to create a moral legibility in which a Manichean distinction of good from evil is clear and recognizable. But this definition is only the stepping-off point for her thesis that melodrama's sphere of influence has recently broadened significantly, notably with the attacks of September 11, 2001. The events were interpreted through a deeper structural mode of melodrama that neutralized cultural, ethnic, gender, and economic differences in favor of the abstract notion of a victimized collective body and American ideals of "freedom" and "democ-racy" in need of heroic redemption. Having evolved from its previous functions, American melodrama began to sanction state power as a necessary and righteous measure against evil (Anker 2005: 25f.). Anker was of course not the first to describe the influences of a certain melodramatic mode of perceiving or experiencing polit-ical reality.[4] Peter Brooks had already entered this path as early as 1976, in his lucid and still inspiring study of the melodramatic imagination:

> As the modern politics of created charisma – inevitably a politics of personality – and self-conscious enactments must imply, we are within a system of melodramatic struggle, where virtue and evil are fully personalized. Rarely can there be the sug-gestion of illumination and reconciliation in terms of a higher order of synthesis. (Brooks 1985: 203)

The modern political leader, according to Brooks, is obliged to do continuous battle with an enemy, no matter whether it is another political power, a force of nature, hunger, poverty, or inflation. From Saint-Just's and Robespierre's murderous Manicheism to President Bush's division of the world into "us" and "rogue" or "villainous" states, the melodramatic pattern seems fully in operation.[5] In the final remarks of his book (on TV culture),[6] Brooks reveals his debt to the theses of Richard Sennett, who in his *Fall of Public Man* (1977) bemoaned the ubiquitous psychologization of the public space. Sennett's psychosociological critique complements Brooks's derivation of psychoanalysis from the spirit of melodrama. I would like to pursue this line of thought further in order to show how everyday life in the Western world (and not only pop culture and politics, Brooks's and Anker's subjects) might be seen as increasingly melodramatic.

Brooks sees psychoanalysis as a realization of melodramatic aesthetics: (1) The nature of conflict in psychoanalysis is a version of melodrama, as it is menacing to the ego, which must find ways to reduce or discharge it; (2) the dynamics of repression and the return of the repressed shape the melodramatic plot; (3) enactment is necessarily excessive: The relation of symbol to symbolized is not controllable or justifiable; (4) in melodrama, evil is reworked in the process of repression and the status of repressed content; (5) the structure of ego, superego, and id suggests the subjacent Manicheism of melodramatic persons; (6) Freud's thought is dualistic, the struggle of *eros* and *thanatos* suggesting an explanation for the fascination of melodramatic virtue and evil; (7) the "talking cure" reveals its affinity with melodrama, the drama of articulation: Cure and resolution come as a result of articulation, which is clarification; both psychoanalysis and melodrama are a drama of recognition that could lead to the cure of souls (both thus becoming equivalents of religion) (Brooks 1985: 201f.).

I would stress this last aspect because it will lead us to the analyses of Eva Illouz and her sociology of "emotional capitalism." Referring to Freud's journey to the United States in 1909, the year that marked the beginning of the transformation of American emotional culture, Illouz writes:

> It is rather strange that many sociological and historical analyses have offered us elaborate and sophisticated accounts of psychoanalysis in terms of intellectual origins, or its impact on cultural conceptions of the self, or in terms of its relationship to scientific ideas, but have overlooked a simple and glaring fact, namely that psychoanalysis and the wide variety of dissident theories of the psyche which followed had, by and large, the primary vocation of reshaping emotional life. (Illouz 2007: 6)

It is a new emotional style that emerges, the therapeutic emotional style. This style is first of all determined by the language of therapy and stresses the importance of the self in everyday life – both in the professional environment and within the family – the self awaits its discovery, not least the discovery of its sexuality, which got connected with language and was well discussed in the flourishing guidebook literature of the 1920s: Life was "psychologized." The most relevant features of this new style for my context are:

1. The world of work has been increasingly emotionalized and feminized ever since Elton Mayo's legendary Hawthorne experiments of the 1920s (human relations approach), which has led to a domination of entrepreneurial workplaces by the doctrine of "communicative competence." Mayo's application of the conceptual tools of psychology to women eventually helped reshape the new guidelines for managing relationships in the modern workplace, as these gradually factored in women's emotional experiences and senses of selfhood, which, as Illouz notes, also indirectly helped redefine masculinity inside the workplace: "the new approach to emotions *softened the character of the foreman*" (Illouz 2007: 15, italics in the text). Emotional capitalism has created a new emotional culture in which the economic self is more emotional than before and emotions are closer to instrumental action, i.e., less protected against misuse due to the amalgamation with the world of work.

2. Another strand of recent developments brilliantly observed by Illouz is the combination of the two cultural narratives of self-help and suffering. In the middle of the nineteenth century, Samuel Smiles's famous book, *Self-Help*, collected stories of men who had escaped poverty and pain to achieve glory and wealth through their own strength – a democratic American narrative (or, to speak with Illouz, an institution "deposited" in mental frames[7]) that promises *to anyone* (150 years ago only to men, but nowadays also to women) a linear rise via diligence and virtue. Freud's notion of the logic of therapy followed a completely different approach: Therapy doesn't proceed in linear-horizontal ways, but figuratively-cyclically, and it will succeed only if it can be turned into social capital – traits that would appeal to the upper classes, but not to workers, who Freud thought would see no benefit from such cures for neurosis. This typical constellation of the nineteenth and early twentieth centuries has been changed fundamentally by the combination of both of these narratives. As Illouz points out, modern civilizational syndromes such as bad parenting, lack of self-esteem, and habitual addictions are "democratic ills" no longer clearly defined in terms of class. "In this process of general democratization of psychic suffering, recovery has strangely become an enormously lucrative business and a flourishing industry" (Illouz 2007: 42). This combination became peculiar or even pathological when during the 1960s personal growth and self-realization turned into ideals under the influence of theorists such as Abraham Maslow and Carl Rogers, who offered the diagnosis that any person who does not engage in change and self-enrichment must be considered ill. Again, Illouz:

Such views of human development were able to penetrate and transform cultural conceptions of the self because they resonated with the liberal view that self-development was a right. This, in turn, represented an extraordinarily enlarged realm of action for psychologists: not only did psychologists move from severe psychological disorder to the much wider realm of neurotic misery. They now moved to the idea that health and self-realization were one and the same. People who had un-self-realized lives were now in need of care and therapy. (Illouz 2007: 45f.)

Only hindsight shows how an incipient critique of capitalism that echoed in the 1960s idea of self-realization in non-material terms gave way to a radical individualization and pathologization of everyday lives. It brought about a completely new market, a business for the soul that nourishes whole cohorts of professionals (therapists, psychiatrists, doctors, consultants) and dominates the media in the form of talk shows of every kind.[8] Like no other place in the public sphere, talk shows rearticulate the claim of cure while at the same time denying its possibility. This paradoxical situation helps the subject become a member of society by letting her perform her suffering. Paraphrasing Warhol, one could say that everyone now has his or her fifteen minutes of public suffering.

Illouz summarizes the most important aspects of the therapeutic narrative: (1) The narrative addresses and explains contradictory emotions (e.g., loving too much and not loving enough); (2) it uses cultural templates of religious narrative that are both regressive (past events are still present) and progressive (the goal is to establish prospective redemption); (3) it makes people responsible for their own psychic well-being, yet it does so by removing any notion of moral fault (insofar as the concentration on childhood and deficient families exonerates people from culpability for an unsatisfactory life); (4) the narrative is performative, reorganizing experience as it tells it; (5) it is a contagious cultural structure because it can be duplicated and may spread to collaterals, grandchildren, and spouses; (6) it is almost an ideal commodity, as it demands no or little economic investment; (7) it emerges in a culture saturated with the notion of rights, in which both individuals and groups are increasingly demanding "recognition" (defined as acknowledgment of and remedy for their past sufferings) (Illouz 2007: 55f.).

A modified citation from Freud can provide the best description of the state that the Western "therapy societies"[9] are in: We are only the master in our own house when it is burning. To put out this fire, at least in the field of work, personality testers and assessment centers attempt to analyze the emotional-motivational structure of employees – a form of individual capital bound even more strongly to the body than taste or appearance, fashion or style.[10] Just as school grades are a measure of cultural capital, these tests try to authorize and canonize a certain emotional style. As Peter Brooks has noted, this is one of the core characteristics of melodrama, and perhaps the essential one. Melodrama offers a world in which people move like actors on stage: They are mastered by imperatives that cannot be controlled or guided, mediated or overcome in any way. Such imperatives can only be acted out. Individuals must accept melodrama's primary roles (father, mother, child) and perform them as elementary mental constellations. The resulting conflicts cannot be understood as occurring *within* the persons, but rather *between* them. Melodrama's internalization of societal claims corresponds to an externalization that brings mental states onto the stage and transforms them into actions. Thus, instead of a "psychology of melodrama," we see a "melodrama of psychology" that refers constantly to what Brooks calls the world of the moral occult – "a repository of the fragmentary and desacralized remnants of sacred myth" structured by Manichean conflicts between good and evil, proceeding beneath the surface of common perception (Brooks 1985: 5).

The melodramatic "moral occult" caters to our world at the abyss that remains after God's death, with its remnants of myth structured by Manichean dualities. This realm, Brooks writes, "bears comparison to the unconscious mind, for it is a sphere of being where our most basic desires and interdictions lie, a realm which in quotidian existence may appear closed off from us, but which we must accede to since it is the realm of meaning and value" (ibid.). The melodramatic mode keeps on producing descriptions that point to things higher, hidden, but nonetheless present and true. Within its schema, touching the forces of light and darkness can be seen as a rebellion against pure reason that tries to live out of the plenitude of being instead of staring into an empty sky. Melodrama aims at this plenitude; desiring an ethical recentering, it produces what Brooks calls a "central poetry": "To the extent that the melodramatic imagination at its most lucid recognizes the provisionality of its created centers, the constant threat that its plenitude may be a void, the need with each new text and performance to relocate the center, it does not betray modern consciousness" (200). Thus melodrama keeps on talking, expressing, searching for conflicts, for true feelings, for the hidden meanings. As a narrative creation, it demands an unconventional life set against repression, against doing without the pleasure principle, against giving up the desire to live a life less ordinary.

With the need to fill the void after Enlightenment's critique of everything comes a certain pressure to uncover the essential underlying structures of so-called "reality": The goal is to reperceive and express the soul in a secularized world. Aesthetically, the most important techniques for achieving this end are polarized conflict, heightening occurrences and events of everyday life, and hyperbole. In the melodramatic imagination, all the gestures, as we (ordinary people) perceive them, refer constantly back to a deeper meaning so that a process of translation is required to draw the moral occult into the light of the "real" reality. This permits interpretation of the commonly available world as a metaphor. But, as Brooks concludes within the context of a discussion of Balzac, "it is not a question of metaphoric texture alone; it is rather that, to the melodramatic imagination, significant things and gestures are necessarily metaphoric in nature because they must refer to and speak of something else. Everything appears to bear the stamp of meaning, which can be expressed, pressed out, from it" (9f.). This way of reading everything metaphorically permits the recipient to enjoy his self-pity and to feel the world in its entirety by experiencing it through what Robert Heilman has called "monopathic emotion" (Heilman 1968: 85). Positioning this strategy within its historical contexts, Eric Bentley interpreted melodrama as the only of four remaining forms of the dramatic (melodrama, farce, tragedy, comedy), adding that of these four classic types, only melodrama preserves feelings in the mode of dreams, while positing the necessity to act them out (Bentley 1964: 195ff.). For Bentley, such dramatization is anti-naturalistic, a point also emphasized by Christine Gledhill in "Signs of Melodrama" (Gledhill 1991: 227). Unlike in realistic novels, the social typification of characters in melodrama does not serve to guide the reader from individuals to society's system as a whole. Its metaphors, its emblematic types, point instead to inner life, to the internalized results of societal or ideological constraints.

The Melodramatic Condition

In a study of the end of Western world supremacy, German journalist Jan Ross set such a reading of melodrama as metaphor in a global political context. He starts from Arundhati Roy's description of George Bush (in *The Ordinary Person's Guide to Empire* [2003]) as the first president who has fully revealed the true motivations of American foreign policy, doing so more clearly than any critical author, activist, or scientist could have dreamed. All his predecessors would have reacted similarly to such an attack as the one on September 11, but in Roy's view what Bush did was bring to light the whole apocalyptic machine of American Empire, as an apparatus that aims at the militant-aggressive implementation of Western principles. As Ross reminds us of Bush's second Inaugural Address in January 2005:

> [The] address only lasted for 20 minutes – but it may have been the most ambitious, exuberant proclamation that has ever been made by an American president or any modern statesman. . . . At the climax of his emphasis the president returned to the image of a "Day of Fire" [9/11] and declared: "By our efforts we have lit a fire as well; a fire in the minds of men. It warms those who feel its power. It burns those who fight its progress. And one day this untamed fire of freedom will reach the darkest corners of our world." This made one shudder at a double meaning – a moment of great, heartrending pathos, and at the same time a document of hubris.[11]

Against the background of the ideas I have presented and rethinking Anker's politically focused theses, it seems clear how much these lines, with their "moral-occult" allusions to the Old Testament, belong to the language of melodrama, and why Arundhati Roy welcomed them as a revelation of political truth. The alleged universalism of the West, its "natural" perspective on freedom and democracy, is here contaminated with a heroic scheme of good and evil – and only this moral world is universal. Of special interest in our context is that Bush's statement combines the two post-revolutionary strands of ethical thought noted above – the moral-occult and the teleological – which are normally clearly separated. Normally, one believes in underlying conflicts, Manicheism and epiphanies of the moral good, or one is a secularized supporter of reason and the growth of an emancipated world; Bush here includes both. In his famous 1992 book *The End of History and the Last Man* (a compilation of the central thoughts of Hegel and Nietzsche), Francis Fukuyama declared this second strand a winner in the global battle of ideas and systems, but his prophecy that the world would thereafter move calmly towards global liberalism, market societies, and democracy would be proved wrong by September 11, 2001 at the latest – not to mention the wars in Yugoslavia, Somalia, Rwanda, and elsewhere. As Ross observes, with 9/11 old fronts had reappeared:

> Bush's inaugural address was armed Fukuyama, apocalypse and messianism instead of the obliviously ongoing logic of history of the Clinton era. In the shape of radical Islam, an obstacle had emerged once again on the way to a universal and homogeneous global culture, just like nationalism, fascism, and communism; the day of redemption had to be postponed once more, and a last truly fierce combat with the forces of darkness had to be survived. (Ross 2008: 139, my translation)

Bush combined the optimism of the emancipation narrative *à la* Fukuyama with the Manichean world view of melodrama, which sees nothing but the eternal battle of good and light with evil and darkness. For in a post-traditional world, we know that in the absence of all gods there will be no salvation, no return to an unclouded good, no Last Judgment (which is why Bush's statement is not a genuinely biblical, but melodramatic interpretation!). It seems as if melodrama has become ubiquitous, not only as the counterpart of the rational-globalized sphere of allegedly emotion-free values, but also politically, in its alliance with paeans of emancipation.

In 1979 – ten years before Haneke's *The Seventh Continent* – the French philosopher Jean-François Lyotard presented his influential report on the postmodern condition. Reading Lyotard's text today, it is astonishing how little, and how implausibly, the text discusses a theme very frequently cited in the discourse of "postmodernity": the end of great (or "master") narratives. To give a short example: Lyotard illustrates his thesis of delegitimation with examples of a loss in credibility suffered by the narrative of emancipation (political narrative/practical reason: just/unjust), but he does not say *why* the traditional narratives of freedom, justice, and emancipation should no longer be self-evident and convincing. This is remarkable, because Lyotard himself positions the pursuit of justice as some kind of master narrative previously declared dead against the threatening danger of pure efficiency thinking, as seen for example in the work of Niklas Luhmann and the *terreur* of his depersonalized systems theory.

Perhaps the special quality of Lyotard's report was not his precise observations – though there were some, such as the reform of the university, the status of lifelong learning/continuing education, the impact of efficiency doctrines on the value of labor – but lies more in the conveyed feeling that something new, a new era of knowledge, was about to start with computers, databanks, and global networks (though he didn't mention, for example, communication via Internet).

Maybe it is because of his subject – "knowledge," which has been differentiated and multiplied in unpredictable ways in the last thirty years – that these "new" times have retained almost nothing of their explicative power – knowledge, understood as judged, weighed information (which means theoretical knowledge in the first place), is quite transient. Feelings, however, are not. And that the narrative of great, kitschy feelings won't die off has been impressively proven by the recent enlargement of the melodramatic mode to a comprehensive *Weltanschauung* encompassing almost all spheres of life. That is what I want to suggest by my term "the melodramatic condition." You can't avoid it; it shapes Western culture.

Haneke's Polemics

I have suggested how many factors enter into the constellation of melodrama: psychologization, feminization, emotional acting-out, narrative excess as pressure on "reality," villainy and good/evil schemes; and I have called melodrama an experience-shaping pattern characterizing all spheres of everyday life, notably including politics. In a last step I would like to further explain the "melodramatic condition" by exploring Haneke's criticism of it.

Pressure on "reality"

Like melodrama, Haneke exerts pressure on "reality": He does not accept so-called objectivity. The pronounced gestural mode of indication that characterizes the Austrian films, in what I've named Haneke's period of autonomy, identifies what the director himself has named "the emotional glaciation of society" as a sociohistorical situation beyond concrete characters. These films' plots are explicitly not about the destiny of individuals, for example, Max running amok; rather, they circulate around the pattern-construction of a single but representative case. Violence thereby becomes an object of distanced – sometimes distant – vision, not of melodramatic feeling. It is not psychology that is addressed, but sociology, as the analysis of stratifications, structures, and systems.

The anti-psychological iciness of Haneke's plots may be working towards something referred to by Illouz when she writes: "If we do not want psychology to pull the rug from under our feet, we should ultimately try to reformulate a critique of social injustices by inquiring into the ways in which access to psychological knowledge may perhaps stratify different forms of selfhood" (Illouz 2007: 71). The films are ungracious with the characters; it is as if they have refused to acknowledge to what degree mental situations help shape selfhood. They are not interested in the psychology of individuals. In the end, their central feature is a cinematic approach that, by stressing the medium's power to show, forces the viewer to look from outside, to observe. A page of text with an interior monologue can transmit as much content and atmosphere as a ninety-minute feature film. Only the narratives, the oft-rehearsed structures of mainstream production, open the inner world of characters – the stereotyped inner world. This is precisely the achievement of melodrama's victim–villain–hero plots: to break through the surface in the double sense of looking from the inside (and not only deploying filmic observation, i.e., pictures taken from the outside) and revealing the underlying melodramatic meaning. It is only via such plots that we can gain access to the emotions of characters, that we can identify, on an abstract meta-psychical level, with their elementary roles. Ordinary melodrama is as little a matter of individual psychology, of concrete persons, as is Haneke's work. This is what renders the melodramatic condition so encompassingly relevant and actual.

Haneke, as an artist of the "critical paradigm," addresses the gap between therapeutic emotional style and individual micro-psychology *systemically* by relying on the visible, the observable (nature of film), instead of trapping his subjects and his viewers in a visually sutured "talking cure." His style resists emotional excess. The particular pressure on reality that Haneke's films exert doesn't allow for a monopathic *jouissance*; rather, it frustrates – which, as is well known, leads to refusal and criticism. Haneke's style is meant to activate resistance, to preserve critical distance, not to engulf the viewer in the melodramatic narrative of archaic feelings and hopes.

In a certain sense Haneke thus could be seen as Lyotard's aesthetic nightmare. Notwithstanding the French philosopher's obvious sympathy for the sublime and its power to lead rationality and thus human understanding to its limitations, there is a deep fear in his *Postmodern Condition*, the fear of losing *the humane* in a world populated by psychic systems caught in communication loops, on the other side of humanism. Haneke's Austrian films are very close to the post-humanist paradigm: He exploits the medium of film to beat psychology out of our minds. It is a violation – and it is meant to be one.

Against the plot

Ever since the beginning of his work for the cinema Haneke has polemicized against the elements of mainstream narratives: schematization, the work's "save-the-world" function, in which a problem is posed and solved by a hero within ninety minutes. This invective against the overwhelming idiom of mainstream cinema could be read more profoundly now as a critique of the narrative features of melodrama. In other words, the notorious rewind of the victim's counter-action in *Funny Games* – the culmination and turning point of the Austrian period – may be the ultimate criticism of the melodramatic villain–hero scheme. How much artistic satisfaction Haneke must have felt editing this sequence!

Anna's struggle against the two killers in *Funny Games* fits perfectly with Anker's scheme quoted earlier, although what Anker lists as points (d) and (e) are not given a very American form (the film has too much silence, too many pauses, is too slow, and does not evince enough cyclical interaction of action and emotion/suffering to create suspense or resolve suffering, nor is the film's aesthetic project to encourage empathy for the victim and anger towards the villain). These could be the reasons why *Funny Games U.S.* so quickly lost the attention of its intended audience.

But Haneke goes much further, amalgamating his criticism of plot structure with a profound analysis of the psychological basis of horror, and thus widening his attack on the melodramatic condition. He does not simply show the archetypical roles into which characters are forced (resident/invader, heroic victim/villain), but also points to the sociology of psychologization identified by such scholars as Illouz. He does so by using the first third of the film to show the abyss of politically correct middle-class language games: They do not work if your enemy uses them instrumentally. His funny guys are transfer pictures, bricolage copies, constructions composed of *Tom and Jerry* and street workers' nightmares (the "victim of society" talking like a social pedagogue who is meant to help him). In the end they cannot be unequivocally related to a specific class or demographic, and this is exactly why Haneke can send them as probes to an "I-acknowledge-you" culture and its emotional style. Peter and Paul's pseudo-polite habits and complacent talk makes them seem friendly, though their body language speaks differently (clumsiness with the eggs, the wearing of gloves). What little it takes, Haneke seems to say, to lull us as spectators, as long as a certain "style" is followed! And how quickly our calm disappears when such "style" is not followed (the Arab man in the metro harassing and spitting on Anne in *Caché*, the tensions arising between Georges and Anne in *Code Unknown*, when Georges refuses to talk).

Acting-out

There has been a lot of talk about the film-within-the-film sequences in *Code Unknown*, especially the "gas chamber" scene and Juliette Binoche's role as an actress within the plot. In my book I've suggested that the episode of the announced killing brings the spectator to her "true" feelings by threatening her vicariously with the most horrible death. Just when she loses all hope, Anne finally seems to show a spontaneous, natural reaction: despair. It seems everything earlier was a game, a mindgame, a psycho-trip. Against the background of my comments on melodrama I'd like to give this thought another direction. The lust for angst that leads us spectators as voyeurs to the characters' ineluctable elimination is strong evidence of our melodramatic impregnation, the enduring lure, facilitated by simple, evident, "true" feelings of good and evil. And in the end we are shocked at how good we feel in the staged world of final combats, in the performance of a perfectly recognizable villainy (though you cannot see the rogue: He's the auto-referential man with the camera) and beautiful victimhood (for example, Anne, though we discover she's an ambivalent character, too). Combats, villainy, and victimhood normally afford great emotions that begin to feel uncomfortable only when the victim lacks the power to stand up, is moribund or already *in extremis*, without any prospect of rekindling the melodramatic combination of action and suffering. What remains is the question of why the horror starts so late: the shiver of realizing how far our minds have been colonized by the melodramatic condition, by the lust for victimhood. Decadence, some might say (Bohrer and Scheel 2007). Or is it the dawning sense that the "real" world is in fact there, in the "moral-occult," in melodrama?

It's a feminized world

A change of focus in Haneke's polemic against the melodramatic condition occurs with the transition from the period of autonomy to that of the tragic. The radical critique of the notion of "reality" and of traditional plot construction is supplemented by remarks on psychologization and feminization. The French films push female figures to the center, but they seem to follow their predecessors in the glaciation trilogy and in *Funny Games* in not being very likable characters. Anne, in *Code Unknown*, is an egocentric career type; Erika, in *The Piano Teacher*, is a pathological post-career type; the Anne of *Caché* is an overstrained wife-of-a-career-husband type. In Haneke's Paris, societal hopes rest on young men from either the third world or the collapsed second world, immigrants to Western culture who have not (yet) been infected with melodrama. One could say that the Marian of *71 Fragments* has grown up to become the Amadou of *Code Unknown* and Majid's son in *Caché*. These boys and men stand for an understanding that does not dissolve joyfully in pain, for a proud positioning in society without being coached by talk show masters in how they could articulate their sufferings – for an honesty of a different kind, one that does not naïvely invest in the hope that everything could somehow turn out to be completely different (and, thus, it seems, being prepared to let go of all principles: One could interpret Anne and her transformations in *Code Unknown* in this way).

These non-white, non-Western European male characters contrast in certain ways with Anne and Erika. For Haneke's critique of melodrama to come full circle, it was almost an over-determined necessity to adapt *Die Klavierspielerin*, because Jelinek's novel combines paradigmatically the illusion of self-help and the deepest suffering. Here, for the first time, Haneke grants his audience cathartic tears at perceiving a hopelessly entangled ego, one oscillating between dominance and submission. Erika is very much an effigy of the melodramatic condition in the sense that the subject matter offered great potential to sustain the turn to affect and to real experience – and perhaps to use her story to demonstrate this world's need for – yet, simultaneously, the remoteness of – any reasonable hope that things will turn for the better (Metelmann 2005: 294). This ambivalence may also be seen in the Anne of *Code Unknown*, who shows emotional reactions in her "real" screen life (e.g., to the screams of the child), while remaining incapable of any "real" feeling of tenderness. All we really see of her emotional situation is her impressive love-accusation monologue (that is: a *text*, "have you ever made somebody happy?," an expression of a melodramatic desire, the great fortune, beyond a stable, psychologically transparent relation) and the changing of the entrance code. In *Caché*, Haneke puts the emotionally restyled relation of the sexes at the level of plot. As a TV anchorman, Georges is himself an active part of the discourse society. He can talk about anything, but he is unable to find any words for his innermost feelings, which circle around the basic problems of guilt and expiation. Anne wants to talk to him, she's well versed in communication, she tries to deescalate, makes him offers – yet she lacks the empathy to really reach him.

What a brilliant critique of melodrama: The hero has to defend himself against the attack of an (invisible) villain, but he can neither act (because in fact he himself is the villain) nor talk (which is what he's obliged to do, in a feminized culture of valuable social exchange). The beautiful woman, in turn, has no real emotional access to her husband, yet she keeps on begging him *to talk to her*! And, at the same time, this arrangement delivers so much ambivalence because already the title *Caché* suggests there is something hidden beneath the surface of reality. Still, in his quasi-melodramatic constellation Haneke denies the excess, the acting-out, the dissolution in the combination of action and suffering. To me this seems a *memento mori*, balancing refusal and affirmation at the highest possible level.

The great divider

In this sense Haneke can finally be called the great divider. He's the one to go back to the pre-postmodern state in his first four feature films, to polemicize also in political terms against the bonding of the narrative of emancipation (autonomy) and that of the everlasting struggle between good and evil (the tragic, not tragedy[12]) by clearly separating them both. But clear separations are harder to find in the period of the tragic, and his position in the French films seems to be comparable to the perspective that Jan Ross suggests to the West after the end of its political supremacy:

> There is a historic prototype for the conversion of the West from an exclusive, once dominant partial culture to a universal ferment, a common property of mankind. This is Hellenism, as the French strategist François Heisbourg has diagnosed: the last days of ancient Greek culture, as the once proud cities Athens, Corinth, and Thebes had been disempowered on a military, political, and economic level, but have pervaded and formed the whole Mediterranean and the Orient, from Spain to the Ganges, with their civilization. The winners of history, Alexander the Great and the Roman Empire, went to the school of the subjected Hellenes, learned their

languages, took over their science, statuary, and architecture. The Greeks, no longer the masters of anyone, not even of themselves, became the teachers of the world. (Ross 2008: 190, my translation)

Viewing Haneke as the ungracious teacher of moviegoers has become a cliché even as it is partly true, although the accusations of moralism have become quieter since *Code Unknown*, perhaps thanks to its self-portrait of the director as a war photographer in crisis ("we need an ecology of images"). This might have something to do with a tendency towards melodramatization of plot which circles around the intangible without utopian references of the kind found in the Austrian films, as I've tried to argue (Metelmann 2003: 191ff., 230ff.). The later films are characterized by a stronger psychological profile, reflecting the cultural impact of women; like ongoing therapeutic conversations, they seem to enumerate things more than to provoke "reality" by presenting a shocking model of it. But they still keep a critical eye on reality; and to this degree, Haneke – the man with the clip control, with the function of sorting – remains an antipode to the melodramatic condition. But now he knows and is showing what rumbles just under the surface.

Can You Help Me, Mr. Haneke?

To put it bluntly, I would say that Haneke can resist the melodramatic temptation less and less. Following the presentation of my paper at the Haneke conference at Boston University in October 2007, the discussion turned to what Haneke might do next. To me as to Haneke, the mini-story in a dream he had described some weeks before in an interview with the *New York Times Magazine* suggested the atmosphere of a possible future movie. As he told the interviewer, he dreamed he found himself on a bus that was careening out of control. Apparently, it was he who was in charge of safety, but for some reason he failed to gain control over the steering wheel, so that the bus ended up running over one person after another on the street. To Haneke, this nightmarish feeling of being helpless to prevent terrible things even if one is responsible is representative of the current situation of the world:

All of us are responsible but unable to change the direction of the bus – everyone in Europe, everyone in the so-called first world, is in that same position. A horrible predicament, almost unbearable if you think about it, but the bus keeps right on rolling. (Wray 2007)

Haneke didn't fail to mention that he might use this dream in one of his films. A year ago I interpreted this dream as a statement of tragic consciousness. Now I would add that it could also be read as a concession to melodrama's specific combination of suffering and – finally, after twenty years of battle! – *more* action. Let's see.

Acknowledgments

I am very grateful to Peter J. Schwartz, Holger A. Klein, Scott Loren, Stephan Dietrich, and Roy Grundmann for comments and help with the translation.

Notes

1   The full quote is: "Ich [Haneke] habe die Absicht, ihn [*Zuschauer* = spectator] *nicht* zu vergewaltigen, und wenn, dann – wie gesagt – zur Selbständigkeit," in Haneke (1991: 213, italics in the text).

2   The debates focused (1) on the origins of the film melodrama, especially of the 1950s, in literal and theatrical traditions (Heilman 1968; Elsaesser 1987; Brooks 1985; Seeßlen 1980); (2) from a feminist point of view on the domestic and feminine as well as the alliance with stardom (Gledhill 1987, 1991); (3) on difficulties of a precise genre definition (Neale 1980; Williams 1998); and (4) on parallels between melodrama and modernity (Singer 2001).

3   Anker (2005: 24). Like her, Singer (2001) proposes a "cluster concept" also involving five key constitutive factors: pathos, emotionalism, moral polarization, a non-classical narrative form, and graphic sensationalism. Two of them are absolutely required: "moral polarization and sensational action and spectacle" (58).

4   Besides Brooks's study Thomas Elsaesser's influential essay (1987) and Linda Williams's book (1998) must be mentioned here.

5   It was the Clinton advisor Robert S. Litwak, head of the International Studies department at the Woodrow Wilson Center, who defined a rogue state as "whoever the United States says it is."

6   Discussing the melodramatic structures of TV serials would require a separate essay. As just one example, I'd like to quote a remarkably self-reflective statement at the end of season two (last episode) of the serial *24*. Sherry Palmer (Penny Johnson Jerald), accompanying Jack Bauer (Kiefer Sutherland) to find the man behind the terrorist attack plans, says to the "hero": "You're an impressive man, but you see everything as either good or bad, just like David [President David Palmer, Jack's only friend and brother in counter-terrorism], and the world is much more complicated than that." Bauer's answer – "No, it's simple, there's a war about to start and you're the only person who can help me stop it!" – could also have been scripted by Peter Brooks (or by George W. Bush's advisory board) to illustrate his thesis of a melodramatic world view.

7   Illouz (2007: 57) refers to the conception of Paul DiMaggio in "Culture and Cognition."

8   Illouz (2003) has dedicated a complete study to these phenomena.

9   Alain Ehrenberg's (1998) lucid study of the exhausted self and depression in society clearly shows that the described phenomena are not exclusively American, but European developments, too.

10 This is again where an entire field of further research opens up that is dedicated to the relation between the work of Pierre Bourdieu and the notion of "emotional capital" – which would also have to take into account concepts such as Franck's "mental capitalism."

11 Ross (2008: 139, my translation). The Bush quote is available at www.guardian.co.uk/world/2005/jan/20/uselections2004.usa (retrieved September 11, 2008).

12 There are different perspectives on melodrama and tragedy. Brooks goes along with Bentley in considering tragedy impossible after the rupture between men and the common body (god/the gods, the holy, etc.). Elsaesser, on the contrary, sees in melodrama *real* tragedies, because its ordinary characters fail pathetically in living their ideals, which find no place in America's everyday life, with the consequence that the disillusioned protagonists even increase the doses of idealism. Georg Seeßlen again denies the tragedy character because (1) tragedy deals with men who still have and believe in gods, whereas in post-sacral times there are only fathers left; (2) tragedy tells of conflicts within the protagonists, whereas melodrama shows conflicts between them; and (3) in tragedy the individual fails because of the law, whereas in melodrama it is the convention they cannot overcome. He summarizes: "The melodrama is more than the secularized form of tragedy. It is the place of the powerless anger that injustice keeps ruling the world and there's no god and no heaven. Orthodox Christians and Marxists do not know what to do with melodrama" (Seeßlen 1980: 25, my translation).

References and Further Reading

Anker, E.: "Villains, Victims and Heroes: Melodrama, Media, and September 11," *Journal of Communication* 55:1 (March 2005): 22–37.

Bentley, Eric: "Melodrama," *The Life of the Drama* (New York: Atheneum, 1964), pp. 195–218.

Bohrer, K. H. and Scheel, Kurt, eds.: "Kein Wille zur Macht. Dekadenz, Merkur." *Zeitschrift für Europäisches Denken* 8/9 (August/September 2007).

Brooks, Peter: *The Melodramatic Imagination: Balzac, Henry James, Melodrama and the Mode of Excess* (New York: Columbia University Press, 1985).

DiMaggio, Paul: "Culture and Cognition," *Annual Review of Sociology* 23 (1997): 263–87.

Ehrenberg, A.: *La Fatigue d'être soi* (Paris: Odile Jacob, 1998).

Elsaesser, Thomas: "Tales of Sound and Fury," *Home Is Where the Heart Is: Studies in Melodrama and Women's Films*, ed. Christine Gledhill (London: BFI, 1987), pp. 43–69. (Originally published in 1972.)

Franck, G.: *Mentaler Kapitalismus. Eine politische Ökonomie des Geistes* (Munich: Hanser, 2005).

Gledhill, Christine: "The Melodramatic Field: An Investigation," *Home Is Where the Heart Is: Essays on Melodrama and the Woman's Film*, ed. Christine Gledhill (London: BFI, 1987), pp. 5–39.

Gledhill, Christine: "Signs of Melodrama," *Stardom: Industry of Desire*, ed. Christine Gledhill (London: Routledge, 1991), pp. 207–29.

Haneke, Michael: "Herr Haneke, wo bleibt das Positive? Interview mit Stefan Grissemann und Michael Omasta," *Der Siebente Kontinent. Michael Haneke und seine Filme*, ed. Alexander Horwath (Vienna: Europaverlag, 1991), pp. 193–213.

Heilman, R. B.: *Tragedy and Melodrama: Versions of Experience* (Seattle: University of Washington Press, 1968).

Illouz, E.: *Cold Intimacies: The Making of Emotional Capitalism* (Cambridge: Polity Press, 2007).

Illouz, E.: *Oprah Winfrey and the Glamour of Misery: An Essay on Popular Culture* (New York: Columbia University Press, 2003).

Lyotard, Jean-François: *The Postmodern Condition: A Report on Knowledge* (Minneapolis: University of Minnesota Press, 1984). (Originally published in 1979.)

Meindl, Harald: "Zum Erhabenen in der Kinotrilogie Michael Hanekes," *Utopie und Fragment. Michael Hanekes Filmwerk*, ed. Franz Grabner, Gerhard Larcher, and Christian Wessely (Thaur: Kulturverlag, 1996), pp. 55–80.

Metelmann, Jörg: *Zur Kritik der Kino-Gewalt. Die Filme von Michael Haneke* (Munich: Fink, 2003).

Metelmann, Jörg: "Die Autonomie, das Tragische. Über die Kehre im Kinowerk von Michael Haneke," *Michael Haneke und seine Filme. Eine Pathologie der Konsumgesellschaft*, ed. Christian Wessely, Gerhard Larcher, and Franz Grabner (Marburg: Schüren, 2005), pp. 283–99.

Neale, Stephen: *Genre* (London: BFI, 1980).

Ross, J.: *Was bleibt von uns? Das Ende der westlichen Weltherrschaft* (Berlin: Rowohlt, 2008).

Seeßlen, Georg: *Kino der Gefühle. Geschichte und Mythologie des Film-Melodrams* (Reinbek bei Hamburg: Rowohlt, 1980).

Singer, Ben: *Melodrama and Modernity: Early Sensational Cinema and its Contexts* (New York: Columbia University Press, 2001).

Williams, Linda: *Melodrama Revisited. Refiguring American Film Genres: History and Theory*, ed. Nick Browne (Berkeley: University of California Press, 1998), pp. 42–88.

Williams, Linda: *Playing the Race Card: Melodramas of Black and White from Uncle Tom to O. J. Simpson* (Princeton and Oxford: Princeton University Press, 2001).

Wray, J.: "Minister of Fear," *New York Times Magazine*, September 23, 2007.

10

"Mourning for the Gods Who Have Died"

The Role of Religion in Michael Haneke's Glaciation Trilogy

Gregor Thuswaldner

Theologians have been captivated by Michael Haneke's oeuvre. While Haneke's films have been read on many different levels, their theological dimension is undeniable, as they tackle central religious themes such as guilt, sin, and predestination versus free will. Haneke in an interview talks about Jansenist ideas decades after his initial encounter with the Catholic Counter-Reformation movement in seventeenth-century France – evidently, he is still fascinated with certain aspects of Jansenism (Grabner 2008: 24). Even though junior and senior Catholic theologians affiliated with the University of Graz were among the first group of scholars to investigate Haneke's films (see Grabner, Larcher, and Wessely 1996), important aspects of Haneke's spiritual cosmos, such as his appropriation of Jansenist theology, his indebtedness to Blaise Pascal, his fascination with biblical images and the context of Austrian Catholicism, which are particularly apparent in his glaciation trilogy, have not been adequately addressed.

The term Jansenism goes back to the Dutch theologian Cornelius Jansen or Jansenius, as he was called before he became bishop of Ypres in present-day Belgium, whose posthumously published book entitled *Augustinus* caused much controversy among the Catholic leadership of France. Jansen was intensely concerned with defeating the heresy of ascetic monk and religious thinker Pelagius (354–418), since he viewed Pelagius' teachings as a threat to the church of his day. Pelagius criticized the doctrine of God's saving grace, because he believed it only led to moral laxness among Christians. Disgusted by the lack of morals he encountered in the church, Pelagius insisted on the individual's role in gaining salvation. In contrast to the official Catholic doctrine, Pelagius and his followers believed that, with God's help, everyone could become morally perfect. Instead of relying on the centrality of God's grace for human conduct and self-definition, Pelagius stressed the importance of adhering to high moral standards. St. Augustine, a contemporary of Pelagius, sharply refuted his theology by emphasizing the corruption of sin and our inability to live up to God's moral expectations. According to St. Augustine, God's grace is the only way to salvation. Paradoxically, eleven centuries later, Jansen viewed Pelagian teachings as the cause of the moral laxity in the church. As religious scholar Marvin O'Connell has pointed out, "All around him, Jansenius seemed to see evidence of a religious culture ready to exalt natural virtue and to ignore the heinousness of sin – and not just among scoffers and *libertines érudits* but among serious practicing Catholics as well. Priests in the confessional abetted a subtle resurgence of the Pelagian poison by coddling their penitents, indulging the whims and vanity of the worldly" (O'Connell 1997: 42).

In his *Augustinus*, Jansen renegotiated the ethico-religious debate's central questions of free will vis-à-vis God's grace. What prompted him was his awareness of an acute lack of ideological guidance in the church. The Council of Trent (1545–63), which provided the theological framework for the Counter-Reformation, had not fully explored these questions (Mason 2000). Despite the Council's attempt to negotiate the tension between grace and free will through its definition of faith – adapting and canonizing Thomas Aquinas's definition of faith "as an intellectual assent to divine truth by the command of the will inspired by grace and the authority of God" (*Encyclopaedia Britannica*) – there was still much room left for different interpretations regarding the relationship between grace and free choice.[1] Jansen's *Augustinus* radically questions the nature of free agency and stresses predeterministic ideas. Jansen was convinced that even though Christ died for everyone, only a select group would eventually be saved. For Jansen, even our own will depends on God's grace, which gives the elect few "not only the power of willing but the will to do what we can as well" (Kolakowski 1995: 15).

The ruling clergy considered *Augustinus* a threat, as its seemingly heretical treatment of sin versus divine grace evoked notions prevalent in Protestant theology, particularly Calvinism. There are, however, significant differences between Jansenistic teachings and Reformed theology. Calvinists, like Protestants in general, emphasize God's grace as sufficient in order to achieve salvation, while Jansenists, here still following official Catholic doctrine, stress the importance of good works. While Calvinists hold that the elect few can not fall from God's efficacious grace, Jansenists contend that grace cannot be taken for granted. Rather, grace is to be bestowed on one by chance. Unlike Calvinists, practicing Christians of the Jansenist type can never be certain of their salvation. Thus, the Jansenistic world view is even darker than the Calvinistic one. In a world where God's grace does not have lasting effects but has chance-like characteristics, one can easily become a pessimist.

Augustinus influenced a pious group affiliated with the nunnery at Port-Royal, which became a stronghold of the Catholic reform movement. Blaise Pascal, a central member of the group, along with his family, was deeply impacted by Jansen's take on St. Augustine's theology, which is clearly echoed in Pascal's *Pensées*; however, the clergy of Port-Royal were even more influenced by Antoine Arnauld's book *On Frequent Communion*, which advocated restricting the offering of the Eucharist only to deeply moral people. In this sense, the Jansenists Pascal was influenced by placed a greater emphasis on proper morality than on Augustine's concept of divine grace and the (heretical) doctrine of predestination.

While Pascal defended Jansenist teachings, most famously in his eighteen *Lettres écrites par Louis de Montalte à un provincial*, and can therefore be called a Jansenist himself,[2] his fragmentary, posthumously published book *Pensées* goes well beyond strictly Jansenist theology. The goal of his unfinished and fragmentary *Pensées* was to provide the church and non-believers with new arguments for the Christian faith.

The broad affinity with Jansenism of Michael Haneke's work and his interest in Pascal in particular do not involve the devotional aspects of the Catholic reform movement. Rather, he, like other lapsed Catholics and dissidents,[3] is more fascinated by some of their theological themes, such as their epistemological skepticism, the role of God's grace, and the question of free will versus predestination. Even though predeterministic tendencies in the glaciation trilogy are undeniable, there are clearly moments when Haneke's protagonists pause and reflect on their actions and reactions. In *The Seventh Continent* (1989) the family's fate seems inevitable at first glance, as Georg contends in his farewell letter to his parents that their lives are not worth living and that it is only consequential to kill his family and himself. This statement is particularly unsettling, as Georg, Anna, and Evi have been living a seemingly normal life, which mirrors the lives of many middle-class families. Haneke refuses to provide concrete reasons, let alone satisfying psychological explanations, for the family's decision to commit suicide. It seems, however, that Haneke's protagonists live out the wretchedness of human existence as described by Pascal:

> We desire truth and find in ourselves nothing but uncertainty. We seek happiness and find only wretchedness and death. We are incapable of not desiring truth and happiness and either certainty or happiness.[4]

For Pascal the reason for our unhappiness is linked to the absence of God in our lives. Referring to an Old Testament book, Pascal writes: "Ecclesiastes shows that man without God is totally ignorant and inescapably unhappy" (Pascal F 75). By the late nineteenth century, this sentiment had lost none of its impact. Commenting on the mindset of modernity, Friedrich Nietzsche in *The Twilight of the Idols* famously stated that "[w]hen one has his *wherefore* of life, one gets along with almost every how" (Nietzsche 1896: 98). In *The Genealogy of Morals* Nietzsche elaborates on the lack of meaning, "the great vacuum" we are confronted with in modernity:

> [Modern man's] own meaning was an unsolved problem and made him suffer. He also suffered in other respects, being altogether an ailing animal, yet what bothered him was not his suffering but his inability to answer the question "What is the meaning of my trouble?" Man, the most courageous animal, and the most inured to trouble, does not deny suffering per se: he wants it, he seeks it out, provided that he can be given a meaning. (Nietzsche 1956: 298)

Thus, the act of self-annihilation Haneke demonstrates in *The Seventh Continent* can be seen as consequently following modernity's assumptions to its conclusion. However, the family's downward spiral may not be completely irreversible. Although all family members have given their consent to die, their mechanistic and systematic self-destruction comes to an abrupt halt when Georg shatters the aquarium. The dying fish foreshadow the family's impending death. As rare as scenes like these are in the trilogy, these moments of self-reflection, which can be seen as grace intervening, could potentially trigger a reversal of the characters' actions. The fact that Haneke's protagonists reject the warnings of their inner voices makes his trilogy even more shocking.

In an interview with theologian Franz Grabner, Haneke compares beauty with the Jansenist's concept of God: "[Beauty] is totally hidden and only draws nearer in an act of grace" (Grabner 2008: 24). While it is true that the concept of a hidden God already appears in the Bible (see Isaiah 45:15 or Job 23:8–9), it is important to note that in the seventeenth century, notions of the *deus absconditus*, the hidden God, were fueled by the emergence of a theological skepticism. For Jansenists and other religious skeptics of that time, belief and skepticism were not diametrically opposed (Lennon 1977: 299). Haneke shares a similar epistemological skepticism, which does not *a priori* exclude religious concepts. This particular strand of skepticism is evident in Haneke's fragmentary cinematic style, which prevents viewers from appling any psychological interpretations of his characters' actions. As viewers we simply do not know enough in order to judge the motivations of Haneke's protagonists. But this lack of information has advantages, as it offers the potential for a certain liberation of thought. Making room for the importation of questions of spirituality in the gaps between characters' actions and their unclear motivations, Haneke's aesthetic of ambiguity makes it impossible to uphold the Enlightenment binary between the secular and the religious.

In interviews Haneke has often pointed out his interest in ambiguity. He is not concerned with providing the viewers of his films with concrete answers; instead, he underscores the complexity of his characters whose actions cannot be traced back to root causes that we explain to ourselves with the help of sociology, psychoanalysis, and other scientific disciplines. Epistemological uncertainty or skepticism is also an important undercurrent in Jansenist theology in general and in Blaise Pascal's thought in particular. According to Pascal, "[m]an is an incomprehensible monster" (Pascal F 420) and our ability to understand the world, let alone the universe, is limited: "For after all what is man in nature? A nothing in relation to infinity, all in relation to nothing, a central point between nothing and all and infinitely far from understanding either" (Pascal F 71). The epistemological dilemma that Pascal describes has theological and ethical consequences. How are we supposed to live in a world in which God is not present? "Pascal," as Diogenes Allen correctly contends, "is not only a seventeenth-century figure, but a contemporary – a person who is writing about *our* present plight. For our problem is that we do not know where we belong or what we are. Our sciences of nature and of people do not cohere with our sense of significance and worth" (Allen 1983: 9). Haneke illustrates this Pascalian point in *The Seventh Continent* when Evi, who had lied in school that she lost her eyesight, is confronted with her mother, Anna, an optician. It becomes clear that it is Anna who is blind to her child's uneasiness. Instead of trying to engage with Evi genuinely and intimately in order to understand her behavior, Anna only wants to find out if – but not why – Evi had pretended to be blind.

Pascal's notion of our fragmentary epistemological capacity is echoed in Haneke's *71 Fragments of a Chronology of Chance* (1994). But the film goes beyond alluding to the French philosopher by exploring the characters' and the viewers' limitations of knowing, as Haneke directly quotes Pascal's famous wager: If God exists, one will be eternally happy, but if God does not exist, one loses almost nothing (Pascal F 223). As Pascal says, the wager "is an argument for the claim that the belief in God is pragmatically rational, that inculcating a belief in God is the response dictated by reason" (Jordan 1993: 1). It is not an attempt to prove God's existence, but, as Peter Kreeft correctly suggests, it "is addressed to unbelievers, to those who are skeptical of both theoretical reason and revelation" (Kreeft 1993: 291). A female student confronts Maximilian with the wager while at the student cafeteria's lunch buffet:

FEMALE STUDENT: If you count on his existence, you'll win everything. If he doesn't exist, you won't lose anything. Then the other one says, why do I have to bet in the first place? I don't want to anyway. Then the one says you don't have a choice; you have to; you're in the same boat.

MAXIMILIAN: That's just your assumption. If I don't want to, I don't have to.

FEMALE STUDENT: Why? It doesn't matter how you look at it, you end up betting against his existence. It would be equally wrong to say that not going to the polls is not a political act.

Maximilian obviously misses the point that, as Pascal, the father of decision theory, underlines in the *Pensées*, the wager is not optional (see Jeffrey 1995). Distracted by the arrival of an acquaintance, who seconds later hands him a gun and munitions concealed in a plastic bag, Maximilian decides not to explore the consequences of God's existence. It is not a coincidence that Haneke links Maximilian's decision not to consider God's existence with his decision to take on the weapon that will ultimately bring about the massacre at the end of the film.

II

While Jansenist ideas are certainly present in Haneke's films, it would be a mistake to reductively confine the director's spirituality only to the teachings of a seventeenth-century Catholic sect. Clearly, Haneke's interest in metaphysics goes well beyond Jansenism, as he explores theological questions such as eschatological ones and others in *Time of the Wolf* (2003) that were of minor interest to Jansenists. In order to understand the spiritual cosmos of the glaciation trilogy, one must also consider the religious context of Haneke's socialization in Austria after World War II, as well as the Austrian setting of these three films.

Even though the open-minded Cardinal Archbishop emeritus Franz König played a major role in easing social and political tensions in the 1960s and 1970s, the religious climate in Austria during the second half of the twentieth century was largely shaped by a reactionary mindset. Austrian Catholic leaders had no interest in coming to terms with the church's unholy alliance with fascism in the 1930s, nor with its role in the Third Reich (see Binder 2002). The majority of authors and directors growing up in postwar Austria experienced the dominating Roman Catholic religion as an oppressive force and turned away from religion. In their novels, plays, and films these artists voiced their fierce opposition to Austrian Catholicism. Thomas Bernhard, one of the most outspoken critics, famously wrote about the parallels he saw between Nazism and Catholicism.[5] When Bernhard found his unique literary voice in the 1960s, he completely turned away from the Catholic Church. Throughout his career Bernhard's protagonists condemned the Austrian manifestation of Catholicism. Murau, the protagonist in Bernhard's last novel, *Extinction*, claims:

> At first I feared the Church, and then I hated it, with increasing intensity. After all, the Church still dominates everything in this country and this state. ... Catholicism still hold the reins in this country and this state, no matter who's in power. Catholics, charlatans, I thought, mendacious curers of souls. We want no more to do with it, we tell ourselves, we're sickened by it all. In this country and this state nothing escaped the Catholic clergy, even today. (Bernhard 1995: 323)

Despite the fact that Bernhard tends to exaggerate the religious and political climate in Austria, it is true that historically the role Catholicism had played in Austria, particularly after the Counter-Reformation, was not questioned until the second half of the twentieth century (see Bukey 2000: 93ff.). Other authors, such as Felix Mitterer, have criticized the abuse of power and the lack of freedom within the church, as well as its patriarchal structure.[6] Fritz Lehner's highly acclaimed film adaptation of Franz Innerhofer's novel *Beautiful Days* (1982) also paints a grim picture of a religion which seemingly abandoned the Christian concepts of mercy and grace. What is surprising, though, is the fact that despite the artists' disdain for official Catholicism, many are still drawn to religious images and ideas.[7] This, of course, is also the case for Michael Haneke.

The glaciation trilogy demonstrates Haneke's interest in biblical themes and religious images and it reflects both Haneke's appropriation of Jansenist theology and the Austrian context. Unlike other Austrian writers and directors, Haneke's critique of the church is very subtle. In *The Seventh Continent* a radio news segment points to the controversial bishop appointments in Austria and Germany – specifically in Salzburg and Cologne – during the late 1980s. The newscaster quotes Norbert Greinacher, a German theologian, who called upon fellow Catholics to resist the Vatican's arrogant abuse of power. While the next headline about the late Austrian right-wing politician Jörg Haider, which abruptly breaks off, seems unconnected, it is hardly a coincidence that Haneke chose a news fragment that links a reference to reactionary Austrian bishops and the reactionary leader of the radical right, who rose to power during the same period.[8] This segment seems to suggest that in Austria both religion and politics reflect a reactionary mindset. But instead of overtly critiquing the Austrian church or an unholy alliance between some of its leaders and the far right, Haneke's films more broadly examine a disenchanted world in which religion plays only a marginalized role.

At the same time, it would be exaggerated to claim that the manifestation of religion in Haneke's films is mainly present in its absence. To borrow a phrase from Paul Ricoeur, Haneke's glaciation trilogy in particular can be described as films depicting "[t]he period of mourning for the gods who have died" (Ricoeur 1974: 448). In other words, Haneke's characters are struggling to cope with the fact that the world they live in lacks any metaphysical meaning. In an interview, Haneke contends that "[i]n a time when God does not exist anymore, a sense of yearning remains. I don't mean [a yearning] for paradise, but for a different image [*Bild*] of the world" (interview on the *71 Fragments* DVD).

In his films religion is hardly a presence in the public space. The dominating world view in the dark and impersonal world Haneke portrays is materialistic, and any manifestations of spirituality, be they orthodox or unorthodox, are hardly observable. Organized religion seems like a relic from the past, a premodern phenomenon, whose presence is more embarrassing than comforting. When Georg drops off Anna in front of her optometry store at the beginning of *The Seventh Continent*, we see pedestrians rush by the store. As Anna enters the door, two nuns appear, who, equally hurried, disappear within seconds. These nuns do not have any mysterious aura or function like the ones Lola encounters in Tom Tywker's *Run Lola Run* (1998). In Haneke's films obvious religious manifestations have lost their original meaning. This is also true for Christianity's most important religious symbol, the cross, which in *The Seventh Continent* only appears as a doodle on the notepad Anna uses when she makes phone calls. Towards the beginning of *71 Fragments* Maximilian B., the student, who at the end of the film runs amok, fails in arranging tangram puzzle pieces to form a cross. Thus, he loses a bet he made with his roommate, a computer science major, who also perfected his tangram puzzle as a computer game. The cross can only be seen as a symbol of death and thus as a foreshadowing of Maximilian's murders. It does not symbolize the Christian's hope in Christ's efficacious redemption, and thus is devoid of any rich religious connotations (Fig. 10.1).

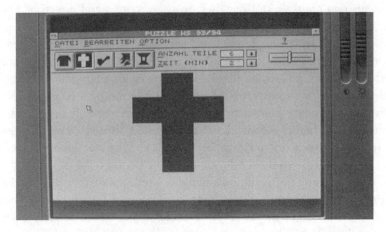

Fig. 10.1   Computer puzzle. *71 Fragments of a Chronology of Chance* (1994), dir. Michael Haneke, prod. Veit Heiduschka.

Even common religious practices, such as praying, have been stripped of religious meaning in Haneke's films. The well-known child's prayer Evi recites in *The Seventh Continent*, "Lieber Gott mach mich fromm, daß ich in den Himmel komm" ("Dear God, give me piety so that I may go to heaven"[9]), does not have any religious significance, but is merely part of her predictable bedtime routine. The patterns of repetition in *The Seventh Continent* evoke a sense of normalcy, but as the story unfolds we learn to question them, as the family seems to function only by performing unconscious habits. Evi's mother expects her to say her prayer every night but she never talks to Evi about religion, nor does Evi ask about God. According to Dorothee Sölle this "naive child prayer . . . does not manifest God's love but utility, the 'handiness' of God" (Sölle 2007: 28). God's only task, it seems, is to transform the praying child into a pious person, so that the child eventually goes to heaven. Sölle questions the motives behind the prayer, as "it expresses a *do ut des* (I give so that you might give) that corresponds to an ideal of capitalism: when I give you something, you in turn must give me something" (Sölle 2007: 41). Apart from these fixed phrases, Evi never voices her desire to become more pious or to be with God in heaven. In his farewell letter to his parents Georg writes about the impression Bach's Cantata "Ich habe genug" ("I have enough") made on Evi during an Easter service at her grandparents' church. She was particularly taken by its aria, which culminates in "Ich freue mich auf meinen Tod" ("I look forward to my death"). Taken out of context, one could think the aria reveals a suicidal message, but instead it contrasts the dismal life on earth with the joys in heaven, which are inseparably linked with the Savior:

> I have enough.
> My sole consolation is

That Jesus be mine and I be His.
In faith I hold on to Him,
Along with Simeon I already see
The joy of that life yet to come. (Bach, BWV 82)

The concept of heaven in *The Seventh Continent*, however, is not connected with a savior but with an exotic image which in the beginning of the film is introduced as an advertisement for Australia (Fig. 10.2).[10] At first glance it bears a resemblance to the description of paradise in the book of Revelation.[11] However, later in the film, the seemingly celestial image of this utopia becomes much darker due to the added motion and sound of the roaring sea and the menacing storm clouds. According to the New Testament scholar N. T. Wright, "[h]eaven in the Bible is not a future destiny but the other, hidden, dimension of our ordinary life" (Wright 2008: 19). Georg, Anna, and perhaps even to a certain degree Evi do not share the hope for an afterlife nor the desire to be united with a savior. Instead, for them the act of self-annihilation becomes the only imaginable salvation from the lives they have led.

The Seventh Continent is not the only Haneke film which references a piece by Bach. In *Benny's Video* (1992) we even get to hear a short segment of the well-known motet "Jesu meine Freude" ("Jesus my joy") twice, which adds an ironic commentary to both scenes. Towards the beginning of the film we encounter Benny and his classmates calmly occupied with a pyramid scheme, as well as with dealing drugs, while practicing the motet with the high school boys' choir.

Defy the old dragon,
Defy the jaws of death,
Defy also fear!

Fig. 10.2   "Welcome to Australia." *The Seventh Continent* (1989), dir. Michael Haneke, prod. Veit Heiduschka.

> Fume, World, and stomp:
> I stand here and sing
> In complete serenity. (Bach, BWV 227)

Taken out of context the original religious meaning of Bach's piece is completely lost. The defiance the boy choir sings about has nothing to do with resisting death or the devil, but instead the students are demonstrating their rebellion against their parents and teachers. Towards the end of the film we see the students perform the motet publicly with Benny's parents in the audience. The performance takes place shortly after Georg and Anna have hosted a party, even though they are hiding the body of the student Benny has killed in their apartment. Since we are shown close-ups of the parents, the lyrics seem to reflect the parents' apparently fearless state of mind. The scene suggests that the parents believe they have effectively succeeded in covering up their son's murder. The line "I stand here and sing in complete serenity" can be read as a commentary that they do not fear any impending punishment. At the same time, the scene makes clear that religious art, music, and rituals are drained of their original meanings and erstwhile functions – now all they do is accompany bourgeois pageants.

It is hardly a coincidence that Benny and his mother escape to Egypt, while the father is supposed to take care of the dead body. The complex role Egypt plays in *Benny's Video* resembles its multifaceted images in the biblical narrative.[12] Haneke clearly alludes to the Holy Family's flight to Egypt in Matthew's Gospel (see Matthew 2:13–23). While Joseph and Mary rescue Jesus from King Herod's mass killings of new-born babies, Benny and his mother try to repress Benny's murder in an exotic setting. The fact that Benny's mother finally breaks down in tears towards the end of their stay reminds one of the prophet Jeremiah's warning not to flee to Egypt in order to evade judgment, as it would only cause the fugitives to suffer (see Jeremiah 42–3).

Flipping though Egyptian TV stations, Benny pauses when he unexpectedly finds a documentary on Baroque organ music, which becomes the unusual soundtrack of his brief time in Egypt. The fact that Benny is mesmerized by this church music can be seen as another example in Haneke's films for God's grace unexpectedly intervening. At first glance it seems ironic that both Benny and his mother have their closest encounter with Christianity in Egypt, a country dominated by Islam. However, in church history Egypt has a prominent place, as it served as a catalyst for the Christian gospel in the first centuries and it produced some of the most important Church Fathers, such as Origen of Alexandria (ca. 185–ca. 254).[13] The fact that we see Benny's footage of his visit to a Coptic church points to his at least aesthetic interest in an earlier manifestation of Christianity than the one he is used to. But the different aesthetic experience of Christianity in Egypt does not lead Benny to ask about God, nor does he acknowledge his sin.

Since Haneke's allusions to religion are mostly subtle, the guard in *71 Fragments* appears as the exception to the rule, as he is by far the most religious character in the trilogy. In one scene, the guard takes Jesus's recommendation in Matthew 6:6 to heart: "But whenever you pray, go into your room and shut the door and pray to your Father who is in secret; and your Father who sees in secret will reward you." Before brushing his teeth he begins his morning routine in the bathroom with prayer:

> Please, dear God grant that the little one will live long and that she stays healthy. And help me to live long and to stay healthy. And help Maria to become a happier person and help me to become a better and happier person. And grant that I don't have a terminal or life-threatening disease and grant that there won't be a Third World War or a nuclear catastrophe in this and the next generation and please help the ones who suffer in this world. And I thank you for everything, dear God and Savior.

This formulaic, short, and hastily uttered prayer – it lasts only twenty-five seconds – suggests that he prays the same words on a continuous basis. While both his religious sincerity and humility are beyond reproach, the content of his limited theology is questionable and reminds one of the utilitarian character of Evi's aforementioned prayer. God's main role, it seems, is to prevent illnesses and apocalyptic catastrophes in his daughter's and especially his own life. While he acknowledges his and his wife's unhappiness, concerns for her health do not enter his mind. Even though he does not explicitly ask for God's forgiveness for his sins, his intercession to become a better person implies that he does not live up to his or God's expectations.

It is obvious that the daily prayer does not have an immediate effect on his relationship with his wife, as both appear emotionally distant the same morning. Apart from that, the guard demonstrates his faith in God and at least some hope that his relationship with his wife will improve. This scene can be read as a meditation on the three cardinal virtues, faith, hope, and love: "And now faith, hope, and love abide, these three; and the greatest of these is love" (1 Corinthians 13:13). It is interesting to consider the immediate context of this well-known verse. Before St. Paul's teaching on love, which is the main theme of this passage, finds its culmination in the aforementioned verse, he briefly acknowledges the fact that our ways of knowing are limited: "For now we see in a mirror, dimly, but then we will see face to face. Now I know only in part; then I will know fully, even as I have been fully known" (1 Corinthians 13:12). St. Paul seems to suggest that faith, hope, and especially love are the remedy of our epistemological limitations. In the dinner scene that follows, we witness the guard's clumsy attempt to reveal his love to his wife, as well as her initial inability to correctly interpret his intention. The dismal state of their marriage becomes obvious after the guard, who had been drinking, tells his wife that he loves her. Since we know from his prayer that he honestly hopes to become a happier and better person, this does not come as a surprise. However, his wife does not know how to decipher this simple speech act. She is confused about the intended meaning and even more worried about the effect the statement is supposed to bring about. He obviously interprets her reproachful question, "What are you trying to achieve with that?," as a slap in the face and counters her verbal attack physically. Even though at first she tries to get up and leave, she overcomes her initial desire, and stays and eventually caresses his hand. Both are aware of the dysfunctional nature of their marriage and their inability to show their love for each other.

This moving scene seems to suggest that love may overcome the problems the characters in Haneke's films suffer from. However, it is a rare scene in the director's oeuvre. On the surface, the gloomy endings of all three films of the glaciation trilogy suggest that Haneke's view of the fragile status of spirituality in modern society and his appropriation of the Jansenistic view of predestination come close to pessimism and even nihilism. However, the fate of the characters in his films is hardly inevitable, as their decisions are, ultimately, based on choice. While Haneke cannot be called a moralizing director in the conventional, narrow sense, he clearly challenges the moral consciousness of his audience. In an interview, Haneke points out that he wants his viewers to feel "obligated to do something against what I show them on the screen. I don't offer solutions, only questions" (Grabner 2008: 13). Unlike Austrian authors from Franz Kafka to Thomas Bernhard and beyond who tend to combat pessimistic notions with irony that borders on sarcasm, Haneke chooses to shock viewers into making moral decisions which are diametrically opposed to the decisions made by his characters. As reviews of Haneke's works attest, it may not be exaggerated to compare the effect Haneke's trilogy has on viewers to a secular Damascus experience.

In the glaciation trilogy Haneke confronts his audience with the "malaises of Modernity" (Charles Taylor), the uneasiness of living in a disenchanted world. Negotiating the consequences of the metaphysical void, Haneke's role as a director reminds one of how Paul Ricoeur saw the philosopher's task: "The philosopher's responsibility is to think, that is, to dig beneath the surface of the present antinomy until he has discovered the level of questioning that makes possible a mediation between religion and faith by way of atheism. This mediation must take the form of a long detour, it might even appear as a path that has gone astray" (Ricoeur 1974: 448). Even though religion is neither uncritically nor explicitly embraced in the trilogy, Haneke's films suggest that the void that the absence of religion has caused may only be filled again with religion. As one might expect from Haneke, though, his films do not provide an answer to whether, let alone how, a return to religion can be achieved.

Notes

1   Jansen was not the only sixteenth-century Catholic theologian who attempted to tackle issues of free will versus determinism. In 1588 the Spanish Jesuit Luis de Molina

published *De Concordia liberi arbitrii cum donis divinae gratiae* ("On the harmony of free will with the gifts of divine grace"), which was vehemently opposed by Jansenists.

2 Scholars disagree on this point. The Catholic philosopher Peter Kreeft tries to dissociate Pascal from his Jansenist affiliation, while others like J. Lataste cannot but see Pascal as a defender of Jansenism. See Kreeft (1993: 14ff.) and Lataste (1911).

3 It is interesting to note that dissidents, especially former Catholics, have been attracted to Jansenism, while practicing Catholics have often voiced their disdain for various aspects of this particular reform movement. William Doyle, the author of an exemplary study of Jansenism, begins the preface to his book as follows: "The unbelieving son of a lapsed Catholic, brought up as a 'non-playing Anglican,' is perhaps not the most obvious person to write about tangled episodes in the history of the Catholic Church" (Doyle 2000: x). In his review of Doyle's book, Richard Lebrun "detect[s] a certain tone of reprobation" in Doyle's descriptions of the Jesuits who opposed the Jansenists. It seems impossible for scholars not to take sides. The eminent sociologist (and practicing Catholic) Charles Taylor oftentimes belittles the pious group as a "hyper-Augustinian" sect in his groundbreaking book, *A Secular Age* (Taylor 2007: 511).

4 Pascal, F (= Fragment) 401. All subsequent citations of Pascal's book will appear in the main text in parentheses.

5 Bernhard famously compared Salzburg to a "terminal disease" and described it as a "lethal soil with its archepiscopal architecture and its mindless blend of National Socialism and Catholicism" (Bernhard 1985: 79).

6 See Mitterer, *Stigma, Kinder des Teufels* (1989), *Verlorene Heimat* (1992), *Krach im Hause Gott* (1994).

7 This is also true for recent films such as Ulrich Seidl's *Jesus, du weißt* (2003) or Wolfgang Murnberger's adaptation of Wolf Haas's *Silentium* (2004).

8 Haneke could be called prophetic, since some bishops, who were appointed at that time, such as Kurt Krenn of St. Pölten, aligned themselves with Haider in the 1990s, years after the release of *The Seventh Continent*. See Bailer and Neugebauer, "The FPÖ of Jörg Haider."

9 This English rendition of the "dreadful children's prayer" (Dorothee Sölle) can be found in Nancy Lukens-Rumscheidt's translation of Sölle's posthumously published *The Mystery of Death* (see Sölle 2007: 28, 41).

10 Haneke ironically juxtaposes Austria and Australia. Austrians are fully aware of the fact that their country is often confused with Australia, which is echoed in the well-known souvenir T-shirt slogan "Austria – We don't have kangaroos."

11 Revelation 22:1–2. In the interview found in the special features section of *The Seventh Continent* DVD, Haneke states that the image is a collage of three different images.

12 The earliest mention of Egypt in the Hebrew Bible already foreshadows the ambiguous relationship Jews have had with Egypt. On the one hand Egypt served as a safe haven for Abraham and Sarah, but on the other hand Sarah was almost added to Pharaoh's harem. See Genesis 12:10ff.

13 According to Henri Crouzel, Origen's greatness as a theologian is matched only by that of Augustine and Thomas Aquinas (Crouzel 2000: 503).

References and Further Reading

Allen, Diogenes: *Three Outsiders: Blaise Pascal, Søren Kierkegaard, Simone Weil* (Cambridge: Cowley, 1983).

Bailer, Brigitte and Neugebauer, Wolfgang: "The FPÖ of Jörg Haider – Populist or Extreme Right-Winger?" www.doew.at/information/mitarbeiter/beitraege/fpoeenglbn.html.

Bernhard, Thomas: *Extinction*, trans. David McLintock (Chicago: University of Chicago Press, 1995).

Bernhard, Thomas: *Gathering Evidence*, trans. David McLintock (New York: Knopf, 1985).

Binder, Dieter: "The Christian Corporatist State: Austria from 1934 to 1938," *Austria in the Twentieth Century*, ed. Rolf Steininger, Günter Bischof, and Michel Gehler (New Brunswick, NJ: Transaction, 2002), pp. 72–84.

Bukey, Evan Burr: *Hitler's Austria: Popular Sentiment in the Nazi Era 1938–1945* (Chapel Hill: University of North Carolina Press, 2000).

Crouzel, Henri: "Origen," *The Oxford Companion to Christian Thought: Intellectual, Spiritual, and Moral Horizons of Christianity*, ed. Adrian Hastings, Alistair Mason, and Hugh Pyper (Oxford: Oxford University Press, 2000), pp. 502–4.

Doyle, William: *Catholic Resistance to Authority from the Reformation to the French Revolution* (New York: Macmillan, 2000).

Encyclopaedia Britannica Online Library: "Roman Catholicism," library.eb.com.ezproxy.bpl.org/eb/article-43673 (retrieved January 24, 2009).

Grabner, Franz: "Der Name der Erbsünde ist Verdrängung: Ein Gespräch mit Michael Haneke," *Michael Haneke und seine Filme: Eine Pathologie der Konsumgesellschaft*, second revised and expanded edition, ed. Franz Grabner, Gerhard Larcher, and Christian Wessely (Marburg: Schüren, 2008), pp. 11–24.

Grabner, Franz, Larcher, Gerhard, and Wessely, Christian, eds.: *Michael Haneke und seine Filme: Eine Pathologie der Konsumgesellschaft*, second revised and expanded edition (Marburg: Schüren, 2008).

Grabner, Franz, Larcher, Gerhard, and Wessely, Christian, eds.: *Utopie und Fragment: Michael Haneke's Filmwerk* (Thaur: Kulturverlag, 1996).

Haneke, Michael: Interview (2005), booklet, *The Seventh Continent*, Kino Video DVD.

Haneke, Michael: Interview (2006), booklet, *71 Fragments of a Chronology of Chance*, Kino Video DVD.

Jeffrey, Richard: "Decision Theory," *The Cambridge Dictionary of Philosophy*, second edition, ed. Robert Audi (Cambridge: Cambridge University Press, 1995), pp. 207–9.

Jordan, Jeff, ed.: *Gambling on God: Essays on Pascal's Wager* (Lanham, MD: Rowman & Littlefield, 1993).

Kolakowski, Leszek: *God Owes Us Nothing: A Brief Remark on Pascal's Religion and on the Spirit of Jansenism* (Chicago: University of Chicago Press, 1995).

Kreeft, Peter: *Christianity for Modern Pagans: Pascal's Pensées, Edited, Outlined, and Explained* (San Francisco: Ignatius, 1993).

Lataste, J.: "Blaise Pascal," *The Catholic Encyclopedia* (New York: Robert Appleton Company, 1911). Retrieved September 22, 2008 from *New Advent*, www.newadvent.org/cathen/11511a.htm.

Lebrun, Richard: Review of William Doyle, *Catholic Resistance to Authority from the Reformation to the French Revolution* (New York: Macmillan, 2000), www.h-net.org/reviews/ showrev.cgi?path=55251012840980.

Leisch-Kiesl, Monika: "Es sind Fragen aufgetreten und offen geblieben, von denen ich hoffe, daß sie nicht allzu schnell beantwortet werden können," *Michael Haneke und seine Filme: Eine Pathologie der Konsumgesellschaft*, second revised and expanded edition, ed. Franz Grabner, Gerhard Larcher, and Christian Wessely (Marburg: Schüren, 2008), pp. 319–40.

Lennon, Thomas M.: "Jansenism and the *Crise Pyrronienne*," *Journal of the History of Ideas* 38:2 (April–June 1977): 297–306.

Mason, Alistair: "Jansenism," *The Oxford Companion to Christian Thought: Intellectual, Spiritual, and Moral Horizons of Christianity*, ed. Adrian Hastings, Alistair Mason, and Hugh Pyper (Oxford: Oxford University Press, 2000), pp. 334–5.

Mitterer, Felix: *Stücke 1* (Innsbruck: Haymon, 1987).

Mitterer, Felix: *Stücke 2* (Innsbruck: Haymon, 1992).

Mitterer, Felix: *Stücke 3* (Innsbruck: Haymon, 2003).

Nietzsche, Friedrich Wilhelm: *The Birth of Tragedy and The Genealogy of Morals*, trans. Francis Golffing (New York: Doubleday, 1956).

Nietzsche, Friedrich Wilhelm: *The Case of Wagner; The Twilight of the Idols; Nietzsche Contra Wagner: The Twilight of the Idols; Nietzsche Contra Wagner [The Antichrist]*, trans. Thomas Common (New York: Macmillan, 1896).

O'Connell, Marvin R.: *Blaise Pascal: Reasons of the Heart* (Grand Rapids, MI: Eerdmans, 1997).

Pascal, Blaise: *Pensées*, trans. W. F. Trotter (New York: E. P. Dutton, 1958).

Price, Brian: "Sontag, Bresson, and the Unfixable," *Post Script: Essays in Film and the Humanities* 26:2 (Winter–Spring 2007): 81–90.

Ricoeur, Paul: "Religion, Atheism, and Faith," *The Conflict of Interpretations: Essays in Hermeneutics*, ed. Don Ihde (Evanston, IL: Northwestern University Press, 1974), pp. 440–67.

Seeßlen, Georg: "Strukturen der Vereisung: Blick, Perspektive und Gestus in den Filmen Michael Hanekes," *Michael Haneke und seine Filme: Eine Pathologie der Konsumgesellschaft*, second revised and expanded edition, ed. Franz Grabner, Gerhard Larcher, and Christian Wessely (Marburg: Schüren, 2008), pp. 25–44. [English translation in this volume.]

Sölle, Dorothee: *The Mystery of Death*, trans. Nancy Lukens-Rumscheidt (Minneapolis: Fortress Press, 2007).

Taylor, Charles: *A Secular Age* (Cambridge, MA: Harvard University Press, 2007).

Wright, N.T.: *Surprised by Hope: Rethinking Heaven, the Resurrection, and the Mission of the Church* (New York: Harper, 2008).

PART II
The Television Films

11

A Melancholy Labor of Love, or Film Adaptation as Translation

Three Paths to the Lake

Fatima Naqvi

Michael Haneke has shown an affinity for a specifically Austrian modernist lineage in his literary adaptations: Roth, Kafka, and Bachmann have been the points of departure in his own literary "crossings over" (*über-setzen*). These authors all wrote "multifocal" works: works that reflect simultaneously on the virulence of racism in Austrian history while nonetheless longingly recalling the lost multiethnic, multicultural Austria-Hungary (cf. Rothberg). I would argue that Haneke's affinity to them arises from a particular historical imperative to "never forget" the Shoah. He interprets this as an injunction to interrogate the psychological dispositions that made fascism possible and that continue into the present, excavating older ways of thinking that either competed or symbiotically connected with these problematic dispositions in the first half of the twentieth century. In his effort to countermand what some have seen as a current (postmodern) willingness to reject mourning or melancholia – to abandon our lost objects under a regime of detachment (see Ricciardi 2003) – he subscribes to an aesthetic and ethic of bereavement in his adaptations. By doing so, Haneke participates in a larger social longing for a return to history (cf. Ryan 2004; Scribner 2003). With his own partiality for the early modern Joseph Roth, the high modern Franz Kafka, and the late modern Ingeborg Bachmann, he picks up on these writers' aesthetic and ethical impulse to dwell on the lost object.[1] Here, I would like to discuss Haneke's film adaptations as a form of elegiac translation, drawing on Walter Benjamin and Sigmund Freud. Melancholic loss, posited as a first principle and an *a priori* without which film adaptations cannot exist, does not renege on the promise of a historically situated *Trauerarbeit*. Melancholic loss becomes the precondition for mourning's possibility.

In this essay, I dwell first on Benjamin's ratiocinations because I would like to take seriously the creative possibilities of translation, including mistranslation. Engaging in my own "misreading" of an English version of Benjamin's essay, "Die Aufgabe des Übersetzers," I outline a general theory of literary adaptation as an estranging act of translation in part I. Film adaptation from literary texts, transposing the building blocks of language to those of film, becomes a melancholy labor of love that must necessarily lose the original to come into being. Loss is not surmounted in a finite process of *Trauerarbeit*, but becomes instead the instigator for an unending filmic return to and departure from the literary text. In envisioning an epistemological horizon within which the movement between media becomes possible, the essay also contributes to a refined understanding of what truly modernist adaptations are. In part II, I refine my argument in respect to Haneke's work in particular, looking at his adaptation of Ingeborg Bachmann's story "Drei Wege zum See" ("Three Paths to the Lake"). Finally in part III, I turn to Haneke's signature fragmentation and argue that it is not simply a slick quotation of illustrious predecessors, but the director's insight into the technique of mournful film translation.[2] In his films, the repetition of melancholia is invested with an erotic impulse at odds with a cynically self-knowing culture under the sway of late capitalism.

I

In a fragmentary dialog for Parisian radio, labeled "La traduction – Le pour et le contre," Walter Benjamin notes the estranging effect an unusual translation can have on an unsuspecting reader (VI: 157–60). Probably developed in conversation with Günther Anders and published only posthumously, the piece continues Benjamin's reflections from his seminal introduction, "Die Aufgabe des Übersetzers" (1923), accompanying his own Baudelaire translations. In "La traduction," two nameless speakers discuss the merits, pitfalls, and potential of translation. The first recounts an odd experience: While leafing through a French translation of Nietzsche, he senses that certain passages are no longer there. These passages, he explains, at one time commanded his sustained attention, and so his astonishment is all the greater. It is not that he cannot find them, he responds to his conversation partner's query, but that – face to face with the once well-known words – he does not recognize them. "Aber als ich ihnen ins Gesicht sah," he says, "hatte ich das peinliche Gefühl, sie erkennen mich ebensowenig wie ich sie erkenne." The complete lack of recognition even precludes temporary misrecognition; the intimately familiar has become entirely unfamiliar and the well-known unknown. He adds that his astonishment, his *Befremden*, was not caused by a shoddy translation. In fact, the translator and his product are held in high esteem (a fact the dialog partner cautiously puts forth). The first speaker quickly moves to dispel the negative connotations his use of the word *Befremden* may evoke. He continues that the Nietzsche passages are now embedded in a decidedly French context. This new horizon represents the marked advantage of this translation: "Der Horizont und die Welt um den übersetzten Text selbst war ausgewechselt und selbst französisch" (VI: 158). The speakers briefly debate this last point. The first interlocutor argues for the conditioning and constraining fact of the mother tongue, the second maintains that the "horizon" points away from the national characteristics of any given text to a world of thought beyond (a particularly comforting thought, one surmises, given the historical milieu of 1935–6).

This passage is interesting for a number of reasons. First, it shifts the criteria by which a translation's merits are judged. Faithfulness to the original, the criterion by which one customarily evaluates translations, is here beside the point. The translation's act of rendering strange an original, its *Verfremdung*, elicits a salutary puzzlement that has nothing to do with the displeasure implicit in the German *Befremden* or with the alienation, *Entfremdung*, symptomatic of modernity. The anthropomorphized text stands across from the reader, and both are strangers to one another (*fremd*); this strangeness becomes the precondition for a new type of understanding and recognition (*Erkenntnis* as derived from *erkennen*).[3]

Secondly, in outlining such an extraordinary conception of translation, this excerpt also gives an inkling of the problems an estranging translation can bring with it. What occurs when the altered "world" around the text so changes the original that misunderstandings ensue? This possibility must have occurred to Benjamin, who notes the pros and cons of translation on a separate sheet addended to "La traduction" (see Benjamin's "Was spricht . . ." IV: 159). International progress in the sciences and the transcension of linguistic parochialism belong to the advantages, while a disregard for nuances and the brutal rendering of mental images are classed as disadvantages. After listing the clear possibilities and definite insufficiencies of translation, Benjamin mentions cases that test translation's boundaries. At the border of the areas occupied by music – Benjamin's verdict: translation unnecessary – and by lyric poetry, which in Benjamin's judgment is the most difficult genre to translate despite its proximity to music, the philosopher-critic constructs another liminal case: "(Wert schlechter Übersetzungen: produktive Mißverständnisse)."[4] His punctuation suggests some hesitation about entertaining the counter-intuitive idea that a bad translation may have heuristic value, since this is the only jotting, apart from subclauses further explicating main points, which he puts in parentheses. What is more, the sentence fragment hints at the productive capacities of a doubled misunderstanding. After this cryptic comment Benjamin immediately remarks that the fact of translation necessarily brings with it a misunderstanding of the original: "Das Faktum daß ein Buch übersetzt wird schafft in gewissem Sinn schon sein Mißverständnis."[5] A mistranslation must augment a primary, unavoidable, and indispensable misunderstanding. A mistranslation, one could extrapolate, multiplies exponentially the possibility of understanding – paradoxically through misunderstanding the original. However, the type of mistranslation Benjamin imagines here is different from the spurious work of certain naïve translators, whom he takes to task elsewhere. They would deny the difference between translation and original as they seek to substitute the translation for the original, to place their work in lieu of the work on which they rely.[6] By contrast, mistranslation in Benjamin's view potentially expands our own horizons, while we are immersed in the new horizon of a translated text (cf. also Stam 2000: 62–3).

My choice of Benjamin's essay "Die Aufgabe des Übersetzers" to construct a cognitive, emotional, and topographical approach to film adaptation may be unusual, especially in light of the fact that Benjamin wrote more explicitly cinematic pieces.[7] Benjamin's translation theory has been used to discuss the translation of written texts from one language into another, including Benjamin's own work on Baudelaire (Schlossman 2001; Weidmann 2001). More often, it has been used to document the untranslatability that becomes either the *a priori* or aporia of all translation and it has been embedded within analyses of Benjamin's own philosophy of language (Jacobs 1993; Düttmann 2001; Menninghaus 1980). While the term "translation" has been loosely applied to adaptation – most recently in Robert Stam's insightful essays "Beyond Fidelity: The Dialogics of Adaptation" and "The Theory and Practice of Adaptation" – no one has discussed the pertinence of Benjamin's notoriously difficult essay to film studies.[8] I aim to do so here, as I argue that the tired trope of carrying-over, of *über-setzen*, deserves renewed attention. The transcendence implicit in Benjamin's essay, a messianic feature that has embarrassed readers (most notably Paul de Man), presents additional problems to anyone utilizing Benjamin's insights for a secular interpretation of films based on literary texts.[9] I will take into account the theological implications as well.

Many thoughtful film critics and scholars writing on adaptation share Benjamin's desire to liberate translation from its subservient role. As a temporally secondary occurrence, adaptation falls prey to the depreciatory appraisal of everything that is not original and originary. In their attempt to shift the discussion away from elusive ideas about fidelity and to expand the domain of the "frequently most narrow and provincial area of film theory" (Andrew 1992: 420), these scholars have argued against the prejudices accompanying what is often seen as a derivative phenomenon. While they have made inroads in dislodging an entrenched iconoclastic bias, preconceptions about adaptations remain. Acutely affected by the negative valuations are television adaptations, a privileged conduit for word-to-image transfers in the German-speaking world because of the clout and resources of public television stations. Even directors themselves are occasionally partial to the literary predecessors on which their films rely. Michael Haneke, for instance, argues that the limited and limiting TV format sullies what he perceives as a pure relation between image, word, and sound (Haneke, "Interview"; Grissemann 2001: 181). "Fidelity" rather than "freedom" is often the operative term within reflections on the subject. Benjamin will return to this binary coupling throughout the foreword accompanying his translations of Baudelaire, in order to better mark his divergence from this misleading opposition.

In order to reconceptualize translation, Benjamin introduces amatory overtones into his theoretical reflections, steering the discussion away from the parameters tradition has set: He conceives of translation as a labor of love. Translation becomes an erotic undertaking that moves beyond moralizing interdictions against too much freedom.[10] He suggests that love for the original and for the goal – harmonization with a pure, paradisial language that existed before man's Fall into history – guides the translator's hand, as the translator turns his attention to the syntax of the original rather than its meaning. In a paragraph in which he emphasizes the difficulty of a translation theory that values form over sense, Benjamin introduces a cabbalistic image that expresses his transcendental conception of language at the time of writing. This segment is notable for its stress on the loving efforts of the good translator:

> Wie nämlich Scherben eines Gefäßes, um sich zusammenfügen zu lassen, in den kleinsten Einzelheiten einander zu folgen, doch nicht so zu gleichen haben, so muß, anstatt dem Sinn des Originals sich ähnlich zu machen, die Übersetzung *liebend vielmehr* und bis ins Einzelne hinein dessen Art des Meinens in der eigenen Sprache sich anbilden, um so beide wie Scherben als Bruchstück eines Gefäßes, als Bruchstück einer größeren Sprache erkennbar zu machen. (IV.1: 18; emphasis mine)

This passage offers a synopsis of the essay as a whole. The translator should privilege contiguity and metonymy (implicit in the idea of a translation's details "following" an original) over identity and metaphor (implied in the negation of the clause, "doch nicht so zu gleichen haben"). He must also aim to capture a way of meaning, the "Art des Meinens," a tonal quality, rather than the content, the "Gemeinte" Benjamin mentions earlier (IV.1: 14). By doing so, the translator reveals that all language – that of the original as well as of the translation – partakes of God's pure language. He does not put together the divine vessel of Adamitic language, a vessel shattered with the Fall.[11] Instead, focusing on the shards, the translator emphasizes the broken nature of post-lapsarian language in both texts. These fragments are the words themselves, whose inherent strangeness he exacerbates.

Love is present not only in the translator's labor, impelled by his regard for the original, but also exists between the texts themselves. They live and die according to a cycle generally only ascribed to organic life (IV.1: 10–11). However, the text does not fall prey to a timeless organicism, where nature trumps art's historicity. The loving relationship between original and translation, albeit approximating a natural intimacy, is firmly embedded in history. It is within history that the translation reveals one of its purposes. It "actualizes" the text from the past in the present epoch.[12] Actualization, I might add, is in its basic premise analogous to film adaptation – both conjure up the complex interplay of organic and historic vicissitudes. A film adapts an existing text to a new cultural climate, modes of production, standards of reception, and so on, creating a new constellation of past and present (cf. Stam, 2005b: 3).

In order to adapt a text for his contemporaries and bring it into the present historical age, the translator must consciously foreground his departures from the original. Fidelity no longer means being true to the original's meaning. Nor does it require adherence to an archaizing language when the original stems from a bygone era. Rather, fidelity is an othering process that obfuscates as much as it clarifies. Benjamin, expanding on the implications of his redefinition of fidelity, turns to a simile rather than a metaphor. A comparison (*Vergleich*) expands on what he means by the phrase "doch nicht so zu gleichen haben" that I quoted above. Describing translation's relation to meaning, Benjamin writes:

> Wie die Tangente den Kreis flüchtig und nur in einem Punkte berührt und wie ihr wohl diese Berührung, nicht aber der Punkt, das Gesetz vorschreibt, nach dem sie weiter ins Unendliche ihre gerade Bahn zieht, so berührt die Übersetzung flüchtig und nur in dem unendlich kleinen Punkte des Sinnes das Original, um nach dem Gesetze der Treue in der Freiheit der Sprachbewegung ihre eigenste Bahn zu verfolgen. (IV.1: 19–20)

He here envisions the relationship between sense in the original and sense in the translation as an extension of the translation's loving approximation of the original's way of meaning. The transmission of meaning is eschewed – the content is only touched upon in the new text, just as a tangent only fleetingly touches a circle's circumference. As a complement to the image of the shattered vessels of divine light in the first quotation I discussed, the tangent and its caress of the circle evoke not the completion and spherical nature of the whole vessels filled with divine light, but the open-ended nature of the translator's task. Extending into infinity, the line's properties remain unchanged, as do the circle's. However, the point of contact is all important, as it defines the geometric figure. A tangent suggests self-transcension; in this it is reminiscent of Rainer Maria Rilke's "intransitive love," a concept delineated more than a decade earlier. For Rilke, intransitive love leads to the lover's transcendence of his or her finite being, precisely by loosing the relation to a particular love-object. Indeed, for Benjamin the relationship between the translation and the original is like that between polygamous partners in an open marriage, where the laws of fidelity do not hinder the freedom of flux. This love, which knows neither the confinement of the subject nor the constraint of the object, ultimately gestures beyond itself.

In the English variant of this essay, a psychoanalytic term dispels the amorous inclinations guiding the translator as well as the translation. It enables the creative misunderstanding whose mechanism I discussed earlier. Let me juxtapose the two variants of the quotation about the fragmented vessel in which this Freudian term appears. The newer translation from 1996 reads:

> Fragments of a vessel that are to be glued together must match one another in the smallest details, although they need not be like one another. In the same way a

translation, instead of imitating the sense of the original, must lovingly and in detail incorporate the original's way of meaning, thus making both the original and the translation recognizable as fragments of a greater language, just as fragments are part of a vessel. (Benjamin, "Task," 2004: 260)

Certain modifications have transpired, as a glance at Harry Zohn's 1968 version reveals:

Fragments of a vessel which are to be glued together must match one another in the smallest details, although they need not be like one another. In the same way a translation, instead of resembling the meaning of the original, must lovingly and in detail incorporate the original's mode of signification, thus making both the original and the translation recognizable as fragments of a greater language, just as fragments are part of a vessel. (Benjamin "Task," 1985: 78)

Some smaller grammatical and lexical changes as well as an important semantic substitution have occurred – the "way of meaning" has taken the place of "mode of signification." Plain language replaces the structuralist-sounding phrase, itself very much in keeping with structuralism's popularity in the decade in which the essay was first translated. However, the Freudian "incorporate" (the German einverleiben) has remained in the older and newer, revised translation. The translation still "must lovingly and in detail incorporate" the original, rather than "develop in accordance with," "conform to," or "assimilate" the original. I offer these alternatives for Benjamin's German verb anbilden, which borrows from Romantic and Humboldtian terminology and philosophemes (Menninghaus 1980: 37–8). Anbilden calls to mind the organicism he evokes throughout the essay in his parlance of fruit and fertility, seeds and kernels, and maturation – a natural ground Benjamin ultimately undermines (Jacobs 1993: 130–2).[13] The only connection between Benjamin's verb anbilden and Freud's einverleiben lies in the latter's lexical root, Leib. Both words point to an organic substrate upon which the ego or the physiologically conceived text attempts to grow. Anbilden also suggests a late eighteenth- and nineteenth-century ideal of Bildung, with its underlying ideal of complete evolution and self-realization. The fact that Benjamin at other times draws on distinctly psychoanalytic terminology makes it all the more surprising that the revised translation keeps the psychoanalytic "incorporate," rather than choosing an English word more faithful to the language-philosophical implications of anbilden.[14] Benjamin employs the very term einverleibend in his 1916 essay "Über die Sprache überhaupt und über die Sprache des Menschen." There he uses it in relation to God's language, a language that creates in the act of naming: "Mit der schaffenden Allmacht der Sprache setzt er [der Schöpfungsakt] ein, und am Schluß einverleibt sich gleichsam die Sprache das Geschaffene, sie benennt es" (II.1: 148). In this case, compounding the conundrum, the translator Edmund Jephcott opts for the gentler "assimilates" in the recently published Selected Writings 1913–1926 (I: 68).

"Incorporate," in contradistinction to "assimilate," evokes no benign associations. It is the term James Strachey brings into play in his translation of Sigmund Freud's "Triebe und Triebschicksale" from 1915. Freud, as is well known, models incorporation on physical ingestion. Incorporation comes into play in the ego's dialectical development with its environs. The self, in an early, narcissistic stage, seeks to incorporate the object outside itself which gives pleasure. Incorporation, Freud stresses in "Triebe und Triebschicksale," indicates a type of love that seeks to destroy the object's autonomy. In this regard, it is ambivalent – love entails the loss of the object as it is. Freud also opts for the term *einverleiben* in his essay "Trauer und Melancholie," written shortly before "Triebe und Triebschicksale." In a pathological melancholic state, which Freud juxtaposes with a salutary mourning process, the ego regresses to the same narcissistic phase of oral ingestion, identifying with the lost object by introjecting it. Identification with the object is an early form of object-choice; it manifests itself in the desire to literally take in the other: "das Ich . . . möchte sich dieses Objekt einverleiben, und zwar der oralen oder kannibalischen Phase der Libidoentwicklung entsprechend auf dem Wege des Fressens" ("Trauer und Melancholie," 436). The incorporation of the other into the self has become, as Kathleen Woodward scathingly notes, something of a "theoretical piety (if not banality)" in discussions of grief drawing on Freud's work (1990/91: 108 n.3). However, I would like to retain a degree of fidelity to Freud's conception in order to imagine the integration of otherness in the process of self-constitution. I will elaborate on such a conception of melancholia further on in my argument.

How is one to understand the aggressive intrusion of "incorporation" where it seems unwarranted? Perhaps melancholic incorporation reveals something about the mechanism behind translation itself. Are not translation as well as melancholia predicated on ambivalence rather than unadulterated love? If so, does narcissistic identification of the successor text with its predecessor (a precondition for the painstaking travail of translation) lead to the emergence of such hatred as well as love? Maybe only because of narcissistic identification do conflicted feelings come into view – on the part of the translator, translation, and reader. Hatred emerges as one of love's excrescences, a hatred that the profession of a loving labor previously masked.

The English word "incorporate" avoids the transmission of the original's sense in favor of a more ambiguous and thereby implicitly richer term befitting our own ambivalent epoch. Clearly the revised essay, in keeping with Benjamin's conception of translation, performs his polemic against faithfulness to an original's meaning. It thereby renews the work in the age of its fame – one need only consider Benjamin's academic currency (IV.1: 11). The text is actualized for the present with its psychoanalytic implications, acknowledging a profound ambivalence. With the added ambiguity of the psychoanalytic variant, translation's love does not discomfit a contemporary reader. There is, after all, something generally embarrassing about the concept of love – in contrast to trauma or violence – in critical analyses. When love does appear, an adjective such as "courtly," "platonic," or "melancholic" often modifies it, classifies it, and establishes a suitable lineage. The few who, like Niklas Luhmann or Ulrich Beck, write about love often contain it within system-theoretical and sociological models. The injection of a Freudian term into the translation essay tones down Benjamin's love of translation, for translation, and in translation.

What could it mean to conceive of literary adaptation as a loving Benjaminian translation tempered by a Freudian melancholy? First of all, the idea of loss in translation is brought to the fore and reevaluated. Loss is not a reason for general lament, as it is in so many accounts deploying "an elegiac discourse . . . lamenting what has been 'lost' in the transition from novel to film, while ignoring what has been gained" (Stam 2005b: 3). Indeed, loss becomes the condition for the possibility of any and every adaptation. Attempts to incorporate the beloved original are undertaken in the full knowledge that they can never succeed entirely, for the melancholic successor text is unable to absorb the predecessor fully. Melancholic attachment means the inability to orient oneself solely toward the new; put more positively, it means a persistent return to a still present past. The memory of the original is kept alive and returned to without surcease, creating a situation in which the undead haunts the living. While this life-in-death must be denied in melancholia, it may be acknowledged in translation. The coming into being of the translation, however, signals the vacillation between mourning and melancholia and perhaps even the transition to *Trauer* (the former is a process, which leads to a new love-object, rather than a state of perpetual concern with a lost beloved object).

Second and less abstract, such a conception of adaptation further quells the futile discussions of fidelity to an anterior source. A film would be judged not by its ability to mimic certain subjective or objective criteria of the literary text such as period, sociological milieu, or other verifiable facts (number of characters, names, and so on), but by its ability to estrange them. Faithfulness in melancholic translation, as I outlined, is an othering, purposefully alienating process. Within the brief moment when the trace of literature in the film is recognized, a different emotional-cognitive response can be imagined. This would ground itself less in the moralizing categories of fidelity and betrayal than in the ethical categories of alterity-in-sameness and sameness-in-alterity. I do not mean to be precious here; I do, however, want to take seriously the tonal qualities that may bind together original and translation. These are qualitative aspects that we often do not take into account when weighing certain quantitative elements of a film against its literary precursor. There may be a similarity within this atmospheric difference that deserves our sustained attention.

Third, it becomes epistemologically defensible to treat film and literature as separate media, but as continuous languages. A Mallarmé quotation in Benjamin's essay hints at such a continuity of thought between different languages: "Les langues imparfaites en cela que plusieurs, manque la suprême: penser étant écrire sans accessoires, ni chuchotement mais tacite encore l'immortelle parole, la diversité, sur terre, des idiomes empêche personne de proférer les mots qui, sinon se trouveraient, par une frappe unique, elle-même matériellement la vérité" (17). Benjamin leaves the French quotation untranslated, assuming not only that the reader is conversant in French as well as German, but that his ideas can be expressed in a thought-world lying outside and beyond both languages. Hans Jost Frey sees the embedded quotation as a performative element drawing attention to the multiplicity of languages: "Nun erscheint das Zitat an einer Stelle, die von der Integration der Einzelsprachen zur wahren Sprache handelt, und es bespricht selber die Vielheit der Sprachen und das Fehlen der einen höchsten. Das fremd-sprachige Zitat stellt also im Gesamttext die Situation her, die er bespricht" (2001: 154).[15] Benjamin works on the assumption that the sense of his essay emerges despite the polyglot nature of the argument, because thinking remains outside the dif-ferences of language. Reflection on the one pure, integrative language – although it must take place in concrete languages – transcends the boundaries established by them. Dudley Andrew, separating verbal from film narrative, claims as much in regard to the movement between literature and film, drawing on E. H. Gombrich and others: "We can and do correctly match items from different systems all the time: a tuba sound is more like a rock than like a piece of string; it is more like a bear than a bird. . . . We are able to make these distinctions and insist on their public character because we are matching equivalents" (1997: 33). The homology between literature and film, and the movement between both as separate signi-fying systems, becomes epistemologically possible, since they refer to a common signified. There is a certain metaphoricity involved in these kinds of transfers, one I will discuss in the next section.

The issue that remains unaddressed in these ruminations, however, is the reli-gious dimension of Benjamin's essay when applied in such an obeisant manner to film studies. The theological horizon that pure language implies cannot be eliminated without doing the original essay an injustice. However, in the process of actualizing the essay, an etymological and topographical redefinition of translation becomes necessary. Translation stems from the Latin *transferre* (past participle: *translatus*); the German *über-setzen* is the direct transposition of both morpheme and lexeme. The word indicates a horizontal movement, a carrying over from one side to another. As such translation harmonizes with the term "tran-scendence," for which philosopher Emmanuel Lévinas also stresses a vertical dimen-sion. For him, transcendence indicates not only a "movement of crossing over (*trans*), but also of ascent (*scando*)," as Pierre Hayat notes in his introduction to Lévinas's *Alterity and Transcendence* (1999: ix). Lévinas renews the spiritual concept, endow-ing it with a decidedly secular aspect. For him, transcendence becomes a foundational moment in intersubjective relations. The subject, confronted with absolute alterity in the face of the other, is called into question, and brought to its own limits. The *I* can only recognize itself in and through the *you*. Translation shares the inclusive impulse Lévinas ascribes to transcendence. Its dynamic is, as I have argued, dependent on melancholia, whose narcissistic structure implies a presence of the other within the self. The other's presence makes of melancho-lia a process that is less self-contained and closed off from the outside than one would suspect. The "being 'in us' of bereaved memory," Jacques Derrida writes in relation to melancholia, "becomes the *coming* of the other" (1986: 22). By extension, the melancholic translation recognizes itself in and through the original. Transcend-ence, conceptualized in this manner, participates in the estranging effort under-taken by the Benjaminian translation. Through *Verfremdung*, transcendence elicits the salutary *Befremden* necessary for *Erkenntnis*. This recognition can only occur when the translation and the original regard each other with the gaze of strangers in a moment of transcendence, *fremd* to one another except for a gentle caress.

II

Haneke, as I stated at the beginning, has worked with well-known literary texts from the beginning of his career. Ranging from his adaptation of Ingeborg Bachmann's *Drei Wege zum See* (*Three Paths to the Lake*, 1976), Peter Rosei's *Wer war Edgar Allan?* (*Who Was Edgar Allan?*, 1984), Joseph Roth's *Die Rebellion* (*The Rebellion*, 1992), and Franz Kafka's *Das Schloss* (*The Castle*, 1997) – all made for television – on to Elfriede Jelinek's *Die Klavierspielerin* (*The Piano Teacher*, 2001) for cinema, Haneke has demonstrated a proclivity for modernist literary works by fellow Austrian artists, or Austro-Hungarian, as the case may be.[16] Haneke's fruitful exploration of the possibilities inherent in translation culminates in his adaptation of *Die Klavierspielerin* (awarded *Grand Prix du Jury*, best actor, and best actress awards in Cannes 2001). *Three Paths to the Lake*, televised on the fourth anniversary of Bachmann's death, stands out as a particularly melancholic trans-lation, not only for its occasion or subject matter (death and exterritoriality), but – more importantly in terms of this essay – also for its style. In the TV film *Three Paths to the Lake*, Haneke begins the translatory work that he will continue in all his later films.[17]

Bachmann's "Drei Wege zum See" is the closing story within a volume devoted to the problems of *translatio* and fittingly entitled *Simultan*.[18] The eponymous story of the German-language collection – translated as "Word for Word" in English – is specifically concerned with the dilemma of a simultaneous translator named Nadja. Recounted with a smattering of languages, the third-person narrative revolves around the Babel and babble of tongues. The protagonist's translations imperil her; the concomitant embeddedness in language and in history is an ever-present danger to such a borderliner between languages.[19] Nadja's ruminations recall Benjamin's belief in the fallen nature of all historical languages and evidence Bachmann's intense involvement with Benjamin's work (see Weigel 1999: 99–106; Bannasch 1997: 203–14). Bachmann makes much of the translator's double-bind situation:

... sie rieb sich beide Ohren, wo sonst ihre Kopfhörer anlagen, ihre Schaltungen automatisch funktionierten und die Sprachbrüche stattfanden. Was für ein seltsamer Mechanismus war sie doch, ohne einen einzigen Gedanken im Kopf zu haben, lebte sie, eingetaucht in die Sätze anderer, und mußte nachtwandlerisch mit gleichen, aber anderslautenden Sätzen sofort nachkommen, sie konnte aus "machen" to make, faire, fare, hacer und delat' machen, jedes Wort konnte sie so auf einer Rolle sechsmal herumdrehen, sie durfte nur nicht denken, daß machen wirklich machen, faire faire, fare fare, delat' delat' bedeutete, das konnte ihren Kopf unbrauchbar machen, und sie mußte schon aufpassen, daß sie eines Tages nicht von den Wortmassen verschüttet wurde. (295)

She ... rubbed her ears at the spot where she usually wore her headphones, where the switches were thrown automatically and the language circuits were broken. What a strange mechanism she was, she lived without a single thought of her own, immersed in the sentences of others, like a sleepwalker, furnishing the same but different-sounding sentences an instant later; she could make machen, faire, fare, hacer and delat' out of "to make," she could spin each word to six different positions on a wheel, she just had to keep from thinking that "to make" really meant to make, faire faire, fare fare, delat' delat', that might put her out of commission, and she did have to be careful not to get snowed under by an avalanche of words. (14)

When Nadja thinks in terms of a relation *between* all currently "broken" languages (implied in the *Sprachbrüche*, the literal "breaks in language," that become apparent in the process of translating), it exacerbates her inability to reflect on her situation. Even her relative safety when she is a perpetuum mobile of meaning, translating content, depends on a precarious moment of disavowal. When she thinks in terms of a self-presence of language, Nadja's psychical integrity is equally endangered. An identity between the way of meaning and what is meant *within* a language jeopardizes her professional usefulness within the economic cycle underwriting her lucrative career.

"Drei Wege zum See," however, is concerned with translation in another, more abstract sense. The elegiac short story deals with non-synchronous personalities who try to carve out a space for themselves within postwar European society. The protagonist Elisabeth returns to her Carinthian *Heimat* and revisits her past in memory, only to find all physical and psychical routes of return blocked. The suicide of the protagonist's lover, son of the fictional Trotta from Joseph Roth's *Die Kapuzinergruft* (*The Capuchin Tomb*), and an all-pervasive longing for the vanished Austrian Empire mark the hundred-page-long text. The dark tenor, as Sigrid Weigel notes, befits the final story in *Simultan*, which – completed before Bachmann's premature death in Rome – acquires something of the status of a last testament (Weigel 1999: 297–409; cf. also Dusar 1994: 297–308).

Haneke utilizes the melancholic impulse of the longish short story, exploiting the modernist, non-synchronous tensions within Bachmann's "Drei Wege zum See" in his adaptation in order to create an aesthetic of estrangement. The establishing shot in the film already renders foreign the original. Whereas the written text begins with a description of a map of the Kreuzberglgebiet in southern Austria and its three paths to the Wörthersee, Haneke's film starts with a close-up of softly rippling, sun-dappled waves. The topographical impulse – which generates the story – is kept, but the metaphorical resonances of the *Wanderwege* as trails through life are heightened. As Axel Corti's voice-over intones the opening lines of the written text (394), a disjunction emerges between spoken word and visual cue: The film shows water rather than land. The film works on multiple registers, of course, and its fidelity to the literary text, whose beginning is quoted entirely and without emendation, is counteracted with this aqueous beginning. Water is the site for a symbolic crossing-over into a past with which the protagonist only belatedly and partially identifies. The lack of solid ground beneath our feet (water fills the frame and no shore is in sight) participates in the water motif Bachmann employs in "Simultan." It heightens our perception of the disorienting fluidity of a language and identity that can never be fully self-present (cf. Craig 2000: 48–9). Elisabeth's walks along the trails and her ambulatory anamnesis are continually interrupted in the story and the film. The literal and abstract blockages subvert any unproblematic notions of belonging and being native: "Das Leitmotiv der Wanderwege bedeutet hier also nicht eine Allegorie des Lebensweges [I.I], vielmehr verwandelt erst ihre Zielverfehlung die Wege in Signaturen, aus denen Geschichte(n) lesbar werden" (Weigel 1999: 399). On the one hand, we are provided with an image of an ultimately illusory clarity in the landscape, through which the reader cannot move. On the other, we encounter an engulfing, shape-shifting fluid, which offers the viewer no ground but lots of surface for projection. Topography in both cases becomes the generating impetus for multifaceted, plural histories, ambiguously refracted through the errant protagonist's refractory mind.

Translation adaptation, as my preceding discussion intimates, works within a strongly metaphorical register (we noted this in Benjamin's case). This kind of translation requires a certain *Bildhaftigkeit* within the process of *Anbildung*. For this reason, the metaphorical readings of the establishing shot in *Three Paths to the Lake* can and should be further multiplied. In what has become a customary self-reflexive gesture in films, water signifies the developing fluid out of which photographs – a major point of discussion and contention in the narrative – and film itself emerge. The translation from one medium to another, implicit in this close-up of developing fluid, is dependent on the desire for incorporation. The water seems to spill over the frame's edges, seeking to absorb the original without remainder. Water also beckons toward the desired transcendence of pure language and the translucency of pure translation (according to Benjamin, true translation is "durchscheinend," IV.1: 18). Freighted with the Christian symbolism of baptism and rebirth, a recurrent motif in Haneke's oeuvre, this signifier of plenitude underscores the religious underpinnings of transcendence. Haneke alludes to the sacred dimension, while simultaneously investing transcendence with a secular aspect.[20]

The visual self-referentiality about translatory loss is also brought to the fore in the film's thematic and visual concern with photography. *Three Paths to the Lake* dwells on a film's components – the single shots of the finished product. If Benjamin stresses the importance of the individual units that make up the complete work, using Hölderlin's word-for-word translations of Sophocles as an example, then Haneke (in his stress on the pure image) repeatedly hones in on the photos that comprise film at the rate of twenty-four images per second. He shows Elisabeth, a professional photojournalist, in the context of her work. Just after she has come back to Klagenfurt, she looks at a portrait photo of her brother and his bride. As the camera zooms in on the black-and-white photo, music abruptly sets in on the soundtrack. Kathleen Ferrier's tremulous rendition of "Hark! The Echoing Air" from Purcell's *The Fairy Queen* signals the beginning of memory, and the film cuts to a flashback. The narrative delves into the brother's wedding ceremony in London, the celebratory dinner, and the couple's departure on their honeymoon. From the discrete black-and-white portrait photo comes narrative film, and the original unit is incorporated into a larger whole. Photos are translated into a filmic memory of a past that was perceived as incomplete; however, they do not signal a wholesale or wholesome recuperation of the past.

At times Haneke's film suggests an organic memory, structured like the human psyche around lacunae and impelled by the dialectic between remembering and forgetting. While photos can be the building blocks of a new translation, creating moving visuals from frames, *Three Paths to the Lake* also hints that a supplementary structure is the essence of all translation predicated on loss. Photos do not correspond in undistorted, undisplaced form to filmic memory – for example, we never see the exact scene in which the portrait photo of the brother and his wife was taken. They require supplementation on the auditory plane to become effective (hence Purcell). The book makes this explicit: "Elisabeth versuchte, da die Fotos nicht aufschlußreich genug waren, eifrig zu erzählen" (402) ("Because the photos were not sufficiently informative, Elisabeth attempted to give an enthusiastic report," 125). These lines are not recounted in the voice-over. In order to thematize and circumvent the problem, *Three Paths to the Lake* fragments the original's content and creates narrative segments out of embedded photos. It repeats seminal scenes from different angles, shifting points of view. Revisiting episodes such as Elisabeth's extended stay in a London hotel, the film performs its desire for rapprochement with the original. What is told in relatively linear fashion in the novel (which avoids extreme fragmentation) cannot be so straightforwardly recounted in the adaptation. The film purposefully elicits the *Befremden* of the viewer, who is confronted with the same segment twice or thrice. He or she shares in the film's melancholic loss and its inability to turn away from the loss. The original is approached tentatively, and elements of sense are captured in fleeting instants. Reapproximation and fragmentation, *Three Paths to the Lake* insists, must characterize an adaptation. The closure implicit to *Trauerarbeit* is held at bay; precisely the hesitancy to present a final version of events is what lends *Three Paths to the Lake* its televisual power.

Dissonances belong to what I have described as Haneke's aesthetic of estrangement and are necessary within melancholic translation.[21] Haneke's translatory thrust is evident in the thematization of cinematic storytelling – or, better said, its perpetual questioning. Axel Corti's voice-over narration explicitly discusses the role of photography in the segment devoted to Elisabeth's education and career. On a visual level, the film problematizes this very account in the moment of its telling. The short story itself runs chronologically through the incisive markers along her journey, from photographer's apprentice to jet-setting photojournalist. About Elisabeth, Bachmann writes: "Sie fuhr mit [dem Fotografen] Duvalier nach Persien, Indien und China, . . . [sie] lernte . . . alle die Leute kennen, die Herr Matrei, Gott und die Welt' nannte, und Picasso und Chagall, Strawinsky und Julian Huxley, Hemingway wie Churchill wurden für sie aus Namen zu Bekannten und Personen, die man nicht nur fotografierte, sondern mit denen man essen ging" (413) ("She traveled to Persia, India and China with Duvalier, and . . . she met all the people Herr Matrei always referred to as 'Who's Who'; Picasso and Chagall, Stravinsky and Julian Huxley, Hemingway and Churchill stopped being mere names to her and became people you didn't only take pictures of: you went out to eat with them," 137). The film flits from still to still, roughly recounting the same stages in the journey in stenographic shorthand. A photo of the Great Wall stands in for China, barren mountain ranges and a caravan of camels for Iran. However, the film brazenly juxtaposes a photograph of Marilyn Monroe and Arthur Miller when Corti's voice-over, citing directly from the written text, mentions Ernest Hemingway. The disjunction between the measured, neutral soundtrack and the incongruous picture calls into question any standards of judgment adhering to bygone notions of fidelity as a one-to-one transmission of content. Also, when the protagonist's father, perusing wedding pictures, lauds Elisabeth and remarks that it is good to have a photographer in the family, the photos in his hands give lie to his words – they include the supposed photographer! No photo is absolutely verifiable in relation to an element within the short story (or even to a reality created within the story itself).

Such disjunctions and dissonances convey a distrust of the building blocks of cinema, and Haneke's film also questions the conditions for translation and the possibility of adaptation *per se*. Estrangement perhaps even contaminates the director's relationship to the materials with which he works. Three embedded photographs in the montage of black-and-white stills of Elisabeth's trajectory show jostling photographers clambering over and onto one another. The photos offer a meta-commentary on the rapacious nature of filmic incorporation, which spare no effort to capture the past for the present. Conversations about the anthropophagic nature of photojournalism, culled from the short story, are inserted in numerous scenes in *Three Paths to the Lake*. In these, Elisabeth's lover Trotta questions her desire to enlighten the world about its ills and shortcomings. He attacks her belief in the ability of photography to jar people into moral action as cynical and exploitative. For him, such photos are demeaning, since they do justice neither to the victimized objects in front of the lens, nor to the humanity of the viewing subject. The lovers' discourse, restaged numerous times in different venues, establishes that mechanical reproduction is not the purpose of photos, whether in the service of photography or of film. The auditory replication of their conversation manages to capture something the images of Elisabeth and Trotta cannot, as they argue during work, after sex, while traveling. It lends particular urgency to their debate, and Haneke's film takes their words to heart. The relationship of the photos in *Three Paths to the Lake* to the film itself is clearly not one of simplistic rendering via *abfotografieren* (Trotta's derogatory term implying the facile re-presentation of reality, 417), but of Benjamin's *anbilden*. The embedded pictures are personal photos, travelogues, and snapshots of famous acquaintances and not the exploitative images of suffering children Trotta assails for their banal evil.[22]

This central problem – the relation between images, suffering, and the dissemination of others' pain – will recur in Haneke's later film *Code Unknown* (2000), more than a quarter of a century after he first broaches the subject. Discussing a Walker Evans-like series of metro portraits he has taken, the character Georges questions his motives. Like Elisabeth, he, too, is a photojournalist. Like her, he asks whether the mechanical reproduction of scenes of torture, massacre, and grief has an enlightening purpose or simply participates in the cruelty it condemns. A marked shift has taken place in his thinking, the viewer suspects, since Georges was introduced with a photomontage from Kosovo reveling in scenes of carnage and grief. The second photo series of people from all walks of life, while still beholden to a montage technique and an aesthetic of spontaneity, evinces an interest in local heterogeneity (which may nonetheless give rise to interracial, interreligious conflict in Paris), rather than far-off ethnic conflict. The close-ups eschew the naïve reproduction of violence, which Georges advanced earlier. Returning to the ethics of photography, *Code Unknown* carries on a dialog with *Three Paths to the Lake* across time, practicing the Romantic potentialization Benjamin lauds as translation's goal (IV.1: 257).

III

Haneke's somber closure of *Three Paths to the Lake* emphasizes melancholic loss on multiple levels, while it also underlines the fact that an adaptation's complete absorption of the original is beyond reach. The final image of the film turns back to the opening shot of the lake; this time the water is enveloped in evening shade. The title is again superimposed on the rippling, darkened waves. Nothing has come to a clear end, although everything seems to be ending – as the preceding scene of Elisabeth's reflections on the fundamental asymmetry between the sexes and her disturbing dream of bleeding to death intimate. On the soundtrack, Corti's voice-over recounts the dream as Elisabeth lies down in her pitch-black room. The film then cuts to the undulating waves. No resolution has been found on a filmic level for the problems of delayed memory work, personal loss, and historical disappearance posed within the written narrative (and there, too, left open). The translucency of pure translation, as Benjamin himself recognized, is impossible for all texts but one, the Bible. In Bachmann's and Haneke's case, complete transparency cannot be attained when the original and the translation meet in the topographic realm that has been the generating impulse for both. The transfer from one medium to another is necessarily partial.

By remaining true to the syntax of this early film, in which he first broaches the issue of melancholia, Haneke continues his adaptation work in his later films. Over time, meaning accrues to particular, resonant images such as the water shot I have been analyzing. As the water metaphor from this first film is carried over into later works, the metaphoric impulse – tied to reflections on the film medium but also to the historical end of the Austro-Hungarian Empire – is embedded in other contexts. Particularly in Haneke's trilogy from the late 1980s and early 1990s (*The Seventh Continent*, *Benny's Video*, and *71 Fragments*), the aqueous "transfers" recur in epiphanic moments, where children are confronted with human transience. These life-and-death instants shatter the desolate bourgeois existence the children have previously known. Thus the transcendent beginning of *Three Paths to the Lake* resonates in a shot at the outset of Haneke's *The Seventh Continent*, when a billboard fills the screen. On the "Welcome to Australia" poster, an ethereal landscape confronts the viewer. Rolling waves surround a bluish mountain range; from the strip of sand adjoining the breakers, a few extraterrestrial-looking rocks jut into the foreground. This utopian Australia complements – and eventually replaces – the dystopian Austria the family members inhabit and to escape from which they commit suicide. The sign bespeaks deliverance, extending a hope that this world withholds from the protagonists. The desire and necessity for translation becomes a literalized wish for *Über-setzung* to a distant continent that exists only in fantasy. In another segment of *The Seventh Continent*, the Pascalian desire for departure (which also always implies a return) – "vous êtes embarqués" – is condensed into a similar, breathtaking image (see Horwath 1991: 15). Shortly before her willed suicide, the little girl has a vision of a white boat strung with garlands, gliding past the junkyard in which she stands. In Haneke's *Benny's Video*, teenage Benny, after having committed a murder and fled to Egypt with his mother, witnesses floating white boats in the night, as Bach's organ music from the TV fills the room and signals his redemption (cf. Metelmann 2003: 100). However, while these images have been tied to social anomie in the industrialized West and have occasionally been linked to Austria's repression of its fascist past (Metelmann 2003; Derobert 1993), I postulate that they remember a historical loss – that of the multilingual, multi-ethnic empire the present state of Austria once was. Haneke combines this anamnesis with the transhistorical acceptance of loss in melancholic technique. The acknowledgment of such multifaceted loss already dampens the hues in *Three Paths to the Lake*'s final shot without dimming its later translatory potential.

Notes

1   In *The Ends of Mourning: Psychoanalysis, Literature, Film* (2003), Alessia Ricciardi persuasively argues that modern art is beholden to an aesthetic and ethic of bereavement, which we should emphasize today. Within modernism's bereavement and its indebtedness to lost objects inheres utopian potential, in her opinion, countermanding modernity's speed, modernism's fetishization of the new, and postmodernism's superficial consumption of the old as fashion. Successful mourning work, Ricciardi writes (siding with Freud against Lacan), requires a "form of repetition . . . that, unlike the repetition-compulsion of the death drive, is benign and opens up the possibility of a renewal of the object" (25). What she describes as a bit-by-bit recuperation of the past through the psychic effort of mourning is what has gone missing in a "postmodern politics of transience and detachment" (46).
2   This narrative fragmentation, utilized first in his film adaptations, is later carried over into Haneke's glaciation trilogy, *The Seventh Continent* (1989), *Benny's Video* (1992), and *71 Fragments of a Chronology of Chance* (1994). The two-second-long black leader in *71 Fragments*, for example, obstructs the viewer's access to a linearly unfolding plot and continually reminds him or her of the lacunary relationship that a translation has to an original.
3   In Werner Hamacher's extended reflection on *erkennen* and Benjamin's transcendental language philosophy, he relates recognizability (*Erkennbarkeit*) to communicability (*Mitteilbarkeit*), and recognition (*Erkenntnis*) to communication (*Mitteilung*) (2001: 174–6).
4   The period, inserted within the parentheses in the English translation published 2002 (I: 251), is not present in the German edition and adds a definitiveness lacking in the original (VI: 159; cf. German editors' note VI: 635).
5   The comma before the subordinating clause is absent in the original (VI: 159).
6   Irving Wohlfarth explains the goal of bad translators: "Es sind gerade die schlechten Übersetzer, die Vermittler, die an unmittelbare Lösungen glauben. Anstatt die reine Namensprache durchscheinen zu lassen, bringen sie die unreinen Zeichensprachen auf gemeinsame Nenner und erzeugen anstelle einer mittelbaren Unmittelbarkeit deren schlechte Parodie – eine unmittelbare Mittelbarkeit" (2001: 112).
7   His *Kunstwerk im Zeitalter seiner technischen Reproduzierbarkeit*, with its emphasis on the liberating possibilities of film, or his montage-method in the *Passagen-Werk* may seem more fruitful embarkation points for a journey into film adaptation. Anne Friedberg (1993) utilizes Benjamin's "Kunstwerk" essay and *Passagen-Werk* to construct her theory of the virtual, mobile, and gendered gaze emerging in modernity. See also the essays on Benjamin and film in Gumbrecht and Marinnan (2003) and Andrew's volume on the influence of Benjaminian thought on contemporary discussions of the image. In his introduction, Andrew argues that cinema lies between Benjamin's storytelling and translation (Andrew 1997: 5).
8   On the issue of adaptation more generally see Stam (2005a, 2005b); also Naremore (2000); Serceau (1999); Rentschler (1986). For earlier works: Richardson (1969); Bluestone (1961).
9   Paul de Man tries to rewrite Benjamin expurgated of Judaism in his chapter on the translator-essay in *The Resistance to Theory* (1986: 73–105). On de Man's relation to Benjamin's messianism, see Weigel (1997: 105–9).

10 Numerous commentators have noted the amorous overtones of Benjamin's essay without discussing the implications of this love; see Wohlfarth (2001: 113), Düttmann (2001: 146), Schlossman (2001: 284).

11 Benjamin's image of the broken vessel is derived from cabbalistic sources. According to the Gnostic Isaac Luria, all divine light has been scattered with the breaking of the heavenly vessels. See also Scholem (1977: 71, 77).

12 On the "actualization" of texts in Benjamin's sense through dialectical images, see Weigel (1997: 213–17) and Gilgen (2003: esp. 60).

13 Carol Jacobs suggests "form" for *anbilden* in her translation (1993: 136).

14 In *Entstellte Ähnlichkeit*, Weigel recovers Benjamin's use of the Freudian-inflected words *Bahnung, Unbewußtes, Verdrängung, Innervationen*, and *Entstellung* (1997: 38, 44–9).

15 Frey calls the assumption into question that a thought-language exists beyond finite languages (2001: 155).

16 His first TV adaptation was based on James Saunders's radio play *After Liverpool* and entitled *Und was kommt danach?* (1974). For a complete filmography, see Grissemann (2001: 213–17).

17 In a personal interview with the author, Haneke also professed particular esteem for Bachmann's writing (Haneke, Interview).

18 In the English translation from which I quote, the title is simply rendered as *Three Paths to the Lake*.

19 For a Derridean reading on the interrelationship between language, history, fascism, and gender in "Simultan," see Craig (2000: 39–60).

20 On the religious dimension of Haneke's early works, see Grabner (1996).

21 Under the heading "Being strange to oneself and to another," one could imagine a discussion of the relationship between the characters of Haneke's *Three Paths to the Lake* and Bachmann's original. If the opening of Bachmann's text explicitly thematizes the protagonist's sense of dislocation, recounting her foreignness in a London hotel filled with Pakistani, Spanish, Indian, Philippine, and African staff and guests (103), Haneke's film takes this sensation and magnifies it in its rendering. A long shot of an airplane taking off in broad daylight, then Elisabeth's trip by train to Klagenfurt, thereafter a taxi ride home – the viewer participates in the protagonist's frenetic pace toward her childhood home. However, as the camera shares her point of view, focusing on the city monument of the *Basilisk*, a long shot interrupts the journey. Standing behind an opening door, the camera moves forward abruptly into a bathroom, revealing a black man. He stands naked in the spacious bathroom and sternly cries toward the camera to "get the hell out." The image of the nude man remains unexplained. Further on in the film, the flashback discussed above places this episode within the segment of Elisabeth's stay in the London hotel. The scene is repeated with slight alterations – the camera's angle as well as the man's intonation has changed, and Elizabeth has been partially included in the frame as the door is pushed open. While Elisabeth's sense of alienation is underlined by another tracking shot, revealing a spying African waiter and nasty giggling maids in one of the hotel's endless corridors, the doubling of the bathroom scene revolving around nakedness and blackness bespeaks a larger alienation. The film, aware of its own loss and estrangement from its source, is forced to repeat in an effort to assimilate the original, displacing its estrangement onto problematic signifiers.

22   For Elisabeth the strange nature of his assertions – ungrounded, as she at first believes – ultimately distances her from her job, as she begins to take on Trotta's views. It also estranges her from him, since she sees his argument as a part of his untimely nature. But his temporal alienation becomes a part of her, so that she, too, becomes unmoored from her age.

References and Further Reading

Andrew, Dudley: "Adaptation," *Concepts in Film Theory* (1984), rpt. in *Film Theory and Criticism*, ed. Gerald Mast et al., 4th edition (New York: Oxford University Press, 1992), pp. 420–8.

Andrew, Dudley, ed.: *The Image in Dispute: Art and Cinema in the Age of Photography* (Austin: University of Texas Press, 1997).

Bachmann, Ingeborg: "Drei Wege zum See," *Simultan*, in *Werke*, ed. Christine Koschel et al., Vol. 2 (Munich: Piper, 1978[a]), pp. 394–486.

Bachmann, Ingeborg: "Simultan," *Werke*, ed. Christine Koschel et al., Vol. 2. (Munich: Piper, 1978[b]), pp. 284–317.

Bachmann, Ingeborg: *Three Paths to the Lake*, trans. Mary Fran Gilbert (New York: Holmes and Meier, 1989), pp. 117–212.

Bannasch, Bettina: *Von vorletzten Dingen. Schreiben nach "Malina": Ingeborg Bachmanns "Simultan"-Erzählungen* (Würzburg: Königshausen and Neumann, 1997).

Beck, Ulrich and Beck-Gernsheim, Elisabeth: *Das ganz normale Chaos der Liebe* (Frankfurt am Main: Suhrkamp, 1990).

Benjamin, Walter: "Die Aufgabe des Übersetzers," *Charles Baudelaire, Tableaux parisiens* in *Gesammelte Schriften* IV.1, ed. Tillman Rexroth (Frankfurt am Main: Suhrkamp, 1991), pp. 7–21.

Benjamin, Walter: "On Language as Such and On the Language of Man," trans. Edmund Jephcott. *Selected Writings 1913–1926*, ed. Marcus Bullock and Michael W. Jennings, Vol. 1 (1996; Cambridge, MA: Belknap, 2004), pp. 62–74.

Benjamin, Walter: "The Task of the Translator," trans. Harry Zohn. *Selected Writings 1913–1926*, ed. Marcus Bullock and Michael W. Jennings, Vol. 1 (Cambridge, MA: Belknap, 2004), pp. 253–63.

Benjamin, Walter: "The Task of the Translator," trans. Harry Zohn. *Illuminations*, ed. Hannah Arendt (New York: Harcourt, Brace, 1968; New York: Schocken, 1985), pp. 69–82.

Benjamin, Walter: "La traduction – Le pour et le contre," *Gesammelte Schriften* VI, ed. Rolf Tiedemann and Hermann Schweppenhäuser (Frankfurt am Main: Suhrkamp, 1991), pp. 157–60, 729–30.

Benjamin, Walter: "Translation – For and Against," trans. Edmund Jephcott et al. *Selected Writings 1935–1938*, ed. Howard Eiland and Michael W. Jennings, Vol. 3 (Cambridge, MA: Belknap, 2002), pp. 249–52.

Benjamin, Walter: "Über Sprache überhaupt und über die Sprache des Menschen," *Gesammelte Schriften* II.1, ed. Rolf Tiedemann and Hermann Schweppenhäuser (Frankfurt am Main: Suhrkamp, 1991), pp. 140–57.

Bluestone, George: *Novels into Film* (Berkeley: University of California Press, 1961).

Craig, Siobhan S.: "The Collapse of Language and the Trace of History in Ingeborg Bachmann's 'Simultan,'" *Women in German Yearbook* 16 (2000): 39–60.

de Man, Paul: *The Resistance to Theory* (Minneapolis: University of Minnesota Press, 1986).

Derobert, Eric: *"Le Septième Continent, Benny's Video*: Désagrégation et impuissance," *Positif* 388 (June 1993): 22–4.

Derrida, Jacques: *Memoires for Paul de Man*, trans. Cecile Lindsay et al. (New York: Columbia University Press, 1986).

Dusar, Ingeborg: *Choreographien der Differenz: Ingeborg Bachmanns Prosaband "Simultan"* (Cologne: Böhlau, 1994).

Düttmann, Alexander García: "Von der Übersetzbarkeit," *Walter Benjamin: Übersetzen*, ed. Christiaan L. Hart-Nibbrig (Frankfurt am Main: Suhrkamp, 2001), pp. 131–46.

Freud, Sigmund: "Instincts and their Vicissitudes," *Standard Edition of the Psychological Works of Sigmund Freud*, trans. and ed. J. Strachey, Vol. 14 (London: Hogarth Press, 1957), pp. 117–40.

Freud, Sigmund: "Mourning and Melancholia," *Standard Edition of the Psychological Works of Sigmund Freud*, trans. and ed. J. Strachey, Vol. 14 (London: Hogarth Press, 1957), pp. 243–58.

Freud, Sigmund: "Trauer und Melancholie," *Gesammelte Werke*, Vol. 10 (Frankfurt am Main: Fischer, 1973), pp. 428–46.

Freud, Sigmund: "Triebe und Triebschicksale," *Gesammelte Werke*, Vol. 10 (Frankfurt am Main: Fischer, 1999), pp. 210–32.

Frey, Hans Jost: "Die Sprache und die Sprachen in Benjamins Übersetzungstheorie," *Walter Benjamin: Übersetzen*, ed. Christiaan L. Hart-Nibbrig (Frankfurt am Main: Suhrkamp, 2001), pp. 147–58.

Friedberg, Anne: *Window Shopping: Cinema and the Postmodern* (Berkeley: University of California Press, 1993).

Gilgen, Peter: "History after Film," *Mapping Benjamin: The Work of Art in the Digital Age*, ed. Hans Ulrich Gumbrecht and Michael Marrinan (Stanford, CA: Stanford University Press, 2003), pp. 53–62.

Grabner, Franz et al., eds.: *Utopie und Fragment: Michael Hanekes Filmwerk* (Thaur: Kulturverlag, 1996).

Grissemann, Stefan, ed.: *Haneke/Jelinek: Die Klavierspielerin* (Vienna: Sonderzahl, 2001).

Gumbrecht, Hans Ulrich and Marrinan, Michael, eds.: *Mapping Benjamin: The Work of Art in the Digital Age* (Stanford, CA: Stanford University Press, 2003).

Hamacher, Werner: "Intensive Sprachen," *Walter Benjamin: Übersetzen*, ed. Christiaan L. Hart-Nibbrig (Frankfurt am Main: Suhrkamp, 2001), pp. 174–235.

Haneke, Michael: Interview with the author, Vienna, May 27, 2003.

Haneke, Michael: "Schrecken und Utopie der Form," *Frankfurter Allgemeine Zeitung*, January 7, 1995.

Hart-Nibbrig, Christiaan L., ed.: *Walter Benjamin: Übersetzen* (Frankfurt am Main: Suhrkamp, 2001).

Hayat, Pierre: "Philosophy between Totality and Transcendence," introduction to Emmanuel Lévinas, *Alterity and Transcendence*, trans. Michael B. Smith (London: Athlone, 1999), pp. ix–xxiv.

Horwath, Alexander: "Die ungeheuerliche Kränkung, die das Leben ist," *Der Siebente Kontinent: Michael Haneke und seine Filme*, ed. Alexander Horwath (Vienna: Europaverlag, 1991), pp. 11–39.

Jacobs, Carol: *Telling Time: Lévi-Strauss, Ford, Lessing, Benjamin, de Man, Wordsworth, Rilke* (Baltimore: Johns Hopkins University Press, 1993).

Luhmann, Niklas: *Liebe als Passion: Zur Codierung von Intimität* (Frankfurt am Main: Suhrkamp, 1992).

Menninghaus, Winfried: *Walter Benjamins Theorie der Sprachmagie* (Frankfurt am Main: Suhrkamp, 1980).

Metelmann, Jörg: *Zur Kritik der Kino-Gewalt: Die Filme von Michael Haneke* (Munich: Fink, 2003).

Naremore, James, ed.: *Film Adaptation* (London: Athlone, 2000).

Rentschler, Eric, ed.: *German Film and Literature: Adaptations and Transformations* (New York: Methuen, 1986).

Ricciardi, Alessia: *The Ends of Mourning: Psychoanalysis, Literature, Film* (Stanford, CA: Stanford University Press, 2003).

Richardson, Robert: *Literature and Film* (Bloomington: Indiana University Press, 1969).

Ryan, Judith: "Modernism and Mourning," *A New History of German Literature*, ed. David E. Wellbery (Cambridge, MA: Belknap, 2004), pp. 723–8.

Schlossman, Beryl: "Pariser Treiben," *Walter Benjamin: Übersetzen*, ed. Christiaan L. Hart-Nibbrig (Frankfurt am Main: Suhrkamp, 2001), pp. 280–310.

Scholem, Gerschom: *Von der mystischen Gestalt der Gottheit: Studien zu Grundbegriffen der Kabbala* (Frankfurt am Main: Suhrkamp, 1977).

Scribner, Charity: *Requiem for Communism* (Cambridge, MA: MIT Press, 2003).

Serceau, Michel: *L'Adaptation cinématographique des textes littéraires: Théorie et lectures* (Liège: Editions du CÉFAL, 1999).

Stam, Robert: "Beyond Fidelity: The Dialogics of Adaptation," *Film Adaptation*, ed. James Naremore (London: Athlone, 2000), pp. 54–76.

Stam, Robert: *Literature Through Film: Realism, Magic, and the Art of Adaptation* (Malden, MA: Blackwell, 2005[a]).

Stam, Robert: "The Theory and Practice of Adaptation," *Literature and Film: A Guide to the Theory and Practice of Film Adaptation*, ed. Robert Stam and Alessandra Raengo (Malden, MA: Blackwell, 2005[b]).

Stam, Robert and Raengo, Alessandra, eds.: *A Companion to Literature and Film* (Malden, MA: Blackwell, 2004).

Weidmann, Heiner: "'Wie Abgrunds Licht den Stürzenden beglücket.' Zu Benjamins Baudelaire-Übersetzung," *Walter Benjamin: Übersetzen*, ed. Christiaan L. Hart-Nibbrig (Frankfurt am Main: Suhrkamp, 2001), pp. 311–24.

Weigel, Sigrid: *Entstellte Ähnlichkeit: Walter Benjamins theoretische Schreibweise* (Frankfurt am Main: Fischer, 1997).

Weigel, Sigrid: *Ingeborg Bachmann: Hinterlassenschaften unter Wahrung des Briefgeheimnisses* (Vienna: Zsolnay, 1999).

Wohlfarth, Irving: "Das Medium der Übersetzung," *Walter Benjamin: Übersetzen*, ed. Christiaan L. Hart-Nibbrig (Frankfurt am Main: Suhrkamp, 2001), pp. 80–130.

Woodward, Kathleen: "Freud and Barthes: Theorizing Mourning, Sustaining Grief," *Discourse* 13:1 (Fall/Winter 1990/91): 93–110.

12

Michael Haneke and the Television Years

A Reading of Lemmings

Peter Brunette

Since the late 1980s, Michael Haneke's theatrical features have alternately thrilled, frustrated, and infuriated international art cinema audiences. It is illuminating to compare these films and the reactions they provoke to Haneke's early made-for-TV films, which have rarely been screened since their original airing in Germany and Austria and are completely unknown to American viewers. As this essay will argue, some crucial aesthetic differences exist between Haneke's TV work and his theatrical features, yet many of his overarching themes remain the same.

What I want to focus on here is perhaps his most accomplished work of this period, the two-part made-for-television film (both parts are full-length films), completed in 1979, entitled *Lemmings* (*Lemminge*). Part One, called, with that familiar, bitter irony that Haneke aficionados know so well, *Arcadia* (*Arkadien*), is set twenty years earlier, in 1959. Part Two, *Injuries* (*Verletzungen*), is set in the present day, that is, in 1979. Tellingly, both parts of this frequently difficult film are precisely and unflinchingly labeled "Ein Film von Michael Haneke," an unmistakable proclamation of the auteurist aesthetic underpinning them, quite unlike the directorial anonymity that accompanies made-for-TV films in most other countries, as well as the bulk of TV fare in Germany and Austria.

The two parts add up to a single, often very powerful and thoughtful film that is, even at its most predictable and schematic moments, thoroughly competent and always immensely watchable. The full frontal female nudity (along with the occasional glimpse of male genitalia) and the self-consciously, resolutely down-beat *Weltanschauung* unashamedly expressed in this thirty-year-old television production underscore, once again, the vast gulf that has always separated European television from its unrecognizable American cousin.

What I found in this film, as I expected, was the familiar Haneke moral/social critique of Western consumerist society. What surprised me, however, was that the critique was much fiercer, and yet at the same time much more formally conventional than in the later films that Haneke has subsequently become known for. For example, the precise, challenging, and often purposely cold formal techniques of the so-called glaciation trilogy (*The Seventh Continent*, 1989; *Benny's Video*, 1992; *71 Fragments of a Chronology of Chance*, 1994), which have become so well known since the director's ascension to international celebrity, are nowhere to be seen. Yet on the other hand, the bitter intensity, even anger, of the social critique in *Lemmings* goes far beyond anything in these later films. In other words, while Haneke's critique in this film seems occasionally so strident that it recalls the less palatable side of the director's work and personality – the hectoring scold and unassailable moral arbiter (think, perhaps, of *Funny Games*, 1997) – the cinematic technique itself is most often completely unremarkable.

The most obvious explanation for the lack of formal fireworks is related to the television medium itself, where money is always scarce and aesthetic experimentation, as with mainstream Hollywood cinema, needs to be kept to a minimum to attract the largest possible audience. Television aesthetics and spectatorial address are also, of course, determined by the viewing situation – non-theatrical, domestic, distracted, only partial attention – and by its product – serialized soap operas, news items, and entertaining sitcoms with laugh tracks. Hence, the emphasis on the close-up, serialized, dialog-driven narratives chopped up into small, easily consumable bits. In Germany and Austria, specifically, TV's *Bildungsauftrag* (educational mandate) also compelled programmers to commission literary adaptations and social problem films, which require conventional dramatic handling and a clear-cut *mise-en-scène* that caters to social and psychological realism that is generally (though not automatically) narrower in aesthetic terms than art cinema and even post-classical Hollywood cinema.

The reasons behind the overwhelming, often excessive bitterness of the socio-ethical critique are more complicated. For one thing, it is probably a mistake to analyze Haneke's work of any period solely in terms of the thematic protocols of international art film production or, at the opposite end of the spectrum, made-for-television features. Rather, the profound unhappiness that engulfs so many of his characters – in the TV work but even in the later films – has to be understood as closely related to that which infects the characters of his countrywoman and Nobel prizewinning writer Elfriede Jelinek, who also concentrates on horribly lost souls who seem to act out their frustrations and near-enigmatic malaise to an extent that seems counter-intuitive and self-destructive. Ulrich Seidl, another Austrian filmmaker who is a decade younger than Haneke, can probably also be included in this group, given the immensely powerful, but overwhelmingly dark and despairing vision of such films as *Tierische Liebe* (Animal Love, 1995), *Hundstage* (Dogdays, 2001), and *Import/Export* (2007).

Obviously the "causes" of such similar, dark views of the world, and especially of Austria, will always be complexly over-determined. Ultimately, however, I think it can be plausibly argued that much of it is traceable to Austria's particular relationship to the events before, during, and after World War II, especially regarding the country's complicated, never resolved, never even examined relationship to Hitler (who was of course born in Austria) and the Nazi party. Other countries, like France, have had their own postwar devils to wrestle with, especially in terms of the elaborate discourses of "victimhood" that have had to be generated by each social collective, but Austria has had particular difficulty justifying its warm embrace of the *Anschluss* while all the while claiming bragging rights as Hitler's "first victims." In addition, of course, the Austrian population and military suffered much more severely than the French (for whom the war was essentially over by May 1940), and we see the scars of this ambiguous, compromised, and far from noble suffering in both Haneke and Jelinek. It should also be added, in passing, that the autobiographical element might also be profitably taken into account in trying to understand a film like *Lemmings*, given the fact that the characters who populate it are the same age as the director who created them and come from the same town (Wiener Neustadt) in which he grew up.

Part One, set in 1959, is drenched in American rock 'n' roll and populated by deeply dissatisfied Austrian teenagers. The crisp cutting and almost metallic images that Haneke later became famous for in a film like *71 Fragments* are in short supply in both parts of *Lemmings*, and, as mentioned earlier, the paucity of means normally afforded to a television director is painfully in evidence. Hence, for example, zooming is used to focus the audience's visual attention or to substitute for editing, which would be far more expensive, another device usually associated with television's limited financial means. Minor reframings of characters within scenes are often accomplished through a small, awkward zoom rather than through camera movement, and cutting is always kept to a minimum, though here it seems to be an economic choice rather than an aesthetic choice, as in the later films. All thematically significant dialog is captured in the traditional manner, in an extreme close-up, which is usually the stopping point of a zoom.

The camera occasionally undertakes fairly elaborate pirouettes to change angles on a character in a tight space, say, in a bathroom, but these movements seem motivated, once again, more as cost-saving measures than for their thematic import. One salient, striking visual device that is used in almost all Haneke's later theatrical films – that of concentrating for long minutes on objects and the material facticity that surrounds his bourgeois characters before showing us their faces, thus preventing us, in a quasi-Brechtian fashion, from identifying with them until well into the film – is almost completely missing here. Instead, we are more conventionally introduced to all the characters' faces and entire bodies from the first moment they enter upon the scene.

Part One opens with a group of shots of an anonymous town (later identified as Wiener Neustadt), in what will later become Haneke's familiar deep blue-black, as if to suggest that what we are about to see concerns an entire town, maybe even an entire country, and not just the specific individuals we will meet. Paul Anka's "Lonely Boy" blasts on the soundtrack, like a more benign version of John Zorn's extreme punk music that will rudely interrupt the opera arias at the beginning of *Funny Games* some twenty years later. What follows is a long tracking shot of a string of vandalized cars, with only the most minimal agency – an anonymous hand pulling off a hood ornament – shown, though this image will return and be explained at the end of Part One. Haneke thus employs a conundrum-like circular metaphor (question raised at the beginning, answered at the end) that will reappear in Part Two.

We next see some young girls doing their homework and, significantly, discussing issues of authority found in the Ten Commandments, especially but not only the parental variety (a sample from their textbook: "We should obey all authorities because their legitimacy comes from God"). When they turn to another commandment they are studying, "Thou Shalt Not Commit Adultery," a tittering embarrassment ensues. So two central themes of the film – sexual repression and the older generation's authority or lack of it – are stated and linked from the very beginning. Slightly later, we will return to the girls who take turns silently reading about sex (they're too embarrassed to read the passage out loud), smoking illicit cigarettes, and moonily dancing with each other to Brenda Lee's "I'm Sorry."

Class resentment makes an appearance early on as the working-class father of a charming young man named Fritz makes disparaging remarks about his well-to-do friend Christian – it's obviously not only the teenagers who are angry – but as with most of Haneke's later films, the political divisions are factually posited as one more point of conflict rather than explored in depth.

We next briefly meet Mrs. Leuwen, the mother of two of the central teenage figures (Sigurd and Sigrid, both confusingly called "Sigi" throughout) who is confined to her bed, a state of affairs with obvious symbolic meaning, like that of her crippled husband, as we will shortly see. The next cut is to a dancing school attended by all the principal teenage figures we will meet, and significantly, they resemble automatons as they follow the dancing teacher's robotic count. At this point the first of a series of shocking white and red titles bursts onto the screen, as in *Funny Games*. The first one is "Lemmings," and the immediate cut back to the dancers implies that they constitute a perfect example of the title we have just read. The principal couples are introduced in this manner as we cut suddenly back to a second red title, "Part I: Arcadia," then back to the dancers, and then finally to the identification of Haneke as auteur.

At this point, Haneke foists upon us an explanatory, rather heavy-handed title card in case we don't get the full import of the film's title itself: "Lemmings: a type of vole. Compact bodies. 7.5–15 cm long. In recurrent migrations that often lead to the ocean, where the lemmings drown, decimating their own kind in collective suicide." The pointed bluntness of this information, which some might label pretentiousness, is mitigated by its obviously "scientific" tone, as though what we are about to see is a dispassionate intellectual demonstration conducted by Haneke. Its effect is also enhanced by the utter lack of sound that accompanies and thus underlines it.

Later in the film, Mr. Leuwen, the father of Sigurd and Sigrid – he too is crippled, both literally and figuratively – even goes so far as to thematize the meaning of the title in a speech he makes to his daughter Sigrid that is obviously intended to be the central moral pronouncement of the film: "You are all lemmings. They burrow into their own filth. Completely absurd. And you all have but one goal: To croak as soon as possible!" In Part Two, Sigrid, twenty years later and now grown up, will repeat her father's words to her friends.

Haneke's proclivity for self-contained vignettes, rather than fully elaborated, seamlessly sequenced scenes, a proclivity that he will put to such good use in the later films, particularly the multi-part narratives *71 Fragments* and *Code Unknown* (2000), is already in evidence here, and the film alternates quickly, somewhat like a melodrama or even a soap opera, from story to story. Fritz, a talented high school student of modest means, is having an unhappy affair with Gisela, the wife of his Latin professor, whom he greatly admires. His friend Christian, who comes from a well-to-do family, is trying to persuade his girlfriend Eva to sleep with him. In this pre-pill, pre-sexual revolution era, both women of course get pregnant and, in a repressive country in which such women are ostracized or, if they are students like Eva, actually expelled from school, their condition hangs constantly over their heads and determines all their actions. Eva will have to abandon all hope of further study, and the professor's wife Gisela, also known by Fritz as "the shepherdess" (a pun on her last name, Schäfer, which means "shepherd" in German), is shown in a horrifying scene repeatedly jumping off a table and pounding her abdomen in an effort to abort her pregnancy. This entire scene unfolds in virtually a single long take, and thus looks forward to the extensive use the director will make of this technique in the later films.

Intergenerational conflict abounds and the young people are never just in trouble or even unhappy in this film, but clinically depressed, full of rage, and often suicidal. But these symptoms are already present in their parents. After Sigurd, in an extreme close-up, has woundingly asked his crippled father whether he has ever really *liked* anything in his life, Mr. Leuwen smashes his son's dinner plate with one of his crutches, out of pure frustration with an offspring who prefers to smoke cigarettes while listening to "Puff the Magic Dragon" than to speak civilly to his father. Similarly, Gisela confesses to Fritz while they're in bed after sex that she wants to destroy everything around her, including all the furniture. "It obstructs me. Confines me. Makes me dependent." Haneke is always careful to limit himself to merely hinting at the causes of these inchoate expressions of intense, violent dissatisfaction, without ever offering specific social or psychological explanations. Rather, all seems part of a sickly *Zeitgeist* whose causes are multiple but difficult to pinpoint.

Sexual frustration looms large, but one wonders whether it hasn't always done so, in every generation of the modern era, without necessarily leading to insanity and suicide. Perhaps Haneke is suggesting that the frustration regarding repression and rules insisted upon by a discredited older generation was at its height right before the advent of the sexual revolution and the collapse of authoritarian structures that would come with the 1960s.

The professor is humiliated in class by the public revelation of Fritz's affair with Gisela, and when he confronts her with the truth, she rushes to the sink and throws up. After slapping her, he casually lights her cigarette. Eva is willing to sleep with Christian to "be like other couples" and to "give him what he wants," but in the event is deeply depressed by her experience, even before she finds out that she is pregnant. Sigurd spies on the neighbors through the window, while rubbing his groin, then heads straight to the bathroom – avoiding the blinking red light, his bedridden mother's signal that she needs something – presumably for a rousing session of masturbation. By this point we fully realize, as we focus for a long time on the fruitlessly blinking red light while Sigi remains in the bathroom, this is definitely not 1979 American television.

A mild foretaste of Haneke's patented use of sudden outbursts of inexplicable violence (*Code Unknown*; *Caché*, 2005) comes when Sigurd playfully gets his family's maid Anna to try to strangle him in the bathroom, then applies a sharp jiu-jitsu blow to her waist that leaves her shocked and in tears. Meanwhile his sister Sigrid is playing lovely classical music on the piano. The juxtaposition of sick unwhole-someness and idealistic aesthetic beauty recalls a standard cinematic topos in postwar European films of the "contradictions" the Nazis were capable of, most notably captured in Rossellini's *Rome, Open City* (1945), where Nazi officers play Beethoven on the piano in a room next to the torture chamber.

In a long tracking shot that will also become a staple in Haneke's formal reper-toire, Christian and Eva discuss whether or not to have sex. Christian does not insist, but Eva seems to think it's important to "do everything that is necessary." Subsequently, they have their awkward sexual encounter, in a brilliantly sketched scene in which Haneke captures the crippling ignorance and vulnerability of this pre-sexual revolution moment as powerfully as does Ian McEwan in his novel *On Chesil Beach* (2007). With so many obstacles and pitfalls to avoid, and with so much at stake socially speaking, sex has come to seem something enormous to them. Later, post-coitally in bed, Christian asks if she is disappointed. "No, not really," she replies, "just sad." But when he goes to the bathroom, she begins sobbing because she is afraid that he will no longer respect her. "I feel so guilty, I just wanted to make you happy."

The love-making between Fritz and Gisela is just as sad, as a cut to them in bed, with Fritz turned coldly away from her, makes abundantly clear. He is irritated when she cries – virtually every love scene in the film is accompanied by female tears – but then confesses that he needs her too, because he has "no one else." In an odd detail, Gisela keeps knocking her head on an overhanging bookshelf and the tension this produces (either intentionally or by accident of *mise-en-scène*) adds to the nervous tension of the scene. Fritz wars with his working-class mother and father, of whose "vulgarity" he is deeply ashamed, when his beloved professor sends a letter informing them of their son's perfidy with his wife. Fritz's

father can only respond with imprecations and physical violence. Once her pregnancy is discovered, Gisela tries to abort her fetus through a variety of desperate
and dangerous means. Their final breakup comes during a conversation in Gisela's
car, parked in a lonely spot in the forest. Haneke beautifully and wordlessly concludes this scene with three purposely alienating shots: First, a two-shot of them,
staring straight ahead (like the zombie figures of *The Seventh Continent*) through
the windshield that reflects the trees to the point of obscuring the two figures;
second, a more distant shot, in which the humans can no longer be seen, from
the upper right; and finally, an even more distant shot from the upper left.

Eva's pregnancy leads her to threaten suicide while walking with Christian, in
the same tracking shot as before, and she becomes obsessed with a news item about
a young girl who killed herself by sticking knitting needles in an electrical outlet.
As with many of Haneke's subsequent characters, the newspaper article says that
the reasons for her suicide are "unknown." Christian tries to argue her out of it,
saying he wants to talk to her "reasonably," a motif that will continue to gather force.

Sigurd, once he is revealed as the source of the vandalism of all the fancy Mercedes
that we saw at the beginning and during the middle of the film, will actually accomplish the suicide that Eva attempts but fails at. This act comes after a wild rock
'n' roll party which features, along with Little Richard's "Tutti Frutti" and Fats
Domino's "Blueberry Hill," a lot of heavy petting and complaisant parents, who
nevertheless do not like their automobiles vandalized.

Following Sigurd's death, the Leuwens question Sigrid closely, trying to understand why their son and daughter, who has also been involved in the vandalism,
have spent so much time destroying things (Fig. 12.1). The father is simply unable
to comprehend something so "unreasonable," and this is obviously an important
point for Haneke, this gap between generations in understanding and in the dif-
fering criteria (or lack of them) for making ethical judgments. Looking forward
to something that appears frequently in the theatrical films (and in Haneke's interviews about them), Sigrid can only say, "I don't know why we did it. It was fun."
After Mr. Leuwen speaks the crucial bit of dialog about the younger generation
being nothing more than lemmings who wallow in their own filth and seek death
as quickly as possible, Sigrid tells him that Sigurd's last words, as he lay dying
after jumping off the roof, were, "Another cripple in the family!" Hearing this,
Anna, the servant, smiles silently to herself.

Similarly, Eva's father, another member of the older generation still committed to the rule of reason (though it must always be remembered that this "rule
of reason" also produced the Holocaust), reiterates again and again to Christian,
while they're having a beer together (and while Eva is simultaneously trying to
electrocute herself in the basement) that it simply "makes no sense" why Sigurd
would vandalize all those cars for "no reason," especially since he was so well off.
When Christian replies that maybe he did it "in protest," the older man can only
very reasonably ask "against what?" Christian's cryptic, existentialist reply, which
dumbfounds Eva's father, is "against everything."

Fig. 12.1 Sigrid (Eva Linder) and her parents. *Lemmings* (1979), dir. Michael Haneke, prod. ORF and SFB.

It is also during this scene that Eva's father reveals a crucial (if somewhat implausible) piece of historical information that goes some way toward explaining *something*, or at least seems to, especially given how long Haneke has withheld it. This is the revelation that Mr. Leuwen is crippled and Mrs. Leuwen mentally unbalanced and bedridden because, while being strafed by an allied airplane during the war, they threw themselves over their children's bodies to protect them. Nevertheless, the very fact that Haneke withholds this revelation so long indicates that it can never be more than a partial explanation of the children's personal alienation or, even less, that this sort of guilt-inducing sacrifice, now unthinkable, can explain the anger of an entire generation. Perhaps Haneke has introduced this historical detail merely to heighten the contrast between generational attitudes toward duty and other values, since one can scarcely imagine the younger generation acting in such a self-sacrificing fashion to protect their own children.

It also seems to resonate with some of the material worked by Elfriede Jelinek, especially in *Wonderful, Wonderful Times* (1990 English translation of *Die Ausgesperrten*, 1980), in which the tyrannical father has lost his leg in the war. Yet the father's brutality in the Jelinek novel can never provide a sufficient reason for the children to have become such cruel and hateful sociopaths, nor can this wartime anecdote of the strafing ever explain the "inexplicable" anti-social actions of Sigurd and Sigrid. Again, the alienation of the present generation seems to have taken on a viciousness that ultimately transcends reason and thus defies understanding.

Though Haneke is parsimonious with explanations that emanate from within the form and content of the film itself, or from an invisible directorial consciousness, the characters themselves are perversely voluble, especially in *Lemmings*, Part Two: *Injuries*. They are always ready to offer extensive verbal evidence about how bad they feel without simultaneously experiencing the need to probe – except in the vaguest, most unconvincing fashion – why they feel this way. Thus, when asked by Christian what it's like making love to the professor's wife, Fritz declaims, "I don't believe we can do anything else beside serve ourselves with the bodies of others. The closer we get, the more that one thing leads to another. The only thing that one really feels is sadness, maybe. Or maybe longing" (Fig. 12.2). The origin of such a self-serving attitude, however, is never suggested, even indirectly. Consumerist society, the legacy of World War II and the Holocaust, social and sexual repression, the Cold War? Yet Haneke is right that unhappy people, especially an entire generation, rarely understand the reasons for their unhappiness. And as the director has insisted over and over in later interviews, no novel or film can ever fully explain anything.

Part One ends with Sigrid going off to Vienna presumably to make her way in the world and to escape the cloying provincialism that seems, at times at least, to be a principal enemy for all the young people. On a whim, Christian travels part of the way with her and they jokingly "break the rules" by smoking in a

Fig. 12.2 Christian (Rüdiger Hacker) and Fritz (Wolfgang Hübsch). *Lemmings* (1979), dir. Michael Haneke, prod. ORF and SFB.

non-smoking compartment. Christian confesses guiltily to Sigrid that he didn't really try to prevent Eva from killing herself. He too would like to go away, he says, but he and Eva have decided to leave school and get married. "Why can't you just get an abortion?" Sigrid asks. "We're in Austria, in Neustadt!" he replies bitterly. "How do you abort a baby here? You're traveling forward and I'm traveling backwards." But then he jokes that it's only an optical illusion, referring to the fact that she is sitting facing the direction in which the train is moving, while he is on the opposite side. He then blurts out, "I don't think I can bear it any longer, this whole mess." "I think you should try," she suggests softly. "Yes, but you're going away." His last ironic comment to her, after he has gotten off the train to return to Neustadt, is that "I don't think it was an optical illusion after all."

The final shot of Part One of the film is Christian waiting in an interim train station. The visual field of the extremely foreshortened long shot is stuffed with entrapping lines that hold him firmly pinned in physical, and by clear implication, psychological position. He is little more than a dot amid the multiple horizontal and vertical lines that seem forever inescapable. For the first time in the film, we hear not American rock 'n' roll on the soundtrack, but what sounds like traditional Austrian folk music.

Part Two, set in the present day of 1979, is more directly, and less ironically, subtitled *Injuries*. In fact, it begins dramatically with a car crashing into a tree, but we don't know who the occupants are. In this way, perhaps, the scene is meant to apply symbolically to the fate of the entire group or generation from Part One, whom we will now be watching two decades later. We next cut to a woman in bed. We naturally think it's someone who's been injured in the accident, but then we discover a man sleeping next to her, who turns out to be her husband. So it's not the survivors of the accident, after all, and this is only the first of many conscious reversals that seem to indicate that the individual characters aren't really important in themselves, only insofar as they collectively represent this "injured" generation. (In a similar fashion, Haneke names virtually all his main characters in the theatrical films varieties of "George" and "Anna," and has referred to the pair of malefactors in *Funny Games* as "artifacts" rather than real characters.) This dynamic also looks forward to Haneke's penchant for withholding character and narrative information in order to demonstrate that things are not always what they seem. By a delicious irony, however, when the crash is shown again at the end of the film, it turns out to be this very woman, now safely lying in her own bed, who is indeed the victim of the crash.

The woman, we learn later, is in fact Eva from Part One, though what confuses things for the viewer is the fact that she, like all the other characters, is now played by a different actor. (Beside the obvious practical implications of this choice, it is also one more way for Haneke to make the characters "typical" and generic rather than individualized.) We watch as the family goes through its bourgeois morning ritual that Haneke so loves to document in so many of his films, though now, unlike in the later films, we see their full bodies and are allowed

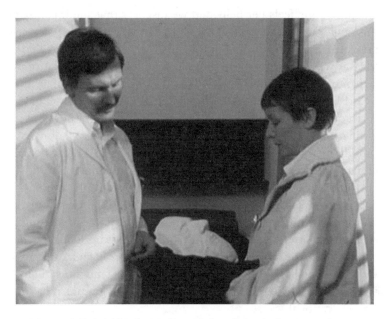

Fig. 12.3 Fritz and Sigi (Elfriede Irrall) with her father's death mask. *Lemmings* (1979), dir. Michael Haneke, prod. ORF and SFB.

to begin to relate to them. Setting the tone is their son's retelling of a fearsome nightmare he has had in which there was "no one to rescue me," and a bit later Eva has to slam her door shut on the hand of an aggressive panhandler, causing the first of many "injuries." The family is so nice and wholesome-seeming that of course we expect something awful to happen to them. And we won't be disappointed.

We are next reintroduced to Sigrid (Sigi), who is now pregnant, and who has returned home from Vienna to deal with the aftermath of her father's death. She meets Fritz, who has become a physician in the hospital, and is presented with a death mask of her father, in white plaster, that her father has requested following an old custom no longer much in use (Fig. 12.3). She says, coldly, "it makes no difference to me that he's dead," though this sentiment is belied to some extent when she suddenly breaks into tears. In any case, even though she escaped to Vienna twenty years earlier, and even though she now refuses to view his body, his presence/absence impinges on her life. She also has a bizarre encounter with a clergyman who accidentally drops and breaks the death mask, perhaps signaling the ultimate irrelevance of the older generation, now departed. It is the young people who have taken their place, perhaps becoming very like them in the process.

When Sigrid returns to her family's opulent apartment, all of the furniture is covered with white sheets and will remain that way throughout the film. Even the phone that she tries to use is dead. Nothing more clearly indicates the death of the older generation and the unwholesome vacuum they have left in the lives of their offspring. She feels her belly and we discover that she is pregnant, and it is upon this single fact that the bulk of the film's thematic meaning will come to rest. Bach's mournful "Sarabande from Suite #5 in C Minor" is heard on a non-diegetic solo cello, as it will be several more times at significant, contemplative moments.

We next move back to Eva, who, we discover, is having an affair, though her husband Christian is as yet unaware of it. She tells Christian that "I have the feeling that I am on a very thin rope. I can keep my balance right now, but the smallest thing will cause it to snap and then everything will collapse. I don't know what to do. Nothing matters to me any more. You, the children. I don't notice it when you're all here, but when I'm alone I just sit here, I don't feel anything. I feel like a stone. I try to feel something for myself, but there's nothing there."

In the meantime, Fritz and his wife Bettina (who was present only briefly in Part One), along with Christian and Eva, are invited by Sigi to a reunion dinner. Fritz's wife Bettina bitterly attacks her husband and ends up suddenly cutting him on the hand, in yet one more instance of the signature Haneke gesture of unexpected and thus shocking violence. She denounces the smugness of all gathered, but again, Haneke seems to regard her rage as a historical given that has no specific, but only a generational, cause.

She is brought back to her senses by a quick slap from Sigi (another moment of sudden Hanekean violence), and after she apologizes, Sigi recounts to those assembled her father's speech about the lemmings, from Part One. Truth to tell, this over-emphasized repetition of the father's words seems a bit heavy – especially if you've just watched Part One – but it works nonetheless. After Fritz and his wife leave, Christian agrees with Bettina's assessment and says that Fritz has become "vain, cold, and indifferent." He continues, "We're all too scared to let out our rage. I guess I delude myself into thinking that it's possible to keep together what fell apart long ago." Christian refuses to say any more because he doesn't want to "hurt" anyone, using the verb *verletzen* from the subtitle of Part Two.

Sigi's answer is to have a child, she says, but Christian bitterly replies that "we brought three into the world so that it would 'help' against the tedium, our fear, or the devil knows what. There is nothing, absolutely nothing, that we can be proud of, that we can hold on to. Unfortunately." Inchoate teenage protest in other words has turned into a desire for some sort of accomplishment, but this generation is too enervated to achieve it. (And by showing that having children has done nothing for Eva and Christian, Haneke also subtly undercuts the potentially cloying symbolism of Sigi's child as panacea for all unhappiness.)

However, the vagueness of Christian's explanation for their unhappiness ("tedium, our fear, or the devil knows what") is made more concrete in several scenes that follow closely. For example, at a training session for the police, Christian hears an ultra-graphic, yet passionlessly delivered technical explanation of what happens to the inhabitants when an atomic bomb is dropped on a city. Moral issues are completely excluded and probably never even occur as a valid point of discussion to the majority of the participants. Christian walks out, however, and throws up over and over. (He has spoken earlier to Eva about seeing a doctor because he has been vomiting and thus it is ultimately impossible to tell whether his reaction in this specific instance has a physical or moral cause, or both.)

The film moves back to Eva. When her lover Peter leaves her, she is disconsolate and hospitalized, and subsequently is reunited with Fritz, who has come to visit her. Explaining her affair to Fritz, in a tight close-up, she says that "I was trying to buy some warmth with a little sex. I couldn't figure out the source of indifference [in Christian], and Christian didn't care and didn't take it seriously. He can't show his sympathy. We're freezing next to each other and it's not very funny. We're like two kids in front of a pile of toys which are very precious and complicated but nobody taught us how to play with them. Either we leave the pile of toys alone or we break them all." She then proposes to a startled Fritz that they begin an affair. Later, when Christian tries belatedly to show some "warmth" to her with some forced sexual attention, she rebuffs him.

Sigi takes an Antonioni-like walk through the city where she encounters some children fighting, a dead cat with vividly bright blood leaking from its mouth, and a bucket falling off a roof that almost hits a small girl. She is obviously anxious, perhaps about what Christian has said about the meaninglessness of it all, and goes back to her family's apartment, where all the furniture remains covered with white cloths, offering a perfect, visually empty accompaniment to the sad Bach cello piece we hear once again on the soundtrack.

Eva and Christian have a fight about Eva going out, obviously on a date with Fritz. She tells Christian that she doesn't care if they divorce, and she doesn't even care whether he gets the children either. After a loveless tussle and some low-grade violence from her husband, she arrives at Fritz's apartment. On the television, in perhaps another stab at a more concrete "explanation" of the depressing state of these *verletzte* lives (and parallel to the atomic bomb from the earlier scene), is a report about the Jonestown tragedy in Guyana, where hundreds have died blindly following their leader's command to commit suicide. Here Haneke seems to be treating the television news media as a neutral source for disturbing content, rather than as a major cause of the lack of genuine communication that afflicts contemporary society, as he will in the later films. Eva asks for a cognac, which is the same drink she had chosen during her first sexual encounter with Christian, in Part One, which was fully as awkward as the present one.

Literalizing things even more is a copy of one of the versions of Francis Bacon's disturbing *Study after Velazquez's Portrait of Pope Innocent X* (1953), which improbably adorns Fritz's bedroom (Fig. 12.4). Fritz makes things perhaps a bit too earnestly explicit by claiming that this painting "fits our situation nowadays, the situation of all of us. He screams, but behind the glass." Eva rhetorically and somewhat implausibly asks, "Why do we all hurt each other? Why can't we live without hurting others? Why can't we treat one another gently?" Fritz responds that there are only two possibilities: "Indifference or injuring [*verletzen*] others and getting injured oneself." His wife Bettina, he says, has told him he is incapable of love, but actually

Fig. 12.4   Fritz and Eva (Monica Bleibtreu) stand in front of Bacon's *Pope Innocent X. Lemmings* (1979), dir. Michael Haneke, prod. ORF and SFB.

he is good at it precisely because he is so indifferent. "Despite everything," he concludes, "we should try to be friendly." When Fritz and Eva decide to sleep with one another, Bacon's blurred pope is momentarily right behind and between them. In bed, Eva begins to cry, and then apologizes for it, and Fritz chastises her. "You need to unlearn having a bad conscience if you don't feel anything," he lectures, and recounts a story about killing his father's canary in order to make himself stop feeling bad about a teacher he had a crush on. At this point Haneke purposely makes another link among the characters – thus once again making them varieties of a type rather than specific individuals – by having Eva blow her nose in the sheet, which is what Gisela did after having equally sad sex with Fritz in Part One. Eva tearfully complains that "someone else is living my life for me, I'm not there." The mournful Bach cello piece concludes this sad scene and makes a mockery of their passion.

Sigi next goes back to the priest in the hospital for help, but finds him in an apartment overflowing with empty wine bottles. She tells him, in a TV-style close-up, that she has now decided she doesn't want the baby, because it won't help and everything has just gotten worse. "Don't you feel it, father, when you see people in the street, when you talk to your friends, you see that cold rage in their faces? That hate. How can a child grow up in that environment, how can I justify that? I can't even turn on the TV without crying. How can the announcers stand to say such things without screaming or crying? I know there are good and delightful things, but the fact is that everything hurtful and bad sticks out better in your memory."

She confesses to him that she tried to kill herself eighteen months earlier, while driving in the Alps, and recites a presumably authentic statistic that the suicide rate of children between the ages of eight and twelve has gone up 70 percent during the last year. The priest replies that, unfortunately, the church cannot help the hate she feels in herself and others. "The worst is that we are robbed of our self-respect, robbed of the life around us, because we are only allowed to live without dignity," he opines. "And that only we ourselves are to blame for losing it. The Middle Ages are over, no one relieves us of our guilt anymore." Nevertheless, Sigi seems to have drawn some solace from the mere encounter with the priest, another human being with whom she has connected, at least, if not a convincing spiritual advisor, and makes a little joke: "Don't worry, with a kid in your belly, especially one so big, you can't really kill yourself."

This minuscule but nevertheless measurable turn toward life, at least in her case, is reinforced in the following scene in which, lying in bed at night, she decides to get up and, using binoculars, surveys the simple, banal, but possibly decent, maybe even good, life that is going on around her in the various apartments through whose windows she can see.

The other half of the binary that Haneke is clearly offering us, that of Eva and Christian, has no potential for redemption and remains murderous. Christian, now seriously ill, morally blackmails Eva into going away with him for two weeks without the children so that they can be reconciled. After a dissatisfying consultation with Fritz, who unhelpfully recommends that she simply do what she wants to do, she reluctantly agrees to go on the trip with Christian. We watch as she and Christian leave the children at their grandparents' house and drive off in their car. After he inexplicably pulls off onto a side road, the car picks up speed and Christian crashes its right side into a tree. (It is difficult to determine whether Christian is attempting a murder-suicide or just trying to murder his wife.) We suddenly realize that this is the shot with which Part Two began, making everything that follows in the film, technically speaking, a flashback. An ambulance pulls up as we see, in the foreground, Eva's head sticking out through the broken windshield.

Then we cut suddenly to the sound of a woman screaming, whom, in the general collapse of individual characters into each other to represent an entire generation, we at first take for Eva in an emergency room somewhere, especially when the only thing we see on the visual track accompanying the screaming are some cold-looking instruments. The camera pulls away to reveal Sigi, not Eva, putting an oxygen mask to her face, and then continues to pull away to an empty long shot, until we understand that, all the while screaming horribly, she is giving birth. What is most bitter here is that, in the terms of the opposition between Eva and Sigi, even choosing life and birth over death means "hurting" someone or oneself. The soulful Bach cello piece returns.

In the final scene of the film, snow falls softly on a long, narrow road. People are riding horses and a man is purposefully striding toward us. It's Christian, with his left arm raised in a rigid sling, in a kind of grotesque parody of a Nazi salute

Fig. 12.5   Christian's "Nazi" salute. *Lemmings* (1979), dir. Michael Haneke, prod. ORF and SFB.

(Fig. 12.5). He shouts orders to passing recruits. "Am I dead for you?" he yells at them. "Politeness doesn't exist anymore for you! Why are you in this academy? You believe that nothing matters anymore. Attitude is dead. Honor is dead. Dignity is dead!" It seems clear that he has now become the previous generation which he and his fellows have so despised. We hear jet planes flying over, as the camera moves into an extreme close-up and then freeze-frames on a grotesque shot of his open, angrily contorted mouth. "But what still matters?" he shouts. "What matters? WHAT MATTERS???"

After the angry posing of this question – which this two-part film has taken nearly four hours to demonstrate is thoroughly unanswerable – we hear, under the freeze-frame, the command "Platoon march" issued by another voice, presumably that of the new generation that will challenge the earlier generation now represented by Christian. The sound of heavily tramping boots, redolent of another common metaphor of fascism, predominates, and the freeze-frame of Christian's screaming face turns into the familiar violent red of the title card of the film. Suddenly displayed against this red field is "LEMMINGE" in bold white letters, almost as a final, fruitless attempt at an explanation or answer, and the film comes to an end. The juxtaposition of the automaton-like boots and the title recalls the opening of the film, in which the title was applied to the younger generation learning, like robots, how to dance. Haneke seems to be suggesting that this new, as yet unseen generation, in other words, has the potential for being even more dangerously unhappy than his own.

13

Variations on Themes

Spheres and Space in Haneke's Variation

Monica Filimon and Fatima Naqvi

In Michael Haneke's two-part television drama *Lemmings* (1979), a strange painting becomes the site of verbal foreplay, the discussion revolving around it a prelude to intimacy. The doctor Fritz Naprawnik (Wolfgang Hübsch) tells the woman who has just entered his apartment for a rendezvous that his Francis Bacon painting *Study after Velazquez's Portrait of Pope Innocent X* (1953) is an appropriate allegory for contemporary life. The dematerializing papal figure that looks as if it were falling in a black void – mouth agape with horror and impotence – embodies, in his view, the individual's isolation and inability to communicate with others. To his soon-to-be lover Eva Beranek (Monica Bleibtreu), Fritz argues that the image "rather precisely describes our situation"; the pope is "screaming, but as if from behind glass." Responding to her incredulity, Fritz comments further on the relationships established "behind glass." "I think," he tells her, "that there are only two possibilities: indifference or injuring, injuring others and getting injured oneself." The same scream of helplessness is invoked at the end of the film when the jilted husband Christian Beranek (Rüdiger Hacker) – who is responsible for Eva's death in a car accident – finds himself alone in his pain. He is dismissed both by the impersonal state for which he works (its disembodied voice orders the army to march) and, more relevantly, by his children who play around him, apparently unaffected by their mother's death. Whether the characters' "screaming" passes beyond the glass of the television and whether one needs to injure others or oneself in order to feel alive in a state whose institutions do not engage in a direct dialog with the individual – these are the major themes of this film that are reprised in Haneke's later work.[1]

Modulations of these themes are to be found in Haneke's television production *Variation, or "Utopias Exist – Yes, I Know"* (*Variation oder "Dass es Utopien gibt, weiß ich selber!"* [1983]), on which we will focus in this essay. *Variation* is the unspectacular drama of two middle-aged people who abandon their respective partners for a love affair. The film is, however, spectacular both in the short-lived achievement of its protagonists – who manage to open up to each other – and in what becomes the director's long-term commitment to questioning the capacity of television (and, by implication, film) to imagine a new kind of intimate sphere with transformative potential for the withered public sphere. In *Variation*, the filmmaker suggests that a restructuring of the public and private spheres is possible. The illusionistic relationship between the diegetic spaces within the film and the extra-diegetic space creates an opening toward the viewer, who is actively involved in the creation of this other sphere.

Sites of Engagement

The definition of the public and private spheres owes a great deal to their close metaphorical relationship to real sites and locations. In reflecting on this connection, Haneke's early works for television partake of a larger concern of the postwar period: The changing character of the public and private spheres as they relate to physical space becomes the locus of intense debate among German academics beginning in the late 1950s. In works such as Hannah Arendt's *The Human Condition* (1958; translated in 1960 into German as *Vita activa* by Arendt herself), Jürgen Habermas's *The Structural Transformation of the Public Sphere* (*Strukturwandel der Öffentlichkeit*, 1962), and Alexander Mitscherlich's *Die Unwirtlichkeit unserer Städte* ("The Inhospitality of Our Cities," 1965), the imbrications of space and society are analyzed at length.[2] At the outset of his discussion of the transformation of the bourgeois public sphere, Habermas points out the difficulty in defining categories such as "public" and "private." He resorts repeatedly to physical space in order to anchor his argument about these abstract entities, as in the following example at the beginning of his work:

> We call events and occasions "public" when they are open to all, in contrast to closed or exclusive affairs – as when we speak of public places or public houses. But as in the expression "public building," the term need not refer to general accessibility; the building does not have to be open to public traffic. "Public buildings" simply house state institutions and as such are "public." (Habermas 1989: 1–2)

Habermas bemoans the disappearance of the intimate sphere by way of his reflections on architecture, which serves as a direct expression of the disintegration of the critical, participative public. In the manner in which Habermas uses specific sites to make and qualify arguments about the social realm, so too does Haneke rely on physical spaces in his film to make larger claims about human interactions. These spaces navigate between public and private spheres and attempt to carve out something approaching the intimate sphere of past centuries. Habermas identifies the intimate sphere as the "core" of the private sphere. It is originally the locus where the individual's subjectivity forms by means of interaction with others (1989: 55). In its most positive definition, Habermas claims, the intimate space is where "human beings who, under the aegis of the family, were nothing more than human" (1989: 48). Habermas admits that the bourgeois public sphere arises out of the illusory idea that the intimate sphere is somehow separate from market forces. Nonetheless, this intimate sphere is an indispensable realm of illusion. Note the recurrence of the verb "seem" in the following definition of this sphere:

> It seemed to be established voluntarily and by free individuals and to be maintained without coercion; it seemed to rest on the lasting community of love on the part of the two spouses; it seemed to permit that non-instrumental development of all faculties that mark the cultivated personality. The three elements of voluntariness, community of love, and cultivation were conjoined in a concept of the humanity that was supposed to inhere in humankind as such and truly to constitute its absoluteness: the emancipation (still resonating with talk of "pure" or "common" humanity) of an inner realm, following its own laws, from extrinsic purposes of any sort. (1989: 46–7)

Haneke represents this intimate sphere of the family in all of his films as the potential crucible for a new kind of public, albeit one that has given up on overt socio-political goals. Even when the passive consumption of packaged ideas has replaced the ordinary citizen's analytical and negotiating agency in the latter half of the twentieth century, the utopian allure of the familial intimate sphere persists. Haneke's films of the mid-1970s and early 1980s partake of a wider German trend, whereby political issues recede from public consciousness to be replaced by an engagement with private problems. This "new inwardness or new subjectivity," of course, thereby paradoxically moves the private squarely into the purview of the public.

In Haneke's films, the physical impossibility of a real space in which individuals can interact face to face is shown repeatedly; what remains is the supposedly one-way "space" of the television (interestingly, Haneke has to date refrained from examining the interactive, hyperreal space of the Internet). *Variation*, at the beginning of the director's career, sketches the collapse of the public and private spheres into one another. Haneke addresses the solitary individuals in front of the television "glass," constructing an imaginary space of dialog for them and so bridging the gap between the viewers' private screening rooms and the public nature of the film. In this way, *Variation* attempts to make viewers aware of a new, simultaneously intellectual and intimate sphere, both public and private, between the filmic text and themselves. The film, like its protagonists, constantly oscillates between creating social closeness between viewers and characters and dissociating them from each other, between encouraging social bonding and rendering it impossible.

Setting the Stage

Variation opens with an extended prologue in which the major themes of the film are introduced. In the first segment, the dislocation of voices and sounds corresponds to the breaking down of the private and public distinction. Sound bridges connect the initial shots before the title is shown and introduce all the major figures and their locale, which takes on particular importance. Viewers meet the busy, yet gloomy, Berlin; Georg (Hilmar Thate) and his soon-to-be lover Anna (Elfriede Irrall) discuss his sister Sigi's (Eva Linder) childhood fear of gigantic, all-surveying angels; family photos of Georg, his wife Eva (Monica Bleibtreu), and Sigi are shown; Georg, Eva, and Sigi argue about Goethe's drama *Stella*, which explores the question of whether individuals can be happy in a familial threesome; and, finally, Sigi returns to her room to play the cello. Sounds located somewhere else invade most of the frames. Georg's interview about his sister's childhood fears is superimposed on the montage of different views of Berlin; Anna and Georg's earlier dialog played on a tape recorder overlays their silent meeting in the present; Sigi's cello playing accompanies the slow pan over Georg, Sigi, and Eva's family photos; and, at the end of the prologue, Eva's reading of the count's story from *Stella* follows Sigi into her room when she starts practicing her instrument. By way of the sounds, the other person is constantly present in his or her absence; the sounds carry the distant and recent past into the present-tense frame of the image. In this way, they function as mediators in the here-and-now of the frame, suggesting that, without the intercession of an acoustic element, the individual cannot connect to the city (in Georg's case in the first sequence), another individual (in Georg and Anna's case), or even the self (in Sigi's case). The personal stories that are verbalized segue into the public realm, as becomes clear particularly in Georg's story about his pupils, with which the film opens. By expressing their "very personal fears" in paintings and drawings about the apocalypse, the children take part in a larger social dialog. Their works, we find out at the end of the film, are to be exhibited in a gallery.

The destabilization of the viewers on an acoustic and visual level is both the necessary by-product and the price for their participation in the film. In the first sequence of the film, the intimate and the public are already so imbricated that they also call each other into question. The otherwise public space of the hectic city is revealed to be part of the characters' intimate vision, an impression that the story of Sigi's childhood conveys. She feared over-sized angels, who could discern her every move. The gradual reduction in camera distance from the extreme long overview of the city to a street-level long shot of indifferent passers-by reinforces this perception. Georg's present voice creates, as mentioned, a disjunctive acoustic temporality, injecting the little girl's 1960s fears into 1980s Berlin. With the camera, the already disoriented viewers visually advance toward the city in the absence of any reassuring anchor.[3] The viewers have to choose between identifying with the huge angel in the story, whose syncopated descent into the middle of the crowd throws them into a hostile city, or identifying with the middle-aged male voice, which offers a more narrow, human view. This first film segment, opening with a blank frame, fades into the blinding image of the sun, so that viewers are also enjoined to move between identifying with an omniscient Father-voice coming from beyond and suggested by the sun, and dissociating from it since they cannot make sense of the connection between Berlin, the voice, the child's anxiety, and the conditions for the telling of this particular story. The lack of a clear-cut narrative agent in these shots and the disquiet arising from omniscient surveillance certainly comment on the aftermath of German terrorism and express a general uneasiness toward any ultimate "Father" force. However, the shots also serve as a meta-reflection on the paradoxical nature of Haneke's filmic storytelling. While the viewers are actively involved in the reconstruction of the narrative, the conditions for the witnessing of such a narrative are uncongenial. Their purportedly democratic participation is constantly threatened by the intrusion of an omniscient perspective.

In this manner, the film creates a willfully disorienting space impregnated with emotion from the outset. The city is presented as a social product in which the perceived, material space of the streets and buildings is redefined through the characters' imagination and traumatic experiences and so takes on the qualities of what Edward Soja has called a "Thirdspace," a "fully *lived space*, a simultaneously real-and-imagined, actual-and-virtual . . . locus of structured individual and collective experience and agency."[4] This is no longer merely the everyday, material space of the apartment building in which an interview takes place or the abstract space of the girl's fears, but also one of constant inquiry into the personal and collective history whose social "products" the figures in the film are. This kind of perspective opens up the metropolis to subjective exploration on the part of the characters involved in determining the emotional significance of familiar but ever-shifting spaces. It also opens the metropolis to the viewers whose inhabitation of the filmic space is filtered through emotions they share with the protagonists. Georg and Sigi, for instance, are intimately connected through the phantasmagoric vision of the watching angel, and viewers share in their intimacy through the haptic descent of the camera onto street level.

It becomes very difficult to sustain this insinuated closeness, however, when Haneke calls attention to filming as a public, recording act in the next segment. The fatherly voice "naturally" telling the story of childhood existential fears is revealed to be a mechanical voice on a tape. The cut to the close-up shot of the tape recorder becomes a subtle comment on the man-made character of any (hi)story, personal or collective, and also on the individual's necessarily indirect relation to it via analog modes of reproduction. If viewers attribute the voice on the tape to the man they see on the screen, it is merely because they are trained to connect space and time, image and sound. Such connections are contingent.

The camera – which had been pulling us more and more into a terrestrial environment – moves away from the first characters it encounters, Georg and Anna, who are listening to the tape. Instead, the camera turns its attention to the children's drawings, showing how they imagine the apocalypse and what images plague them at night. The close-up tracking shot along their drawings suggests a more immediate, authentic access to the Thirdspace of collective experience via their works than by other, analog means. The children's drawings also reduce the viewers' apprehension about the state of the isolated individual at this historical juncture: All the drawings are of public spaces under threat. From the global atomic "mushroom" cloud, to the neighborhood attacked by fighter planes, to the globe clutched in one claw, and, finally, to the row of people struck by lightning, no human being faces the terrible end alone. In each child's imagination, refracting the conditions of the Cold War and ecological catastrophe, there is a vision of shared humanity that is besieged. Georg's disappointment with older children, who "[have] already learned to show nothing of themselves," suggests that the process of acculturation actually produces children's awareness of an external, critical public for their most private emotions and a resulting sense of alienation from others. In Georg's view, contemporary Western culture eventually does away with the innate feeling of belonging, within one's most private self, to a collective. This minor thematic strand in *Variation* takes on greater importance in Haneke's later cinematic oeuvre, where children are both more prescient and sentient in regards to changes in their environs than the emotionally stunted adults around them.[5]

Not only the tape recorder, but the family photos of the next scene also bemoan the lacking intimacy, to which the children's drawings still attest. The dissolve from one set of images into another provides a telling contrast – the tracking shot continues to the right, highlighting the change in media. The drawings give way to family photos, whose sharp lines and clear dimensions lack the drawings' aura of authenticity and immediacy, as well as the sense of a collectively lived experience that gave the children's pictures their force. The staged photos introduce the viewer to the fabricated narrative of the middle-class family, whose memories are organized around the proper musical education expected from the children in a bourgeois household.[6] The portrait photos are exhibited as a measure of familial cohesion and conventional humanity.[7] The camera finally focuses on two particular photos, one of Georg and Sigi smiling and the other, to the left, of Eva, Georg's wife, looking protectively to the right, her gaze "missing" the two siblings. The members of the family are in this manner framed separately, but the couple that defines the present state of affairs is an incestuous one: The brother and sister are divorced from the wife. As viewers are soon to find out, the three seem to form an unconventional family in which the roles are fluid. A careful inspection reveals the parents' absence from the photos and raises the question of the kinds of intimacy a family can achieve in their absence. In light of the post-1968 moment in which *Variation* was made for Sender Freies Berlin (SFB), Haneke injects his generation's working-through of the parents' involvement with fascism into a present that is deemed deficient perhaps because the parents are missing.[8]

The final clues of the prologue relate to the viewers' implication in the collapse of public/private distinctions and their role as audience. These hints are embedded in this last, less ambiguous scene, which is, as such, different from the preceding ones. Viewers are at once part of the public performance and outside it, on the screen and in front of it, part of the audience, but also beyond it.[9] The family album is followed by a long shot of the interior of a house, with the stairs featured prominently on the left and a long hallway to the right. The house is in darkness and, as characters come in and move into one or the other rooms, the camera remains fixed on this transitional space. The viewers' perception of filmed theater is further reinforced by the way in which the different sections of this "stage" are lit at different moments, drawing attention to the deliberate implementation of theatrical devices within the televisual medium. Although two-dimensional, the characters are enlivened by the impression of three-dimensionality associated with theater. In addition, the film borrows the simultaneity of experience that characters/actors share with their audience and which, in this case, reinforces the witness position already attributed to the viewers in the initial segment. (The film returns to this staging of the viewers' role in the final segment.)

By making clear the reference to theater, *Variation* continues the self-reflexiveness Haneke introduced earlier; it ascribes to television a preeminent role in the establishment of a public sphere in a post-theatrical age. Eva and Georg have returned from a performance of Goethe's *Stella* (1776/1806), and they are involved in an amicable dispute about the two endings of the play. The literary debate about Goethe's variations is reproduced within the private space of the family on screen, which transfers to television the role literature played in the construction of the public sphere by means of literary debate in Habermas's account. In *Variation*, the discussion revolves around whether three people can willfully enter a *ménage à trois* and achieve happiness. Georg considers the second ending of the play, in which the three lovers commit suicide, more realistic, while Eva supports the version exalting a shared three-way love. Haneke's film is a variation on this theme, for the characters will not resort to violence, nor live happily ever after. At this point, Eva is optimistic because she has been sharing her husband with his sister and the threesome is agreeable to her. The film opens up their intimate spheres to issues that are, ultimately, of public relevance: Can people "feel humanity" toward each other, as the count and wife do in Goethe's play, and come to terms with each other's desires, or is this impossible?

The utopia of shared love is subtly questioned from the beginning of the scene. At no point do the three characters share the same frame, and they barely share the space of their cluttered, but homey, kitchen.[10] The argument does not lead to a better understanding of each other's viewpoints and, implicitly, to the strengthening of the intimate sphere: Sigi refuses to get involved, Georg is partly amused by Eva's insistence on getting to the heart of the story, and Eva seems relentless to demonstrate that she is right. Georg does not follow Eva's reading, but instead constantly interrupts her with offerings of food. The surface harmony of the household comes from Sigi's self-withdrawal to the upper regions of the house and from the characters' passive acknowledgment of each other. They all listen, but none of them hears what the other has to say.

The act of listening moves into the foreground at the end of the prologue, and the soundtrack indicates the public function of music. As Eva continues reading, Sigi returns to her room and starts playing the cello. What seemed to be non-diegetic music in the shot of the family photos is revealed to be the sister's music. When Eva's reading overlays Sigi's room, it renders the space private; when the room becomes the site of a performance, it suddenly becomes public, as in a concert. For the third time, the film collapses private/public distinctions. First, the intimate space of Anna and Georg is created through a public, recorded inter-view and, second, the apparently private space of the house is "staged," is turned into theater, for an audience external to the film narrative. The intimate sphere of the bourgeoisie – with which Haneke is always and exclusively concerned – is repeatedly shown to be the public sphere, with and against the signs of decrepi-tude in Habermas's analysis of its structural transformation. The TV public is reminded of its critical function in the creation of this public sphere, which in turn is supported by a seemingly intimate sphere. That this self-critical, self-reflexive, and self-productive function becomes difficult to carry out for the viewers has hope-fully become clear.

Two in a Bubble

The opening shots of postwar Berlin suggest that all spaces are remapped in the postwar period, resulting in ambiguous relationships within inherited, obsolete notions of social spheres and physical structures. However, the peaceful coexis-tence in non-bourgeois relationships that is envisioned in *Stella* appears, in parts of the film, like a realizable goal, especially where Georg and Anna deepen their relationship. In certain moments, the intimate becomes public; a form of "public intimacy," to borrow the title of a book by Giuliana Bruno, comes into existence between the lovers. Anna and Georg's love affair takes place in public places, and their most tender moments are always in front of others. Subway trains, a half-built cultural center, flights of stairs, phone booths, the post office, or a café become sites of close interaction, while the bathroom, the living room, or the bedroom fail to fulfill their expected role.

Indeed, certain moments in the film seem to redraw the public and private spheres along lines the controversial German philosopher Peter Sloterdijk envisions in recent work. In his three-part work *Sphären* ("Spheres," 1998–2004), he redescribes the intimate sphere that Habermas outlined forty-five years earlier; Sloterdijk literal-izes this discourse. In his first volume, entitled *Blasen* ("Bubbles," 1998), Sloterdijk does so by concretizing the metaphor of the sphere, in order to show that all human relations are essentially circular and contained. Bubbles, in his view, surround human beings, whether they are the embryo's amniotic sac, the child's soap bubbles, or the Trinitarian sphere of medieval church imagery. Such bubbles form basic morphological entities; with them, people give shape to their experience of being-in-the-world and conceive of themselves as intimately connected with one another. In his not unproblematic reflections, Sloterdijk supports his theories with allusions to fine art, and a series of art historical reproductions (Hieronymus Bosch, Masaccio, Dürer) is embedded in the book. While the relationship of image to text is not explicated, it seems to be one of illustration, that is, the two people who are slipping in and out of a gelatinous bubble in Bosch's *Garden of Earthly Delights* seem to underline the assertion on the facing page that "[people] always have their existence exclusively in exhaled, divided, torn, reconstituted space. . . . If people are *here*, so largely in spaces that have opened for them, because they have given them form, content, expansion, and relative permanence by living in them" (1998: 46). Haneke's early television works, in which torn-up, fragmented urban space serves as an analogy of the dissolution of intimate relationships, engage in a quest for whole, complete spaces[11] – spaces morph to fit the people moving in them, as they search for their complementation or supplementation through one another. The incompleteness of space, as a result, lets the viewers draw certain inferences about the characters' inability to create meaningful bonds with others.

The site of Anna and Georg's spiritual communion, where they recognize their mutual vulnerability, is important in this regard. Georg searches for Anna at a lecture on the individual's role at the end of the twentieth century. The lecture is part of an opening ceremony at the inauguration of a cultural center. The edifice, however, is still under construction. The striking use of transparent plastic sheets for walls and ornamental, potted trees heighten the segment's artificiality – both suggest a fake, unfinished setting. The frozen attitude of the audience, still attired in warm outerwear, is contrasted with the mobility of the camera, which careens through the full auditorium, finally coming to rest behind the podium. Georg bursts through the plastic partitions as if into a bubble, to quickly transport Anna out of the space and into another, contiguous space, where they can constitute their dyadic relationship. Here Anna and Georg are captured in a compelling two-shot as light streams in through a plastic partition separating them from the auditorium. Their own translucent membrane surrounds and shields them. The speaker's voice from offscreen resonates with this image: He quotes a Brecht text stressing the importance of being a "good lover" in some unspecified "future." The two characters then abandon the weighty intellectual debate about the future for a journey through the porous building. The camera moves rapidly with them in the search for a secluded room. As Anna and Georg make their way up the stairs, their newly found emotional closeness is visually captured in a long, overview shot of a rounded flight of stairs. This second bubble shot in *Variation* suggests, to some degree, the coziness of a Sloterdijk sphere (which is always displaced by and replaced with

Fig. 13.1   Anna and Georg in a "bubble." *Variation* (1983), dir. Michael Haneke, prod. SFB.

others). The recognition of another person's special presence gives rise to a visually arresting image.[12]

Telling Stories of the "Occidental Crisis"

The moment of storytelling is essential both to the consolidation of the nascent intimate sphere between the two characters and to a certain closeness between viewers and characters about the developing affair. Anna starts to recount the story of one of her authoritarian teachers, whose tales remain vivid in the minds of his former students. In Haneke's films of the 1970s and 1980s, the adults are weighed down by memories of loss and are cut off from an emotional involvement with past generations – as such, Anna is not worried about how and why her teacher suddenly disappeared. These adults feel trapped or "condemned" like the boy thrown into the dungeon in the teacher's story. It is not difficult to discern a parallel between the adventure story and the situation of the society depicted in these films, which grapples and denies its own "being-in-spheres." Its occidental crisis articulates itself in a number of ways in *Variation*, ranging from failing modes of interpersonal communication, the relationship established when people look at each other, and on to the connection with plant life in the urban environment.

Without light, without sound, without another human being, the boy in the story is trapped in a cell, where a "loss of orientation" results, as Anna explains. As Anna reveals her fear of never finding an answer to her questions, the camera slowly tracks in from a long shot of the protagonist framed within the rectangular light coming through the window to a close-up of her insecure expression at the end.[13] The light, which places Anna in the center of the frame, reproduces the screen in front of the viewer, thus contributing to the fusion of private and public spaces. The intimate space created between Georg and Anna is consciously opened up to public viewing. The prolongation of the narrative binds the listeners/viewers to the narrator, and points to the importance of continuation within television's narrative economy: Only if viewers' curiosity about the next plot twists is piqued do they remain invested in the continued circulation of such stories within society (as Haneke had seen with his two-part *Lemmings* four years earlier). The ending of such a series can be perceived as a kind of sentence ("sentenced" like the boy in the story). But Haneke himself shows that this narrative economy does not necessarily have to function in this way: In the dark, a true intimacy can be achieved, one that concentrates on the narrating voice and not on the images' light. The frame goes black; we only hear Georg and Anna whisper to each other about their partners and love lives. Georg's match lights the scene only briefly. The whispering, the heavy breathing – lovemaking and storytelling are brought together in this scene. When Georg leaves the building later, non-diegetic music (a rarity in Haneke's case) heightens the moment's beauty and the happiness that results from a narrated, shared intimacy.[14]

The narrative act, the presence of the storyteller, and his audience revive a type of intimacy that Walter Benjamin considered gone with the rushing, ever-expanding modern world, in which one no longer feels the constant presence of death within the lived space. The encounter with death, for Benjamin as for Haneke (whose debt to the German-Jewish philosopher has yet to be systematically explored), used to be the source of the conscious encounter with the self and with the community of others who share the same terror of extinction. For Benjamin, the individual's consciousness of a shared space guarantees memory and, implicitly, one's awareness of mortality, the very reason for the storyteller's authority.[15] In *Variation*, Haneke places his characters in the vicinity of an emotional and spiritual death that comes with isolation and the frustrating incapacity of creating or preserving the longed-for nearness to others. The use of offscreen sounds and voices internal to the story, as well as the overhead point-of-view shot, constantly insert the viewers as witnesses into the text. In this particular sequence, one learns not only of vanishing people but also of Anna's anxiety vis-à-vis imprisonment and death. Her story reinforces Georg's initial story and his sense of vulnerability to inexplicable events. Through Georg's offscreen voice, viewers are inadvertently asked to identify with him, since his position across from Anna is similar to theirs; when Anna looks offscreen at Georg, she seems to be addressing us. In this way, Haneke achieves a fleeting moment of shared exposure to death. The characters' anxieties and fears are unveiled not only to themselves and each other, but also to the viewers inserted as the unseen witnesses.

At this moment, Anna seems to be searching for a sign of understanding in Georg's face – and, by extension, in our faces. Francis Bacon's *Study after Velasquez's Portrait of Pope Innocent X*, with which we began our essay and which plays such a prominent role in Haneke's *Lemmings*, is reproduced in Sloterdijk's *Blasen*, to suggest that all human beings profoundly depend on seeing each other's face in everyday life. Bacon's image of individual horror presumably contrasts with the positive relationships human beings form with one another in the act of facing one another (again, the relationship between text and image remains untheorized in Sloterdijk's book): "The assertion that people have their faces not for themselves but for others counts for the whole older history of human faciality," Sloterdijk writes in a somewhat awkward formulation, drawing on Emmanuel Lévinas. He continues: "A face first is visible to the gaze of the other; as a human face, it possesses the ability to return its own being-looked-at-ness with looking-at-the-other" (1998: 198). For Sloterdijk, theories of auto-eroticism and narcissism deny the fact that the experience of self-reflection was not widespread until the nineteenth century, with the mass production of mirrors. Self-knowledge based on a confrontation with the self can only take place in and around the reciprocated gaze. The self-constitution through the face of the other occurs at the end of the above-mentioned segment, when Georg's match captures the lovers in a two-shot: The intensive gaze in the eyes of the other leads to a declaration of love. Only now can Anna take pleasure in her own image in the next segment, when she laughingly removes her makeup in front of the mirror.

Nonetheless, the scream of the isolated individual in Bacon's study remains the model for Haneke's interpersonal relationships in the film; intimate public bonding does not last. The Baconesque cry rupturing such fleeting ties of commonality comes from the hurt partner – particularly from Anna's companion, the actress Kitty (Suzanne Geyer), who wants to be loved "a little bit more" and whose screaming face congeals into a distorted expressionist mask. In the interior spaces of the shared apartment, a theatrical, outward-turned intimacy cannot be kept alive, despite the actress's efforts to exteriorize her inner life.[16] As Bruno shows in an essay from *Public Intimacy* entitled "Fashions of Living: Intimacy in Art and Film," the realm of the home (*domus*) becomes a battleground in the desired domestication of the partner.

The lesbian couple live in an expansive *Altbau* (a late nineteenth-century building with spacious, high-ceilinged apartments, characteristically popular during this period with students, intellectuals, and a certain segment of the bourgeoisie) that is invaded by plants. At one point, the quarreling lovers collapse into their own jungle. There is a particular morbidity about the repeated use of potted plants to enliven closed spaces, whether it is the lecture hall where Georg looks for Anna, Georg and Eva's living room, the café in the final scene, or even the city in the few shots Haneke takes in order to suggest the arrival of a new season. Eva finds

Anna's letter for Georg in the mailbox in a medium shot of the hallway in which oversized, tangled plants frame her fragile figure. Kitty reproaches Anna for her empty civility ("You confess your sins to me and then all is forgiven, right?") in a medium shot in which the vegetation completely obscures the background window. The plants' domestication fails, as do the attempts to domesticate the partner. The seeming naturalness of all familial relations is repeatedly called into question by the all-encroaching flora.

Here, too, one could see parallels to the account Sloterdijk offers in *Blasen*: where our post-human age looks to artificial means of personal supplementation (Sloterdijk gives the example of Andy Warhol and his tape recorder, which Warhol calls his "wife"), earlier cultures sought mythical answers to the question of the "foundational alliances of souls." He points to the images of the tree of life, the *arbor vitae*, which symbolized the integration of human beings into a communal "inner world space" (*Weltinnenraum*).[17] In a strange series of shots before the final scene in *Variation*, where the four partners meet and speak past one another in a kind of split-screen mutation, the plant symbolism intrudes as a kind of narrative excess. Before the final meeting of Anna, Kitty, Georg, and Eva in the restaurant, the film includes a series of shots showing parks and boulevards with water fountains springing up against glass-and-steel buildings, of men transporting potted trees in cars or through botanical gardens, and highways carved across oases of vegetation. The viewers are reminded that such a controlled environment is only a poor substitute for the natural world. Similarly, the rhetoric of civility only masks the lack of genuine attachment. We are reminded that these trees no longer have the spiritual meaning that earlier societies accorded them. This denatured nature hardly conceals the highways and broad boulevards that cut through the wounded, degraded environment. In the same way in which Anna's empty civility hides the lack of empathy (Kitty looks in the mirror at the end of their fight, because she cannot see herself in the other), the trees are meant to hide the city's inhospitability.

The denatured city acts back on the people who live in it. In his political pamphlet *Die Unwirtlichkeit unserer Städte*, Alexander Mitscherlich underlines this chiastic relationship between humans and urban environments: "People create a living space in cities, but also a field of expression with thousands of facets, but in a reverse manner the city's form shapes the social character of its inhabitants" (1965: 9). The chiastic relationship between urban space and communal well-being is no longer perceived as such. This is amply evident in the functional separation of living from working quarters, nature from architecture, and in the pseudo-attempts at integration in *Variation*. The lack of contrasts in the depicted urban regions changes our perception of the nature in it. According to Mitscherlich, everything that reminds us of nature looks like it has been technically altered, as if it were packaged.[18] In such spaces, there is no possible public intimacy. Only an "unboundedly intrusive intimacy" or "complete lack of interest" reigns ("*schrankenlos zudringliche . . . Intimität*" or "*vollkommene ... Interessenlosigkeit*," 98). The oscillation between extreme aggressivity and hyperemotionality on the one hand

and disinterest and coolness on the other is shown in the contrasting manner in which the two women play their roles. Suzanne Geyer's Kitty tends toward such intrusive intimacy, whereas Elfriede Irrall's Anna leans toward disinterest.[19] In the interaction between Anna and Kitty, Haneke reveals an entire society's incapacity for public intimacy.

Kitty chases an illusion of wholeness with the other that has already long escaped her, and desires a supplementation that necessarily fails. Her shriek at the end of the scene (or Christian Beranek's primitive yawp in Lemmings, Part Two) signifies the horror and helplessness of her postwar generation to defend the ideal of human closeness in an age in which the desire for a clinical break from the past has alienated individuals from their common memories and sites of personal connection. Blinding white light dominates the scene, especially in the shots in which Kitty is framed against the window. This cold light opened the film and characterizes the final scene in the café: the light of Benjamin's "sanatoria and hospitals," of perfect but detached civility, of surveillance and alienation.[20] Haneke repeatedly uses this light in scenes where couples confront one another, such as the piano teacher and her student in The Piano Teacher, or in Andreas Pum's final confrontation with God in The Rebellion (1992).

In the last scene in Variation, this blinding whiteness is used to show the alienating "socio-spatial dialectic" (Soja 2000: 8) of the city and its inhabitants. Kitty climbs to the second floor of the café where all the former lovers have agreed to meet. The whiteness surrounding her denies this public space any potential for the kind of intimacy we have been outlining. This segment is a visual representation not only of the dissolution of public and private spaces, but also of the disturbing effect this dissolution has on the intimate sphere.[21] Filmed in the clinical light of previous scenes (versus the rainbow spectrum of past storytellers), the characters demonstrate their incapacity to engage with each other "without hurting each other all the time" (as Anna remarks in her argument with Kitty and Eva says to Fritz in Lemmings). The private battles are carried into the public space, where Kitty and Eva provoke Georg, and where Georg reacts to both women with open dislike. A theatrical element is inserted again, when the table becomes the setting for a staged scene. Kitty refutes Anna's efforts to mind her place in public; she literalizes Anna's admonition "not to make a scene" and insists that she is witnessing the "strangest/funniest private comedy." She denies the distinction between public/private. Tellingly, Anna, who attempts to maintain the obsolete dichotomies, cannot find the clarity she strives to have: the whiteness of the toilet, to which she retires to write Georg a quick departing note, returns us to the whiteness of the opening shot. This will hardly be the place for self-cognition. She even declines to look in the mirror: "I understand nothing," she writes, "not even myself."[22]

Eva, her voice coming from offscreen, complements Kitty's meta-filmic role when she triggers the filmic space of Sigi's suicide attempt. When she points to the source of Georg's decision to come to the meeting, namely his desire to calm a "guilty conscience," we suddenly see the bathroom where Sigi tried to kill herself. The parallel cutting between the café and the bathroom where Sigi is performing a carefully calibrated suicide is actually a cross-cutting collapse of the two spaces into one, neither public, nor private – this hybrid space is unmistakably intimate to all the characters and, implicitly, to the viewers. Sigi's attempted suicide belongs to a previous time and place, but her detached meticulousness and paced manner provide a conspicuous contrast to the apparent nonchalance with which the characters chat about their daily lives at the table. These two spaces "cue" each other perfectly: Anna and Georg cannot find an apartment for themselves because feelings of guilt toward their former partners trouble them. The immediate cut to the white tub Sigi prepares for herself visually indicates another source of their restlessness. The answer to the "occidental creativity crisis," the "abendländische Kreativitätskrise" in Georg's words, lies precisely in forgetting the victims of the search for intimacy. The sudden cut from Georg to Sigi's glass of pills implies a brutal search for self-realization through the other that does not take into account the fragility of the relationships that have already been established. The lack of self-confidence on the part of the abandoned Eva and Kitty, conveyed through a filmic transgression, echoes Sigi's lack of self-esteem and wish for death.

The suicide attempt marks the social unconscious of the meeting and of the film as a whole. The older generation fears or feels guilty about the emotional breakdown of the younger generation, yet rarely confronts this fear (the children's drawings being a notable exception). Instead of focusing on one character at a time, Haneke forces them on the screen simultaneously (as he will later in *Code Unknown*), and the viewer has a hard time following the cacophony of voices. Snippets from each monologue nonetheless reveal each character's innermost fears: Eva tells of her attempt to regain sexual self-esteem by trying to sleep with another man, while Kitty talks about the offer to play in a televised production and thus restore the professional self-esteem she exclusively based on Anna as her private spectator. The public space of the frame, in the sense that it is open to myriad viewers, registers two different private spaces (of Eva and Georg on the one hand, and of Anna and Kitty on the other) and two intimate spaces, one of the visible "victims," Eva and Kitty (seated side by side), and the other of the invisible "aggressors," Georg and Anna (seated across from them). Both are ultimately collapsed into one common, intimate space of pain via Sigi's act. Paradoxically, the only intimate sphere all characters achieve rests not on their vulnerability as victims of an alienating, dividing end of the millennium, but on their aggressivity as perpetrators of further social dissolution.

The possibility of shared responsibility vis-à-vis the future is short-lived. Anna cannot find a rational explanation for her own feelings and decides to leave Georg at the end of the meeting. The party breaks up and, as Eva, Kitty, and Georg leave, the overview long shot of the entrance to the café and the melancholic, non-diegetic piano notes supplementing it reintroduce the viewers as god-like witnesses, at once connected to the characters and their complicated emotions and thoughts and divorced from them. The ending is a shot sequence of all characters isolated within their respective spaces. Georg wanders through the city and becomes a spectator of Woody Allen's *Annie Hall*, Sigi calls somebody from the clinic where she is still a patient, Eva takes off her makeup in the bathroom at the end of the day, Kitty acts on stage, and Anna looks blankly ahead at the wheel of her car. Whether public or private spaces, these locations are largely widowed of their intimate potential and function as places of self-alienation. Viewers share the characters' confusion about the proper course of action that would reconcile the individual's need for self-fulfillment through intimate connection with others and the feeling of moral responsibility toward those with whom one shares memories and the physical space of a house.

Haneke, however, refuses to provide a univocal ending, opting to move the viewers into the foreground and, through this gesture, empowering them. The last segment renders visible their placement, which has constantly been brought to the fore through the film's self-reflexivity. In the movie theater where *Annie Hall* is playing, viewers are positioned on the implicit theater screen; *Variation's* character Georg and his fellow viewers become the possible audience for the now fictionally embedded witnesses. Haneke's camera becomes a storyteller who refuses closure and dissolves the public and the private into each other. Like the figures in *Variation*, viewers are isolated within a multitude: All share the film's screen space and yet remain within their own private rooms in front of the TV. Any intimate sharing is only momentary (for the duration of the film), and the enduring community of all private viewers ultimately remains an unrealizable goal. The camera can only suggest the possibility of establishing an intimate sphere with its viewers – who are left to return the embedded audience's gaze, to confront the other's face. Haneke's later films will turn up the soft volume of the non-diegetic music in *Variation*, so to speak, and "scream" to provoke further self-questioning.

Notes

1 This conglomeration of themes has contributed to the prevalence of the phrase "glacia-tion of emotion" – a phrase Haneke himself employed to describe his first works for the cinema – being used as a kind of shorthand to describe Haneke's oeuvre.

2 Where English translations of the cited German texts are available, we have used them; in the absence of translations, we have offered our own.

3 The identities of the man who is speaking and of the girl whose story he is telling remain unknown at this point; by the end of the prologue, viewers can deduce that the two are Georg and his sister, Sigi. Furthermore, the vision of the city cannot be clearly attributed to either of them as Sigi "speaks" to the viewers through Georg and Georg, in his turn, "speaks" through Haneke's camera.

4 See Edward Soja's description of "Thirdspace" in *Postmetropolis* (2000: 10–11, empha-sis in original) and in *Thirdspace: Journeys to Los Angeles and Other Real-and-Imagined*

Places (1996). In the latter work, Soja proposes a new way of thinking about space that should take into consideration the interrelatedness of space, the social, and the historical. Resorting to Henri Lefebvre's discussion of space as the interweaving of the "perceived," material space, the "conceived," imaginary space, and the "lived" spaces which are a combination of the previous spaces, Soja suggests that "Thirdspace" extends beyond a simple mixture of the physical and mental spaces. Some of the examples of the "Thirdspace" mode of thinking that Soja offers are bell hooks's redefinition of the interrelated spaces of gender, race, and class, Foucault's "heterotopias," or the "border work" of postcolonial feminist writers (Soja 1996: 8–12).

5   Haneke, in contradistinction to his character, evinces a more benign view of childhood repeatedly, especially in *The Seventh Continent* (1989), *71 Fragments of a Chronology of Chance* (1994), *Time of the Wolf* (2003), and *Caché* (2005).

6   Michael Haneke's commentary on vacuous traditions that no longer befit an age finds ample expression in other films, from *Lemmings* to *Funny Games* (1997) or *The Piano Teacher* (2001). Music is not capable of encouraging a community of emotion, but becomes merely an empty form used only for social prestige.

7   The tracking shot also includes a snapshot of young Sigi posed somewhat scornfully in front of the camera, which marks a rupture with the previously coherent display of controlled poses.

8   *Lemmings* is a deeper exploration of the same themes: broken families, absent fathers, sickly mothers, or inappropriate, surrogate parents raise children who are incapable of relating to each other and who are likely to transmit this attitude to their own children. Symptomatically, this situation reflects on the restless 1970s and 1980s generation of Germans and Austrians who challenged representations of the past with which their parents found it difficult to cope. The situation is not singular to German-language cinema: Spanish cinema of the 1970s, for example, dealt extensively with the effects of a "silent" past on future generations (Victor Erice's *The Spirit of the Beehive*, 1973) or Carlos Saura's *Cría cuervos . . .* , 1976) are well-known examples in this regard.

9   This impression is further reinforced by the use of two "projector" lights on the stage (the rotund moon sparkling in each snowflake when Eva and Georg come into the house and the lamp by the door).

10 This kitchen space is tight, with its pots and pans hanging everywhere, the radio sharing the countertop with bowls and silverware, the ironing board leaning against the patterned tile of the wall. The apparent warmth of this lived-in space will give way to the clinically cold, almost empty family kitchen in *Benny's Video* (1992), the uncomfortable country-house kitchen and its traps in *Funny Games*, the oppressive, tension-ridden country kitchen in *Code Unknown* (2000), or the contrast between Georges and Anne's gadget-laden, modern kitchen in *Caché* (2005) and Majid's messy, cheap kitchen in the same film. In its transformation throughout the films, the kitchen, as one of the most intimate spaces in the home, signals changes in the private sphere.

11 Similarities can be discerned to Mitscherlich's description of functioning cities in *Die Unwirtlichkeit unserer Städte*, which he – like Sloterdijk in his model of human interaction – codes feminine and dyadic: "In her great examples, she [the city] is clearly a maternal lover [*eine Muttergeliebte*]. A being, with which one is in love, from which one cannot separate oneself; one remains her child or her tender visitor eternally" (1965: 31).

12   However, Haneke also induces a feeling of apprehension in this scene, undercutting the positive associations through his perspective. The scene is shot as if from a closed-circuit television camera. The director's preoccupation with the erasure of private/public distinctions surfaces, as this erasure tilts into a form of social control (one need only think of the closed-circuit monitoring within Benny's apartment in *Benny's Video*).

13   The shot is remarkable in its multiple layers of frames that function almost like Chinese boxes. The unfinished tale of the boy is wrapped within the narrative about another unfinished story – that of the teacher's fate – which is, in turn, framed within the fragmentary account of Anna's life and further encased within the story of the couple.

14   As Georg climbs down a flight of stairs with snow sparkling under the streetlight, the Antonioni-inspired poetry of the shot further reinforces the complicity with the viewer. If there is a utopia, this is its most pregnant moment in the film. The non-diegetic nostalgic piano music that is here associated with Georg nevertheless continues the apprehensive chords heard when he and Anna were climbing up the stairs in the abandoned building, in what we described as the Sloterdijk-inspired bubble shot. If the latter may have been motivated by the story (the two pass by a radio when the music is first heard), the intensity with which the music follows the protagonists through the building is psychologically subjective, as is the intensity of the non-diegetic music following Georg down the snowy stairs. Through this use of music, the film emotionally and mentally connects the protagonists and the viewers, contributing to the fusing of the private and the public.

15   In contrasting the Middle Ages and the modern world, Benjamin comments: "There used to be no house, hardly a room, in which someone had not once died. . . . Today people live in rooms that have never been touched by death, dry dwellers of eternity, and when their end approaches they are stowed away in sanatoria or hospitals by their heirs. It is, however, characteristic that not only a man's knowledge or wisdom, but above all his real life – and this is the stuff that stories are made of – first assumes transmissible form at the moment of his death. . . . This authority is at the very source of the story" (1968: 94).

16   Kitty's over-emphatic gestures remind viewers of the transgressive act of watching others' emotions, even when they are being consciously acted out for a public.

17   Cf. Sloterdijk, where he takes this tree symbolism into the realm of mass politics and fascism (1998: 402–17).

18   Cf. Mitscherlich (1965: 52).

19   At the beginning of the conversation, Kitty pulls the scarf she has just been given as a present over her face in a forceful movement of self-effacement, one eventually contradicted by her desire to make Anna feel guilty. Her attacks continue, motivated by her impotence to change anything. She nervously swallows down the cake Anna brought for her birthday, indicating her frustration at Anna's emotionally vacant gesture and the need to incorporate any sign of affection Anna can still offer. She expresses her painful incapacity to breathe at the thought of Anna's actions, but, at the same time, she stands up and with her towering stature dwarfs her partner. After Anna's passive aggressive comment, "Sometimes I don't know myself why I am still here," Kitty becomes menacing and ends up attacking the food again, which,

by now, has also become a sign of her lack of self-control. She cries, sobs, bangs her head against the wall, and physically attacks Anna, but also pauses, collected, to check her face in the mirror, only to resume her reproaches. She ends up almost physically choking Anna. Elfriede Irrall, in contrast to Geyer, plays Anna in a subdued and minimal manner, befitting the cliché of the disillusioned postwar individual. She has been married before, wants to be fair but cannot, and, like Kitty, keeps pursuing an ideal of intimacy that she senses she can only achieve temporarily. Like the boy in the dungeon, Anna feels "condemned" to loneliness and fragmentariness. She lives in a demystified world, and even Kitty's outcry at the end – following the latter's exclamation "What should I say when you don't hear me?!" – cannot reach her.

20   Detached civility is also what prevents Eva and Georg from truthful communication. Their own argument reveals the extent to which the disappearance of the intimate sphere rests on the aggressive dissolution of even the slightest demarcation between the private and the public spheres. Confronted with Georg's decision to leave, Eva tries to reach him: "We've talked about our work, our interests, but we've never talked to each other." When Georg is submitted to what he feels is an interrogation, a sensation amplified by the use of high-key lighting on his face and the absence of back or fill light, he admits that the intimacy he shares with Anna is not necessarily built on rational communication (in fact, they talk "about everything and nothing"), but goes beyond words and, one may add, could have come from their common consciousness that one has only limited access to such utopias. Anna and Georg's intimacy is forged on their fear of loneliness while Eva and Georg's intimacy is further broken through the seemingly public-style interrogation.

21   In the other bedroom scene, the nightmare of finding Kitty with her wrists slashed in a tub of water wakes Anna, screaming with horror and guilt, yet unable to share her experience with Georg. In this manner, the private space of the bed becomes the site of very personal nightmares that connect individuals to emotional spaces outside the intimate sphere they have momentarily achieved. With the arrival of guilt, in itself a sign of moral connectedness to the other, as well as of a guilt not shared with the other (no similar nightmares "visible" on film trouble Georg), the intimate sphere is done away with once again. Paradoxically, the guilt of being unable to preserve one intimate sphere ends up subverting the other intimate sphere that seemed plausible in the beginning. Once again, the film alternates between the hope of community and the authenticity of shared emotion and the impossibility of achieving them, even in small measure.

22   In the film, emotional intimacy also comes as a reaction against public surveillance. Georg and Anna meet mostly in public places (the train, the conference building, the school, or the post office in the end) or in private places invaded by public voices. Furthermore, the two shots of Anna and Georg in bed are revealing. In one of them, a letter from Anna's mother, which is conveyed as an old woman's querulous and disapproving voice-over, inserts the implied public into the extremely private moment. Public scrutiny is likely to undermine the closeness the two achieve. Although viewers never see the sister to whom the letter is written, she is, in a way, part of the audience, which also makes the viewers the expected moral judges of the affair.

262 MONICA FILIMON AND FATIMA NAQVI

References and Further Reading

Benjamin, Walter: "Der Erzähler: Betrachtungen zum Werk Nikolai Lesskows," *Gesammelte Schriften*. Vol. 2.2 (Frankfurt am Main: Suhrkamp, 1977), pp. 435–65; "The Storyteller: Reflections on the Works of Nikolai Leskov," *Illuminations*, ed. Hannah Arendt, trans. Harry Zohn (New York: Schocken Books, 1968), pp. 83–111.

Habermas, Jürgen: *Strukturwandel der Öffentlichkeit* (Darmstadt: Luchterhand, 1962); trans. Thomas Burger and Frederick Lawrence, *The Structural Transformation of the Public Sphere: An Inquiry into a Category of Bourgeois Society* (Cambridge, MA: MIT Press, 1989).

Mitscherlich, Alexander: *Die Unwirtlichkeit unserer Städte: Anstiftung zum Unfrieden* (Frankfurt am Main: Suhrkamp, 1965).

Sloterdijk, Peter: *Sphären*, 3 vols. Vol. 1: *Blasen* (Frankfurt am Main: Suhrkamp, 1998).

Soja, Edward W.: *Postmetropolis: Critical Studies of Cities and Regions* (Malden, MA: Blackwell Publishing, 2000).

Soja, Edward W.: *Thirdspace: Journeys to Los Angeles and Other Real-and-Imaginary Places* (Cambridge, MA: Blackwell Publishing, 1996).

14

Projecting Desire, Rewriting Cinematic Memory

Gender and German Reconstruction in Michael Haneke's Fraulein

Tobias Nagl

Michael Haneke has gained a reputation for being a "difficult" or "dangerous" director who would rather *not* make a film than compromise aesthetically. Depending on where we are coming from, Michael Haneke appears as the ultimate wet dream or, respectively, a nightmare of auteur theory. A well-read and self-styled media theorist, Haneke, like no other contemporary director, has provoked intellectually inclined critics to abandon the comparatively modest stakes of academic film studies and to seek shelter in the vaults of continental philosophy: References to Heidegger, Plato, Leibniz, Adorno, Derrida, Spinoza, Debord, Baudrillard, Sylvère Lothringer, or Virilio abound in the reception of Haneke, not to mention the curious interest he has awakened among professionally trained theologians. Critics, especially in the highbrow German press, have praised him for the way he challenges what they see as "conventional viewing habits" through distancing effects, long takes, visceral shock, and a negative aesthetics which requires active spectatorship in an increasingly threatening and "exploitive" audiovisual media environment. This discourse on the properties of "media" is characterized by a strong ontological dimension; yet at the same time it displays what Martin Jay has described as the "denigration of vision" in twentieth-century European thought. Referring to Umberto Eco's seminal reflections on "apocalyptic and integrated intellectuals" and their attitude towards popular culture, Alexander Horwath in an important 1991 essay already pointed to the profound ambivalences in Haneke's auteurist self-fashioning and suggested the possibility that Haneke might be both "apocalyptic" and "integrated": "apocalyptic enough to consider mass culture and TV with its hysterical hustle an agent of dulling" (Horwath 1991: 35), but integrated enough to place his critique in the same mass communication channels. Or, as the *New York Times* writer John Wray has asserted in an article ingeniously entitled

"Minister of Fear," it is "one of the greatest paradoxes" of Haneke's position that "the methods he despises are the only ones at his disposal" (Wray 2007).

Such ambivalences are already quite visibly in place in his German and Austrian television dramas or *Fernsehspiele*, which Haneke started directing in 1974 with his Godardian TV debut *After Liverpool* (*Und was kommt danach . . .*). The filmic form of the state-funded made-for-TV movie or television drama, writes Jane Shattuc in her study of Fassbinder's television works, must be considered one of "the major indigenous genres of West Germany," which has certainly played a key role in German film funding structures. Due to the obligation of German TV stations to adhere to a notion of education or *Bildung*, many of the *Fernsehspiele* were literary adaptations and were characterized by strong "high-cultural connotations" (Shattuc 1995: 39). At the same time, the made-for-TV movie also allowed its makers a great deal of artistic freedom and increasingly became a site of formal experimentation. But despite the growing critical realism and auteurist concerns with original scripts which characterized the genre during the heyday of the New German Cinema in the 1960s and 1970s,[1] the *Fernsehspiel*, because of its didactic imperatives, nevertheless remained a much despised format: In 1978, the film critic and director Hans-Christoph Blumenberg, for example, famously proclaimed in the weekly *Die Zeit* that television remained a "journalistic not an artistic medium" (Shattuc 1995: 3). One could argue, as Jane Shattuc has, that the *Fernsehspiel* in its aesthetic form is more closely related to classic Hollywood film and is German only in its content and subject matter – yet this judgment seems too hasty, especially in regards to the more experimental productions, such as Haneke's adaptations of modernist literature (*Three Paths to the Lake*, 1976; *Who Was Edgar Allan?*, 1984). For Alexander Horwath, on the contrary, the *Fernsehspiel*, caught in its contradictory position wedged between the avant-garde and commercialism, appears as an attempt to catch up on something that German-language film industries in the 1950s and 1960s had missed – the creation of a *künstlerische Erzählfilm*, an aesthetically ambitious, yet popular narrative film form.

Fraulein (*Fraulein – Ein Deutsches Melodram*), produced and broadcast by the Saarländischer Rundfunk in 1986, was released at a crucial transitional moment in German TV and film history. As a movement, the New German Cinema had collapsed, while state-funded TV was already facing the challenge of cable TV networks that were tentatively introduced in several cities during the so-called "Orwell" year of 1984, the second year of Helmut Kohl's conservative chancellorship. That year also saw the popular success of Edgar Reitz's fifteen-hour TV series *Heimat*, an oversized *Fernsehspiel* which chronicled the history of a small Hunsrück village from the end of World War I to the reconstruction period of the 1950s. *Heimat*, which also received a brief theatrical release, rewrote the conventions of the discredited *Heimatfilm* in a compellingly stylized New German Cinema aesthetics, sparking an international critical debate on historical memory and its representation – or, better: non-representation – of the Holocaust. The *Heimat* series resonated with a growing interest in oral history and attempts of

Fig. 14.1   Johanna (Angelica Domröse) looks out of the projectionist's booth. *Fraulein* (1986), dir. Michael Haneke, prod. Saarländischer Rundfunk.

the New German Cinema generation to come to terms with a traumatic past. Moving from political history to what Félix Guattari had called the "micropolitics of desire," the attention paid to the lived memory of ordinary Germans was also a driving force behind Fassbinder's FDR trilogy, especially his *The Marriage of Maria Braun* (1979) and *Lola* (1981), which Michael Haneke in an interview described as "undigestable dishonesties" (Grissemann and Omasta 1991: 198). As I will argue in this essay, both *Heimat* and *The Marriage of Maria Braun* constitute an important intertext for *Fraulein*.

According to Haneke, *Fraulein* was a deliberate attempt to create a "counter-film" against the heroizing of German postwar mentalities which he saw at work in the renewed interest in 1950s popular culture from fashion to music during the first years of Kohl's "spiritual and moral reconstruction" (*geistig-moralische Wende*).[2] Yet *Fraulein* was not Haneke's first period piece about the 1950s. In *Arcadia* (*Arkadien*), Part One of his 1979 breakthrough *Lemmings* (*Lemminge*, ORF), the director had already dealt with teenage angst and discomfort in postwar Austria. The film already expressed the later thematic obsessions of the filmmaker: isolation, breakdown of communication, illness, violence, and suicide. It also prominently showcased a stylistic device for which Haneke became famous – the reliance on the long take. Perhaps as a result of the subject matter and in homage to the 1950s social melodrama, *Lemmings*, Part One, however, also contains carefully composed shots that look like they could be straight out of Nicholas Ray or Douglas Sirk.

For example, in the establishing shot we see affluent and existentialist teenage rebels meticulously framed in the rear-view mirror of one of the cars they have just vandalized, while we hear Paul Anka's "Lonely Boy" as accompanying soundtrack. Thomas Elsaesser once remarked that Edgar Reitz's *Heimat* had been "not so much a review of German history as a review of German *film* history" (Elsaesser 1985: 12). *Fraulein*, too, translates the meditation on history into a self-referential inquiry into audiovisual representation. Whereas *Heimat's* female protagonists are obsessed with the image of Zarah Leander (at crucial points they watch Carl Froehlich's film *Heimat* [1938] in their local movie-house and imitate Leander's exotic hairstyle displayed in Detlef Sierk's Puerto Rican fantasy *La Habanera* [1937]), Haneke's *Fraulein* revolves around a female cinema operator and projectionist whose fantasy life unfolds under the imagined – sometimes benevolent, sometimes erotic – gaze of Hans Albers, one of German cinema's most powerful leading men in the 1930s and 1940s. Despite Albers's *private* refusal to be photographed with leading party officials, he appeared as Nazi cinema's answer to Clark Gable, Humphrey Bogart, and Fred Astaire. And it is exactly this symbolic distance of his star persona to state power that granted him moral integrity in the postwar period and allowed Albers to reemerge as an icon of German integrity restored, everyday "resistance," and patriarchal authority in the shadow of the Holocaust. What remained a constant during Albers's career, which encompasses three different political regimes, was his status as an object of female fan culture, consumerism, and erotic investment: Already in *Mädchen in Uniform* (Leontine Sagan, 1931) we see a group of school girls marveling at one of Albers's star photos.

Haneke collaborated on *Fraulein* with scriptwriter and novelist Bernd Schroeder, the well-known recipient of the prestigious Adolf Grimme TV award, husband of the "quality" talk show host Elke Heidenreich, and ghost-writer for political comedian Dieter Hildebrandt and singer-songwriter Reinhardt Mey. To any reader familiar with the cultural topography of post-1968 Germany, these professional and personal affiliations alone mark Schroeder as a representative of a social democratic, humanist bourgeoisie that in the early 1980s had already seen its best days gone by and that increasingly came under attack from a new wave of "postmodern" cultural producers who almost viscerally detested its complacent moralism, lack of humor, and didactic imperatives. Schroeder had been the driving force behind highbrow literary adaptations such as Ludwig Thoma's novel *Münchnerinnen* (ZDF, 1974), co-wrote (together with Heidenreich) a *Fernsehspiel* on the existential challenges faced by retirees (*Die Herausforderung*; SWF, 1975), but ultimately failed to successfully translate his contributions to the genre into a wider recognition of his literary works. In 1975, Schroeder described his ambitions as follows: "I do not want to create art. I want to transport information, critical information, topics that can be researched journalistically through the medium of the *Fernsehspiel*, i.e. in a mediated and indirect manner" (Neudeck 1975: 19, as quoted in Hickethier 1980: 304).

The subject matter of *Fraulein* falls squarely into such a "documentary" or "critical realist" framework: It is based, as Haneke later explained, on a "true" story that Schroeder had picked up somewhere in the Ruhr region. Set in 1955, *Fraulein* thematizes the domestic life and romantic interests of the projectionist Johanna Kersch (Angelica Domröse), a single mother whose husband Hans (Peter Franke) has been missing since the end of the war. Johanna is having an affair with André (Lou Castel), a former French prisoner of war who now makes a living in seedy wrestling clubs under the pseudonym "The Black Mask" and occasionally helps out in the Kersch construction business. Since the end of the war, the family business has been run by Hans's materialist brother Karl (Heinz Werner Kraehkamp), who tries to persuade their mother (Margret Homeyer) and Johanna to declare Hans dead. When Hans unexpectedly returns from a Russian POW camp after Adenauer's historic negotiations in Moscow, Johanna's world is ruptured. After ten years of imprisonment, Hans is sick and delirious and unable to work. Although Johanna continues her affair with André secretly, her French lover suddenly leaves without warning. Johanna's son Mike (Michael Klein), a *Halbstarker* (juvenile delinquent), dies in an explosion when he and his friends are trapped by the police, while her daughter Brigitte (Mareile Geisler), a prototypical *Fräulein* of the reconstruction period, marries her GI boyfriend (Bob Anderson) and relocates to the US. When Hans finds out about Johanna's former relationship with André, he turns so bitter and cynical that she kills him in his sickbed so that she can be free to reunite with her lover. She drives to France, only to learn that André has a family and children. After sleeping with André in an anonymous hotel room, Johanna decides to return to Germany. While she is on the road in the shiny convertible left behind by her daughter's boyfriend, we see a short flash-forward, which shows Johanna turning herself in to the local police, no doubt in her German hometown. In a rather ambiguous ending which at first glance might be read as an indication of the insanity of Haneke's female protagonist, she is then reunited with André in a roadside café, while watching television. André mysteriously reappears and smiles. With a grin he grunts, "Good that you were driving that car" (the economic miracle wagon which is easy to recognize). Her French lover then claims to have murdered his wife and Johanna bursts into delirious laughter.

It is not hard to see why Haneke and Schroeder called *Fraulein* a "German melodrama," given its focus on female suffering and desire and a narrative that is built around many key tropes and discourses that make up Germany's cultural and cinematic imaginary of the 1950s: the independent "rubble woman" and the debate concerning female sexuality and domesticity, the returning war veteran and the ruination of patriarchal authority which is replaced by non-German masculinities, the emergence of youth cultures, and the Americanization of everyday life. But whereas scriptwriter Schroeder intended to create "a loveable apotheosis" of the woman behind the economic miracle, Haneke later claimed that he himself aimed at a "radical critique" (Grissemann and Omasta 1991: 198). This critique, however, is not so much historical – like Edgar Reitz's *Heimat*, Haneke's film is surprisingly free of any overt reference to the question of German guilt or the connection between psychic repression and economic reconstruction – as enacted in stylistic terms, through a reworking of cinematic references. The idiosyncratic fascination of *Fraulein* results precisely from this struggle between Schroeder's kitsch and Haneke's attempt to undermine and deconstruct the cliché of the image.

It is important to note here that except for its explosive, ambiguous ending which is in color, *Fraulein* was shot in stylish black and white. The grainy black-and-white stock and filtered photography not only point to Fassbinder's *Die Sehnsucht der Veronika Voss* (1982). The practice of alternating between black-and-white and color processes is also reminiscent of Reitz's *Heimat* and of the postmodern, palimpsest-like surface aesthetics characteristic of Martin Scorsese's *Raging Bull* (1980), Francis Ford Coppola's *Rumble Fish* (1983), Maurizio Nichetti's *The Icicle Thief* (1989), and Wim Wenders's *Wings of Desire* (which was released one year after *Fraulein*). But the promise of color spectacle is a self-referential sign in the film, which opens with a close-up of a film poster, advertising Hans Albers in the "AGFA-Color" *Farbfilm* epic *Münchhausen* (1943, Josef von Báky) (Fig. 14.2). Haneke's film begins and ends with images from *Münchhausen*, resulting in a circular structure similar to the narrative framing of the two explosions in *The Marriage of Maria Braun*, a film which *Fraulein* implicitly if not explicitly references.

Set to the chaotic babble of the heavily accented voices of André and Johanna's daughter's American GI boyfriend, the uncanny first shot of *Fraulein* – a cut-out

Fig. 14.2   Film poster showing Hans Albers in *Münchhausen* (1943). *Fraulein* (1986), dir. Michael Haneke, prod. Saarländischer Rundfunk.

detail of a *Münchhausen* movie poster – displays a painted medium close-up of Hans Albers in his characteristic wide-eyed pose, riding on a cannonball in one of the most famous special effects sequences of the film which unwillingly, according to Eric Rentschler, acknowledged the complicity between the cinematic apparatus and the German war machine in Nazi cinema (Rentschler 1997: 379f.). This shot, perhaps the finest moment of *Fraulein*, is both highly disturbing and playfully ironic. If there was ever an actor who represented a male and muscular zest for action and testosterone-driven adventure in the first decades of German sound film, it was Hans Albers. Here, he is frozen in a moment of dramatic action, appearing almost castrated without the weapon on which he is crashing into the Sultan's castle. Winking at the audience, this phallic connection between the cannonball and, literally, Albers's balls was already acknowledged in Joseph von Báky's fantasy epic in a brief visual dirty joke when Albers during his magic carpet ride momentarily loses control of the much bigger cannonball and his naked thighs are revealed for a few seconds of celebrating masculinity as spectacle.

On another level, by opening the film with a *painted* image of Albers, *Fraulein* not only deconstructs the myth of *Münchhausen* as one of German cinema's greatest achievements, but also quotes the film in another, more direct fashion. *Münchhausen* itself opens with a shot of a *painted* portrait of Albers in the role of the famous baron, whose eyes in an animated trick sequence twinkle at the spectator, thus establishing a secret collusion between the spectator, the yearning hero, and the illusionary power of cinema. In *Fraulein*'s opening shot, this icon of a blonde German masculinity, however, is not addressing the audience through his twinkling blue eyes, but is gawking incredulously as if caught in the act while we hear foreign accents offscreen. Scripted by the banned writer Erich Kästner under a pseudonym, *Münchhausen*'s plot celebrated the subversive power of deception and lies and, in its spectacular use of AGFA color stock, *Münchhausen*, like *Kohlberg* (Veit Harlan and Wolfgang Liebeneiner, 1945), *Immensee* (Veit Harlan, 1943), *Die Goldene Stadt* (Veit Harlan, 1942), or *Frauen sind doch die besseren Diplomaten* (Georg Jacoby, 1941), also attempted to counter Hollywood's innovations in creating escapist spectacle. Expressing Nazi science's larger struggle "to remake the world synthetically in a quest for mastery over nature," as Esther Leslie put it in a fascinating study of art and the chemical industry (Leslie 2005: 191), in *Münchhausen* AGFA color was part of an attempt to arm the home front with a new cinematic wonder weapon in the struggle for ideological support of the war effort. *Fraulein*'s first shot does not just subtract the color from Albers's *Münchhausen* in a modernist gesture, it also marks this subtraction as lack by carefully framing the line *Farbfilm* (color film), whereas both Albers and the title of the movie are cut off. After a few seconds, the camera zooms out and tilts down, while we hear the haunting Doo Wop classic "Little Darling" by the white American vocal group *The Diamonds* on the soundtrack and the title of Haneke's film appears in glaring red letters. Tracking back and reframing the entire theater in a long shot, the camera shows André, Johanna, her children, and her daughter's GI boyfriend in a convertible and, respectively, a Goliath tricycle. After a few lines of further dialog they leave and Johanna enters the theater.

Yet this is not the only instance where Baron Münchhausen is brought into the life of the protagonist and projectionist, establishing a link between German history, desire, and cinematic fantasy. After Johanna has finished cleaning the lounge of the theater, she wistfully studies the illustrated press kit of *Münchhausen*, and it seems that only in these moments when she is alone in the cinema, absorbed by cinephilia, is she granted something like happiness. But unlike the female spectators in Reitz's *Heimat*, who imitate Zarah Leander's style and gestures at home in front of the mirror, showcasing a non-voyeurist proximity to the filmic image (as described by Mary-Ann Doane in her theory of female spectatorship [Doane 1982]), Johanna's relation to the screen as a projectionist is mediated, distanced, and controlled. She is never shown in the auditorium with other patrons; instead, we see her controlling the spectacle from the sanctity of her booth, peering down at the audience or screen through a small peephole. The spontaneous and sometimes embarrassing emotional responses of the audience, shown in an unflattering light, are depicted time and again through a series of slow tracking shots across the auditorium. The first film Johanna projects with the assistance of her French lover André (who through most of the film wears a tight tank top) is, of course, *Münchhausen*. What we as viewers of *Fraulein* see is footage from the iconic cannonball sequence, rendered not only in black and white, but at a diminutive distance at the other end of the auditorium, belittling Albers even more. The deconstruction of the Albers image, already inaugurated in the opening sequence, is carried out further in *Fraulein* in a later sequence with footage from the "rubble film" *Und über uns der Himmel* (1947), which was also directed by Joseph von Báky. This second "film within the film" is clearly used as an ironic intertextual commentary on the legacy and continuation of Nazi cinema in the reconstruction period. In *Und über uns der Himmel*, Albers stars as a *Heimkehrer*, a returning war veteran, who soon becomes successful as a black market dealer and runs into moral conflict with his uptight son. Described both as a "rubble film" and as a star vehicle in the contemporary press, *Und über uns der Himmel* was relatively successful at the box office, although many reviewers decried von Báky's commercialism as risk-averting and indicative of a troubling continuation of "old ways" (Shandley 2001: 160–74).

Despite its sentimentality and moralism, which critics have repeatedly pointed to, one of the most striking sequences of *Und über uns der Himmel* contains a series of what Jaimey Fisher has called "rubble shots," which can be read as a symptom of a deeper representational crisis in German cinema (Fig. 14.3). Such panorama shots of lone veterans and *Heimkehrer* wandering through bombed-out cityscapes, Fisher argues, are not just important with respect to their historical referentiality, nor should they simply be understood as socio-cultural signifiers of "realism"; these shots also express the emergence of a lacking, passive, or "marginal" masculinity, which Kaja Silverman has described in terms of male masochism and male specularity (Silverman 1992: 52–121). According to Fisher, the crisis in gender identities

Fig. 14.3   "Rubble shot" from the film *Und über uns der Himmel* (1947). *Fraulein* (1986), dir. Michael Haneke, prod. Saarländischer Rundfunk.

resulting from historical trauma translates cinematically into what Gilles Deleuze has described as a renunciation of the "movement-image" centered on male action and desire in favor of the neo-realist "time-image" dominated by passive, meandering, and disoriented males who lack a mastering gaze. European postwar cinema and Italian neo-realism in particular, as Deleuze writes on the magisterial first pages of *Cinema 2*, can be characterized as a "cinema of the seer," that is, defined by a "build-up of purely visual situations" in which "the character has become a kind of viewer. He shifts, runs and becomes animated in vain, the situation he is in outstrips his motor capacities on all sides, and makes him see and hear what is no longer subject to the rules of a response or an action. He records rather than reacts. He is prey to a vision, pursued by it or pursuing it, rather than engaged in an action" (Deleuze 1989: 3). By dislodging the male subject from a privileged specular position, such lingering "rubble shots," inhabited by overwhelmed and melancholic protagonists, effectively revise the scopophilia, denial of castration, and mastery that feminist psychoanalytic film theory has associated with the "male gaze." Since these autonomous, dispersed shots of ruins invert the specularized, objectified images of women in classical narrative cinema, they simultaneously reinstate a socio-cultural castration at the heart of hetero-normative masculinities that is usually neither visible nor acknowledged and, thus, signal "the twilight of the active, desiring male subject" (Fisher 2001: 98).

To return to the rubble "film within the film," *Und über uns der Himmel* ends with a moral call to arms, yet it features Albers in an unfamiliarly broken role, performing Theo Mackeben's melancholic title song while slowly crossing the bombed-out Potsdamer Platz with its industrial rubble women: "Es weht der

Wind von Norden. Er weht uns hin und her. Was ist aus uns geworden? Ein Häufchen Sand am Meer. Der Sturm jagt das Sandkorn weiter, dem unser Leben gleicht" ("A wind blows from the north. It blows us back and forth. What has become of us? A small pile of sand on the beach. The storm throws the grain farther, just like our lives"). Mackeben's song (with its initial melancholic melodic structure that is then resolved in an "optimistic" sixth note jump) resembles, as Fred Ritzel has convincingly demonstrated, not only the "endurance hits" (*Durchhalteschlager*) of the war period such as Michael Jary's "Ich weiss, es wird einmal ein Wunder geschehen" ("I Just Know that a Miracle Will Happen"), but also the memories of age-old folk songs and Nordic myths, expressing feelings of German victimhood, ignorance, and the need for psychic self-preservation in the face of the "catastrophe" that the war and its "humiliating" end had come to represent.[3]

The most iconic image of this sequence in von Báky's film appears at the end of the song when the lyrics move from melancholia to the notion that "life has to go on." This shot, which has been used as footage in countless TV documentaries to represent postwar Berlin, shows several rubble women who are pushing a cart which is painted with the bold letters "No time for love." The renunciation of female desire and the call for national reconstruction go hand in hand.

It is quite telling to see what use *Fraulein* makes of this sequence, which was reedited by Haneke and drastically altered in its meaning. Footage from *Und über uns der Himmel* appears in the first third of the film after Johanna has received a letter from the Association of Returned War Veterans, announcing the homecoming of her husband Hans. It is no coincidence that her mailbox resembles a bird's cage, since this letter makes Johanna and her two teenage children feel trapped rather than redeemed. Johanna begins to remove the photos and wrestling trophies of her lover André from the living room, while her daughter, melodramatically framed in a doorway, bursts into tears in a painful long take. On the soundtrack we hear Albers's song, and then *Fraulein* dissolves into Haneke's reedit of the rubble sequence. The cart with the "no time for love" graffiti now appears directly at the *beginning* of the sequence with the more melancholic part of the song, thus not celebrating the heroic deferral of female desire in the name of national reconstruction but commenting on the sadness signified by the return of the father. But this is not the only modification Haneke makes to the rubble film sequence and its chronology. Interestingly, Haneke edited out almost all shots in which von Báky showed muscular German men cleaning up the rubble and rebuilding a new Germany. In Haneke's version, the sequence becomes a fantasy scenario of female desire, in which the faded glory of a broken Hans Albers is the closest we get to something like a phallic masculinity.

The masculinity of Johanna's lover André in the film is also severely undercut or undermined by the fact that he is not only a foreigner, but also a former prisoner of war. Although he tries to assume responsibility for Johanna's children, André appears boyish when he is fooling around with her teenage son. For Johanna, it seems, he occupies the position of a plaything, rather than assuming the role of a potential provider for her family. At night, he works as a half-clad wrestler, wearing a tight fantasy costume, which marks him as a spectacle and marginalizes his authority even more. The war veteran Hans, on the other hand, is also dislodged from a privileged specular position; often he simply stares vacantly in an emptied-out domestic sphere, smoking one cigarette after another. Almost in a caricature of the family construction business which his brother is running, Hans stays at home and builds small models with matches and glue. When he and Johanna spend their first night together after over ten years – they stare at the ceiling in an awkward struggle – he makes his first and only attempt to cast an erotically charged gaze on Johanna, mumbling: "I want to see you." Johanna, who is lying motionless on their over-dimensioned bed, lifts her nightgown over her head and displays her naked body in an alienated gesture which Haneke underscores by showing the whole sequence in one high-angle long take from the top of the ceiling, followed by an ironic cut, a clip from the revue film *Schlagerparade*, in which the Swedish starlet Bibi Johns is performing her song "Das mach' ich mit Musik." Later, when Hans learns of Johanna's affair with André, Haneke cuts from a close-up of Hans to his crotch and we see how urine is slowly running down his legs. On a narrative level, Johanna's sexuality with André is represented in a more joyful light, but the bliss Johanna might be feeling is undercut by Haneke's disjunctive editing and his penchant for close-ups which stress the sheer technicality of the sexual act. In one of the montage sequences toward the second half of the movie, Haneke's rapid editing and avoidance of point-of-view shots even blurs the differences between the two men entirely and it becomes unclear who is touching her.

Critics have often mentioned that in Fassbinder's films power relations are played out in what has been called the "field of vision" (Jacqueline Rose). Rereading the psychoanalytic film theory of the 1970s, Thomas Elsaesser has argued that the work of Fassbinder is exhibitionist rather than voyeuristic, pinpointing that his characters perform *for* and are read *through* the look of an "other." This holds especially true for the heroines of Fassbinder's FDR trilogy (*The Marriage of Maria Braun*, *Veronika Voss*, *Lola*) who are victims of the objectifying look of men and constitute themselves as subjects through becoming objects of male vision. These heroines are also aware of the power of woman as spectacle and know how to deploy this power to achieve their own ends. This is where we can mark Haneke's strongest deviation from the Fassbinder text. In *Fraulein* Johanna can *project*, but she can't *perform* for a male other. She controls the image, but she doesn't become the image for a male audience. In the alienated postwar landscape, the available masculine positions are too weak to fully recognize Johanna as a desiring subject. As Georg Seeßlen has pointed out, it often appears as if there is no mediation between close-up and long shots, between individuality and the social in Haneke's filmmaking (Seeßlen 1996). Unlike Fassbinder's *The Marriage of Maria Braun*, the melodrama in *Fraulein* remains a broken promise, despite the generic conventions and ingredients that are firmly in place. Johanna neither becomes a Maria Braun, a "Mata Hari of the Economic Miracle," nor is she in any sense a 1950s material girl, the *Fräulein* of the film's title:

There is no drama of intersubjectivity that arises from the look of the characters, no spectacular rise and fall, no morality. Consider the climax, the crime of the disembodied, alienated narrative: Johanna kills her husband. The perspective could not be more disengaged: In a high-angle shot she pulls the intravenous drip in a barely noticeable move, a cinematic whisper; within seconds it is over.

In the final moments of the film, however, we see Haneke foreground a less disengaged cinematic subjectivity, as he scripts a fantasy "release" of our protagonist/ projectionist from her war-torn husband and Germany as postwar reconstruction body. As we see in the opening shot of *Fraulein*, all escape routes are marked as fantasy, linked to the heroine's cinephilia and her obsession with Hans Albers. Even after André's photographs are discarded, Albers's star photo continues to take center stage, prominently displayed in the lounge of the "Roxy," Johanna's small-town movie palace. And it is significant that the only eyeline matches in the film are used when Johanna looks at or calls upon Albers in moments of desperation or joy. One of the most prominent intersubjective eyeline matches occurs at the end of *Fraulein*, after Johanna jumps into her convertible on a return home voyage, leaving André behind in France. On the 1950s TV set in the French roadside café, we see dreary news reports and then suddenly someone at the counter changes the channel – the next "transmission" Johanna sees is in color, nothing other than the spectacle *Münchhausen*. In clever editing, Albers now seems to stereoscopically stare directly at Johanna instead of his movie partner Brigitte Horney (Figs. 14.4, 14.5). In these last few seconds, when *Fraulein* switches to color, André reappears and as a final fulfillment of cinematic fantasy, claims to have murdered his wife. The unexpected plot twist reminiscent of a Sirkian *deus ex machina* is both underscored and questioned by the sudden switch to color. In the last shot we see Albers climb into a hot-air balloon and then disappear into the night on his way to the moon – Johanna bursts into a fit of mad laughter and "The End" appears in bright red letters on the screen, echoing both the color and the typography of the film's title (Figs. 14.6, 14.7). In light of Haneke's later writings on violence and media (Haneke 2008), this ending offers itself to a reading as a critique of the

Figs. 14.4 and 14.5   Albers "stares" at Johanna and Johanna looks at Albers. *Fraulein* (1986), dir. Michael Haneke, prod. Saarländischer Rundfunk.

Figs. 14.6 and 14.7   Albers in *Münchhausen* and Johanna bursts out laughing. *Fraulein* (1986), dir. Michael Haneke, prod. Saarländischer Rundfunk.

"illusionary potential" of the cinematic apparatus that links insanity and the "culture industry" and, in an almost Brechtian fashion, flattens out the image through the use of competing sign systems (image/writing), while pointing to the "scripted" and circular nature of fantasy.

Yet, I would argue that this is neither the only nor the best way to understand the often contradictory and idiosyncratic nature of Haneke's early TV works. In a compelling reading of *The Piano Teacher* (2001), Jean Wyatt has pointed out how Haneke's adaptation of Elfriede Jelinek's modernist novel in fact deconstructs the high/low culture division that seems so crucial to the director's later hermetic style and snobby aesthetic preferences.[4] Through the ironic juxtaposition of sound and image, of sublime music and pornographic images of a perverse or "abject" sexuality, Wyatt argues, we are "exposed to the shocks of *jouissance*" (Wyatt 2005: 455). Such a structural oscillation between what Wyatt calls "the scenario of romantic desire," which compels identification, and the "surprises of *jouissance*" seems characteristic of *Fraulein* as well, and it deliberately links this problematic to the question of gender identity, popular culture, and cinephilia. It is not just that mass culture, and cinema in particular, in *Fraulein* is explicitly coded as feminine, it is also positioned as waste, trash, or *abject*. In one of the most powerful scenes of the film we witness the destruction of Johanna's movie theater, where the images she projects and adores implicitly or explicitly speak of a wasted, marginal, and ruined masculinity that threatens patriarchal reconstruction. Cinema itself becomes an abjected cultural object of a bygone era, if we think of *Münchhausen*'s ridiculous and outmoded rerun in a provincial 1950s theater and its final funeral on the small TV screen of a roadside café in the middle of nowhere. It is this special relationship to cinema as an abject object (always-already lost) that is characteristic of cinephilia. From this perspective, we might argue that *Fraulein*'s ending does not signal so much a critique of "false" identification, but that in this final moment of the film we also get a glimpse of the heroine's humanity, agency, and *jouissance* which *Fraulein* had been hiding for such a long time. In a famous reversal of Godard, Haneke repeatedly stated that "a feature film is twenty-four lies a second." This statement seems hopelessly nostalgic at a historic moment when cinema has ceased to function as the prime producer of dominant ideologies and "meaning." In its detailed and playful execution, *Fraulein*'s final sequence suggests that a negative aesthetics is not the only possibility to rescue cinema as a site of utopia. Through the eyes of cinephiles, however, this utopia might not be "truth" anymore. As Johanna's blissful, physical laughter in *Fraulein* indicates, we might have to locate it somewhere else.

Notes

1 Knut Hickethier (1980: 222–311). See also Hickethier (1993). On the Austrian *Fernsehspiele* of the 1970s and 1980s, see Georg Haberl (1996).
2 Stefan Grissemann and Michael Omasta (1991: 198, author's translation). In the German culture wars of the 1980s, references to the 1950s were not only made by the conservatives in their attempts to undo the trauma of 1968 and revive outmoded Cold War ideologies but were a very common, ironic feature of the postmodern "politics of style" characteristic of the post-punk generation and the *Neue Deutsche Welle* (New German Wave). See Siepmann, Lusk, and Holtfreter (1983); Diedrich Diederichsen (1985); *Rendezvous unterm Nierentisch. Die Wirtschaftswunderrolle* (Germany 1986/87, dir. Manfred Breuersbock).
3 For the entire lyrics of the song and a very valuable reading of it in the context of Nazi and postwar *Schlager*, see Fred Ritzel (1998: 295–7).
4 This cultural elitism becomes most obvious in Haneke's use of popular music. In *Fraulein* popular songs and *Schlager* are not credited at all. In *Funny Games* (1997), Haneke plays with the "shock" value of heavy metal as one of the most "abject" pop musical styles. But what we hear as a sonic contrast to the classical music in the film's famous opening sequence, in fact, comes from the American avant-garde composer, improviser, and jazz saxophonist John Zorn. Haneke is aware of Zorn's background and, as he explained in an interview, intended to use Zorn as an example of another artist who has parodied a popular genre (metal) just as he himself parodies the thriller genre. The problem is that Haneke can only think of Zorn's postmodern approach in terms of parody or distantiation. I would argue that Zorn has a different goal in mind, that it is possible to be equally invested in metal, jazz, and the classical avant-garde. To use Jameson's distinction: What is at stake is precisely the difference between pastiche and parody. See also Christopher Sharrett (2004).

References and Further Reading

Assheuer, Thomas, ed.: *Nahaufnahme: Michael Haneke, Gespräche mit Thomas Assheuer* (Berlin: Alexander Verlag, 2008).
Deleuze, Gilles: *Cinema 2: The Time-Image* (Minnesota: University of Minnesota Press, 1989).
Diederichsen, Diedrich: *Sexbeat. 1972 bis heute* (Cologne: Kiepenheuer and Witsch, 1985).

Doane, Mary-Ann: "Film and the Masquerade: Theorizing the Female Spectator," *Screen* 24 (September/October 1982): 74–87.

Elsaesser, Thomas: *Fassbinder's Germany: History, Identity, Subject* (Amsterdam: Amsterdam University Press, 1996).

Elsaesser, Thomas: "Memory, Home and Hollywood," *New German Critique* 36 (Autumn 1985): 11–13.

Fehrenbach, H.: *Cinema in Democratizing Germany: Reconstructing National Identity After Hitler* (Chapel Hill: University of North Carolina Press, 1995).

Fisher, Jaimey: "Who's Watching the Rubble-Kids? Youth, Pedagogy, and Politics in Early DEFA Films," *New German Critique* 82 (Winter 2001): 91–125.

Grabner, Franz, Larcher, Gerhard, and Wessely, Christian, eds.: *Utopie und Fragment: Michael Hanekes Filmwerk* (Thaur: Kulturverlag, 1996).

Grissemann, Stefan and Omasta, Michael: "Herr Haneke, wo bleibt das Positive? Ein Gespräch mit dem Regisseur," *Der Siebente Kontinent: Michael Haneke und seine Filme*, ed. A. Horwath (Vienna: Europaverlag, 1991), pp. 193–213.

Haberl, Georg: "Kinospiel am Bildschirm. Der österreichische Fernsehfilm als ästhetisches Problem," *Der neue Österreichische Film*, ed. G. Schlemmer (Vienna: Wespennest, 1996), pp. 359–69.

Haneke, Michael: "Gewalt und Medien," *Nahaufnahme: Michael Haneke, Gespräche mit Thomas Assheuer*, ed. T. Assheuer (Berlin: Alexander Verlag, 2008), pp. 155–63.

Hickethier, Knut: *Das Fernsehspiel in der Bundesrepublik. Themen, Form, Struktur, Theorie und Geschichte* (Stuttgart: Metzler, 1980).

Hickethier, Knut: "Dispositiv Fernsehen, Programm und Programmstrukturen in der Bundesrepublik Deutschland," *Institution, Technik und Programm. Rahmenaspekte der Programmgeschichte des Fernsehens*, ed. K. Hickethier (Munich: Fink, 1993), pp. 171–244.

Hoehn, M.: *GIs and Fräuleins: The German American Encounter in 1950s West Germany* (Chapel Hill: University of North Carolina Press, 2002).

Horwath, Alexander, ed.: *Der Siebente Kontinent: Michael Haneke und seine Filme* (Vienna: Europaverlag, 1991).

Horwath, Alexander: "Die ungeheuerliche Kränkung, die das Leben ist. Zu den Filmen von Michael Haneke," *Der Siebente Kontinent: Michael Haneke und seine Filme*, ed. A. Horwath (Vienna: Europaverlag, 1991), pp. 11–39.

Jay, Martin: *Downcast Eyes: The Denigration of Vision in Twentieth-Century French Thought* (Berkeley: University of California Press, 1994).

Kreuzer, T. and Thomsen, C. W., eds.: *Geschichte des Fernsehens in der Bundesrepublik Deutschland: Die Programme 1952–1990*, 5 vols. (Munich: Fink, 1994).

Leslie, E.: *Synthetic Worlds: Nature, Art, and the Chemical Industry* (London: Reaktion Books, 2005).

Neudeck, R.: "Notizen aus der Provinz. Das Fernsehspiel-Porträt: Bernd Schroeder," *Medium* 5:10 (1975): 14–19.

Rentschler, Eric: "Germany: Nazism and After," *The Oxford History of World Cinema*, ed. Geoffrey Nowell-Smith (Oxford: Oxford University Press, 1997), pp. 374–82.

Ritzel, Fred: "'Was ist aus uns geworden? Ein Häufchen Sand am Meer': Emotions of Post-War Germany as Extracted from Examples of Popular Music," *Popular Music* 17:3 (1998): 293–309.

Rose, Jacqueline: *Sexuality in the Field of Vision* (London: Verso, 1986).

Schlemmer, Gerd, ed.: *Der neue Österreichische Film* (Vienna: Wespennest, 1996).

Seeßlen, Georg: "Strukturen der Vereisung," *Utopie und Fragment: Michael Hanekes Filmwerk*, ed. Franz Grabner, Gerhard Larcher, and Christian Wessely (Thaur: Kulturverlag, 1996), pp. 37–54.

Shandley, R. R.: *Rubble Films: German Cinema in the Shadow of the Third Reich* (Philadelphia: Temple University Press, 2001).

Sharrett, Christopher: "The World That is Known: An Interview with Michael Haneke," *Kino-Eye: New Perspectives on Austrian Film* 4:1 (March 8, 2004), www.kinoeye.org/04/01/interview01.php. [Interview reprinted in this volume.]

Shattuc, Jane: *Television, Tabloids, and Tears: Fassbinder and Popular Culture* (Minneapolis and London: University of Minnesota Press, 1995).

Siepmann, E., Lusk, I., and Holtfreter, J., eds.: *Bikini. Die Fünfziger Jahre. Kalter Krieg und Capri-Sonne* (Berlin: Elephanten Press, 1983).

Silverman, Kaja: *Masculinity at the Margins* (New York and London: Routledge, 1992).

Wray, J.: "Minister of Fear," *New York Times*, September 23, 2007.

Wyatt, J.: "*Jouissance* and Desire in Michael Haneke's *The Piano Teacher*," *American Imago* 62:4 (Winter 2005): 453–82.

15

(Don't) Look Now

Hallucinatory Art History in Who Was Edgar Allan?

Janelle Blankenship

When *Who Was Edgar Allan?* (*Wer war Edgar Allan?*) premiered on Zweites Deutsches Fernsehen in 1986, German reviewers were baffled, spoke of the film as a "plot-poor puzzle" (Kopka 1986, my translation), a "Venetian-mystification crime thriller" (*Münchener Abendzeitung*, 1986, my translation), or a "celebration of understatement" (Böbbies 1986, my translation). Despite its shortcomings, its puzzling, circular nature and indeterminacy, critics were also quick to identify that what the film accomplished was to endow an aesthetic and filmic sensibility to the *Feindmedium* (vilified medium), television (Horwath 1991: 27). Haneke himself referred to *Who Was Edgar Allan?* (1984) as aesthetically the most rigorous or challenging of his TV films (Grissemann and Omasta 1991: 207). Although ORF announced Haneke's literary adaptation to the Austrian press as a "schmaler Film" ("minor film")[1] and tried to prevent it from being screened at the Berlin International Film Festival, the film was received with great acclaim when presented as part of the "Panorama" platform for new talent. Efforts to promote theatrical release failed, however, as the rights could not be obtained for Ennio Morricone's film score, one of many appropriations or quotations within the "text" – a haunting refrain taken from Morricone's own soundtrack for Bernardo Bertolucci's 1976 historical epic *1900/Novocento* (Traversa 1994: 206).

Haneke's mysterious crime thriller is an intriguing and puzzling adaptation of a postmodern novel by Austrian author Peter Rosei.[2] Critics have described Rosei's early works as Kafkaesque, characterized by radical pessimism, a melancholic world view,[3] and a shifting narrative perspective. Resonating with Haneke's "cinema of provocation," Rosei's earliest work also "contains graphic depictions of death, destruction, and threatening environments" (Schwarz 1992: 69). Yet there are more profound affinities between the author and the director. One can argue that what perhaps drew Haneke most to this Austrian writer was Rosei's interest in the "constructed" nature of narrative (Schwarz 1992: 65). In an interview, Rosei stated that he considered Edgar Allan Poe to be a model for his own "constructed" and self-reflexive narration, acknowledging the importance of Poe for his own under-standing of literary production: "Poe at that time helped me a great deal, above all through his poetics. Poe is one of the sharpest critics of divine inspiration. He says literature is essentially something constructed" (ibid.).[4] The German literary scholar Bianca Theisen has identified this self-reflexivity as a key feature of Rosei's take on the detective genre:

> Bringing together autobiographical fiction with the detective story by charting a quest for identity onto the conventions of detection, Peter Rosei's *Wer war Edgar Allan?* (*Who was Edgar Allan?*, 1977) corresponds to what critics have called the "metaphysical detective story." The term, first coined by Howard Haycraft to characterize Chesterton's paradoxical stories of crime and redemption, has come to label the parodic play on the generic limits of detective fiction in postmodern texts. The rule-governed, highly coded narrative closure of traditional detective fiction gives way to meta-fictional, self-referential texts that draw on the matrix of detection the way that modernist texts employed myth, in order to address "unfathomable epistemological and ontological questions: What, if anything, can we know? What, if anything, is real? How, if at all, can we rely on anything besides our own constructions of reality?" Rosei's narrative offers a graphic exercise in this kind of postmodern epistemology of uncertainty. The narrow, labyrinthine alleys and canals of a desolate Venice here offer the map for a frightening foray into the dark territory of a consciousness increasingly confused and corrupted by narcotics. A young drug addict tries to pin down the mysterious identity of a stranger who seems to be involved in several murders and linked to a drug ring. (Theisen 2003: 55)

Within this "graphic exercise" in a "postmodern epistemology of uncertainty," Rosei attempts a "dynamic cross-cutting of images" (such as falling snowflakes and a raging tidal wave), creating a "stereoscopic view" of an "atomized reality" (Theisen 2003: 108).[5] In this sense, Rosei as an author who was influenced by both Poe's "poetic calculus"[6] and Deleuze and Guattari's notion of "rhizomatic" textuality[7] views himself as a "detective, natural scientist and ethnographer" (Schwarz 1992: 67). Paratactic description, fragments of speech, and repetition build an uncanny grammar of uncertainty and circularity in the narrative, weaving a web of intrigue around both our student dropout protagonist and the mysterious elderly gentle-man named Edgar Allan. In one moment of hallucinatory over-identification, the phantasmagoria of the literary figure Edgar Allan Poe and the mysterious presence of the German-American gentleman are conflated in the mind of the protagonist. The student superimposes their identities: "As if the paroxysm could be intensified to an even greater degree, in the maelstrom of my consciousness, the real figure of Allan was coupled to that of the poet Poe, long passed away, and I saw both as one. I saw a gigantic figure, half protecting, half threaten-ing, bend down towards me and now the question rang entirely different, utterly unsolvable – I was asked, the figure asked – so Who was Edgar Allan?"[8]

Rosei's novel was published at a decisive moment in German literary history when "new subjectivity" (*Neue Subjektivität*) gave way to postmodernism in the late 1970s. Whereas the new subjectivity (whose authors include Peter Schneider and Nicolas Born) had emerged as a critique of both literary modernism and post-1968 politically engaged writing, focusing on private, personal dreams and fantasies and using often autobiographical forms, postmodernist German literature (whose authors include Peter Süsskind and Christoph Ransmayr) often uses parody, pastiche, and genre formula to playfully transcend high/low dichotomies. *Wer War Edgar Allan?* exhibits features of both tendencies: It focuses on moments of extreme interiority, but also self-consciously utilizes the generic framework of the detective novel and literary allusions. In addition to Poe, the dense intertextual references woven into the novel include Johann Wolfgang Goethe, Charles Baudelaire, Robert Louis Stevenson, and Albert Camus (Theisen 2003: 137). It is also worth noting that 1977, the year of the novel's publication, was marked by a series of assassinations and kidnappings committed by the ultra-left-wing Red Army Faction (RAF) and the subsequent annulment of civil rights and institutionalization of state surveillance during the "German Autumn." The same year marked a key rupture in German intellectual history. The prestigious Merve publishing house gave up its subtitle "International Marxist Discussion" and began to publish the first German-language translations of Foucault, Baudrillard, Deleuze and Guattari, as well as Lyotard, thus paving the way for the German reception of French poststructuralist theory and postmodernism.

In 1984 Haneke turned to the labyrinthine, fragmented, and iterative structures of Rosei's novel to stage his own game of uncertain identities. The German-Austrian co-production closely follows the plot structure of the novel, thematizing the mysterious murder of a contessa and the drug-induced hallucinations of a German art student in Venice who becomes obsessed with a German-American gentleman named Edgar Allan (Rolf Hoppe). Paulus Manker, who also stars in Haneke's earlier production *Lemmings* (1979), plays the young German art student, a melancholic and blasé character who lives in complete isolation, dividing his time between artistic studies and drug and alcohol excess. On occasion, he sobers up and dresses up as a young gentleman to seek out social interaction in cafés. In his inebriated and drugged state, Rosei's narrator is haunted by reflections of his elderly acquaintance Edgar Allan. He first meets Edgar Allan in a café, where they discuss the mysterious murder of the contessa and the drug cartel of Venice. The student begins to suspect that Edgar Allan is indeed implicated in the crime or connected to the narcotics underworld.

Figuring as more than mere aestheticized decay, Venice in the film (similar to the setting portrayed in Nicholas Roeg's 1973 Daphne du Maurier adaptation *Don't Look Now*) serves as an enigmatic crime scene and a topography Haneke utilizes to deconstruct stable identities of the self. The opening shot creates an atmosphere of mystery and intrigue, as the camera tilts down to follow a white scarf that an unknown woman has dropped into the dreary waters of a canal from the balcony

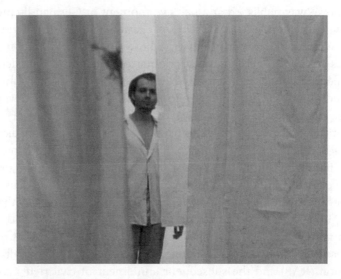

Fig. 15.1   The student (Paulus Manker) wanders through the Venetian underworld. *Who Was Edgar Allan?* (1984), dir. Michael Haneke, prod. ZDF and ORF.

of a white palazzo. The labyrinth of alleyways, arcades, clotheslines, canals, cafés, betting parlors, and halls of the university leads our young addict on a frenzied search for lost and deferred meaning. We follow the student drifting through the Venetian underworld in search of cocaine (Fig. 15.1). In close-up, we see the student snort cocaine and then visit a bar, where Edgar Allan appears as an uncanny mirror reflection. Further hallucinatory experiences are intercut with artistic experimentation and visits to the café where our protagonist first meets his German-American acquaintance, "Edgar Allan." As in *Fraulein* (1986), references to cinema form an important subtext and are used to stage a self-reflexive aesthetic. After a hallucinatory experience that leads the student to chase Edgar Allan through the streets of Venice, we see the student briefly stop in front of a cinema, whose marquee advertises Wim Wenders's *The American Friend* (1977). In a perpetual search for clues, our protagonist desperately digs through the trash in the rain, hoping to find a piece of paper Edgar Allan has discarded.[9]

As the film continues, it becomes more and more difficult to distinguish between self, reflection, subject, object, detective, and criminal. At key moments that mark the change of seasons in the film, the student returns to a narrow alley outside his apartment building. He sits exposed to the elements, sketching a sculpted mask while enduring various weather conditions, from sun to rain to snow. Not surprisingly, the protagonist identifies with the mask and sketches out a "self-portrait" of artistic desire as he himself lies on the floor beside the mask, in an impressionist study of sunlight that flows through his studio apartment, illuminating artistic objects in its path. In the final sequence of the film the student walks the streets of Venice during a snowstorm and studies a mugshot on the door of the police station. This criminal sketch bears a strong resemblance to Edgar Allan and also resembles the sketch of the mask that the student has worked on throughout the film. The camera lingers on this mugshot, but then the student shakes his head and continues to criss-cross the city. The plot, which involves numerous drug- or alcohol-induced "sights" or sites of excess, is indeed difficult to summarize. Suffice it to say that the film creates a lyrical portrait of artistic desire and also utilizes a circular self-reflexive narrative to heighten what Haneke in his later work has identified as the "illusory" nature of the apparatus.

The thriller opens, however, with a far more thrilling and dramatic *mise-en-scène*, a low-angle shot of an ornate white palazzo balcony: Police officers appear and disappear, followed by an aristocratic woman dressed in white who peers down into the depths. In a hurried movement, she leaves the scene and a lone scarf drifts down to the dark waters. The intense *photogénie* of this establishing shot is perhaps reminiscent of the 1920s avant-garde, an homage to the white gauzy fabric of Madeleine that blows in the wind before her traumatic live burial in Jean Epstein's *The Fall of the House of Usher* (1928). Haneke finally cuts from a long shot of the investigation and the harsh reality of sirens and searchlights to a symbolic close-up of the white object now engulfed by black and murky waters, set to the eerie refrain of Morricone's film score.[10]

After a fade to black – also a defining feature of the famous opening shot of Roeg's restrained horror classic *Don't Look Now* – we enter the student's apartment, which is now mediated through the powerful gesture of one of Haneke's long takes. The introductory game of search and surveillance is now transposed into traces, remnants, and artifacts of art history, as Haneke explores depth of field and the camera tracks back to reveal more and more derelict studio space. The stifled detective search of Haneke's film catalogs an eclectic collage of torn and truncated images, cut off and alienated from an unimaginable or inconceivable whole. These images – often of body parts such as eyes and ears – are now tacked up on the walls of the student's studio apartment with other art history documents and ephemera (slides, photographs, sketches, film strips). The student's art history collection is completed by traces of the sculpted bodies of the statuesque exterior, fragmented plaster body parts, cornice moldings and masks, and architectural plunder pillaged from the labyrinthine city (Fig. 15.2).

Rosei's novel begins and ends with broken memory and the broken materiality of writing – the narrator states that the material used for his story consisted of fragments of first literary attempts, diary notes, and miscellaneous paperwork, including letters and bank receipts (Rosei 1992: 45). Instead of emphasizing a broken textuality, Haneke utilizes artifacts and ephemera of art history – sketches, slides, fragmented photographs, and fragmented sculptures in the studio – to translate this broken, paratactic memory and textuality into a visual collage of the disembodied self. Whereas Rosei's text disintegrates into fragments, notes, hallucinatory experiences, and paratactic memory, Haneke's film is structured around

Fig. 15.2   The student's art history collection. *Who Was Edgar Allan?* (1984), dir. Michael Haneke, prod. ZDF and ORF.

images of fragmented media – stills, slides, sketches – parts that desperately call out to be reconceptualized as part of a larger, coherent whole.

As the camera pans back to reveal the interior of the studio apartment, on the left side of the frame we are confronted with a collage of fragmented eyes, perhaps torn out of newspapers and photographs, which in later shots will briefly flutter in the wind. In Rosei's novel trash is constantly blown through the apartment, symbolic of the broken subject who stumbles around Venice in a perpetual drug-induced haze. In Haneke's adaptation, in contrast, what qualifies as "refuse" is both the law or letter of the recently deceased father (an "unfinished" letter fragment, which the student later crumples up and discards in front of a souvenir shop) and the subject of art history itself, now reduced to an incoherent and seemingly indecipherable maze of fragmented notes, film strips, slides, anatomical drawings, charcoal sketches, postcards, and photographs. The maze of images and body parts may mirror the "split" psychological state of the protagonist, who before his father's death studied medicine and anatomy, but is now infatuated with the signs and symbols of art history (Fig. 15.3). Yet how should we read the even more enigmatic "cave-painting" of a horse which is time and again lovingly caressed by Haneke's cinematography? Among the maze of artworks and art historical references that haunt Haneke's film, this equestrian image is a particularly cryptic object that has garnered the attention of numerous scholars, such as Riemer. Haneke

Fig. 15.3 A maze of images and body parts inside the studio. *Who Was Edgar Allan?* (1984), dir. Michael Haneke, prod. ZDF and ORF.

himself has described it as both an "irritant" and an ancient sign of madness (Grissemann and Omasta 1991: 212).

I want to consider the role of the horse as part of a complex system of visual references that serve to question the illusionism of the cinematic apparatus – a concern that ties Haneke's early TV films to his postmodern surveillance thrillers on media and violence (*Benny's Video*, 1992; *Funny Games*, 1997/2007; *Caché*, 2005). I am interested in how the equestrian image for Haneke serves repeatedly in different manifestations as a compelling symbol of the protagonist's interiority and unstable identity, translating the fragmented literary structure of the novel into an often hallucinatory visual language based on what Pier Paolo Pasolini has theorized as "free indirect point discourse." I will also scrutinize how the image of the horse becomes a signifier for the non-subjective, non-human "exteriority" of cinematic technology itself. I would finally like to offer a reading of Haneke's horses as an allegory of cinematic movement and, thus, as a reflection on the "ontology" of cinema and modern perception, which allows us to read the allusions to the horse gallop as part of a larger chain of references in nineteenth-century visual culture and early cinema which are tied to the *fin-de-siècle* detective search for clues and visual evidence that had previously escaped human perception. The animation of equestrian movement is an allegory of cinema itself and its staging of truth and illusion. Haneke utilizes a variety of art history references in this adaptation, above all references to the horse in motion and Giovanni Morelli's method of art history detection, to point to an alternative genealogy of cinema, not film as entertainment but the moving picture as an instrument of detection, a tool for analysis and also illusion. I am thus not so much concerned with tracing the film's plot or its overall visual style, but with analyzing a series of often overlooked details, volatile double entendres, and mirror effects. Instead of performing a linear close analysis, I will unfold this subtext in the form of a theoretical *flânerie* through what might otherwise appear as disconnected moments in Haneke's cinematic reverie. An interesting counterpoint of historical references emerges in a film that at other points seems quite hermetic and sealed, also allowing the viewer to align *Who Was Edgar Allan?* with later concerns of the director, both addressed in his features and his relatively unknown engagement with the Lumière cinematograph in his contribution to the omnibus film *Lumière and Company* (1995).

Haneke himself emphasized that the thematic obsession with the horse, first displayed as a somewhat anachronistic "cave wall" sketch in the studio apartment, does not exist in the novel.[11] It is Haneke's own signature, the ultimate signifier in a never-ending chain of signification pointing to the self-proclaimed insanity and sickness of the male protagonist. When a lawyer, clad in black, shot in deep-focus cinematography,[12] suddenly pays the student a visit, bringing news and documents concerning the death of the student's father, the advocate is forced to sit uncomfortably upright under this equestrian sign. Later the student in this sequence stands in front of the horse, obstructing the sketch from our view, while also conflating his own identity with that of the artistic object. In this introductory sequence, which follows the foreboding crime scene in the opening sequence of the film, we see the advocate grow increasingly awkward and nervous under this sign, yet the student seems empowered. Sitting at his desk, framed by a bricolage of torn images, fragments, and art history ephemera, the student smiles, confessing that he is sick, too sick for a funeral. The lawyer has entered the apartment with news of the death of the student's father. The student, however, decides against traveling to Germany for his father's funeral, stating that he is too ill to travel. Clearly, the relationship between father and son was strained.

In a later sequence of the film we witness in detail the "sickness" of the male protagonist, his drug-induced paranoia and hallucination. After snorting cocaine, the student is haunted by the reflection of his new friend Edgar Allan, whom he met earlier in the Café Florian. When Edgar Allan first introduces himself in the elegant café, he laughs and states, "You think of Poe. So did my father." It is clear that the actor is here speaking both to the student and to the spectator, already playing with and even mocking the audience's expectations. In a stylized hallucinatory sequence, set to an eerie high-pitched wail, the drugged student suddenly believes he sees his German-American acquaintance as a mirror image in a seedy bar. After an extreme close-up of a cassette deck, the music ends and the hallucination begins; already in *Who Was Edgar Allan?* Haneke likes to play with the automatic stop-start button (anticipating *Funny Games*, when the attacker suddenly turns to us to ask "where is the remote" and then rewinds so he can again take control of the media apparatus and outcome of the film). His disjunctive editing, triggered by turning off an analog media device, signals subjective time–space confusion, just as the hallucination marks a departure from the realism of a linear narrative. The student's drinking companion refuses to take amphetamines and scoffs, "I am not sick." He is thus not privy to the sensory overload and optical illusion that haunt the film and Rosei's novel. He, unlike the student, "doesn't see a thing." Delirium is thus engaged by the film in a dual way: On the one hand, it is identified with sickness and deemed pathological; on the other hand, a healthy perspective is identified only as a rarefied outsider view. The nascent movement of cinema or dream of animating the image is also revealed as a modernist sickness or "delirium" in a Deleuzian sense, as a genealogy that is built on fragments and ruptures, not on the smooth space of historical progress and continuity.

Haneke draws upon the novel's interest in perception and "optical illusion" to probe his own obsession with the prehistory and illusionism of the cinematic apparatus, as well as the theatricality of cinematic time and space and the manipu- lation of media, the fast-forward/rewind or acceleration/deceleration of the moving image. The language used to describe the optical illusions in the novel is already proto-filmic. Rosei draws upon the phantasmagoria of "projection" – "illu- sory projections" (*Illusion Projektionen*), "projections of my insanity" (*Projektionen meines Wahnsinns*), and "phantom reproductions" (*Abbildung des Phantoms*) (Rosei 1992: 37, 38, 96) to depict the unsettling impact of the optical illusions and atom- ized view of reality: "In the darkness I saw flying points of light and other optical illusions. A slight shudder took hold of my body."[13] Staging the self-reflexive play of the camera within the labyrinthine movement of Venice's canal system, Haneke translates this drug-induced *flânerie* of urban perception into highly sub- jective close-ups, visual and architectural cues or clues. The boundaries between internal and external vision are blurred, as the protagonist (re)collects and orders his *flânerie*. The architecture of Venice is also obscured by the iconography of dim alleyways, silhouettes, mirrors, and double exposures. The film conjures up doubles, only to dispel them as an illusion.

In another spectacular sequence the director experiments with the "impossible" subjective point-of-view shot that pans 360 degrees to finally face the viewing subject or protagonist. Haneke's stalking camera seems to float above the waters, moving from the dark claustrophobia of a narrow passageway to the open water- ways of the canals, encountering a barge that is transporting four golden horse statues, only to finally turn on its axis almost 360 degrees to face the protagonist who is now in retrospect revealed to be the viewing subject, the origin of the point of view. It is in this logically impossible sequence, where the gaze is momentar- ily disembodied, drifting without being anchored in the physical perception of the protagonist and returning almost violently to confront the protagonist, that we are again faced with the enigmatic equestrian sign or animal cryptology. It is as if the equestrian image self-reflexively triggers the madness of the masterful choreography of this impossible subjective–objective perspective, what Pasolini has described as the neurotic gaze of an ambiguous "free indirect discourse."[14]

As Pasolini argued in his analysis of Antonioni's filmmaking, free indirect discourse creates a "film within a film," "allowing a director to smuggle a formal expression of his/her individual point-of-view into a narrative film by disguising it as the purely formal expression of a character's point-of-view" (Keating 2009). Deleuze also provocatively describes the free indirect point-of-view shot as an ethical camera consciousness or camera Cogito – an alternative to Henri Bergson's alienating "cinematographical consciousness" – which makes the camera "known"/felt:

> A character acts on the screen, and is assumed to see the world in a certain way. But simultaneously the camera sees him, and sees his world, from another point of view which thinks, reflects and transforms the viewpoint of the character. Pasolini says: the director "has replaced wholesale the neurotic's vision of the world by his own delirious vision of aestheticism." It is in fact a good thing that the character should be neurotic, to indicate more effectively the difficult birth of a subject into the world. But the camera does not simply give us the vision of character and of his world; it imposes another vision in which the first is transformed and reflected. This subdivision is what Pasolini calls a "free indirect subjective" . . . We are no longer faced with subjective or objective images; we are caught in a correlation between a perception-image and a camera consciousness which transforms it (the question of knowing whether the image was objective or subjective is no longer raised). It is a very special kind of cinema which has acquired a taste for "making the camera felt." (Deleuze 1986: 74)

In Haneke's later films, such as *Caché* and *Code Unknown* (2000), it becomes apparent that this free indirect point-of-view shot can also be "plugged," sutured onto surveillance as another outside apparatus that spies on the protagonist, initiating an uncanny view of the self from the space of the other. The "free indirect discourse" in *Who Was Edgar Allan?* defamiliarizes or *others* the gaze in a manner which will in later films return as the gaze of the other. Here we are reminded of one of Haneke's primary goals in *Who Was Edgar Allan?*, which is to defamiliarize Venice and avoid replicating the tourist images often associated with the city. As an example of how he estranged the monumental city and its architecture, Haneke in an interview (Grissemann and Omasta 1991: 199) cites his bird's-eye surveillance shot of Saint Mark's Square, now rendered an abstract geometrical grid, similar to the high-angle opening shot of Francis Ford Coppola's *The Conversation* (1974). Haneke's cinematography transposes the fragmented and iterative language of Rosei's narrative into a new cinematic style. Utilizing a hand-held camera, steadicam, and fluid tracking shots, Haneke zooms, pans, and frequently draws upon the long shot, close-up, and slow motion to overcome the limitations of televisuality, but also to estrange the city, documenting it through disconcerting angles and surveillance shots.

Associated more with modernism than with postmodernism at this point in his career, Haneke, in another hallucinatory sequence in *Who Was Edgar Allan?*, again utilizes this self-referential play on vision, point of view, and perception to lure the student and the spectator into a fantasy of "animating the image," as the insane equestrian image takes flight. Here Haneke makes playful reference to the time and motion studies by French physiologist Etienne Jules Marey and American photographer Eadweard Muybridge which historians use to narrate the prehistory of projected moving pictures. In the film's second hallucinatory sequence, it is as if the student meditates on the artistic representation of the horse gallop and the experimental terrain of the time and motion studies pioneered by Muybridge and Marey. At the same time, Haneke's self-reflexive play on horse movement identifies the characteristic "shorthand' of cinematic illusionism, the trick of animating the image.

In a striking series of close-ups, the wide-eyed "sickness" of the student suddenly reveals the techno-origin or quite literally the *Ur-Sprung* (first leap or leap into life) of cinema, as the horse lifts its legs in a flying gallop. At first glance, this leap conjures up Muybridge's 1879 photographs of Leland Stanford's racehorse "taking flight," exposing what Walter Benjamin in his short history of photography terms the opening up of the "new nature" of the "optical unconscious" (Fig. 15.4).[15] However, on closer examination, Haneke's "horse gallop" is not the anatomically correct version but the outmoded incorrect pose, another play on using the camera for truth and illusion. The representation of equestrian movement in the second sketch conjures up not the correct pose of Muybridge's instantaneous photograph of the racehorse Occident with all four legs crumpled beneath its belly like a spider, but the incorrect pose of an elongated gallop, the false representation of the "flying gallop" as epitomized in Géricault's painting *Derby at Epsom* (1821). The student seems to hallucinate art history in a painful close-up, flipping between the two equestrian images. After an extreme close-up of Paulus Manker's eyes (the fulfillment of the taunting series of eyes that underscores the act of artistic seeing within the studio apartment), Haneke cuts to two sketches of the horse, the original "cave drawing" (a variation of the drawing in the opening studio shot) and a second charcoal sketch where equine art "takes flight" (Fig. 15.5). The student blinks and subsequently flips between two artistic objects; the equine object lifts all four hooves off the ground. Woven into the director's self-reflexive play on art history, artistic vision, and perception, this equestrian "animation" is another detective search, Haneke's attempt to "identify" the origin of cinematic movement.

Haneke's understanding of cinematography here not only echoes the "free indirect subjective" discourse of Pasolini, but also Epstein's 1920s notion of *photogénie*, a lyrical mode of enunciation stressing the pure poetry of everyday objects, the shock of a new cinematic perception, and the sublime experience of slow motion and the close-up. Similarly, the protagonist's hallucinatory experiences emerge at

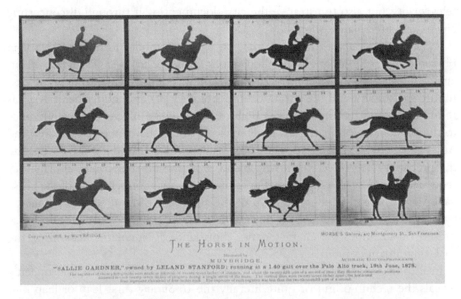

Fig. 15.4 Muybridge's photographs of Leland Stanford's racehorse "taking flight." *Who Was Edgar Allan?* (1984), dir. Michael Haneke, prod. ZDF and ORF.

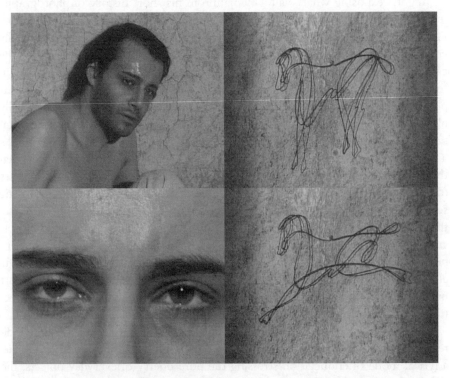

Fig. 15.5 The student in close-up, flipping between the two equestrian images. *Who Was Edgar Allan?* (1984), dir. Michael Haneke, prod. ZDF and ORF.

the crossroads of temporality and technology: Haneke's protagonist sees the image of the horse in flight, but cannot contain or hold the image. A bottle of wine shatters in slow motion. Time *qua* movement is not only animated, it is distorted, reversed, reminding us of the earlier nineteenth-century discourse on series-photography representation as truth or deception. Just as the revolutionary photography of Muybridge was criticized, deemed a "distorted," failed aesthetic by influential artists such as the sculptor Rodin, who famously insisted that he preferred the traditional depiction of a gallop seen in the paintings of Géricault, Haneke seems to use the *photogénie* reverie of the image to self-reflexively point to an earlier art history discourse critiquing the powerful illusionism of the apparatus. One hundred years prior to Haneke's critique of film as twenty-four lies a second, artists critiqued the series-photograph as a fragmented lie, an illusion every fraction of a second.

Describing movement as the "transition" from one attitude to another, Rodin famously asserted that "it is the artist who is truthful" and "photography which lies, for in reality time does not stand still" (Rodin 2009: 32). Rodin continues to argue that the sensitive plate lacks life and vitality, the important tools of the artist:

> If the artist succeeds in producing the impression of a movement which takes several moments for accomplishment, his work is certainly much less conventional than the scientific image, where time is abruptly suspended. It is that which condemns certain modern painters who, when they wish to represent horses galloping, reproduce the poses furnished by instantaneous photography. Géricault is criticized because in his picture *Epsom Races* (*Course d' Epsom*), which is at the Louvre, he has painted his horses galloping, fully extended, *ventre à terre*, to use a familiar expression, throwing their fore feet forward and their hind feet backward at the same instant . . . the sensitive plate never gives the same effect. And, in fact, in instantaneous photography, when the forelegs of a horse are forward, the hind legs, having by their pause propelled the body onward, have already had time to gather themselves under the body in order to recommence the stride, so that for a moment the four legs are almost gathered together in the air, which gives the animal the appearance of jumping off the ground, and of being motionless in this position. Now I believe that it is Géricault who is right, and not the camera, for his horses appear to run; this comes from the fact that the spectator from right to left sees first the hind legs accomplish the effort whence the general impetus results, then the body stretched out, then the forelegs which seek the ground ahead. This is false in reality, as the actions could not be simultaneous; but it is true when the parts are observed successively. (Ibid.)

Rodin argued that Muybridge's photographs of the racehorse gallop do not document, but distort and falsify movement. The magnifying gaze of series-photography is seen to misrepresent reality. Rodin thus interprets the series-photography image as another site of a distorted optical illusion. In Rodin's wake, numerous *fin-de-siècle* artists questioned the validity of series-photography and its new project of modernizing vision. Nearly a century after the Muybridge racehorse takes flight, Haneke self-reflexively inscribes this theme of racehorse motion, animation, and cinematic time into the visual cues and art history references of his adaptation. He unfolds the spectacle of watching the horse in flight as another contested site of a fragmented and distorted artistic gaze: What is real? What is illusion? Subsequently, the racehorse motif in *Who Was Edgar Allan?* (intimately tied to Muybridge's time–motion studies) serves to underscore the hallucinatory nature of animal locomotion and implicates media in a web of deception, again highlighting the "illusionism" of the apparatus. We see the racehorse enthusiast Edgar Allan place sizable bets on three horses with the student as his witness. The music speeds up to document the race of adrenaline as the bets are placed. The next day, the student attempts to bet on the same horses, but is told by a surprised bookie that these horses either "do not exist" or haven't raced in several years. Linear time appears "out of joint" – thus, another "scientific" nineteenth-century obsession that paved the way for the invention of the cinematograph now is linked to the merely subjective realm of hallucination.

In a later sequence of the film the student is seen wandering around the university, looking for the lectures on the art critic Giovanni Morelli, who developed the "Morelli method" that would revolutionize art history scholarship in the 1880s. The student stares at a list of informational flyers in a darkened room that is heavy with high-contrast lighting and oversized shadows. A disembodied offscreen male voice[16] asks: "Are you searching for something?" Yes, the student replies, "I'm looking for the lecture on Giovanni Morelli," only to hear, "But that's been over for 3 months!"[17] The Italian politician and art critic Giovanni Morelli serves as another anachronistic and enigmatic "double" within the film, a "split" character who trained as a medical doctor yet also published seminal work in art history in German under an anagrammatic pseudonym, "Ivan Lermolieff." The Morelli method, contemporaneous with the "birth" of cinema – what Benjamin in Freudian terminology describes as the opening up of the "optical unconscious" – thus appears as another search for clues that perhaps holds the key to reading or interpreting the film's self-reflexivity. Morelli's anagrammatic pseudonym and the fragmented modernism of Morelli's method are certainly fitting references for Haneke's own forensics game which speculates on how to adapt, identify, and at the same time unwind traditional narrative structures, spectator/viewer positions, and key elements of filmmaking.[18] Morelli famously sought to identify the characteristic "signature" of painters through scrutiny of minor details that revealed artists' *unconscious short-hand* and conventions for portraying, for example, hands and ears (fragmented body parts frequently displayed by Haneke in the student's art studio).[19] Morelli's technique was a major breakthrough of scientific thought in the nineteenth century, inspiring not only Carlo Ginzburg, the father of "micro-history," who returned to the Morelli method in the 1970s to ground his study of the past that starts with seemingly insignificant, minor details, but also Sigmund Freud (who used Morelli's method in his 1914 study *The Moses of Michelangelo*).

Like Muybridge's time–motion studies, Morelli's art historical methodology can be read as an allegory of detection that works through fragmentation. In Haneke's detective crime thriller the flying gallop is the fragmented signature of cinema, the modernist sickness that Haneke self-reflexively has to identify. However, it is important to point out that within the larger hallucinatory sequence of Haneke's film, the moving picture of the horse in flight (resembling a rudimentary thaumatrope or thumb flip book) is itself only a prelude to another more dramatic play on cinematic illusion and paranoia. After observing the "primitive" animation of the cave-painting, the spectator sees Haneke unveil another trick of "disjoined editing." In a lap dissolve, Edgar Allan walks down a passage with his back turned to the spectator. Before he reaches his destination or recedes into the depth of the image a dissolve shows the same character in reverse, walking out of the depth of the frame toward the spectator – for a brief moment Edgar Allan is a double exposure, a split subject heading in two opposite directions, exploding the representation of cinematic space. The sequence finally leads to another self-reflexive moment, an homage to a New German Cinema director, Wim Wenders. As the protagonist rushes out into the rain, desperate to locate his American friend, Haneke quickly cuts to a cinema and a marquee advertising Wenders's *The American Friend*. We see our student struggle in vain to find the written "trace" of Edgar Allan, looking through the crumpled papers and receipts in the trash can outside the cinema. Yet it is the spectator who makes the link and sees the title of Wenders's "film within the film," a doubling of the "American friend" as well as a doubling of the desire that gradually unfolds between the two characters.[20]

The self-reflexive aesthetic, double exposures, and hallucinatory art history in Haneke's filmmaking lead to either the constant danger of a vicious loop or circle – media repetition, reversal, or doubling – or the micro-fragmentation of a modernist Morelli detection. But Haneke continues to unfold the horse gallop motif in the film, tying it to delusion, paranoia, and hallucinatory perception. If we read the thaumatropic representation of the horse as part of the larger narrative of race-horses in the film, the insider reference to the railroad magnate Leland Stanford, who hired the series-photographer Muybridge to record his racehorse Occident with all four hooves in the air, becomes more apparent. Indeed, Haneke himself suggests that this is a "film about film," filtered through the lens of art history. In the second gambling sequence, the betting parlor is framed by a gigantic painting which again takes certain features from Géricault's elongated horse body depicted in *Derby at Epsom*, but which also seems to "correct" the pose. In the final betting sequence, however, the movement of the horses is again distorted through the magnifying techniques of both slow motion and close-up cinematography, as the student and Edgar Allan return to the betting studio and the student demands to know the truth behind Edgar Allan's previous visit. Although Rosei's novel seems to suggest that it could have been a covert drug deal that took place in the betting studio (thus, not an actual bet), the film is slightly more ambivalent. There are simply no answers. The agent tells the student that he must be mistaken

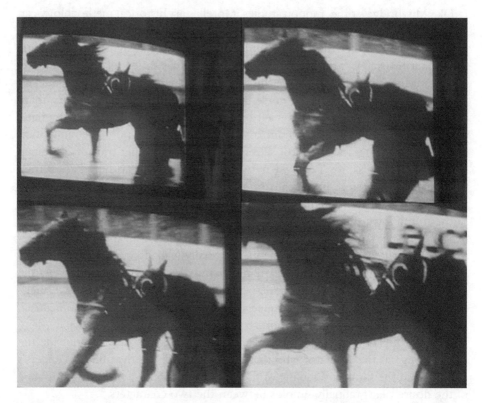

Fig. 15.6   Slow-motion images of the horse race. *Who Was Edgar Allan?* (1984), dir. Michael Haneke, prod. ZDF and ORF.

– perhaps he has fallen prey to an "optical illusion." Edgar Allan reminds the student that "he should be more careful next time." The agent clearly denies having had a transaction with Edgar Allan at the studio, although he recognizes Allan and greets him by name. With tears welling up in his eyes the student turns his attention to a black-and-white TV monitor, which presents the audience with a close-up, slow-motion analysis of the horse race (Fig. 15.6). It is only at this point in the film that the horses are finally set into "motion" or animated in proper "cinematic" form (although it is no longer in the medium of the charcoal sketch or cave-paintings). Yet this animation occurs only within the smaller frame and "counter-medium" of the television and takes place in a sequence which again emphasizes a disjunctive temporality or anachronism, a mis-meeting or misreading between the student and Edgar Allan. As we see in the television monitor, Haneke's horses do not gallop – they move in fragmented slow motion, evoking an effect that Georg Lukács in his late aesthetic theory calls the "disanthropomorphization" and estrangement of the photographic image.[21]

Unlike the explosive shift to color analyzed by Tobias Nagl in this volume in the context of the televisuality in the final scene of Haneke's *Fraulein*, in *Who Was*

Edgar Allan? the monitor's spectrality showcases staccato black-and-white images that do not speak to desire or *jouissance*, but rather emphasize the notion of a *lack* implicit in any melancholy misreading. As tears of anger and disappointment well up in the student's eyes, it becomes obvious to the spectator that the bond between Edgar Allan and the art history student is shattered. Haneke has stated that *Who Was Edgar Allan?* is a film about a homoerotic relationship (Grissemann and Omasta 1991: 198) and the slow-motion camera seems to "distort" and disfigure this relationship.

On a historical register as well, there is a sense of melancholy and paranoia in Haneke's use of TV screens and computer monitors in *Who Was Edgar Allan?*. Already in 1984, Haneke was channeling contemporary fears concerning the rise of a control society that were quite pronounced in Germany in the wake of that Orwellian year, with the movement to boycott the *Volkszählung* (the national census, which took place in 1983). The device we see pictured in the film is thus less a television set than a surveillance screen or electronic monitor, an apparatus that screens movement and "monitors" identity. In the control society documented by Haneke's camera, computer monitors have created an alien-nation. After the student attempts suicide and is taken to the hospital, the image fades to white and there is a cut to an ominous close-up of a computer screen: The calculated blips of the computer keys entering information are accompanied by an offscreen female voice that asks: "Are you a foreigner? Alien?" As in *Fraulein*, there is no *Heimat* and the notion of a "return" is presented in an ironic light. The lawyer in the film asks the exiled German protagonist: "Werden Sie nach dem Studium nach Hause zurückkehren?" ("Will you return home after your studies?") "Irgendwann" ("At some point") is the uncertain reply.

The television set is again scripted into Haneke's haunted screen as part of an anachronistic play on early cinema and older media artifacts in his 1995 tribute to the original Lumière cinematograph in the collection *Lumière and Company*. To commemorate the centennial of the Lumière Brothers' first "motion picture," international filmmakers were invited to direct their own one-minute Lumière film. Using the restored original camera of 1895, each director offered his or her own experimental tribute to early cinema. Haneke not surprisingly is somewhat of an anomaly within this collection: He uses the Lumière camera to tape contemporary news broadcasts on the UN, hockey, soccer, nuclear disaster, speed-trap surveillance equipment, and the weather in Germany. Instead of restaging the arrival of a train (Patrice Leconte) or breakfast with baby (Spike Lee), Haneke films TV, presenting the viewer with a fast-paced montage of televised news clips from March 19, 1995, in honor of the first tour of the Lumière cameraman on March 19, 1895. The Haneke–Lumière camera captures everything from the political to the mundane, featuring news clips on items as diverse as gun laws and inflatable dolls. After the experiment, Haneke also admits that media is always already a past incarnation, a melancholy event that calls out to be misread, misappropriated, manipulated.[22]

Notes

1 In Austria the airing of *Who Was Edgar Allan?* received terrible ratings; ORF viewer levels were at an all-time low (Traversa 1994: 206). Haneke, however, gained viewers in the 1990s when he returned to TV and the "Krimi" to write a script for a 1993 episode of the TV crime series *Tatort*. This conspiracy thriller concerned the mysterious death of an engineer who produced parts for a nuclear power plant. The episode, entitled "Kesseltreiben" ("Witch-Hunt"), premiered on March 7, 1993 and reached over 11 million viewers. Haneke in his interview with Grissemann and Omasta states: "One has to *use* television. For the Saarländischen Rundfunk I even wrote an episode of *Tatort*. Theme: Crime in the Nuclear Power Industry. Nowhere else have I had as many viewers as with *Tatort*. One can use the genre in order to challenge the spectator intellectually and morally" (Grissemann and Omasta 1991: 206, my translation).

2 Born in Vienna in 1946, Peter Rosei originally studied law at the University of Vienna and for a short time also worked as an assistant to the painter Ernst Fuchs, the artist who founded the Viennese School of fantastic realism. Rosei's prolific career includes numerous acclaimed novels, plays, radio plays, and poetry.

3 This overbearing melancholia is certainly not the only side to Kafka's writing. I would echo Deleuze and Guattari, who argue that the "Kafkaesque" view oversimplifies his multifaceted narrative, which also carries within itself seeds of desire and ecstasy.

4 "Poe hat mir damals sehr viel geholfen, vor allem durch seine Poetik. Poe ist ja der schärfste Feind der Inspiration, von irgendwelchen numinosen Kräften. Er sagt, Literatur sei essentiell etwas Gemachtes."

5 In an interview, Rosei stated that one of his goals in the novel was to "montage consciousnessness." See Theisen (2003: 106).

6 Poe's "poetic calculus" is a synthesis of mathematics and poetic reason, illustrated for the reader in the cryptic tale "The Purloined Letter" (1844). A detective named Dupin finally locates a hidden object, a love letter, not by probing the dark secrets or recesses of an apartment, but by examining that which is languishing on the surface, in plain sight, a letter that has been turned inside out or "purloined."

7 In *A Thousand Plateaus*, Deleuze and Guattari use the concept of the "rhizome" as a metaphor for their own writing, which they differentiate from the tree and the root. A rhizomatic text is a non-hierarchical, open structure that has no center. They argue that a rhizome "has no beginning or end. It is always in the middle, between things, an interbeing, an intermezzo" (Deleuze and Guattari 2004: 27–8). In *Who Was Edgar Allan?* this non-hierarchical media awareness or the laying bare of the illusionism of the apparatus also becomes obvious in the film's only direct reference to one of the most astute observers of nineteenth-century media and namesake of its title: Edgar Allan Poe. In a moment of self-proclaimed madness near the end of the film, the protagonist in a meticulously composed tracking shot narrates Edgar Allan Poe's own trickster tale, "Hop Frog" (1849). In a dramatic long take, the camera slowly tracks back to reveal the film studio of *Who Was Edgar Allan?*, another derelict space, complete with camera equipment, lighting, props, equine statues, searchlights, and the police siren seen in the film's dramatic opening. As Haneke confirms in an interview,

this long take is another playful, ironic gesture that critiques the artifice of the apparatus. The film ends with another slow, painful tracking shot, pulling the viewer away from the ideological apparatus or screen of entertainment; as we become aware of the frame, we are again implicated in the frame-up, film as truth and deception.

8   Since no published translation of the original exists, I have offered my own translation. The original reads: "Und so, als könnte der Paroxysmus noch gesteigert werden, verband sich im Wirbelstrom meines Bewusstseins die reale Gestalt Allens mit jener des längst dahingegangenen Dichters Poe, und ich sah beide in eins, sah eine riesenhafte Gestalt halb fürsorglich, halb drohend zu mir sich herunterbeugen, und nun, um vollends unlösbar zu sein, tönte die Frage anders – ich wurde gefragt, die Gestalt fragte – und so: Wer war Edgar Allan"? (Rosei 1992: 59).

9   In another self-reflexive sequence of the film, the camera tracks back as Manker narrates Edgar Allan Poe's trickster tale "Hop Frog" to reveal Haneke's own film studio (see note 7 above). The self-reflexive camera showcases the set of the 1984 detective thriller with all the props and camera equipment strewn haphazardly throughout the open space. In the final sequence of the film, we witness another elaborate tracking shot, as the frame of the film is minimized on our screen, reminding us that the spectator has also been "framed," like the television set itself. This final moment of the film seems to anticipate Laura Mulvey's theoretical insight, that the grammar of the film frame itself is an anachronism, a holdover from celluloid.

10 Haneke has described *Who Was Edgar Allan?* as the most musical and least static of all his films: "In no other film did I have as many tracking shots and the cameraman, who hated 'tracking,' almost gave up. [But] the pull of the story should also translate visually. One thing leads to the next. This film is permanent movement" ("In keinem meiner Filme bin ich soviel herumgefahren, und der Kameramann, der eigentlich Fahrten haßte, verzweifelte. Der Sog, den die Geschichte hat, sollte auch optisch umgesetzt werden. Einer verfolgt den anderen. Der Film ist eine permanente Bewegung") (Grissemann and Omasta 1991: 199, my translation). Haneke thus views it as "not a coincidence" that this film, out of all of his TV works, "comes closest to being cinema" (ibid., my translation).

11 Although the horse does not appear in the novel as an obsession or "art history" object, Rosei's narrator does describe a memory he has of observing a beautiful horse and then discovering later that the dealers had fed the horse arsenic. The horse was apparently "ruined in its final moment of beauty," like the slow-motion movement of the horses on the monitor that serve to deconstruct and "disanthropomorphize" the image. Haneke in his interview with Grissemann and Omasta claims that the "horse symbol" is not present in the novel.

12 Deep-focus cinematography is also used frequently in Haneke's adaptation of Franz Kafka's unfinished novel, *The Castle* (1997).

13 Rosei (1992: 73, my translation).

14 The "zoom" is another example of Haneke's "cold formalism" that could also be interpreted as a form of modernist *écriture* that can be subsumed under the category of "free indirect subjective" discourse. See Gilles Deleuze (1986), Pier Paolo Pasolini (1988), and Patrick Keating (2009).

15 Walter Benjamin (1977; 1969: 237).

16   See Libby Saxton's discussion of offscreen space in Haneke (Saxton 2007). Brigitte Peucker
     makes the important point that sounds in Haneke frequently occur in voice-over or
     issue from offscreen, yet "refuse the homogenizing effects of extradiegetic music"
     (Peucker 2007).

17   The enigmatic way Haneke introduces art history, without explaining it to the viewer,
     and also introduces a character who is in the process of deciphering and studying
     these references seems to anticipate certain moments of "testing" that we see in later
     films such as *Funny Games*. Critics such as Thomas Elsaesser have used the concept
     of "mind games" to describe crisis scenes in films from *Fight Club* (David Fincher,
     1999) to *Funny Games*. I would argue that it is important to differentiate between
     the incessant and self-imposed "test drive" in Haneke and the unreliable rules of
     "mind games" played in his films. See Thomas Elsaesser (2009) and Avital Ronell
     (2005).

18   In this context it is worth pointing out that the scriptwriter of *Who Was Edgar Allan?*,
     Hans Brockner, is also a pseudonym for both Haneke and Peter Rosei.

19   On Giovanni Morelli's art history method of detection (primarily used to identify
     fakes/frauds), see Carlo Ginzburg (1980). Ginzburg points to the importance of the
     "unconscious" in Morelli's art history method and praises his "medical diagnosis" that
     picks up on details unnoticed by the normal eye.

20   This particular scene probably alludes to another hallucinatory film reference in Peter
     Rosei's novel *Von hier nach dort/From Here to There* (1978). A young male protagonist
     goes to the movies in heavy rain and leaves his umbrella inside the theater; he
     subsequently hallucinates that the ticket counter has stolen his umbrella and used it
     as a parachute (Rosei 1992: 120).

21   "Photography as a point of departure is in and of itself disanthropomorphic. Film
     technique is the first mimetic reflection of reality to reverse this disanthropomorphism
     and approximate the image of normal visibility of everyday life . . . Yet it is still not
     an aesthetic. There is even the possibility that film technique will slip back into dis-
     anthropormorphism, for instance slow motion" (Lukács 1963: 490, my translation).
     Lukács's diatribe against the apparent distortion of "subjective time" is part of a larger
     debate on the ideology of modernism.

22   Here we get a glimpse of one of the theoretical idioms or strategies that is dominant
     in Haneke's later work, the purposeful pedagogy of anachronism, the use of outdated
     or outmoded media devices in an ironic play on the audience's own use or abuse of
     desensitizing media. Out-of-place artifacts shock the spectator into a new awareness,
     not only of the history of media forms, but also of our own dependency on these
     devices.

References and Further Reading

Benjamin, Walter: "A Small History of Photography", trans. Phil Patton, *Artforum* 15:6
     (February 1977): 46–51.
Benjamin, Walter: "The Work of Art in the Age of Mechanical Reproduction," *Illumina-
     tions*, ed. Hannah Arendt, trans. Harry Zohn (New York: Shocken Books, 1969).
Böbbies, Peter: "Ein Fest der leisen Töne," *Die Welt*, January 14, 1986.

Deleuze, Gilles: *Cinema 1: The Movement-Image*, trans. Hugh Tomlinson and Barbara Habberjam (Minneapolis: University of Minnesota Press, 1986).

Deleuze, Gilles and Guattari, Félix: *A Thousand Plateaus: Capitalism and Schizophrenia*, trans. Brian Massumi (Minneapolis: University of Minnesota Press, 2004).

Elsaesser, Thomas: "The Mind-Game Film: A New Genre, or an Old Ontological Doubt?," *Puzzle Films: Complex Storytelling in Contemporary Film*, ed. W. Buckland (Oxford: Blackwell, 2009), pp. 13–41.

Enzberg, P.: "'Einfach unterwegs sein': Zur Wahrnehmungsproblematik und zum Problematischen der Wahrnehmung bei Peter Rosei," *Dossier 6: Peter Rosei*, ed. Gerhard Fuchs and Günther A. Höfler (Graz and Vienna: Droschl, 1994), pp. 33–63.

Frey, Mattias: "*Benny's Video, Caché*, and the Desubstantiated Image," *Framework: The Journal of Cinema and Media* 47:2 (Fall 2006): 30–6.

Ginzburg, Carlo: "Morelli, Freud, and Sherlock Holmes: Clues and Scientific Method," trans. Anna David, *History Workshop* 9 (1980): 5–36.

Grissemann, Stefan and Omasta, Michael: "Herr Haneke, wo bleibt das Positive? Ein Gespräch mit dem Regissuer," *Der Siebente Kontinent. Michael Haneke und seine Filme*, ed. Alexander Horwath (Vienna: Europaverlag, 1991), pp. 193–213.

Haneke, Michael: "Beyond Mainstream Film," *After Postmodernism: Austrian Literature and Film in Transition*, ed. Willy Riemer (Riverside, CA: Ariadne Press, 2000), pp. 159–70.

Horwath, Alexander, ed.: *Der Siebente Kontinent. Michael Haneke und seine Filme* (Vienna: Europaverlag, 1991).

Keating, Patrick: "Pasolini, Croce, and the Cinema of Poetry," *Scope: An Online Journal of Film and TV Studies* (February 13, 2009), www.scope.nottingham.ac.uk/article.php?issue=jun2001&id=276&section=article.

Kopka, C.: "Ein spannungsarmes Rätselspiel," *Westfälische Rundschau*, January 14, 1986.

Lukács, Georg: *Eigenart des Aesthetischen* (Neuwied am Rhein: Luchterhand, 1963).

Mulvey Laura: *Death 24X a Second: Stillness and the Moving Image* (London: Reaktion Books, 2006).

Pasolini, Pierre Paolo: *Heretical Empiricism*, ed. Louise K. Barnett, trans. Ben Lawton and Louise K. Barnett (Bloomington: Indiana University Press, 1988).

Peucker, Brigitte: *The Material Image: Art and the Real in Film* (Stanford, CA: Stanford University Press, 2007).

Riemer, Willy: "Iterative Texts: Haneke/Rosei, *Wer war Edgar Allan?*," *After Postmodernism: Austrian Literature and Film in Translation*, ed. Willy Riemer (Riverside, CA: Ariadne Press, 2000), pp. 189–98.

Rodin, A.: "Movement in Art," *Rodin on Art and Artists: Conversations with Paul Gsell* (New York: Dover, 2009), pp. 32–6.

Ronell, Avital: *The Test Drive* (Bloomington: Indiana University Press, 2005).

Rosei, Peter: *Beiträge zu einer Poesie der Zukunft. Grazer Poetikvorlesung* (Graz and Vienna: Droschl, 1995).

Rosei, Peter: *Drei Romane: Wer war Edgar Allan? Von Hier nach Dort. Das schnelle Glück* (Stuttgart: Verlag Klett-Cotta, 1992).

Rosei, Peter: *Wer war Edgar Allan?* (Salzburg: Residenz Verlag, 1977).

Saxton, Libby: "Secrets and Revelations: Off-screen Space in Michael Haneke's *Caché* (2005)," *Studies in French Cinema* 7:1 (February 2007): 5–17.

Schwarz, W., ed.: *Peter Rosei. Gespräche in Kanada* (Frankfurt am Main and New York: Peter Lang, 1992).

Theisen, Bianca: *Silenced Facts: Media Montages in Contemporary Austrian Literature* (Amsterdam: Rodopi, 2003).

Thomas, J.: "Haneke's New(s) Images," *Art Journal* 67:3 (2008): 80–5.

Traversa, I.: "Strategie der Fragezeichen: Multiperspektivisches Erzählen in Michael Hanekes Verfilmung von *Wer war Edgar Allan?*," *Dossier 6: Peter Rosei*, ed. Gerhard Fuchs and Günther A. Höfler (Graz and Vienna: Droschl, 1994), p. 206.

16

Bureaucracy and Visual Style

Brian Price

This essay concerns eleven shots in Haneke's adaptation of Franz Kafka's *The Castle* (1997). Taken together, these eleven shots – structurally similar, but not in any sense identical – thematize the problem of bureaucracy in visual terms. They both invoke and solve a problem of bureaucracy, namely, the long-standing difficulty political theorists have had defining it. As Claude Lefort so succinctly states: "Bureaucracy confronts us as a phenomenon of which everyone speaks and believes to have experienced in some way, and yet this phenomenon strangely resists conceptualization" (1986: 89). This is a problem, I propose, that Haneke seems to understand rather well, and his understanding is that of a visual artist, one who thinks in and with images. We all believe that we know a bureaucracy when we see one, as Lefort suggests, but how can one *see* a bureaucracy? Isn't the point of bureaucracy that it can never be seen, that the logic of bureaucracy must never be revealed? How, then, might something that is meant to be suppressed – that cannot function unless its organizing logic is secreted – be rendered in visual terms? What these eleven shots propose, I will argue, among other things, is a solution for the theorization of bureaucracy in terms of visual style and *as* visual style. It is a questioning after the visuality of bureaucracy itself.

It is for this reason, in particular, that I concern myself here solely with Haneke's adaptation of Kafka's novel, rather than engaging in an extensive consideration of the relation *between* novel and film. The plot of Haneke's film is obviously derived in important ways from Kafka's novel and indeed follows it very closely. The film, like the novel, recounts the story of K., a land surveyor who has been summoned to "The Castle" for employment, only to arrive at an extended series of frustrated encounters with residents of the town and employees of the Castle to which he has been summoned, with people who fail in almost every instance to countenance both his "advanced" standing as a land surveyor and – most of all – his place in the system that has supposedly requested his services. K.'s journey begins in a village taproom filled with peasants – all of whom are suspicious of K.'s claim to belonging. Already wearied from his journey, K.

demands recognition and clears, in the meanwhile, a space to sleep on the floor. K.'s goal is to contact Klamm, his alleged superior, the one who knows both K.'s advanced standing and his reason for being there. Klamm, of course, never appears – only Barnabas, a messenger with whom we see K. frequently interact in his efforts to reach Klamm. But as K's journey progresses, K.'s standing as land surveyor is never recognized and he is forced instead to accept lower forms of employment and shelter, as when he takes work as a janitor and sleeps with his newly won fiancée, Frieda, on the floor of a classroom with his two hapless assistants in tow, one of whom will come to be Frieda's spouse by the end of the film. In other words, every effort K. makes to be recognized as land surveyor – every attempt he makes to move forward – results in the dissolution of what has come together in a process of searching, or the worsening of a lot that was already quite low. The more K. asks, the less he learns.

For Haneke, this confusion – as it is for Kafka – is the work of bureaucracy. And for both Haneke and Kafka, the active production of disinformation that belies the "working" of any bureaucratic form is related to technology. For Kafka, though, it is a question of the telephone – this technological form that promises contact, but only at a distance. For instance, the narrator of Kafka's novel, echoing K.'s wonder upon his arrival at the taproom, puts it clearly: "So there was a telephone in this village inn? They were certainly well equipped" (Kafka 1998: 3). In other words, the phone – as a form of new technology – would seem to promise contact, when what follows is only a *mise-en-abyme* of disinformation. For Haneke, however, the organizing logic of bureaucracy is best understood in visual terms. Thus to understand the nature of bureaucracy itself – which causes K.'s undoing (and our own) – Haneke directs our attention to the visuality of bureaucracy itself by insistently depicting K.'s failed movements in the form of eleven tracking shots – a series of shots that will work, as I have said, to produce a philosophical under-standing of bureaucracy that has eluded political theorists thus far.

I shall begin my investigation, then, with a description of the eleven shots I have in mind as an answer to the paradox articulated by Claude Lefort. What binds these shots together – the logic that unites them in my account here – is that they are all lateral tracking shots. Each of these tracking shots, save for two, occur out-doors and record the movement of K. between bureaucratic spaces, the various sites in which K. will make his appeal for his belonging in the Castle as land sur-veyor. Each instance is also a single take and should be understood as a unified movement in space, one that is most often disconnected from the scenes of bureau-cratic appeals that appear between these instances, which are largely rendered in a more fragmentary and conventional form (shot/reverse-shot constructions, shorter durations between shots). To emphasize this point, each tracking shot is most often preceded and followed by a cut to black, a pause that disrupts the continuity of the visible.

The lateral movement of these tracking shots best describes the character of K.'s struggle as forward momentum continually interrupted. In his frustration with the perpetual display of disinformation, K. is driven – as we all can be – to move forward. But "forward" and "backward" are spatial directives implied only by the lateral reach of the tracks. Tracks, as we know, can be placed anywhere. They guarantee nothing more than lateral movement, movements that are precise, calculable, and largely inflexible. One can go right or left, forward or backward. It is only the determination of the frustrated K. that gives us a sense of moving forward, even when moving forward – as a spatial directive that implies progress in roughly metonymic terms – means going backward. Indeed, the irony implicit in each tracking shot is that the tracks laid do not go on, definitely, from one place to another; rather, they are fragments. They guide and record movements through space, but only to a point. They do not secure a path between two places like the railroad system from which they are borrowed. The tracks begin and end in definite points, but those points are in no sense determined by place, or by fixed and predictable destinations. In this way, and as we will see, the tracking shot echoes the spatial logic of bureaucracy.

But first, the list:

1. The shot begins on bodies in motion. The camera is initially trained on a teacher who is surrounded – to the left and the right – by schoolchildren, his students. The camera follows the movement of teacher and students and moves from left to right, until K. enters the frame from screen-right. At that point the camera pauses, but does not cut. It remains stationary as K. and the teacher speak. It is a less than cordial exchange in which the teacher asks K. if he is on his way to the Castle and tells him to remember that the children are innocent. As K. moves on, the camera retreats in the opposite direction and follows him as he moves left. K. pauses almost immediately after commencing with his travels and the camera rests with him, only to begin again its track to the left as K. carries on. The screen goes black.

2. After the fade-to-black that follows shot one there is another tracking shot. This time we see K. carrying on with his walk. The camera follows right to left as K. moves through a field of snow that shows no path. In voice-over, the narrator tells us: "The road didn't lead to the Castle, it only made towards it, then turned aside as if deliberately, and though it didn't lead away from the Castle, it got no nearer to it either."

3. The camera follows K. from right to left. The shot begins in the middle of K.'s walking. The shot, that is to say, begins in motion. K. sees Barnabas and pauses. The camera observes the pauses, is guided by K.'s movements in most instances. Barnabas enters the frame and the two men begin a conversation about the frequency and effectiveness of K.'s potential communications with the Chief. They begin to walk and the camera follows both men; it carries on in its leftward trajectory. At the end of the shot, the camera pauses with Barnabas as he tells K. that "we're home" and invites him inside. The path to Barnabas's home runs perpendicular to the path described by

Haneke's tracking equipment. K. follows Barnabas down the perpendicular path but the camera cannot follow. The screen goes black.

4. The camera tracks K.'s movement from right to left, pauses briefly as he says "good evening" to a group of men burning what appears to be furniture, but one cannot say what kind of furniture, or even that it is furniture; it appears most legibly as a structure in flames. K. continues left and so does the camera. The shot ends as K. follows a short and winding path that is also roughly perpendicular to the tracks. It does not follow him inside and the screen goes black.

5. The shot begins with K. as he walks, this time from left to right. It follows his introduction to Pepi, the barmaid at the taproom – Frieda's replacement. Frieda, of course, left her job for the sake of her relationship with K., one that K. began solely in an effort to obtain access to Klamm, Frieda's former boss (we think) and former lover (we think) and higher up in the bureaucratic chain (K. thinks). As the camera continues to track right, K. arrives at a coach and pauses. The camera remains fixed on K. as he waits, pacing slowing, and finally sits. This shot does not resolve itself with a cut to black. Haneke cuts instead to a shot of K. sitting inside of the coach and stealing a sip of brandy, having been encouraged to do so by the coach driver. K. then meets Klamm's assistant, who has come to ask a few questions. After a few cuts that document the exchange, the tracking shot resumes again. This time, however, it follows Klamm's assistant and moves from left to right and lasts only a couple of seconds. The screen goes black.

6. After a brief meeting with Klamm's assistant, the screen goes black and the tracking shot resumes. This time it moves left to right and follows K. as he runs through the snow and after what he takes to be Klamm's coach. Once he catches up with the coach, it turns and heads down a road that is perpendicular to the tracks. Neither K. nor the camera follows the coach. Instead, K. and the camera reverse direction and move now from right to left. As K. and the camera move slowly left, we hear the shouts of K.'s assistants, who are moving in the direction of K., but from left to right. Both enter the frame but neither K. nor the camera stops to observe them, as they have in K.'s previous encounters. It is only when K. and the camera run into Barnabas a moment later that both pause. Barnabas hands K. a letter from Klamm. As he begins to read the letter, all four men – Barnabas, Arthur, K., and Jeremiah – all line up in a row facing the screen and placed in the order, right to left, in which I have named them. The composition emphasizes the lateral character of the tracking shot. Once it is revealed that Klamm has praised the assistants (Arthur and Jeremiah), both break the lateral formation, hug each other, run screen-right (the camera does not follow), and then return and circle around and between Barnabas and K. in an imperfect 8, a rounded formation that runs afoul of the linearity of the tracks. The shot begins to move leftward as K. and Barnabas carry on their conversation, pauses briefly as they stop, and resumes again as Barnabas follows after a frustrated K. The shot pauses again as K.

pleads with Barnabas to make an appeal on his behalf for a meeting with Klamm. The assistants find their way back into the frame and the screen goes black.

7. On his way to see Barnabas, K. is seen moving right to left. The camera, once again, follows his movement, pausing only when K. arrives at the snowy pathway to Barnabas's house, which is perpendicular to the tracks. K. goes down the path and the camera does not follow. The screen goes black.

8. The camera tracks from right to left as K. walks slowly. It pauses with K. as he notices one of his assistants peering through a window. His assistant tells him that Arthur, the other assistant, has left and filed charges against him. As K. is told that Frieda has returned to work in the taproom, K. reverses direction and starts walking right to left. The camera follows. The camera pauses briefly as Barnabas reappears and swears to K. that his request to see Klamm was successfully delivered – not to Klamm, of course, but to his secretary. As Barnabas begins his story the camera and K. resume their rightward trajectory. Barnabas walks in front of K. and backwards, so that he can face him directly as they move. Jeremiah runs past them and K. hurries his pace – and thus the camera's – in order to stop him.

9. Shots 9 and 10 admit some variation – or what will initially appear as variation. The shot begins inside the boarding house and just after K. has confronted Frieda and Jeremiah, who are now living together in one room as a couple. This tracking shot begins, unlike the ones that precede it, indoors. At first, it appears not to be one. As the shot begins, Haneke's camera is fixed on K. who sits and drains a bottle of brandy. As K. begins to stand, the camera tilts upward, dictated, as always, by K's movement. The camera then carries on in a lateral tracking shot from left to right as K. goes in search of Erlanger, the secretary, K. presumes to be living in this boarding house and finds instead Bürgel, whom he wakes and engages in a quiet and frustrated conversation. The camera remains fixed on the two from afar and then eventually cuts inside and to a shot/reverse-shot construction of the two speaking. The close-ups within the sequence move closer and closer to their respective subjects. The camera does not, as usual, cut to black.

10. At the conclusion of the conversation between K. and Bürgel, K. reenters the hallway and begins his movement from left to right. The camera, once again, follows him and he is joined by what appears to be one of Klamm's assistants who is in the room adjacent to Bürgel's. As the two move in step with the camera that tracks right, the man speaks to K. about Frieda, the politics of the taproom, and what might frustrate Klamm. The shot cuts as the man prepares to exit the boarding house, but Haneke does not cut to black. Instead, he cuts to the other side of the door and shows us the man entering back into the snowy outside.

11. The camera tracks right to left with K. and Gerstäcker, as they head to the latter's house. The camera movement is continuous and stops only when the screen goes black, which also interrupts the voice-over narration. Things end

as abruptly as they began and always *in medias res*. The screen goes black and then is followed by a text: "this is the end of Franz Kafka's fragment."

A few initial observations about these eleven shots. What you will already have noticed is that taken together they figure inconsistencies within repetition. The form of the tracking shot – its fixed lateral path – is what recurs in every instance. At times, the shots are fluid, graceful, and uninterrupted, as we see in 2 and 11. They feel confident; the uninterrupted movements give us a sense that K. knows where he is going and that he is moving in the right direction, which is what we all want to feel when we are negotiating our existence in a bureaucracy. The demand might get heard, so we hope and we carry on.

More often, and in every other instance, the camera pauses and reverses direction, preserving in visual terms K.'s indecisiveness and uncertainty. K. wants nothing more than something decisive, but his movements – which are mimicked by the camera's lateral tracking – reflect an uncertainty about which way is best. It is these shots in particular that should make us wonder which way is forward. For most of us (I presume) the presence of the Castle, if we believe it can be entered, feels to the left. This is the direction indicated by the first tracking shot – even though it pauses – and is repeated in 2 and 11, our only instances of unbroken motion. And it is important to note that in the final shot of the film K. believes that Gerstäcker is going to help in his quest for Klamm, that is, that he is once again back on the right track and headed toward the Castle. Gerstäcker, of course, has only offered him some other work, an odd job. By then, K. cannot hear anything other than what he wants said.

With the exception of shots 9 and 10, all of Haneke's tracking shots are situated outside, and as I have already suggested, occur as documents of K.'s efforts to arrive at the next level of bureaucracy where his case will be properly heard. Or so he supposes.

The insistence on the lateral range of the tracking shot lends this trope its force: the notion that one must keep moving forward, push ahead, and do so all in an effort to find the proper inside of bureaucracy. The inside, presumably, is the thing that cannot be represented spatially in coordinates that are identical to the "outside." That is, if we believe that something has an "inside," then we have to assume that it is different – at least in representational terms – from what is "outside." However, in shots 9 and 10, the tracking shots reappear, as I have described above, inside the boarding house. The boarding house is a confusing space; it is simultaneously a site of domesticity and official labor. It shows no distinctive signs that would render the difference in obvious terms. The appearance of the tracking shot within that structure only further complicates the matter. It adds another set of terms that will be conflated with the already existing terms (i.e., domesticity and labor) and their valences and implications.

In other words, we have come to think of bureaucracy, throughout the film, as an inside – as a series of interrelated insides, even if that relation is none too obvious. The outside, of course, is the space recorded by the tracking shot – the recurring path K. follows in an effort to detect the logic of the spaces inside. The variations with the repetitive structure of the tracking shot merely register the degrees of anticipation, frustration, and certainty K. feels at any given moment of his searching. However, when Haneke brings this trope inside, into a space that is already conceptually confused, as he does with the shots inside the boarding house, the distinction between inside and outside also erodes. The spatial logic of inside and outside is what gives one hope; it denotes, in graphic terms, the possibility of one's entrance or one's exit; indeed, that the distinction itself will be obvious and clean. As Haneke proposes it here, however, bureaucracy has neither an inside, nor an outside. Seen as such, spatial metaphors for bureaucracy are doomed to failure, conceptually and affectively. To be, in Haneke's world, is to be bureaucratized; it is to be thrown in a world in which our identity is already given, and given strictly for the sake of what that identity allows someone to take from us, even as we do not recognize the identity that preexists us in any given bureaucratic form. Bureaucracy is always a matter of domination. And just as Haneke conflates domesticity and labor, inside and outside, bureaucracy very harrowingly becomes conflated with existence. *To be is to be a bureaucrat, or to be subject to one whose presence and logic will never be located, but defines you all the same.*

If we return, then, to Lefort's suggestion that bureaucracy is something that we all believe we have experienced and yet are incapable of conceptualizing, we are prepared for what I would describe as the paradoxical effect of bureaucracy, for a consideration of the way in which the failure of conceptualization is precisely the success of any bureaucratic form. The paradox of bureaucracy – or, rather, the paradoxical effect of bureaucracy – begins with our assumption that any given bureaucratic system, machine, or form is orderly, much as K. himself assumes. It is something, we suppose, that can be reckoned with precisely because we believe the bureaucratic form before us to be founded on reason. The agony we are suffering when the word first comes to our lips – *this stupid bureaucracy, that stupid bureaucrat* – is owed to a realization that we are not yet recognized by a system that is functioning without our feedback, without reference to the truth we would like to submit to this system, knowing full well that the system in question is going to decide our fate in this particular instance and that it will do so mechanically. If we can give it the proper information – the correct spelling of my name, a missed digit in my social security number, evidence that will prove irrefutably that I could not have committed the crime of which I am being accused – we believe we can afford to be at ease about the workings of the system. I can be at peace with the ways in which I am being determined by this or that bureaucratic form. It can even work to my advantage. It is only upon the failure of that system that I begin to perceive my alterity, my being apart from a system that is going to define me incorrectly as other and at the expense of my freedom, stability, or upward mobility. However, for most of us, when we experience this moment of bureaucratic failure as the outside of a system – indeed, when we see ourselves for the first time as an *outside* – we nevertheless persist in our belief that the system can become legible and thus enterable. We repeat a course of action with only a slight variation. If we remain patient and persist in our efforts to correct the error that is working its way through a system that is certain to exist, then we will be able to discover the logic that animates this system – its founding reason. In other words, we believe that an order exists and that it is only our failure, as potential perceivers of a hierarchy that temporarily eludes us, that makes the conceptualization of bureaucracy impossible.

It is an understanding of bureaucracy – or, at least, of the feeling of overwhelming disenfranchisement that fosters the success of any bureaucratic form – that likewise comes forward in Michael Haneke's *The Castle* in expressly visual terms. It does so precisely because the image itself participates in a new mode of bureaucratic organization, one whose complications Haneke seems necessarily unable to conceptualize. However, before arriving at a fuller analysis of the conceptualization of bureaucracy that Haneke's film proposes, it would pay to consider some of the ways in which bureaucracy has been understood in political theory, as well as the spatial logic that each attempt to theorize bureaucracy takes for granted and thinks of, in turns, as structure.

Contingency and Structure

Lefort makes no claim that the one who suffers from bureaucratic procedure is going to be the one to conceptualize it. His concern is, instead, with the way in which political philosophers have failed to conceptualize something that we all claim to have experienced. How, in other words, can we experience something that eludes definition? What would it mean to do so? However, the failure of conceptualization is precisely the problem of bureaucracy as we experience it in everyday life and precisely at the moment in which we are forced to confront our alterity to that system. Moreover, it is the very failure to conceptualize, I propose, that fosters the experience of repetition within a bureaucratic system, even if repetition with difference only produces in us an increased sense of alterity. But this failure is also the reason why we persist in our movements, much like K. in his tracking shots, despite the failure of repetition to produce a productive communicative act – a face-to-face encounter that will result in the clarification we desire and that will produce, in turn, the result we have always assumed any bureaucratic form to be capable of producing.

In Lefort's view, bureaucracy is something that resists conceptualization despite being something that we all claim to have experienced precisely because it is a contingent formation and is thus susceptible – as a system – to the unforeseeable specificities of time and place. Or as he puts it:

The bureaucracy, in my view, is a group which tends to make a certain mode of organization prevail, which develops in determinant conditions and flourishes by virtue of a certain state of the economy and of technical development, but which is what it is, in essence, only by virtue of a particular kind of social activity. (1986: 113)

As Lefort sees it, bureaucracy is always related to domination; indeed, it is the very way in which one group perceives, in political and thus imaginative terms, the possibility of its own coming to power, an acquisition of authority that will depend, in turn, on a system of maintenance – deflection, deferral, and rank – that is an operation of bureaucracy once authority has been established. Bureaucracy is not something handed down from generation to generation as a structure that admits no variation through time. Rather, it is an act of world-making. Or as Lefort puts it: "by recognizing its distinctive historicity, one is able to grasp, at the horizon of its activity, a world which it would like to mold in its image and constitute as the dominant class" (115).

Lefort's ontological conception of bureaucracy – his insistence on thinking bureaucracy at the moment of its appearance in relation to a culture that makes a particular bureaucratic form possible – solves a number of problems, and does so without making any totalizing or universal claim about what bureaucracy *is*. Primarily, Lefort's understanding of bureaucracy as a form that is both contingent and constitutive is a corrective to more structural and universal definitions, especially as they have appeared in the thought of Hegel, Marx, and Weber – three of the most important thinkers of bureaucracy. As Lefort has argued, despite their obvious differences, each of these thinkers conceives of bureaucracy as something external to the social, as a system unaffected by the historical conditions in which any given bureaucratic structure functions.

Consider, for example, the model proposed by Max Weber. According to Weber, a bureaucracy suggests a division of labor within a pyramidal structure, an interlocking system in which everyone understands his or her role as laborer and – moreover – understands his or her own identity within that system. To participate in a bureaucracy is to know one's place in a system and how to advance in that system if one should choose to. For this reason, Weber cannot help but be agnostic on the character of bureaucracy itself, as something ontologically well defined. The being of that structure is apparent and thus the identity one assumes as a participant in the structure is equally clear and capable, as such, of being renegotiated, insofar as negotiation implies promotion to a new role, to an identity that is knowable in advance.

Moreover, bureaucracy is strongly related to democracy and impersonal forms of social organization. A bureaucratic structure is, in Weber's analysis, what came to replace charismatic rule, where all power relations were preserved by force and determined by the will of a single leader invested with absolute authority. Or as

Weber suggested in *Domination and Stratification*, "In the Roman manorial system, it was preferred to entrust slaves with the direct management of money because of the possibility of inflicting torture" (1994: 71). For Weber, the model of charismatic authority is ultimately vulnerable to revolt, depending as it does not on a law of relations external to any given participant in that power structure, but on strictly affective investments. In other words, the slave may one day come to realize that the money is actually in his possession and that the torture inflicted to produce allegiance might yield positively different results; namely, revolt instead of obedience, wealth instead of poverty.

Weber's notion of bureaucracy, by contrast, is a more rational form of authority, one that depends upon a stratified system of specialized labor, responsibility, authority, and – most importantly – secrecy. The pyramidal form well defines the logic and class structure of bureaucracy and the skill set of a particular worker within that structure determines his or her place within that hierarchy. It is an impersonal structure – much like law itself, with which it is practically and logically intertwined – precisely because what is defined in each instance is a limited set of responsibilities. The properties of the job are defined ahead of any given worker who will come to occupy it. Moreover, any given job entails nothing more than knowledge of what happens in that job. A worker on the lower and widest level of the bureaucratic pyramid contributes something to the very top of that structure, but knows not how or why. Specialized labor is what both affords one entrance into a bureaucratic form and makes possible a logic of secrecy that maintains the well-functioning of a stratified system. For the slave living under charismatic authority, there are no secrets beyond the one he keeps: the very possibility that he will keep the money and fight back. In a bureaucratic form, what remains hidden from the worker below is the very conversation about what might take place. Silence and ambiguity are good for productivity and the secret is the very thing to which the worker does not have access.

Seen as such, secrecy has to be understood as the generative mechanism of bureaucracy as a paradoxical form. The levels of any given bureaucratic structure are always knowable in advance; what is not knowable, however, is what gets said in the spaces or levels that one does not yet inhabit, even though the terms and conditions of mobility are calculable, at least formally. A bureaucratic structure, then, is simultaneously transparent and opaque. If it were only transparent, stratification would not endure; more likely, it would become as vulnerable to revolt as earlier and more charismatic forms of social organization. The structure appears to us as a model of egalitarian openness; a fixed totality that can be perceived by way of an architectural metaphor (hence, the pyramid). However, what happens within that structure is both interpretive and out of view; it cannot be represented, like the architectural analogy of the pyramid, as a fixed form. It is fluid, whispered, and off the record.

This is partly why Weber comes to understand bureaucracy as a transcendental structure impervious to the specificities of the social at any given moment in time, as "one of the most difficult social structures to destroy," owing to a process in which " 'communal action' is transformed into rationally organized 'societal action' " (1994: 92).

In other words, a bureaucratic form is something that is imposed communally and affects the organization of the social, in turn. Whatever discontent might appear in the realm of the social, whatever demands get made there at a particular time and place, will do little to disrupt it. The emergence of bureaucracy can be located historically, but not its disappearance. Once we have entered into it, it is impossible to change, and is so by virtue of a repetition that leads to perfection and a practice of secrecy that secures the continued existence of what gets perfected. As Weber suggests:

> This is due to the fact that it is based on specialized training, the technical specialization of work . . . In the event of a work stoppage, or if work is fully interrupted, the resulting chaos is not easily controlled by improvising with replacements from among the governed. (92)

Although Weber does not say so, the reason that the structure remains in place is that bureaucracy itself takes on the character of a metaphysical ideal. We cannot resist it precisely because we do not exist, ontologically speaking, without it. It is who we are and who we are will be repeated through time, owing to the durability of the model that has arrived and that will never fail. No one will revolt against it precisely because what we would be rejecting is our sense of self, that which constitutes us most fully and prior to our arrival. The bureaucratic form may have emerged in a moment of contingency (or at least the appearance of contingency), but once in place it will only ever generate itself, again and again.

It could very well be that bureaucracy will never disappear – as Weber imagined – but it is not likely that it will carry on in the pyramidal form that was supposed to endure, much like its namesake. If we follow Lefort and understand bureaucracy as a group that works to make "a certain mode of organization prevail . . . but is what it is, in essence, only by virtue of a particular kind of social activity," then we are in a better place to comprehend the way in which any given bureaucratic form takes shape at a particular time, or how it might actually be capable of making the adjustments necessary to sustain itself when the demand made by any bureaucratic form exceeds the competence of the set of specialists that it has both produced and relied upon. What Lefort's understanding of bureaucracy as a contingent form should make clear is not that bureaucracy is guaranteed to disappear (although any given instance of it is as likely to as not), but that it will be transformed in time and because of time and the specificity of place. In other words, bureaucracy can only survive if we (the "we" that maintains an interest in domination, that is) assume that the social needs to be reimagined politically at the very moment in which an older form appears to be on the wane. We might call it revolution, insofar as one model of governance and social organization (whether public or private) is being entirely replaced, but the term itself does not promise that bureaucracy will be the thing rejected, only its current and necessarily obsolescent form. What Lefort's contingent bureaucracy might offer to post-Marxist theories of capital is the recognition that bureaucracy, like capital itself, is adaptive and the result of a collective imagining of another way, even when another way implies an expansion of the promise of the former system by the abandonment of the structure in place. The new form can only be built on the rusty and discontinuous limits of the old, on a ground that was not, as it turns out, one at all.

This is what has been happening since at least the early 1990s, particularly in the moment that we might describe as post-Fordist, or as a transitional period in global labor practices and international commerce that has brought nearly to an end the techniques and modes of social organization made possible by Taylorized forms of labor and a pyramidal form of bureaucracy that maintained the well-functioning of that system. In *The Culture of the New Capitalism*, Richard Sennett describes this moment as a transition from a pyramidal structure of bureaucracy to one that more closely resembles the discontinuous structure of an MP3 file. The shift in the structure of bureaucracy happens precisely because the state of the economy has been radically changed by the emergence of the Internet, the casualization of labor, and the increasing importance of shareholders – who can now access information about their holdings instantaneously and from well outside of the corporation, and are thus capable of controlling the interests of a corporation in a way that far exceeds the slow authority of the manager-on-site. This is what Sennett describes as a shift from a top-down model to a more lateral conception of authority; it is also the era of the hostile takeover, which happens digitally, from afar, and unexpectedly:

> Due to the emergence of sophisticated shareholder power, corporate generals at the top of the chain of command were not the generals they once were; a new source of lateral power had emerged at the top, often literally foreign, often otherwise indifferent, to the culture that long-term associations and alliances had forged with the corporation. (Sennett 2006: 39)

The indifference Sennett describes here is related, in his account, to the ways in which the traditional pyramidal structure understood time as both steady, linear, and calculable. Careers and investments, in that model, were planned long term. Both were imagined as a series of steps that one takes slowly and deliberately, knowing just what those deliberations will yield: upward mobility in one's career and a steady and predictable expansion of a company's assets. In Sennett's view, the pyramidal model also created loyalty to a job and to one's colleagues, where the new digital, MP3 culture is predicated on anonymity, non-linearity, and the notion of quick money where once there was investment.

The logic of the MP3 model of bureaucracy works as follows:

> . . . in an MP3 player, what you hear can be programmed in any sequence.
>
> In a flexible organization [the new model], the sequence of production can also be varied at will. In high-tech software producing firms, for instance, the institution might focus on some promising, innovative bit of imaging work, then go back to build the routine code support which simplifies the imaging, then go forward to think through commercial possibilities. This is task-oriented rather than fixed-function labor. Linear development is replaced by a mind-set willing to jump around. (48)

The worker, then, is no longer a specialist. He must be capable of multiple and seemingly unrelated tasks, of being "task-oriented" rather than "fixed-function," a shift in labor practices required by an approach to capital that prefers quick money to long-term investment. Simply stated: Discontinuity and instantaneity come to replace linearity and duration and do so not for the sake of the end of bureaucracy and the expansion of capital, but for its proliferation. Sennett's conception of bureaucracy, like Lefort's, presumes the goal of any bureaucracy to be domination. The MP3 model might appear more flexible and participatory (anyone can check their investments in the minute, manage them online), but it does not do away, in Sennett's conception, with centralized authority. It is merely harder to locate: "In an MP3 player, the laser in the central processing unit is boss. While there is random access to material, flexible performance is possible only because the central processing unit is in control of the whole" (51).

While Sennett's MP3 model attests to the contingent character of bureaucracy – and marks quite well a shift in the global economy that has been afforded by its adaptability – what remains consistent across both Weber's account and Sennett's, and curiously so, is a use of spatial metaphors to describe and comprehend the logic of bureaucratic form. The pyramid (Weber) is replaced, in the new economy, by a lateral conception of indifferent and foreign authority (Sennett), which leads to a non-linear conception of bureaucracy: the logic of discontinuity afforded by the model of the MP3. However, there is still a center, it is just that it is harder to access because the metaphor complicates spatiality. It renders space in terms of discontinuity, but only – we must presume – at the level of appearances.[1] Power, in other words, must still coagulate, but it can only do so by means of dissimulation and dispersal.

The Bureaucracy of Visual Style

If we return once again to Lefort's suggestion that despite the fact that we all believe that we have experienced bureaucracy, it nevertheless eludes conceptualization, we can say, then, that the reason it does so has to do with the inadequacy of spatial metaphors, all of which presume to provide us with a cognitive map of social relations, to borrow Fredric Jameson's phrase. If we look at the precession of metaphors in my account alone, what appears is a structural collapse: We begin with a pyramid, which keeps its widest and most lateral dimension at the bottom. It is the space of entry, a space of the lower class and the least powerful. In the MP3 model, Sennett provides us with a reversal of the spatial metaphor. The widest lateral portion is now at the top and depicts the offshore investor, casualized labor, and the hostile takeover. The new top-heavy MP3 model crushes the limited support upon which it temporarily sits – which is what the metaphor is meant to signify to begin with. Once the pyramid collapses by virtue of this new digital MP3 model, the entire structure disappears and is rearranged in more discontinuous, non-linear terms. And while the MP3 model is non-linear and discontinuous, it still maintains a center; in Sennett's metaphor, the laser. The MP3, however, is not an instance of discontinuity without limits. Rather, the laser at the center – the ephemeral figure of power – implies the one that creates and understands the logic of any instance of bureaucratic formation.

The MP3, however, is not rhizomatic, insofar as rhizomatic form implies – in the terms proposed by Deleuze and Guattari – an "acentered, non-hierarchical, non-signifying system without a General and without an organizing memory" (Deleuze and Guattari 1987: 21). This is certainly how Deleuze and Guattari figure Kafka's conception of bureaucracy. Consider the way they describe "The Metamorphosis" as a spatial visualization of bureaucracy:

> The bureaucratic triangle forms itself progressively. First, the director who comes to menace and to demand; then the father who has resumed his work at the bank and who sleeps in his uniform, demonstrating the external power that he is still in submission to as if even at home he was "only at the beck and call of his superior" and finally, in a single moment, the intrusion of the three bureaucrat lodgers who penetrate the family itself, taking up its roles, sitting "where formerly Gregor and his father and mother had taken their meals." And as a correlate of all of this, the whole becoming-animal of Gregor, his becoming beetle, junebug, dungbeetle, cockroach, which traces an intense line of flight in relation to the familial triangle but especially in relation to the bureaucratic and commercial triangle. (15)

In Deleuze and Guattari's account, the other of any given bureaucratic formation is the one most capable of flight by way of mutation and metamorphosis. However, it is worth emphasizing Sennett's point here that discontinuity is a feature of the metamorphosis of capital itself. The flight is not a flight away *from*, but a flight *toward* another bureaucratic formation. Or to be more precise, one can no longer say what is toward and what is away, as the frustrated movements of Haneke's K. so aptly describe. As we have seen, no single bureaucratic formation persists unchanged through time; not, at the very least, while capital still appears capable of reinvention. The line of flight is nothing more than the becoming of capital and its attendant bureaucratic form as most recently instanced by the MP3. The MP3 may have *become* but it is not an endless line of flight. Rather, the algorithmic code – in practice and as metaphor – is a contingent totality. It is a structure with finite capabilities, even though it appears aleatory and inconsistent. One simply needs to know how to read it, to be capable of thinking an abstraction that is knowable even when it is elusive. To be able to think it is to be capable in turn of producing in contingent terms a new form of domination. If there is no center, the possibility of domination disappears, even though any actually existing center must be concealed. By center, of course, I can only refer to a spatial metaphor that is itself contingent and describes in every version of its appearance a mode of unification, as well as its founding and operative logic. The point of any successful bureaucratic formation, though, is to make "center" appear as a failed metaphor, as an instance of conceptual failure – as something that cannot orient our thinking spatially, despite the spatial directives it requires in order to be productive to thought and our search for a positive communicative exchange, the face-to-face encounter with the one that continually eludes us.

However, to speak here of the successive failures of spatial metaphors is to describe a progression that takes place – teleological developments that occur in a continuous and causal fashion even if the latest model appears to us in a non-linear form. Indeed, it presumes a shift that takes place in total and all at once. It would also be to presume that bureaucracy has an inside, a logic that guides its metamorphosis; or, a spirit.

This, of course, is what is also so often presumed in Marxist accounts of capital that persist in believing that capital contains within itself the conditions of its own demise. As Ernesto Laclau and Chantal Mouffe have argued, such models of economic determinism are themselves beholden to a teleological conception of the movement of capital. If we presume that capitalism will *necessarily* be the source of its own undoing (whether by way of the falling rate of profit, or some other means), then we will likewise have to suppose that capitalism is not a contingent form. As such, our efforts to change it will come to nothing. It will simply fall of its own internal volition; its inside. By contrast, if we believe capital to be a contingent form – and if we should like to put an end to it – then the shift that takes place can only come from a constitutive outside, which is precisely how Laclau and Mouffe have thought the possibility of revolution and the end of capital against more orthodox Marxist conceptions of economic determinism. What this would mean, then, is that "inside" and "outside" are only ever constitutive (Laclau and Mouffe 2001: 98). One has to believe in one's alterity; one has to be able to imagine oneself *as* outside precisely in order to imagine an opposed inside; something that is changeable precisely because what is "inside" has no true outside. To insist otherwise would be both to deny the efficacy of resistance (our continual search for the source of bureaucracy) and to wait instead for a teleological becoming, the line of flight that is not an escape from bureaucracy but a metamorphosis into a new bureaucratic system – another bureaucracy whose shape I don't yet know, but towards which I am moving. In which case, we will only ever perceive ourselves to be outside without end; our being will only ever be defined by a system whose functioning escapes us ceaselessly and does so expressly for the sake of domination. Dispersion, as Sennett's MP3 suggests, is another form of collection. It is also a collectivity that must remain secreted if it is going to function.

This brings us back to Haneke's adaptation of *The Castle* and to the special position of tracking shots 9 and 10, which take place inside the boarding house. If we take seriously the idea that the film's recurrent trope of laterality depicts the outside of the bureaucracy – a space K. is eager to traverse in order to find his way to the proper inside – we can see tracking shots 9 and 10 as the instance in which inside and outside are conflated, when "inside" is being expressed in the very trope that has been defining bureaucracy's "outside." And as I have already mentioned, that conflation follows on the convergence of domesticity and public labor that we already see in this mixed-use boarding house. The camera movement of shots 9 and 10 is like that of the other tracking shots – it is one that we recognize as outside, both architecturally and psychologically. The other tracking shots occur outdoors and are always records of K.'s travels between indoor spaces, where the proper negotiations with the bureaucracy are meant to occur. In shots 9 and 10, inside and outside, private and public are not only conjoined, but are rendered conceptually indistinct in the moment of their conjugation. Conceptually, then, these scenes pose two distinct problems. On the one hand, the failure of the distinction between inside and outside should be the very thing that allows one to understand bureaucracy as a contingent form; on the other hand, to do that is to begin to find one's way out, even if only by imaging "outside" as the moment of recognition of an alterity *that can be changed*. One cannot find one's way out until one has understood that the distinction between inside and outside is necessarily constitutive and contingent. However, to render inside and outside as indistinct by virtue of their very distinction is to be able to think in productive terms the failure of a linear conception of space. Not to think it – or to be incapable of thinking it – is to accept the "inevitability" of bureaucratic form and the continual morphing that occurs teleologically and without our agency. To be caught in a bureaucracy becomes analogous to being defined by an essence that precedes and determines us; that is, it becomes analogous to metaphysics. *I will never know for sure.*

It is important to remember, however, that the visibility of conflation itself in these two shots – the inside that is also outside – is owed to a differential operation. The stylistic distinctiveness of the tracking shot makes us aware of its repetition and consistency – that it keeps occurring and always outdoors (with the exception of 9 and 10). That is, it draws its conceptual clarity – a clarity that is owed to the precision with which conceptual indistinction and spatial disorientation can be visualized – from the shots that precede and follow it. It is defined, in other words, by a differential system that is partially closed; it is fixed, but only contingently so. The eleven tracking shots are equivalent, but not identical, and as such they can be understood as the meaning that comes by way of unification in a field of difference, of the possibility of any shot whatsoever. The repetition of the tracking shot is what allows us also to understand the meaning of the other shots within this system that do not resemble them. In this way, what we might say is that Haneke's eleven shots suggest a totality that produces and is produced in turn by difference, as any system of enunciation would be. The repetition of the tracking shot in each case is what allows us to perceive difference in each and to arrive at meaning: To be caught in a bureaucracy is to be trapped in a form in which the structuring principle is simultaneously transparent (i.e., the tracking shot; the pyramid; the MP3) and opaque (i.e., the impossibility of fixing that structure in an effort to pin down the bureaucrat himself and resume one's well-being within that system).

What this implies is that bureaucracy is to be understood as a contingent totality, both as Haneke expresses it in visual and equivalential terms and as it functions in the world. In a more recent explication of the logic of hegemony and the chain of equivalence, Ernesto Laclau describes the contingent character of any totality – what prevents it from enduring without end – in these terms:

> In *Emancipation(s)*, I asserted that the totalizing instance is an object that is at the same time necessary and impossible. It is necessary because identities, being strictly differential, can only become true identities if the system that embraces them all is a closed or saturated one – otherwise there would be an unlimited dispersion of meaning. But that necessary object is also impossible: the tension between equivalence and difference, which are the contradictory conditions of its constitution as an object, cannot be eliminated; there is no square circle that can provide the bases for the logical articulation of these two poles. It is this combination of necessity and impossibility that makes possible the transition from ground to horizon. If we had only the "necessity" side of the equation, the totality would be representable in a direct way and, as the underlying positive foundation of every partial differential arrangement, it would have the status of a ground. If we had only the dimension of "impossibility," there would not be any signification whatsoever. (Price and Sutherland 2009)

Laclau, of course, is referring to the way in which any given hegemonic formation – which is central in his view to the very possibility of social change – comes to disappear. He is addressing the way in which a totality is required in order to produce signification and meaning, especially in a chain of equivalence in which difference will be deemphasized for the sake of meaning. In other words, for a chain of equivalence to form, we will have to deemphasize our differences for the sake of that unification, however temporarily. Unity can only ever be achieved on the basis of a shared partiality – what is not shared is what stands outside of a given chain of equivalence, or hegemonic formation. What prevents any given hegemonic formation from hardening into a universal form and obtaining the status of ground is that the tension between equivalence and difference, which can produce meaning and collectivity, is also what makes possible its collapse. Equivalence and difference is another way of expressing the relation, as Laclau suggests, between the necessary and the impossible, which he articulates as the absence of "a squared circle" that would guarantee the foundation of a fixed and universal system. Laclau, of course, is speaking of hegemony. However, his discussion is also entirely germane to our consideration of bureaucracy as something that is transparent and opaque, necessary and impossible. On the one hand, one could say that any bureaucratic formation is hegemonic, in the negative sense, and derives its negativity from the way in which it secretes its logic behind an apparent and disorienting structure, disorienting because what appears to us is the difference deemphasized and not the logic that forges a chain of equivalence. What bureaucracy secretes is its impossibility, despite the fact that what we long for when trapped in that structure is access *to* the impossible.

The impossible squared circle, finally, is what Haneke makes most plain with the visual style of the tracking shot. In addition to conflating inside and outside in 9 and 10, these tracking shots also include within the repeated structure of lateral movements images of failure and indirection, and the abandonment of linearity within a linear form. Consider, for instance, shot 7. The camera follows K. from right to left and pauses only as K. turns and heads down the path to Barnabas's house that runs perpendicular to the tracks. In other words, K.'s movement will defy the lateral course of the tracking shot, which, in a larger sense, provides the terms of repetition that allow us to understand difference (and thus meaning). But, of course, K.'s movement – his visit with Barnabas – fails to produce meaning, insofar as meaning is to be understood here as access to the logic of the bureaucracy; the source and nomological principle of what collects. The lateral tracking shot – this camera movement made possible by the equipment of an earlier moment in the history of industrialization – is incompatible with the movements that necessarily occur off the tracks, in an elsewhere that bears no stable spatial logic *as yet*. Sometimes those movements are perpendicular and often they are more winding, more curvilinear. The tracking shot can only move one way. The source and logic of a bureaucracy (the laser) appear to be in a direction quite opposed to it in graphic terms. In other words, the lateral path of the tracking shot, which provides us – by virtue of repetition – with the trope of "moving forward," fails K. again and again, and does by virtue of a spatial incompatibility. The winding path goes in a direction the track cannot follow and thus the logic of the trope itself fails. But in its failure, Haneke can describe the impossible in visual terms: two incompatible movements and spatial descriptions that are seen at the same time. What we are watching is the square that refuses to be circled. And if the square cannot be circled, what we have before us is a contingent conception of bureaucracy offered in visual terms, and precisely because the tracking shot can feature incompatible movements at once.

What Haneke's eleven shots offer to us, then, is a way of understanding the work of bureaucracy as the failure of conceptualization itself. On the one hand, this is quite promising, insofar as this failure is what prevents any given formation from enduring indefinitely. What Haneke shows us in this account is a bureaucracy in transition, the moment of its passing in time – and owing to the character of its time – and a passing that appears like a structure in flames, present in its soon-to-be former phase but undergoing a metamorphosis into another form that is not yet apparent. Indeed, what is most innovative about these shots – what they contribute most strongly to political theory – is an image of the messiness of the transition itself. In other words, the movement of spatial metaphors that we saw above, and that derive from the history of theoretical reflection on bureaucracy, provides us with an image of the clean break – of a form of bureaucracy whose beginning and ending is clearly visible. By contrast, Haneke's shots suggest that the dissolution of any social formation is never total and something that happens all at once. Indeed, what this uneven field of dissolution makes possible for the bureaucrat to come is a space of hiding, a residue that distracts us. If we were all to collectively witness and be capable of comprehending in spatial terms a shift from one bureaucracy to another, we would already be capable of preventing it from working.

More skeptically, then, I would argue that Haneke's eleven tracking shots offer an understanding of bureaucracy as an inverted hegemonic formation. If a socially productive conception of hegemony depends on the deemphasization of difference for the sake of unification, then bureaucracy creates unity also by way of the deemphasization of difference. But where hegemony shows its unity as the representation of what is to come and what is currently missing, bureaucracy is a unity that occurs but secretes the logic of its organization. What appears is everything that remains outside of a unity that we cannot see but is present just the same; moreover, what appears – if we can truly say that bureaucracy is an inverted hegemony – is a remainder that has no logic of its own. What appears is what falls outside of the logic of bureaucracy. Hence, the failure visualized in Haneke's eleven shots. K. is no doubt looking in the wrong places, because the role of the bureaucrat – if he is to be successful in constructing and maintaining his authority – will be to imagine a logic that appears ahead of what anyone else can or has currently seen. In this sense, the problem of bureaucracy requires one to think about thinking, to be capable of imaging a series of relations that bear no necessary relation to what appears before.

Another way to state the problem is to wonder whether the movements I am describing as tracking shots (and as eleven in total) are not actually executed with a steadicam; that is, with a different technology altogether, one that emerges at a different moment in the development of capitalism and bears no relation, as equipment, to the era of industrialization. The steadicam can produce any move-ment whatsoever, which includes straight lines. The camera is not harnessed to tracks. In this case, I would have had to be on the set to know what Haneke used – to have been there at the moment in which the logic appears – to know with total certainty. An image secretes the logic of its origin; what appears is not what produced it. The image itself is disinformatic; transparent *and* opaque. But also, the site of production is itself only ever a fragmented experience – a piece that will appear in a whole that only the director will know, and even then only notion-ally. A bureaucracy is something that always appears too late, despite the fact that we all feel that we have some understanding of it. Its full conceptualization is possible but only according to the inexorable logic of the bureaucrat to come and the structure that does not yet exist, but will. The problem it poses to polit-ical philosophy, then, is the recognition that the ability to think abstraction – to think ahead or behind of what appears – is also to possess the means of domination. What cinema can do is to give us the mixed signs of transition, a rendering of two worlds that are necessarily incompatible but visible as decline. However, decline is not, as I have said, a clean break. What Haneke's eleven shots suggest most of all is that bureaucracy has no clear beginning, middle, or end. The spatial logic of a bureaucratic structure can be imagined, but only as failure and indistinction, as the superimposition of competing and contradictory logics. And as we have seen, the failure of a fully closed and durable system is precisely what the bureaucrat to come requires in an effort to erect a new and seemingly unknowable form.

Acknowledgments

I would like to thank Roy Grundmann, Scott Krzych, and Meghan Sutherland for their very incisive comments on this chapter.

Note

1   And as Scott Krzych has suggested to me, the spatial metaphor of the MP3 is further complicated by the fact that one regularly uses MP3s without knowing in the slightest how they actually work. It is an odd feature of our relation to technology, one that echoes the essence of bureaucracy itself: We can be proficient in our use of something – we can follow its rules – without knowing how something comes to be in the first place. The rules will tell us nothing about origin.

References and Further Reading

Deleuze, Gilles: *Kafka: Toward a Minor Literature*, trans. Dana Polan (Minneapolis: University of Minnesota Press, 1986).

Deleuze, Gilles and Guattari, Félix: *A Thousand Plateaus: Capitalism and Schizophrenia*, trans. Brian Massumi (Minneapolis: University of Minnesota Press, 1987).

Kafka, Franz: *The Castle*, trans. Mark Harman (New York: Shocken Books, 1998).

Laclau, Ernesto and Mouffe, Chantal: *Hegemony and Socialist Strategy: Towards a Radical Democratic Politics*, 2nd edition (New York and London: Verso, 2001).

Lefort, Claude: "What is Bureaucracy?," *The Political Forms of Modern Society: Bureaucracy, Democracy, Totalitarianism* (Cambridge, MA: MIT Press, 1986), pp. 89–121.

Price, Brian and Sutherland, Megan: "Not a Ground, but a Horizon: An Interview with Ernesto Laclau," *World Picture* 2 (Autumn 2008), www.worldpicturejournal.com (accessed January 14, 2009).

Sennett, Richard: *The Culture of the New Capitalism* (New Haven, CT: Yale University Press, 2006).

Weber, Max: *Sociological Writings*, ed. Wolf Heydebrand (New York: Continuum, 1994).

PART III

The German-Language Theatrical Features

17

Structures of Glaciation

Gaze, Perspective, and Gestus *in the Films of Michael Haneke*

Georg Seeßlen

The cinema has made us accustomed to two standard forms of presentation that are sometimes positioned against each other, sometimes woven into each other. One of them is a mythical mode of presentation maintained especially by popular genre cinema and Hollywood film in particular. In a mythical mode of presentation, a person or a plot fragment attains credibility through aesthetic convention and the return of canonical elements ranging from the fairy tale to the Western film. The hero in a Western is credible because, on the one hand, he behaves as every hero in a Western, and, on the other, he carries with him in his saddle bag the dreams and fears of our childhoods. The other mode of narration is what we call psychological realism. A figure or a plot fragment become credible to us because they behave more or less the way we are accustomed to seeing in our everyday realities and lived experiences, or at least in what we consider these to be. Naturally, here, too, convention plays a decisive role. Psychological realism is no less obfuscating than mythical narrative; both structure and limit our gaze at the same time. And both guarantee to make the cinema an outrageously productive machine for stilling our desire for visual gratification and our hunger for experience, at the same time that they prevent, to a certain degree, the cinema from unfolding its own artistic possibilities.

In both these forms of narration, the cinema provides, more than anything else, reassurance, no matter in what virtuoso and occasionally threatening manner it might play with its technology and how derisively it might at times treat representations of reality. In the mythical mode of narration there is always the unambiguous clarification of good and evil. We create evil through a condensation of our unprocessed and fear-laden impulses – monsters, rogues, veiled images of the enemy – and we create the heroes who will, in turn, eradicate these evils. The principle of the mythical mode of narration is thus a kind of deliverance, a surrogate war, which always ends in our favor. On the flip side, psychological realism puts before our eyes the basic explicability of the world, constructing what, for the bourgeois age, has come to be the most important perceptual aid – the unambiguousness of the person, the composition of biography completely from a logic of cause and effect. For us the most comprehensive derivative of this is still the melodrama, in which the construction of the unambiguous character accompanies a moral rigor that does not allow gradations between good and evil – a cinema in which morality and terror, as we know them from the original melodramas of the time of Rousseau and the French Revolution, go hand in hand. The melodrama is morality without transcendence and mercifulness.

Hence, a cinema that wants to liberate its own aesthetic from its self-inflicted immaturity would be expected to have perhaps three relatively consequential modes of defense:

1. it must be anti-mythical;
2. it must be anti-psychological (at least in the sense of the unambiguous reconstruction of the biography); and
3. it must be anti-melodramatic.

Of course, being anti-mythical, anti-psychological, or anti-melodramatic in no way means completely ignoring myth, psychology, and melodrama. Rather, at issue is an awareness with regard to delimitation and to the move of liberation, because myth, psychology, and melodrama are as much as ever the foundations of our communication, from every advertisement to the coverage of war. Taken together, they probably constitute the language whose boundaries are also the boundaries of our world. Hardly any filmmaker has found a film language that is so consequentially anti-mythical, anti-psychological, and anti-melodramatic as Michael Haneke has, whose works no less continue to critically examine myth, the psyche, and morality.

In recent years, this world, without making it too concrete, has changed in such a way that the crisis of this language of myth, psychology, and melodrama has become highly visible; and Haneke's feature films are, among many other things, a direct account of this crisis. We have an inkling of the kind of coverage that, as is the case with the Gulf War, performs a virtual, mythical, and markedly melodramatic war about which we cannot decide if it is indeed taking place, or which, as in the case of the former Yugoslavia, denies us any production of sense, resolution, explanation, and morality. At several internal sites of war we learn that the bourgeois construction of reliable biography has ceased to function. Humans are no longer identical with their social location, or, put differently, the use of the social symbols of money, goods, habitus, mode of trafficking, and so on, can no longer be explained through a mythical construction of *Heimat*. The characters in Haneke's films belong more to an income bracket than to what was formerly known as class. The human being of post-industrial society requires the ability to change *Gestalt*; we will no longer be able to presume that a human is without doubt self-identical. Thus, what we see on the list of casualties is what we call identity. And obviously, it is precisely the awareness of this loss that leads to ever greater attempts at arbitrarily and violently reconstructing identity, be it by attempting to define oneself via ever more differentiated subcultures, through the ever-increasing accumulation of symbols of wealth, or through the reconstruction of national or even racial identity as a barbaric substitute for social location. An additional casualty of this loss is the predictability of social conflicts, the ability to endow them with something like a melodramatic morality and, above all, the predictability of violence. There is no lack of clarity as to the great potential for violence that post-industrial society is bound to bring forth, but at the same time it is somewhat arbitrary at what point it will erupt or whether it will occur as self-destruction or as an irrational explosion. Violence has left the ghetto as a social space and the biography as an individual space; the most telling perpetrator of violence is the person who runs amok – or the vapid serial killer – people, that is, in whose violence we can recognize neither completely rational causes nor completely rational goals.

Of course, mainstream cinema, too, responds to such losses and casualties. It explodes its narrative forms and plunges into an unconscious delirium of sensations. But unlike mainstream cinema, Haneke is not concerned with the bizarre fascination of irrational violence, but rather with a new form of research – a cinematic determination of structure which is the foundation for all of this. It is obvious that a cinema that seeks to overcome the traditional narrative forms of myth, biography, and melodrama must redefine itself in every detail. Thus, in what follows I would like to attempt to explain at least some of the aspects of this new film aesthetic and make accessible the critical discourse of cinema as best I can.

In the classical film narrative, the actor or actress on the screen is present to me as an audience member in four very different ways:

1. As himself, a person whom I can find more or less meaningful, more or less likable, but of whom a piece remains, in every guise, of a primary, unmistakable identity, which also exists outside of the filmic image.
2. As the presentation of a principle, of a moral-historical dilemma, as archetype of a movement, a class, a profession, as portrayal of the principle of fairness, childlikeness, innocence, or passion, as it were.
3. As representation of a second, imaginary biography which is just as complete as the first and consists of an internal component – what must have happened to the character prior to the story – and an external component – what happens to a character in the plot of the film.
4. The character on the screen is also my counterpart. He is, to a certain degree, ME. He is the guise I assume in the realm of adventure and cathartic movements.

These four forms of audience identification and control over the filmic image, which, by the way, are never more perfectly bound together in film than by the function of the star, are consistently denied in Haneke's feature films. The audience does not primarily discover what is present in these figures on the screen, but rather what is absent in them. Their material presence does not cast a complete biography; and one can neither distance oneself from them as outrageous exceptions – they are much too regimented in their living circumstances, too normal – nor can we identify with them in the sense that we are taken by the feeling that we would have behaved similarly in a similar situation, which, as far as I am concerned, is the case with Michael Douglas in *Falling Down* (Joel Schumacher, 1993). And the only principle that they demonstrate is that of orderliness, material ascent, and emotional impoverishment which, however, only make them into a perfect reflection of their environment. One might say that the primary tragedy of Haneke's figures is that they are so identifiable with their environment that there can be no more individual identity. The question as to what individual and society are in a biography cannot be answered for them. And in the act of violence that, as it were, is devoid of any motive, we can see more than anything that society and the individual have lost touch with one another. For the audience, this concurrence in Haneke's films leads to the egregious physical presence of the actor, if we even want to call him that, and the absence of the usual mechanisms of distantiation and identification poses first and foremost an enormous challenge. The question of who is actually up there on the screen and how I relate to him via my gaze is no longer answered by the film but rather referred back to myself.

The characters on the screen are not performing emotions. It is not emotions that are enacted before us but, if anything, concrete gestures – attempts to retrieve via ritual that which was lost. It is just as difficult for the audience to condemn the figures for their lack of emotion, in a manner we know from classical cinema where the emotionless person is always the bad person and sooner or later will be punished. This begs the question: Where in this world should the feelings come from? By the same token, the close observation of material things and the camera's power for intimacy prevent the flight into a primarily metaphorical understanding of the characters that does not see them as representatives of concrete reality, but as symbols. In other words: Once it has overcome its limitations, the cinema can devise a completely new form of the presence of an ambiance, which does not exist in traditional aesthetics and, through its tension between intimacy and alienation, can initiate completely new modes of exploration. Haneke's filmic figures are at once completely normal and completely enigmatic in such a way that we can no longer establish the cultural separation between the self and the foreign. In this way, they also give back to the audience the foreignness of the self. The cinematic image consistently establishes familiarity and foreignness at the same time, and since neither myth, nor biography, nor melodrama offer to resolve this contradiction, all we are left with is the search for structure, for the relations between words, between things, between gestures. But this search would lead nowhere, if Haneke's films did not provide for such a wealth of structural image and sound materials.

I want to attempt, then, to briefly describe this structural wealth, the aesthetic method, and the categories of cognition without losing myself too much in speculation and interpretation.

Camera

As a rule the camera is employed functionally; one critic has rightly compared it to an instrument of examination. Above all, it resists that movement which overcomes the distance between audience and representation. Again and again it is in search of the close-up of the sign, the indicator. Very different from the camera in mainstream cinema, it refrains from trying to overcome the mundane limitations of perception through tricks, instead describing precisely these limitations of perception, the reduction of the perceptual field. When the camera looks at a switched-on television, it disappears into it. It lingers for a long time on objects which do not necessarily have to be at the center of the action, which are momentarily not even in use, or whose meaning is derived from their position on a semiological plane, in a system of affinities, to put it structurally. This endows the shot with enormous photographic value; it is subordinated neither to the story nor to the effect, and it runs counter to mainstream cinema inasmuch as the image does not disappear at its moment of consumption. For me, one of the uplifting aspects in the films of Michael Haneke is that one does not get the sense of seeing images in a state of disappearance, but images in a state of emergence. The photographic shot provides a stability of the image that does not simply cause one shot to replace the other, but to overlay it. This is of course also served by the deployment of fades to black between individual scenes, especially pronounced in *71 Fragments of a Chronology of Chance* (1994), which further underscores that one shot, while over, is not replaced by the next. On the other hand, however, this way of distinguishing shots also tells us that we should not give in to the illusion of a complete spatial and chronological continuum. The shot obtains an autonomy that, of course, also bestows a sense of duration and underscores the fragmentation of the whole.

At first glance, this behavior of the camera is more objective, almost cold. It only registers exactly what is, neither rising above the action nor looking away in an exercise of discretion – the replacement of the factual with the symbolic, as it were. And, on the other hand, therein lies its unique humanness. It refuses not only identification and excess, but also premature judgment. The camera is not the judge, it shows what is the case. And it denies any deceit through beautiful images that have long become second reality. Gianni Amelio has made a statement in this regard that Michael Haneke would likely agree with; namely, that the filmmaker of today finds his primary objective not in finding interesting images, but, on the contrary, in trying to avoid all the images that besiege him. Thus, the incredibly difficult objective of film is, on the one hand, to find images that have not yet been distorted – not yet aesthetically lacquered – and, on the other hand, to find distorted images, images of life in the distorted world. The composition of the images in the films of Haneke is always unsettling and open, but never harmonious and never filled in a way we know from the industry of the senses. Emptiness is a significant element of their composition.

The camera is close to the body, but it is painful that there is no mediation between the close-ups and the long shots which, on top of that, are mostly of narrow spaces. There is virtually no relationship between a person's lonely individuality and his societal determination, unless we draw it ourselves. The camera discretely dissects things, bodies, and social rituals.

Colors

The predominant colors – at least in the trilogy – are cold blue and nocturnal gray, against which contrasting colors carry the function of signals and leitmotifs. In *71 Fragments*, the red of the jacket of the Romanian boy runs through the overall blue-gray constellation and this red, in turn, is taken into Anni's story, which then continues, overlays, and comments on the story of the Romanian boy. Not coincidentally, this use of red that is associated with the children represents something like a claim of life and love against the coldness of the environment, but more essential to Haneke's aesthetic, I think, is the structural connection of two occurrences whose internal affinity cannot be explained purely in phenomenological terms.

The colors in the other feature films, too, are mostly deployed photographically. That is, they are clearer and more intense than would be required for the mere ascertainment of moving objects and people. As with the shots, something resistant also adheres to the colors. They seem, as it were, to refuse to disappear.

A further part of the anti-mythical mode of narration is the denial of certain ambivalences, and the emphasis on the materiality of texture within color. This is the case with blood for Haneke – consider *Benny's Video* (1992) or the ending of *71 Fragments* – which is never to be regarded as a magical complement to red, the color of life. It is a coarse, thick, murky, and, in *71 Fragments*, even a black fluid that suggests neither sacrifice nor redemption.

Topography

Haneke's figures can be seen as being in a state of ordered enclosure, so to speak. The states of inside and outside, one could also say the relationship between the

I and the world, seem to be even more strongly pitted against each other, as they aspire to reconverge on another level through the electronic media. Often the films begin with a description of this state of an I, a perception that cannot reach the world. Thus, we are shown the darkened room of the protagonist in *Benny's Video*, into which the world can enter only by way of the television set and the video camera. Or as in *The Seventh Continent* (1989), where the very first image from the interior of a car in the carwash describes the delimitation of perception.

The gaze through windows and doors is essential to perception, but precisely therein lies the limitation of this perception. Through this limitation, the information systems of image and sound are further separated; especially in *71 Fragments* it happens again and again that we see something but hear nothing and vice versa. In this way, each shot also becomes a philosophical parable about the recognition of the Other in the world. As a viewer I could describe the situation this way: An I is in search of the world and is time and again confronted with the contradictory and fragmentary nature of what the world wants to share of itself. At the same time, this world presents itself in a state of torpidity, of glaciation. More than anything else, it speaks of its uninhabitability. Thus the observing I is, to a degree, referred back to itself; that boundless world of signs and symbols, as the world was viewed under the romantic gaze, which we have never lost, no longer exists.

Haneke's films take place in a world which is at once undeniably ours, and at once its own negative utopia. There are no nice relics here, no more niches that could support yet another form of cognition. The basically Janus-faced nature of the media world – an all-encompassing system of control and reduction on the one hand and the unleashing of internal floods of images on the other – is slanted towards the former. Media control plays an important role in all three films of the trilogy; and in all three cases it is probably important that it renders the human both perpetrator and victim. Again and again people switch functions; they are at once the observers and those being observed; sooner or later even they themselves enter the medium, and with that the structure of inside and outside, of I and world, falls yet again into a fatal circulation. In the end, everything one can experience about the world is the wrought and debased image of oneself.

Thus, the purpose of the filmic image in Michael Haneke is not to create meaning but, on the contrary, to create an open space for the questions of the viewers. In the end everything is completely open and there are a number of possible interpretations for the conclusion.

Rituals

The central perspective in the trilogy is directed toward the family, an institution which originally had to intercede between the individual and society and, in the structure of glaciation, is bound to have this contradiction as its actual content.

It contains rituals of community, hierarchy, and world experience, for instance in the vision of a common journey. In *The Seventh Continent*, the journey to Australia is still a real utopia. In *Benny's Video* the journey is an escape after everything has already happened. In *71 Fragments* there are only tattered hints of journeys, and, on the other hand, the journey of the small Romanian boy is but a flight for survival, at the end of which lies little in the way of paradise. Eating together is a ritual in which harmony and sensualism once more converge in an image, but, at the same time, it tends to be the beginning of the point of departure for catastrophes. In the middle of this redemptive ritual repressed feeling erupts without being able to become language. The ritual nature of everyday life prevents even the positive rituals from being redemptive; rituals are the only thing that holds the groups together. But in every ritual the individual experiences his failure vis-à-vis the community, in every ritual language experiences its failure against the dictate of silence. In all the films of the trilogy there are scenes at a child's bed, which, tellingly, is consistently shown as being positioned against the wall in an acutely restrictive, nearly prison-like, even somewhat cave-like situation. These are scenes where parents want to speak with their children but have no answers to their questions.

One of the most moving scenes in *71 Fragments* is the married couple's meal, where the silence is interrupted by the husband's sentence, "I love you." His wife retorts by asking if he is drunk. He admits that he is and yet wants to explain that he wanted to present something like a gift with this sentence. But she insists on finding out exactly what it is about this sentence. And when she does not let up, the husband slaps her in the face with the back of his hand. The wife wants to jump up and run away. Yet, she cannot. In the silence that hovers over the rest of the meal her hand seeks out his arm.

I do not think that a love story in the age of glaciation could be told more beautifully, nor can one describe more precisely why it cannot unfold. The sentence "I love you" brings up all of the buried emotions in both of them and leads into the catastrophe because the sentence must remain completely foreign, like a tremendous provocation.

Indeed, emotion and ritual remain estranged from each other: As happens in *71 Fragments*, in the middle of the rituals of having dinner, watching television, people burst into tears, and the others, more or less silently, watch this outburst, which, like the renewed outbreak of violence, can hit anyone at any time and which, like the latter, ultimately won't change anything.

Language and the Body

Haneke's characters use language like signs; it is essentially foreign to them, which is why the gestures, facial expressions, and language of the characters do not achieve the kind of unity we know from the heroes of classical narrative cinema. They use language as something external to themselves. Body, language, and biography exist, as it were, in separate worlds. The more language there is in the media, the less language people themselves have. And the more language is eaten up by ritual, the less remains for dialog.

Again and again we also see the loss of the body, such as in the empty mechanics of table tennis practice, in its numbness. The act of violence which appears so enigmatic may thus be, among many other things, something of a desperate reflex to the loss of the body. The body understands itself as imitation of the matrix of media images. And this loss also accounts for the cold casualness, the unmoved curiosity, with which people react to violence, for they can react toward the body of another only as if toward an image that one can turn on or off.

In Haneke's films, where there is language there isn't a body, and vice versa. That is, the loss of body and language is not a mutual loss, but rather a loss of each against the other, such that the one cannot help reconstruct the other. In Haneke's film, body language functions just as little as language functions as an element of sensuousness. For this reason, too, the statement "I love you" makes his characters so helpless. Not only do they not know what I am, what love is, what you are. They also do not know how to relate this sentence to their lives. They have only learned to distance themselves through language from themselves and others, and for this reason they must despair with every sentence that would describe the reverse motion.

Perspective

In almost every image in Haneke's films, limitations of perception, but also the shock of perception, become painfully apparent. Often it happens that the camera does not capture the central action, but rather only registers indirect effects. Relationships between people are conveyed through the exchange of materials and signs, such as money or weapons, and not in a physical wholeness. The presence of an object – for example, a killing device – proves more fatal to people than the rupturing of biography, of recognition, or of the word. The thing has crowded out the person as the subject of the action. The gun is the subject of the plot in 71 *Fragments*.

People talk to each other not in interrelated images, but rather in absurd metaphors; they must travel far outside themselves, even in language, in order to get close; yet, on the other hand, they are hopelessly removed from themselves and each other when they endeavor to formulate simple emotional truths or wishes. The most fruitful scenes of alienation in the films of Michael Haneke are determined by the sentence "I love you."

Mode of Communication

The loss of body, intimacy, and worldly experience is pitted against the excessive influence of the media. Thus, people evade one another and then catch one another again in the web of media. The loss of body and language leads to the attempt to send each other messages by way of an electronic medium, as is the case with Benny, who is unable to admit directly his deed to his parents and, instead, silently presents them with the recording of his manslaughter after the news. The attempt to control one another via the image replaces the emotional relationship. People are blanketed by a permanent stream of news and barely decipherable messages. It is the meta-stratum of the global village in which we find ourselves.

Sound

In Haneke's films it is often the driving perception; we often already hear something of which no image has yet reached us. We register the cruelty of the action, mostly through the soundtrack. Here and there it can function as an alarm signal against the familiar order of images, against their seeming innocuousness.

That film exists as image and sound is seen by the director as an enhancement: "That is," he says, "not only twice as much, but rather ten times as much, because one has a counterpoint. Nothing needs to run parallel. Rather, one can implement it very precisely." This also constitutes the use of music in a double sense, one aspect of which is background, counterpoint, and illustration, while the other is commentary, as with Alban Berg's violin concerto "To the Memory of an Angel," which was dedicated at once to Alma Mahler-Werfel's daughter and his own upon her death. Thus it accompanies the mesh work of death of the family in *The Seventh Continent*. Even in ignorance . . .

Time

What often intensifies the pain while watching Haneke's films is the almost unbearably drawn-out lingering on an agonizing scene, be it one of violence, one of a desperate attempt to communicate, such as the telephone call of the old man with his daughter in *71 Fragments*, or a point of heavy silence.

The scene of the telephone call of Otto Grünmandl takes eight minutes in a static shot. Here the attention is so closely focused on the dialog, which, of course, only moves in circles, that one actually tends to underestimate the duration. The scene with the ping-pong game, on the other hand, is perhaps a bit shocking for the audience in that, for that moment, cinematic time becomes real time and the observation of an otherwise trivial process strangely sensitizes us for its defamiliarization. The film does not kill any more time here, but rather makes time conscious.

I want to point out one more aspect regarding the motive of time which is personally important to me. If one views Haneke's films in the context of his television work, then what unfolds is certainly also something of a generationally comprehensive chronicle of "not seeing," of misconduct, and especially of concealment in Germany and Austria after the world war. The behavior of the two generations which Haneke describes, namely, that of the first postwar generation and then its children, has as its imaginary place of origin not only the development of the industrial, medial society, but rather also the persistence of fascism in its repression, which passes on the inability to speak. Haneke never uses this as a theorem in an invasive way, but he does hint at it time and again. Thus, in *The Seventh Continent*, for example, one hears about a Nazi trial from the radio. Benny's parents are people who react in their orderliness and in their repression to fascist guilt, and so on.

We may detect a beginning of this glaciation, which reached its climax in the trilogy, in the two-part television film *Lemmings* (1979). The film describes the phase of self-discovery in the 1950s, when liberation was bound to fail because the actual moral framework of the religious-conservative bourgeoisie did not allow the old society, and a mass society abandoned by all of its gods, to live together in anything other than repression. Thus, suicide is the only remaining radical gesture that pervades the story of the director's generation and the morality of the next. At the time, he stated in an interview: "Our fathers either never came back from war with their ideals or they were quickly forced to ignore the breakdown of their world in order to go on living. That is, to continue to live their lives in an upright way, in the middle of the twentieth century they had to act as if the nineteenth century had never ended, as if God, Emperor, and Fatherland were still living, just under a pseudonym." This labor of repression was continued by the next generations in the other films in a certain way. At the same time, a vague fear of living without a real sense of abode resulted in the hapless furnishing of a synthetic home.

That also means: The icy silence that emanates from the children in the trilogy is the final consequence, the response to a process of repression which began after the war, and amplified the guilt from one generation to the next.

The loss of a life in the story and the space also lead to a loss of symmetry, and just as in his images Haneke tries to avoid traditional harmony in composition. From film to film symmetry is called more and more into question. Even after several viewings, the fascinating thing about *71 Fragments* appears to be the withholding of a harmonious symmetry (which demands a great knowledge of symmetry from the artist). The number 71 alone is one of the most asymmetrical things imaginable. It is a composition of unevenness, of non-resolution, which is present in all of these films – a polyphony of symmetry.

Narrative Mode

The narrative mode is anti-mythical because it strictly refuses the classical three-act form – conflict, sacrifice, resolution – even though all of Haneke's films cite it, in some cases repeatedly, as an oblique possibility. Perhaps the question of the sacrifice, which is no longer either accepted or understood, is central to the metaphysical level of the films.

The narrative mode is anti-psychological because the characters are not self-explanatory.

And it is anti-melodramatic because, as Haneke puts it, it is "more or less a coincidence who the victim [is] and who the perpetrator [is]." In all of his characters there is the impulse towards goodness. They could neither be fully trusted nor be completely condemned.

In Haneke's films there is no image flow. In traditional narrative cinema each filmic image already contains a connotation of the next one; it wants to make us believe that it is the only one that would have to come now, and film production knows enough tricks to attain this interlocking of images which let us forget how much each filmic image is an arbitrary excerpt and how much this cut would constitute a break. In contrast, Haneke positions the sequences next to each other, even separates them in *71 Fragments* through fades to black in order to make it clear to us that meaning does not reside organically in the images but analytically in our heads. He contrasts the seamless aesthetic of the Hollywood film with the consciousness of the fragmentary.

Each take in Haneke's feature films breaks from conventional rhythm; since *Lemmings*, he has been known for those long takes in which the audience itself must recognize the internal movement and which contain not a trace of mannered staticness. In his later films the takes often break off in order to avoid harmonious triads and to provide space for a dissonant editing technique. The latter could justifiably be characterized as deconstructive inasmuch as it draws attention to detail and, in contrast to the principle of invisible editing, makes the cut visible as the very loss of the image.

The films do not, in fact, simply construct an emotional *Endzeit*, an apocalypse of emotions, but rather they practice, in the words of the director, a negative utopia in the sense of Adorno. They leave open the option of regaining the original freedom. To put it in the words of Max Scheler: "Man has the 'world,' has an open sphere of things around him, he is 'open to the world'; he can even concretize himself, he has self-consciousness, and this concretization of the self, and acquisition of distance to the self, makes him capable of saying no to himself and to the phenomena inside him, potentially turning him into a moral being." The loss of morality, that is, not the occurrence of immoral actions, but action which no longer relates to morality, which is what Haneke's films are about, is related back to its structural condition – namely, the loss of the world, quite directly shown in the images as the loss of "world openness" and as the loss of the ability of self-concretization. Even that is quite directly palpable in the images of the films, in the characters' futile attempts at obtaining self-awareness.

If one looks again at the motives in Haneke's films – the family as the space of glaciation, isolation, and also loss of the world; the reification of the world; violence as the last, nonsensical consequence; unconscious alienation; the loss of the possibility to live and of world topography; that civil war of signs and messages which is always there before catastrophe strikes – then their ongoing structure can be read as an anti-mythical representation of a process of isolation which ranges from the loss of the world and the ideational repression of the war generation to the material repression of the postwar generation, its failed liberations and its new petrification, all the way to the medial repression of the third generation. And in every generation the process of isolation, and of the loss of the world and the I, must happen more rapidly and radically because repression is quasi-accumulating. If the family of the war generation still constitutes a context of power and ideology, the family of the next generation is but one of consumption and acquiescence. And the family of the third generation, the one the film trilogy is about, is reduced to a context of cover-up and repression – a ritual media context.

What no longer happens in this world of non-perception and non-communication is education. Not in the sense of an external adjustment to circumstances, but in the sense of knowledge about the historicity of life. All three films of the trilogy are about children, who are completely left to themselves by families and pedagogic institutions – not by malicious people who have somehow lost their benign socio-democratic models, but by the institutions themselves. These children resume the absence of speech and are abandoned without constituting an I – which is what, by the way, distinguishes them from the rebellious children of the New German Cinema from Fassbinder to Klick and even more so from Truffaut's reconstruction of the romantic gaze onto Antoine Doinel. This is why there is no real liberation for them outside the family and the pedagogical institution. Our experience of the foster care of the children in *71 Fragments* is completely ambivalent. The institution that clothes and feeds them gives them neither world openness nor self-confidence. Thus, their rebellion does not lead them out of these institutions, but only into their center.

In order to comprehend this loss of education in the structure of glaciation, it might be a good idea to recall the opening of Lessing's *The Education of Humankind*. There he writes: "Education is for the individual person what the revelation is for the entirety of humankind." Accordingly, education would be a passing on of the utopia. The absence of enlightenment, or, speaking materialistically, the absence of a historical project, is thus still preserved in the structures of glaciation. The final paradox in every attempt at communication, in every image of the films of Michael Haneke, is that the concealment of the past leads to a disappearance of the future. Evidently, Haneke's characters only know the present as a period of life. Nothing about them lives in the past and nothing for the future, which is why every attempt at intergenerational communication is condemned to failure. The old man in *71 Fragments* can only live his present maliciousness and desire for closeness; between him and his family there is no other life in the past and no other life for the future.

In the end the question remains, as it were, as to how to describe the anti-mythical, anti-psychological, and anti-melodramatic narrative mode of Michael Haneke. I would most like to call it a philosophical-heretical one. It is philosophical because it asks questions about the fundamental conditions of perception and communication, thereby entertaining a post-Adorno negation; the explanation – but even more so the hope – does not lie in the film, but rather in the fact that the film exists and challenges the audience to adopt an attitude beyond resignation and cynicism. To be reminded of the ability to say "No." The difference between *Benny's Video* and "Man bites dog" lies less in socio-critical acuity than in the attitude towards cynicism and the ambition to imbue the images with philosophical depth. The enlightening and humane power of Haneke's films lies in the fact that both their micro- and macrostructures reject any kind of acquiescence with the status quo. And it is a heretical mode of narration because it resists, in a rarely seen manner, the conventions of popular culture, which have long since become something like a third religion, but also because it resists trite and traditional ways of explaining the world.

With that we are again at a beginning; in Michael Haneke's first film, *After Liverpool (Und was kommt danach . . .)* [1974], Jean-Luc Godard is quoted as saying: "The philosopher and the cineaste have a certain way of life in common, which consists of a generation's very own view of the world."

This view is certainly marked by the experience of loss which entitles one to anything except sentimentality. Thus one can view Michael Haneke's films as those of an enlightening pessimist, but this is only one side of the truth. The other is that the exactness of observation does not disavow, that the director loves his characters. Only in this way can he perhaps permit himself such dangerous closeness to them, which is completely without impertinence. If one sees several of his films one after the other, one quickly recognizes how much tenderness is behind such seemingly cool observation. To the question as to what he wants in the cinema, Haneke responded: "Precise films," and he named Bresson, Tarkovsky, Bergman, Cassavetes, Iosseliani, Scorsese, Woody Allen – in that order.

Thus, what remains to be written, then, is the history of the cinema of precision. Here myth is being replaced by philosophy, the structural research. The place of psychological realism and its convention is taken by the acuity of observation, which is dedicated precisely to the small and hidden things, the naturalized details of reified life. And what takes the place of melodrama is the moral dialog between film and audience.

Translated by Timothy Dail

18

The Void at the Center of Things

Figures of Identity in Michael Haneke's Glaciation Trilogy

Peter J. Schwartz

> *Heute ist alles so transparent, ich weiß nicht, ob ich mich da richtig ausdrücke, jedenfalls ist alles aus Glas und aus so durchsichtigem türkisen Plastik, und es ist irgendwie körperlich unerträglich geworden.*[1]

I would like to begin with a shot from *Benny's Video* (1992). Having murdered a girl he's met randomly and about whom he knows next to nothing, Benny rifles her red cloth bag on the floor of his room, clearly looking for clues to identity. In a high close-up over his shoulder, we watch him sort though notebooks and folders, then impatiently empty the bag, find a wallet and within it a single banknote and a folded snapshot of someone in a blue bathrobe, cropped oddly headless, holding a cat. He inspects the image, first upside down and then right side up, discarding it with a gesture that suggests a failure to find it intelligible. He shifts more folders, revealing a high school physics textbook and then a small wooden sphere – a Russian nesting egg – which he twists open to find a second, and then, within that, a third; the third egg is empty (Fig. 18.1). Dropping the pieces onto the physics book to complete a still life in the emblematic *vanitas* style, he hangs his hands in defeat for a moment, then gets up from his seat and crosses the pile, departing the frame. The matryoshka metaphor complicates the Christian and pagan sense of the egg as a symbol of life or the soul to suggest that the thing Benny seeks may be (like the Günter Grass self-as-onion) a matter of shells within shells – and perhaps that the physics of murder is no proper path to the metaphysics of selfhood.[2]

What is Benny looking for? It's not simply a matter of knowing a name. One has to ask why he kills the girl. The film opens with his (and our!) fascination with the moment of death. The postmortem inventory of the bag's contents echoes

Fig. 18.1   The empty egg. *Benny's Video* (1992), dir. Michael Haneke, prod. Veit Heiduschka and Bernard Lang.

his slo-mo replay of slaughter; what Benny wants from the egg is what he has sought in the death of the pig. This is also the thing that his parents won't give him: One could call it closeness, but it is more. Two shots in the film connect the boy's fascination with killing to a desire for carnal – sexual – contact: the teasing foreplay with the bolt gun preceding the murder, and the scene in which Benny, lying awake, overhears his parents copulating. His eavesdropping on the secrets of sex is revisited with the tape, through the bedroom door, of his parents' discussion of corpse disposal, of the secrets of killing. The film links Benny's curiosity to his family's inability to communicate, verbally or emotionally – to their coldness of feeling (above all the father's) and to its objective correlative, the aesthetic coldness of their environs, especially of the kitchen. The kitchen is marked by the parents' continual absence, by the high-design coldness of spotless black glass, by the social pretension and sad overkill of expensive equipment used to prepare frozen pizza and cups of yogurt and milk. Benny's aggressive pantomime here with the girl ("What's this? – A policeman in the subway!") suggests that the glaciation the room implies *must* turn desire for contact to violence – confuse sex and killing – as it soon will.

The scene between murder and cleanup in which Benny sits and eats yogurt is one of several in which he is centered within an expanse of glass. The day after the murder, we see him sitting before a pane overlooking the tracks in a railway station; shortly after, he is filmed in a barber's mirror, with the barbershop window onto the station hall as backdrop (Fig. 18.2). In a bathroom mirror, we watch his father take him to task for the haircut. Throughout the film, Benny is bracketed by semi-reflective surfaces of metal or glass, often doors. The framing suggests a portrait, yet the backgrounds belie this intention. The boy's relations to self, to the world, and to others – the social selfhood of which portraits normally

Fig. 18.2   Benny (Arno Frisch) in front of the barber's mirror. *Benny's Video* (1992), dir. Michael Haneke, prod. Veit Heiduschka and Bernard Lang.

speak – are a house of mirrors, translucencies, transparencies, opacities, and simulacra. Here Haneke develops vocabulary used more sparingly in others of his films. In *Caché* (2005) we see Georges often framed before bookshelves – both real ones at home and studio fakes made of plastic – as in the typical scholarly bookjacket photo. In *71 Fragments of a Chronology of Chance* (1994) a semi-reflective café window lets Bernie's sale of a pistol mingle visually with the movements of passersby, meshing the transaction with normal life and commerce, and thus suggesting the social duplicity of a thriving market for the means and media of violence. A similar play with windows in *Benny's Video* points to an origin of the figure in Robert Bresson (*L'Argent*, 1983), perhaps with an admixture of Fritz Lang's signature shop displays (*M*, 1931; *The Big Heat*, 1953; *Scarlet Street*, 1945).[3] Walking home from Ricci's the morning after the murder, Benny pauses before a jeweler's shop in a pedestrian zone. There his image merges with the display as a well-dressed middle-aged couple enters the glass in between; he exits frame right as for a few more seconds we watch his reflection moving off left. The shot echoes Bresson's reflection of Yvon Targe in a toy-shop window as he pursues an old woman he will later kill, itself possibly a nod to Hans Beckert in *M*. In Haneke, as in Lang and Bresson, semi-reflective shop windows express torn selfhood with *Doppelgänger*, while at the same time revealing desire (for money, commodities, sex, blood) as a source of the split. But Haneke seems to ask a question that Lang and Bresson do not: Who *is* this person?

All the shots I have named – in the kitchen, in the station, the barber's chair, the bathroom mirror – ask this question, the question all portraits pose. Since its inception in northern Europe in the fifteenth century, the painted portrait, a bourgeois genre, has employed backgrounds consisting of arrays of objects – most often interiors, though also landscapes, or a combination of both[4] – to characterize individuals placed before them. The practice is common enough now in art and film to appear self-evident, but its origins are in fact linked with the rise of the bourgeois subject. Jan van Eyck's famous portrait of the merchant Giovanni Arnolfini and his wife (1434) may have been the first painting to show subjects in a domestic setting; the Flemish and Florentine practice of setting a subject before a distant landscape seen through an open window seems to have been an invention of the 1460s. Both conventions derive from mid-century Flemish votive painting (Jan and Hubertus van Eyck, Rogier van der Weyden, Hans Memling), which used objects within interiors as well as landscape symbolically to communicate information about an increasingly bourgeois donor clientele. Building on Flemish models in the first half of the sixteenth century, German painters – Hans Holbein the Younger especially, but also Albrecht Dürer and Lucas Cranach the Elder – expanded the formula by investing landscape backgrounds in portraits with personal symbolism[5] or decorating interiors with professional attributes meant to characterize bourgeois sitters.[6]

Haneke varies this model with backgrounds that signal middle-class social status, yet which also warn of their failure to *give* identity. (Besides the kitchen we have the parents' conspicuous dining-room wall full of art, before which Benny, eating alone, is also centered.) The blankness of such backdrops expresses the void in Benny, their opacity, transparency, and reflectivity miming the hall of mirrors through which his sense of self and reality flows. Haneke is hardly the first in the German tradition to link an empty center of selfhood with problems of media, taste, commodities, and desire. Let me quote from a text of 1774: "Ah, this void! this terrible void I feel in my breast! – I often think that if only I could hold her to my heart for once, just once, that void would be entirely filled."[7] The void that Goethe's young Werther feels at this stage in his sorrows is one he has sought to fill in a number of ways, all of them typical of his class. A bourgeois, he seeks to distinguish himself – in expressions of taste and feeling, in clothing and conduct, as an artist and as a lover – from other bourgeois, as well as from members of other classes (aristocrats, common folk). It is likewise class-typical that he constructs a narrative for his life by identification with literary narratives, above all the Bible, Homer, Ossian, Goldsmith, and Rousseau. In the course of the novel, the distinctions collapse and the narratives out themselves as illusory; suicide – a messy suicide – is the result. What Werther's end shows is on the one hand a failure of differential self-definition to compensate lack of positive content (a product, perhaps, of the composite nature of the German *Mittelstand* as a class), and on the other a fatal consequence of reality's misdescription by media. In the German context, the shaping of senses of self by the media – the shaping, or the misshaping – is a *Sturm-und-Drang* topos, a late eighteenth-century product of bourgeois cultural ascendance. We see it not only in *Werther*, but also in Faust's complaints at being prevented by books, technological instruments, tradition – and, *nota bene*, distortions of sunlight through colored glass – from touching nature directly. "Still this old dungeon, still a mole! / Cursed be this moldy walled-in hole / Where heaven's lovely light must pass, / And lose its luster, through stained glass. / Confined by books, and every tome / Is gnawed by worms, covered with dust, / And on the walls, up to the dome, / A smoky paper, spots of rust; / Enclosed by tubes and jars that breed / More dust, by instruments and soot, / Ancestral furniture to boot – / That is your world! A world indeed!"[8] The Georges of *Caché* is a descendant of Faust's nightmare student the *Bildungsbürger*, that nineteenth-century calcification of the late eighteenth-century attempt to weld together an unwieldy aggregate of urban patricians, craftsmen and merchants, businessmen, lawyers, physicians and clergymen, bankers, professors, and schoolmasters as consumers of culture – of media – in common. This is a part of the cultural capital that Georges has denied Majid ("You deprived my father of a good education"). Haneke questions its efficacy as a guarantor of selfhood and social power with the pullback shot in the recording studio that makes Georges shrink before his backdrop of plastic books – a reversal, possibly, of the famous zoom to Mabuse's gaze in Lang's *Dr. Mabuse, the Gambler* (1922), and hence also of its enunciatory power.[9] The books figure similarly in the mirror behind Anne as she challenges Georges while he slumps on the sofa ("Maybe you could share your great wisdom") – bookless, defensive, emasculated, his dissimulation clearly exposed.

Yet the unstable dependence of the bourgeois subject on its own signs of status is in evidence in German art before 1774. It is represented iconographically in one of the earliest bourgeois portraits extant, Hans Holbein's portrait of the Steelyard merchant Georg Gisze (1532) (Fig. 18.3). The picture is one of the first to employ a professional *mise-en-scène* to signal bourgeois social status – and what it signals is both solidity and insecurity.[10] Holbein's portrait, painted in London, sets Gisze in what seems an office, amidst objects both representative and symbolic: On the carpeted table before him are scissors, a quill, a signet ring and a metal signet, a pewter writing set *cum* change dish, a ledger, a timepiece, a vase bearing flowers; behind him on shelves and walls correspondence, another account book, two more signet rings and four red wax seals, a gilded spherical string dispenser, keys, a balance, a further signet hanging by a chain. The letters bear Gisze's merchant mark, a personal emblem used to identify goods as a merchant's product or property; his device – *Nulla sine merore voluptas*, "No joy without sorrow" – is written on the office wall. The ambivalence of this motto – and a certain unease in Gisze's features – have been correlated with ambiguities in the depiction of his environment: The room's perspective is irregular, quill and writing set seem poised to fall from the table, balance and seal from their shelf. One scholar suggests that "Holbein must here be making a concealed comment on the mental state of his sitter," another that what is signaled may be anxiety about the plague, then raging in London, or a more general concern with the insecurity of fortune (Campbell 1990: 34; Holman 1980: 142). Yet despite the expressiveness of Gisze's physiognomy, the attributes point to a mental state conceived not as a matter of individual psychology, but psychosocially. It has been observed that the Renaissance

Fig. 18.3   Hans Holbein the Younger, *The Merchant Georg Gisze* (1532). Oil on oak panel, 96.3 × 85.7 cm. Bildarchiv Preussischer Kulturbesitz/Art Resource, NY.

iconography of fortune (to which Gisze's sphere may perhaps refer) reflected above all the worries of merchants, who stood equally to rise or fall precipitously by her graces.[11] The medicinal flora at Gisze's elbow may point to fear of a threat to life, as some have argued, but the several signs of imbalance point to a threat to the very sense of self that the setting is meant to affirm. Finally, the profusion of signets and marks suggest some anxiety as to their function.[12] Here again, as with Benny and Werther, we perceive attributes of identity possibly signaling their own inadequacy.

This ambivalent mode of signaling may typify moments of what might be called social-semiotic disorganization. The early 1530s – in Germany, the era of the original Faust – saw not only plague in England, but also religious, social, and economic unrest. The decade is further characterized by sumptuary legislation defending distinctions threatened by social disorder by linking rank rigidly to outward signs. Holbein's English portraits reflect the attendant anxieties: One can peg his sitters' status precisely based on sartorial semiotics.[13] In the age of Werther, the weakening force of such legislation (as part of a more general "disorganization of symbolic orders") allowed its replacement by the new dynamics of the fashion system, as well as by J. C. Lavater's physiognomic anchoring of semes of selfhood in facial features rather than dress.[14] There are similar forces at work in Weimar Germany's fascination with social typology, evident for example in the revival by Otto Dix, August Sander, and other portraitists of Holbein's technique of marking status with background, in Siegfried Kracauer's practice of reading films as social hieroglyphs, in Adorno's and Walter Benjamin's pages on bourgeois interiors, and in writing by Béla Balázs on film's "physiognomy of things" – not to mention advancing police methods and Nazi racial metrics.[15] More recently, the 1980s and early 1990s – the years of Haneke's trilogy – see the rise of a new identity politics and problems of social coding provoked by globalization, the collapse of the Iron Curtain, and third world migration to first world countries, conditions amply reflected in the director's French films (*Code Unknown*, 2000; *Caché*).

A further factor that links all these eras is suicide. The correlation is statistical, but arguments could be made for substantive connection. Austria's historically high suicide rates reached a postwar peak in 1986 (Katschnig et al. 2001: 16), and it is not hard to see Haneke's *Seventh Continent* (1989) as a comment on this phenomenon. The 1530s, the 1770s, and the years around 1930 all saw comparable spikes in the incidence and in the public discussion of suicide (Bobach 2004). The scholarship on suicide has made clear that although the delict is peculiarly polyvalent – people kill themselves for all sorts of reasons, and the reasons established seldom seem quite to explain the act – it tends also to be socially indexical: As Emile Durkheim observed, "the relations of suicide to certain states of environment are as direct and constant as its relations to facts of a biological and physical character [are] uncertain and ambiguous" (Durkheim 1951: 299). Haneke's film asks us to respect the complexity of motivation behind the horrific events it describes – he has called the film a response to the ready reductions of the press and the narrative simplifications of mainstream filmmaking – while at the same time demanding an effort at comprehension (Grabner 2005: 35). The film's question is: *Why does this family commit suicide after destroying everything that they own?* In other words, not only: Why do they commit suicide? but also: Why do they first demolish their *mise-en-scène*? Haneke disarms pat answers not only by having his actors play unemotively, but also by lingering as he does on the demolition; there is no facile way to get from here to psychology. We are forced by the *mise-en-scène* to consider the indexicality of the event, to ask how these deaths follow from such a life, from the spaces and things and ways it consumes and inhabits – the car, carwash, and garage, the road, the bedroom, the kitchen; the food, the furniture, books, records, clothing, fish tank, TV, toothbrushes, sleeping pills; the school, the optometrist's shop, the factory interior. The drama – to use a phrase of Antonioni's – is plastic: The things and the spaces play as much of a role as the people who move in their midst.[16]

Haneke has spoken more of his debt to Robert Bresson than of any to Antonioni, yet *The Seventh Continent* certainly bears the imprint of both directors. The debt is formal and thematic, as well as transformative: Haneke builds on their work (and combines their techniques) to achieve new effects. Bresson's signature framing informs nearly all of Haneke's feature films, beginning with *The Seventh Continent*, in an adaptation of the aesthetic of fragmentation through which Bresson aimed to disrupt ("denarrativize") traditional filmic narrative.[17] Colorful close-ups of money in circulation derived from *L'Argent* appear in all three films of the trilogy, as do truncated verticals (of doors especially, but also of bodies in action, often in interaction with objects). Jean-Louis Provoyeur has suggested that Bresson's fragmented bodies "denarrativize" motivation by isolating actions from facial expression and hence from the signs of intentionality of which traditional narratives weave psychological explanations.[18] Haneke's framing of the repeated morning ritual sequence of *The Seventh Continent* not only "denarrativizes" the family's actions (it does do that), but it also frames their activity as a headless inter-action with meaningless objects. There is such framing in *71 Fragments*, including the morning ritual sequence of the armored-truck guard Hans Nohal, but here objects retain some sense (Nohal's gun is still a professional attribute), whereas in *The Seventh Continent* the things seem to float free of sense. The effect is heightened by disconnection in the montage between close-ups and long shots, as Georg Seeßlen observes: "there is virtually no relationship between a person's lonely individuality and his social determination, unless we draw it ourselves" (Seeßlen 2005: 53). Or as Haneke notes of Bresson: "What is omitted is the pretense of any kind of wholeness, including that of man's representation – the torso and the extremities come together only for fleeting moments; they are separated, set equal to objects and at their mercy, the face becomes one part among many, a motionless, expressionless icon of melancholy for the loss of identity."[19] This description recalls Albrecht Dürer's engraving *Melencolia I*, its subject "surrounded by the instruments of creative work, but sadly brooding with a feeling that she is achieving nothing"[20] – with the difference that for these bourgeois the objects informing identity are no longer the tools of the artisan, scholar, or merchant, but consumer goods, a more volatile type of cultural capital. Nor does the workplace have any longer a clear relation to selfhood. Neither Georg's factory, nor the numbers he runs, lets us know what he does there. Such depiction renounces Holbein's semantics of identity the way *Caché* does Lang's of control. If Haneke's Benny is Georg Gisze drained of the warmth of selfhood by the lamination of his environment, then the family S. is Gisze decapitated, a trio of selves without physiognomies beyond what their spaces, objects, routines have impressed upon them. This is why, with a sledgehammer, the film equates an implosion of selfhood with the social-semantic bankruptcy of things.

Yet the way these spaces, objects, routines are employed as *mises-en-scène* is reminiscent less of Bresson than of Michelangelo Antonioni. Comparing Haneke's trilogy with Antonioni's great tetralogy within the frame of a general likeness between the *Vergletscherung* (glaciation) of one and the other's *malattia dei sentimenti* (malaise of the feelings), Jörg Metelmann has noted echoes, in *The Seventh Continent*, of Antonioni's *Red Desert* (*Il deserto rosso*, 1964): Ugo's and Georg's industrial workspaces, children feigning illness for parental attention (Antonioni's Valerio, Haneke's Anna), and a common concern with man's disappearance as man before the backdrop of modern technologies. Drawing on Gilles Deleuze's poetics of the *espace quelconque* (any-space-whatever), he shows affinities in the films' figurations of human dislocation within the anonymous urban, mercantile, and industrial "non-places" of postwar Western society (Metelmann 2003: 222–52). To this I would add not only Haneke's use of touches of red in a blue-gray palette to signal emotional heat – as with the bag Benny rifles, or the coat Marion steals in *71 Fragments*, not to mention the blood – but also a code from *Red Desert*, that of shallowness vs. depth. The interrelation of figure and ground, of people and things, is a constitutive part of Antonioni's visual idiom.[21] In the tetralogy, he accentuates such relation by frequently using lenses of long focal length to flatten depth of field. *Red Desert* was a milestone in the expressive use not only of color, but also of such lenses, used not only to produce abstract color compositions within the frame, but also to place the characters (as Antonioni put it) "in contact with things."[22] By compressing depth, the long lens enhances our sense that objects on different planes belong visually, and perhaps meaningfully, to a single pictorial plane.[23] As David Bordwell has noted, *Red Desert* constructs a thematic contrast between "the thin, dingy planes" of the industrial wasteland through which its characters move and "the sparkling depth" of Giuliana's imaginary island beach (Bordwell 1997: 248). Other scenes too are figured in depth: The car's arrival at Ugo's factory, which brings a moment of contact between planes as Giuliana buys a sandwich from one of its passengers, a political agitator; her desperate glance up the empty street in front of the shop in the Via Alighieri; her near-suicidal drive to the end of the wharf by the orgy shack; the echo of her beach-fantasy boat in the freighter outside her son's window. The planar compression achieved with long lenses would seem to signify Giuliana's entrapment within a mental and physical wasteland, while the film's visions of depth – arrivals, departures, beach, ships, perhaps death in fog and water – suggest a utopian wish for release. The film expresses this aurally too, in the boat horns we hear – or hear Giuliana hearing – periodically in the distance. These horns are an obvious intertext in *The Seventh Continent*, as is the boat that appears to Evi in the car lot. (Benny also sees ships, in Egypt.) Less obvious perhaps are Georg's farewell glance up and down his empty street and the inviting chthonic pinkness of the recurrent Australian beach, likely an echo of Giuliana's. For Haneke, too, flatness appears to signify entrapment, depth a promise of exit; yet he is clearly less sanguine even than Antonioni about possibilities of exit.[24] The depth of his beach is – paradoxically – flat: a poster, a screen, an image only, seductive and fatal. The film's final montage, intercutting the beach, TV no-signal static, and flashbacks to earlier moments of life with reverse shots of the dead or dying Georg, restates the title's implicit identification of death with a deceptive dream of flight.[25] Haneke has observed of his characters that "they destroy their possessions and everything that's theirs with the same intensity, the same methodicalness" with which they go through the motions of everyday life in the waking sequences: "They devote themselves completely to it. And it could be an act of liberation, but the way they do it shows that it's not a liberation for them. And for me, that's the saddest thing in the film" (Haneke 2005). The final montage confirms this message. Here nostalgia for depth comes up short, hits the screen, the film's last insistent shot the white noise (in the script: *Bildrauschen*) of a late-night TV *Sendeschluß*. Same thing with Anna's long look out the window after slapping Evi, an ironic echo of Giuliana's visionary moments: Anna sees a street – the same empty street as her husband will see – through a gate. It is Evi who sees a ship, only to be distracted by the car dealer's test drive. The sequence is not unlike Benny's one direct, beautiful vision in Egypt of ships floating at anchor at night, a shot bracketed by hotel channel-surfing frustration and Benny's video of a road – two dreams of escape, both conditioned by media. These are moments of longing and wishing that things could be different: utopian moments – for us. Benny may not care for his vision's organ soundtrack, but *we* do; Evi may not hear Alban Berg's violin concerto, but we ache at the requiem for a child (Metelmann 2003: 76–7; Assheuer 2008: 118).

These are romantic visions, recalling the characteristic conjunction of music, moonlight, and *Sehnsucht* found in Novalis, J. H. Wackenroder's "Oriental Fairy Tale of a Naked Saint," or the poems of Joseph von Eichendorff. The German romantic dream of merger in oneness – in God, love, art, the *Volk*, nature, death – was historically a response to increasing complexity in modern economic, social, political, and media systems, a reaction that aimed for relief in ecstatic dissolution. Haneke explores this dream (which we are still dreaming), approaching it with suspicion, yet still investing it with some hope. The death of the family S., he admits, could have been a liberation. What makes it not one is the way they do it: as methodically, as mechanically, as they've lived their lives, and as much captive to media snares as before. And as cold: a *Liebestod* without love. Worst of all, the attempt to escape is determined by what is to be escaped. This irony, too, is romantic. The word *Bildrauschen* contains the verb *rauschen*, to rush, as do brooks or leaves: a trope typical of Eichendorff and Novalis, for whom nature's rushing holds out a promise of immediate (non-verbal, asemic) experience or cognition, which may however produce self-destruction. The screen before Georg at the end is the leering death mask of such a promise, with antecedents already in Eichendorff ("Das Marmorbild," 1818; "Der Schatzgräber," 1834).

The transition from bourgeois identification through signs of vocation to consumerist self-definition has early roots – Werther, a failure as a creator, signals selfhood through reading and fashion choices instead, and the sociologist Colin

Campbell has identified a "romantic ethic" of modern consumerism running along-side the Protestant work ethic[26] – but the form that Haneke gives the problem is very much of the twentieth century. Especially, one could say, of the 1960s, which set the terms of debate on spectacle, media, and consumerism: There is a reason why writers on Haneke often cite Baudrillard, Debord, McLuhan, Adorno.[27] In film and literature, one sees parallels in Ugo Gregoretti's bitter send-up of consumer culture *The Free-Range Chicken* (*Il pollo ruspante*, a segment of the collaborative film *Ro.Go.Pa.G.*, 1963, which ends one family's buying jag with a car crash), or Georges Perec's novel *Les Choses* (1965, translated as *Things: A Story of the Sixties*, 1990). The parallels with Perec are especially strong.[28] *Les Choses* opens with a patently cinematic pan across an interior that will reveal itself as a fantasy of bourgeois social arrival: "Your eye, first of all, would glide over the grey fitted carpet in the narrow, long and high-ceilinged corridor. Its walls would be cup-boards, in light-colored wood, with fittings of gleaming brass."[29] Perec's six-page description of this interior articulates a sense of self and social belonging of which the real lives (and the real apartment) of his protagonists, a young couple employed in advertising, fall very short. Puzzled and overwhelmed by the complex task of differential self-definition through cultural goods, they flee Paris to take teaching work in Tunisia. Expecting something like *Casablanca*, they end up in the non-descript southern city of Sfax. Here the signs lose their syntax: Their apartment is big but their things make no sense there, the town and its people are unintel-ligible – "opaque" – and they come to feel they no longer know quite who they are. This could be a liberation, but it is not.

Like Haneke's Egypt, Australia, Romania, Perec's Tunisia confutes the roman-tic projection east of a utopian sphere of reduced complexity. For the German romantics, the Orient was a dream of the dissolution of difference, a fantastic coun-terpoint to modernity's waxing intricacy. Too often, in fact, the dream turned to one of self-dissolution in death, in suicide. The death of the family S. literalizes this connection: they destroy their things, then themselves, because what they seek in "Australia" is escape from the social-semantic system their things trap them in. If René Girard is correct to assert that violence proceeds from crises in social dis-tinction, then this might explain not only the violence with which they proceed, but also Haneke's linking such violence with the semiotic bankruptcy of goods and media in affluent societies (Girard 1977). But does this explain Maximilian, the student who runs amok in *71 Fragments*? This film is less about selves in inte-riors than the other two, but there is one scene that employs the vocabulary: Maximilian's endless ping-pong. Here the drab back wall suggests an evacuation of self, while the net in the foreground expresses entrapment.[30] The dehumaniz-ing effect of Max's mechanical training recalls the – headless – buck vaulting shot in *The Seventh Continent*, itself an echo of that film's morning ritual sequences. These sport scenes express the peculiarly modern feeling of what Günther Anders once called "Promethean shame," the embarrassment of modern man that he cannot match – in efficiency, strength, productivity, beauty, longevity – his own

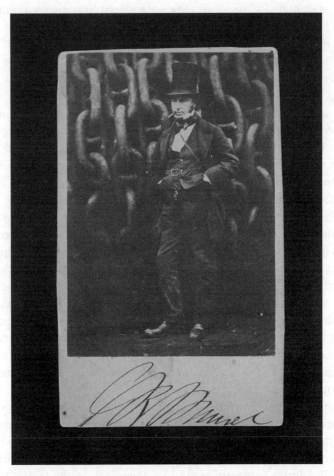

Fig. 18.4   Robert Howlett/London Stereoscopic and Photographic Company. *Isambard Kingdom Brunel and the Launching Chains of the Great Eastern* (1857). Harvard Art Museum, Fogg Art Museum, on loan from the Historical Photographs and Special Visual Collections Department, Fine Arts Library, Harvard College Library, Bequest of Evert Jansen Wendell, 120.1976.1929.

technological products (Anders 1956: 21–95). The century's ambivalence on this subject is well expressed in the history of cinema, from paeans to mechanization (Eisenstein's *General Line*, 1929; Dovzhenko's *Earth*, 1930; Dziga Vertov's *Man With a Movie Camera*, 1929) through schematized ambivalence (Lang's *Metropolis*, 1927; Chaplin's *Modern Times*, 1936; Riefenstahl's *Triumph of the Will*, 1935) to later dystopias (the *Qatsi* and *Matrix* trilogies, Gilliam's *Brazil*, 1985). Lang's *Metropolis* showed the seduction to self-immolation inherent in modern technology; in *Koyaanisqatsi* (1982), Godfrey Reggio followed Antonioni in using long lenses to turn industrial landscapes into wasted *paysages-état-de-l'âme* or signifiers of states of

Fig. 18.5   Man before his machine. *Koyaanisqatsi* (1982), dir. Godfrey Reggio, prod. Francis Ford Coppola.

mind, transmuting the powerful sense of identity expressed in Robert Howlett's portrait of the industrialist Isambard Brunel before the launching chains of his ship the *Great Eastern* (1857) to subservience, conflicted dependence, human fragility-by-comparison, a near-extinction of self (Figs. 18.4, 18.5). This is a story of how the things we have made – our narratives, our technologies, our families and societies – not only make us, but may destroy us. Modern man's Promethean claim is that he has made himself. Haneke shows where we're botching the job.

Acknowledgments

I would like to thank Antien Knaap for information on Northern Renaissance painting, Greg Williams and Roy Grundmann for their helpful comments on drafts of this essay, Andrei Molotiu for a good book tip, Jonathan Zatlin for making "things" click, and Alexandra Payne-Rancier for getting me thinking about Holbein and Otto Dix.

Notes

1   "Today everything is so transparent, I don't know if I'm expressing myself correctly, in any case everything's made of glass and from this transparent turquoise plastic, and it's become somehow physically unbearable" (Kracht 2002: 25).
2   Compare Jan Svankmajer's use, in *Lekce Faust* (1994), of an empty eggshell discovered inside a loaf of bread to signify Faust's loss of his soul, perhaps an inverted Easter metaphor.

3   On Lang's shop windows, see Gunning (2000); also McArthur (1992: 75–6).

4   According to Erwin Panofsky, these two genres develop in synchrony: "Since the out-
doors and the indoors are complementary aspects of one substance, namely, space,
important advances in landscape painting are always accompanied by analogous
advances in the interpretation of the interior" (Panofsky 1953, vol. 1: 57).

5   See, for example, Cranach's pendant portraits of the humanist Johannes Cuspinian
and his wife (ca. 1503, Oskar Reinhart Museum, Winterthur, Switzerland).

6   The convention would peak with such quasi-emblematic "books of the trades" as
the *Ständebuch* of Jost Ammann (1568) and the *Afbeelding der Menselijke Bezigheden* of
Jan Luyken (1694). On early bourgeois portraiture see Campbell (1990: 109–37).

7   Goethe (1989: 96) (*The Sorrows of Young Werther*, letter of October 19).

8   Goethe (1961: 95–7) (*Faust I*, lines 398–409).

9   See Gunning (2000: 109). I owe this insight to comments by Tom Levin at the October
2007 Haneke conference at Boston University.

10   Its recognized antecedents, besides the transitional works of the brothers Van Eyck,
are portraits by Quentin Metsys (*The Moneylender and his Wife*, 1514, Louvre; *Portrait
of Erasmus*, 1517, Galleria Borghese) and Jan Gossaert's *Portrait of a Merchant* (ca. 1530,
National Gallery of Art, Washington, DC). On Metsys, see Campbell (1990: 165 and
plates 178, 179); for Gossaert ("genannt Mabuse"), see Holman (1980: 141).

11   See Doren (1924; on the ball as a symbol of fortune in Holbein and Dürer, see esp.
n. 135, p. 137), and Warburg (1992). On the Baroque tradition, see Henkel and Schöne
(1996: emblems 1796, 1797, 1799, 1800, 1801); also Heckscher (1985).

12   Merchants' marks are apparently runic in origin, and sometimes heraldic in character. Their widespread use dates to the fifteenth century, and is connected historically
with the influence of the Hanseatic league. See Girling (1964).

13   Thus for example Gisze, a merchant, wears silk, but not gold, a prerogative of
royalty and the nobility. With certain of Holbein's bourgeois subjects (Gisze,
the astronomer Nicolaus Kratzer, the humanists Thomas More and Erasmus), the
semantic burden is displaced, so to speak, to expressive interiors, whereas his portraits of nobles and royalty concentrate social indices almost exclusively in clothing,
the monochrome backgrounds sometimes containing plants with heraldic (not
professional) significance. See Baldwin (1926: 10 and 154ff.).

14   On the disturbance of symbolic orders ca. 1800, see Wellbery (1985).

15   Benjamin (1982), section "I" ("das Interieur, die Spur"), vol. 1, pp. 269–80; Kracauer
(1947); Adorno (1997); Balázs (1986: 61–9). On the Weimar period see in general
Schmölders and Gilman (2000).

16   Jean-Luc Godard: "So the drama is not just psychological, but plastic." Antonioni:
"Well, it's the same thing" (Antonioni and Godard 1996: 295) (interview on *Red Desert*,
1964).

17   See Provoyeur (2003: 107–48).

18   Provoyeur (2003: 118). On Bresson and Haneke see also Leisch-Kiesl (2005).

19   Haneke (2008: 153). See the translation in this volume.

20   Klibansky et al. (1979: 320). Haneke's citation in his film *The Time of the Wolf* (2003)
of Dürer's apocalyptic watercolor of 1525, *Landscape Flooded with Waters from Heaven
(Dream Vision)*, points similarly to a threat of evacuation of meaning from the world.
On melancholy as a bourgeois phenomenon, see Lepenies (1969).

21 See for example Gandy (2003); Bernardi (2002: 180–8).
22 "A large proportion of *Il deserto rosso* was shot with lenses of focal length from 100 mm. upwards" (Salt 1992: 259). See also Sears (2003: 278), and Chatman and Duncan (2004: 79–82).
23 This is one of the major devices in Godfrey Reggio's *Koyaanisqatsi* (1982), in which the optical flattening of people against machines signals a mostly unhealthy interdependence.
24 Or of accommodation; see Antonioni's interview with Godard (Antonioni and Godard 1996).
25 The screenplay's less ambiguous original title was simply *Australien*. See the facsimile in Horwath (1991: 42).
26 Campbell (1987). On Werther and consumerism, see Purdy (1998: esp. 147–79).
27 Much of what Baudrillard wrote on violence in affluent societies in his *La Société de la consommation* (1970: 272–9), for example, could have been written by or about Haneke himself.
28 I am not making an argument for influence, but for affinity. I asked Haneke in September 2007 if he was familiar with these two works; he said he was not.
29 Perec (1990: 21). "*Les Choses* commence par un panoramique latérale. C'est un mode d'écriture qui est très influencé par le cinéma, surtout au niveau de montage, des successions d'images, de cette progression qui permet d'arriver sur un objet et puis, une fois qu'on est dessus, d'oublier complètement le reste" (Perec 2003: 215).
30 A device common also in Antonioni and Lang.

References and Further Reading

Adorno, Theodor W.: *Kierkegaard: Konstruktion des Ästhetischen*, ed. Rolf Tiedemann (Frankfurt am Main: Suhrkamp, 1997).

Anders, Günther: *Die Antiquiertheit des Menschen: Über die Seele im Zeitalter der zweiten industriellen Revolution* (Munich: Beck, 1956).

Antonioni, Michelangelo and Godard, Jean-Luc: "The Night, the Eclipse, the Dawn" (interview, 1964), *Michelangelo Antonioni, The Architecture of Vision: Writings and Interviews on Cinema*, ed. Carlo di Carlo, Giorgio Tinazzi, and Marga Cottino-Jones (Chicago: University of Chicago Press, 1996), pp. 287–97.

Assheuer, Thomas: *Nahaufnahme: Michael Haneke; Gespräche mit Thomas Assheuer* (Berlin: Alexander, 2008).

Balázs, Béla: *Der sichtbare Mensch, oder die Kultur des Films* (Frankfurt am Main: Suhrkamp, 1986).

Baldwin, Frances Elizabeth: *Sumptuary Legislation and Personal Regulation in England* (Baltimore: Johns Hopkins University Press, 1926).

Baudrillard, Jean: *La Société de la consommation* (Paris: SGPP, 1970).

Benjamin, Walter: *Das Passagen-Werk*, ed. Rolf Tiedemann (Frankfurt am Main: Suhrkamp, 1982).

Bernardi, Sandro: *Il paesaggio nel cinema italiano* (Venice: Marsilio, 2002).

Bobach, Reinhard: *Der Selbstmord als Gegenstand historischer Forschung* (Regensburg: Roderer, 2004).

Bordwell, David: *On the History of Film Style* (Cambridge, MA: Harvard University Press, 1997).

Campbell, Colin: *The Romantic Ethic and the Spirit of Consumerism* (Oxford: Blackwell, 1987).

Campbell, Lorne: *Renaissance Portraits: European Portrait-Painting in the 14th, 15th and 16th Centuries* (New Haven, CT: Yale University Press, 1990).

Chatman, Seymour and Duncan, Paul, eds.: *Michelangelo Antonioni: The Complete Films* (Cologne: Taschen, 2004).

Doren, Alfred: "Fortuna im Mittelalter und in der Renaissance," *Vorträge der Bibliothek Warburg 1922–1923*, ed. Fritz Saxl (Leipzig: Teubner, 1924), pp. 71–144.

Durkheim, Emile: *Suicide: A Study in Sociology*, trans. John A. Spaulding and George Simpson (Glencoe, IL: Free Press, 1951).

Gandy, Matthew: "Landscapes of Deliquescence in Michelangelo Antonioni's *Red Desert*," *Transactions of the Institute of British Geographers* 28 (2003): 218–38.

Girard, René: *Violence and the Sacred*, trans. Patrick Gregory (Baltimore: Johns Hopkins University Press, 1977).

Girling, F. A.: *English Merchants' Marks: A Field Survey of Marks Made by Merchants and Tradesmen in England between 1400 and 1700* (London: Oxford University Press, 1964).

Goethe, Johann Wolfgang von: *Goethe's "Faust,"* trans. Walter Kaufmann (New York: Random House/Anchor, 1961).

Goethe, Johann Wolfgang von: *The Sorrows of Young Werther*, trans. Michael Hulse (London: Penguin, 1989).

Grabner, Franz: "'Der Name der Erbsünde ist Verdrängung': Ein Gespräch mit Michael Haneke," *Michael Haneke und seine Filme: Eine Pathologie der Konsumgesellschaft*, ed. Christian Wessely, Gerhard Larchner, and Franz Grabner (Marburg: Schüren, 2005), pp. 33–46.

Gunning, Tom: *The Films of Fritz Lang: Allegories of Vision and Modernity* (London: BFI, 2000).

Haneke, Michael: Interview with Serge Toubiana (2005), *The Seventh Continent*, Kino Video DVD.

Haneke, Michael: "Schrecken und Utopie der Form," Thomas Assheuer, *Nahaufnahme: Michael Haneke; Gespräche mit Thomas Assheuer* (Berlin: Alexander, 2008), pp. 135–53. [English translation in this volume.]

Heckscher, William S.: "Goethe im Banne der Sinnbilder: Ein Beitrag zur Emblematik," *Art and Literature: Studies in Relationship*, ed. Egon Verheyen (Baden-Baden: Valentin Koerner/Duke University Press, 1985), pp. 217–36.

Henkel, Arthur and Schöne, Albrecht, eds.: *Emblemata: Handbuch zur Sinnbildkunst des XVI. und XVII. Jahrhunderts* (Stuttgart: Metzler, 1996).

Holman, Thomas S.: "Holbein's Portraits of the Steelyard Merchants: An Investigation," *Metropolitan Museum Journal* 14 (1980): 139–58.

Horwath, Alexander, ed.: *Der Siebente Kontinent: Michael Haneke und seine Filme* (Vienna: Europaverlag, 1991).

Katschnig, Heinz, Ladinser, Edwin, Scherer, Michael, Sonneck, Gernot, and Wancata, Johannes: *Österreichischer Psychiatriebericht 2001*. Part 1: *Daten zur psychiatrischen und psychosozialen Versorgung der österreichischen Bevölkerung* (Vienna: Im Auftrag des Staatssekretariats für Gesundheit im Bundesministerium für Soziale Sicherheit und Generationen, 2001). www.bmgfj.gv.at.

Klibansky, Raymond, Panofsky, Erwin, and Saxl, Fritz: *Saturn and Melancholy: Studies in the History of Natural Philosophy, Religion and Art* (Nendeln/Liechtenstein: Kraus Reprint, 1979).

Kracauer, Siegfried: *From Caligari to Hitler: A Psychological History of the German Film* (Princeton, NJ: Princeton University Press, 1947).

Kracht, Christian: *Faserland* (Munich: dtv, 2002).

Leisch-Kiesl, Monika: "Es sind Fragen aufgetreten und offen geblieben, von denen ich hoffe, dass sie nicht allzu schnell beantwortet werden (können): Michael Haneke – Robert Bresson," *Michael Haneke und seine Filme: Eine Pathologie der Konsumgesellschaft*, ed. Christian Wessely, Gerhard Larchner, and Franz Grabner (Marburg: Schüren, 2005), pp. 347–68.

Lepenies, Wolf: *Melancholie und Gesellschaft* (Frankfurt am Main: Suhrkamp, 1969).

McArthur, Colin: *The Big Heat* (London: BFI, 1992).

Metelmann, Jörg: *Zur Kritik der Kino-Gewalt: Die Filme von Michael Haneke* (Munich: Fink, 2003).

Panofsky, Erwin: *Early Netherlandish Painting: Its Origins and Character*, 2 vols. (Cambridge, MA: Harvard University Press, 1953).

Perec, Georges: "Entretien avec Gabriel Simony" (1981), *Entretiens et conférences*, Vol. 2: *1979–1981*, ed. Dominique Bertelli and Mireille Ribière (Nantes: Joseph K., 2003), pp. 208–26.

Perec, Georges: *Things: A Story of the Sixties*, trans. David Bellos. In *Things: A Story of the Sixties and A Man Asleep*, trans. David Bellos and Andrew Leak (Boston: Godine, 1990).

Provoyeur, Jean-Louis: *Le Cinéma de Robert Bresson: De l'effet de réel à l'effet de sublime* (Paris: L'Harmattan, 2003).

Purdy, Daniel L.: *The Tyranny of Elegance: Consumer Cosmopolitanism in the Age of Goethe* (Baltimore: Johns Hopkins University Press, 1998).

Salt, Barry: *Film Style and Technology: History and Analysis*, 2nd edition (London: Starword, 1992).

Schmölders, Claudia and Gilman, Sander, eds.: *Gesichter der Weimarer Republik: Eine physiognomische Kulturgeschichte* (Cologne: Dumont, 2000).

Sears, Roger, ed.: *Making Pictures: A Century of European Cinematography* (New York: Abrams, 2003).

Seeßlen, Georg: "Strukturen der Vereisung: Blick, Perspektive und Gestus in den Filmen Michael Hanekes," *Michael Haneke und seine Filme: Eine Pathologie der Konsumgesellschaft*, ed. Christian Wessely, Gerhard Larchner, and Franz Grabner (Marburg: Schüren, 2005), pp. 47–56. [English translation in this volume.]

Warburg, Aby M.: "Francesco Sassettis letztwillige Verfügung," *Ausgewählte Schriften und Würdigungen*, ed. Dieter Wuttke (Baden-Baden: Valentin Koerner, 1992), pp. 137–63.

Wellbery, David E.: "Die Wahlverwandtschaften," *Goethes Erzählwerk: Interpretationen*, ed. Paul Michael Lützeler and James E. McLeod (Stuttgart: Reclam, 1985), pp. 291–318.

19

How to Do Things with Violences

Eugenie Brinkema

But, I said, I once heard a story which I believe, that Leontius the son of Aglaion, on his way up from the Piraeus under the outer side of the northern wall, becoming aware of dead bodies that lay at the place of public execution at the same time felt a desire to see them and a repugnance and aversion, and that for a time he resisted and veiled his head, but overpowered in despite of all by his desire, with wide staring eyes he rushed up to the corpses and cried, There, ye wretches, take your fill of the fine spectacle![1]

In 1975, when Jean-Louis Baudry returned to Plato's *Republic* in order to locate in the founding text of Western metaphysics an anticipation of cinema's simulation machine, he did not turn to the above moment. Instead, he famously wrote of Book VII's Allegory of the Cave, the defining idealist parable for the lure of illusions taken for the real.[2] In Baudry's account – and in the apparatus, ideological, and psychoanalytic film theory that followed in the 1970s and 1980s – image and recorded sound were (in different ways) aligned with the illusory, the fraudulent, the degraded, the removed, the absent. To this day, the Allegory remains a privileged model for articulating cinema's relationship to the mediation of the real. By contrast, the brief aside quoted above – made in the context of a discussion of reason, affections, the irrational, and the appetitive – offers a very different scenario of vision centered around precisely what is missing in the Allegory: embodiment, ambivalence, passion, and affects such as disgust and horror. The prisoners in Plato's cave take cast shadows and rebounding echoes for reality itself, and fail to realize the cheat, the lie, the dim dimness of their perceptions. There is an illumination higher than the enabling condition of shadowy representation, and it is only through suffering into that blinding light that one sheds degraded appearance for the nobler cloth of idea and truth. But the case of Leontius offers a reversal of the shadows-taken-for-things model of vision and knowledge – here, vision is irrefutably, unpleasantly immediate, present, insistent. Instead of deceiving or placating, vision speaks of a revolting truth: the desire to gaze upon the abject sight of the dead. The final line – the affective cry from the depths of the tortured and distended body – is an address to the eyes themselves: There, ye wretches, take your fill. Look. Here. This is this.

Although the event with the corpses lacks the Allegory's elegant parallels to the dark, static, immobile frontality of cinema, we can nevertheless glimpse in this alternative model another scene of how vision functions, how eyes address the world and are, in turn, addressed by and through it. In place of structure-passivity-illusion-deceit-shadows-echoes-imprisonment, here we have something like event-activity-truth-embodiment-immediacy-ambivalence-affect. If the history of metaphysics is itself a history of other scenes – inscribed into it by the logic of substance, permanence, being, and the tyranny of first principles (what Nietzsche angrily called the philosophers' "hatred of even the idea of becoming"), each necessitating degraded others – then this imagining otherwise of eye-work suggests that a non-metaphysical, supremely immanent model of vision is inscribed within, and pushes against the skin of, resists and stresses the tense edges of, metaphysics. This seeing without enlightenment is marked not by remove or distance but by a horrific overproximity to the tiny horrors of the real (and a reluctant, persistent ecstasy); it is a seeing that is of violence done and is itself violent, is itself doing violence.

Michael Haneke's *Benny's Video* (1992) tensely hovers between these two models of vision in the philosophical mythology of the West. On the one hand, it everywhere suggests a Platonic view of imaging in which there is an outside at a remove from the scene of appearance and shadows, often setting up formal binaries between interiority/exteriority, darkness/light, sound/image – even if only to trouble those binaries and the epistemologies they sustain. At the same time, there is a form of seeing in *Benny's Video* that aligns with the Leontius model: a vision that is immediate, insistent, and insistently present, not removed at all; a vision that hurts, that is aligned with violence and that is violent in its phenomenological and ethical dimensions. While Benny's affectlessness is at a far remove from the passion spoken to the wide staring eyes of Leontius, the images of *Benny's Video* (and many of Haneke's other films) create a counter-narrative to that coldness, one blushing with tortures to the flesh that do not go unseen but that compel the eyes to look on the face of death.

For the moment, I want to risk stating the obvious (to stave off the greater risk of leaving these things unsaid) – *Benny's Video* is, above all, about a death (each time *a* singular death, though there are at least four: the pig's, the girl's, Benny's grandfather's, which likely took place, and Benny's grandmother's, which likely did not); about death as an ungraspable, meta-phenomenological limit and death as a plastic banality; about the murder that produces the cruel central death (a messy murder, a time-consuming, sloppy ending of being); about things that can and must be done with corpses (the post-*Psycho* problematic); about the family and the nation, and the guilt that binds them; and about video, film, and other proliferating technologies of mediation. More broadly, it is a meditation on the image, on violence, on the image of violence and the violence of the image, and most broadly it concerns presence and absence, simultaneity and distinctness, and the messy reversibility of cause and effect.

Critical work on *Benny's Video* has focused on the historical context of postmodernity that seems to account for Benny's wildly complex media environment, saturated with too many horrific images and all the signs of late capitalist visual decadence. The dominant critical theme, despite important differences in the literature, is that there has been a collapse of the mediate and the real, a fall to the recuperative logic of the same. Thus, even when he is not explicitly invoked, the traces of Jean Baudrillard's simulacrum smudge the pages that read Haneke's text. For Baudrillard, one of the most horrific transformations of postmodernity is the exorcizing of the powerful fantasy of the double as a copy distinct from the self, "a perfect duplicate" of one's own being. The transformation of this fantasy into cloning's pure repetition commutes "the operation of the double from a subtle interplay involving death and the Other into a bland eternity of the Same" (1993: 114). Baudrillard seems to be the ideal diagnostician of Benny's world: a subject incapable of thinking difference or otherness, and doomed to the pure repetition of equalized images on a homogeneifying screen that flattens the news, horror films, home videos, and snuff into each other. This critical impulse to diagnose a logic of the same has informed so much of the work on *Benny's Video* that it is the rare text that does not invoke some plaint about a lost origin and lost differences in its analysis of mediation, the image, the real, and violence.

However, behind theories of media convergence in the age of the spectacle lies the fantasy of endlessly translatable experiences. Is this not the oldest dream of metaphysics, the possibility that within this homogeneified mediascape resides a culture predicated on a universal language of all-image-all-the-time? In a sense, Haneke criticism does not *diagnose* a world in which images and the real are collapsed as much as *desire* that world, for the flattened logic of the universal screen supports the most comforting of promises: that against this we can position some otherwise originary real. An awkward collusion thus exists between Haneke criticism and the figure of Benny himself, one predicated on respective avowals of metaphysical tropes in the attempt to suggest that that classical model is now obsolete in the modern age of media.

The antinomies of *Benny's Video* criticism are: (1) Benny is an anti-psychological symptom of familial breakdown and emotional numbing in postmodern late capitalism and Benny is a fully psychologized, Oedipally rebellious child whose guilt over the murder ultimately leads to a redemptive revenge against his parents and a moral/theological salvation; (2) *Benny's Video* deconstructs the dangers of media violence by deploying sound to affectively shock the viewer back into a recognition of taken-for-granted horrors and *Benny's Video* perfectly conforms to the seductions of media violence by flattening and flatly repeating its own violent events and is thus identical to the object it critiques; and (3) *Benny's Video* deploys the modernist language of fragmentation, alienation, and provocation to critique a postmodern mediascape that treats images as reality and *Benny's Video* performs the postmodern collapse of images and reality to suggest that no exteriority or critique is possible from within late surveillance society.

Consider the third antinomy: The initial claim is exemplified by Brigitte Peucker's argument that Haneke's films employ modernist techniques (formal rigor and anti-psychological characterizations) to violently move spectators. While the images are often bereft of violence, the assaultive realism of sound "wages war against the inauthenticity of postmodernity" (2007: 131). The coldness of mediation run amok is countered by the warmth of the affective jolts experienced by the sensitive plane of the spectatorial body. Thus, while Peucker argues that "*Benny's Video*, the film, revolves around a postmodern consciousness for which representation and reality are nearly indistinguishable" (135), difference and possible critique are engaged on the level of a very real spectatorial working-over. This claim rests on the notion that *Benny's Video* is about a world in which representation and reality are increasingly indistinguishable, and violence has to escape representation altogether to make itself directly and assaultively present to the senses via affect. By contrast, the second half of the antinomy is represented by Fatima Naqvi's discussion of victimization and violence in postmodernity, in which the proliferation of images flattens, compromises, or otherwise indifferently equalizes a now-interchangeable series of encounters with the world. The failure of inter-subjective recognition involves amplifying invisibilities and co-optations because "in the all-encompassing mediatization to which *Benny's Video* is part one and *Funny Games* the sequel – there is such a pervasive sense of non-recognition in a culture of images" (2007: 65).

When Kant grappled with his famous antinomies, his resolution involved critiquing the methodological and metaphysical errors that made both halves of the contradictory claims equally demonstrable. The shared assumptions in the above antinomies are equally metaphysical, searching for a locus of truth in either the figural idea of Benny or the literal psychology of Benny, a sign of the possibility of critique or the failed self-inscription of futile attempts at media deconstruction. I suggest that the critical error (whose identification leads to the possible resolution of these aporias) is the failure to interrogate how key terms in each argument – "image," "mediation," "violence" – are treated in Haneke's film. It is because violence and the image are treated as separable items in criticism (the one, the medium; the other, the object of mediatic capture) – and this is nowhere more true than in criticism that suggests a postmodern collapse of the real into the spectacle – that *Benny's Video* is viewed as both a diagnostic of a problematic and a preeminent example of that problematic. Contra the view that more images in Benny's world equals greater homogeneity and a flattening logic of the same, I contend that media proliferation produces ever more distinctness, more difference, and that the violence of form is neither modernist (not a metaphorically violent alienation) nor overpresently real (in the sensorial attacks of horrible sounds) but the violence of the image, multiplied and extended and expanded. In this essay,

I argue that Haneke's effort in the film is to make the image synonymous with violence, and violence synonymous with the image, not as a historical claim about postmodernity but as an ethical claim about representation's potential.

At this point, surely it is expected that the writer will oblige with a plot summary to frame the discussion of the film. You no doubt want to learn all about little Benny and his naughty little films. But I believe that it is an error to read *Benny's Video* from narrative's left to right of forward progress (for it puts linear time in question) of events-that-take-place (for it puts the event in question). For *Benny's Video* is a series of shapes, not events; structures, not subjects. Consider, instead, the two dominant forms of the film, one effecting a logic of space and the other a logic of time. Imagine a darkened rectangle in the aspect ratio of the cinematic screen, almost completely black, so that shape and texture come to presence by even darker lines tracing where matter may be taken up thickly in the room. Behind this room in diegetic space, but squarely in front of the spectator for whom all retreats into perspective present themselves on the same flat screen, there is an entry into another space marked by a blinding, almost washed-out light. Sometimes this structure cashes in the promissory note of offscreen space, leading through the depths into the light – so begins the film as the dark gives way to an overexposed sunlight, captured on grainy video, the light which gives no warmth but bounces instead off the mass of the pig that in the future – but not yet, not yet – will reel back in the throes of a death captured by light but uncaptured in substance on the film within the film. Other times, however, the structure is flattened into its elements in a tableau of negative space and line: The twice-seen, ultimately damning, shot from inside Benny's room at night as his parents worry over the logistics of corpse disposal and reputation management is preceded by Benny's request to keep his door and the living room door open. The result is a frame of almost entirely absented space: a thin vertical sliver of light from the door in the upper left third of the image, a short perpendicular streak of light at the bottom edge of the opened door, and only the faintest cast illuminated triangle.

The aesthetic language of the film is entirely based around these vertical light lines and tall thin rectangles of luminosity. Benny's room is a study in upright forms: lined-up videotapes cut the *mise-en-scène* into hundreds of little black bars, as though the markers of a prisoner's interiority in relation to some exteriority had been refigured, barring bars now folded fully into the room they bind. Tall lockers structure the room alongside the elongated windows covered with shades from which the thinnest thread of light continually makes its tensile edge known. Even at the moment of flattest squareness – the empty frame of Benny's room in which he has just silenced the girl, her corpse the substance of the offscreen space for a frame that speaks violence only through its absence – the video screen's image of lockers descending in height, creating a slant of receding vertical blocks, is a cruel mockery of Renaissance perspective at the moment when the human is no longer the measure of space but the blunt corpse excepted from it.

Things substitute for that sliver of light, and it is importantly neither aligned with transcendence nor privileged as the "real." The question of the film is whether the perpetually animated television screen, with its blue-cold light, is a substitute for the light at the end of the hallways and rooms that pepper the film – is it identical to those spaces-beyond that illumination designates elsewhere, or is it a degraded approximation of that light, set in contrast to the rays of the sun that ever threaten to burst from behind the flat shades that press them out? Peucker reads Haneke's signature shot as calling attention to "the materiality of the cinematic medium . . . for the light that permits the image enters the 'dark chamber' from which it is shot through a partly opened door, which suggests the work of the shutter that admits light into the camera itself" (2007: 137). The repetition of this shot, first at its "original" moment and then as evidence against Benny's parents, blurs "postmodern and modern velleities." The modernist investment in the materiality of film is set alongside the indeterminate ontology of those images. To this argument, I would add that this image also evokes a logic of light and darkness that is saturated with the visual language of classical metaphysics. It could be argued that postmodernity precisely allows for the co-existence, and ultimately co-optation, of these various registers of representation, but I resist the notion that these registers are flattened into each other, that they must be victim of the logic of the same.

The crudest visual sketch of classical metaphysics is the horizontality of lighted sky above the darkened mass of the earth, separated by a line traveling from left to right splitting the elements and hierarchizing the valuation of each realm. (It is no coincidence that the Allegory of the Cave is the tale of ascending move-ment from the depths of cold, damp, lizard-ridden earth into space-above.) Haneke's insistent vertical rectangles of light evoke the divided metaphysical world, but, now, quite literally, turned on its side. Instead of the hierarchy of above/below, dark and light are co-present, co-extensive, side by side in difference but not pri-ority. If light is beyond or other, it is not aligned with idealism or supersession; indeed, into that light are the horrors of the earth: where the fat pig will die, where the parents' cruelty will calmly articulate its reason. A reading that seeks redemp-tion, confession, or salvation in the end of the film might note that in Egypt the world is turned a crucial ninety degrees and on film for the first time is the shock-ing appearance of the horizon, of set planes of sky, sea, and earth in their proper hierarchized order.[3] This reorientation of the divided world is underlined by shots taken through the bus windows as the travelog commences, each horizontal rect-angle replaced with another as Benny and his mother take their tour of what is now, literally, a different world.

But this spatial reorientation does not promise transcendence or hint at redemp-tion, and that is in part because of a second form that structures and shapes *Benny's Video*. If the first dominant form of the film is the antechamber of darkness that shapes the world-on-its-side of perverted metaphysics, the second structure takes the form of the pyramid. Though they are ignored in much criticism, or mentioned only to describe the narrative bookends, the pyramid schemes in which Benny and his sister attempt to participate are crucial for thinking about temporality and causality in the film as a whole. Any pyramid scheme – including the classic "Airplane Game" version in the film – involves an exchange of money for the exponential enrollment of other members; it definitionally offers neither product nor service. It has, and this is why it is always a scam, no end benefit; it is unsustainable and it is purposeless. The pyramid-scheme structure has often been mentioned in relation to late-stage capitalism in relation to the non-delivery of products and services in the new global market and the inevitable benefit to early entrants at the expense of later entrants. Late capitalism is no doubt the historical context for Benny and his family, but I am not suggesting that this scheme is invoked multiple times in the film merely to suggest themes such as social decay, excess material goods, and the exploitation of workers, for tropes are not the issue in this anti-psychological formalist film. Instead, the pyramid must be taken in its literal dimension: as a shape, as a theory of hierarchization, and as a specific form of troubled temporality.

The pyramid scheme is invoked three times, like all proper betrayals. The second embedded video that the audience encounters after the initial images of the slaughter is amateur footage of Benny's sister's pyramid scheme party; later, in the locker room at school, Benny tries to solicit participants in his own scheme; finally, after the return from Egypt, Benny's sister has a second party, now with parental approval, and the plane gets off the ground. The pyramid scheme structuralizes a hierarchy premised on exploitation in place of transcendence and truth; like the games in Haneke's *Funny Games* (1997) wagered with the complicity of cinematic inscription – games the family cannot fail to lose – it ensures the success of the few over the losses of the many. It suggests one thing more regarding causality and temporality: Because there is no end benefit produced by the scheme, income that should properly be the result of a service or product is acquired in advance from recruitment alone. The pyramid's reversal of profit before product involves an effect that precedes its cause, both an affront to Hume and to narrative cinema's love of forward temporality. If the possibility of an effect before its cause is anathema to the metaphysician, it is not a problem for the modern physicist who takes for granted backward causation, cyclical time, and their consequence – that the fixity of the past is not guaranteed.

This uncausal logic evokes another in *Benny's Video* – that of video technology, in which any and every effect can be made to precede its cause through the wild potentiality of the rewind button. Peucker reads the scene in which Benny rewinds and then replays in slow motion the taped moment of the death of the pig as a desire to control "narrative flow and time . . . in order half-seriously to interfere with the inevitability of its narrative and to reverse 'reality'" (2007: 136). I suggest, instead, that it is not simply the case that the manipulation of the incomprehensible image evokes an attempt to interfere with the inevitability of the event, but that in the forward temporality of the meta-film, *Benny's Video*, the effect of the pig's fall in advance of its resurrection in advance of finitude makes the death of the pig into a fundamentally different event. It makes every death of the pig a death-in-process of the pig, makes every death a dying. There is no inevitability to the visual narrative, though certainly that is the animating myth of video log-ics; instead, what the rewind function does is produce an aesthetic of backward causation that undermines the fixity of the past instead of and against securing it. The pig is both alive and dead; alive then dead; dead then alive; and none of those orderings are privileged or, in fact, existent, independently of their visual presentation in the images given over to the spectator to Haneke's film. The tem-poral foldings of *Benny's Video* suggest that an event does not have materiality outside of its representations and, therefore, that the manipulation of represen-tation does not just interfere with the inevitability of any one narrative, but undermines the inevitability of narrative as such.

Against the critical preference for the logic of the same, Haneke's is an aesthetic of distinctions, differences, effects that precede their cause, and images that con-vey intensity over signification. Critique is made possible not by examining character or narrative but by theorizing the film's form: structures of negation that are subtractive, not additive, entropic, not progressive. Haneke has general-ized of his work, "I believe that every art form works with structures, and structures are produced by repetitions. Without exception the repetitions and variations in my films have their basis in music" (2000: 161–2). Certainly, this substitution of repetition for development aligns Haneke's modernism with the larger aesthetic shifts of the serial and post-serial twentieth and twenty-first centuries. While *71 Fragments of a Chronology of Chance* (1994) takes a "contrapuntal form," as Haneke avows (as does *Code Unknown*, 2000), *Funny Games* is Haneke's most Cagean piece, marked by interruptions, digressions, and even a dared invitation to abandon the diegesis altogether – and, also, yes, a playfulness that shocks. (To round out the idiosyncratic analogy, perhaps *Time of the Wolf* [2003] is Haneke's visual trans-lation of Xenakis's murky sound mass.) But *Benny's Video* can be understood through none of these signifiers: Its structure is not post-Wagnerian counterpoint, neither wild Cageanism nor a cloudy nod to Xenakis. For *Benny's Video* repeats. It repeats in a very specific way. In the auteurist-authorized taxonomy of structural allusions to musical form, *Benny's Video* is Haneke's Morton Feldman work.

Haneke occasionally employs the repetition of minimalism, a repetition with little difference (or little differences), as in his detailed attention in *The Seventh Continent* to fragmented, identical repeated motor gestures of routinized activi-ties. That repetition draws connections, forms an organic totality. Now, though, a different repetition: irregular, halting, awkward, a non-metronomic repetition that does not theorize sameness but uses repetition to introduce difference, dis-tinctness, fragments, and breaks. Feldman's compositional desire in works like *Rothko Chapel* (1971) was to present sounds as such – his Husserlian cry: To the sounds themselves! – but in an entropic trajectory of decay rather than amplification and growth, as if to undo listeners' memory in "intervals that seem to erase or cancel out each sound as soon as we hear the next" (2000: 7). Rejecting an aesthetic priority of sublation and persistence over negation and absence, Feldman wanted to express "where the sound exists in our hearing – leaving us rather than coming toward us" (25). Repetition functions to produce discontinuity, to repeat *so that things might become absent*, so that not hearing, barely hearing, frustratedly hearing becomes the basis for an aesthetics of refusal, withholding, and impermanence. In place of a logic of repetition as additive, Feldman's repetition subtracts, depletes musical material through iteration, a compositional technique often described as "negation." Figuring repetition as an absenting force requires repudiating the assumption that repetition is always *of* presence and *for* presencing. In place of a climax, Feldman's dream for a piece was to die a natural death, formal finitude being the telos of a repetition on the side of absence in these compositions of decomposition.

Haneke's aesthetic in *Benny's Video* is what I term "negative repetition"; it iterates in order to deplete, reappears via a logic of non-presence, cancels events out, introduces discontinuities and distinctnesses. Fully repudiating the logic whereby repetition ensures sameness, continuity, and progress, Haneke's Feldmanesque treatment of structural repetition everywhere promises that it too, formally, will die – though not a natural death. *Benny's Video* repeats; "VCR logic," Mattias Frey's term for the endless playability that subtends the film, is a logic of rewind, play again, pause, slowly press on, pause again, rewind to the beginning this time, now faster, faster on to the end, to the snow, to the final static. The very ontology of the title is a repetition in question, as much by its possessive structure as its singular noun, for there are many of Benny's videos, objectally cluttering the *mise-en-scène* and circulating as embedded texts within Haneke's film, itself yet another object of the title. There is the repetition of the footage of the pig, the repetition of that slaughter in the murder of the girl, and the repetition of its videographic documentation (each of these a literalization of Bazin's definition of obscenity as the replay of a recorded moment of real death).[4]

Consider the fecundity of these repetitions (they are not mutually exclusive):

- Technological repetition; spectatorial repetition. The identical repetition of an event, ontologically and phenomenologically repeated for diegetic viewer and extra-diegetic spectator, made possible through mechanical reproduction (intertextually, this includes the embedded televisual footage, available for rebroadcast within the diegesis; it also includes some of the screenings Benny puts on for his parents, footage the audience has already seen and now sees, identically, again; extra-textually, it includes Haneke's own film, distributed and repeatable without difference).
- Technological repetition; spectatorial difference. The repetition of an event that maintains inscriptive homogeneity but is recontextualized through its distribution and conditions of exhibition (this includes the repetition of the pig slaughter video in the twin contexts of Benny's private viewing and his exhibition of it as an object of both history and futurity for the girl prior to

her death; it also includes the repetition of identical video clips deployed as markedly different objects: to shock or provoke, as to his parents; to trap or accuse, as to the police).

- Mimetic repetition; the repetition of the event. These are resemblances, mockeries, performances. Every event comes into presence as a narrative appearance in the film through the occurrence of multiple reappearances. Three pyramid schemes. Four deaths. Four interrogations: Benny's of the girl, replete with a parody of a head-tilted, chain-smoking interviewer; Benny's parents of him after the revelation of the murder tape; the one that never takes place, by the principal of Benny; and the flat querying by the police at the end.
- There are countless other repetitions on a structural level: minimally, there are the architectural recurrences of Benny's room, the school, the video store, Benny's room, the living room, the bathroom, Benny's room, and so forth; the repetition of Bach and the agonies of the dying girl in a sonic fold of return; the repetition of the spoken *"so halt"* ("whatever," "because"), signifier of causelessness; finally, the repetition of actors, in *Funny Games*, and, more ephemerally, the repetition of surveillance from *Benny's Video* to *Caché* (2005), in which the latter film's absent cause leaves room for a now-grown Benny to spectrally occupy that space.

The result of this wild particularizing of the gesture of repetition in *Benny's Video* is that repetition ensures distinctness and difference over and in place of continuity and sameness. Recurrence, replication, and reappearance function within an overriding logic of *negative repetition*. In place of an affirmative production of contiguity and history, negative repetition brings to presence fragmentation and the break, non-identity, divergence and dissimilarity. Negative repetition escapes both the classical logic of development and the modernist logic of fragmentation; it resists all dialectics and possibilities for sublation to, instead, fold upon itself at multiple sites of difference and distinctness. Contra the critical view that Benny's world is ethically toxic, flat, homogenized, and standardized, the formal language of Haneke's text introduces everywhere multiple, irreducibly distinct, generatively self-showing differences.

I opened this essay by invoking two divergent models of vision in play in *Benny's Video* because criticism privileged the Allegory model over, and at the expense of, the Leontius form. Indeed, it is in criticism that most rigorously interrogates Haneke's film from the viewpoint of the image in postmodernity that the logics of the Allegory are most fixedly invoked. The second model of a vision that is too close, too real, and that is itself violent – shaking wide open eyes to their retinal core – is the ground for my argument: That, far from suggesting that the contemporary image has become a substitute for reality, at the risk of an ethical and political loss, *Benny's Video* offers a model of the image as co-extensive presence, as the site for generative potential, and as an opening up of forces that bring forth the truth of force. Violence is not a mute, brute subject or reified object of mediatic contemplation for either Benny's video(s) or *Benny's Video*, but is revealed as a problematic of the image just as the condition of the image is aligned with violence. Far from critiquing a world in which the real and the mediate are confused and blurred – and far from figuring Benny as a monstrous symptom of this condition – *Benny's Video*, as I will argue below, opens up "the image to violence and violence to the image."

I take the above phrase from Jean-Luc Nancy's essay "Image and Violence," first published in *Le Portique* in 2000 and reprinted in his 2005 collection on the arts, *The Ground of the Image*. Because Nancy treats the problematics of image and violence outside of the overly limiting language of postmodern media analysis, his work offers theorists a way out of the impasses of the logic of the same and the binary of mediation versus the real. To move past this impasse, Nancy first deconstructs the legacy of the Situationists. The critical tendency to regard Benny's immersive media environment as either the symptom or cause of his loss of affect and attendant loss of ethical responsibility represents the insistent pressure of a version of Situationism in visual studies; we might call this the Debordification of Haneke criticism. For it is Guy Debord's 1967 *The Society of the Spectacle* that leaves its sticky theoretical fingerprints all over the claims that Benny is at a remove, that his experiences with reality are mediated and therefore flattened, that he experiences reality through the images he takes in on the singular screen in his darkened bedroom. On the surface, Debord seems to anticipate Benny's impersonal alienation from family and culture; his homelessness and rootedlessness; his movement between the institutional registers of family, school, law (touring Foucault's disciplinary sites); and how he mirrors back the world of images in place of acting. And so Debord's legacy has been employed: Frey reads *Benny's Video* through the lenses of "Baudrillard, Virilio, Augé, Foucault, and Deleuze," positioning Benny in late capitalism's wandering "supermodernity" of non-places, encountering everywhere a simulacrum in which images stand in for objects, feeling the weight of the virtual over the actual.[5] In a later essay, Frey claims that the film creates "a flat line of reality or unreality, a total conflation of the actual and the virtual. Benny experiences news, commercials, feature films, the pig video, and finally his own slaying of his classmate as all equally unreal" (2006: 32). As in the earlier critical antinomies, note the theoretical dominance of the Situationist assumption that postmodernity involves a trade in images and a subsumption of the real into the spectacle.

The critique I am mobilizing against this critical urge first appears in the title essay of Nancy's *Being Singular Plural*. As Nancy writes, "The denunciation of mere appearance effortlessly moves within mere appearance, because it has no other way of designating what is proper – that is, nonappearance – except as the obscure opposite of the spectacle" (2000: 51). The ground of Situationism's "version of Marxist critique" is that some real, true reality has been replaced with a spectacle or economy of appearances that disrupts, hides, or distorts that real. Nancy takes this critique to task for the understanding of appearance as only ever "mere" or "false" appearance ("surface, secondary exteriority, inessential shadow

. . . semblance, deceptive imitation"). Critical work remains obedient to metaphysics in its refusal to regard "an order of 'appearances,' preferring, instead, authentic reality (deep, living, originary – and always on the order of the Other)" (52). Against the recuperation of some origin or authenticity (as in all appeals to distantiation through reflexivity), Nancy insists that we must figure the relation of appearance to truth in an entirely different way, not as a replacement of the latter by the former but as a "co-appearance" in which beings appear only as their appearing to others. Thus, "there is no society without spectacle; or more precisely there is no society without the spectacle of society"; in short, "society is the spectacle of itself" (67). Nancy's reversal of metaphysical assumptions requires a new conceptual understanding of representation, image, spectacle, and appearance.

Film theory too is in thrall to Platonism, in part because of the comfortable alliance between Situationist critiques and their Marxist offspring (the stubborn residue of Althusser, Brecht, and all manner of ideology theorists in visual studies) and the assumptions of metaphysics from which we are not yet free. Any opposition between an originary or essential truth (call it art, consciousness, reality, violence, ethics) and appearance or spectacle rests on this classical divide. *Benny's Video*, most of all among Haneke's work, tempts criticism into making an argument based on an Other–Same relation that pits some form of reality against some form of appearance/spectacle – this is Haneke's explicit auteurist aim, in his oft-stated call to shock the viewer into a recognition of their complicity in the contemporary media environment, and it is also the tease of Benny's line that death is reducible to the "ketchup and plastic" of the movies. But this is the last lie, the final violence, of *Benny's Video*. For if criticism succumbs to this lure and produces a reading that preserves (or even insists on) the proper, originary, or necessary distinction of appearance from the real, then the film theorist, even as she imagines producing a reading that calls for ethical responsibility in the face of mediation's numbing, occludes the force that subtends representation. In essence, metaphysical criticism lets Benny and *Benny's Video* off the hook for the force of images, participates in a writing-over and forgetting of the violence of all images as such.

Nancy's recent work on visual arts and the cinema fully theorizes this non-metaphysical reading of representation, requiring a radical reevaluation of the universe of both Benny and Haneke. Nancy argues that the image is sacred because it is "separate, what is set aside, removed, cut off"; his word for this separateness is *"the distinct."* The distinct is at a distance, detached, "placed outside and before one's eyes." The image is irreducibly distinct because what it is to be the image is to be separate from the thing which is the invisible ground of the image by being in-visible. The image effects a cut with continuity: "The image is a thing that is not the thing: it distinguishes itself from it, essentially" ("The Image – The Distinct," 2). The image not only presents its distinctness from the thing, it also distinguishes itself by "the force – the energy, pressure, or intensity" of the image's distinction from the thing. The image does not depict this pressure but rather *is* the intensity of this distinction – "this intimate force is not 'represented' by the image, but the image is it, the image activates it, draws it and withdraws it, extracts it by withholding it, and it is with this force that the image touches us" (5). That touch brings spectators into the image, involves a mutual regard that is both a look and a recognition. Thus, the image is not an imitation (for mimeticism reinscribes the appearance/original binary) but the resemblance from which the thing is detached. The image is *obvious*, it offers evidence and is evident; the distinct is visible "because it does not belong to the domain of objects, their perception and their use, but to that of forces, their affections and transmissions. The image is the obviousness of the invisible" (12).

This abstraction of the image as the distinct is given its own theoretical force in Nancy's writing on violence, which opens with a double move: First, "images are violent," as they assault in their intensity or quantity; second, there is an omnipresence of "images of violence" that are "indecent, shocking, necessary, heartrending" ("Image and Violence," 15). These founding principles are the self-same as those at play in *Benny's Video*: The latter is the premise of the narrative, while the former is Haneke's avowed aim in his own images to the spectator to a "Haneke film." Nancy's interrogation of what links "the image to violence and violence to the image" begins by defining violence as "the application of a force that remains foreign to the dynamic or energetic system into which it intervenes." Violence "denatures, wrecks, and massacres that which it assaults," and "takes away its form and meaning" while exhausting itself "in its raging" (16). Thus, violence is force, but a "pure, dense, stupid, impenetrable intensity," and that which exercises itself "without guarantor and without being accountable." Instead of serving truth, violence "wants instead to be itself the truth"; likewise, the history of philosophy suggests truth's own violence ("already truth forces Plato's prisoner to leave the cave, only to dazzle him with its sun"). Finally, violence is monstrous, but also monstrative: Violence demonstrates, it "exposes itself as figure without figure." Here, the visual returns, for violence makes an image of itself. In all cases of violence's imposition (divine violence, the torturer's violence) violence must *show*, must leave a mark or a trace and make its wound visible: "it consists in imprinting its image by force in its effect and as its effect" (20). The worst form of violence involves a specifically visual desire:

> Cruelty takes its name from bloodshed (*cruor*, as distinct from *sanguis*, the blood that circulates in the body). He who is cruel and violent wants to see blood spilt. . . . He who is cruel wants to appropriate death: not by gazing into the emptiness of the depths, but, on the contrary, by filling his eyes with red (by "seeing red") and with the clots in which life suffers and dies. (24–5)

Because "the image disputes the presence of the thing," each image is also monstrative; like violence and truth "the image is of the order of the monster" (22). Cruelty hunts a "little puddle of matter," and every image "borders on such a puddle" (25). Thus all of Haneke's films – but also all film, all images – are ever at a risk of giving in to this order and becoming, in the end, horror films.

Like Benjamin and Deleuze before him, Nancy ends with two violences (perhaps a trace of the metaphysical in his own work; its seductions are not entirely avoidable): the groundless violence of art and the violence of blows that provides its own ground. The one associated with art is a "Violence without violence [that] consists in the revelation's not taking place, its remaining imminent"; it is a revelation "that there is nothing to reveal." By contrast, the other "violent and violating violence reveals and believes that it reveals absolutely" (26). The question for *Benny's Video* is whether it attempts to reveal or suspend revelation, whether the revelation does not take place, or whether it imagines it reveals absolutely. I contend that Haneke has the knowledge Nancy values, that "there is nothing to reveal." The *mise-en-abyme* of security cameras capturing Benny in his final exchange with (and brief, flat "Sorry" to) his parents does not make recourse to an exteriority – it does not, as much criticism suggests, figure the complicity of a network extended to the spectator and infinitely unattributed eyes of surveillance. Rather, that frame is not a last or final frame, but *yet another* frame, unhierarchized above the other frames but "imminence infinitely suspended over itself" (26). Critique does not issue, then, from appeals to a degraded real now lost in the infinite proliferation of screens, frames, cameras, and ontologically promiscuous image types; critique involves the suspension of this revelation, the presencing of the groundlessness of any revelation. (In this sense, the sublimely open ending of *Caché* and the refusal to psychologize or ground the killers' accountability in *Funny Games* are other instances of Haneke's infinite suspension of revelation.)

This suspension involves the coming to presence of a number of generative terms: intensity, difference, distinctness, each aligned with a violence that multiplies (a "violence without violence"), whose forces proliferate the new instead of closing down into reductive completeness. In place of criticism that hegemonizes the same, we should regard *Benny's Video* as an endless opening up of an infinite number of non-forthcoming revelations. The postmodern landscape, littered with televisual, video, and cinematic images, is an explosion of differences, distinct images, and possibilities for an endless series of forays into the world. Instead of a retreat from some originary, non-appearing real, Haneke gives Benny a world of too many openings, a world in which the violence of every image is too forceful and present not in retreat from the possible but fully onslaughtedly forward into it. What Benny gives up, at the end of the film, is not an object to the courts nor his parents to the law – what he gives up, and what he gives up on, is the image. The ultimate problem with *Benny's Video* is not that violent images are flattened together (the correlative problem is not that images flatten a reality) because both the image and violence produce generative differences and deploy the force of the distinct. The proliferation of images in postmodernity is *not* a problem of the same, but a fecundity of distinctnesses. The point is not that one should not look at images of violence – the point is to look, that one must look, that the image has a force that one must contend with and *regard*. Giving up (on) the video does not suggest redemption or salvation. Benny is neither victim nor monster: He is a coward. He does not commit enough to the force of images and he fails to remain accountable to the implications of violence's monstration. Haneke is not Benny because he does not refuse this responsibility.

The title is a trap, as many titles are: The named video does not belong to Benny as an object or property, even less so is it an item of exchange or circulation, a product or pedagogical device. *Benny's Video* should be read as *Benny's Vide-o*, *Benny's I-see*, but also Benny's "I look," "I observe," even "I understand." Nancy plays again and again on the French *égard et regard* – to look, and to regard, each of which involves "watching and waiting, for observing, for tending attentively and overseeing," and also respecting, observing, considering, being open to something's power and accountability (2001: 38). The video images that Benny regards open up onto the real and evidence themselves; we can therefore now reread the images of the pig's death as perfectly materializing Nancy's argument that "Death is part of life, instead of making life part of (or parted from) something other than itself. Death *is neither* the opposite of life *nor* the passage into another life: it is the blind spot that opens up the looking" (18).

This is why Nancy describes film as "an opening cut in the world onto this very world." Rejecting the taking of metaphysics for the cinema, Nancy folds the metaphor inwards, arguing:

> That is why the recurring attempt to compare cinema with Plato's cave is inaccurate: precisely, the depths of the cave attest to an outside of the world, but as a negative, and this sets up the discrediting of images. . . . Film works the opposite way: it does not reflect an outside, it opens an inside onto itself. The image on the screen is itself the idea. (2001: 46)

To resolve the antinomy that *Benny's Video* either perfectly replicates the postmodern mediascape (to critique it) or perfectly replicates the postmodern mediascape (falling prey to it), I argue that *Benny's Video* does not attempt to discredit images, either to critique them or to collude with them. The film has been mistaken for a metaphysical tract in which representation must refer (or fail to refer) to some outside; Benny's videos instead open up the inside of representation to itself, as does Haneke's meta-film. In proliferating images, and in producing difference in place of homogeneity, Haneke's texts bring forth the force of the violence of all images. The evidentiary force of images that open up onto the real, the aesthetic force of images that recruit spectators to their intensity, and the ethical-political force that fails to offer revelation in order to produce "violence without violence" is amplified, instead of mitigated, by the *mise-en-abyme* of representations and frames. It is more images, and not fewer, that the world presents and that presents the world. Thus, late modernity, with its explosion of images, is a bringing forth of the possibility for critique and not the closing down or death of critique.

But could that be embraced – even at the cost of accounting fully for the force of images, especially the one with which the film opens, the obscene, horrible image of the instance of death? Perhaps thinking the new after *Benny's Video* involves a promise to *Vide-o*. Haneke asks us to regard, without horror, without paralysis, with neither the guilt nor burden with which it was first offered, "This is this." Imagine affirming: There, ye wretches, take your fill of the fine spectacle.

Notes

1 Plato, *Republic*, IV 435–442 (Plato 1989: 682). The Greek used to describe the sight is *kalon* (fine or beautiful). The affects I invoke above – disgust, horror, desire – are only part of the spirited story; Socrates reads the event in relation to anger, and many commentators figure it principally in relation to self-disgust and shame (including sexual shame). Despite the fact that the event involves unburied corpses (with echoes of *Antigone*) and notably takes place outside the borders of the city, the appetitive and even aesthetic elements co-opt its political or civic dimensions; as a result, some critics point to Leontius' apolitical demeanor in the scene as its most shocking element.
2 Jean-Louis Baudry (1975). This article, along with Baudry's 1970 "Cinéma: effets idéologiques produits par l'appareil de base" (*Cinéthique* 7–8), comprised the foundation of apparatus theory. Together, they also insisted on the centrality of metaphysical and philosophical thought to film studies, invoking Husserl, Plato, and the entirety of the history of idealism to grapple with identification, spectatorship, representation, and ideology. Both articles are widely reprinted in translation; see *Narrative, Apparatus, Ideology*, ed. Philip Rosen (New York: Columbia University Press, 1986).
3 Peucker and Wood argue that the flight into Egypt suggests the possibilities for rehabilitation, if not redemption, though they formulate this shift and its limitations differently (Peucker 2007: 137; Wood 2007).
4 See André Bazin (2003).
5 See Mattias Frey (2002).

References and Further Reading

Baudrillard, Jean: *La Transparence du Mal* (Paris: Editions Galilée, 1990); trans. James Benedict, *The Transparency of Evil* (London: Verso, 1993).
Baudry, Jean-Louis: "Le dispositif: approches métapsychologiques de l'impression de réalité," *Communications* 23 (1975).
Bazin, André: "Death Every Afternoon," *Rites of Realism: Essays on Corporeal Cinema*, ed. Ivone Margulies, trans. Mark A. Cohen (Durham, NC: Duke University Press, 2003).
Feldman, M.: *Give My Regards to Eighth Street: Collected Writings*, ed. B. H. Friedman (Cambridge, MA: Exact Change, 2000).
Frey, Mattias: "*Benny's Video, Caché*, and the Desubstantiated Image," *Framework* 47:2 (Fall 2006).
Frey, Mattias: "Supermodernity, Capital, and Narcissus: The French Connection to Michael Haneke's *Benny's Video*," *Cinetext* (September 2002).

Haneke, Michael: "Beyond Mainstream Film: An Interview with Michael Haneke," *After Postmodernism: Austrian Literature and Film in Transition*, ed. Willy Riemer (Riverside, CA: Ariadne Press, 2000).

Nancy, Jean-Luc: *Être singulier pluriel* (Paris: Editions Galilée, 1996); trans. Robert D. Richardson and Anne E. O'Byrne, *Being Singular Plural* (Stanford, CA: Stanford University Press, 2000).

Nancy, Jean-Luc: *L'Evidence du film: Abbias Kiarostami/The Evidence of Film*, trans. Christine Irizarry and Verena Andermatt Conley (Brussels: Yves Gevaert, 2001).

Nancy, Jean-Luc: "L'image – le distinct," *La Part de l'œil*, 17–18 (Brussels, 2001); trans. Jeff Fort, "The Image – The Distinct," *The Ground of the Image* (New York: Fordham University Press, 2005).

Nancy, Jean-Luc: "Image et violence," *Le Portique* 6 (University of Metz, 2000); trans. Jeff Fort, "Image and Violence," *The Ground of the Image* (New York: Fordham University Press, 2005).

Naqvi, Fatima: *The Literary and Cultural Rhetoric of Victimhood: Western Europe, 1970–2005* (New York: Palgrave Macmillan, 2007).

Peucker, Brigitte: *The Material Image: Art and the Real in Film* (Stanford, CA: Stanford University Press, 2007).

Plato, *Republic*, IV 435–442, *The Collected Dialogues of Plato, Including the Letters*, ed. Edith Hamilton and Huntington Cairns (Princeton, NJ: Princeton University Press, 1989).

Wood, Robin: "Michael Haneke: Beyond Compromise," *CineAction!* 73–4 (Summer 2007): 44–55.

20

Between Adorno and Lyotard

Michael Haneke's Aesthetic of Fragmentation

Roy Grundmann

Within the canon of Michael Haneke's cinema, *71 Fragments of a Chronology of Chance* (1994) and *Code Unknown* (2000) have a special status. Rather than having their stories revolve around a small, homogeneous group of characters (commonly in Haneke, the nuclear family), each film expands its dramatis personae to a larger, more diverse set, whose individual narratives are linked only loosely. This mode of storytelling is marginal not only within Haneke's body of work. A recent comprehensive study of multicharacter constellation films in global cinema stops short of identifying a seamless cinematic history for this model, singling out isolated precursors instead, as well as pointing to television's serialized productions for strong affinities (Tröhler 2007). It seems, however, that films with multicharacter constellations and multistrain narratives have become more prominent over the past two decades and have developed into a fledgling trend.[1] The main assumption projected by this trend is that a film, by featuring a large cross-section of characters, can most effectively represent the complexity, heterogeneity, and interconnectedness of the modern world. Its myriad stories are most democratically told through a dehierarchized narrative structure and a decentered aesthetic capable of conveying the fragmented mode in which this fully globalized, fully mediatized world experiences itself.

Several recent examples within this trend also reference a range of social, cultural, and political problems related to globalization. Generically, these films are just as likely to take the shape of socially minded crime dramas about inner-city ethnic strife or the global drug trade, urban melodramas about the clash of differently marginalized protagonists, or social-realist studies about some aspect of transnationalism or diasporic life, such as the precarious existence of migrants or the hardships of refugees. The films thus reflect the fluctuating demands of genre and

evolving standards of realism even as their stylistic idiosyncrasies and political investments clearly identify them as auteurist creations. In this sense, many multistrain
narrative films show the influence of European art cinema, even if they belong
to the post-art cinema era and have been made outside of Europe.

Haneke's two multistrain narratives are closely aligned with European art cinema
and European history. They reflect that cinema's long-standing concern with such
traditional first world problems as urban alienation, the anonymity of contemporary society, and the social anemia of the middle class. But they also reflect more
recent historical phenomena, such as the various repercussions of the fall of the
Eastern bloc, of Europe's advancing political and bureaucratic integration, and of
its colonialist legacy. What they share thematically with other multistrain narrative films is the depiction of a dual social phenomenon: On the one hand, there
is an ever-expanding social stratification within and across national and cultural
hemispheres; on the other hand, this potentially isolating tendency is offset by the
films' tracing of similarly elaborate patterns of contingency between individuals,
groups, and social layers. In addition, a depiction of the fragmentation of human
experience and the pluralization of contemporary social structures seems to
demand a dispersion of the films' narrative structures, so that thematic complexity
is reflected in and rendered by a similarly complex web of narrative contingencies. In 71 Fragments and Code Unknown, these narrative contingencies are part
of a comprehensive aesthetic of fragmentation. While this aesthetic provides a
scaffold for conveying impressions of human multitude, this is not its primary
purpose. Instead, form itself is foregrounded. It remains connected to contents,
but it also becomes contents unto itself. This particular approach to fragmentation, and the ways in which it helps Haneke articulate a range of specific and
long-standing concerns about art, aesthetics, and philosophy, are the subject of
this essay.

Introduction

71 Fragments features two married couples whose stories are juxtaposed but who
never meet during the film, two unrelated children whose stories intersect only
indirectly as they become successive targets for adoption by one of the couples,
an embittered, socially isolated pensioner and his daughter who works in a bank,
and a university student who ends up running amok in the bank and shooting
several of these characters. As already indicated by its title, 71 Fragments divides
its narrative into distinct parts, which it separates by fades to black. The film
isolates its characters from one another by placing them into these segments, so
that any two of them rarely cohabit one and the same shot, and it further "traps"
them through framing and a minimally moving or altogether static camera. By
contrast, the claustrophobic components of Code Unknown are partially countered

by fluid camera movements, which make the film appear less rigid in the way it presents its large cast. It includes a Parisian couple consisting of an actress and a photojournalist whose relationship is deteriorating, the photojournalist's younger brother and their father, who are already alienated from each other, a Romanian street beggar and her family that awaits her back home when she is deported from France, and an African man and his family who live in Paris. Rather than compartmentalizing these characters through a stark, superimposed visual grid in the manner of 71 Fragments, Code Unknown sets them in relation to one another by interlinking their stories as a sprawling, open-ended web of heterogeneous relations that seem to branch out from the film's initial scene. The overall effect here is less one of imprisoning isolation than of dislocation and itineration.

Given both films' thematic concern with the Janus-faced state of industrial civilization (thoroughly functionalized and hyper-networked, yet socially microspheric and alienated), their underlying frame of reference is constituted by the intersecting historical forces of modernity and postmodernity. In Haneke's cinema, these forces are more than mere commonplaces. They are cast as destructive syndromes of society's advanced rationalization, fragmentation, and despiritualization, whose wide-ranging symptomatology receives further thematization in both films. One of the themes singled out in 71 Fragments and Code Unknown is the phenomenon of injury, whose various instances befall the characters on an interpersonal as well as a broader, social level. Linked to it is another theme – the more abstract phenomenon of injustice, which is likewise identified as existing on the level of the individual (often involving certain ethical conundrums and spiritual crises) and between groups (produced through society's advanced rationalization and its cultural and political fragmentation). Injury and injustice function as tropes through which Haneke depicts a pervasive crisis of accountability for the individual on the part of a radically fragmented, incoherent world for which a common horizon has vanished and all positions and relations are thoroughly relativized.

71 Fragments and Code Unknown reinforce the depiction of this crisis of accountability through their fragmented narratives and visuals. In fact, fragmentation acquires a meta-critical function in both films. It facilitates a self-reflexive attempt at making film assume its own accountability – which, as I shall explain with reference to Haneke's artistic investments, philosophical interests, and moral convictions, may here be understood as art's accountability to the world, and which thereby also comes to redefine film's artistic value. In this sense, then, what sets 71 Fragments and Code Unknown apart from other recent multistrain narrative films that concern themselves with similar social and cultural themes are the specific aesthetic functions and philosophical implications that Haneke accords fragmentation. It is through fragmentation that Haneke's multistrain narratives explore their own status as art in relation to a larger, likewise fragmented reality they are part of. What becomes of further interest to us is the theoretical foundations that underscore this exploration and inform Haneke's self-reflexive deployment of form.

Notwithstanding the historically specific forms it has taken, the fragmentation of reality is central to both the modern and the postmodern age. Its social manifestations and subtending symptoms have long become the subject of philosophical debates on ethics, aesthetics, and representation. Proceeding from the perspective that Haneke's work is situated at the intersection of modernism and postmodernism and, hence, should be discussed in relation to both, my essay intends to contribute to a widening discourse that seeks to relate his cinema to the theories of two philosophers in particular, Theodor W. Adorno and Jean-François Lyotard.[2] While each is firmly anchored in his respective area – Adorno embodies high modernist theory and Lyotard has been deemed one of the most important thinkers of postmodernism – their philosophical projects have, in fact, been compared to each other for their overlapping interests and shared concerns.[3] As both their projects indicate post-Hegelian philosophy's dissolution of the concept of unity, they also reflect how both philosophers consider fragmentation to be central to our understanding of reality and art's relationship to it. Adorno's and Lyotard's respective theories exemplify the different ways in which modernist and postmodernist thought has grappled with this phenomenon. Modernism abounds with declarations that the center is either dispersed or obscured, or that it is altogether absent and can no longer be retrieved. However, few enunciations within modernist art, literature, and theory evince acceptance of this state. The absence of the center registers negatively in modernism – that is, as a marked loss.[4] Thus, in their very understanding of reality as shattered, modern art and modernist thought still exhibit what Wolfgang Welsch has called a "Ganzheits-Melancholie," a melancholic yearning for wholeness and unity (2002: 176). While postmodern art and philosophy hardly deny the shattered state of reality, what distinguishes the postmodern from the modern is a shift in attitude to this reality. It registers in a greater acceptance of the state of fragmentation and a different conceptualization of loss. Rather than regarding the scattered pieces of reality as life's broken shards and, thus, as evidence of damage and destruction, postmodernism considers them pieces of a mosaic, but without the expectation that these are to form a higher ordering principle. "Ganzheits-Melancholie" is thus replaced with "Vielheits-Interesse" (an interest in plurality and the manifold), to cite Welsch's likewise appositely chosen correlative term (ibid.).[5]

There is no clearer indication of modernism's deep ambivalence towards the condition of fragmentation than Adorno's aesthetic theory. On the one hand, the stringency with which it is imbued clearly shows that Adorno had no hopes of retrieving any notion of unity or a center: Only shattered art can honestly reflect the shattered reality of contemporary life (AT 19, 189).[6] On the other hand, Adorno's philosophy is still cast within the horizon of bringing together what can no longer be actually united.[7] In a critique of Hegel's notion of spirit (the teleological striving for coherence), Adorno suspends art between the necessity to cohere and the interdiction to do so, lest method and meaning become objectifiable and, thus, serve the subject as proof of a false totality (AT 101).[8] Art cannot but synthesize the manifold of empirical reality, but it must do so non-violently, that is, by abjuring any total-ization of meaning (AT 190). This idealist goal is something Adorno defines as an act of justice – justice towards the heterogeneous – and he makes it rest on art's paradoxical task of elevating the negation of synthesis to its operational principle (AT 155).

Adorno thus still understands the fragment in relation to a whole, whose irre-trievable loss fuels his notion that humanity is in need of compensation and that this compensatory function can fall only to art. More particularly, at issue for Adorno is the task of reconciling humanity with nature, which can be accomplished by art only in a utopian moment.[9] Because Lyotard, by contrast, refrains from archaeologizing the fragment as a leftover from destruction, he feels no need to recruit it into a negative teleology of impossible reassemblage, whose goal of sponsoring meaning is simultaneously upheld and deferred. But if Lyotard does not conceive of fragmentation in etiological terms, his notion of fragments as autonomous segments far from implies any belief in their harmonious integra-tion. Their irreducible specificity places them in a relation of incommensurability to one another that constitutes the radical heterogeneity of language and the always already deferred status of reality (D 179–81, 195).[10]

While a notion of fragmentation is thus at the heart of both philosophers' thinking, it is worth noting the differences in their underlying concepts of reality. Understanding these will also help us account for Haneke's evolving approach to fragmentation. Within Adorno's theory of art and aesthetics, empirical reality can be engaged by art only obliquely, via negative dialectics. While the pervasive objectification of the world through processes of rationalization com-pels Adorno's progressive-teleological modernism to declare authentic meaning (*Sinnstiftung*) a strictly utopian possibility, the necessity to judge is still regarded by him to be paramount. But society has all but lost its capacity for judgment. This task now falls to art. According to Adorno, it is by seeking to obtain justice that art can fulfill its accountability to the world – if only by becoming ever more hermetic. For Lyotard, the radical heterogeneity of the world makes its verification altogether impossible. Art's accountability to the world is no longer the seeking of a (however utopian) justice, but the never ceasing proclamation that justice is impossible to obtain (D 184). Whereas in Adorno's concept of fragmentation the condition that determines human relations is that of *alienation*, Lyotard's reformulates this mode as a non-pathogenic *alienness*, an irreducible otherness. His terms harbor connotations not so much of social illness as of social strife. They suggest that Lyotard regards language and society as being essentially agonistic (D 193, 194). Lyotard's concept of radical socio-linguistic heterogeneity is not devoid of a notion of justice, but due to heterogeneity's irreducible nature and absolute presence, justice can never be achieved. Its inher-ent impossibility echoes as an ideal that is gleaned only in actions that are the effects of its absence – that is, in grievances, lawsuits, or potentially violent com-plaints and defenses.[11]

If *71 Fragments* and *Code Unknown* constitute two examples of cinematic fragmentation, a comparison of their aesthetics reveals differences that can be related to Adorno's and Lyotard's respective philosophical positions. Generally speaking, *71 Fragments* represents the world as a shattered totality that finds its just and honest representation in scattered, disjointed scenes of loss, destruction, and dysfunction. In *Code Unknown*, destroyed coherence is recast as uneasy, chafing heterogeneity, which the film dramatizes in scenes depicting the incommensurability of speaking positions, and which is visually rendered by a camera that, while moving fluidly, is keenly aware that justice towards the individual is impossible. However, of interest is not only the significant extent to which both films can be compared to Adorno's and Lyotard's philosophies. Perhaps even more important are the impulses they present towards a critical reinvestigation of these philosophies.

My discussion of *71 Fragments* constitutes the larger portion of this essay. I use the film to discuss the different positions Adorno accords art and film, a territory fraught with conceptual discrepancies and displaced biases. My first step will be to compare the film's aesthetic of fragmentation to Adorno's modernism. While this step is motivated by the existence of certain affinities between Haneke's notion of film and Adorno's notion of art, these will have to be assessed against the limits of this comparison: Haneke's film – and film as a medium – falls outside the idealist aesthetic-philosophical standards that guided Adorno's thinking about modern art. Given the irreducible nature of these limits, a discussion of Haneke's films would here seem to suggest the necessity of parting with Adorno. Yet, I will argue that it is worth keeping Adorno in the picture. Rather than declaring him altogether lost to a discussion of (Haneke's) film, my further analysis of *71 Fragments* will indicate a continued dialog between the filmmaker and the philosopher, and more particularly with the latter's late essay "Transparencies on Film" (1966). I use *71 Fragments* as an occasion to read Haneke's cinema with regard to three areas that Adorno touches on in his essay, but that, at the same time, remain underdeveloped: cinema's affinity with subjective modes of experience, a stronger emphasis on the role of the spectator, and the need to understand anew what Adorno defines as the sociology of the cinema. I argue that Haneke's spectatorial address and his use of certain formal devices reanimate some of the ideas Adorno tentatively outlined in this essay.

In this sense, *71 Fragments* may be understood as an interlocutor to Adorno's film theory, whose potentially useful but dormant aspects the film may be said to activate "from below." What I hope will emerge in this discussion is not only an elucidation of the relationship between Haneke and Adorno, but also a reassessment of Adorno's own relationship to film. It has been noted that the "Transparencies" essay, by dislodging film from its subsumption under the function of mass culture, to a certain extent contradicts the impression that film, for Adorno, represented a lost cause. My discussion of Adorno's reconsideration of the medium seeks to bring out what I think are specific inflections in Adorno's relationship to film. Loss certainly remains the predominant vector here, but my reading of the "Transparencies" essay in relation to Haneke's cinema argues that loss may also create the potential for conceptual transformations and departures. At issue will be the idiom that is dearest to Adornian aesthetic theory – the notion of autonomous art. The "Transparencies" essay indicates that Adorno, when turning his attention to film, was struggling with the absence of the notion of autonomy – a struggle that kept him from considering the medium's potentials to a greater extent than he might have. The nature of Haneke's interlocution, I argue, is not that his cinema seeks to restore autonomy to film as a medium, but that his filmmaking works towards developing what art historians have recently termed the autonomy of aesthetic experience. I consider this notion of autonomy as a decidedly paradoxical – because non-essential – vector of aesthetic theory. Towards the end of the essay, I will discuss Haneke's second multistrain narrative, *Code Unknown*. I read the film in terms of Lyotard's theory of radical socio-linguistic heterogeneity and I outline some characteristics of its redefinition of concepts of justice and irreconcilability and the implications these redefinitions have for the function and status of artistic representation. Aiming to identify certain areas of correspondence between Lyotard and Adorno via a discussion of Haneke's work, I hope to provide more insight into the position of Haneke's cinema at the intersection of modernism and postmodernism. Finally, I briefly point to certain problematic areas in Haneke's representation of difference, which I likewise attempt to relate back to Lyotard's theory of injustice and incommensurability.

An Aesthetic of Fragmentation

71 Fragments begins with a written announcement, displayed against a black background: On December 23, 1993, nineteen-year-old student Maximilian B. shot three people to death in the branch of a Vienna bank and shortly thereafter killed himself with a shot to the head. This announcement is followed by the superimposition of a date – "12. Oktober 1993" – the point when the film's story begins, two and a half months before the horrific events. But this date actually appears over the beginning of a television news sequence. Unlike several others that will follow in the course of the film, this first newscast is not integrated into the diegesis (as an item that would be watched by any of the protagonists on their TV sets at home), and its contents – a string of reportages about civil war and political unrest in various parts around the globe – seems not directly related to the narrative. Upon completion of this seemingly stand-alone sequence, the narrative's various strains begin to unfold. The first is that of the refugee boy Marian's flight from Romania and his vagrant life in Vienna. Another depicts the theft and the illicit trafficking of army weapons, one of which is bought by Max and ends up becoming his killing tool. There are also two stories about married couples: The first shows Hans and Maria, whose drab working-class existence and humdrum marriage are compounded by concerns about their sick infant; the second is about the Brunners who, desperately trying to adopt a child to fill their comfortable but empty bourgeois lives, initially pursue the orphan girl Anni, but then reject her in favor of Marian. Also interspersed is the story of the lonesome, bitter pensioner Tomek, whose social interaction with the world is limited to telephoning his daughter or talking to her across the counter in the bank in which she works.

The tension between the film's austere, self-consciously divisional structure and that structure's pregiven parameters has a certain gestural character. Through it the film announces itself as a modernist work. It downplays representational plenitude and, instead, valorizes formal asceticism; it second-guesses notions of linearity and closure and, thus, deprivileges the role of denotation; most importantly, it suspends causality and questions coherence in its exploration of the conceptually rich contrast between the fragment and the whole. But while this contrast arguably determines the aesthetic structure of the film, how exactly does it suggest an analogy to Adorno's notion of the fragment and how far may such an analogy be carried? Surely, the contradictory concepts of chronology and chance in the film's title suggest a certain affinity to Adorno's high modernist notion of the fragmented, open-ended, aporetic work of art. It may even bring to mind his claim that art must turn against itself internally, that it must bring reality into appearance as unreconciled and antagonistically torn (AT 189). I agree with Harald Meindl that Haneke is very methodical about fragmenting his images.[12] Haneke does seem to be inspired by Adorno's credo that art must allow its elements to unfold their own dynamic both *for* and *against* the purpose of their synthesization. In fact, the film may be regarded as Haneke's most literal attempt at simultaneously initiating and frustrating the production of meaning by questioning the compatibility between the individual fragments and their relation to the larger framework. But even if we, for a moment, leave aside Adorno's very specific definition of art's elements in our initial look at the film's fragmented structure, we are compelled to note that the dual process of sponsoring and frustrating meaning is a commonplace in modernist aesthetics. Within the domain of film alone, it has centrally shaped the aesthetic of numerous examples of European art cinema, with its visual and narrative ambiguities, elliptical storytelling, disjointed editing, and symbolic and oneiric treatments. While certainly modernist, this quality is too broad to account for how Haneke's films may be said to differentiate themselves within the tradition of art cinema of which they are also a part. Nor does this quality help us establish a closer analogy to Adorno, for it does not account for the specifications Adorno's *Aesthetic Theory* made for art – specifications, it should be remembered, from which film remained categorically excluded.

To explain the nature of Haneke's modernism – and to lay the foundation for what I believe will eventually validate an analogy to Adorno – let me start with Haneke's relation to art cinema. I indicated earlier that Haneke's films go beyond these conventions by promoting formal structure to a state where it acquires a certain independence from content. David Bordwell has described this pattern as characteristic of parametric cinema. It suggests the immanence of structural laws in a work and thus emphasizes that there is a level of perceptual order that coexists with or even trumps representational meaning (1985: 283). *71 Fragments* shows strong similarities to what Bordwell calls the "ascetic" or "sparse" variant of this cinema, which he sees embodied by the films of Bresson and Ozu (285). Haneke's film displays its divisional structure from the beginning, its fragments producing a "recognizably pre-formed style" (ibid.). In a relatively short time span, the film rotates through a limited number of settings, which are identified as repetitive along with a likewise limited number of shot types and ways in which the characters and the camera move. This formal organization effectively serves the demands and exigencies of the multistrain narrative, playing into the story's episodic structure and compounding its ellipticality through the omission of information and the sense of distended time. Parametric cinema does not completely abjure realism and symbolism, as Bordwell points out (282). I would argue that, in *71 Fragments*, their deployment actually supports the film's parametric nature, as they help generate the generic representativeness of characters' actions and of the settings in which these occur.

For example, the catastrophe in the bank, instead of galvanizing the characters into social interaction (as is the case, for example, in the disaster film genre), foregrounds the alienated state of the site where it occurs. The bank symbolizes capitalist society's advanced dysfunction, which, as the film suggests, is not primarily constituted by the unequal distribution of wealth but by the fact that all human relations have come to be defined by rationalized, alienated processes of exchange. These are so pervasive that they defy isolation. In their profoundly irrational nature, the shootings thus serve the film at once as a symptom of the crisis of modernity and, staying true to modernity's very spirit, as a signifier of enigma that obviates symptomatology's traditional explanatory role. Indeed, it is Haneke's focus on symptomatology – most of his films have what I would call a "symptom layer" – that makes his highly controlled and limited reliance on realism and symbolism fully evident. Consider, for example, how *71 Fragments* depicts the symptomatology of injuries – one of Haneke's favorite symptoms – by classifying them between individual case study and rote representativeness. The student Max, who eventually deals a lethal injury to several people, is an injured person himself. Max's fatal act does not remain completely unexplained – stress and humiliation are identified as key factors in his behavior. But since the insights into his psyche remain minuscule and his story is even more scattered and sparse than the other stories, the symptoms of his impending breakdown never assume the role they have in conventional realist and genre films.[13] Suffering and causing injuries also characterizes the relationships between Hans and Maria and between Tomek and his daughter, both of which the film treats as diagnoses of the dynamics of mutual alienation, manipulation, and placation. This depiction of injury does not deny the characters their individual subjectivities, but it replaces point-of-view shots with a strictly external perspective. The same approach is taken with Anni.

The film establishes a causal link between fate and psychology by inscribing her orphan status into her dour, standoffish demeanor, which, in turn, suggests her diminished odds of finding foster parents. But by alluding to pop culture (the *Little Orphan Annie* cartoon), the film suggests that her orphan story is more common than Marian's, and it counters the melodramatic aspects that are incurred by turning her injury into an individual case study.

71 Fragments thus effectively harnesses the tension between representational content (which is always unique on some level) and formal structure (whose austere repetitiveness here strives to make form independent from content). Notwithstanding its modernist aspiration to formal distinction, it is through the film's form that the theme of injury is rendered concrete, that it becomes palpable as a pervasive social phenomenon or, if you wish, a syndrome. The film's sociological vein is just strong enough to impute a causal logic between injury and other social ills, such as violence, which Haneke's cinema is also concerned with. By this logic, rationalized and profit-oriented society's violation of the indefeasibility of human existence – of what defines humans as unique – compounds the injuries and injustices caused by the decay of traditional frameworks of meaning (personal-familial as well as social and moral). As a result, those qualities that make each person unique – his or her irreducible otherness – become transformed and reappear in pathological form. Otherness manifests itself in certain states of alienation and hostility and resurfaces in monstrous outbursts of violence.

While *71 Fragments* evinces the formal qualities of parametric cinema, the issues it is concerned with clearly reflect the traditional interests of the more broadly defined category of art cinema. But to place the film in this lineage has ambiguous consequences, for it must be acknowledged that art cinema's topics have remained more or less the same since the 1960s. They now appear as little more than clichés. On the other hand, it is precisely the citation of serious concerns *as* clichés that Bordwell has identified as the specific provenance of the more narrowly defined parametric cinema. Its elaborate anatomies necessitate a reliance on received situations, predictable plot patterns, and well-worn subjects so as not to distract spectators' attempts to apprehend and appreciate form (1985: 285).[14] The same might be said for the relation between form and content in Haneke's glaciation trilogy. As his films place the phenomena of injury and injustice in relation to what I have termed the crisis of accountability, they evince a socially critical impulse known from art cinema, while facilitating the kinds of moral, ethical, and spiritual inquiries that are associated with parametric modernism. The films of the trilogy thus capture the crisis of accountability on several levels. Diegetically, this crisis registers in the characters' state of glaciation. But this state then becomes a basis from which to explore broader and more abstract issues, such as the moral implications of the passing of guilt from parents to children, the ethical responsibility to think historically, and the precarious attempts (including artistic ones) to preserve or recapture a largely eroded spirituality.

71 Fragments involves its spectators in these questions and sparks their interpretive activities by extending its concern with the crisis of accountability from the thematic to the formal level. To this effect, and in a manner typical of parametric cinema, the film exploits specific formal and narrative binaries, such as between close-ups and long shots, on- and offscreen space, cause and effect, and chance and determination. Consider two of the film's narrative strains – its depiction of weapons trafficking and its portrayal of Hans and Maria's glaciated lives. The highly condensed content of each of these two strains is generated by semantic gaps created by elliptical editing and the contrast between extreme close-ups and tightly framed minimalist long shots. In the depiction of Hans and Maria's morning routine, each close-up (hands lighting the stove, putting the kettle on, etc.) constitutes a radical reduction of perspective that, despite its connotative framing, frustrates resemanticization. Conversely, the long shots through the apartment's door frames convey a sense of distance that collapses in on itself, turning into its opposite – an impression of narrowness that, while likewise suggesting a "beyond," constitutes a similar semantic vacuum. For us to judge these two characters and their world requires an awareness of our own assumptions about them and, thus, implicitly requires judging ourselves. In the story about the weapons, the close-ups of broken padlocks and of bags filled with loot seem to become a very part of the criminal chain of exchange – the individual shots seem to perform this type of exchange as much as they depict it. Rather than rehearsing (or exacerbating) the form–content split, the aesthetics of the weapons story demonstrate how parametric cinema is actually more likely to effect a self-reflexive collapse of form and content. The film in this instance not only despectacularizes the crime story it tells, it also identifies itself as being an integral part of the world it shows.

These aesthetics indicate that Haneke's films account for their own position in the world – as stories, as artifacts, and as commodities. And they ask audiences to develop an awareness of their susceptibility to generic conventions and their behavior as consumers of entertainment. Thus, while the shootings at the end of *71 Fragments* may be the final consequence of the weapons trafficking, the film does not exploit the assassination voyeuristically, nor does it trivialize it by presenting it as the story's freakishly singular outcome. Denying Max's motivations the status of dramatic fulcrums or narrative causes, the film foregrounds the deeply engrained desire for explanations and the quick-to-emerge impulse for establishing narrative causality. In this sense, if there is a "reason" behind Max's irrational act – namely, that the world no longer makes sense to him – the purpose of this rote explanation is mainly to make clear to spectators that Max's position is not so different from their own, as they, too, struggle to put together the pieces of a puzzle. As both experience modernity's crisis of accountability in their own way, the puzzle of the cross that Max attempts to piece together early on in the film becomes a self-reflexive icon that binds protagonist and spectator as alter egos.

Our discussion of *71 Fragments* in terms of parametric cinema may help us resituate the film in relation to Adorno's notion of modernist art. As we have seen, the film's form is unable to establish full-fledged autonomy from its content; but that its gesturing in this direction (and the aesthetic impact this gesture has) should trigger associations with Adorno may be more understandable now. Indeed, similar comparisons have been considered for other instances of parametric cinema. Bordwell opens his discussion by entertaining a possible analogy to the serialism of high modernist music. He cites Noël Burch's important assertion that film "is made first of all out of images and sounds; ideas intervene (perhaps) later" (1985: 278). But Burch further argued that, while style is thus as much subject to structuration as narrative, "a film cannot be organized as rigorously as a musical piece, for the former is not susceptible to mathematical schematization and is usually committed to concrete representation" (279). For Bordwell, this means that parametric cinema has to pare down its structure into more cognitively manageable elements. Something similar holds true for *71 Fragments*: While insisting on the relatively high degree of variability of its fragments in relation to a larger whole, the film, which, after all, remains an example of narrative cinema, must make these available for synthesization and it must simplify its structure.[15]

The limitations of the analogy between parametric cinema and high modernist seriality are suggestive with regard to the relation between Haneke's notion of film and Adorno's notion of art. For Adorno film did not have the same kinds of aesthetic potentials as abstract painting, serial music, and other forms of high modernist art. Indeed, he did not consider film an art in the strict sense of the term, because he felt he could demand of art that its formal and semantic openness be much more radical than film's. This raises the question as to what, for Adorno, constitutes the specificity of art and its elements. According to Adorno, it was the sensuous-expressive mimetic qualities of empirical reality itself, whose "unruly" nature causes a work's internal contradictions and caesurae, that comprise something of an artistic essence. Only if art engages them without usurping them can it declare itself to be reality's humble interlocutor (AT 155). On the surface, it would seem that film's medium-specific capacity to record reality lends it a privileged ability to capture precisely these qualities. But this conclusion amounts to a misunderstanding of Adorno. At issue is Adorno's concept of the beauty of nature which – and this is the downfall of the analogy to film's recording capacity – is not to be understood as referring to a mere object whose beauty art must capture. Rather, the term "beauty of nature" aims to define all that is "naturally beautiful" within art – in other words, those laws that constitute the internal dynamics of an artwork, its divergent elements (AT 197).[16] For Adorno, as Wellmer explains, "art does not imitate the real but, at best, those aspects of the real that already point past reality" (1985: 15).[17]

Within Adorno's theory, what is of interest to art about the real is never the real as such but something potentially synthesizable – an aesthetic value. Precisely by virtue of its privileged capacity to record empirical reality does film resist transposition to such a value. Or, put the other way round: Paradoxically, it is the visual immediacy of film that requires translation into artistic expression. What Miriam B. Hansen has called film's "obtrusive referentiality of the image flow" (1981/82: 194) obstructs the production of an inner logic of purely aesthetic elements and makes the production of artistic expression contingent on further artistic inter-vention.[18] Film can never fully achieve the artwork's status of autonomy, making it contingent on the vector of artmaking as socio-political practice. Adorno's dif-ferential conception of film and art would thus seem to present an impasse with regard to further comparisons to Haneke. Yet, declaring the case closed would pre-clude an understanding of the more nuanced specifications Adorno actually does make for film – and an opportunity, too, to explore Haneke's cinema as an artistic project that in crucial ways continues, complements, and corrects Adorno's in the area of thinking about film and mass culture. In addition, while for Adorno film and art may exist in two different theoretical registers, these remain indirectly con-nected. I submit that Haneke's cinema implicitly illustrates this connection.

To begin this discussion, I believe it is worth acknowledging that when one speaks of Haneke's affinities to Adorno, one has in mind, perhaps more than anything else, a certain affinity of attitudes. The first that comes to mind is un-doubtedly the interest Haneke shares with Adorno in the aesthetic integrity of high modernist styles of classical music, which finds a correlative in their shared condemnation of the culture industry. Another one can be found in Haneke's assim-ilation of Adorno's characteristically modernist melancholia or, more precisely, his oblique yearning for a totality whose irretrievable loss his modernism nonethe-less staunchly affirms.[19] But what may arguably be regarded as the most import-ant affinity of attitude is the view that art should be accountable to the world. For Adorno, this accountability was primarily articulated through the progressive-teleological nature of his aesthetic theory, which, as Wellmer has pointed out in his reading of Adorno, expected art to raise the level of its resistance to integra-tion in proportional relation to the recipient's advancing sophistication (1985: 69). For Haneke, who is well aware of the limitations of the analogy between film and Adorno's notion of art, this teleology by contrast translates into a broader, morally inflected attitude towards film's responsibility to the spectator: Regardless of how any given spectator might respond in any given viewing, placing him/her into an obliging position is the least an artwork can do.[20] Taking the spectator to task must be held up as the irreducible standard that guides the responsible auteur's approach to filmmaking.[21]

Befitting this moral framework, *71 Fragments* turns its concern with the crisis of accountability into a "virtue" for itself, making it the fulcrum of its self-reflexive aesthetic. Renouncing the role that bourgeois society traditionally assigns to art (to provide answers, to offer coherent meaning, and, thus, to soothe), Haneke, in his attempt to redefine film's accountability, clearly looks to Adorno in defining it as an accountability to the world. This attitude, when put into cinematic prac-tice, registers first and foremost as a vexation with spectators. They become aware that the establishment of an overarching meaning is a desire on their part that Haneke's films may acknowledge but do not endorse. However, by assigning the production of meaning to the spectator, Haneke's cinema thus also implies a crucial departure from Adornian thinking. His films self-reflexively suspend spectators precisely at the point of their frustrated desire for synthesization, whereby their encounters with the enigmatic aspects of the work become unlocked from the text-centered dialectics of deferral and negation that dominate Adorno's theory. The very fact that spectators of a Haneke film experience their desire to reach a verdict as an increasingly questionable project indicates that they are being "unweaned" from relying on synthesization and following its teleological under-pinnings. Whereas Adorno conceived of meaning as emerging entirely from within the artwork's divergent elements, which the recipient could at best hope to retrace, Haneke gives the spectator more freedom, but also more responsibility. The work, as I will argue further below, certainly retains its own significance, but the recovery and appreciation of preestablished aesthetic constellations – in other words, the retracing of text-immanent dialectics – becomes an increasingly thankless task in viewing Haneke's films, and it has to compete with numerous other specta-torial activities.[22] While in Adorno's theory it is art that is internally at cross-purposes, in Haneke's cinema, it is the spectator.

From Text to Spectator

As might be expected, the shift in emphasis from text to spectator, as significant as it is, does not constitute a complete renunciation of Adorno on Haneke's part. In the last decade of his life, Adorno himself made such a move, albeit in a tentative manner. He had always remained convinced that film's artistic processes, unlike those of art, are ontologically and historically inseparable from its techniques of mass reproduction and exhibition. For many years, this conviction had been supported by another, no less totalizing view, articulated during his years in exile in the United States: that film is largely synonymous with the culture industry, whose main rationale was the commodification of folk culture and myth into an ideology of conformity, and whose main goal was the reproduction of the spectator as con-sumer.[23] If these two views on film never became completely disengaged in Adorno's thinking, his essay "Transparencies on Film" gestured towards loosening their over-determined bind.[24] In it, Adorno ventures into areas that indicate his willingness to consider film outside the binary of autonomous art and jaundiced mass culture. As becomes clear in the course of his argument, Adorno proceeds on two distinct levels – a medium-specific and a historical level – and the fact that these are only superficially connected suggests how difficult it really was for Adorno to accord film a genuinely progressive potential. The essay's engagement with film's medium-specific devices is relatively cursory. The reason, one may speculate, is not that Adorno was ignorant of how they function, but that few of them lent themselves to his model of dialectics that continued to inform his thinking on the whole.[25]

The various internal tensions that produce the essay's tentative openings, but also its partial foreclosures, are signaled by the word "transparencies" in its title.

Miriam B. Hansen has pointed out that the term's ambiguity produces several connotations. It refers to the area of specularity and the visual – by alluding to reflections, slides, and other projected images – but also implicitly references politics through its invocation of the banner (1981/82: 193). That Haneke's cinema does not lend itself to the second connotation would, at first glance, seem to constitute another affinity with Adorno; yet, crucial differences exist. While Adorno personally resisted extending his theoretical work to political practice (196), the authoring of his essay against the background of his friendship with Alexander Kluge, and its publication within the context of the rise of the Young German Film as an alternative film practice, point to Adorno's political affinities and the broader political motivations and dimensions of his life-long project. And even though Adorno's views on film were, for decades, over-determined by his culture industry argument, he was, as Hansen points out, quite aware of cinema's theoretical (and, thus, implicitly political) potential in its ability to juxtapose images in montage: "Only through montage which negates the affirmative appeal of the image and interrupts the chains of associative automatism can film become a medium of cognition" (194).

Yet, Adorno's relation to montage is complicated. Whereas *Aesthetic Theory* extols the virtues of montage through the example of dadaist collage techniques (AT 155), "Transparencies on Film" alludes to dadaist montage experiments for the cinema as being a filmmaker's false friend, as they replace dialectics with shock effect (Adorno 1981/82: 203). Rather than explicitly referencing classic examples of cinematic montage or the inherently montage-oriented films of his friend Kluge, Adorno prefers to keep his discussion of montage consistent with the investigatory categories of *Aesthetic Theory*. These shape his view that film is of interest only if it can wrest its mimetic impulses – which Adorno locates on the level of pure movement, prior to all content and meaning (ibid.) – away from manipulatory influences. This process is contingent on montage's capacity for delivering film's mimetic elements to synthesization. As becomes evident in the "Transparencies" essay, Adorno clearly favored intellectual over affect-oriented reception: Whether in film or in art, montage must be strictly epistemologically defined. Ideally, film editing must produce a series of discontinuously moving images, a kind of interior monologue that he analogizes to the aesthetic qualities of modernist art. As film is not capable of producing these qualities as directly as other media, avant-garde writing is upheld as an ideal to be achieved by film (201), while avant-garde music becomes a model to be emulated by and combined with film (203). Consistent with the utopianism that informs all of his thinking, Adorno stops short of proposing anything more concrete; however, the essay's thrust suggests that only montage can transform film images into a mental language, potentially enlisting film's mass stimuli in the service of emancipatory intentions (203).

However modified to the theoretical parameters of his subject, Adorno's reasoning not only champions intellect over affect, but reattaches film's properties to the principle of dialectics. Revealing every image as writing, dialectics, as Hansen notes, is solely capable of eschewing the pitfalls of decoding signs by putting in place a modernist *écriture* (1981/82: 196–7). The notion of *écriture* is crucial for Hansen's understanding of Adorno's concept of montage, because its mode of "critical deciphering" (197) would seem to grant more agency to the spectator. It would thus also, at least potentially, keep at bay the long-standing and frequently renewed charge that Adorno's notion of dialectics confines the recipient to the task of retracing the work's inner structure. *Ecriture* also informs Hansen's exegesis of Kluge's attempt to put dialectics to emancipatory use. But while Kluge stands as an important historical instance of exploring the potential of dialectics for the cinema, his is a very specific dialectics, which found expression in an equally specific historical model – the concept of the alternative public sphere. To explain Adorno through Kluge has had the implicit effect of making it harder to see the significance of Adorno's notion of film in relation to a broader spectrum of modes of cinematic production and reception.[26]

However, Adorno's preference for intellect over affect, situated as it is within a theoretical discourse of medium specificity, stands in tension with his historical perspective on the cinema. After having observed the culture industry for over three decades, Adorno cannot but accord the spectator at least a tentative freedom from the manipulative impact of dominant entertainment. One of the "Transparencies" essay's crucial revisions is the observation that ideology is always in need of reconfirmation and that meaning is never closed. The reason for this instability is the irrepressible presence and unpredictable role of spectatorial libido (Adorno 1981/82: 201). The viewer's fundamentally desirous predisposition, as Adorno acknowledges in his reconsideration of the unstable effects of the culture industry, has turned out to be too unruly to make the act of reception and consumption completely predictable. Yet, given the essay's acknowledgment of the historical role of bodily presence and functions, reconfining spectatorship to the workings of a purely mental language seems, at least, counter-intuitive. The relation between the medium-specific and the historical argument in Adorno's essay is informed by a mind/body split. Adorno's discussion of film resembling a mental language is related to his claim that film has a unique ability to "base itself on subjective modes of experience which film resembles and which constitutes its artistic character" (ibid.). "Subjective modes of experience" here clearly refers to mind, intellect, and epistemology. But there is no reason why it cannot comprise libidinal impulses and somatic responses more consistent and broader in scale than the fleeting moments of happiness that comprise Adorno's notion of affect (which emerge in the interstices of the process of synthesizing a work's internal impulses); nor can their triggering be neatly attributed to one specific aspect of film – their production owes something to the spectatorial processing of both form and content. This fluidity is more easily acknowledged in Adorno's historical argument, which defines the sociology of the cinema as that which comprises the public's desires, expectations, and customs of consumption. However, even as a definitive answer eludes us, one suspects that Adorno's inclusion of the role of the spectator's affective and, hence, unpredictable responses to films in this historical evaluation is over-determined by his association of content with mass culture (201).[27]

What I would like to propose, then, is to relate Adorno's notions of film's affinity to subjective modes of experience and of the sociology of the cinema to Haneke's films, so as to explore the duality of affect and intellect, of film's epistemological and sensory dimensions in ways that make their positions in Adorno's theory appear less binary. I certainly do not want to deny that dialectics play their part in Haneke's cinema – they do, but we need to be clear that dialectics are not facilitated primarily through editing.[28] We should further acknowledge that Haneke's films remain more thoroughly committed to representational content than Adorno's progressively revised notion of film is prepared to envision[29] – no matter whether we regard content as "mere" *suyzhet* or as always already rendered into (often antithetically organized) form. As I shall argue, it is through both form and content, through their separate but also combined effects, that Haneke's films seize on the cinema's affinity with subjective modes of experience. They rehearse but also go beyond Adorno's concern with mental activity in the synthesization of art's divergent mimetic materials. They involve epistemological activity but they also produce a broad scale of (often negative) affects that include, but are not limited to, anticipation, anxiety, dread, disgust, frustration, and disorientation. Haneke's films thus complement and expand Adorno's notion of aesthetics to levels that fall outside the purview of the traditional parameters of aesthetics. They move into the territory of aisthesis, which has been characterized as being determined by two clusters of processing stimuli: affect, sensation, and feeling on the one hand; cognition, perception, and insight on the other (Welsch 1990: 11).

While my analysis of Haneke's cinema thus takes Adorno into a different direction from Hansen's, it nonetheless remains inspired by her remarks on the implications of the term "transparencies" in the title of Adorno's essay. The formal arrangement of static scenes in *71 Fragments* shows a certain structural similarity to the division of Adorno's essay into a series of "unconnected – though not unrelated – aperçus" (Hansen 1981/82: 193). From a perspective that reads Adorno's revised notion of film primarily through Kluge's cinema, this comparison may seem strained. Yet, Haneke's affinity to Adorno may not be contradicted *per se* by the fact that his films do seem to constitute a more continuous image flow than can be found in more orthodox examples of dialectical cinema (which tend to define dialectics mostly through dense montage). When Haneke selects individual scenes from this flow and displays them as singular dispositifs capable of developing a lasting affective and mnemonic presence within the spectator, they suggest a further analogy to "transparencies," which Hansen also mentions – namely, to slides (ibid.). Indeed, to take the analogy further, many of them have a high degree of recognizability and a self-denigrating plainness to them. They don't have the ascetic glamor of Antonioni's images; they seem more muted, like Bresson's, and show their affinity to his choice of common motifs. As such, their visual quality is not to be understood in analogy to the high degree of communicativeness attributed to Hollywood images. On the contrary, "transparency" signals the overt inscription of mediation, motivation, and intention. The commonplace impression of many of these images works against the cinema's fetishizing tendencies, while their status as derivative reflections (ibid.), to round out the analogy, bespeaks their position as motifs that circulate through Haneke's work as a whole.

These analogies suggest that Haneke's cinema may be productively compared to the way Adorno understands the cinema's capabilities and potentials. Haneke's films seize on the basic cognitive properties and affective qualities that render and structure their diegetic world – the disruptive effect of fades to black, the cognitive dissonance of the cut and of the reframed image, the duration of the take, and the stark contrast between a lack and a sudden excess of action. Thus, certain cinematic devices – particularly the long take and the reframed image – are explored both for and also beyond their capacity to yield epistemological results. They are of interest for the way in which they "charge up" the viewing situation as a whole, forcing one to rethink the terms of what one means when one talks about film viewing as an "aesthetic experience." Viewing the image for content certainly remains central to this experience. But content, in Haneke's films, must always compete with form. This tension creates a gap between film's basic mimetic elements and the received modes of their synthesization. The long take and the reframed image enable spectators to infer that filmic content is not identical with its basic material substrate. I say "infer" to stress that the implications of this effect are cognitive-affective as well as intellectual. The hybridity of Haneke's approach affects both components of spectatorship. It causes spectators not merely to question the image, but to question themselves as readers. Plunging spectators into a crisis of judgment, Haneke's films intervene in the sociology of the cinema without trying to transcend it.

The long take and the image known as *mise-en-abyme* – the shot that makes us watch an act of watching and tells us so[30] – are particularly notable for their capacity to carry cognitive as well as affective markers. They are proof that Adorno's binary notion of film's medium-specific and sociological dimensions can be moved closer together; they can be understood in relation to an expanded notion of aesthetics that includes but is not limited to epistemology, and that identifies sensory experience as a knowledge category of its own. Let us first consider *71 Fragments'* central use of the long take. If the long take as a stylistic staple of realism aids rather than abates film's mediation of reality, Haneke uses it in ways that further amplify film's combined sensory and epistemological capacity. A typical instance is the scene of Hans and Maria's interaction over supper. When Maria is flabbergasted by her husband's completely unexpected declaration of his love for her, her reaction triggers his embarrassment and an act of physical violence. After the initial shock of having been slapped in the face has passed, Maria decides not to leave the table and, instead, briefly yet forgivingly puts her hand on Hans's arm. The tensions at work in Hans and Maria's interaction between alienation and intimacy, aggression and vulnerability, and affect and affectlessness have a heightened, slightly unreal character or, if you will, a latent absurdity that is highly typical of select moments in Haneke's films. It owes to the fact that Haneke's long takes carry instances of excess – an element of visual poetry, a tinge of the surreal, a dimension of the grotesque. Content is defamiliarized; intellectual processing becomes tinged with affect. However, my intention here is not to place the excess of this scene under the traditional rubric of cinematic shock. While the scene draws on the depiction of sudden violence for the production of affect, this isolated moment feeds into a larger dynamic of latent but prolonged, and slowly increasing, spectatorial estrangement. It is this quality that underscores the gap between form and content in the scene. Going beyond its surface realism, the scene subverts any sense of neutral observation, while also leaving the exact nature of its motivation unexplained. While the scene does not foreclose the attribution of social conflict on the diegetic level, the elements that Adorno calls social antinomies are revealed in the gap between this content and its slightly "unreal" representation. Rather than objectifying time (as was Adorno's charge against Antonioni's long takes [1981/82: 201]), the scene subjectifies time for the audience. By triggering anxiety in the spectator, the long take makes the viewing situation its main subject.[31]

A further example of Haneke's cinema that brings this critical self-awareness to the fore is the scene that features the video of Max's performance in a game of table tennis, accompanied by the voice-over of the coach's commentary (Fig. 20.1). The coach's scathing comments neutralize the video's pedagogic potentials; he prefers to use it for discipline, punishment, and humiliation. The video's negative functions are underscored by the duration of the long take, but this effect is complicated by the scene's self-conscious framing of the video monitor, which subjectivizes the visuals. While seemingly clear in its contents, the scene becomes epistemologically aporetic. It constitutes another instance of the crisis of judgment. This effect is produced in part through overt manipulation of the spectator: The scene encourages spectators to be skeptical about the harshness of the coach's critique, while not providing enough information to help them judge whether Max merits such criticism and how he might respond to it emotionally. However, the scene is exemplary of a more pervasive production of cognitive dissonance that brings Haneke's cinema into closer proximity with Adorno. The scene illustrates that for Max, like for many of Haneke's characters, glaciation is not merely a form of social malaise. It is more specifically the condition of the characters' own impulse for self-domination – their *Herrschaftsgedanke*. What Haneke wants to explain to us is that his characters, who are well-educated and relatively prosperous middle-class subjects, are highly efficient at putting this impulse into practice. We need to understand that Max's use of the video as a training tool is consensual and, possibly, initiated by him. As such, it represents the very instrument of his self-oppression.[32] The family suicide in *The Seventh Continent* is described by Horwath as a compulsively ritualized sequence of planned actions, whose fetishistic, far from liberating destruction of previously fetishized items foreshadows death (1991: 13).

Fig. 20.1   Video of Max's performance in the table tennis game. *71 Fragments of a Chronology of Chance* (1994), dir. Michael Haneke, prod. Veit Heiduschka.

What Max's table tennis video and the family suicide share in common, then, is a demonstration of Adorno's observation that the subject becomes the victim of the totalizing effects of its own acts of synthesization and objectification.[33] But while Haneke's films diegetically trace this self-domination to its final, destructive stage, they also attempt to follow Adorno's mandate that art has to negate the very dynamic of domination that it renders visible.[34] It must negate, defer, and negatively dialecticize its own inevitable participation in this dynamic. Thus, *The Seventh Continent* eschews a falsely totalizing and objectifying depiction of the suicide and, instead, replicates the mode of destruction through its fragmentation of the visual field through close-ups and cuts.

But Haneke's strategies for following this mandate vary. While montage plays a fairly important role in the suicide scene in *The Seventh Continent*, in Haneke's subsequent films it becomes increasingly replaced with other devices, such as the use of video. This use of video is exemplary of how Haneke's films force us to see their subjects through their tools of self-oppression, whose formal and content components he pries apart, treating them as art's constitutive but antithetical elements. This is most elaborately put into practice in *Benny's Video* (1992) and *Caché* (2005), where video assumes a negative role in the diegesis (it becomes the subject of *Kulturkritik* in *Benny's Video* and is associated with threat and antagonism in *Caché*). But it also functions as our main cognitive channel through which we view both films. Thus, I would argue against the charge that video for Haneke is inherently negative. It is a tool – one among many – for Haneke to demonstrate how Hegelian *Geist* is transformed into self-oppressive instrumental reason. A further discussion of these two films' use of video would go beyond the parameters of this essay. While Haneke certainly merits critical attention as an intermedially motivated filmmaker, his deployment of video is not the only significant element. As I will argue below, another device, the reframing of the image, is just as important. This device helps shape a scene's psychological, aesthetic, and philosophical dimension. It can become a visual distillation of the many facets that emerge in the course of a character's story.

Consider the story of the orphan girl Anni, which the film distills into a particularly potent *mise-en-abyme*. Once again focusing on the depiction of symptoms, the story concerns itself with the nature of Anni's injuries, but without providing background information on the character. The film deflects spectatorial identification away from the girl and towards the characters who respond to her, particularly her potential foster mother, Frau Brunner. When she rejects Anni for Marian, whose handsome boyishness and "exotic" alienness have greater appeal to her, spectators are thrown into moral conflict.[35] They empathize with Frau Brunner's decision, while, at the same time, recognizing Anni's tragedy. In contrast to Marian, whose own reorphanization at the end of the film technically compares to Anni's, but whose "rise-and-fall" parable feels more rounded and complete, Anni simply gets dropped from the narrative. Without even a perfunctory sense of closure (unlike Marian, Anni is neither directly nor indirectly affected by the shootings), her story is identified as unassimilable.[36] The film's treatment of the character as an alien body that it cannot but reject is integral to its analysis of the corrosive forces of modernity. These forces pervert inalienable humanity into a kind of human alienness, creating a population of injured monsters.

In Anni's case, this perverse transformation finds visual expression in the remarkable shot that depicts her seated on the rim of the bathtub in the orphanage's bathroom[37] – a minimalist, deceptively simple-looking tableau that combines the symbolism of art cinema with the meta-critical, ethico-philosophical tendencies of parametric cinema (Fig. 20.2). The shot's thick framing reveals only a small section of the space, and the girl's perpendicular position in relation to the camera obscures her face. The erection of visual barriers around a luminous center, enhanced by the distance of the object to the camera, symbolizes her internal rift, torn as she is between her need for affection and her maintaining of a protective armor. On this level, the shot summarizes the manner in which the film has morally implicated spectators in Anni's fate. We realize that our acutely felt spatial distance from the character does not relieve us from answerability: We are part of the very humanity that, if invisible to her, has nonetheless betrayed her and will continue to do so.[38] Another dimension of this shot is more philosophical. The image's charged interplay between light center and dark margin, and between granting and denying visual access, throws into relief the visual dynamics of access itself. It is fair to say that access is one of the Enlightenment's greatest obsessions and most questionable legacies. Late modern instances of it consist of elaborate technologies and ideologies that perform a kind of leveling – and, ultimately, a denial – of precisely those features that constitute the unique qualities of each human being. The shot's *mise-en-scène* theatricalizes the camera's "struggle" to access the

Fig. 20.2   Anni (Corina Eder) seated on the rim of the bathtub. *71 Fragments of a Chronology of Chance* (1994), dir. Michael Haneke, prod. Veit Heiduschka.

girl. It barely reaches her, and what it captures appears foreboding and needy at the same time. This suggests that the (lack of) attention Anni has received in her life has had a dehumanizing effect on her. The shot, in fact, comes close to identifying visual objectification as being incommensurable with the girl's humanity. Her humanity is available only obliquely, as an unreconciled fragment that hauntingly questions film's capacity for a realist anthropological humanism. As the shot articulates this self-questioning through its contradictory visuals, it comes close to proffering a correlative to Adorno's notion that the fragment is not the disrupted but the incompatible. No question: Even in this scene, film remains subsumed under its inherently representational capacity. Yet, Haneke forges the visuals of this shot into a dialectic whose radical skepticism reflects Adorno's view that it is in the aesthetic expression of the unreconciled where art may find its designation to perform acts of justice.

The shot of Anni in the bathroom self-consciously inscribes us as viewers. Not only are we watching and made aware of doing so. We are also made aware of the specifically aesthetic nature of this dispositif. Bracketed by fades to black, it is presented as an autonomous fragment, an aesthetic object in its own right. It is about itself as an object, but also about our relationship to it. This it conveys to us by virtue of its reflexive specularity and its ostentatious perspectivism. Despite their seeming redundancy and excess, Haneke's *mises-en-abyme* do not provide clarity but enigma. They install the spectator as the supreme benefactor of the powers of visual access; at the same time, they subversively diminish their yield. Most of the objects to which Haneke's *mises-en-abyme* seek access they also, in one way or another, render inaccessible. The spectator is thus suspended between two antithetical axes, which simultaneously signal authorization and deauthorization of his/her capacity to discern the image. But if Haneke's *mises-en-abyme* thus create what one may term a "phronetic crisis" – the questioning of the ability to pass judgment via the deployment of reason[39] – to misunderstand this rhetoric as an abnegation of reason altogether would be to misunderstand Haneke's relation to the Enlightenment, in whose project, in a further parallel to Adorno, he remains deeply invested. Epistemology, as my analysis has shown, is not obviated by Haneke's images. However, while the deployment of reason implies the possibility of knowledge, Haneke's spectator, even if he/she succeeds in obtaining knowledge, can scarcely rejoice in it. With it comes the realization that one's knowledge is highly contingent on a multitude of factors, not the least of which are one's own subjectivity and partiality. This realization, reinforced by cognitive-affective impulses such as anxiety, dread, or disgust, intersects with and colors the films' epistemological dimension. If one then considers these caveats and qualifications of the spectator's status as epistemological subject in relation to Haneke's interest in religion and spirituality, one might say that knowing entails a kind of "humbling." It means that one accepts one's profound inability to obtain certainty even as one continues in search of it; for this search comprises one's sole agency – it remains at the center of experience.[40]

Aesthetic Experience: Autonomy and Performativity

Haneke's films contribute to a redefinition of what Adorno has characterized as film's affinity with subjective modes of experience. The films' dual targeting of affect and intellect appeals to the spectators' multiple, dispersed, and simultaneous activities of reception. The films succeed in channeling these activities into a concerted and sustained spectatorial engagement – an engagement that begins with but continues beyond the initial viewing, with spectators' revisiting, rethinking, and critically debating particular scenes and shots. We return to a Haneke film not because it was beautiful, but because we have unfinished business with it. We are in the process of "figuring it out," but this process has not come to an end. This pattern belies the received opinion that narrative cinema is unable to resist assimilation into the maelstrom of images and visual fragments that make up our daily existence as subjects of mass culture. In this sense, then, Haneke's films – or, at least, certain "privileged" moments in them, certain scenes we recall for their enigmatic nature and/or for the distinct affects produced in us – also seem to occasion a sense of autonomy that emerges during their viewing; an autonomy, however, that, because of its paradoxical permeability to the outside, is not an essentialist demarcation. This paradox begs some rethinking of the category of autonomy. To the extent that any concept of autonomy indicates a trace back to modernism, it seems to replicate traditional binaries of subject/object, inside/outside, mind/body, form/content, and high art/low art. More specifically within the context of Adornian thought, it refers to the artwork's provisional resistance to being integrated by the viewing subject (integration feeds the subject's totalizing, self-oppressive tendencies of objectification and synthesization). Thus, to reintroduce the very notion of autonomy may seem to invite the misunderstanding that one wants to posit Haneke's spectatorial address as a highbrow/high art gesture to remove the subject from what is deemed the hyperaestheticized postmodern media environment, to rescue it from postmodernism by modernist means. Haneke's films make seeing difficult, and difficulty, after all, is a quality associated with modernism. Yet, if Haneke's spectatorial address may be understood as an intervention in the kind of socio-cognitive crisis that also gets depicted as a theme in his films, this crisis is already very much a modern crisis. Hence, it cannot be solved by an exclusively modernist concept of autonomy, whose orthodoxy would only function as a term of contraction.

At issue, then, is neither the classic notion of the autonomy of the artwork nor the related notion of the autonomy of absolute truth. Nor is the films' occasioning of autonomy to be read as a sign of Haneke wavering between emulating Adorno's "purist" modernism and embracing his own pragmatist variant. Instead, I want to propose that it may be considered the clearest sign of their affinities – a correlative to their respective modernisms that, nonetheless, points to a path towards postmodernism. It may be neither counterproductive nor contradictory to allow the concept of autonomy to remain anchored in modernist aesthetic theory. Albrecht Wellmer has proposed that it may be possible for us to go beyond Adorno without leaving him behind, by relating his notion of the open-endedness of modern art to the postmodern recipient (1985: 27–8), whom Wellmer has characterized as the "more flexible organizational form of a 'communicatively liquified' identity of the I" (28). This recipient's capacity for dynamic change is no longer defined by the mandate to update his/her synthesizing skills to stay abreast of modern art's advancing level of sophistication. It is constituted by an expansion of the notion of reception to the level of affect – or, as Wolfgang Welsch has described it, by a shift from the concept of aesthetics to that of aisthesis, which can encompass affect and intellect, sensation and perception (1990: 11). But if this "communicatively liquified" identity with its capacity for dynamic change is a reality, where exactly does autonomy reside? More importantly still, what could possibly remain its purpose?

The claim that Haneke's films provoke an affective response separate from, but also interfering with, their semantic decoding is not to suggest that the production of meaning in Haneke's cinema is split – as if this were possible – between work-owned hermeneutics and spectator-targeted affect.[41] Recent aesthetic theory, in an effort to understand anew the complex interplay between work and recipient, has sought to privilege neither spectator nor work and has excluded neither epistemology nor affect with regard to its analytical scope. In Juliane Rebentisch's proposition, art exists solely as – and within – the dynamics of form and medium that inhere to aesthetic experience.[42] Rebentisch adds the significant qualification that "medium" no longer designates art's respective means of representation, however unlimited these may be: "What is now meant by medium is the open horizon of possible context constructions, which is given with the specific artwork itself and is, as such, infinite" (2003: 94).[43] If the first part of this definition expands the notion of medium to the potentially infinite construction of contexts the viewing of a work may occasion, this is not least to protect the spectator, relatively recently liberated by postmodernist theory, from reimprisonment by claims of modernist discourses of medium specificity. If the definition's second part nonetheless insists on the continuous significance of the artwork within the scenario of aesthetic experience, it is not to wrest meaning away from the spectator again and restore it to the work. On the contrary, Rebentisch's formulation reflects a concern about the decreasing attention to issues of spectatorship in an era marked by the aestheticization of everyday life – where everyone is a spectator all the time and, hence, where spectatorship is threatened with losing its relevance within theoretical understandings of what constitutes aesthetic experience. Autonomy, in Rebentisch's theory, thus resides neither fully in the work nor in the recipient, and yet it crystallizes from between the two as a specific idiom – a mode of reception whose vectors develop a dynamic that always makes it potentially separable from the recipient's basic stream of cognitive intake.

For Rebentisch aesthetic experience of art means that every context construction that is performed in the course of understanding the work is necessarily referred back to its own contingency (94). This referral mechanism makes the subject experience the act of taking recourse to the object and the act of constructing contexts for its understanding as interrelated, though not necessarily harmonious acts. The uneasy relation between these two acts constitutes the self-reflexive and performative character of aesthetic experience: "Specifically aesthetic is an experience in which the context constructions in relation to an object (and its markings) appear at once (and conflictually so) as evident and contingent" (95). It is interesting that the artistic objects with regard to which Rebentisch has developed her theory of aesthetic experience are installations. For it could be argued that Haneke's deployment of *mise-en-abyme* and the long take, which suspend spectators' aesthetic experience between evidence and contingency, between the impulse to judge and the inability to do so soundly, is not primarily cinematic but installational. More specifically, Haneke uses these devices to combine the time-based nature of cinema with the object-based qualities of art. This tension places the spectator into an unstable subject–object relation, in which he/she is given fewer opportunities to ease into a completely immersive, vicarious, and objectivist mode. To be sure, these modes are never fully absent from Haneke's films either, because the films follow the parameters of narrative fiction films. For them to subvert the sociology of the cinema, they must partake in it. Indeed, it seems that

Haneke's films derive their charge from their unpredictable oscillation between sponsoring immersion and demanding the kind of attention required by installed objects.[44]

The hybrid nature of Haneke's films helps us relate them to Rebentisch's concept of aesthetic experience. Their dual intellectual and affective address expands Adorno's notion of the role of the spectator. By constructing enigmatic form/ content relations and selecting scenes for mnemonic reprocessing, the films make themselves available for broader circuits of generating meaning. They develop what we may term "their work-centered bit" and contribute it to the broader dynamics that constitute aesthetic experience. This part may be described as their truly Adornian moment; but their gesture of thus "offering" themselves to the viewer is already poised to transform this work-centered logic into something else; the reception of the individual work at once potentially extends into broader processes of reception and production. While Adorno's theory remained work-centered, he nonetheless seemed to glean this potential when he stressed the processual nature of art's dialecticization, which manifested itself in prolonged processes of critical debate.

> By reading the spirit of artworks out of their configurations and confronting the elements with each other and with the spirit that appears in them, critique passes over into the truth of the spirit, which is located beyond the aesthetic configuration. This is why critique is necessary to the works. In the spirit of the works critique recognizes their truth content or distinguishes truth content from spirit. Only in this act, and not through any philosophy of art that would dictate to art what its spirit must be, do art and philosophy converge. (AT 88)

However, the only area in which this type of critique could take place, in Adorno's view, was the area of high art. Only high art was capable of resisting processes of synthesization and thus disrupting the subject's totalizing and, ultimately, self-victimizing tendencies of instrumentalization. Thus, what was behind the declaration of the artwork as autonomous was not the protection of the work but of the recipient. To this logic, Rebentisch juxtaposes a notion of the autonomy of aesthetic experience that proceeds from the profound ontological equality of artwork and recipient (2003: 37). There is no overdetermined dynamic of domination through integration; the subject performatively constructs its own relation to the object, marked by a tentative relation to the object and by an ongoing tension between returning to the object and constructing contexts that are occasioned by, yet exceed, this return. The hybrid nature of Haneke's films – their capability of sponsoring, at certain moments, the aesthetic experience of installed objects, while remaining within the basic immersive mode of the cinema – seems to aid this effect. The films' projection in the immersive environment of the cinema aids certain productions of affect and exploits film's affinity with subjective modes of experience: It is the spectator who is installed, however reflexively. This aspect competes with moments in which the condition of installation shifts from the spectator to the object, such as a long take, a tableau, or the overt experience of intervals. If one of the effects of installed objects is what Rebentisch, in the context of installations, calls an *internal* temporalization – the recipient's radically contingent relation to the object helps foreground aesthetic experience itself as overtly temporal – it would seem that Haneke's films complicate this effect. They oscillate between immersive and installed, between passive and active, and between their basic temporality (which determines cinema as a time-bound art) and the internal temporalization of the viewer. The fact that they cannot achieve with consistency the qualities of installed objects of gallery spaces should not cause debates about their insufficiency. They are not gallery objects, nor do they want to be; they are films. But their hybridity may open the workings of Rebentisch's notion of the autonomy of aesthetic experience also to the area of mass culture itself, as opposed to leaving it confined to the space of galleries.

From Judge to Witness, from Truth to Language Games: Lyotard's *Différend* and the Agonistic Nature of the Social

To recognize the hybrid tendencies in Haneke's films and to reconceptualize the paramaters for their unfolding as the territory of aisthesis means to discern the presence of another thinker besides Adorno – Jean-François Lyotard – whose own notion of aesthetics has been characterized as the "aesthetics of impact" (Wellmer 1985: 63). Lyotard does not stand diametrically opposed to Adorno. Indeed, his ideas are widely considered to be a postmodern continuation of Adorno's modernism. With regard to Haneke's cinema this continuation has already been identified in reference to the concept of the sublime. This is how Harald Meindl discusses framing devices, black leader, and reflective surfaces in *71 Fragments* (2008: 102) as well as some of the themes the film shares with *The Seventh Continent* and *Benny's Video*, such as the victimization of children and the omnipresence of suffering (104). In these films, bundled perception commingles with spectatorial dread, formal disruption and a sense of inaccessibility combine with irritating sense perception and discordant overstimulation (ibid.).

   According to Meindl, Haneke's production of the sublime makes his films behave "asocially," but out of a sense of moral responsibility. In this sense, Haneke's films can be read as an artistic mirror in which the influences of Adorno's and Lyotard's respective notions of the sublime converge. For both, the sublime is an instance of casting into language an irreconcilable conflict (Welsch 1990: 134, 144). For Adorno, this process does not lead to articulation but to an aesthetically immanent artistic expression – a silence that speaks volumes – whereas in Lyotard the impossibility of representation is articulated as such, that is, as an announcement of impossibility. Both aspects are present in *71 Fragments'* depiction of Anni's fate. Adorno's notion of the sublime may be related to the *mise-en-scène* of the bathroom shot that shows Anni sitting on the rim of the tub. Irreconcilable conflict is not verbally articulated – it remains a hidden vector, and its mode is that of the dialectic. Lyotard's version is found in one of Frau Brunner's dialog lines: "How can we explain it to her?" Explain what, one is prompted to ask, and the answer is: her decision to reject Anni. As such, the subject is not fully stated either. The sentence constitutes an allusion to that which cannot be said, a linguistic circling of the trauma.[45]

But while Lyotard's announcement of the unsayable replaces the austerity of negative dialectics with the more playfully circling motions of linguistic performativity, this notion does not altogether escape the kind of reification to which any discursive strategy (no matter whether verbalized or visualized) is potentially subject. This problem already drove the progressive-teleological nature of Adorno's dialectics, in which the open forms of modern art and the recipient's raised capabilities for retracing their ever-advancing synthesizing processes became coefficients (Wellmer 1985: 69). Thus my only caveat to Meindl's reading of the sublime in Haneke is that the sublime's effect originates solely from within the work. This reduces aesthetic experience to a stable and recognizable set of formal qualities that, once again, fall under the sway of dialecticization. Language, but also art (which is now conceived of in linguistic terms) both remain subject to this dynamic. As Jacques Rancière has pointed out in a critique of Lyotard's notion of the sublime, the threat of Hegel continues to loom large (Rancière 2007: 134). However, the question of form is not the only problem. If this "threat" that is identified by Rancière affects the domain of representation, it also affects the interdiction of representation and the dynamics of the unsayable.

Before returning to this problem, indeed, in order to return to it, I want to move to an area of Lyotardian thought that is adjacent to the sublime and that can be productively related to Haneke's cinema. It takes as its point of departure the same figure of irreconcilability that, in the case of the sublime, leads to allusion, inference, and the general deferral of meaning. At issue is *Le Différend*, which is often identified as Lyotard's major philosophical work, but which has nonetheless been somewhat eclipsed in the past two decades by a larger interest in Lyotard's more specific notion of the sublime. *Le Différend* is Lyotard's analysis of the radical, incommensurable heterogeneity of the social. The condition that, according to Lyotard, centrally determines language and the social is that of dissent. If language is structured agonistically, so Lyotard argues, then a linguistically conceived society must be, too (D 193, 194). Linguistically, dissent emerges from the fact that there is no highest principle or category of discourse. The adjudication of a conflict according to the rule of one particular category of discourse necessarily entails discarding or ignoring another discourse category which was likewise involved in the conflict. Thus, dissent is about the paradigmatic nature of injustice. As Lyotard argues in *Le Différend*, it is impossible to speak without committing injustice.

The relevance of Lyotard's theory for a reading of Haneke's cinema, particularly his more recent French films, is considerable. *Code Unknown*, *The Piano Teacher*, *Time of the Wolf*, and *Caché* all proffer different dramatizations of Lyotard's insight that the application of one's own specific rule, one's own discursive law, in the case of a conflict between radically different parties, must necessarily lead to irresolvable conflict and to injustice.[46] Politically and historically, the absence of an overarching discourse category has registered in the recent redefinition of the national in the course of the advancing Europeanization of nation-states such as France and the changing face of nationalism in the wake of the fall of the Eastern bloc. Nationalism has become redesignated and has sponsored regionally, culturally, ethnically, and religiously specific dynamics of belonging. Many of Haneke's theatrical features reflect aspects of these permutations. Beyond this general notability, however, *Code Unknown*, whose very title already alludes to the absence of an overarching order of discourse, is of particular interest with regard to Lyotard's theory. The first film Haneke made after his relocation to France, it combines many of the thematic concerns of the glaciation trilogy, such as the alienation between parents and children and the impersonal nature of urban life, with the more specific concerns of his French period, particularly the various facets and repercussions of France's history of colonialism (distrust of African immigrants, multicultural tensions, the historical trauma of colonialist wars and massacres). That *Code Unknown* treats many of its characters slightly too schematically as representatives of one or another of these political, cultural, and historical phenomena has already been pointed out in critical analyses of the film (Naqvi 2007: 237). What merits further interest here are the philosophical implications of the type of conflict that the characters are embroiled in, because they can be related to Lyotard's theory of radical social heterogeneity and agonistic dissent.

Of interest is also Haneke's approach to representing this agonistic conflict, particularly his deployment of the long take as the central component of the film's narrative structure. Unlike *71 Fragments*, which subdivides a few of its takes through cuts (which, technically speaking, makes the number 71 slightly incorrect), *Code Unknown* is composed exclusively of uninterrupted long takes. As in *71 Fragments*, these are separated by fades to black, but in *Code Unknown* they feel less ostentatious. *Code Unknown*'s greater visual fluidity thus also seems to stand in contrast to what I identified earlier as the parametric features of *71 Fragments* – its pared-down and enunciated pattern of shot ranges, angles, and other elements of *mise-èn-scene*. That *Code Unknown* does, in fact, correspond to a second subcategory of parametric cinema, the "replete" variant, which Bordwell juxtaposes to the "ascetic" or "sparse" form, becomes clear if one considers the long take as a strongly articulated stylistic event that makes subsequent deviating procedures recognizable (1985: 285). It is an inventory which "brings many disparate stylistic procedures to bear on the problem of representing character encounters." Bordwell goes on to say:

> Typically, the ascetic option presents a material similarity of procedures across differentiated *syuzhet* passages; the replete option creates parallels among distinct portions of the *syuzhet* and varies the material procedures used to present them. (Ibid.)

While the long take, as I shall argue below, has a seemingly natural propensity for representing conflict as socio-linguistically incommensurable, its specifically parametric deployment in *Code Unknown* also helps identify via comparison the agonistic nature of various social layers and diverse types of interaction in the film's diegetic world. Many of the long take's functions are dazzlingly epitomized by the film's first (and by now famous) long take, which introduces most of the film's key protagonists in a tracking shot through the streets of Paris. The take begins when Anne, an actress, leaves her Paris apartment and is intercepted on the street by Jean, the teenage brother of her lover, Georges. Jean has run away from home and would like to stay with Anne and Georges. Their conversation, which revolves around the conflict between the boy's yearning for freedom and his need to take responsibility, ends with Anne agreeing that Jean can briefly stay at her place, and with the camera now following Jean back towards Anne's apartment. On his way, Jean rudely discards a crumpled pastry bag into the lap of Maria, a Romanian beggar, who sits on the sidewalk by the bakery where Anne had previously bought the pastry. Jean's thoughtless behavior is observed by Amadou, a young man from Mali, who stops Jean and demands he apologize to Maria. An intense physical fight ensues between them, which brings Anne right back into the picture, along with several concerned passers-by and an annoyed store manager. Jean refuses to acknowledge Amadou's charge, and there is a general confusion as to why the fight began and who started it. The two police officers who arrive on the scene claim they are willing to hear the conflicting parties in order to determine what happened. But this seeming impartiality is soon revealed to be a chimera. At issue is the question of identity. Maria is arrested for not having a passport. Jean, it is implied, is commanded to the precinct as well, but his passport is returned to him on the scene. In contrast to Jean, Amadou does not get his passport back, which is surprising, given that he is much more willing than Jean to explain to Anne and to the officers what transpired. This shows that Amadou's status is much more fragile than Jean's. He entered the scene as Maria's defendant, but is soon forced to defend himself and, like Maria, ends up *sans papiers*. It matters little that his own sense of justice (after all, it was he who initiated the conflict with Jean) compels him to help solve the conflict. He is willing to cooperate when asked to come to the precinct – under the condition he is not being forced. However, the officers have little patience for this stipulation, which leads to the fact that Amadou is manhandled into custody.

What, then, is specifically agonistic about the way the film depicts this conflict? As becomes clear from Lyotard's argument, agonism is not about consensus building, but may be regarded as a form of perpetual dissent. The film's depiction of Jean's and Amadou's violent clash on the street implies that there is little prospect for resolution through dialog: Jean's defensiveness and arrogance cause him to reject Amadou as a party to the conflict. And while Amadou, on a superficial level, seems more interested in initiating dialog, the fact that he categorically and vehemently insists that Jean first of all apologize to Maria hardly wins Jean's understanding. Because it puts Jean on the defensive with such force, it has little potential for kindling dialog. We may be tempted to perceive the conflicting parties' resistance to engaging in dialog as counterproductive, perhaps even dysfunctional. But such a reading ignores the agonistic character of the confrontation, which, according to Lyotard, is a socio-linguistically viable form of conflict. To be sure, Amadou's outrage against Jean seems dramaturgically contrived.[47] But notwithstanding its staged nature, the scene arguably proffers a more accurate depiction of how tensions unfold in contemporary multicultural societies (where inequalities relating to race, class, gender, and citizenship are imbricated in each other) than do liberal rhetorics about the constructiveness of social dialog. According to the logic of Lyotard's argument, these rhetorics are deleterious because their teleological and idealist notions of consensus building are blind to many of the concrete problems that make the obtainment of social equality all but impossible (see Stoehr, this volume).

But the particular way in which conflict is visualized in this scene can be read even more closely in Lyotardian terms. Central significance falls to the role of the camera, whose rehearsal of the logic of agonism is threefold. First, one can say that the function of the camera in this scene is performative in that it foregrounds its own labor and admits to the delimiting effect of its purview. It makes a very palpable effort of tracking the characters as they move about, such that its restless panning movements suggest the impossibility of treating its subjects with equality. It must make choices, and these choices automatically produce injustice – to honor one character means to neglect another. But even to pay attention to a particular character does not automatically guarantee his/her "just" treatment. Shades of this dilemma are alluded to when characters exit the frame because they part company or when the camera passes over them in its pursuit of other characters, but also when characters return into the frame unexpectedly, or when they are pulled back into it against their will, as when they are forcefully retrieved by other characters. It is this automatic incurring of injustice that reflects the condition of agonism. The camera further reflects this condition by depicting the unfolding confrontation between Jean and Amadou without resorting to editing as a repositioning device. The absence of shot/countershot patterns, which honor point of view and underscore the notion of dialog, indicates Haneke's intention to eschew the corresponding mandate of a "balanced" presentation of conflict. Instead, the camera implicitly but consistently conveys skepticism that conflict can be adjudicated and justice obtained.

While the absence of point-of-view editing installs the spectator at a distance to the unfolding confrontation, this distance is not a safe distance. The spectator is inscribed into the conflict as a third party, which further constitutes the agonistic constellation as Lyotard defines it (D 34). In this constellation the spectator is a judge, but the judge is "humbled" into a witness position that compels him/her to defer the act of passing judgment and, instead, favor the ethically less compromising act of producing further testimony. This perpetual deferral of justice is not meant to avoid justice altogether but to contain as much as possible the production of injustice. Indeed, to the extent that one may imagine Haneke's implied spectator as a white European spectator, the camera makes this spectator aware of the fact that he/she is part of the power differential portrayed in the scene – he/she is party to the very system of laws that both regulate and exclude Maria's and Amadou's positions. As we watch the conflict unfold, we soon realize that Maria and Amadou have little bearing on the adjudication of the conflict, because their positions are incommensurable with the criteria applied to judge them, which are more closely aligned with Jean's position and, thus, with that of the white European spectator of Haneke's film. The police's bias against Maria and Amadou and the fact that Amadou is not accepted as a prosecuting party but is instantly put on the defensive brings this dynamic fully to the fore. This constitutes what Lyotard defines as a *différend*: "A case of *différend* between two parties takes place when the 'regulation' of the conflict that opposes them is done in the idiom of one of the parties while the wrong suffered by the other is not signified in that idiom" (D 12). In Maria's case, the *différend* is constituted even more directly by the camera itself, which aligns itself with the police officer in bringing her back into the frame. Maria's visualization as a subject is synonymous with her production as a subject before the law. This logic seems inexorable – all that can be done is to testify to its existence, something Haneke hopes to achieve by imbuing the camera with a certain performative zeal that enables our recognition of the dilemma and, at best, its critical reflection.

The camera in *Code Unknown*, which is entirely composed of long takes, translates into movement the agonism of the social that Lyotard conceives of in linguistic terms. For Lyotard, the social is the universe which is formed by all the instances of a phrase. That phrase can be cast in several modes of presentation (such as a cognitive, a question, or a prescription) and further specified in genres of discourse that reflect certain stakes (the intent to convince, to persuade, to affect, and so on).[48] It is already on this basic level, before the emergence of more specific conflagrations, that conflict exists – that is, in the form of the radical heterogeneity of speaking positions. Haneke represents this phenomenon on different levels. Examples are not specific to *Code Unknown* but can already be found in *71 Fragments*. At times, the characters are not even fully conscious of the friction between them. There is, for example, Tomek's phone conversation with his daughter, which Haneke depicts as both a gesture of reaching out and a game of manipulation and evasion. The fact that the scene features only Tomek's side of the conversation constitutes a simple but effective way of illustrating how even seemingly casual conversations adhere to a basic linguistic structuring of conflict. The scene foregrounds how individual phrases reflect certain incommensurable linguistic stakes that determine the dynamic of anticipating, uttering, and linking statements.[49] Conflict thus does not originate in the incidental clash of individual psyches; instead, individual psyches, like conflict, are determined by the basic linguistic structure of the social. This structure also determines the phenomenon of direct or indirect social competition. In *71 Fragments* Anni and Marian's indirect competition for foster parents provides an example. The granting of one person's social viability, particularly through the media, automatically means the neglect and discarding of another's.

However, it is *Code Unknown* that systematically represents the social as agonistic in nature. The film repeatedly demonstrates that inhabiting one and the same space and partaking in one and the same action has very different implications and consequences for its various characters. Exemplary is the scene featuring Maria's deportation from France back to Romania. The camera shows the entrance of an airplane that is being boarded by passengers belonging to diverse professional and socio-economic groups. The last person to board the plane is Maria but she is not on the plane of her own free will. Her presence on the plane is the result of the very absence of certain privileges that enable the presence of her co-passengers, namely, the political right to cross state boundaries and the professional and socio-economic ability to make use of this right. Maria is escorted to the door by two police officers who deliver her into the discreet custody of a flight attendant, so that the other passengers remain unalerted to Maria's "special" status. The implication of this maneuver is that discipline, particularly if performed by or on behalf of the state, produces its own, inadvertent, kind of honesty. It gives the lie to the state's liberal agenda of acknowledging difference for the purpose of furthering tolerance and consensus.

Code Unknown links its depiction of space to the motif of the journey, but space is not represented in the picaresque tradition or as something that is dynamically negotiated by the characters. To the extent that their criss-crossing trajectories exemplify their radical socio-linguistic heterogeneity, space still signfies the inexorability of conflict. There is still a quality of inescapability that adheres to the film's concept of space, even if, in contrast to *71 Fragments*, its entrapping features are qualified by a number of factors. Most importantly, in *Code Unknown* conflict is not constituted by alienation but by alienness. The clearest example is the scene on a Paris metro train in which Anne is baited and spat upon by a young Arab man who is full of contempt for her racial and class privilege and her citizen status. At the same time, his tirade also reflects his unexamined sense of male entitlement and his deeply patriarchal attitude. The purpose of their conflict is to dramatize, not to overcome, the incommensurability of their positions as social subjects, each of which has its own history and specificity.

If there is no highest category of discourse, reality is not objective but is subject to debate. But since the radical heterogeneity of the social curtails the prospect of consensus, reality is constantly deferred. It exists in a state of future definition (D 3, 5, 22, 23, 195). This conclusion brought Lyotard some notoriety. It came to epitomize what critics of postmodern thought regarded as postmodernism's deleterious tendency to relativize reality by reducing it to the inconsequential pluralism

of language games and the random aestheticism and anarchism of ludic performance. Engaging these critiques would exceed the parameters of this essay.[50] Suffice
it to say that such critiques often reflected a deeper resentment towards the general rise to prominence of theatricality and performance in post-1960s culture –
which included the elevation of performativity to a critical-analytical paradigm by
which to analyze such areas as politics, science, and economics, whose seeming
gravitas had made them appear to exist in a higher realm than the ludic and which
had thus been deemed in need of being "protected" from its "diluting" influence.

    The misguided, fallacious nature of such claims is demonstrated by a film such
as *Code Unknown*, which does not dismiss the notion of truth, but foregrounds its
centrality to Western culture and society. Reflecting Lyotard's axiom that truth
awaits verification, many of the conflicts in the film involve characters debating
suspicions, adjudicating truth claims, and verifying evidence. Some of the conflicts
involve debates on the ethical implications of the search for evidence, such as the
argument between Georges and one of his friends that revolves around Georges's
work as a photographer. The film relativizes the ethical status of documentary
photography in two ways: It contrasts liberal-democratic rhetorics of truth-telling
with the commodified status of war photography (but also art photography), and
it situates Georges's candid camera portraits of subway passengers in an ethical
gray zone between voyeuristic lure, which entails disrespect for the consent of
the subject, and the candid photograph's prospect of epistemological authenticity. We may frown on Georges's unblinkingly ambitious pursuit of access to his
subjects. However, when we watch the subway assault by the young Arab man
on Anne – a scene that has repeatedly been hailed for the originality of its visuals and the authenticity of its approach to *mise-en-scène* – we watch it exactly
from the coordinates formerly assumed by Georges's camera. Making Georges's
camera position the enabling condition of our witnessing of social conflict, the
film supplements its critique of the reification of photographic evidence by
acknowledging the link between photographic records and the political (and, by
implication, historical) significance of witnessing.

Conclusion

In his essay in this volume, Tom Conley points out that the function of the long
take at the beginning of *Code Unknown* is to display conflict as a kind of noise.
The film cues us to this association by virtue of a verbal pun that is readable on
the window of a Viennese pastry shop in front of which the conflict unfolds. "*Vienne
... noiserie*: 'let there be noise' or a staging of violence, if indeed *noise* is understood as din and shuffle that mediate discord and conflict of one kind or another"
(Conley, this volume). As my relatively brief analysis of *Code Unknown* has meant
to suggest, the film, far from claiming the possibility of justice, nonetheless insists

on the necessity to bring testimony and on the imperative to hear it. Keeping conflict alive is culturally, philosophically, and politically more viable than reducing it to the task of bringing about a solution through consensus. While *71 Fragments* already contains moments that reflect Haneke's interest in showing the agonistic nature of the social and in relativizing what we commonly call reality, the film is still underscored by the concept of truth, even if this truth is now an increasingly empty horizon. In contrast to *Code Unknown*, the film still emphasizes the necessity of judgment, even if its implied notion of the overarching concept of justice is guided by Adorno's view that justice is only possible if it is pursued via negative dialectics. Both films show similarities in those areas in which Adorno's and Lyotard's theoretical interests converge, namely, in their mutual emphasis of the incommensurable, the uncommunicable, and the inhuman (Welsch 1990: 144). This area of convergence also includes adjacent definitions of art, even if each philosopher accords art a different function. For Adorno, art was the only medium in which irreconcilable conflict could be articulated – by virtue of art's capacity to pay justice to the heterogeneous. For Lyotard, art's function must shift from the obtainment of justice to the articulation of testimony.[51] Art can give expression to the *différend* by virtue of its ability to go in search of new ways of articulating conflict, even if these articulations must necessarily be tentative in nature.

At certain times, however, Haneke's attempt to illustrate the absence of an overarching discourse category in the universe he portrays does not lead to relativism. Instead, it seems to produce the opposite effect. At issue is the quasi-tautological production of otherness that reinforces its given depiction and risks lifting it to the status of overarching truth. This is particularly the case in recent examples of Haneke's oeuvre that seek to demonstrate in implicit manner a character's oppressed status in relation to the larger world of the film. Implicit here means that the audience, rather than gaining privileged access to the character's situation via explicating discourses, encounters him or her through the same signifying economy that channels – or even produces – the oppression he or she experiences. This approach works well for characters such as the student Max in *71 Fragments*, because he is part of the hegemonic body politic. It becomes more problematic with characters such as Maria or the older Arab man on the subway in *Code Unknown* who tries to protect Anne from the younger Arab man. The status these characters assume in relation to the white, Western European norm does not simply produce an elucidating image of subalternity; it always already reproduces the latter as an effect that is, as it were, consolidated in its tautological portrayal. The crux is that some of these characters appear to be created simply for the purpose of showcasing their oppressed status, which does not altogether abrogate the presence of Lyotard's concept of the *différend*, but diminishes it in relation to the larger economy of phrases. But we need to be careful not to generalize here. In certain instances, as with the retrieval of Maria into the frame by the police officer, careful attention to style can counter the effect of tautology. Maria's retrieval into the frame by the officer and on behalf of the camera is in and of itself foregrounded as a yanking movement whose performative nature sponsors spectatorial affect in addition to reflection. In the case of the older Arab man on the subway, the situation is already more complicated. He is summoned into existence only briefly, and for the specific purpose of endowing the discourse of the subaltern with unpredictable nuance (although one wonders on whose behalf), before being "recalled" from existence again.[52]

This dilemma is thrown starkly into relief in *Caché*, in which an Arab man, Majid (played by Maurice Bénichou, the same actor who plays the Arab man seeking to protect Anne in *Code Unknown*), commits suicide by slashing his throat. The depiction of this act, one assumes, is to make us remember France's colonialist oppression and particularly its imperialist war against Algeria. More specifically, it functions as a hyperbolic mnemonic trace to the October 17, 1961, massacre of Algerians by the Parisian police under the command of the former Vichy official, Maurice Papon. The full implications of this mnemonic trace cannot be discussed in the parameters of this essay. However, what merits brief mention in the context of the present discussion is that, as Paul Gilroy has argued (2007: 234), the figure of Majid is reduced to the task of signifying a figure of unspeakable trauma. As *Caché* closely defines Majid's existence in relation to the guilt-ridden, semi-acknowledged memories of his childhood friend, Georges, otherness is called into existence only to be imperiously recalled from it again, and this happens largely for the purpose of uncovering and indicting the Western logic within which the other has been conceived. The film takes Majid's otherness beyond his status as an individual – it points to a whole people, who are imagined primarily in terms of their extermination. A similarly over-determined logic has recently been identified by Jacques Rancière with regard to Lyotard's theory of the sublime. According to Rancière, the sublime's capacity to allude to the unrepresentable facilitates art's engagement with otherness in the same way that Jews' remembering of what is banished from memory constitutes a mnemonic engagement with otherness. For Rancière, this reveals a hidden dialectic in Lyotard's putatively non-dialectical approach.

> Lyotard radicalizes Adorno's dialectic of reason by rooting it in the laws of the unconscious and transforming the "impossibility" of art after Auschwitz into an art of the unrepresentable. But this perfecting is ultimately a perfecting of the dialectic. What is assigning a people the task of representing a moment of thought, and identifying the extermination of this people with a law of the psychic apparatus, if not a hyperbolic version of the Hegelian operation that makes the moments of the development of spirit – and forms of art – correspond to the concrete historical figures of a people or a civilization? (2007: 134)

This critique can be applied to Haneke's cinema, but, once again, it is important not to generalize. As Fatima Naqvi has shown (2009), Haneke's literary adaptations *Three Paths to the Lake* and *The Rebellion* demonstrate a complex and nuanced approach to the textual figuration of historical trauma constituted by the loss of war and empire by the Nazi period and the Holocaust. As in the more recent films, these epiphenomena are explored via ellipses, structuring absences, and other strategies of textual displacement that are the building blocks of dialectics. But while in the literary adaptations the use of dialectic is more overt and pervasive than in the recent films, it does not deploy a metonymic chain between trauma, extermination, and a particular ethnic, racial, or religious group. *Caché*, by contrast, evinces a particular combination of the logic of the sublime (the art of the unrepresentable), as it has been identified in numerous instances of Haneke's cinema, with the logic that conceives of otherness first and foremost in terms of extermination. The latter is traced via the figure of Papon both to the deportation of the Jews to Auschwitz and to the slaughter of the Algerians in Paris, and it is within this associative logic that Majid's suicide seems embedded. However, the debate about *Caché* has barely begun, and this essay can only briefly name some of the pressing questions that emerge. Does Haneke's recent approach to the legacy of colonialism contain a conceptual correlative to the undoubtedly productive ways in which such earlier films as *Three Paths to the Lake* and *The Rebellion* figure historical trauma? Are there ways in which the other in *Code Unknown* and *Caché* is able to gain a momentum that helps it elude the over-determined associative logic by which it is conceived? Might such ways exist undiscovered within the logic itself or are further propositions contingent on contrasting Lyotard's notion of otherness with that of other theorists, such as, say, Lévinas?

My reading of *71 Fragments* in relation to Adorno's distinct if relatable notions of aesthetics and of film has sought to position Haneke as an interlocutor to Adorno. I have argued that Haneke's cinema sponsors a form of aesthetic experience that is both autonomous and performative. This redefined aesthetic experience may be regarded as a supplement to Adorno's delimiting notion of film, not least because it also recasts the function and status of the dialectic while not altogether renouncing it. Certain factors that define the viewer/recipient's performative relation to the art object (such as affect, aisthesis, and the potentially infinite possibilities of context construction) thus help us reposition and, indeed, reimagine film both as a medium and an art form in relation to the notions of art, aesthetics, and representation, as we find them developed in *Aesthetic Theory*. It is hoped that this new notion of aesthetic experience potentially enables new readings of Adorno and establishes new areas of cross-fertilization between his two interests. But as my brief discussion of the representation of the marginalized and the subaltern in Haneke's cinema suggests, to enact a similar move with regard to Haneke's relation to Lyotard is possible only up to a point, which is to note certain similarities between Haneke's representation of multiculturalism and Lyotard's notion of the radically heterogeneous, fragmented nature of the social. Beyond this point, I feel compelled to defer exploring how Haneke's films might be read as productive supplements to Lyotard's theorems. It appears that Haneke's representation of radical heterogeneity in scenarios of multiculturalism evinces its own discursive lacunae and limitations, some of which seem comparable to certain limitations identifiable in Lyotard's associative logic of otherness and the unrepresentability of historical trauma. The debate on the strategies of representation and its discursive limits continues, and Haneke's films will, for a while, continue to assume a prominent part in it.

Acknowledgments

I would like to thank Noll Brinckmann, Fatima Naqvi, and Gregory Williams for their useful and generous comments on this essay.

Notes

1   Among American productions, the most prominent are *Grand Canyon* (Lawrence Kasdan, 1991), *Short Cuts* (Robert Altman, 1993), *Pulp Fiction* (Quentin Tarantino, 1994) and, more recently, *Traffic* (Steven Soderbergh, 2000) and *Crash* (Robert Haggis, 2004). Certain non-US directors likewise seem to have developed a penchant for this model, as is most notably the case with Alejandro Gonzáles Iñárritu and his films *Amores Perros* (2000), *21 Grams* (2003), and *Babel* (2006), which have, in turn, garnered Hollywood's interest and financial investment. Other international filmmakers, such as Pedro Almodóvar, have always displayed a certain tendency for writing films with larger casts. Yet, Almodóvar's model more specifically derives from the TV soap opera, where narrative and character constellation emerge from and are contingent on seriality rather than such intradiegetic factors as event or topography. In American cinema, too, multicharacter constellation films and multistrain narrative models are not always identical. There have always been films with large casts that participate in one and the same narrative (the epic model) or center around a particular event, as in Hollywood's biblical epics, large-scale war movies, or other "cast of thousands" spectacles, often about disasters or competitions (e.g., the road race). These films weave their large casts into a plot unified by action and hierarchized by star parts, to which the term "multistrain narrative" does not fully apply. Multi-generational family dramas and gangster epics such as *The Godfather* (Francis Ford Coppola, 1972) also present a special case. See Tröhler's study for a detailed construction of such concepts as open versus closed collective, ensemble, cross-section, mosaic, and web structures. Haneke's only other films that might be related to multistrain narrative models and multicharacter films are *Lemmings* (1979) and *Time of the Wolf* (2003). But the former's expansive cast and narrative structure are modeled on the television miniseries, while *Time of the Wolf* retains a steady focus on one protagonist, the mother, and on her children, who remain the spine of the film through which the numerous other characters are encountered.

2   See particularly Harald Meindl's essay on the function of the sublime in Haneke's work. To my knowledge, Meindl was the first to relate Haneke's work to Adorno and Lyotard. I am indebted to his pioneering thinking, which has inspired me to understand the

relation between Haneke and these two philosophers in a different way. Meindl's essay performs a Lyotardian reading of *71 Fragments* and *The Seventh Continent* (1989). While Lyotard is at the center of Meindl's essay, he focuses on Lyotard's theory of the sublime, not on *The Différend* and its theorization of fragmentation, agonistic conflict, and injustice. The essay's succinct comparison to Adorno's concept of the sublime is suggestive, but while Adorno's treatment of the sublime constitutes a distillation of many key insights of *Aesthetic Theory*, it serves Meindl to extend Adorno's concept of modern art to film in a rather linear and, thus, problematic manner. Meindl is not the only scholar interested in the relation between Haneke and philosophy. For a further discussion of Haneke's work in relation to Adorno, see Jean Ma's essay reprinted in this volume. Ma's interest in the affinities between Adorno and Haneke focuses on the use of music in *The Piano Teacher* (2001). The film's depiction of the cognitive dissonance of erotic passion through music, which Ma identifies as the film's "principal mechanism of enunciation," invites a comparison to Adorno's theory of music with its claim that music effectively demonstrate's art's capacity to identify and articulate social antinomies without giving in to alienated culture. While for Ma Adorno's concept of art thus yields an affective dimension, my own discussion of affect sees Haneke's films superseding the limitations of Adorno's theory of visual representation and affect. For a critical historicization of Lyotard's concept of the demise of master narratives and for a reading of Haneke's films as a response to what the author considers the ascent of a new master narrative, the melodramatic view of the world, see Jörg Metelmann's essay in this volume.

3   The more successful comparisons between Adorno and Lyotard have been conducted by scholars interested in the deep interpenetration of modernist and postmodernist thought and culture (rather than remaining invested in the concept of the radical break). For two highly useful arguments about the dialectical nature of this interpenetration, see Albrecht Wellmer (1985) and Wolfgang Welsch (1990, 2002). My discussion of the relationship between Adorno and Lyotard and my general remarks on the phenomenon of fragmentation across modernism and postmodernism are indebted to these commentators.

4   This is not least the case because, during the first half of the twentieth century, the experience of loss articulated itself around the destructive impact of cataclysmic events, such as the two world wars, the decline or demise of older political structures (such as colonial empires and monarchies), and, of course, the catastrophe of the Holocaust, which, as a political and humanitarian apocalypse, also triggered a lasting spiritual crisis. But even such arguably "constructive" phenomena as the growth of cities, the rise of mass culture, and advances in technology were registered with profound ambivalence, as they were perceived to cause the fragmentation of experience that leads to a disorientation of the subject. For a summary on negativity and modernism's lost center, see Welsch 2002: 172. While the articulation of loss may be said to constitute the inaugural phase of high modernist art just prior to World War I (literature and film were soon to follow), critical discourses initially remained skeptical of these tendencies. I am grateful to Gregory Williams for pointing out to me an early example of art history's initially negative response to the loss of the center, Hans Sedlmayr's *Verlust der Mitte* (1948), published in English as *Art in Crisis: The Lost Center*. By contrast, more recent literary and psychoanalytic discourses have found a rich source in

Walter Benjamin's and Sigmund Freud's respective bodies of work (both of which are sprawling and decentered) to understand and, ultimately, reevaluate the relationship between loss and negativity. For a discussion of Benjaminian literary discourses and psychoanalysis in relation to Haneke's cinema, see Fatima Naqvi's essay on *Three Paths to the Lake* (1976) in this volume and her comparison of this film to Haneke's *The Rebellion* (1992) (Naqvi 2009). Naqvi's work is partially inspired by Alessia Ricciardi's rereading of modern art as an aesthetic of bereavement (Ricciardi 2003). For a landmark study of Benjamin's theory of modernity, see Buck-Morss (1991).

5   Postmodern tendencies of segmentation and plurality are less easily identifiable through specific historical events. Key phenomena are certainly the rise of postcolonialism and of feminism. Another axis of identification is the rise of new communication technologies. Many of the changes that register postmodern tendencies can be seen to emerge during the decade of the 1960s, which saw a markedly increased interest by the West in forms of racial and sexual alterity. Likewise important during that decade were the rise of youth culture and its discursive revisioning of the category of experience, the breakdown of private and public spheres, and the rise of postmodern art and postmodernist philosophy in general, which enacted a characteristic breakdown of subject and object, theory and practice, and art and philosophy, not least through an interest in making art and theory more performative.

6   All passages from *Aesthetic Theory* will henceforth be referred to as "AT."

7   Welsch points to the tension in Adorno's argument between his impulse to hold on to art's traditional task of reconciliation (which it used to perform by exploring the category of beauty) and what forms the fulcrum of his teleological modernism, his demand that art resist this traditional function, so as not allow society to instrumentalize it (1990: 131).

8   For Adorno, the striving for coherence is art's unavoidable task but also its downfall, as it constitutes a usurpation of art's aporetic tendencies. As Wellmer has summarized it, synthesis – the essence of Hegelian spirit – becomes a system-forming and objectifying behemoth; in its all-encompassing tendencies, instrumental reason comes to dominate rather than liberate the subject (Wellmer 1985: 10). Against this process Adorno posits his concept of negative dialectics, a principle to which the artwork itself is held, so as to help it keep at bay the impulse for totalization that is embodied in any modern system of technocracy and bureaucracy, and that, in the artwork, assumes the character of false aesthetic and structural coherence (epitomized by Wagner's *Gesamtkunstwerk* and its mass culture variants, such as Hollywood).

9   Utopian because art must proceed within the paradox of negating its own tendencies for synthesization. This paradox constitutes the idealism of Adorno's progressive-teleological model of aesthetics. Welsch has noted that the gradual evolution of Adorno's ideas affords a certain internal, implicit shift in Adorno's attitude towards reconciliation. It increasingly becomes an abstract horizon in Adorno's theory, emptied of any concrete possibilities for enactment. However, as Welsch appositely characterizes it, Adorno keeps reconciliation alive as a motif precisely by giving it up as a way of reasoning (i.e., as a logic) (1989: 136).

10   In-text citations from *The Différend* will henceforth refer to it as "D." Characteristic of postmodernist theory, Lyotard's text collapses the distinction between the subject and the mode of its enunciation by overtly dividing its argument into fragments that are

numbered. My in-text citations of the book will thus not reference the page numbers of the English-language translation, but indicate the individual paragraphs. For Lyotard, the radical heterogeneity of language is constituted by the incommensurability of phrase regimes (for example, a question, a prescriptive, a cognitive) and the even greater incommensurability of the genres of discourse in which these present themselves (the mode of the tragic, of the technical, of the didactic, and so on). The articulation of phrases and statements is highly paradigmatic: The utterance of one, at that moment, means the non-utterance of all the others. This makes the articulation of phrases – in anticipation of how they will be received, responded to, and integrated by others – over-determined by larger stakes. Language is inherently prone to conflictual instru-mentalization. It has existential magnitude (D 184). And because it is language that constitutes the social, the social is inherently agonistic – essentially, it cannot agree on reality; in Lyotard's radical linguistics, reality is always deferred (D 188, 193, 194).

11   The key phenomenon that motivates Lyotard's inquiry into the linguistic impossi-bility of justice emerged in tribunals about Nazi atrocities. Within the strictly posi-tivist and empiricist domain of law, survivors' testimonials about the existence of gas chambers were placed within a binary logic that turned into a juridical conundrum: Given the sweeping and perfidiously perfectionist nature of the techniques of mass extermination, survival was technically impossible. Verification of the existence of gas chambers thus seemed to implicitly clash with the very survivor status of the few who did survive the camps. This reasoning has since become the fulcrum of the rhetoric of Holocaust denials. For a critically performative invocation of this conundrum that leads Lyotard to pose the issue of incommensurability, see paragraphs 1 through 16.

12   Meindl ascribes to Haneke's use of fades to black (in both *The Seventh Continent* and *71 Fragments*) a dramaturgical and reflexive capacity. They place spectators into an "excentric" position to the diegesis and they "recalibrate" the spectatorial gaze (2008: 89). Echoing Georg Seeßlen's observations about Haneke's use of close-ups, he argues: "A look, which is forced into observing detail and from which are withheld visual totalities (which would, in any case, be fictitious), observes more, because rather than scanning in cursory manner what there is to see in order to rush onward, it can (or must) take its time" (85). Since Meindl's essay has not been translated, I have offered my own translation.

13   *Falling Down* (Joel Schumacher, 1993) provides a good contrastive example to Haneke's film.

14   As Bordwell puts it: "Not much acumen is needed to identify *Play Time* as treating the impersonality of modern life, *Tokyo Story* as examining the decline of the 'inher-ently' Japanese family, or *Vivre sa vie* as dealing with contemporary urban alienation and female desire" (1985: 282).

15   Haneke's films might be usefully contrasted here to the work of Peter Kubelka, whose flicker film *A.R.N.U.L.F. R.A.I.N.E.R.* (1960) comes as close to serial music as is possible. But even if compared to Kubelka's more mimetically oriented *Unsere Afrikareise* (1966), Haneke's cinema betrays its provenance in the more conventional terrain of art cinema with its investment in realism and symbolism.

16   In German, a subtle but important distinction is possible between "the beauty of nature" (*Die Schönheit der Natur*) and "the naturally beautiful" (*das Naturschöne*). While in the former, which is used by the English-language edition of *Aesthetic Theory*, beauty and

nature are understood as two autonomous objects linked in a possessive relation, in the latter, *Natur* is not exclusively designated an autonomous noun but also works as a dependent qualifier for *Das Schöne*. This translation underscores the attributive quality of "naturalness" by recasting it more openly as a modality that in English can be expressed via the adverb "naturally."

17 As no English translation of Wellmer's important text exists, I have offered my own translation.

18 By contrast, for Adorno, the snippets of reality pasted into dada collages were, in and of themselves, non-representational. The way they come to function within the work's inner logic does not testify to art's creative-organizational prowess, but to its very inadequacy when faced with the task of shaping reality. An admission of defeat cast into aesthetic form, dadaist montage helps art break the pretense of having reconciled itself with the heterogeneously empirical, "admitting into itself literal, illusionless ruins of empirical reality" (AT 155). This statement might be puzzling if one does not pay enough attention to the word "ruin," which adds to literal (empirical) reality an instance of constructedness, however negatively or devolutionarily conceived. If, according to Adorno, what is of interest to art about the real is its transformability into an aesthetic value, then the ruin is such a value. It was this quality that gave Adorno grounds to consider dadaist montage an instance of "the inner-aesthetic capitulation of art to what stands heterogeneously opposed to it" and to formulate his notorious paradox that "the negation of synthesis becomes a principle of form" (ibid.).

19 In the case of *71 Fragments*, it is in the narrative emphasis on modality ("how and why did it happen?") as opposed to outcome ("what will happen?") that this melancholic yearning registers. The film's aesthetic of fragmentation must be connected to the absence of an overarching explanatory principle that might explain the wider contexts, broader circumstances, and deeper reasons for the social syndromes that surface in the film's depiction of symptomatology.

20 Critics and scholars have attributed to Haneke's cinema various forms and degrees of reflexivity that challenge spectators, and, interestingly, these often seem to carry moral and ethical inflections. To begin with, there is Haneke's systematic cultural critique of commodified Western society, which browbeats and moralizes against the spectator, but which, as Horwath noted, also evinces a stubbornness, an integrity signaled by the refusal to eschew personal responsibility for one's actions and one's films. Then there is the ascetic structure of his films, which have frequently been compared to Robert Bresson's work – the will to utter self-discipline and concision, which reflects a desire to participate in truth (Horwath 1991; Leisch-Kiesl 2008). Meindl compares Haneke to several paradigms of ethically inflected reflexivity, ranging from the emancipatory role Brecht ascribed to art to a kind of moral-specular interpellation of the recipient by the work, as posited by both Rilke and Lévinas (2008: 93). Meindl also sees Haneke share an ethical component with Adorno, which is constituted by the artwork's asymmetrical positioning to reality and which leads one to impute a certain asocial character to Haneke's films that help them resist appropriation by society (92). Jörg Metelmann's study (2003) gives ample consideration to early twentieth-century political modernism (particularly Brecht) and to questions of alterity and alienness, which leads back to Lévinas. Mattias Frey has analyzed Haneke's work in relation to Jean Baudrillard's critique of capitalism and mediatization (2002) and, more

recently, to David Rodowick's theory of the desubstantiated image (2006). Stephen Shaviro has read Haneke's *Caché* (2005) as a tour-de-force *mise-en-abyme* of guilt and self-acquittal ("The Pinocchio Theory"). Most recently, Catherine Wheatley has traced a systematic ethical reflexivity in Haneke's films, which she analyzes against the background of the tradition of political modernist counter-cinema and Stanley Cavell's theory that the cinema gives respite from our complicity in the structuring of our world (2009: 40). Perhaps because of the proliferation and the stridency of this tenor of ethical readings of Haneke, there have recently also been ethical critiques of his work, mostly regarding representation of first world anxiety about non-white ethnicities. See particularly Gilroy (2007) and Galt (2010) as well as Lykidis in this volume.

21   According to Haneke's own comments, his move from making television films to making theatrical features has constituted a change with regard to his means of artistic expression, whereby the aesthetic-philosophical distillation of style is viewed as a leap in artistic "value" – evinced through the work's simultaneous gain in clarity and simplicity – in comparison to a more sociologically and pedagogically motivated use of television as a medium. See Stefan Grisseman and Michael Omasta's interview with Haneke, "Herr Haneke, wo bleibt das Positive?" (1991).

22   Indeed, the continuously upheld prospect of a dialectical synthesization of artistic elements may be what ordinarily keeps the spectator from realizing that a result-oriented hermeneutics also entails a potential disavowal of one's own subjectivity, because the spectator becomes logic personified. This disavowal goes hand in hand with the spectator's delusional assumption of the kind of phronetic power that, according to Haneke, the cinematic image should question rather than reconfirm.

23   Miriam Hansen has summarized Adorno's reasoning: "the logic of mechanical reproduction – inextricably bound up with economic dependency and ideological complicity – so completely controls all processes of film production that any concept of artistic technique appears to be subsumed by it" (1981/82: 187).

24   Published in 1966, the essay acknowledges its inspiration by the emergence of an alternative film practice in Germany in the wake of the collapse of the country's established film industry. It is against the background of the rise of the Young German Film, which not only sought to develop a new aesthetic but also proposed a radical renegotiation of production and distribution practices, that one must see Adorno's revisiting of the equation of technique and technology. Rather than merely reembracing the totalizing implications of this equation, Adorno, in Hansen's words, "recasts it as problematic" (189).

25   Adorno's resistance to proffering a systematic and more detailed engagement with film aesthetics may, at least in part, have been prompted by the actually existing artistic and aesthetic heterogeneity within the Young German Film movement, itself only a small part of a contemporaneous global groundswell of efforts to radically renew the cinema. Different cinemas placed different emphases, but most shared an interest in the appropriation of mainstream conventions and cultivated notions of playfulness, spontaneity, and riffing; European new waves shared with the New American Cinema an interest in the improvisational; various Latin American cinemas developed an interest in theorizing and practicing a poverty of means.

26   Montage in Haneke's cinema does not have the highly analytical function it has in other art and avant-garde cinemas that are likewise influenced by Adorno's writings,

such as that of Alexander Kluge. This does not mean that Haneke and Kluge do not merit a more detailed comparison. In his essay in this volume, Thomas Elsaesser briefly compares Haneke's oxymoronic concept of the chronology of chance with one of Kluge's well-known philosophical aphorisms: "Tausend Zufälle, die im Nachhinein Schicksal heissen" ("a thousand coincidences that afterwards, in retrospect, are called 'fate' "). While Elsaesser acknowledges that Kluge's statement is made much more specifically with regard to our inability to account for the historical catastrophe of National Socialism, World War II, and the Holocaust (by asking "how could it have come to this?"), his comparison suggests that Kluge's statement does not lack suggestive force with regard to Haneke's own, more oblique interest in history and its representation. A closer comparison between Haneke's and Kluge's respective notions of history, the public sphere, and modernity's socio-cognitive crisis remains to be undertaken. For a discussion of Haneke's engagement with the concept of the public sphere, see Filimon and Naqvi's essay in this volume.

27   "Society projects into film quite differently – and far more directly on account of the objects – than into advanced painting or literature. What is irreducible about the objects in film is itself a mark of society, prior to the aesthetic realization of an intention. By virtue of this relationship to the object, the aesthetics of film are thus inherently concerned with society. There can be no aesthetics of the cinema, not even a purely technological one, which would not include the sociology of the cinema" (Adorno 1981/82: 202).

28   While there are instances of dialectical montage in Haneke's films (the suicide scene in *The Seventh Continent*), in other instances Haneke uses montage in ways that suggest a subversive citation of hegemonic editing models – for the purpose of enacting a performative critique of them. This constitutes another approach to engaging the sociology of the cinema. Hence the respective sequences in *71 Fragments* and *Code Unknown* that mimic commercial editing structures to make viewers aware of their own normativized responses. *Code Unknown* contains a rooftop pool sequence, which, in Hollywood-style parallel montage, shows an adult couple trying to save a child from falling off the roof, but which is then revealed to be a fictional sequence, a film within a film. *71 Fragments* has a sequence that depicts Max's last hour prior to the shootings which differs markedly from the rest of the film. It primarily functions to accelerate narration and intensify drama, but without yielding the false sense of resolution or explanation provided by mainstream examples.

29   It is also necessary to acknowledge that Haneke's mode of production is historically removed from the models of alternative film practice that seem to have inspired Adorno's revision of his views on film. That it could be compared to it practically, in terms of alternative aesthetics and the creation of an alternative public sphere, is also highly doubtful, but, in any case, exceeds the parameters of the present discussion.

30   This term has been invoked repeatedly in connection with Haneke's films. See Thom, www.plume-noire.com/movies/reviews/hidden.html. For more scholarly citations see Beugnet (2007) and Shaviro ("The Pinocchio Theory"). Also compare Elsaesser's discussion of framing and reframing, theorized in his essay in this volume. For a more systematic discussion of the *mise-en-abyme* that has influenced my own thinking about it as a visual dispositif, see Megan Sutherland's essay, "Death by Television" (2010).

31   In the long take of Max's table tennis practice with the ball machine the quality of excess assumes an even greater intensity. It appears as though the take's indisputably gratuitous length aims to produce negative spectatorial affect as a goal unto itself. By virtue of its "torturous" monotony and duration, the scene turns its affective force onto the spectators themselves, which leads to an ironic redefinition of what Adorno characterized as film's objectifying function.

32   The punishing function of the video of Max's game at a tournament and the vexing duration of the long take of his duel with the ball machine can certainly also be read as a classic Adornian critique of the modern processes of rationalization, which have extended their suspension of individual agency also into the putatively non-alienated area of sports and recreation.

33   For an eloquent summary of this logic, see Wellmer (1985: 10). The subject's tendencies of self-oppressive synthesization find its opposite in the instance of play, because play is an expression of humanity; it indicates the possession of the imaginary before the latter becomes thoroughly instrumentalized. Tentative instances of this can be observed in Haneke's depiction of children. The diabolical abuse of play as the ultimate form of totalizing oppression is, of course, shown in *Funny Games* (1997).

34   "The strict immanence of the spirit of the artworks is contradicted on the other hand by a countertendency that is no less immanent: the tendency of artworks to wrest themselves free of the internal unity of their own construction, to introduce within themselves caesurae that no longer permit the totality of the appearance" (AT 88). It remains important for us to remember that, when it comes to film, these internal caesurae by no means have to be exclusively constituted by cuts.

35   While Frau Brunner's half-hearted acknowledgment of her decision to reject Anni suggests that she is still in denial about it, her fleeting verbalization of the moral dilemma, "How can one ever explain this to the child?," does not go unnoticed.

36   I would assign the nature of Anni's disappearance from the narrative to a different category than the disappearance of Anna in Antonioni's *L'Avventura* (1962). While Antonioni's film does not account for this disappearance, it does provide textual acknowledgment of her absence (the other characters speculate about her whereabouts and go in search of her). In addition, the audience, as Bordwell has pointed out, explain the disappearance in terms of art cinematic conventions of ambiguity and the authority of auteurist creativity (1985: 207). While Haneke's cinema, too, draws on these qualities, *71 Fragments* casts Anni's disappearance not so much as inexplicable or irrational. It remains textually unacknowledged and, thus, follows the film's parametric logic. It is reduced to a structural feature whose effect, while unfolding apropos, is all the more powerful.

37   Bathrooms hold explosive signifying potential in Haneke's cinema for the exploration of links between traumatic aspects of a person's existence and other socio-linguistic and philosophical symptomatologies. In almost every Haneke film there is at least a brief scene of a character who confronts his/her own anguish in the privacy of a bathroom. However, it is particularly the female characters who are portrayed in this setting. Notable examples are *Three Paths to the Lake* (1976), *Lemmings*, Part One (1979), *Variation* (1983), *Benny's Video* (1992), and *The Piano Teacher* (2001). Male examples can be found in *Lemmings*, Part I, and particularly in *The Rebellion* (1992), which constitutes

an elaborate example of the exploration of threatened masculinity and disempowerment through the topography of the men's restroom.

38   Even as the space is identified as her chosen redoubt, it is also coded as being highly
impersonal, antiseptic, and devoid of affection. It thus becomes, among other things,
an apposite metaphor of the functions and limitations of the foster home, signifying
the institution's inadequacy in fulfilling the needs of its inhabitants. While this reading
may strike some as prosaically sociological, we ought to recall that Haneke's cinema
is also one of sociological critique – even if his observations are cast in terms of philosophically inflected *mises-en-scène*. The shot of Anni in the bathroom of the orphanage
is thus one among numerous instances across many Haneke films that show the decline
of social and civic institutions, particularly schools, as a central symptom for a larger
decline of Western society. Many of these instances tie the depiction of their symptomatology to more specific philosophical issues, such as the decline of the imaginary
in human relations, the metaphoric potency of linguistic signifiers, and so on.

39   In fact, the visuals of Haneke's *mise-en-abyme* may be said to qualify a traditional understanding of cinematic fetishism, which refers to the rationalization – and, thus, fulfillment
– of illusion. Proposing an analogy to Haneke's subversive engagement of the sociology of the cinema, one might posit the *mise-en-abyme*'s subversive engagement of
the psychoanalytic foundations of the cinema: The spectator's cognitive activity still
implies the fetishistic reasoning of "I know, but all the same . . ." But in Haneke's
cinema this phrase no longer gives the lie to reasoning (by casting the absence of the
cinematic signifier within the terms of alibi). Now it designates the spectator's realization of the compromised state of his/her capacity to judge the image as a dispositif
of epistemological skepticism.

40   Given Haneke's Protestantism and his interest in religion, this fallibility may certainly
also be interpreted theologically. Such an interpretation would take Bordwell's observation about parametric cinema's sparking of religious readings (1985: 289) one step
further, as it imputes a religious dimension to the viewer, not merely the text. Add
to this the fact that the spectator's dual awareness that, while one is fallible, one's
best bet is still to go on exercising one's judgment, is structured like the Pascalian
wager that is discussed by Max and his fellow students.

41   For Adorno, affect is reduced to fleeting moments of happiness that are conceived to
be a dialectical outcome of the decoding of the work's internal impulses. While Haneke
the Adorno disciple has endorsed the desirability of this kind of affect for the cinema, his own films clearly imply that this is but the most circumscribed view of affect.
What they demonstrate instead is that Haneke the filmmaker is highly aware that
spectatorial affect in the cinema has a much broader range and a constant presence.

42   Rebentisch (2003: 94) is here inspired by Niklas Luhmann's thesis that art is neither
a sign for something else nor mere material form. Rather, art exists purely within
the dynamic of form and medium in aeshetic experience. She qualifies Luhmann's
definition of medium (1995: 195), which, for her, is no longer confined to the (however infinite) capacity of artistic means of expression.

43   As there is, as yet, no English-language translation of Rebentisch's book, *Ästhetik der
Installation*, I have offered my own translation here.

44   The level on which the spectator's reception of Haneke's films might be compared to
a gallery visitor's apprehension of an installed object was pushed into negative hyperbole

with *Funny Games*, which, in the manner of an installation, crystallized for spectators the volatile shifts in their own relationship to the film during a single viewing. Some spectators ended up deciding to leave the object alone by walking out, others were on the verge of doing so, resisted, revised, and reapproached the film, and then possibly still walked out. The hostility towards the film among critics also testifies to dynamics that involve object hatred more than merely a negative response to a movie.

45 Frau Brunner's statement is a correlative to Lyotard's attempt to explain his notion of the sublime with the example of the lost prayer: "My Lord, I have forgotten the prayer, but I can give an account of how the prayer got lost" (Welsch 1990: 147).

46 I am indebted to Wolfgang Welsch's eloquent summary of Lyotard's argument for my own understanding of it.

47 The film is partially based on accounts of people who have told Haneke their experiences of living in Paris, but it is not clear whether Amadou's conflict with Jean represents one such episode, whether it is a compendium of such stories, or whether it is completely fictional.

48 As Lyotard describes it, no phrase is the first and the modes that link the phrase always already take the phrase into account. Any given phrase is put into play by conflicting genres of discourse, and the success or validation of one genre (such as persuasion) is not the one proper to others (such as scorning or rejecting). The multiplicity of stakes along with the multiplicity of genres turns every linkage into a kind of victory of one of the stakes/genres over the others. These others remain forgotten, neglected, repressed possibilities (D 188).

49 As Lyotard puts it, "it is not that humans are mean or that their interests or passions are antagonistic. . . . [T]hey are situated in heterogeneous phrase regimens and are taken hold of by stakes tied to hetergeneous genres of discourse. The judgment which is passed over the nature of their social being can come into being only in accordance with one of these regimens, or at least in accordance with one of these genres of discosurse" (D 196).

50 For a critique of Lyotard's critics, see Welsch (2002: 169). This debate is a long-standing concern of Haneke's. Almost the same debate can be found in the argument between Trotta and Elisabeth in *Three Paths to the Lake*.

51 Lyotard says that this is what is at stake for literature, philosophy, and politics (D 22).

52 The scene's intention is to make the older man's indignancy an index of the conflict's irreconcilability and to illustrate the cumulative historical burden it implies. As part of an older generation of immigrants, the character is made to witness a conflict that is only the latest installment of a history which he has likely experienced first hand and in which he possibly had an active role. The scene implies that Lyotard's redefinition of the position and function of the judge may be in need of complication: In this case, the judge is not part of the hegemonic parameters in which the conflict is embedded, but actually comes from the other, historically and politically underprivileged side. But while the character's behavior may be based on a real-life incident, and while it complicates the stereotype of the angry Arab, it also encourages the viewers to take sides against the young Arab man and to identify with Anne's hegemonic position – and it does so in ways that are not marked by performativity, as was the case with the camera pan that retrieves Maria back into the frame.

References and Further Reading

Adorno, Theodor W.: *Ästhetische Theorie*, ed. Gretel Adorno and Rolf Tiedemann (Frankfurt: Suhrkamp, 1973); *Aesthetic Theory*, trans. and ed. Robert Hullot-Kentor (London and New York: Continuum, 1997).

Adorno, Theodor W.: "Culture Industry Reconsidered," trans. Anson Rabinbach, *New German Critique* 6 (1975): 12–19.

Adorno, Theodor W.: "Transparencies on Film," trans. Thomas Levin, *New German Critique* 24/25 (Autumn 1981–Winter 1982): 199–205.

Arato, Andrew and Gebhardt, Eike, eds.: *The Essential Frankfurt School Reader* (New York: Continuum, 1988).

Beugnet, Martine: "Blind Spot," *Screen* 48:2 (2007): 227–31.

Bordwell, David: *Narration in the Fiction Film* (Madison: University of Wisconsin Press, 1985).

Buck-Morss, Susan: *The Dialectics of Seeing: Walter Benjamin and the Arcades Project* (Cambridge, MA: MIT Press, 1991).

Frey, Mattias: "*Benny's Video, Caché*, and the Desubstantiated Image," *Framework: The Journal of Cinema and Media* 47:2 (2006): 30–6.

Frey, Mattias: "Supermodernity, Capital, and Narcissus: The French Connection to Michael Haneke's *Benny's Video*," *Cinetext* (October 2002), cinetext.philo.at/magazine/frey/bennysvideo.html.

Galt, Rosalind: "The Functionary of Mankind: Michael Haneke and Europe," *On Michael Haneke*, ed. John David Rhodes and Brian Price (Detroit: Wayne State University Press, 2010).

Gilroy, Paul: "Shooting Crabs in a Barrel," *Screen* 48:2 (Summer 2007; special dossier on *Caché*): 233–5.

Grisseman, Stefan and Omasta, Michael: "Herr Haneke, wo bleibt das Positive?" *Der Siebente Kontinent: Michael Haneke und seine Filme*, ed. Alexander Horwath (Vienna: Europaverlag, 1991), pp. 193–213.

Hansen, Miriam B.: "Introduction to Adorno, 'Transparencies on Film' (1966)," *New German Critique* 24/25 (Autumn 1981–Winter 1982): 186–98.

Horwath, Alexander: "Die Ungeheuerliche Kränkung, die das Leben ist: Zu den Filmen von Michael Haneke," *Der Siebente Kontinent: Michael Haneke und seine Filme*, ed. Alexander Horwath (Vienna: Europaverlag, 1991), pp. 11–39.

Huyssen, Andreas: "Introduction to Adorno," *New German Critique* 6 (1975): 3–11.

Jay, Martin: *The Dialectical Imagination: A History of the Frankfurt School and the Institute of Social Research, 1923–1950* (Boston and Toronto: Little, Brown, 1973).

Leisch-Kiesl, Monika: "Es sind Fragen aufgetreten und offen geblieben, von denen ich hoffe, dass sie nicht allzu schnell beantwortet werden (können): Michael Haneke – Robert Bresson," *Michael Haneke und seine Filme: Eine Pathologie der Konsumgesellschaft*, 2nd edition, ed. Christian Wessely, Franz Grabner, and Gerhard Larcher (Marburg: Schüren, 2008), pp. 319–40.

Luhmann, Niklas: *Die Kunst der Gesellschaft* (Frankfurt am Main: Surhkamp, 1995).

Lyotard, Jean-François: *Le Différend* (Paris: Editions de Minuit, 1983); *The Differend: Phrases in Dispute*, trans. Georges Van Den Abbeele (Minneapolis: University of Minnesota Press, 1988).

Meindl, Harald: "Zum Erhabenen im Kinowerk Michael Haenekes: Ästhetisch-theologische Hinweise," *Michael Haneke und seine Filme: Eine Pathologie der Konsumgesellschaft*, 2nd edition, ed. Christian Wessely, Franz Grabner, and Gerhard Larcher (Marburg: Schüren, 2008), pp. 83–112.

Metelmann, Jörg: *Zur Kritik der Kino-Gewalt: Die Filme von Michael Haneke* (Munich: Fink, 2003).

Naqvi, Fatima: "The Politics of Contempt and the Ecology of Images: Michael Haneke's *Code inconnu*," *The Cosmopolitan Screen: German Cinema and The Global Imaginary, 1945 to the Present*, ed. Stephan K. Schindler and Lutz Koepnick (Ann Arbor: University of Michigan Press, 2007).

Naqvi, Fatima: "Postimperiale und postnationale Konstellationen in den Filmen Michael Hanekes," *Österreich 1918 und die Folgen: Geschichte, Literatur, Theater und Film*, ed. Karl Müller and Hans Wagener (Vienna: Böhlau, 2009), pp. 165–78.

Rancière, Jacques: *Le Destin des images* (Paris: Editions La Fabrique, 2003); *The Future of the Image*, trans. Gregory Elliot (London and New York: Verso, 2007).

Rebentisch, Juliane: *Ästhetik der Installation* (Frankfurt: Suhrkamp, 2003).

Ricciardi, Alessia: *The Ends of Mourning: Psychoanalysis, Literature, Film* (Stanford, CA: Stanford University Press, 2003).

Sedlmayr, Hans: *Verlust der Mitte: Die bildende Kunst des 19. und 20. Jahrhunderts als Symptom und Symbol der Zeit* (Salzburg: Otto Müller, 1948). *Art in Crisis: The Lost Center*, trans. Brian Battershaw (Chicago: H. Regnery, 1958).

Shaviro, Steven: "The Pinocchio Theory: *Caché*," www.shaviro.com/Blog/?p=476.

Sutherland, Meghan: "Death by Television," *On Michael Haneke*, ed. Brian Price and John David Rhodes (Detroit: Wayne State University Press, 2010).

Tröhler, Margrit: *Offene Welten ohne Helden: Plurale Figurenkonstellationen im Film* (Marburg: Schüren, 2007).

Wellmer, Albrecht: *Zur Dialektik von Moderne und Postmoderne: Vernunftkritik nach Adorno* (Frankfurt: Suhrkamp, 1985).

Welsch, Wolfgang: *Ästhetisches Denken* (Stuttgart: Philipp Reclam Jr., 1990).

Welsch, Wolfgang: *Unsere Postmoderne Moderne* (Berlin: Akademie Verlag, 2002).

Wheatley, Catherine: *Michael Haneke's Cinema: The Ethic of the Image* (New York and Oxford: Berghahn Books, 2009).

Wiggershaus, Rolf: *Die Frankfurter Schule: Geschichte, Theoretische Entwicklung, Politische Bedeutung* (Munich: Deutscher Taschenbuch Verlag, 1988).

21

Hollywood Endgames

Leland Monk

Michael Haneke's 2007 remake of his own German-language film *Funny Games* (1997) offers an ideal opportunity to measure and assess the current efficacy of a specifically Hollywood style of filmmaking. The original was already addressing itself to an American cinema: The title is in English, the *mise-en-scène* of the lake house is modeled on American interiors, and the killer's direct address to the audience taunts the consumer of mediated violence with his desire to see more. As Haneke observed, "[i]t is a reaction to a certain American cinema, its violence, its naivety, the way American cinema toys with human beings."[1] The stakes are raised considerably, however, when Haneke chooses to make a movie in America about America and, as I will be emphasizing, in Hollywood about Hollywood. It will be the purpose of this essay eventually to determine what the remake of *Funny Games* has to say about Hollywood filmmaking today. First, though, I'd like to consider certain aspects of the Austrian original that hit their mark, the success of which is made more salient and impressive when their re-creation falls short in the American remake.

I

The two versions of the film can be considered together as a kind of controlled experiment. They have the same story and characters; virtually the same script, with some updated colloquialisms ("awesome" and the like); and, unlike most Hollywood remakes, they were made by the same director (assuming, for the sake of the experiment, that this is a constant despite the fact that, as this collection attests, Haneke's work has evolved and matured in the intervening ten years).[2] The changes that have been made are relatively minor. Some concessions have been made to technological "advances": There is reference to a guest bringing his laptop and the film accounts for George's missing cellphone after Ann's is submerged (in the original the mobile phone is attached to the house, not a person). And they try to contact the 911 emergency line with the waterlogged device instead of an acquaintance.[3] The 2007 film is otherwise a doggedly faithful shot-by-shot remake of the Austrian original.

Except for the dogs. In the original the family dog is a German shepherd named Rolfi; in the US version he's a golden retriever not very aptly named Lucky. The choice of breed is important and summarizes for me the very different depictions of class in the two films.[4] Rolfi has an unassuming name (it would be like "Freddy" in English), but German shepherds have a long association with nobility and Germanic/Teutonic grandeur. They are keenly intelligent and make fierce guard dogs; they are frequently used by police and military forces to patrol borders and high-security enclosures; and they are adept at tracking criminals and sniffing out suspects. The dogs were especially favored by the Nazis (Hitler himself had a German shepherd) and they were allegedly trained to identify and track down Jews.[5] Rolfi then represents the fierce and vigilant guardian patrolling the perimeter of this wealthy enclave, his ferocity belied (or disguised) by his just-a-regular-guy name. Lucky meets the same fate as Rolfi (bludgeoned to death with a golf club) and is no more successful at protecting his masters. But the breed's attitude to an intruding Other is very different. Golden retrievers are known for their eager-to-please friendly disposition, which has made them one of the most popular family dogs in the United States. They are amiable and welcoming to *everyone*, strangers as much as their owners, so don't serve as effective guard dogs.[6] The different ways these breeds relate to an outsider suggests something interesting about the way these families understand their position in the social world.

The 1997 German-language version of *Funny Games* has in its cross-hairs a clearly recognizable target: It nails to the screen and eviscerates the cultured and insular European haut-bourgeois couple, one genus of the Hanekean species called Ann-and-George (variously Anna/Anne/Ann and Georg/Georges/George, depending on whether the language is German/French/English). These are the names of the middle-class couples in virtually every original screenplay Haneke has written and they represent the model liberal subjects who, under the pressures exerted on them during the film, have brought home to them the violence, self-interest, and aggression in their own constitution that's allowed them to attain their privileged position and which they ardently disavow in order to think of themselves as, precisely, liberal. In both versions of *Funny Games*, the engines of the couple's destruction are two charming, well-spoken young men, dressed for sport, who assault and destroy them with the appurtenances of their own leisure class, which they wield expertly:[7] the golfer's top-of-the-line driver (Rolfi/Lucky and Georg/e), the hunter's shotgun (Georg/e *père* and *fils*), and the yacht-clubber's sailboat (Ann/a). Although the markers of cultural refinement (familiarity with obscure opera passages and performers)[8] and class privilege (the gated estate of a posh second home, expensive golf and boating equipage) are the same in both versions, these distinctions don't "place" the couple as a very specific type of the upper-level bourgeoisie so readily in America and for Americans as they do in the European class consciousness (which is to say, Europeans tend to be conscious *of* class). In the US, golf and sailing are associated more with the professional and managerial classes than the upper class; and shotguns are used *primarily* to blow someone away.

The remake's depiction of class privilege is no less pointed than the original's but its edge is blunted and blurred by the blandness of a presumed equality in a supposedly democratic sociality. Even in this affluent domain, the United States is, nominally and ideologically, a classless society. In the encounter that initiates the escalating violence, when one of the intruders asks to borrow some eggs, the same scene plays rather differently. In the original, Anna is wary but civil; the civility of her highly civilized demeanor is tested and pushed until it starts to crack. The noble German shepherd, even a sweet one named Rolfi, is always on duty, patrolling the periphery. In *Funny Games U.S.* there's a sense that Ann is constrained to be polite not just by social decorum but by an imperative to treat the stranger (if grudgingly) as an equal. The affable golden retriever is friendly to everyone, on principle. It's not evidence so much as a figure for what I'm trying to characterize here in the different ways Ann/a relates to the intruder, who represents the masses outside that gate. In the original she wraps all four eggs up together in a news-paper – an ovate collective; in the remake she conveniently has an extra egg-tray on hand and places each one in its separate but equal place, a prefabricated dim-ple. Democracy, American style.

A remarkable thing happens to the bourgeois couple in the 1997 version of *Funny Games*: They *become* a couple, in a far more visceral and literal way than is signified by Hitchcock's handcuffs. If at the beginning of the film their identities and rela-tionship are nothing more than the prescripted and preconstituted roles and gestures of a particular social type, if they are altogether generic from the onset, once they are both, literally, shell-shocked by the death of their son they manage to come together, in and as an almost indissociable unit. This happens at the end of the most powerful and affecting scene in the film, a protracted rendering of their unfathomable grief shot in one long take (it lasts more than ten minutes): Anna sits in a chair stunned and immobile for a long time (1:25), then stands and hops (she is bound hand and foot) to the television where she turns off the blar-ing broadcast of a car race; she sits dazed, then finally speaks, "they've gone" (2:39); she tries to cut the rope binding her hands on the TV set, stands, and hops across the room, camera panning left to follow, until she leaves the frame (4:04); Georg rises from the floor, sits there in shock, then starts to sob uncontrollably (5:11); Anna, unbound, hurries in to embrace and finally calm him; "we've got to get out of here," she says (8:13) and awkwardly helps him to his feet; and this is where that new sense of the couple is forged as they become Anna-and-Georg in more than name, bonded together indivisibly (9:22). Anna helps support Georg and, legs bent, crouching over her haunches, she slowly and resolutely walks him with sumo-wrestler-like steps across the room; he is draped over her, dragging his crippled leg; and they are no longer two separate people. They almost literally fuse into

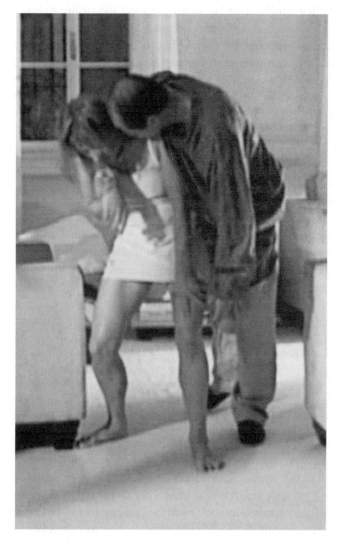

Fig. 21.1   Anna (Susanne Lothar) supports Georg (Ulrich Mühe). *Funny Games* (1997), dir. Michael Haneke, prod. Veit Heiduschka.

a composite entity, melded together by the extremities of pain and loss, united, again quite literally, over their son's dead body (Fig. 21.1).[9]

A similar kind of change happens, subtly, in the way they regard each other thereafter. These feelings are conveyed entirely through look and gesture, in the extraordinary acting of Ulrich Mühe and Susanne Lothar. He seems to see her with new eyes, as though realizing for the first time what a strong and resourceful woman he's married to. When, as she leaves the house to find help (for him;

she could just flee) and he asks her to forgive him, she rushes to kiss and embrace him, as though to say, like Cordelia: no need for forgiveness.

These moments happen in the remake but to little effect. When Ann helps George to walk, she is little more than an inefficacious crutch for her inefficacious husband. When he looks at her in a new way, it's as though he's realized she's not *just* a trophy wife. And his whining plea for forgiveness is just another instance of him being unforgivably weak.[10] Poor George, the American family man, has a much tougher model of manhood to live up to, or fall short of. In American cinema from the early Westerns through *The Desperate Hours* (William Wyler, 1955; remade in 1990 by Michael Cimino) to the recent Harrison Ford Viagra-dose *Firewall* (Richard Loncraine, 2006), the *paterfamilias in extremis* is obliged to (im)prove his manhood by dispelling the invasive threat to his family with a new-found virility that usually takes the form of a virulent violence.

Besides losing in the American context some of the original's point and precision about the vacuous class types that are Anna and Georg, and the suggestions of their subsequent reformation in the crucible of intense suffering, the remake never quite succeeds in forging the link between the actions and motivation of the two games-playing young men and the spectator's desire to watch such a spectacle.[11] Michael Pitt plays the role of Paul either as delightedly *self*-amused at the games he initiates ("That's awesome, really!") or unrelenting and implacable in his execution of them. He looks at the camera and addresses the audience directly, but never manages to make the connection.[12] He and his cohort are like the gods in *King Lear* who, having taken the form of wanton boys, kill us for their sport. Their sport, not the viewer's. The efforts to implicate the spectator mostly fall flat in the remake. Michael Pitt never quite establishes the conspiratorial relation to the audience that the marvelous Arno Frisch achieves, with his ironies and insinuations, his twinkle-eyed amusement at *our* desire to see more, his knowing wink to the camera (sadly omitted in the remake).[13] Viewers of the American version, eager for entertainment, don't seriously entertain the unnerving idea that they have entered into the sport of these funny games simply by watching them unreel. No doubt this failure has as much to do with the impermeability of "the fourth wall" in Hollywood cinema as it does with the performance style of the two actors playing Paul.[14]

If the Brechtian alienation effects of such unconventional and meta-cinematic addresses to the camera/audience in *Funny Games U.S.* don't quite come across, the film's deployment then violation of more conventional cinematic and generic codes (especially those of the suspense-thriller-horror movie) are even more effective in the remake. The location shooting for *Funny Games U.S.* was mostly on Long Island (with on-set filming in Los Angeles), but the provenance of the later film is distinctively the multiplex more than the recreation homes of the wealthy. Haneke has been clear about who he hoped to address with the remake:

> The first film didn't reach the public I think really ought to see this film. So I decided to make it again. The original was in German, and English-speaking audiences don't

often see subtitled films. When I first envisioned *Funny Games* in the mid-1990s, it was my intention to have an American audience watch the movie. . . . But because I made *Funny Games* in German with actors not familiar to U.S. audiences, it didn't get through to the people who most needed to see it.[15]

The film was marketed as a horror thriller in the States but in the event it didn't reach very many of the American mall-kids it targeted.[16] It has so far made a respectable $7.2 million but most of that has been overseas. The domestic take was only $1.2 million (Haneke's 2005 art-house hit *Caché* made three times that amount in US theaters) and half of that was during the opening weekend.[17] Word traveled fast: The number of daily screenings at my local cineplex were whittled away quickly before it disappeared completely. *Caché* had legs but *Funny Games U.S.* had stumps. Those who did see it expecting a typical genre film with lots of gory violence were of course outraged. Their online condemnation of the film has been fierce but has also generated some more thoughtful response urging the disappointed to examine the reasons they disliked it so much.[18] Haneke was no doubt pleased with the intensity, if not the number, of irate responses to the film when it opened. One can almost hear his trademark giggle echoing through the glass-and-plaster arcades of the mall as the *Hostel* crowd who *Saw* and hated the movie violently objected to his antiseptic and remedial version of mediated violence.[19]

The most controversial moment in both versions of the film that finally gives the audience what it wants, psychologically, generically, and cinematically (only to take it away again), is the scene where Ann/a grabs the shotgun and shoots Peter with it, which prompts a distraught Paul to find the remote control, rewind the scene we've just witnessed, and play it again; this time, he takes away the gun from her and a vengeful satisfaction from us. That table-turning shotgun blast is the most Hollywood moment in the film – the trigger-finger implanted in the viewers' brain was just itching for it. And its impact has been enhanced in the Hollywood version with Hollywood special effects. Peter doesn't just get a splattering-blood-packet hole blown through his chest, as in the original; the shot has been digitally enhanced so the hail of hot lead blasts his body across the room and against the wall where it slides to the floor in a crumpled heap, leaving a bloody smear on the wainscoting. Haneke turns up the visceral CGI wattage on this, the most cathartic moment in *Funny Games*, only to hollow out a larger void in the American moviegoer's sensational appetites. The thrilled shouts of affirmation it consistently elicits in the theater then echo more hollowly when that homicidal delight is taken away.

It is curious that in this scene Ann/a doesn't learn from her mistake as Paul does from his. He rewinds the film to intercept the woman's appropriation of the phallic weapon, replaying the bloody death of his accomplice to a different end; so why doesn't she? That is to say, in the playback scene she should leave the shotgun where it is and *grab the remote*! Imagine: She rewinds through all the torment, back before her son's head was blown off, back before her husband was crippled by the golf club, back until Peter comes to the door asking to borrow some eggs. *That's* the time to pull out the shotgun and blow that sucker away – *yeah!* Oops, look at that. I fell into one of Haneke's traps again. See my bloodlust on display! I've obviously, unthinkingly, seen too many splatter films. Shame on me. In Haneke's universe, if one is quick and lucky enough to grab hold of the universal remote, the most – perhaps the only – ethical thing one can do is push the power button, not to exercise remote control over what transpires but to *turn it off*. So Haneke would like to do, I would suggest, with the cinematic apparatus that goes by the metonymic nickname Hollywood.

II

The two films that *Funny Games U.S.* has been compared to most often are George Sluizer's *The Vanishing* (1993), a Hollywood remake, in English, of the director's foreign-language film *Spoorloos* (1988), and Gus Van Sant's shot-by-shot 1998 remake of Hitchcock's classic *Psycho* (1960). *The Vanishing* is notorious for the studio-enforced absurdity of its altered ending. It is awful but also instructive: Like the laughably upbeat ending the studio dictated for Ridley Scott's *Blade Runner* (1982), the tacked-on climax of Sluizer's remake is a travesty of every psychological, aesthetic, and cinematic principle that made the film so compelling and unsettling; and it speaks volumes about what qualifies as a proper Hollywood ending. The Dutch version was an art-house hit about a young man whose girlfriend disappears at a highway rest-stop; he becomes obsessed with discovering what happened to her, even to the point, once he meets her abductor, of submitting to the same fate, whatever it may be. The ending is bleak and terrifying, a revelation worthy of Dostoevsky about the capacity for evil and the end-point of a Poe-like mad love that finds its consummation not before or above but in the grave of the beloved. In the remake, the grave is no dead end. Kiefer Sutherland's character is resurrected, rising from the grave in time to save a damsel in distress, his new girlfriend, from Jeff Bridges' villain by shoving a shovel into his dour grin. It's like Haneke reshot his film to culminate in Ann giving both barrels of that shotgun to Peter and Paul. Oh yeah, and little Georgie was only pretending to be dead.[20]

Haneke agreed to direct *Funny Games U.S.* only if the producers in turn agreed to it being a rigorously faithful shot-by-shot remake, saying in effect about the original: What you see is what you get. This stipulation prevented in advance a Sluizer-like fiasco but it likely also constrained Haneke from making any substantial changes he might have wanted to implement in order to revise – not just offer a revision of – the original, as Hitchcock did with *The Man Who Knew Too Much* (1934, 1956). If Haneke made changes of his own he would perhaps be obliged to make others not of his devising. Even so, he apparently liked having a Hollywood hand offer to feed him so he could bite it; and he snapped at the opportunity.[21] The producers extending Michael Haneke an outstretched and itchy palm holding a check and film contract might be reminded of Lenin's quip about the purveyors of capitalism who would commodify even their own execution: When the Revolution comes, he drily observed, the capitalists will be happy to sell us the rope to hang them with.

Gus Van Sant's *Psycho*, almost universally condemned except by Universal studios, who opened their vaults to him after the success of *Good Will Hunting* (1997), is an under-rated film. Under cover of the same policy as Haneke's remake, a strictly faithful shot-by-shot re-creation of the original, Van Sant managed to interpolate some shots of his own – there is nothing like them in Hitchcock's canonical work – that don't necessarily improve on the original but do provide occasionally brilliant glosses on it. Two examples. When near the end Lila comes upon the mummified corpse of Mrs. Bates in the fruit cellar, the dead woman is facing a well-lit aviary of *live* birds, dozens of them. What is conveyed here is a glimpse into the psychotic mind of Norman Bates, who has staged the psycho-drama of this tableau. Norman regards that desiccated body not just as a relic of the past but as an *egg*, an egg with a future, and someday it will hatch. That's why the corpse is consistently placed in relation to a bare light bulb – it's an incubator, like schoolchildren use to hatch little chicks. Those live birds anticipate the Phoenix-like future incarnation of Mrs. Bates once she finally comes out of her shell.

Another nothing-like-it-in-the-original interpolation appears on screen when Detective Arbogast is attacked on the staircase. Two unaccountable shots appear for a brief moment: With the first slash of the knife across his face we see a nearly naked blindfolded blonde woman turn her head to face the camera (Fig. 21.2); and following the second slash we see a blurred image of what looks like a bovine creature at night on a road, seen through a windshield (wipers sweeping aside rain) from the vantage of a moving car about to collide with it (Fig. 21.3).[22] These

Fig. 21.2   Subliminal image (1): the blindfolded blonde woman. *Psycho* (1998), dir. and prod. Gus Van Sant.

Fig. 21.3   Subliminal image (2): animal seen through a car windshield at night. *Psycho* (1998), dir. and prod. Gus Van Sant.

images flash by so quickly that they work – they were designed to work – subliminally, giving shape to what Arbogast is experiencing in his last moments. The two shots make little sense independently but work together rather like a rebus:[23] The first is I think a seductive but blank-faced figure of death; the second conveys the sudden panic right before your speeding car hits a large animal in the road. Put the two together and what you're sensing through the dying man's eyes is not (just) Norman Bates dressed as his dead mother wielding a carving knife but what he/she/it embodies: the death drive.[24]

I've taken this detour through figurations of the death drive in the latter-day *Psycho* to shine some headlights on a similar theme in both versions of *Funny Games*: The playful duo engaging in blood sports (variously Peter and Paul, Tom and Jerry, Beavis and Butthead) likewise embody the force of the death drive, externalized, for their victims. This is signaled even before the games begin with the music that accompanies the opening credits (starting with the title, in blood-red lettering). The Land Rover's expensive sound system plays the soothing sound of "Care Selve" from Handel's *Atalanta* as the family enters the gated estate. Ann/a and Georg/e have been playing a snobby "name the opera, name the singer" game, little Georgie looking on admiringly. This is the only game we see them play of their own devising and it is an anemic one, implicitly teaching their son how to stockpile and profit from an accumulation of cultural capital. The soundtrack of choice for this self-satisfied nuclear family is then supplanted by a non-diegetic explosion of raw noise, the blaring screams of John Zorn's "Bonehead" and "Hellraiser" – the (supposed) sound of death, destruction, and Satanic evil that will annihilate them. The film emphatically characterizes this music as death-driven (it returns diegetically when Paul stalks little Georgie in the house of the neighbors he has already exterminated), which is a rather phobic, Tipper-Gore version of hardcore metal music.[25]

As Anthony Lane pointed out, the notion that the realm of operatic high culture and thrash metal are separate, opposed, and incompatible spheres is rather antiquated: "The fact is that the George of 2008 would have a bundle of thrash on his iPod, all shuffled up with his Verdi. The howl is now mainstream."[26] A sharper use of musical citation (from the cinematic past) is in evidence on the soundtrack for the trailer that packaged the remake as a suspense-thriller-horror movie. It begins with the lovely aria "Ebben? Ne andró lontana" from *La Wally* made familiar by the French art house hit *Diva* (Jean-Jacques Beineix, 1981), accompanying shots of the happy family arriving at the lake house. As the violent action ensues, we hear another classical piece, Grieg's "In the Hall of the Mountain King" from the *Peer Gynt Suite* that carries its own death charge in the pulsing cadences, which increase in tempo with the manic editing: This is the tune compulsively whistled by the child-molesting killer, played magnificently by Peter Lorre, in Fritz Lang's *M* (1931). The visuals, fast cutting, and narrative shaping of the trailer then target the slasher-movie audience while the classical music is pitched to the art-house crowd and the cineastes who can flatter themselves by noting the cinematic quotations. Neither of these musical extracts is heard in the film.

More interestingly, the impulse, the compulsion to repeat, obsessively, entailed in a shot-by-shot remake (of Hitchcock by Van Sant, of Haneke by Haneke) places the enterprise in relation to the death drive on the formal level as well. Repetition compulsion is for Freud the signal instance of the death drive's instinctual function.[27] In his perverse insistence on the repetition of every shot in the Austrian original, Haneke steered the death drive that inheres in that undertaking on a collision course with the heart of Hollywood, with the idea of making it stop.

It is admittedly difficult to find traces of a specifically Hollywood style of filmmaking in *Funny Games U.S.* since it so rigorously recreates the Austrian original and both films were shot on locations and sets designed to be as generic as the people who inhabit them. I already mentioned the digitally enhanced shotgun murder that amplifies the visceral impact of that Hollywood moment. Another shot incorporates into the film some indication of the more banal and quotidian means of production on a Hollywood project. I am referring to the first exterior shot of the house once Ann has climbed out the window to seek help after the killers have gone. In the original, the shot is quick, clear, and efficient: We see Anna run across the dark lawn away from the house and towards the fence; it lasts 19 seconds. In the remake, we see the house and a lit-up tool shed; there is some clattering noise and we briefly see a silhouette, presumably Ann's, while she is presumably searching for the wire cutters to make a hole in the fence. We never see her running across the grass, never see her distinctly at all, and the shot lasts an interminable 49 seconds. This shot and its length puzzled me for a long time. It simply is not interesting or contributory, in visual, psychological, or narrative terms. It just goes on and on with nothing happening. And then it occurred to me that might be the point. Haneke has said the most frustrating thing about making the film in Hollywood was how long it took to set up and shoot the scenes;

they were constantly waiting around for the crew, with their time-consuming prepa-rations, to be ready on the set.[28] This long dull shot may be referencing how oner-ous and tedious it is, when you're on the clock, to wait around while all the production assistants and technicians tinker with the tools of their trade.

In one major and important respect, the present-day Hollywood means of pro-duction are writ large in *Funny Games U.S.* For these aren't just any Ann/e/a and Georg/e/es: They are Naomi Watts and Tim Roth, and they are tormented by Michael Pitt, the cinematic poster boy for disaffected sociopaths. That is to say, they are movie stars. And it is because of them, especially Naomi Watts, that this Hollywood film got made. Haneke has recently worked with French movie stars like Juliette Binoche, Isabelle Huppert, and Daniel Auteuil, cannily deploying their familiarity to defamiliarize the characters they play in unsettling ways. There are fine actors but no movie stars in the 1997 original (except retroactively: Now that Ulrich Mühe is dead and famous for his role in Florian Henckel von Donnersmarck's *The Lives of Others*, from 2006, he has attained some star qual-ity). Watts, Roth, and Pitt have all made edgy, low-budget independent features with interesting directors but it is their more mainstream performances that most tellingly feed into their roles in *Funny Games U.S.* Naomi Watts starred in *The Ring* cycle, playing a strong mother tormented by intrusive evil in big-budget Hollywood remakes of very successful foreign films; and less overtly, her first big (doubled) role in David Lynch's *Mulholland Drive* brilliantly anatomized the not-very-funny fame games of Hollywood stardom. Tim Roth has played an effete aristocrat in *Rob Roy* (Michael Caton-Jones, 1995) and, on the other end of the golf club, the lead in Robert Markowitz's *Starkweather: Murder in the Heartland*, a 1993 based-in-fact TV movie about the killing spree of two young people that also inspired Oliver Stone's *Natural Born Killers* (1994), the unthinking violence of which Haneke has explicitly criticized in relation to the objectives of *Funny Games*. And Michael Pitt's role as one of the Leopold-and-Loeb-like killers in *Murder By Numbers* (Barbet Schroeder, 2002), with Sandra Bullock, qualified him to play on the team of charming, well-spoken murderers in the remake.

It is the allure of movie star Naomi Watts that is most on display in *Funny Games U.S.*, not least when she is repeatedly stripped bare for the camera – and I don't just mean emotionally. The camera placement is as discreet as in the original when Paul and Peter force her to disrobe early in their sadistic play. But, as countless male commentators have pointed out, Naomi Watts is onscreen in her bra and panties for a very long time (most provocatively, for the duration of that ten-plus minute shot; in the original Anna wears a slip). Derek Elley called this wardrobe change the most notable difference between the remake and the original (along with the longer running time, four minutes) and went on to observe, quite rightly, "where the dramatic focus in the earlier version was evenly balanced between husband and wife, here Watts' Anna [sic] is unquestionably the main protag."[29] Nowhere is she more the plucky heroine than when she manages to get off a shot at her tormentor that doesn't get rewound by the remote controller and taken away from the approving spectator: The projectile is saliva, she spits at Paul shortly before she grabs the shotgun, and there is nothing like it in the original.

Both the 1997 and the 2007 versions masterfully deploy, only to frustrate, the audience's expectations about the slasher film, which is consumed by a predominantly male audience.[30] But I would submit that there is another, less obvious Hollywood genre informing the remake (and not the original): the woman's film. Precursor to but very different from today's chick-flick, with its affirmations of female friendship, agency, and management skills on both the romantic and career fronts, the woman's films of the 1930s and 1940s showed resourceful women in domestic situations suffering unspeakably for the sake of the spectator, also coded female. They starred women with a powerful screen presence (the likes of Bette Davis, Barbara Stanwyck, Joan Crawford), which shone through even when their character was confined to meager and mousy circumstances.[31] The hallmark of these films was female sacrifice, enacted on the big screen by bigger-than-life movie stars, and the universal solvent for all female trouble (the lead's and, by identification, the spectator's) was a good cry.[32]

The iconic publicity image for *Funny Games U.S.* is a portrait of Naomi Watts looking beautiful and abused, one side of her face blotched with tears, making it crystal clear that the remake (unlike the original) is about stripping naked – emotionally, psychologically, physically – the female star (Fig. 21.4).

This emblem for the film is a painterly version of the close-up showing her tear-drenched face, not when she or her family are being physically tortured but just before she is forced to take her clothes off for the eager young men holding them captive. Her son has a pillowcase over his head and cannot see; her humiliated husband looks away. She looks both vulnerable and rather voluptuous, with tousled hair and teeth about to bite those full lips. Female viewers who identify with the tears of the movie star at this moment would likely feel with her that those male spectators (and directors) making such a spectacle of this woman want to see her naked in her suffering and suffering in her nakedness. Whether or not Peter and Paul are lovers, they desire her crying.

The Naomi Watts pictured in that publicity poster, which displays the miseries of her sex dissolving into tears, is the star of a woman's film.[33] Here too Haneke is ascetic to the point of astringency, doing with the woman's film what he does with the slasher film. There is no catharsis, no redemption, no ennobling sacrifice in this version of spectacular female suffering.[34] It is hard to conceive of a classic Hollywood woman's film without an accompanying purse full of Kleenex, all wet and wadded by movie's end. In Haneke's version of the woman's film, Ann Farber drowns but not in tears.

The end Naomi Watts's character meets is a remarkable one for the way it absolutely resists the imperatives of the usual Hollywood ending, no matter the genre.[35] There is one more cinematic tease, when on the sailboat the knife shown in conspicuous close-up in Act I comes back in Act III, only to be intercepted (like the shotgun, like Ann's efforts to flag down a passing car) by the killers. Then

Fig. 21.4   Iconic image: Naomi Watts in the theatrical release poster. *Funny Games U.S.* (2007), dir. Michael Haneke, prod. Hamish McAlpine, Christian Baute, Chris Coen, Andro Steinborn.

Paul unceremoniously dumps her overboard. Even Peter is surprised – they had almost an hour of playtime left. When the funny gamester kisses Naomi Watts's cheek and throws her in the drink (*"Ciao, bella!"*), the film says an irrevocable good-bye to the Hollywood movie star. It's a triumph of auteurism over the means of production as they have operated hitherto in Hollywood: Haneke doesn't just kill off the movie star; Naomi Watts was also the film's executive producer.

III

Let me conclude by being a little more precise about what may seem to be an unexamined term in my discussion, the seemingly monolithic "Hollywood." I don't just mean by that designation a particular place or industry. I don't just mean a now superannuated studio system that made some high-quality films on the assembly-line model in the sweatshops of the so-called dream factory. I don't just mean the more contemporary L.A.-based post-industrial, multi-national, multi-media corporations that broker deals with the agents of so-called free agents to put together film deals. Hollywood, as I understand it, is a filmmaking regime that one might call, after Althusser, an ideological state-of-mind apparatus.[36] In the larger project from which this essay is extracted, I am specifically concerned with the genealogy and cultural work done by what we call a "Hollywood ending," the kind of ending to a film that satisfies the imperatives of a Hollywood view of the world by being unrealistically happy, upbeat, and optimistic. Along with these "feel-good" attributes, the Hollywood ending ultimately upholds the social order. If there is loss, it is redeemed; if there is death, it registers as ennobling sacrifice. Such deprivations finally yield a handsome payoff in life-lessons, extended human sympathy, and narrative meaning. This sense of an ending, then, is always more or less ideological, by which I simply mean that it offers false narrative (re)solutions to real social problems.

The 2007 remake is an interesting test case for the ideological force of the Hollywood film apparatus and its demands for a feel-good ending. Here are the results of our uncontrolled experiment and some provisional answers to the question: Can the body of Hollywood cinema readily assimilate antibodies with such fierce resistance to its immune system as a compulsively repeating *Funny Games* and its stubbornly perverse writer-director? It is quite a remarkable thing that the film actually got made, as is. It may not be sporting of him, but Haneke (like Peter and Paul with the golf club, shotgun, and sailboat) expertly wields the expensive equipment of the Hollywood players, those producers of the Hollywood state-of-mind, against them. In its rigorous challenge to the ideological machinery of the Hollywood ending, Haneke's film suggests another sense of that phrase: Hollywood, ending. The end of Hollywood filmmaking as we know it would mean in this case: spectacular visual effects used to evacuate the craving for sensationally mediated violence; the death of the movie star system, without tears; and the deployment of established film genres only to come up with a new formula that frustrates their altogether conventional expectations. *Funny Games U.S.*, Haneke's first (perhaps only) Hollywood film, has a very different sense of an ending that anticipates what a post-Hollywood cinema might be like. *Ciao, bella!*

Notes

1   Interview with Stuart Jeffries (2008).
2   The projected remake of *Caché* (2005) by another director, Ron Howard, will no doubt provide an interesting counterpoint to *Funny Games U.S.* I expect we'll see Hollywood filmmaking reassert some of its most conventional practices.

3   A lost detail: That acquaintance is named Peter, which is also a pseudonym for one of the homicidal intruders, suggesting their "friend" might not be as helpful and friendly as they hope.

4   Of course the choice might also have been determined by the availability of a dead and not yet stiff dog for Lucky's last, sickening appearance in the film, as the dog's corpse spills slowly out the back of the family Land Rover.

5   As Roy Grundmann pointed out to me, the Nazis' affiliation with German shepherds is satirized in Alexander Kluge's film *Yesterday Girl* (1966).

6   These traits are culled from many of the available descriptions and histories of the breeds. My favorite German shepherd profile: "He has a keen sense of humor and enjoys playful games yet, in defense of those he loves, can become a frightening adversary that one would be well advised to keep clear of" (www.germanshepherds/th http://www.germanshepherds.com/theegsd/history). I don't think Rolfi gets the joke of *Funny Games*. Which prompts me to ask: What *is* funny about these *Funny Games*? Only Paul seems to be in on the joke, and only in the original. I would say the comedy, though tenuous, resides in the darkest, the pitch-perfect blackest of black humor. When Peter and Paul vacate the vacation home because the bloody murder of little Georgie has used up the parents' potential to provide more fun ("They're spent"), it's both appalling and hilarious that they call out, like perfect houseguests, "Thanks for the driver! I'm going to put it back in the bag, okay? Thanks, have a nice evening. See you. *Ciao!*" This voice-over accompanies a lurid (and not very subtle) image of mediated violence: A car race is on television, the screen splattered with the boy's blood.

7   Although Michael Pitt and Brady Corbet in *Funny Games U.S.* do not seem very comfortable handling the boat.

8   Naomi Watts is never so unconvincing in the film as when she's trying to sound knowledgeable about Baroque opera.

9   I admit to sharing Haneke's critical regard for the Anna-and-Georg types that populate his films. In this one long exceptional take, however, they separately and together earn my deepest respect. I can't say the same for the American Ann and George.

10 I'm not (just) airing my own prejudices here. I do think the original is a more powerful, more powerfully acted film. But reviewers (e.g., Derek Elley and Anthony Lane) and moviegoers (in the form of online commentary) regularly complain about how weak and ineffectual is Tim Roth's portrayal of George. For the audiences with whom I've seen *Funny Games U.S.*, the funniest – perhaps the only funny – moment in the film is the image of George pathetically blow-drying the battery of his wife's cellphone. For these viewers, his manhood is a joke.

11 Dana Stevens observes in *Slate*: "the direct-address interludes come off as fatuous and hectoring" (www.slate.com/id/2186550). Anthony Lane says of them: "we don't feel nearly as chastened or ashamed as Haneke would like. We feel patronized, which is one of the worst moods that can beset an audience" (Lane 2008: 93).

12 I don't mean simply to trash Pitt's performance. As several critics have observed, he brings a fresh-faced charm to his portrayal of Paul that makes his horrendous actions all the more scarifying. Unlike Arno Frisch in the role, though, he is charming despite, not because of, his killer nature.

13   Also omitted: Paul's remark, when Georg wants it all to be over quickly, that "We're not up to feature film length yet." The line might have been dropped because it has a double vector, calling attention not just to the audience's desire for (as Paul goes on to say, in both versions) "a real ending, with plausible plot development"; the omitted line also highlights the writer-director's desire for more funny games to fill out his feature film, even as he self-consciously foregrounds and immanently critiques American cinema's appetite for blood and death offered up for consumption like extra-buttery popcorn.

14   "Fourth wall" is an inexact term carried over from the theater. Laura Mulvey more precisely summarizes the cinematic conventions, perfected during the classical Hollywood period, that are violated when Paul looks at the camera to remark the viewer's stake in the proceedings: "There are three different looks associated with cinema: that of the camera as it records the pro-filmic event, that of the audience as it watches the final product, and that of the characters at each other within the screen illusion. The conventions of narrative film deny the first two and subordinate them to the third, the conscious aim being always to eliminate intrusive camera presence and prevent a distancing awareness in the audience. Without these two absences (the material existence of the recording process, the critical reading of the spectator), fictional drama cannot achieve reality, obviousness and truth." As Mulvey makes clear, the art and craft of classical Hollywood cinema were designed to totally naturalize those moving pictures projected onto the big screen (Mulvey 1975: 17).

15   Jeffries (2008).

16   The official Warner's website begins and ends with two blood-splattered images nowhere seen in the film: a drop of blood trickles slowly down and off the end of the golf club; Michael Pitt and Brady Corbet, in tennis whites, stand side-by-side looking (in Pitt's case) quite menacing, their bloodied white gloves prominently displayed. We then hear him announce "It's playtime again!" (which no one says in the 2007 version – they are the only English words spoken in the 1997 original), after which the screams and screeches of John Zorn's music play endlessly. Studios today don't just fund and produce a feature film; they make it and market it. *Funny Games U.S.* was marketed as a splatter film. See wip.warnerbros.com/funnygames.

17   www.boxofficemojo.com/movies/?id=funnygames.htm.

18   See www.imdb.com/title/tt0808279.

19   Both Jeffries (2008) and John Wray (2007: 46) mention Haneke's distinctively goofy laugh, a delighted response to audience outrage.

20   More coming attractions: Besides Ron Howard's version of *Hidden* Hollywood, already mentioned, Géla Babluani's Hollywood remake of his own bleak and harrowing *13 Tzameti* (2005), scheduled for release in 2010, will no doubt provide further grist for my mill, the mechanisms of which are more explicitly detailed in section III of this essay.

21   Not that he drew much blood. The critique of Hollywood cinema the film offers is incisive but, for better or worse, the film failed in the only way that matters in Hollywood, at the box office.

22   Several commentators have remarked on these moments in the *Psycho* remake, usually associating the aviary of live birds with the butterflies (moths, really) in *Silence of the Lambs* (Jonathan Demme, 1991) and the intrusive images during Arbogast's murder with cutaway shots in other Van Sant films, as when Mike suffers narcoleptic

attacks in *My Own Private Idaho* (1991). No one to my knowledge has adequately explained them.

23   In an example of montage that Lev Kuleshov would find salutary, I remembered this moment from my first viewing of the film several years ago as a single shot: The woman was in the road and had horns!

24   For a brilliant discussion of the death drive in Hitchcock, see Lee Edelman (2004); and for the death drive in Hitchcock's *Psycho*, see Slavoj Žižek (1992). To my mind, the best cinematic illustrations of the death drive link the operations of the psyche and the cinema to the American automobile: in film noir, the two automotive death drives that end *Out of the Past* (Jacques Tourneur, 1947) and *Chinatown* (Roman Polanski, 1974); and in David Lynch's work, *Lost Highway* (1997), *Mulholland Drive* (2001), and, yes, *The Straight Story* (1999).

25   The killers are also associated with another bane of our mediated existence for the suburban moms of adolescent boys who harbor feelings of rage, aggression, and a fixation on death, the video game. When they return to the Farber home for more play, Michael Pitt's character says invitingly, "Player one, level two," then hurls the annunciatory golf ball at George. In the original, as I've already noted, Paul says in English, "It's playtime again!" before throwing the ball.

26   Lane (2008).

27   See Sigmund Freud (1961). As Laplanche and Pontalis observe about the compulsion to repeat:

> Freud sees the mark of the "daemonic" in these phenomena – the mark, in other words, of an irrepressible force which is independent of the pleasure principle and apt to enter into opposition to it. It was starting from this idea that Freud was brought to wonder whether instinct might not have a regressive character, and this hypothesis, pushed in turn to its logical conclusion, led him to see the death instinct as the very epitome of instinct. (1973: 98)

28   During a master class at Boston University, October 17, 2008.

29   Derek Elley (2007).

30   Carol Clover (1992) makes some trenchant observations about the male audience of slasher films.

31   Thinking about *Funny Games U.S.* within the framework of the woman's film might help to account for Tim Roth's weak performance: He is George Brent to Naomi Watts's Bette Davis.

32   Molly Haskell (1987) provides an excellent overview of the films and conventions of the genre. Mary Ann Doane (1987) examines female spectatorship in/of those films. Jeanine Basinger (1993) navigates the complicated mixed messages of the genre, reporting on three decades of movies addressed to women.

33   And some viewers have responded in a generically appropriate way. One presumably female reviewer (judging by the accompanying photo) at Netflix observed:

> Naomi Watts is at her absolute best as a mother terrified of the boys harming her husband or her son. As always, Watts is selling you her complete vulnerability, utterly willing to show you her soul and really dig in deep. If you rent this movie for no other reason, I would recommend it for her performance alone.

This observation by "Sway," on page four of the member reviews, is number 35 of, to date, 1,168 postings, an archive both deep and superficial indicative of the way viewers did and (mostly) did not engage with *Funny Games U.S.* Most, it seems, were pulled in by the film's cast and put off by the execution of its principles. See www.netflix.com/Movie/Funny_Games.

34   Robert Koehler remarks another genre and its subversion at work in the original, which was noted by a few Austro-German critics: "the *Heimat* film and its extolling of home-based bourgeois values." Koehler discusses "the Trojan Horse of thriller conventions" deployed in both versions and praises the remake for "[t]he arguably courageous attempt by Haneke to effectively smuggle his polemical work of antigenre into the commercial mainstream of American movies" (Koehler 2008: 56, 57).

35   Of course the death of Naomi Watts's character is not the actual end of the film. In the last scene, we see the killers start their sport anew with another wealthy household, suggesting that these end-games are ongoing.

36   Louis Althusser (1977).

References and Further Reading

Althusser, Louis: "Ideology and Ideological State Apparatus," *"Lenin and Philosophy" and Other Essays* (London: New Left Books, 1977).

Basinger, Jeanine: *A Woman's View: How Hollywood Spoke to Women, 1930–1960* (New York: Alfred A. Knopf, 1993).

Clover, Carol: *Men, Women, and Chainsaws: Gender in the Modern Horror Film* (Princeton, NJ: Princeton University Press, 1992).

Doane, Mary Ann: *The Desire to Desire: The Woman's Film of the 1940s* (Bloomington: Indiana University Press, 1987).

Edelman, Lee: *No Future: Queer Theory and the Death Drive* (Durham, NC: Duke University Press, 2004).

Elley, Derek: "*Funny Games*," Sundance Reviews posted on October 20, 2007, www.variety.com/index.asp?layout=festivals&jump=review&id=2471&reviewid=VE1117935140&cs.

Freud, Sigmund: *Beyond the Pleasure Principle*, trans. James Strachey (New York and London: W. W. Norton, 1961).

Haskell, Molly: "The Woman's Film," *From Reverence to Rape: The Treatment of Women in the Movies* (Chicago: Chicago University Press, 1974; reprinted 1987), pp. 153–88.

Jeffries, Stuart: "Master Manipulator," *The Guardian*, March 31, 2008, Arts Section, p. 23.

Koehler, Robert: "*Funny Games*," *Cineaste* 33:2 (Spring 2008): 55–7.

Lane, Anthony: "Recurring Nightmare," *The New Yorker*, May 17, 2008, pp. 92–3.

Laplanche, J. and Pontalis, J.-B.: *The Language of Psychoanalysis*, trans. Donald Nicholson-Smith (New York: W. W. Norton, 1973).

Mulvey, Laura: "Visual Pleasure and Narrative Cinema," *Screen* 16:3 (Autumn 1975): 6–18.

Stevens, Dana: "Michael Haneke's *Funny Games*: Feel Like Being Tortured by a Movie?," www.slate.com/id/2186550.

Wray, John: "The Minister of Fear," *New York Times Magazine*, September 23, 2007, pp. 46–9.

Žižek Slavoj: "'In His Bold Gaze My Ruin Is Writ Large,'" *Everything You Always Wanted to Know About Lacan But Were Afraid to Ask Hitchcock*, ed. Slavoj Žižek (London and New York: Verso, 1992), pp. 209–72.

PART IV

The French-Language Theatrical Features

22

Class Conflict and Urban Public Space

Haneke and Mass Transit

Barton Byg

This essay will compare Haneke's scene of class confrontation, paranoia, and threat of violence in the Paris metro from *Code Unknown* (2000) with two other "canonic" uses of "cross-section" groups of people in a public conveyance: the debate over colonialism in the S-Bahn scene at the end of Bertolt Brecht and Slatan Dudow's left-wing Weimar cinema classic, *Kuhle Wampe* (1931), and Pepe Danquardt's 1993 short film *Schwarzfahrer*, which, in addition to winning numerous festival awards, has been promoted for international educational use, especially by German teachers, for its purportedly "anti-racist" narrative. My premise for this comparison arises from a number of sources. Its proximate inspiration was a presentation at Washington University and subsequent book chapter by Fatima Naqvi on the very scene in *Code Unknown* I will treat here.

For several years now, these three pieces of film have become inextricably connected in my thinking about cinema. One connection I make in any scene set in a subway car, tram, bus, airplane, gondola, or ship is the aspiration of film to provide a "cross-section" of all of society. It may be the case that the photographic image itself, particularly of the human face, the close-up, or portrait, tends to claim a "representativeness" or typicality by its very nature, and photography has developed these associations throughout its history. Bill Nichols, in *Representing Reality*, insists on the centrality to the function of cinema of both our own experience of living in a body and the development of a system by which images of the body become generalizable.

"The cinema in general cannot leave the incarnation of characters or social actors to the viewer's imagination. An indexical bond prevails between the photographic image of the human body and the more abstract concept of historical or narrative agency," he writes (1991: 233). The image of the body is "a cultural examplar, icon, fetish, or type" (243). And elsewhere, asserting that documentary film "exerts a relentless demand of *habeas corpus*" (232), he continues: "Victims and martyrs float in the timeless realm of the illfated or exemplary."

This points toward a seeming contradiction, however. The exemplary quality of an image implies a limit – separating the individual from the mass it stands for. The image limit becomes a boundary to another world, and the static freezing of a living thing as an image implies the ultimate Otherness. To quote Nichols once more, "These terms all uphold Otherness as a precondition for their existence rather than overcome it." But, he finally asks, "How . . . can the body be both an agent and an object? How can it be testimony to life and evidence of death?" (234).

The "cross-section of society" was also a goal of the cinema since the very beginning, with the Lumière company boasting early on that films had been brought into their catalog from virtually all continents of the world. Similarly, the modernist project of August Sander, for instance, to document the "countenance of the age" (*das Antlitz der Zeit*) I have in another essay linked to the Cold War cross-section of humanity presented by Edward Steichen's Museum of Modern Art project *The Family of Man* – surely one of the best-selling photography books of all time as well as an exhibit in Moscow at the height of the Cold War. Finally, the latest installment of Michael Apted's *7-Up* (*49-Up*) appeared in 2005, extending the impulse to document a cross-section of society into the long-term project of a multi-decade chronicle, whose first installment was released in 1964.

Here is what I see is at stake in the cross-section enterprise in the context of the Cold War, both in the form of a contemporary "slice of life" cross-section and a long-term extension of the form: The assertion that photographic images of individuals *inevitably* reveal something about the typical in society – and thus have a social, scientific, and political relevance – points back to that landmark example of these assertions for photography, August Sander's *Citizens of the Twentieth Century*. Sander intended to assemble through portraits an exhaustive cross-section of all social types in Weimar Germany. John Berger has written as follows about the enduring representative character of Sander's photos:

> They each look at the camera with the same expression in their eyes; insofar as there are differences, these are the results of the sitter's experience and character – the priest has lived a different life from the paper-hanger; but to them all Sander's camera represents the same thing. . . . Sander's approach to his subjects had the result that their vanity and shyness dropped away, so that they looked into the lens telling themselves, using a strange historical sense: *I looked like this*. (Berger 1990: 31)

Despite the fact that there are a number of narratives operating in *Code Unknown*, I would argue that at key points in the film, its images also carry this photographic, documentary weight. As representatives of social experience, the images of the film's characters present more than the phenomenon of actors acting as they present their faces to Haneke's camera.

In the face of the tumultuous social change of the 1920s, August Sander's project attempts to present a stable image of society by way of rather conventional, bourgeois methods. The power of Sander's work today arises in part from the ambivalence they reveal: a belief in the emergence of a new society as capitalism seemed in collapse and the search for a refuge in the depiction of an essential *Germanness* (Keller 1994: 15).

Edward Steichen's exhibition "The Family of Man" reveals a similar endeavor to present a cross-section of humanity, but at a much higher level of technology. After the devastation of World War II and in the shadow of the atomic bomb, these images were to confirm the unity of humanity in the eyes of the American middle class, despite the anxieties of the Cold War. The progression from Sander to Steichen also reminds us that the apparatus producing long-term or cross-section films is neither historically nor ideologically neutral. Steichen's use of portrait photography was explicitly connected to the Cold War context both in its technical and aesthetic origins (as Eric Sandeen has analyzed them) and in its own content and function. The exhibit was part of the Moscow exhibition of technical accomplishments from the United States that was the backdrop for Khrushchev and Nixon's famous "Kitchen debate." And the ultimate threat to stability presented by the Cold War was visible on the central panel of the exhibit (but not reproduced in the popular book version): a photograph of the mushroom cloud of an atomic explosion (cf. also Byg 2001: 133–4).

From the Lumières' short films gathered from all the world, it was also just a short step to the *Kammerspielfilm* (chamber film), where the "typical" is presented in a closed world both in spatial and social terms. But with the City Symphonies of the 1920s we are already nearer to the theme of this essay: *Berlin – Symphony of a Great City*, *Man with a Movie-Camera*, *Rien que les heures* – these films, I would argue, posit a unity between the cinema itself and the representation and self-representation of the city which colors our perception of Haneke's city views. How Haneke comments on, and extends or contravenes this "totalizing" project is one of the questions I wish to pose.

What all these "cross-section" films have in common, I am positing, is an expectation of conflict, violence, even catastrophe, which forms the external limit that gives structure to their internal organization: For *The Family of Man*, it is the mushroom cloud (and we see a child's drawing of a mushroom cloud early on in Haneke's 1983 film *Variation* as well). For Cavalcanti's *Rien que les heures* it is the abjection of a lone, poor old woman on the street. For *Berlin*, it is the suicide, but also the vortex of advertisements, fireworks, and amusements (and Danquart's *Schwarzfahrer* seems to quote the mechanical and geometrical anomie of the streetcars passing each other from Ruttmann's work as well). For *Man with a Movie-Camera* the violent limit is perhaps the close-up of the carbon arc of the film projector itself.

Other precedents for this "cross-section of humanity" and its link to destruction are found in literature and myth, social history, and film history. Aside from the anthropological or cinematic cross-section that the history of cinema presents us, a narrative convention in literature is a randomly chosen group of people confined in a traveling vessel. In literature, the examples here are legion, from Noah's Ark to the ferry of Charon across the River Acheron to the land of the dead. This resonates with the medieval satire *Das Narrenschiff* ("Ship of Fools") of 1494, by Sebastian Brant (and the novel and film borrowing the name in the twentieth century). After Brant describes 110 assorted representative follies and vices that flesh is heir to, the fools do not go to the land of the dead, but rather to the island of Narragonia, the island of fools. Linking it perhaps in the images of social and colonial outsiders to the cross-sections we have seen here, the *Literary Encyclopedia* calls *Das Narrenschiff* "the first book in European literature to mention 'naked men on sparkling gold islands' in the New World."

Other social cross-sections in literature would be *Pilgrim's Progress*, *Canterbury Tales*, and, regarding destruction as an organizing aesthetic principle, Kleist's *Erdbeben in Chile* ("Earthquake in Chile") and Thornton Wilder's *Bridge of San Luis Rey*. First published in 1927, the latter is very much contemporary with the City Symphonies and the work of August Sander. Wilder's presentation of the catastrophe as an *image* on the one hand, and as a sociological and philosophical puzzle on the other, seems relevant here.

Part 1 of Wilder's text, "Perhaps an Accident," begins thus:

> On Friday noon, July the 20th, 1714, the finest bridge in all Peru broke and precipitated five travellers into the gulf below. . . . The bridge seemed to be among the things that would last forever; it was unthinkable that it should break. . . . People wandered about in a trance-like state muttering; they had the hallucination of seeing themselves fall into a gulf . . .
>
> Brother Juniper . . . happened to witness the accident. Anyone else would have said to himself with secret joy: Within ten minutes myself. . . . ! But it was another thought that visited Brother Juniper: Why did it happen to *those* five?
>
> If there were any plan in the universe at all, if there were any pattern in a human life, surely it could be discovered mysteriously latent in those lives so suddenly cut off. Either we live by accident and die by accident, or we live by plan and die by plan. And on that instant Brother Juniper made the resolve to inquire into the secret lives of those five persons, that moment falling through the air, and to surprise the reason of their taking off.
>
> It's the hallucination that haunts the average person; it's the image of those five falling through the air, that occupies Brother Juniper. (Wilder 1928: 3–6)

Closer to my chosen locus for the social cross-section in urban space, though, is E. M. Forster's 1908 story "The Celestial Omnibus." Here, a boy discovers a fantastic nocturnal omnibus down a dark alley, under a sign that reads "To Heaven." Taking the fantastic ride by night, he discovers the living souls who are the authors and characters of the books his didactic tutor Mr. Bons has been forcing him to read (Achilles is there, too, by the way). The unimaginative Mr. Bons, unable to "see with the heart" as the boy is, demands to return home halfway through the journey they take on the omnibus together, and falls, literally and not in fantasy, to his death on the city street, crying, as he falls, "I see London." The fantasy fiction ends with the Greek word TELOS – then the story's register shifts to the journalistic, ending with a newspaper notice of a body found on a London street (Forster 1923: 83).

The class conflict, paranoia, and fear of disaster I'm locating in these social cross-sections are also found in the social history of mass transit, particularly the history of the Paris omnibus. Here I'm relying primarily on the work of Masha Belenky on the omnibus and modernity.

Belenky cites three examples of nineteenth-century reactions to the advent of the Paris omnibus in 1828. Foremost is the 1842 text by Edouard Gourdon called "Physiologie de l'omnibus." Only fourteen years after the inception of omnibus service in Paris in 1828, Gourdon writes: "If I seek a personification of society, I find it entirely – truly and rightly, with its anachronisms, its nonsense, its cretinism, its folly and its self-respect – in the omnibus. . . . Everyone passes through the omnibus – to make a history of the omnibus is to make a history of society" (cited in Belenky 2007: 411). Belenky also renders an excerpt from an 1856 letter by Gustave Flaubert as follows: "Since the invention of omnibuses, the bourgeoisie is dead; yes, it sat there, on the people's seat, and it stays there, resembling the rabble in their souls, in their looks, and even in their clothes."[1] And finally, according to Belenky, "There is a Guy de Maupassant short story from 1884 called 'The Dowry,' in which a young petit-bourgeois woman from the provinces takes a Parisian omnibus and is overwhelmed by the proximity of lower-class passengers – who are metonymically represented through their various unpleasant odors" (cf. Belenky 2007: 418).[2]

All of Belenky's descriptions of the omnibus apply to the conveyances we've seen in the films I am discussing here. It is "emblematic of changing perceptions of time and space, it appears as a ravenous monster whose enormous size and indiscriminate palate fostered chaos and disorder, both on the streets of Paris and within the established social order" (408–9), it represented "the erotics of the public, yet menacingly intimate space" (414), offering what Maupassant termed an *"intimité rapide"* – a rapid intimacy (ibid.). It brought the classes together, but was primarily needed to serve the "ever-increasing need for working people to circulate throughout the city"; as its name says, it was "for everybody" (409). "It traveled along fixed routes and had no pre-assigned stops." The names of the vehicles were exotic and evocative: "Les Algériennes (in reference to the Algeria campaign, which was about to begin), Les Sylphides, Les Gazelles, Les Ecossaises: The deductive names, evocative of the feminine, the ephemeral, the mysterious, the exotic and the fleeting" (410).

Belenky's final citation of Gourdon is strikingly cinematic in its description of the omnibus as a fantastic monster: "The lanterns of the omnibus throw green and yellow reflections across its voyagers, attaching to a visage here and there, a hat, a profile, a cravat, a hand, and outlines them vigorously in the night." And later: "We have become Lilliputians, then something of darkness and uniformity, then nothing at all: the rays of the lantern no longer reach us" (417).

In contrast to these various violent borders to society, or the threat of loss and the abyss implied by the "cross-section" experience described here, Marc Augé's "ethnological" description of the metro seems almost optimistic. Augé's emphasis on flow, correspondences, and a resulting "social totality" does not have the cinematic positing of a violent inside/outside construction I am outlining here.

A journey to the beyond is suggested by the cross-section – conflict between insider and outsider, uncertainty and negotiation regarding status and identity, and a realm of conflict and paranoia that may lead to violence and even death. Looking at each example we could ask why they always include the far-flung, bringing the issues of globalization into the local realm of public space. Who actually provokes the threat of violence – by their words or actions or even by their very presence? What comes from the outside – either news, images, or people themselves? Or is the source of conflict the result of the power and class differentials themselves, become visible because they are seen through human representatives in an intimate yet public space? *Kuhle Wampe* sets the parameters here, with a social cross-section strikingly reminiscent of August Sander: Class, space, confinement, range of attitudes, indifference and engagement, interest, belligerence, colonialism, and capitalism, all are present.

As perhaps the most directly "Brechtian" work in film history, *Kuhle Wampe* is famous for its fragmented narrative and analytic, almost geometric arrangement of plot developments. It begins with a family facing unemployment and poverty in Weimar Germany, and very early on the son in the family is shown committing suicide after being unable to find work. Subsequent narrative strands follow the eviction of the family from their home, their settlement in a lakeside tent colony called Kuhle Wampe, and the vicissitudes of the relationship between the young woman Anni (played by Herta Thiele) and her lover Fritz (played by Ernst Busch). Rather than neat plot resolutions, however, the film ends with the young couple joining a workers' athletic event outside Berlin. A final scene depicts a debate over the world economic crisis conducted by a cross-section of society in an urban railway car as its occupants return to Berlin. As a variety of political positions are voiced, the speakers are arranged in shots composed in a documentary, analytical style, with the camera "dissecting" the interior to reveal the range of social positions. Global politics is thus placed within the geometric dynamics of an enclosed mass-transit space.

The colonial is made physical, not through the presence of physical bodies, but through the topic under dispute – an agricultural product: coffee. "If we had colonies, we would have coffee, too," says one man. "We grow so many grapes along the Rhine, why not some coffee?," says another. The threat of violence comes from the verbal assertion that there is a problem that arises from the international arrangement of the economy: *"Hetze,"* the colonialist calls this debate. And the leftist youth calls the same man's own position *Hetze* – incitement.[3]

Pepe Danquart's film *Schwarzfahrer* has become emblematic of the contemporary German processing of ethnic conflict arising around migration, but in ways

I find very problematic, especially in contrast to Haneke's films. Danquart's film won an Oscar® in 1994 for Best Short Film (live action), was screened at more than sixty film festivals all over the world (Berlin, Cannes, Sundance), and won over thirty awards.

The plot of the film is both simple and clever: A group of people wait on a plaza for a tram, and then get on. Among them is a white man in jacket and tie whose motor scooter will not start and seems to fear being late for work; he boards the tram without a ticket. Since the tram is rather full, a young black man takes a seat next to an old white woman over her objections. She is wearing rather too much make-up or powder, which makes her seem all the whiter and even unstable, as her rant of racist clichés quickly confirms. Speaking to no one in particular, but loudly, she accuses "them" of all manner of moral and physical improprieties, including overpopulating the planet and overrunning the country. Almost all the other passengers do their best to ignore the situation, with a few exceptions. A boy of seven or so seems to find the person of color fascinating and observes the exchange closely; an older man nods in passive agreement to some of the woman's remarks; the two "Turkish boys" are seen from the other end of the car, reacting to the woman's taunts from time to time, with some implied threat of aggression on their own part. In the mild disruption caused when a uniformed man boards the car to spot-check for tickets, the black man surreptitiously and quickly grabs the woman's ticket and devours it, then calmly displays to the checker his own monthly transit pass. In a scene of general hilarity to film audiences, the woman implausibly protests that "this negro has gobbled up" her ticket, and is thus expelled from the tram as a "fare dodger" (Schwarzfahrer) while the really guilty party, the white "businessman," is able to breathe a sigh of relief. The black man, too, is able to travel on – resuming his gaze out the window.

In instructional materials, distributed by Inter Nationes and the Goethe Institute, an overview of the film is given, from which I will cite two excerpts: First, "The clear satirical emphasis justifies the film's clichés and unmasks them. This begins with the stark juxtaposition of old and young. It is the older people who are shown to be intolerant. . . . That reality looks different and racist positions are not a generational question is no argument against the satirical method." At the same time, the text continues, "Schwarzfahrer presents a microcosm of a silent majority who simply ignore what is happening."[4]

The workbook for students of German and film goes on to present a list of characters, for whom the language learners are to provide descriptions of appearance and speculation on their daily activities. The translation of the title as Black Rider, rather than the other translation seen on the film, "fare dodger," emphasizes the skin color of the victim/protagonist, but only the "two Turkish boys" are identified according to ethnicity by the list of characters in the exercise. "Young Turkish Germans" is not an option supplied by the worksheet, nor does it attempt to describe either the black passenger or the older white woman who taunts him. He is merely "one of the young men listening to music" as the tram arrives.

Although this highly effective and entertaining short film shares some of the themes of the other works treated here, I believe it does so in a way that fails to question its own satirical presumptions, despite the apologies offered by the instructional worksheet. The problem is that the film is presented as transparent in its depiction of a social interaction, while I would argue that it is the film and its reception (even its employment for German instruction) that should be subjected to scrutiny. For instance, the cleverness of the film allows the audience to distance themselves from the apathetic passengers, even though, as the elderly woman helplessly pleads with the man in uniform, "they all saw" what was happening. Furthermore, the aggression against an outsider, expressed by the old woman, could be felt to be more than enough provocation for physical aggression by the purported "outsiders" as the film's closed-off space presents them – the young man next to her and the two young men at the other end of the car. In the end, albeit in comic and mild form, physical violence *is* perpetrated by the purported non-European, yet a predominantly white audience is allowed to identify both with this revenge fantasy and with the stability offered by the relative remoteness of the East German setting and the marginalized taunter, and the benign intervention of the man in uniform. (The more neutral epithet used by the old woman, *Neger*, which could translate as "negro," is even escalated into the most offensive N-word in the English subtitles.) The "black rider" is presumed by the speaker to be non-German, but the teaching materials don't raise the possibility that he could be an Afro-German – or even from the former GDR where the film is set. The actor who plays this character, Paul Outlaw, is actually American. And in none of the teaching materials or general critical commentary I have seen for the film is any attention called to the fact that East Berlin is clearly the location (identifiable by the trademark Alexanderplatz TV tower in establishing shots and the very presence of streetcars – long ago replaced by buses in West Berlin).

The passivity of the "silent majority" is presented by the film, and may be the socially critical aspect, implying a readiness to stand by silently while witnessing injustice against someone perceived as "foreign." But it is unclear where the *agency* demonstrated by the African American rider in the film will lead outside the confines of the narrative. If the impact of the film is to unify the audience in opposition to racism as verbally pronounced in public by female retirees in East Germany, it is not taking many risks. I suspect, on the other hand, that the function of its wide reception has been to portray Germany and especially its film culture as globally hip and non-racist – but at the expense of the film's characters and East Berlin.

If there is a subtle liberatory message in the film, I find it not in the unflattering cross-section of the people on the tram or the comedy of audience solidarity against overt racism, but in the longing expressed by the few shots between and outside the trams. For instance, the dark-skinned character exchanges inscrutable, almost blank, gazes with another lone rider, a white man of approximately the same age, riding in the other direction. These images and the gaze that links them are outside the narrative space of the film, and don't tend toward comedy at all.

Comedy, one might conclude, is not a satisfactory filmic resolution to either racism or urban anomie.

In Haneke's *Code Unknown*, similarity to the history of documentary photography is found in the urban cross-section the film presents in its structure, in the highly flattened and two-dimensional construction of its street scenes and camera motion, and in the incorporation of documentary elements themselves. Prior to this film, Haneke had set dramatic turning points for two other films in the subway or tram: In *The Rebellion* (1992), the protagonist's confrontation with a privileged military officer riding in a tram precipitates the revolt of the title – perhaps because it is in the space of public transport that status inequality is most visibly manifest in urban society. In *Variation*, Georg and Anna are literally thrown together in "accelerated intimacy" in a crowded subway car, with a shot composition virtually identical to the image of a young couple in the urban railway car of *Kuhle Wampe*.

In *Code Unknown* all the themes traced so far are present, but reduced, often only suggested. The images of death and catastrophe from Georges's war photography are juxtaposed with his cross-section photographs of faces, which he surreptitiously collects on the subway. Here, the "accelerated intimacy" gives way to a distanced intimacy – technical, surreptitious, yet also human and even moving.

But the confrontation between Anne and two young Arab men in the subway returns to both the theme of violence and "accelerated intimacy." The threat of violence comes from one of the young men – largely in verbal form – and culminates in a reciprocated violence of an older "non-white" man who comes to Anne's defense – resulting again in a poignant and contemplative "accelerated intimacy."

Naqvi describes the scene (the fortieth) in both narrative and cinematic terms. As a narrative: "Now a young man of North African descent confronts Anne on the subway, flirting with her. When she refuses his attentions, he mocks the other passive passengers. He follows her as she remains silent and finds another seat; eventually he spits in her face" (2007: 240). It is relevant that most of the verbal aggression of the young man is accessible by means of the soundtrack, since he is virtually invisible in the distance at the end of the subway car. His taunts of Anne for being racist in her refusal to engage with a "little Arab looking for a little affection" are delivered in vivid, fluent, and highly inventive French – with a great deal of sociological sophistication about the contradictions of class and race. But since we are unable to see his face clearly as he speaks, this invective almost hovers over the subway car like a voice-over narration – especially since Anne and the other passengers are silent all the while. Naqvi connects the film language in this scene with the "camera's lack of identification with any of the figures" in the film:

> It also remains at a distance from them in long shots, emphasizing on a metalevel what the young Arab perceives as a lack of human respect. He, too, is shown first at a great remove, in a long shot where he and Anne take up less than a quarter of the screen, both caught in the vanishing point of the subway car (the camera

moves slightly, but, like the other passengers, refrains from involvement). In a reverse projection, the beautiful Anne becomes at once supermodel and arrogant high-society woman for him. He returns the contempt he assumes she has for him, following her down the aisle, sitting next to her in the foreground, then suddenly pivoting in his seat and spitting in her face. Anne's contempt, which was perhaps latent previously, will presumably be engendered or strengthened by the young man's actions. Only the intervention of a nonwhite stranger, who kicks the ruffian as he dashes out of the subway car and yells in Arabic, may modify her negative perceptions. (241)

I believe one can go further than Naqvi here in seeing the violence and exclusion on the one hand and the "accelerated intimacy" and class solidarity on the other in cinematic and photographic terms. Unlike *Schwarzfahrer*, Haneke's framing is reminiscent of *Kuhle Wampe* in using geometry to intensify our awareness of the construction of social and physical space. First, the young man's last taunts – and his final physical threat to attack – go across the boundary between onscreen and offscreen. The fact that almost all of the sound in the scene seems to come from "off" exaggerates the dramatic tension. But the young man's space is marginalized in all cases – from the distance of the long shot, to the edge of the close-up space (in the same long-shot frame), to finally and irrevocably offscreen left. In contrast to this dramatic transgression of the frame's edge, however, are the carefully framed images of Anne and her defender as the confrontation reaches its peak and after it has subsided. These, like Georges's photographs, are reminiscent of August Sander's work, and are equally evocative. Much social information can be read in the moments of relative stasis, tense as they are, first when the young man sits next to Anne and looks out the window, or when the image frames only his hand at lower left. The older man's hand on his own chest, calling attention to the worker's undershirt beneath, offers by contrast a social mediation. The hand is a gesture of peace but also a tool and a potential weapon, yet the man can presumably identify to some degree with all sides of the dispute. But as he prepares to confront the threatening youth, the older man across the aisle from Anne removes his glasses in a gesture reminiscent of the depiction of the suicide's leap in *Kuhle Wampe*. In that film, the young man carefully protects objects of value before jumping from the window – setting his mother's potted plants aside and placing his watch carefully on the windowsill. As a notable example of Brecht's "social gestus," the action underscores the irony that the boy's labor, and thus his life, has no value while the physical objects do. Removal of the glasses in Haneke's metro scene reduces the man's body to an instrument – either of attack or defense – and his kick at the young man further mediates between Anne inside and the youths outside the car. The exchange of looks between Anne and her defender is intense (they avoid letting their eyes meet), as is the verbal acknowledgment of solidarity – Anne's quiet "thank you." Both the allies look miserable and Anne even begins to weep.

This visual expulsion of the young man from the car – as a suggestion of his Otherness, jettisoning him into the void – arises from the logic of cinema itself, especially in the framing practices reminiscent of the silent cinema and the documentary considerations of film and photography in that era. As with *Kuhle Wampe* and *Schwarzfahrer*, the outsider is more physical and three-dimensional while the insiders are present mainly as images. This is even underscored by the young man's threat of violence coming first from extreme distance in deep focus and finally in the form of an offscreen voice. His attack is to spit in Anne's face, while the attack in *Schwarzfahrer* is for the young black man to devour the old woman's ticket (after having eaten nuts during the ride). The Other's physicality is expelled in *Code Unknown* in the too-close foreground and offscreen into an unseen and fundamentally unrepresentable space. The "portrait" character of the images, as in the social cross-sections I have been discussing here, is juxtaposed with a geometric stress on the border to the outside of the cinematic space.

Here I will conclude with the assertion again that the organizing principle of the cross-section that is represented within the car is the catastrophe that resides outside it.

To use two terms from Bill Nichols, the Other is either death or history: When a film moves along the axis of structural options away from myth or narrative in the direction of discursive dispersal, the anxiety and threat of instability increase. As Nichols asks: "How . . . can the body be both an agent and an object? How can it be testimony to life and evidence of death?" (1991: 234). "Death is the deduction or cessation of something within, unseen" (237). Death – or perhaps history – is the otherness of the offscreen. Here Nichols quotes Fredric Jameson: "History is *not* a text, not a narrative, master or otherwise. . . . History is what hurts, it is what refuses desire and sets inexorable limits to individual as well as collective praxis." Nichols concludes: "A magnitude of excess remains. It is a specter haunting what can be said or written" (231).

The man and the woman looking straight ahead after the violent confrontation on the metro return to documentary, and the composition invites the viewer to read them as portraits. Naqvi's emphasis on extra-cinematic possibilities of this shot confirms this, since they are speculations on the portraits and the situation, not on any exposition that has been provided. The man may have intervened because "he is embarrassed by the behavior of a fellow Arabic-speaker, or, alternatively, he has perhaps been the recipient of humiliating treatment as a member of a minority" (2007: 242). Still a third possibility is that he feels forced, against his will, to threaten violence against a younger "foreign" male as a way of affirming his identification with Anne (and with the presumed viewer of the film) in terms of age, education or profession, and class. The hybrid combination of the worker's undershirt with the briefcase and glasses places him in a position between the insider and the outsider in this circumstance.

At the conclusion of the scene, it is their portraits, however, that we are left to contemplate. Naqvi stresses that we could read some ethnic and experiential background into the mere casting of Maurice Bénichou as the male commuter; on the other hand, the evening out of the narrative structure and visual style of the film diminishes, in her view, the "star" quality of Juliette Binoche (Naqvi 2007: 250).

For these reasons, I have been insisting on the relevance of documentary and portrait photography for an understanding of the economy of images in *Code Unknown*. An example is the juxtaposition of the "photomontages" of the character Georges with the other scenes in the film. The first is in color, showing in fragmented framing the bodies of female victims of violence in Kosovo. These images are challenged in the dialog of the film, which asks whether they actually can have an effect in the world, since they compete in an economy of instantly transmitted, similar images. Naqvi writes here of the "paradox of incommunicability": "The images do not evoke a sense of difference from other conflicts" (2007: 246). This dilemma, however, is narratively juxtaposed with the cross-section photos Georges takes secretly in the subway, which are presented to the viewer carefully framed in black and white – "endowed with a quiet dignity" (247). These photos occupy a space that I would argue is both local and global, but to which the violence of Kosovo is narratively outside. Naqvi sees a potential alternative to the indifference of the global media here: "[T]he new portrait series shows an interest in – and not indifference to – the local and the immediate, in its extreme diversity" (247).

But the documentary cross-section these photos represent is crucial here. We do not see them as a part of a narrative, or even as cause-and-effect results of Georges's actual actions of photographing. They are portraits from a place but also signs of the "non-place" that is the subway. Their presentation explicitly calls attention to their existence as portraits – suggestive of August Sander or, for Naqvi, Walker Evans (247). They are also documents of the fiction film's own incompleteness, since they are the work of the photojournalist Luc Delahaye (252).

I believe it is the separateness of these cross-section portraits from the external violence that structures the film which allows the film to, as Naqvi puts it, "partially restore the trajectories that have brought the people in the photo series together in the Parisian Métro, a fragmentary restoration of lives beyond national borders" (248). Augé, too, places in the metro the social-scientific observation that people, as members of a social totality, "only gain self-consciousness by gaining consciousness of others" (2002: 39). The presence of a diverse assemblage of solitary travelers in the metro is, for Augé, made possible by a "contractual" arrangement – all have a ticket to ride, all are going somewhere. Aggression and violence, however, are even here the implicit and structuring alternative: "The theme of insecurity in the Métro would not be so widespread, nor the reactions to any provocation or aggressive behavior so spirited, were not the idea of contractual consensus essential to the definition of this institution" (44).

For Haneke's subways, as for urban spaces in general, such a contractual consensus is fragile indeed. The code that would explain the connections between inside the narrative and outside is unknown. But beyond that, the unknown code that shows the otherness of violence at the edges of visual space in the mass-transit conveyance – the pain of history – is unknown in fundamental cinematic, representational, and urban terms. But that, too, is the faint reassurance the film can offer us.

Acknowledgments

For valuable suggestions and feedback on this essay I am grateful to Masha Belenky, Roy Grundmann, Robert Sullivan, Evan Torner, and my co-panelists at the "Cinema of Provocation" conference: Odile Cazenave, Tom Conley, Alex Lykidis, Leland Monk, and Kevin Stoehr.

Notes

1 Private correspondence with the author, October 10, 2007, citing Flaubert's letter to Louise Colet, 1856 (my translation).
2 Quotation here from private correspondence with the author, October 10, 2007.
3 English from the DVD subtitles, DEFA Film Library/University of Massachusetts Amherst, 2008. *Hetze*, however, is translated as "agitation" on the DVD.
4 My translation. The original German is as follows:

> Die erkennbare satirische Verdichtung rechtfertigt die Klischees des Films und demaskiert sie: Das beginnt bei der pauschalen Kategorisierung von Alt und Jung; es sind die älteren Menschen, die hier der Intoleranz bezichtigt werden, während die Jugendlichen die schimpfende Frau einfach ignorieren und der kleine Junge ihrem Opfer zulächelt. Dass die Realität anders aussieht und rassistische Positionen keine Frage von Generationen sind, ist kein Einwand gegen die satirische Methode. . . . Gleichzeitig führt "Schwarzfahrer" den Mikrokosmos einer schweigenden Mehrheit vor, die das Geschehen einfach ignoriert.

References and Further Reading

Augé, Marc: *Un ethnologue dans le métro* (Paris: Hachette, 1986); *In the Metro*, trans. Tom Conley (Minneapolis: University of Minnesota Press, 2002).

Belenky, Masha: "From Transit to *Transitoire*: The Omnibus and Modernity," *Nineteenth-Century French Studies* 3:2 (2007): 408–21.

Berger, John: "The Suit and the Photograph," *About Looking* (New York: Pantheon, 1990), pp. 31–40.

Brant, Sebastian: *Das Narrenschiff. Literary Encyclopedia*, www.litencyc.com/php/sworks.php?rec=true&UID=22997.

Byg, Barton: "GDR-Up: The Ideology of Universality in Long-Term Documentary," *New German Critique* 82 (2001): 126–44.

D'Alessio, Germana: *Goethe Institut Arbeitsblatt: Deutsche Spielfilme der neunziger Jahre* (Munich: Goethe Institut, 2000).

Forster, E. M.: "The Celestial Omnibus," *The Celestial Omnibus and Other Stories* (New York: Alfred A. Knopf, 1923).

Keller, Ulrich: "Sander und die Portraitphotographie," *August Sander – Menschen des 20 Jahrhunderts – Portraitphotographien 1892–1952* (Munich: Schirmer/Mosel, 1980/1994), pp. 11–18.

Naqvi, Fatima: "The Politics of Contempt and the Ecology of Images: Michael Haneke's *Code inconnu*," *Cosmopolitan Screen: German Cinema and the Global Imaginary, 1945 to the Present*, ed. Stephan K. Schindler and Lutz Koepnick (Ann Arbor: University of Michigan Press, 2007), pp. 235–52.

Nichols, Bill: *Representing Reality: Issues and Concepts in Documentary* (Bloomington: Indiana University Press, 1991).

Sandeen, Eric: *Picturing an Exhibition: The Family of Man and 1950s America* (Albuquerque: University of New Mexico Press, 1995).

Steichen, Edward: *The Family of Man: The Greatest Photographic Exhibition of All Time, 503 Pictures from 68 Countries, Created by Edward Steichen for the Museum of Modern Art* (New York: Museum of Modern Art, 1955).

Wilder, Thornton: *The Bridge of San Luis Rey* (London: Longmans, Green, 1928).

23

Multicultural Encounters in Haneke's French-Language Cinema

Alex Lykidis

Michael Haneke's French-language films, *Code Unknown* (2000), *Time of the Wolf* (2003), and *Caché* (2005), are all concerned with the increased immigration into and multiculturalism[1] of contemporary Western European societies, and France in particular. And yet, these films seem qualitatively different from other contemporary European films about immigration and multiculturalism, such as Stephen Frears's *Dirty Pretty Things* (2002) or Michael Winterbottom's *In This World* (2002). Haneke himself provides a clue as to the nature of this difference when he says: "The interest of the spectator comes from the precision of what's shown. [My characters live] in a predominantly bourgeois milieu – this is the milieu I know best. And I speak of what I know."[2] What Haneke is admitting to here is that his work manifests a consistent and pervasive class (and racial) particularism. His French-language films focus on the lives of white, affluent Western Europeans affected by the multiculturalism of their society more so than on the lives of immigrants or minorities. This is why this essay will discuss the impact of multicultural encounters on Haneke's bourgeois protagonists rather than his cinema's representation of immigrants and minorities *per se*.

While always representing bourgeois existence as fragile and under assault, Haneke's cinema has increasingly externalized the catalysts for the breakdown of bourgeois social order. In earlier films such as *The Seventh Continent* (1989) and *Funny Games* (1997), the danger posed to bourgeois protagonists emerges claustrophobically from within their own familial and class ranks, with no external force able to either threaten them or rescue them from self-destruction. In his French-language films, by contrast, Haneke situates the threat to bourgeois existence in the real or imagined agency of immigrant or minority characters. The preoccupation with the trauma of multicultural encounters in his French-language cinema is therefore not a token acknowledgment of cultural difference but rather a more precise formulation of the dynamics of bourgeois crisis and anxiety that have concerned Haneke throughout his career.

The representation of multicultural encounters through the modality of crisis makes its first appearance in Haneke's cinema in the Egypt trip sequence of *Benny's Video* (1992). In this sequence, Benny travels with his mother to Egypt while his father covers up the murder Benny has committed back in Austria. The trip seems to be designed to absolve Benny of any guilt or shame he might feel about his heinous act, and to strengthen the strained bonds of trust between the family members. The first few scenes of the trip establish the insularity of Benny and his mother from the landscape and people of Egypt. In scenes reminiscent of another Austrian film, Peter Kubelka's *Unsere Afrikareise* (1966), Haneke juxtaposes images in which Europeans are isolated from the landscape and the people of Africa with sounds that are unable to encompass the complexity of the assembled scene. While on a tour bus, Benny is framed off from the landscape he gazes at disinterestedly, and in a later scene, Benny's mother asks him to get out of the way as she films a row of buildings, signaling how in her mind Benny does not belong in the same shot with something indicative of the local culture. Her 360-degree pan shows the ambition of her gaze, her desire to capture everything, to provide a comprehensive record of the local landscape. The droning voice of the tour guide on the bus functions similarly to the cackling and crude exclamations of the safari participants in *Unsere Afrikareise*, demonstrating the insufficiency of European discourse to capture the local realities of Africa.

In the final scenes of the Egypt trip, sound is used contrapuntally to signal the dialectic tension between bourgeois subjectivity and those forces which mark the limits of that subjectivity. While resting in his hotel room, Benny flips through the television channels, finally settling on a station playing Western liturgical/choral music (presumably, Benny chooses this because it is the least unfamiliar of sound options available to him). With a cut, we are taken to a bustling public marketplace, but the liturgical music continues, shifting from diegetic to non-diegetic sound, an expression, perhaps, of Benny's desire to extend the insularity and protectedness of the hotel room to the much more unstable and threatening space of the public marketplace. The liturgical music functions to contain the unruly sounds of the market, to colonize the foreign space with European culture. Here, as in the earlier scenes, the local population is kept in the background, captured primarily in long or full shots, marking the success of the containment that the sound bridge initiated. Two scenes later, we are back in the hotel room and this time Benny has chosen an Arabic-language pop song to listen to on TV, the first moment when the local culture threatens to overwhelm the aural or visual economy of the film. At the end of this scene, Benny's usually stoic and impassive mother breaks down uncontrollably. This is an enigmatic moment, and we can certainly interpret her breakdown as a delayed reaction to the heinousness of Benny's crime and to her complicity in its cover-up. But her breakdown may also be seen as a response to the failed demarcation of European space from non-European space, reminiscent of the final scene of Ousmane Sembène's *Black Girl* (1966), and a harbinger of the traumatic multicultural encounters that will become the dominant theme of Haneke's later films.

This essay will concern itself with the representation of such encounters in three of Haneke's French-language films: *Code Unknown*, *Time of the Wolf*, and *Caché*. I will consider the extent to which these representations both reflect and challenge the assumptions of contemporary French anti-immigrant discourse. The destabilization of bourgeois order within the diegesis of these films is mirrored by Haneke's deliberately ambiguous narrational style, which mires spectators in levels of uncertainty and anxiety similar to those experienced by his bourgeois characters. I will consider how the unease felt by Haneke's bourgeois characters and spectators alike relates to the much more profound insecurity experienced by immigrants, undocumented workers, and minorities in contemporary France. The ambiguity of Haneke's cinema can be explained as a reflection of real-world uncertainties or as a result of authorial expressivity, and in the final part of the essay I will discuss the stakes of these possible explanations for the immigrant and minority issues of interest to us here.

Modes of Address: Insecurity and Ambiguity

Whereas in the Egypt sequence of *Benny's Video* bourgeois crisis is triggered by cultural difference in the most diffuse and sublimated way, the representation of multicultural encounters in Haneke's French-language films seems to explicitly reference contemporary anti-immigrant discourses and debates. In the period between 1945 and 1970, French postwar reconstruction and high rates of economic growth kept the demand for immigrant labor high. Immigrants were encouraged to come to France through a series of immigration initiatives coordinated by the National Immigration Office (ONI), or entered the country on tourist visas and gained legal residency by obtaining work upon arrival. In both cases, they were not allowed to obtain French citizenship, without which they were not able to combat the discrimination they faced in matters of housing, employment, health care, and education. Despite their importance to the French economy, immigrants during this period were without political representation or legal recognition, neglected by the state and largely invisible to the rest of French society.[3] It was amidst the economic downturn of the 1970s that immigrants gained notoriety as social problems and threats to national security. During this time, a series of laws was passed aimed at establishing centralized and more restrictive immigration protocols, expedited repatriations, and assimilation of immigrants into the normative culture.[4] By the 1990s, it had become clear that, across party lines, immigration controls and assimilationism were the twin pillars of immigration policy in France.

Because these increasingly draconian immigration controls had to be legitimated before the public, the representation of immigrants and their situation suddenly became an important tool for both the government and the opponents of its policies – and thus extremely political. During this period, immigration was presented as a threat to national cohesion, national identity, and the security of national borders. The multiculturalism of French society was described and understood increasingly via the rhetoric of insecurity, as Jane Freedman notes:

> Immigration has become an issue that is now perceived very much in terms of "security," both in terms of the need to limit entrance to the country and in terms of the push to further integrate settled immigrants and ethnic minority communities . . . Immigration has been linked with economic difficulties – unemployment and deficits in the welfare budget, rising crime, the threat of terrorism. More fundamentally, perhaps, immigration has been seen as a threat to the very basis of national social and political cohesion, undermining French national identity and thus calling the nation-state itself into question. (2004: 8)

Opponents of immigration described it as an "invasion," a notion expressed in a 1991 article written by ex-President Valéry Giscard d'Estaing in which he stated: "the type of problem with which we are now faced has moved from one of immigration to one of invasion."[5] This type of rhetoric led the French public, when asked in polls, to routinely overestimate the number of immigrants in the country, to falsely assume that their number continues to increase, and to want fewer of them to remain in France. In fact, as a proportion of the overall population, the number of immigrants has remained relatively stable since the 1970s. The major shift has been in the percentage of immigrants of non-European origin versus those of European origin. The former are deemed less assimilable and hence less desirable, and are referred to as *immigrés* (immigrants) or *clandestins* ("illegals") instead of the less pejorative *étrangers* (foreigners) reserved for immigrants of European origin. This rhetoric of invasion, unassimilability, and illegality, apart from legitimating the exclusionary policies of the French state, has also led to widespread discrimination against immigrant and minority populations in civil society.[6]

The feelings of insecurity and anxiety felt by the French public are, according to Max Silverman, also the result of the "confrontation between [colonial] structures (institutions/ideologies) and the post-colonial migration of people and products."[7] During the colonial period, Algerians and other colonized people were legally designated as second-class citizens in their own countries and ghettoized so as to minimize their contact with the French colonizers. The French colonies were governed by a spatial, economic, political, and psychological Manicheanism, famously analyzed by Frantz Fanon in *The Wretched of the Earth*.[8] In the postcolonial period, the (continued) migration of people from the ex-colonies to France, their reunification with their families, reproduction in the country of the colonizer, and their heightened economic and political power have undermined colonial-era hierarchies and contributed to the anxiety felt by the French public. In this way, we can think of the feelings of insecurity over immigration and multiculturalism in France partially as a result of the loss of colonial privileges and partially as a result of a carefully orchestrated campaign by the dominant classes to legitimate exclusionary state policies.

The unease over immigration is also a function of the increasing prominence in contemporary French society of the children and grandchildren of immigrants, who destabilize older, primarily economic and individualist notions of immigrant identity. In the period before 1970, immigrants were seen in relation to their labor function, defined by their status as temporary workers, without families or the rights of citizenship and under the permanent threat of deportation in the case of loss of employment. Perceived in this way, immigrants did not seem to pose a threat to the dominant institutions, classes, and cultures of French society. However, many were eventually married or reunited with their families, and their children became citizens under the right of *jus soli*, which automatically grants citizenship to anyone born on French soil. Members of this new generation typically define themselves in terms of permanent, social, and familial categories rather than temporary, employment-based, and individual categories. They therefore stake a more formidable claim on the rights and privileges associated with French citizenship than previous generations, whose members were typically isolated, atomized, and without legal recourse. The 1993 repeal of the automatic granting of citizenship to children of immigrants and the recent emphasis of anti-immigrant discourse on residential spaces, such as the ghetto and the *bidonville* (shanty town or slum), rather than the workplace, signal these shifts in definition and the threat they are seen to pose to the interests of France's dominant classes.[9]

The representation of immigration and multiculturalism through the language of loss – loss of national cohesion, identity, security, and colonial-era privileges – is reflected in Haneke's French-language cinema, whose bourgeois protagonists are repeatedly stripped of their rights and privileges – life, private property, privacy, protection by the law, epistemic agency, and mastery of language. The rhetoric of "invasion" and emphasis on residential spaces in recent anti-immigrant discourse is referenced in *Time of the Wolf* and *Caché*, which feature home invasions that threaten the livelihoods and private property of the films' central characters. Immigrant and minority characters are perceived by Haneke's bourgeois protagonists as isolated figures, disconnected from their familial and communal milieu, reflecting anachronistic postwar conceptions of immigrants. Amadou's coming to the defense of Maria in *Code Unknown* and the surprising appearance of Majid's son during the police raid (and later at Georges's office) in *Caché* are disconcerting to bourgeois characters and audiences alike because they signal unforeseen allegiances that contest atomized bourgeois preconceptions of immigrants and minorities.

The postcolonial breakdown of spatial demarcations and social hierarchies is in evidence in the subway scenes of *Code Unknown* and the encampment scenes in *Time of the Wolf*, wherein bourgeois characters are forced to occupy spaces shared by people of different ethnic and class backgrounds. The perception of non-European immigrants as unassimilable is embodied by Majid in *Caché*, the unnamed boy befriended by Eva in *Time of the Wolf*, and the subway youth in *Code Unknown*, characters whose seemingly inscrutable agency confounds their bourgeois counterparts. Haneke's bourgeois protagonists often display a mastery of language when speaking amongst themselves, evident, for example, in the recounting of the disingenuous anecdote about the old lady and her dog told during the dinner party scene in *Caché*. During multicultural encounters, however, they tend to lose their ability to deceive, persuade, or intimidate others verbally, finding themselves either rendered mute (Anne in the subway in *Code Unknown*), outmaneuvered (Georges in his confrontations with the bicyclist and Majid's son in *Caché*), or cut short by violence (Anne's husband in *Time of the Wolf*). In all these ways, multicultural encounters are experienced by Haneke's bourgeois characters as sites of a traumatic loss of privilege and agency.

The opening scene of *Time of the Wolf* highlights many of these traumatic forms of loss. We see a family of four – Georges and Anne Laurent, and their children Ben and Eva – drive up to a cabin in the countryside. Upon entering the cabin, they are confronted by a man with a shotgun, his wife and child by his side.[10] After a brief exchange, the man with the shotgun shoots Georges dead and orders Anne to take her children and leave the cabin immediately. The invasion of the Laurents' country home is framed by Georges as a violation of his rights, when he tells the man with the gun: "What did you think – that this was not private property?" In the moments leading up to his death, Georges, remaining calm and level-headed, attempts to reason with the armed man, believing to the last that he is in control and that he can persuade him to accept a compromise. His final words are: "I propose this: we bring in our things, we eat . . ."[11] Devastatingly, it is at this exact moment that the man decides to kill him. The framing of the home invasion as a profound violation is partly a function of its position at the beginning of the narrative, when it is least expected. Camera placement enhances the unpredictability and inscrutability of the shooter's actions. The first interior shot shows the Laurent family entering the cabin in darkness. Positioned in the middle of the cabin, the camera does not show us the shooter or his family, so we have no forewarning of what is about to happen. We are as surprised as the Laurents when the shooter first speaks and begins to make his demands on them. During the verbal exchange before Georges is killed, the camera is placed in-between the two families, facing one or the other so that we hardly ever see the two families in the same shot. The in-between camera placement leaves spectators in a precarious position, showing us only half of the action and situating us dangerously near the line of fire.

This scene demonstrates that the anxiety felt by bourgeois characters in Haneke's cinema is mirrored by the deliberate ambiguity[12] of his narrational and compositional style, which imparts on spectators similar levels of uncertainty and unease. Following Georges's murder in *Time of the Wolf*, Anne scrambles to find some food and shelter for her family, a mission made more difficult by the post-apocalyptic conditions that prevail in the countryside. The precariousness of their situation is symbolized in a later scene when Ben's pet bird escapes from his clutches; as it flies wantonly around the shed they are staying in, its provisional freedom after a life of captivity parallels the Laurents' own plight, who find themselves free from the norms and expectations of their past life but also devoid of its privileges. Ben's frantic attempts to recapture the bird constitute a displaced expression of the family's anxiety, his nose bleed a symptom of their collective trauma. As Anne searches for food and later for Ben, who disappears, the screen is cloaked in the darkness of night, as it is later with morning fog. In the darkness, we are like Anne, attempting to piece together what is happening on the basis of limited information. The anxiety that we feel due to our limited vision is heightened by the traumatic sounds that frequently accompany these moments of darkness, such as during a later scene when we hear the anguished screams of a woman as she buries her child in the forest at night. Haneke modulates the level of light in accordance with the level of familiarity felt by his bourgeois characters during their social encounters. In the first well-lit interior scene of *Time of the Wolf*, Anne meets Bea (A meets B), a similarly-aged, urbane Parisian woman, with whom she shares a cigarette and casual conversation.

The ambiguity of *Caché* stems from a series of narrative enigmas that never get resolved: How is it possible that Georges walks by the person recording video footage of his apartment without seeing him or her? Given that both Majid and Majid's son deny their involvement in the videotaping and harassment of Georges, how did anyone manage to get into Majid's apartment to record the footage of Majid and Georges's discussion? If not Majid or his son, who is the culprit? What was the purpose of sending Georges the footage? Is Anne having an affair with Pierre? What do Pierrot and Majid's son discuss at the film's conclusion? By thwarting our investment in narrative coherence, Haneke situates us in the same predicament as his bourgeois protagonists, struggling to comprehend an increasingly inscrutable and unpredictable social world. In Haneke's universe, we are cautioned against making assumptions about what we see and hear, as narrative events are frequently revisited from a different perspective, destabilizing our earlier interpretations of them. In *Time of the Wolf*, Georges's murderer shows up with his wife in the encampment where Anne, Eva, and Ben are staying. After Anne accuses him of Georges's murder, he vociferously denies the charge. His denial sounds so heartfelt that it perhaps makes us question, even if for a moment, the murder we had earlier witnessed. If doubts do arise, they are facilitated by the lack of establishing shots in the murder sequence (other than a brief over-the-shoulder shot early on), which prevents us from recalling a moment in which both families occupied the same space. In *Caché*, each iteration of the video surveillance footage exhibits different ontological properties: video versus film, playback versus "live," footage taken by the harasser versus images of the diegetic world taken by Haneke. Each new instance of the footage causes us to reconsider our earlier interpretations, adding to the unsolveable mystery at the heart of the narrative. What is most destabilizing about each new appearance of the footage is that its ontological status is not immediately clear to us, and must be reconstructed on the basis of new information, such as the sound of Georges and Anne's voices or the signs of rewinding or fast-forwarding, which suddenly reveal its status as video playback.

There are two scenes in *Code Unknown*, in which Anne (Juliette Binoche) is shown pursuing her profession as an actress, which exemplify the ambiguity of Haneke's narrational and compositional style. In the first scene, Anne is in a room and we hear the voice of a man tell her that she has fallen into a trap. The man goes on to tell Anne that she is a prisoner and that she has been captured because he wanted to see someone die before his eyes. Even though the opening moments of the scene involve what in hindsight seem to be screen directions toward an actress, the intensity of Binoche's performance (she cries profusely at the end of the scene) and the lack of other markers that would distinguish the profilmic space as a film production set make it difficult for us to be sure what we are watching. In a later scene, we see Anne shoot the scene of being trapped in a room again, only this time Haneke shows us the cameraman and the set and we are made to understand that what we had seen before was a rehearsal for this film. A similar effect is created in a second acting scene in which we see Anne with a man in a pool. They are playfully interacting underwater when their attention is directed towards the ledge. We discover that a small boy, their son, is dangling perilously on the ledge and in danger of falling off. Anne and the man rush to the boy and save him from danger. We soon realize, however, as we see Anne and the man dubbing their dialog for the scene in a sound studio, that what we have just witnessed was another one of Anne's acting scenes.

By luring us into initially interpreting these acting scenes as diegetic "reality," Haneke cautions us against mistaking interpretation for objective truth or social construction for essence. He reveals the role of desire, subjectivity, and projection in the production of knowledge, promoting an epistemological relativism that reminds us of the opacity of social experience.[13] We realize that we are neither capable of single-handedly defining complex social realities nor have the right to do so. This challenges the universalism of European political discourse, which takes two primary contemporary forms. First, the purported universal validity of "European values" is invoked to legitimate European expansion. Ulrich Beck and Edgar Grande's definition of European cosmopolitanism calls for "the constant enlargements of the [European Union] and the export of its norms and rules."[14] Second, universal human rights rhetoric has been used to legitimate Western acts of aggression, such as the invasion of Iraq and the bombing of Serbia, that violate international law.[15] By providing us with limited narration, revisiting scenes so as to challenge our initial assumptions, and leaving key plot questions unresolved, Haneke reveals the limits of European bourgeois paradigms in explaining contemporary multicultural realities.

In the acting scenes of *Code Unknown* we can also find eerie parallels to the increasing insecurity of immigrants and minorities in French society. In the first acting scene, Anne is ensnared in a trap under false pretenses. As soon as she enters the room her right to life, privacy, and freedom is taken away from her. In this way, the scene mirrors the false postwar promises of the French state, which encouraged immigration in order to fuel reconstruction and growth but then denied immigrants the rights of citizenship. In the second acting scene, the precariousness of immigrants' rights, which have been alternately granted and taken away through a schizophrenic series of legislative acts since the 1970s, is symbolized by the child's near-fall from the balcony. In another scene we see Anne give an impassioned audition which is followed by a protracted silence from her adjudicators. While we see the casting director and his staff convene in deliberation after Anne's performance, she cannot see them in the dark, evoking the political disenfranchisement of French immigrants and minorities, who are hypervisible to the state, but the state as a tool for their empowerment remains inscrutable and out of reach.

Why do these parallels to the immigrant experience befall Anne? While the spectatorial impact of these scenes is great, their emotional effect on Anne is revealed to be minimal as we see her comfortable and laughing in the second iteration of the imprisonment scene and in the sound studio portion of the pool scene. The diegetic significance of these scenes, therefore, pales in comparison to the impact of deportation on Maria or of arrest on Amadou. We are initially lured into overvaluing our own emotional response, influenced by what we perceive to be Anne's powerlessness and distress. But when her distress is revealed to be a sign of her acting prowess, and is immediately followed by laughter and levity, the difference between the bourgeoisie's luxury to rehearse temporary deprivation through art and the constant struggles of those on the margins of society is revealed. The relief felt after realizing that what we have witnessed are harmless depictions of Anne acting reminds us of our (and her) privilege at being able to escape these realities once the fiction is over. This point of contrast is common in Haneke's cinema, differentiating between the real or perceived insecurity of bourgeois characters and the more profoundly circumscribed lives of immigrant or minority characters.

Haneke's narratives are often punctuated by momentary exposures to societal suffering on a scale that challenges the solipsism of bourgeois protagonists and spectators alike. In *Caché*, Georges and Anne's frantic search for Pierrot is set against the background of a news story about coalition forces in Iraq and the Abu Ghraib prison scandal. In *Time of the Wolf*, after Georges's death, Anne and the children visit her neighbors to ask for their help. After receiving little assistance, they come across an apocalyptic tableau consisting of a raging bonfire in whose center can be discerned the carcasses of several horses, suggesting the magnitude of deprivation and desperation that surrounds them. Later, the Laurents' situation is put in perspective by a Polish couple repeatedly accused of crimes and threatened with expulsion from the camp, whose young child dies despite its mother's public pleas for assistance. Life in the encampment is contextualized by the unnamed boy living on its outskirts, whose own social location is (perhaps willingly) even more marginal and precarious. The contrast drawn between the insecurities of bourgeois existence and the deeper deprivations of immigrant or minority experience allows Haneke to reconstruct what Lydia Morris has described as the stratification of rights in contemporary European societies. The rights of immigrants and minorities in contemporary Europe are dependent on their position in relation to a series of competing discourses and interests: national immigration controls and citizenship laws versus international minority and immigrant rights provisions, the interests of transnational capital versus those of nation-states and minority rights advocates, discrimination along the axes of gender and race versus universalist invocations of human rights, and so on. What results is social stratification, with citizens, residents, and undocumented workers occupying positions on a sliding scale of rights and privileges, with further subdivisions according to gender, race, and national background.[16] It is this social hierarchy that Haneke allows us to reflect on in those moments when the personal stories of his bourgeois protagonists are framed against a background of more profound social devastation and deprivation.

In *Caché*, Haneke induces spectators to become invested in the whodunit machinations of the narrative, only to systematically unravel this pretense by revealing its basis in the troubled subjectivity of the film's protagonist, Georges. This is achieved through the interweaving of Georges's childhood memories of Majid into the playback of the surveillance footage sent by Georges's harasser. These memory-images, along with the partial confessions coaxed out of him by his wife, Anne, help us to reconstruct Georges's culpability in the childhood expulsion of Majid from his family home. Majid's story is also situated in a broader historical context when we discover that his parents were possibly killed in the infamous slaughter of Algerian immigrants by Paris police on October 17, 1961. All this makes us question the righteousness of Georges's quest to find his harasser, culminating in the two meetings between Georges and Majid, when we come to realize that Georges's anxiety over his harassment is incommensurate with the unbearable torment of Majid's lifelong suffering. Majid does not come across as a harasser but as a victim, casting doubt on Georges's memories of Majid as a menacing child and on his current accusations against him. As in *Code Unknown*, we are lured into initially overvaluing the apparent distress of the film's bourgeois protagonist, only to later realize that it is a function of bourgeois privilege (the catharsis of acting, the legacies of colonialism). By miring us in the flawed and incomplete images of the world produced by the distorted lens of bourgeois consciousness, Haneke exposes the racialist and exclusionary core lurking underneath the pretense of universality of French republicanism.[17] As Max Silverman summarizes it:

> The idea of a common and trans-historical culture defining the French nation has been a powerful means of racialising the "French people" . . . [there has been a] continual

presence of an ambivalent discourse of culture in the formation of the modern French nation-state; its effect has been both to preach inclusion according to universalist criteria and to practise exclusion through racialising the French community and its Other. (1992: 9)

The contemporary rhetoric of insecurity, which has argued for the supposed unassimilability of immigrants of non-European origin, has further racialized French national identity. Indeed, despite the seeming colorblindness of republicanism, French citizenship has always been predicated on the assumption that immigrants and new citizens will assimilate into the dominant culture. In the 1980s, a consensus was reached across party lines that immigration was a national crisis whose solution required the state "to integrate or assimilate immigrants into French society through an application of universalist principles which reject any type of recognition of community or ethnic difference."[18] Both the insistence on assimilation and the rejection of some groups as unassimilable demonstrate what Alec Hargreaves calls the "hard core of contingency lurking behind the principled exterior of French republicanism."[19] It is this hard core of contingency that the class and racial particularism of Haneke's cinema brings to the fore. Georges's zealous pursuit of Majid, which appears to precipitate Majid's suicide, demonstrates how the illusion of insecurity at the heart of bourgeois subjectivity motivates retributive policies and actions that create real-life insecurity for immigrants and minorities. As Freedman asserts:

> Paradoxically, whilst the debate over immigration has portrayed policies and legislation designed to limit immigration as safeguarding France's security, it might be argued that these same laws and policies have created an increasingly vulnerable and insecure situation for many of those of immigrant origin currently living in France. And not only has the security of immigrants been affected negatively by increasingly exclusionary policies, the very construction of the discursive boundaries between the French "us" and the foreign "them" in current rhetoric and debates over immigration [has] had an effect in increasing insecurity for migrant and ethnic minority communities living on French territory. (2004: 8)

Modes of Authority: The State and Authorship

Ambiguity has long been associated with art cinema. But it is argued that art films recuperate narrative coherence and mitigate against the radical and destabilizing potential of their ambiguity through recourse to one of two modes of authority: verisimilitude and authorship. Under the logic of verisimilitude, ambiguity is explained as a reflection of real-life uncertainties and instabilities.[20] The uncertainty and instability of our lives are a function of many factors, including levels of material scarcity and economic exploitation, spatial arrangements and social hierarchies, and relations to natural environment and political authority – the state and its accordant institutions and laws. As we will see, the state plays a particularly import-ant role in the production of uncertainty and instability in Haneke's cinema, but not in the way we might expect. To understand this better we need to consider the extent to which Haneke's cinema reflects the symbiotic relationship between the dominant classes and the state in contemporary France.[21]

The close relationship between the state and France's dominant classes dates back to pre-revolutionary times, when the loyalty of the noble classes was obtained through the sale of tax collection and military and fiscal offices. In this way, the state "absorbed ever greater layers of the population into its orbit: political accu-mulation was thus a defining feature of the *ancien régime* state."[22] The expansion of the state bureaucracy in the Napoleonic era did nothing to loosen the bonds between the state and the nobility. New state positions were dominated by pre-vious officeholders, with mobility for the lower orders of civil servants severely limited.[23] When, in the 1850s, the French state was finally oriented toward capitalist development (its parasitic taxation of the peasantry and expansionist war campaigns having impeded capitalist development until then), it shifted its allegiance from the nobility to the bourgeoisie.[24] Other than a brief period of crisis in the period after World War I, the bourgeoisie has enjoyed unrivaled access to state offices and privileges ever since. As Ezra Suleiman states:

> the gradual democratization of [French] society has scarcely affected the ways in which the society's elites are selected, the nature of the elites' organizations and their dominant position in the society. The post-aristocratic ruling groups, as we will see, have managed to preserve themselves and their institutions and to remain singularly unaffected by the profound transformations that have been making their mark on the society. (1978: 4)

The reproduction of bourgeois power has relied on the close ties between elite schools, the *grandes écoles*, and state civil service institutions, the *grands corps*. In the postwar period, there has been greater coordination between corporate and state elites, as an increasing number of white-collar workers move from public to private sector positions, a practice known as *pantouflage*, creating a direct pathway for elites from the *grandes écoles* to the leading economic, political, and cultural institutions of French society.[25] The integration of economic and political interests is also a legacy of colonialism, whose political regimes were explicitly constructed to protect and promote the elite economic interests of the metropole. The importance of the *grandes écoles* is evidence of a postwar shift in the primary mech-anism by which the French state secures the interests of the dominant classes, according to Pierre Bourdieu, relying more on ideological than on repressive state apparatuses (in Althusser's terms):

> physical coercion and repression [gave way] to the milder dissimulated constraints of symbolic violence, with the police and prison system, privileged by adolescent

denunciation and its extensions in scholarly discourse, becoming less important in the maintenance of the social order than the school and authorities of cultural production. (Bourdieu 1996: 386–7)

The postwar trend away from repressive mechanisms of rule ended in the 1970s and 1980s, when elite political consensus mandated stricter immigration controls, loss of rights, repatriation, and assimilation for immigrants and undocumented workers (*sans-papiers*). This system of exclusions has led to heightened levels of societal violence, a vicious cycle of police order, institutional, ideological, and structural violence, and reactive violence by the victims of state repression. This violence has been fueled in part by the repatriation and reintegration of colonial settlers, many of whom instilled in the postcolonial French state the virulently racist and hierarchical "administrative methods and habits" acquired during the colonial period.[26]

What we see, therefore, is that the close relationship between the dominant classes and the state has been a constant feature of modern French history, a stability owed in large part to the close coordination between private and public sectors. Heightened levels of state violence have ensured that the increasing multiculturalism of French society does not threaten this close relationship and the privileges it provides. In Haneke's cinema, this closeness is repeatedly called into question, with bourgeois characters often unable to rely on the state apparatus to secure their interests. In *Time of the Wolf*, the apocalyptic events that form the film's distant backdrop have destroyed traditional state structures, forcing survivors to establish their own institutions of law and order, administration and welfare. While the *ad hoc* state that emerges retains many of the characteristics of prior state forms, such as their propensity for the abuse of power, it also proves to be a less reliable ally to bourgeois interests. When Anne accuses the man who shot Georges of his murder, she has no proof other than her own eyewitness testimony, and is unable to persuade the camp's *ad hoc* judiciary to punish him in any way. In *Caché*, Georges has difficulty convincing the police to take any preemptive measures in response to the threatening videotapes and drawings he has received in the mail. When Anne suggests that Georges take a cop along with him when he visits Majid's apartment, Georges responds: "They'll just say: 'Try knocking on the door and if someone jumps out and tries to kill you come see us again.'" After Pierrot's disappearance, Georges tells Anne: "The police aren't interested except in the kidnapping. For the tapes we need proof. We would have to follow bureaucratic channels – reports, lawyers. The cops don't care if it's linked." We might also interpret Georges's pronouncements of police indifference as a reticence on his part to get the police involved, perhaps fearing that they would somehow take Majid's side. These examples illustrate that the feelings of insecurity and uncertainty induced by Haneke's films are partially a result of the removal of the state as a site of authority at the service of bourgeois characters.

Haneke's cinema, however, also highlights the persecutory role of the state in the lives of immigrant and minority populations. In *71 Fragments of a Chronology of Chance* (1994), a homeless Romanian boy lives outside the purview of the state, escaping police capture and scavenging for food and shelter. But he is eventually captured and adopted by an Austrian family who think of him as more compliant than their previous foster child. When his adopted mother is killed in the climactic scene of the film, the boy is left in her car waiting helplessly. His stasis amidst the violent energy of the rest of the scene signals the precarious suspension of immigrants between state parochialism and state abandonment, between assimilation and exclusion. In *Code Unknown*, the state intervenes in ways that exacerbate the social, economic, and political inequalities between the characters in the film. This is most evident in Amadou's arrest, Jean's non-arrest, and Maria's deportation at the film's outset. In *Caché*, during his search for the truth Georges becomes a vigilante, zealously pursuing Majid, pronouncing him responsible for his harassment and ultimately impelling him to a (self-imposed) sentence of capital punishment. The irony is that Georges's actions seem to only heighten his feelings of anxiety and guilt.

The representation of the state in Haneke's cinema, therefore, takes two primary forms: an abnegation of its historical affiliation as the instrument of the dominant classes and a confirmation of its historical function as persecutor of immigrant and minority populations. How can we make sense of this seemingly contradictory representational schema? By decoupling state oppression of immigrant and minority populations from elite interests, Haneke is contesting the ethical and practical merits of relying on the state to preserve colonial-era social inequalities and divisions. State oppression of immigrant and minority characters does little to prevent the traumatic multicultural confrontations experienced by Haneke's bourgeois protagonists. The police are conspicuously absent when Anne is confronted on the subway in *Code Unknown*, during Georges's altercation with the bicyclist in *Caché*, or after Georges is killed in *Time of the Wolf*. In Haneke's cinema, the state is incapable of neutralizing the charged encounters, exchanges, and contestations that animate an increasingly multicultural civil society. By disarticulating bourgeois feelings of insecurity from the exclusionary and persecutory policies of the state, Haneke dismantles one of the principal arguments of contemporary French anti-immigrant discourse.[27]

The other mode of authority that we can use to explain the ambiguities of Haneke's cinema is authorship. Under the logic of authorship, ambiguity is explained as a manifestation of authorial expressivity. The most conspicuous moments of authorial commentary in Haneke's French-language films are his codas: the sounds of rhythmic drumming as a deaf boy signs to an unseen audience in *Code Unknown*, the shots of the countryside taken from inside a moving train in *Time of the Wolf*, and the shot of the front steps to Pierrot's school in *Caché*. These are some of the most discussed and analyzed scenes in Haneke's entire oeuvre.[28] All three codas seem to represent the possibility of transcending the conflicts and deprivations that have dominated the films up to that point. In *Code Unknown*, the sounds of rhythmic drum play, evoking an earlier scene in which deaf children play the drums together, and the confidence with which the boy signs to his unseen audience suggest a possibility for cooperation and understanding despite the obstacles to communication. In *Time of the Wolf*, the view from inside a moving train suggests that the Laurents and other camp residents might have managed to leave the camp, the beauty and lushness of their view giving us hope that it will deliver them from their life of scarcity. In *Caché*, the conversation between Pierrot and Majid's son provides us with hope that the younger generation will resolve the seemingly insurmountable differences that have divided their parents. All three codas can be seen as expressions of the characters' desires to reach such a point of transcendence, a mark of their utopian longing more so than a prediction that this state can or will ever be reached.

Haneke's codas are cautious articulations of an ideal set of values, practices, and outcomes–cooperativeness, dialog, delivery from want. The universalist ambitions of these codas seem to go against the rigorous particularism and epistemological relativism of the rest of the narratives. Utopian articulations run the risk of affirming the pernicious use of universalist rhetoric in contemporary European political discourse, which we have already discussed. But we might also read the universalism of Haneke's codas more favorably. The values embodied in them are dialogic and contingent, dependent on an engagement with difference, rather than on its collapse as is the case with assimilationism. In line with Immanuel Wallerstein's call that we "universalize our particulars and particularize our universals simultaneously and in a kind of constant dialectical exchange," Haneke's codas can be seen as one side of a dialectic, the other side of which is the consistent class particularism of his narratives, which immerse us claustrophobically in the fears and anxieties of bourgeois characters.[29] By showing us the limits of bourgeois subjectivity and the structural inequalities of French society, and only situating their transcendence in the indeterminate futuricity of his codas, Haneke challenges the egalitarian pretensions of French republicanism without giving up on the principle of equality itself.

Haneke's authorship also manifests itself as an antagonist to the interests of his bourgeois protagonists. The acting scene in *Code Unknown* in which Anne becomes "imprisoned" is indicative of this antagonism because it conflates three figures: Haneke, the director of the film Anne is acting in, and the man who is imprisoning the character played by Anne. The confusion over whether Anne is acting or not during this scene creates a corresponding confusion over the "author" of the camera's gaze: Is it Haneke, the director of the film Anne is acting in, or her imprisoner? The director's instructions come from an unseen offscreen location, similar to the one occupied by her imprisoner, and also by Haneke as the director of *Code Unknown*. The director reads out the lines of the imprisoner character, thus further conflating their two identities. In this way, Haneke associates the scene's acts of imprisonment and deception with his authorial mark on the text.

Haneke's authorship is antagonistic to the bourgeois protagonist in *Caché* as well. If we are to revisit the unresolved questions from the film listed earlier, we will see that many of them are concerned with the placement of the camera that is recording the footage sent to Georges by his harasser. How does Georges walk right past the camera without noticing the camera operator? How is there a camera in Majid's apartment recording the conversation between Georges and Majid, given that Majid and his son profess non-involvement in the tapings? These questions can be resolved if the operator of the camera taking the footage is Haneke himself (which, of course, he is, in his capacity as director of *Caché*). Indeed, Haneke encourages such an interpretation by including an iteration of the same static shot of Georges and Anne's apartment near the end of the film, after Georges's confrontation with Majid's son, that is not explained in the narrative as one of the harassing tapes. More broadly, a conflation between Haneke and Georges's harasser occurs due to the alternation between footage taken by the harasser and this same footage being viewed by Georges or Anne, such as between the two iterations of the footage taken at night, shown to us first as it is being recorded and then a second time as it is played back by Georges. This suggests that Haneke has access to this footage independently of Georges, since we do not only see the tapes sent to Georges but also are privy to the original instances of their recording. We can conclude that Haneke is either the harasser or knows who he/she is and chooses not to tell us.

The antagonism of Haneke's authorial presence also manifests itself through shifts in camera position and point of view. In *Caché*, when Georges persuades the police to visit Majid's apartment in search of Pierrot, and to their surprise Majid's son answers the door, the camera is positioned behind Georges and the police officers, and thus aligned with their point of view and their objective to find Pierrot (Fig. 23.1). But later, when Majid's son approaches Georges in the lobby of the television station where Georges works, the camera is positioned behind

Fig. 23.1 Georges (Daniel Auteuil) visits Majid's apartment in search of Pierrot. *Caché* (2005), dir. Michael Haneke, prod. Andrew Colton and Veit Heiduschka.

Fig. 23.2   Majid's son (Walid Afkir) confronts Georges at the television station. *Caché* (2005), dir. Michael Haneke, prod. Andrew Colton and Veit Heiduschka.

Majid's son, aligned with his point of view and his objective to better understand the man who precipitated his father's suicide (Fig. 23.2). In this moment, the perspective of the film escapes Georges's flawed subjectivity and realigns itself with that of someone who Georges interprets as an antagonist to his way of life.

Haneke's construction of an antagonistic authorial textual presence runs the risk of leaving audiences with a false sense of plenitude, preventing us from recognizing the insufficiencies of art cinema for the representation of immigrant and minority issues. The power of Haneke's cinema stems from its class and racial particularism, which challenges the pretense of universality of European political discourse and French republicanism, reveals the limits of bourgeois paradigms in explaining multicultural realities, and reconstructs the stratification of rights in contemporary European societies. On the one hand, this class specificity, by denying audiences access to the subjectivities of immigrant and minority characters, who occupy marginal positions within Haneke's narratives, stifles the potentially deleterious implications of identification that seeks to collapse rather than understand difference.[30] On the other hand, the immersion in bourgeois subjectivity precludes a whole universe of possibilities for the representation of European immigrants and minorities. As Paul Gilroy says with regard to *Caché*,

> When the Majids of this world are allowed to develop into deeper, rounded characters endowed with all the psychological gravity and complexity that is taken for granted in ciphers like Georges, we will know that substantive progress has been made towards breaking the white, bourgeois monopoly on dramatizing the stresses of lived experience in this modernity. (2007: 234)

Yet such well-rounded depictions have their own problems, given the inability of empathetic identification to articulate the ethical responsibilities of spectatorship across axes of difference. As Michele Aaron notes, empathetic identification induces self-righteous feelings of "moral-ideological rectitude" in spectators, preventing them from understanding how they are implicated and ethically responsible for what they are witnessing on screen.[31]

What is missing from this discussion is a consideration of European minority cinemas, such as Beur cinema, whose politics of self-representation goes beyond both Haneke's class and racial particularism and the empathetic identification central to Stephen Frears's films, for instance.[32] What matters is that each of these modes of representation acknowledges its own limitations. It is this acknowledgment that is short-circuited by the antagonism of Haneke's authorial mark on the text. The ambiguity of Haneke's narration destabilizes narrative coherence and implicates audiences in the ethical ramifications of his narratives. The construction of Haneke as antagonist to his bourgeois characters reinscribes coherence into the text, comforting us with the thought that, in the final instance, Haneke will heroically intervene to restore ethical order. Instead, we should interpret Haneke's cinema through the prism of its particularism that, through its own inadequacies, brings to our attention the marginalization and neglect of minority cinemas in Europe. The limits of bourgeois subjectivity in Haneke's films should be seen as a refraction of the limitations of art cinema itself.

Notes

1 I am using the term "multiculturalism" to denote the racial, ethnic, and cultural diversity of a particular society, and the phrase "multicultural encounters" to denote the meeting between two or more people of different racial, ethnic, cultural, or class backgrounds. My use of the term "multiculturalism" should not be confused with "multicultural policies" of specific nation-states, which typically encompass state support for minority cultural and arts programs, educational and language initiatives and media, legal recognition of minority group rights, favorably differential treatment of minority groups based on their distinct cultures and traditions, and the promotion of greater representation of minorities in government, education, and other fields. These policies have, for the most part, not been adopted in France, whose republican definition of citizenship is hostile to any communal or group-based articulations of identity and rights. For more on multiculturalism, see Amy Guttman (1994). For more on the hostility to multiculturalism in France, see Alec Hargreaves (1997).

2 Excerpt from a French-language interview with Michael Haneke conducted by Serge Toubiana, included in the special features of *The Seventh Continent* DVD released by Kino Video (author's translation).

3 Max Silverman (1992: 46–9).

4 These laws were the Marcellin-Fontanet circulars of January and February 1972 which linked the right to residency to active employment, leading to the expulsion (without

the right to appeal) of long-time French residents who became unemployed; the suspension of immigration in the July 5, 1974 circular and the suspension of the right to family reunification which had previously allowed family members to join their spouse/parent in France if he or she was already a resident (this circular was deemed unconstitutional in 1975 and replaced with a circular implementing stricter criteria for family reunification); the 1977 Stoleru repatriation law and the 1980 Bonnet law against illegal immigration aimed at reducing the numbers of immigrants in the country through forced or financially incentivized repatriation and through the predication of residence permit renewal on active employment; the 1983 *aide à la réinsertion* policy aimed at precipitating voluntary repatriation; a 1984 decree predicating family reunification on "proof of adequate housing and financial resources"; the Pasqua Laws of 1986 and 1993 which gave greater powers to police and prefects to carry out expulsions, made criteria for residence permit renewals and family reunification even stricter, limited immigrants' access to health care and social security benefits, and eliminated the automatic granting of French nationality to children of immigrants born in France. See Silverman (1992: 53–7, 60–7); Jane Freedman (2004: 34–46).

5   Quoted in Freedman (2004: 17).

6   Freedman (2004: 15–20).

7   Max Silverman notes that the social, cultural, and economic gains made by immigrants from the ex-colonies have "been accompanied by an increased effort to distance them from the idea of France and present them as a problem. The line separating 'two worlds' – the 'metropole' and the colonies, the dominant and the dominated – has become increasingly blurred in this period." Silverman contends that this breakdown of colonial-era hierarchies and demarcations is "a source of profound anxiety" for France's dominant classes (Silverman 1992: 107, 110). For more on the legacies of French colonialism, see Alec Hargreaves (2005); Patricia M. E. Lorcin (2006).

8   Frantz Fanon (1963: 37–43).

9   Silverman (1992: 109–11).

10 The intruders in this scene do not appear to be of a different ethnic, racial, or national background than the Laurents, but they do seem to be of a different social class. In the apocalyptic conditions that prevail in *Time of the Wolf*, the stability of the social hierarchy that preserves class distinctions has broken down. So while this home invasion does not constitute a multicultural encounter *per se*, it replicates the social dynamics that inform multicultural confrontations in the rest of Haneke's cinema, namely, the rise in power of previously marginalized groups and the experience of this by the bourgeoisie as a traumatic loss of rights and privileges.

11 All dialog excerpts are based on the French-language dialog as it is heard in the DVD releases of the films (based on subtitles and author's translations).

12 Ambiguity has long been associated with art cinema. For Robert Self, the absence of clearly defined characters and situations in art cinema creates aporias for viewers to contemplate, if not quite resolve: "[T]he art film text is consciously indeterminate, refusing to give its materials secure meaning or to establish the viewer in the position of interpreter. The texts of the art cinema exist quite explicitly as puzzles to be solved by the viewer, but puzzles also constructed to prevent easy solution" (Self 1979: 76–8).

13 For more on the position of epistemological relativism within multiculturalism debates, see Satya P. Mohanty (1997: 14–15).

14 Ulrich Beck and Edgar Grande (2007: 10).

15 For more on the invocation of universal human rights rhetoric to legitimate Western illegal acts of aggression, see Danilo Zolo (2002). For a historical perspective on the universalism of European thought, dating back to the earliest periods of imperial conquest, see Immanuel Wallerstein (2006).

16 Lydia Morris (2002).

17 As Alec Hargreaves states: "In abolishing the system of Estates, which had institutionalized personal and social inequalities on a group basis, [the 1789 Declaration] asserted instead the principle of universalism, i.e. the equal treatment of all individuals whatever their origins." Yet social equality existed in France only in theory, with women denied the vote until 1944 and the practice of slavery in the colonies contradicting the rhetorical universalism of republicanism until 1848. In the interwar period, wartime mortality and low fertility combined with anti-Semitism to fuel anxieties about the ability of the nation to regenerate itself without losing its cultural identity, culminating in the institutionalized racism of the Vichy regime. In the postwar period, republican universalism sat uneasily alongside the racial hierarchies informing the treatment of colonized subjects in Algeria and the other colonies (Hargreaves 1997: 186). See also Erik Bleich (2004: 168); Herrick Chapman and Laura L. Frader (2004: 2–5).

18 Freedman (2004: 2–3). The brief flirtation of the French left with multiculturalist ideas, with the notion that minority groups have a "right to be different," ended when this rhetoric was hijacked by the right in the 1980s to argue for an exclusionary definition of French culture and identity. For more on this, see Hargreaves (1997: 194).

19 Hargreaves goes on to say that the "openness of the republican tradition stops where cultural differences begin . . . While seemingly open to outsiders, the ideology of assimilation is indeed deeply ethnocentric" (1997: 183, 198).

20 The two primary meaning systems used by audiences to explain the ambiguity of art cinema, according to David Bordwell, are verisimilitude (Bordwell uses the term "realism") and authorial expressivity. The former explains textual phenomena as representations of the real world while the latter explains them as expressions of the filmmaker. Art cinema spectators interpret textual ambiguity as verisimilitude (life is this way), and if that fails to explain it, they attribute it to authorial expressivity (this is what the filmmaker is trying to say); whatever aspect of the text seems excessive under the logic of one meaning system is assumed to belong to the other. See David Bordwell (1979).

21 As Ezra Suleiman remarks, "few societies have succeeded in institutionalizing their elite-forming mechanism to quite the degree that France has" (Suleiman 1978: 4).

22 Colin Mooers (1991: 56).

23 Mooers (1991: 74–5).

24 Mooers (1991: 95–6).

25 Suleiman (1978: 11–12, 229).

26 For more on the colonial legacies and heightened violence of the French state, see Étienne Balibar (2004: 35–42).

27 The decoupling of state power from bourgeois interests in Haneke's cinema is in line with much contemporary scholarship on the relative autonomy of the state. While liberalism assumes that democratic states reflect the interests of all sectors of society, and that this is ensured by the egalitarianism of democratic processes, Marxist

thinkers have long argued that the state is primarily determined by and acting in the interests of the dominant classes. Structuralists such as Nicos Poulantzas amended this orthodox Marxist position by arguing that the state remains relatively autonomous from class factional interests so that it can unify and politically organize the dominant classes. The expansion of scholarship on the state to include considerations of culture, gender, race, and sexuality tends to support the description of the state as relatively autonomous. For instance, the work of Stanley Greenberg shows how racial ideology often becomes a form of state dogma above and beyond the interests of capital. For Stuart Hall the state is pluricentered and multidimensional, not necessarily serving the interests of one class faction, but rather a site where the multiple political and related networks of power are condensed and transformed into a practice of regulation, normalization, and domination over particular classes and other social groups. See David Held (1984); Akhil Gupta and Aradhana Sharma (2006); Stanley B. Greenberg (1980: 390); Stuart Hall (1985).

28   See, for instance, Mark Cousins (2007: 223).

29   Wallerstein (2006: 49). Wallerstein's call for a dialectical exchange between particularism and universalism echoes Satya Mohanty's contention that we must respect cultural difference while retaining a moral universalism, constructed out of the diverse experiences and points of view of all members of multicultural societies. These universal values need to be worked out through epistemic cooperation rather than be imposed on minority cultures by dominant groups (Mohanty 1997: 240).

30   The emphasis on bourgeois characters is most attenuated in *Code Unknown*, but even in this film the protagonist is undoubtedly Anne, played by Juliette Binoche.

31   "The films that trace each gradient of the moral high ground to intone the grandeur of their protagonists' actions, be they noble or dastardly, underwrite their moving tales with cast-iron allegiances between the spectator and the tragic but triumphant hero . . . Just as ethical reflection was connected to recognition of the other, and a taking of responsibility for this recognition and of one's own desires, so such films are unethical precisely because they seem to foreclose recognition and responsibility as well" (Aaron 2007: 113–14).

32   For more on Beur cinema, see Carrie Tarr (2005); Peter Bloom (2003).

References and Further Reading

Aaron, Michele: *Spectatorship: The Power of Looking On* (London: Wallflower, 2007).
Balibar, Étienne: *We, the People of Europe? Reflections on Transnational Citizenship* (Princeton, NJ: Princeton University Press, 2004).
Beck, Ulrich and Grande, Edgar: *Cosmopolitan Europe* (Cambridge: Polity Press, 2007).
Bleich, Erik: "Anti-Racism Without Races: Politics and Policy in a 'Color-Blind' State," *Race in France: Interdisciplinary Perspectives on the Politics of Difference*, ed. Herrick Chapman and Laura L. Frader (New York: Bergahn Books, 2004), pp. 162–88.
Bloom, Peter: "Beur Cinema and the Politics of Location: French Immigration Politics and the Naming of a Film Movement," *Multiculturalism, Postcoloniality and Transnational Media*, ed. Ella Shohat and Robert Stam (New Brunswick, NJ: Rutgers University Press, 2003), pp. 44–62.

Bordwell, David: "Art Cinema as a Mode of Film Practice," *Film Criticism* 4:1 (Fall 1979): 56–64.

Bourdieu, Pierre: *The State Nobility: Elite Schools in the Field of Power* (Stanford, CA: Stanford University Press, 1996).

Chapman, Herrick and Frader, Laura L.: "Introduction," *Race in France: Interdisciplinary Perspectives on the Politics of Difference*, ed. Herrick Chapman and Laura L. Frader (New York: Bergahn Books, 2004), pp. 1–19.

Cousins, Mark: "After the End: Word of Mouth and *Caché*," *Screen* 48:2 (Summer 2007): 223–6.

Fanon, Frantz: *The Wretched of the Earth* (New York: Grove Press, 1963).

Freedman, Jane: *Immigration and Insecurity in France* (Aldershot: Ashgate, 2004).

Gilroy, Paul: "Shooting Crabs in a Barrel," *Screen* 48:2 (Summer 2007): 233–5.

Greenberg, Stanley B.: *Race and State in Capitalist Development* (New Haven, CT: Yale University Press, 1980).

Gupta, Akhil and Sharma, Aradhana, eds.: *The Anthropology of the State: A Reader* (Malden, MA: Blackwell, 2006).

Guttman, Amy, ed.: *Multiculturalism: Examining the Politics of Recognition* (Princeton, NJ: Princeton University Press, 1994).

Hall, Stuart: "Signification, Representation, Ideology: Althusser and the Post-Structuralist Debates," *Critical Studies in Mass Communication* 2:2 (June 1985): 92–6.

Hargreaves, Alec, ed.: *Memory, Empire, and Postcolonialism: Legacies of French Colonialism* (Lanham, MD: Lexington Books, 2005).

Hargreaves, Alec: "Multiculturalism," *Political Ideologies in Contemporary France*, ed. Christopher Flood and Laurence Bell (London: Pinter, 1997), pp. 180–98.

Held, David: "Central Perspectives on the Modern State," *The Idea of the Modern State*, ed. Gregor McLennan, Stuart Hall, and David Held (Milton Keynes: Open University Press, 1984), pp. 59–60.

Lorcin, Patricia M. E., ed.: *Algeria and France, 1800–2000: Identity, Memory, Nostalgia* (Syracuse, NY: Syracuse University Press, 2006).

Mohanty, Satya P.: *Literary Theory and the Claims of History: Postmodernism, Objectivity, Multicultural Politics* (Ithaca, NY: Cornell University Press, 1997).

Mooers, Colin: *The Making of Bourgeois Europe: Absolutism, Revolution and the Rise of Capitalism in England, France and Germany* (London: Verso, 1991).

Morris, Lydia: *Managing Migration: Civic Stratification and Migrants' Rights* (London: Routledge, 2002).

Self, Robert: "Systems of Ambiguity in the Art Cinema," *Film Criticism* 4:1 (Fall 1979): 74–80.

Silverman, Max: *Deconstructing the Nation: Immigration, Racism, and Citizenship in Modern France* (London: Routledge, 1992).

Suleiman, Ezra N.: *Elites in French Society: The Politics of Survival* (Princeton, NJ: Princeton University Press, 1978).

Tarr, Carrie: *Reframing Difference: Beur and Banlieue Filmmaking in France* (Manchester: Manchester University Press, 2005).

Wallerstein, Immanuel: *European Universalism: The Rhetoric of Power* (New York: New Press, 2006).

Zolo, Danilo: *Invoking Humanity: War, Law and Global Order* (London: Continuum, 2002).

24

Haneke's Secession

Perspectivism and Anti-Nihilism in Code Unknown *and* Caché

Kevin L. Stoehr

Truth and Perspective

In *Caché* (2005), after Anne (Juliette Binoche) shows her husband Georges (Daniel Auteuil) a sheet of paper with the crude image of a bleeding boy drawn on it, they watch a video sent with the drawing. Anne asks her husband what seems to be bothering him, and he simply replies, "Nothing." He repeats this type of response as he continues to conceal his speculation about the specific cause of their trouble.

"Nothing" is a frequent response by characters to the inquiries of others in several of Michael Haneke's films, particularly in situations when the truth is difficult to communicate or when an individual becomes indifferent to the need to share the truth. In *Caché*, "nothing" becomes an almost mechanical reaction to questions about what is really going on, as when the husband Georges chooses to refrain from voicing his speculations concerning the recent acts of terrorism against his family.[1] Georges's personal decision to omit the truth also echoes the collective "forgetting" (i.e., intentional ignoring) of the French police's massacre of Algerians in Paris in 1961, a tragic event that has direct as well as indirect consequences for almost everyone in the film. One may question whether the omission of the truth is a genuine falsehood, but Haneke frequently explores the consequences of refusing to communicate the truth, regardless of whether one wants to call the original decision to conceal the truth a "lie" or not.

Caché is a movie about the collision between personal perspectives and the consequences of not telling the truth about one's personal viewpoint. There is one intriguing scene in which Georges and his wife Anna emerge from a police station, pass between two vehicles, and are almost hit by a man on a bicycle. The man riding the bicycle is clearly meant to represent a member of an immigrant minority group and the verbal confrontation that ensues illustrates an overall social tension between different races and socio-economic classes. The scene anticipates the later emergence of the character Majid (Maurice Bénichou), whose Algerian parents were killed in the above-mentioned massacre when he was a boy. Georges and Anne quickly forget the encounter with the foreigner after they have returned to their car. But this scene does raise the question, due to the very debate over who was to blame for the near-miss and potential accident: *Whose* perspective is *correct*? Is there a way to adjudicate here, or is the best moral choice to assume, as Anne suggests as a way to end the confrontation diplomatically, that both parties may be to blame for the near-accident and subsequent misunderstanding?

As is evident from his films, earlier television productions, and selected interviews, Haneke is interested in exploring the ways in which cinematic art can raise philosophical questions about the nature of truth. He is also concerned with the moral, psychological, and existential consequences of the choices we make in telling, not telling, distorting, repressing, or doubting the truth. I wish to do some excavation work here in speculating about Haneke's underlying epistemological concerns, and more especially those dealing with the effects, both positive and negative, of certain decisions that we make in communicating or not communicating the truth. Haneke's films raise illuminating philosophical questions and, more particularly, they can be fruitfully related to the principle of perspectivism and to theories of communicative ethics.

For Haneke, truth is always *human* truth, an activity of truth-*telling*, which is of course a basic requirement of human communication, at least in most everyday situations. In communicating we often put our values and choices into question, since by communicating we open ourselves to the possible judgments of others and therefore to the moral and social consequences of saying or not saying what we think is true. We communicate ourselves rightly or wrongly, authentically or inauthentically, sanely or insanely. And when we give others an occasion for doubting our attempts at communicating, either because we have practiced deception or simply refused to communicate in the first place, then there is a danger that this will breed a deep form of skepticism about our intentions. Such doubt, in turn, may result in the kind of mistrust that can completely disrupt a personal relationship.[2]

For example, in *Caché*, Georges asks his wife Anne for her trust after he has refused to disclose his suspicions that are related back to his own childhood utterance of a falsehood. Anne retorts with disbelief: "*I* have to trust *you*? Why not the other way around for once? . . . That's your idea of a sound relationship? Based on mutual trust?" She obviously expects him to practice what he preaches. And there is a brief but touching scene in *Code Unknown* (2000) that deals explicitly with the importance of truth-telling. Here an immigrant taxi driver listens as his young son explains why he got into trouble at school (Fig. 24.1). The father marches the boy into the kitchen, away from the noisy voices of the rest of the family, and gives him a chance to explain precisely what happened. We can guess from the details of the boy's story and from his authentic way of delivering the small details that he is telling the truth, and his father appears to sense this also. Here, honesty is *felt* and the morality of truthfulness is the primary theme.

Fig. 24.1   A father (Djibril Kouyaté) asks his son Demba (Domeke Meite) to tell him the truth about a recent incident at school. *Code Unknown* (2000), dir. Michael Haneke, prod. Marin Karmitz and Alain Sarde.

Haneke tells us that he is a "humanist" because he is an artist, someone who attempts to communicate. Haneke has proclaimed in an interview: "Refusing to communicate is a terrorist act that triggers violence."[3] In certain ways, deception and omission are acts of violence against the truth and therefore against the very basis of human communication. Communication has its inherent limitations, especially when we mean much more than we can say or, on the other hand, when we say more than we really mean. Either way, there are obstacles to the goal of mutual understanding and these forms of disjunction lie at the heart of many of Haneke's film narratives. For example, the young deaf mute girl in the prologue to *Code Unknown means* much more than she *says*, especially since what she "says" is given in sign language to a movie audience that by and large does not understand this particular language. Her gestures mean so much, in fact, that upon viewing the film for a second time, we surmise that she might be trying to communicate a horrible fact about her daily existence at home.[4]

As Haneke's films demonstrate, epistemology and ethics are inescapably interwoven. His recurring evocation of questions about the nature and moral consequences of truth is evident, for example, in his letter to producer Marin Karmitz, dated March 14, 2000, which was included in the liner notes to the Kino Video DVD of *Code Unknown*. Haneke expresses here the difficulty of trying to "sum up in a few sentences" the essential intention behind the film as well as his idea of overarching themes. He states that if one were to list the "obvious ideas" in the film – he cites "the Babylonian confusion of languages, the incapacity to communicate, the coldness of consumer society," and "xenophobia," with a crucial "*et cetera*" after the list – one would arrive at a "mere string of clichés." He suggests that "there is little that can be said outside the aesthetic framework of the film," since the movie must speak for itself *as* a film. Haneke informs us that he does not view himself as a "forger of opinions" whose positions on the themes should interest anyone.[5]

It is remarkable, however, how much Haneke does indeed communicate about his films, given his occasional resistance to outright analysis of them. In personal interviews, as in the case of those with Serge Toubiana for the Kino DVD versions of his films, Haneke does not seem hesitant to speak of overall themes and to engage in an analysis of his films, even beyond one scene. In speaking of his film *Caché*, for example, he announces its overriding theme as the question of how a character deals with guilt. Later he suggests yet another theme, which is a familiar one in the Haneke canon: that of emotional coldness as a personal response to our contemporary bureaucracy-governed and technology-driven society.

While Haneke's letter to the producer concerning *Code Unknown* is mainly a letter that rejects the invitation to comment on the film in a sweeping manner, he does point to the kind of philosophical (especially epistemological and hermeneutic) questions that "triggered and motivated the project" in the first place. Haneke suggests that, while such abstract questions have been "chosen in an arbitrary and incomplete way," he hopes "that they evoke something of the intellectual climate" that led to the making of *Code Unknown*. The following are several of these questions that point to Haneke's philosophical interests, as articulated by the director himself in the above-mentioned letter:

> Is the truth the sum of what we see and hear? Can reality be represented? To the observer, what makes the represented object real, credible, or more precisely, worthy of being believed? . . . In the world of moving pictures, are illusion and deception twins or merely closely related? . . . Is the fragment the aesthetic response to the incomplete nature of our perception? Is editing the simulation of the whole? Is precision an aesthetic or a moral category? Can allusion replace description? Is that which is off-camera more precise than that which is on?[6]

Such questions imply a consideration of different conceptions of truth and they also inquire as to how cinematic art – and not merely *Code Unknown* as a particular film – relates to such a consideration. Truth can be defined in multiple ways, but the following are five basic conceptions of truth that are important to have in mind if we are to take note of the underlying epistemological concerns in Haneke's films.

First of all, "truth" may be defined as a correct mental representation of reality, as for example in traditional Enlightenment thinking, particularly in the empiricist mold. Truth is taken here to be the correspondence between mind-dependent perceptions/concepts and mind-independent objects. Secondly, "truth" may be defined as a coherent and holistic system of propositions, as for instance in Hegel's dialectical ordering of philosophical categories. But Haneke frequently challenges or even rejects these kinds of truth-models that allow for the possibility of any absolute objectivity or universality. He consistently reminds the viewer, either in terms of film style or narrative approach, that more than one viewpoint is always possible, and that some absolute measure for evaluating multiple perceptions of a given object or event is never available.

For Haneke, a singular perception or concept or proposition is never enough to capture "the whole truth," even if we were to presuppose that anything like "the whole truth" does indeed exist. The style and content of Haneke's films typically refute the assumption that any such form of coherence or totality in the form of a "big picture" is possible or accessible. If anything, the narrative structures and visual strategies adopted in a majority of his movies suggest that the world can only be given to us in bits and pieces whose ultimate ordering is unattainable. Haneke is a filmmaker and screenwriter who consistently thwarts our traditional quest for closure – not merely our desire for happy endings, but our affinity for neat resolutions that seemingly help us to interpret the entire movie in an "accurate" and "complete" fashion. Since that type of closure is typically unavailable in everyday life, Haneke makes indeterminacy and open-endedness essential aspects of his cinematic approach.

The remaining three conceptions of truth are a bit closer to Haneke's overall philosophical concerns. As a third option, "truth" may refer to a form of revelation or disclosure, a non-objectified event that occasions the very given-ness or "presencing" of meaning. Truth, under this view, is a kind of gathering-place or "clearing" for the emergence of signification, as is emphasized in Martin Heidegger's and Hans-Georg Gadamer's hermeneutic approaches.[7] All artists as communicators and meaning-makers may be said, in fact, to adopt such a general conception of the truth, simply by virtue of their chosen vocation as artists. However, as a *conscious philosophical orientation*, this approach is demonstrated most clearly by a filmmaker like Haneke, one who is quite willing to slow down his narrative to allow for emphasis on small, seemingly contingent but significant moments of meaning-making. Haneke is a director who is aware that truth and meaning arise most tellingly in terms of the irreducible details of a particular situation. This kind of revelation of meaning may occur not only for a film character but also for a viewer, and these visually poetic, almost ornamental "grace notes" – shots or scenes that do not appear to be tied closely to the plot but which create room for interpretation and speculation – draw attention to the idea that truth first arises, not in an explicit proposition or articulated system of categories or correspondence between the mental and real, but rather in the emergence of a situation's everyday meaningfulness, where a subject or self is open and attuned to such meaning. As with the ambiguous shot of the populated front steps of a school at the conclusion of *Caché*, Haneke calls attention to those seemingly chance moments that are opportunities for various possibilities of meaning to gather, with no single perception or interpretation being the absolutely correct one.[8]

The fourth idea of truth, and the one that is most essential for our purposes here, is that of *perspectivism*. This is the idea that truth always results from one's personal viewpoint or orientation so that any claim to absolute coherence or correctness must be discarded. This conception is not incompatible with the previous view of truth as the basic emergence of meaning in a given context. Friedrich Nietzsche, for example, teaches us that our knowledge is always subjective, determined by a given point of orientation, and that our perceptions must be judged according to the standard of whether they are life-enhancing or life-negating for a particular individual in a particular situation or series of situations. It is clear from his interviews and from his films that Haneke is a perspectivist in the Nietzschean vein, one who attempts to overthrow the notion that objective or universal truth is possible. For instance, in his interview with Toubiana regarding *Caché*, Haneke declares, after discussing his intentional use of ambiguity in the film: "The truth is always hidden . . . It's like in reality . . . We never ever know what is truth. There are 1,000 truths. It is a matter of perspective."[9]

A fifth conception of truth (which might be labeled as "dialogical") derives from more contemporary theories of "communicative" or "discourse" ethics. Following the general logic of such influential discourse ethicists as Karl-Otto Apel and Jürgen Habermas, "truth" is defined here either as the *resulting consensus* of an intersubjective dialog or, following Seyla Benhabib's suggestion, as the actual *process* of dialog, as a shared activity that aims at the goal of mutual understanding.[10] In addition, the dialog in question may be governed by certain normative constraints, such as Habermas's idea of the necessary conditions or presuppositions of an "ideal speech situation." As articulated by Benhabib, such constraints include "universal moral respect" for all interlocutors and the need for "egalitarian reciprocity" to guarantee that all dialog participants have equal or "symmetrical" rights within the overall conversation.[11]

The dialogical model of truth is closely aligned with the aforementioned perspectival and hermeneutic models and in some ways integrates them, though this must be qualified. The very conception of truth as intersubjective and dialog-generated, whether as process or result, depends in part on the interplay between various perspectives, as well as on the very emergence of meaning that is occasioned by this interplay – hence the compatibility of this model of truth with the perspectival and hermeneutic conceptions of truth. For some thinkers, the dialogical approach also permits the goal of *universalizability* in that such a model invites deliberation about the types of norms and institutions that *all* participants in a human speech community would agree are in their common best interests. But the dialogical model of truth becomes incompatible with the perspectival and hermeneutic approaches where the former's claim to universalizability conflicts with the latter two approaches' potential rejection of that claim. When it comes to the question of these models' inter-compatibility, one must examine how strictly an interpretation of the dialogical model adheres to the universalizability principle and how strictly an interpretation of the other models adheres to the idea that given perspectives or meaning-situations are irreducibly particular and therefore non-universalizable.

Given the possible truth-models described above, it is my thesis that Haneke's films offer a general and cumulative indication that he is a hermeneutic-minded perspectivist (a blend of the third and fourth models above) who acknowledges the irreducibility and limitations of personal viewpoints. And while he illustrates the dangers of non-communication and the corresponding need for dialog and mutual understanding (courtesy of the fifth and final model above), Haneke nonetheless appears to reject the goal of universalizability that is inherent in the thinking of some (though not all) discourse ethicists. He rejects this principle not so much because it is an impossible or chimerical goal, which it may well be, but more especially because it derives from the same type of detached, abstractionist, and reductive Enlightenment thinking that has led to the kind of impersonal and conformist society that Haneke clearly critiques. In showing us the dangers of non-communication as well as dishonesty and personal inauthenticity, Haneke thereby advocates a kind of discourse ethics, but one that (as Benhabib has proposed) revolves around the value of the dialog process itself, not upon the absolute need for some resulting and overly generalized consensus among *all* possible interlocutors.[12]

Haneke as Perspectivist

To take but one example of Haneke's recurring narratives and cinematic strategies that evoke the idea of perspectivism, *Code Unknown* is in many ways a series of fragmented vignettes that revolve around one incident, an event that causes different perceptions and perspectives to fuse or collide. This emphasis on the fusion or collision of viewpoints – Haneke's way of stimulating reflection on the overall theme of multiculturalism in contemporary "Western" societies – generates personal consequences that reverberate throughout the film. The multi-perspectival approach is also evident in the movie's subtitle: *Incomplete Tales of Several Journeys*.[13]

Haneke's films reveal time and again that truth is always given to humans in the same way that the world is presented to a movie camera: from given angles that afford different and limited points of view. Following from this, and given the nature of a particular perspective as subject-related and context-dependent, Haneke stresses two different ways in which one's perspective on "the truth" of a situation, as an initial basis for communication, can lead to negative moral, psychological, and even existential consequences.

First of all, a perspective may be defined falsely as being somehow detached from a given context or situation and also divorced from any particular person, such as a "globalized" or "ideal" viewpoint that makes pretense at objective and universal validity. This is the type of viewpoint that has become so mediated by superficial interpretation or mass commercialization or technological production that it no longer appears to be a *personal* perspective at all, but rather a way of viewing things that is collective, impersonal, and seemingly context-free. Here a person's viewpoint becomes "unrooted," so to speak, from the situational assumptions, values, and interests that give rise to this point of orientation in the first place.

A viewpoint that is conceived as being detached from its living context or *Lebenswelt* (to steal a term from Husserlian phenomenology) is often the product of some abstract form of mediation. For example, an explanatory framework may eventually become interpreted as a mere theoretical construct with no practical connection with the world of everyday life. A sense of detachment from one's personal situation can also result from the use of some artificial medium (television, cinema, Internet, etc.), a medium that is used to perceive and interpret that which otherwise would be actively experienced by one's five senses in a direct relationship with the physical or social world. This is evident, for example, in Haneke's frequent use of television news footage as well as his emphasis on televised or photographic images of violent events, as in *Benny's Video*, *Code Unknown*, *Caché*, and *Funny Games*. Such a sense of detachment implies a psychological withdrawal from the concreteness of everyday life via impassive spectatorship. And a similar kind of abstractionism is engendered by the globalization and homogenization of information that is mediated in a seemingly instantaneous manner through trans-regional media such as television and the Internet.

On the other hand, even if a perspective is defined correctly as rooted in (rather than detached from) a particular context, the perspective itself may be conceived as stagnant or fixed – and therefore as implicitly untrue to the inherent "flux" or dynamic nature of an individual's existence. This can happen, for example, when a given perspective is determined by some unchanging ideal or set of values. A person may choose to adhere to a *seemingly* permanent point of view – perhaps because of a need for a false sense of comfort or security – and thereby fail to recognize that other, more life-enhancing perspectives are possible.

In sum, whether due to the detachment of a perspective from its living context, as with abstraction and artificial mediation, or due to the fixation of a perspective to the exclusion of other possible viewpoints, there arises *inauthenticity*, a kind of self-deception about the fleetingness, finitude, and situated individuality of all perception and knowledge. A perspective that becomes dogmatic and that is no longer true-to-life leads in many instances to a person adopting a corresponding self-conception.

Let us turn in more detail to the ways in which Haneke points to the dangers involved in adopting or adhering to certain kinds of perspective. Again, in selected instances the director utilizes self-reflexive techniques that dramatically *detach* the viewer from the immediate "living" narrative-context in which he/she formerly felt situated or engaged. This forces the audience into a clear awareness of watching as well as actively interpreting a film rather than allowing one's imagination to remain *in* the narrative alongside the characters. In the latter role, the film viewer is merely a passive spectator who has temporarily forgotten her own role as a film viewer. Through his way of positioning the spectator, Haneke implicitly summons us to consider the deceptions – or perhaps merely the illusions – involved in mainstream filmmaking and film spectatorship. He intends to liberate the viewer and to make her conscious that she is able to step back autonomously from a given narrative and think about her role in relation to the deceptive *or* truthful nature of this narrative.

Haneke accomplishes this type of autonomy-via-detachment through two methods. First, he occasionally and conspicuously utilizes the "film-within-a-film" technique to make the viewer aware of her situation *as* a viewer, either by emphasizing the presence of video, film, or television within the film or by radically manipulating his movie narrative.[14] Here, we become more aware of our role as film viewers by watching others (movie characters) in this role. Secondly, and less conspicuously, Haneke plays up, even to the point of over-playing, the use of fragmentation and ambiguity in the cinematic presentation of his narrative, to the point that the audience becomes conscious of the fact that perspectives and scenes are being delivered quite selectively and strategically. Here, fragmentation and ambiguity are used in an artificial "consciousness-raising" manner. By intentionally detaching the viewer's consciousness from the immediate narrative context in a way that calls the viewer's attention to her relation to the film, Haneke aims at getting his viewer to think about the degree to which the story being presented expresses the truth of the situation at hand, or the truthfulness and authenticity of the character at hand, or else the lack thereof.

In terms of Haneke's more blatant use of the "film-within-a-film" method of provoking the viewer's self-consciousness, let us consider three clear examples, one from *Caché* and two similar ones from *Code Unknown*. In the opening of the former film, a static film shot lingers unconventionally far past the opening credits – credits that are so small and difficult to decipher that one wonders if there is a subliminal message here that images will count far more than words in this film. We soon learn, however, that the perspective of Haneke's camera at the start of the film coincides with the perspective of a terrorist's camera, a camera that has recorded the exterior of a family's urban home. But this perspective also coincides with that of the married couple, Georges and Anne, who are now watching that footage or shot. Once it becomes evident that we are watching the same images that the main characters in the film are seeing, and that they are watching a shot of their own home from the viewpoint of a camera belonging to someone who wants to disturb their seemingly tranquil bourgeois existence, then we are bound to consider the question: *Whose* perspective are we adopting, *why*, and how does this viewpoint give us any important *knowledge* that will prove relevant for the narrative that is about to unfold? We are forced in a way to consider the overall significance and truthfulness of a perspective *as* a perspective, along with its inherent limitations and possible moral implications.

The other two examples, from *Code Unknown*, are the scene in which Anne (Juliette Binoche) realizes that she is trapped in a room, reacting with more and more anguish to an invisible interlocutor, and the scene in which the same character rushes from a rooftop swimming pool to the nearby ledge of the high-rise in order to rescue a child who dangles there precariously. Both scenes are quite realistic, performed excellently by Binoche, and involve a growing sense of suspense in the audience through Haneke's clever (and quite Hitchcockian) manipulation of our imaginative empathy. And both scenes, increasingly unnerving, conclude with the viewer's sigh of relief as Haneke reveals to us that we are merely watching actors rehearsing or shooting scenes.

Haneke frequently reminds us of the truth that we are film viewers, even though we would like to think that he has no need to do so. Utilizing a form of Romantic irony that presupposes a critical and sometimes disorienting distance between audience and artwork, Haneke is willing to undermine the "truth" of the narrative to which the audience has attuned itself.[15] Haneke occasionally violates the trust of the viewer, in terms of the viewer's trust in the narrative itself, so as to provoke reflection on the very idea of detachment from a coherent plotline. And this is a form of detachment that may be viewed as analogous to what we often experience when our own lives no longer smoothly follow some neatly ordered narrative that we have created for ourselves to give our lives meaning. By subverting and undermining the viewer's trust in the traditional idea of a coherent story-flow, one that seeks some form of closure, Haneke creates a cinematic parallel to the occasional disruptions of our familiar patterns of trust, communication, and truth-telling. By doing so, the director provokes our critical reflection on these familiar patterns and asks us once again to consider the ways in which truth-claims are highly dependent on the individual person, perspective, and context.

On the other hand, there is a frequent tendency in Haneke's films to engage the viewer in a narrative in which she is stimulated to reflect upon the errors and dangers that are inherent in maintaining only one singular perspective – as if it were some absolute (and absolutely truthful) viewpoint that reflects a (seemingly) unchanging context. He typically shows a film character who eventually suffers as a result of adopting such a static and exclusive perspective. This occurs, for example, when we are shown families who cling to the illusion of normalcy or permanence even amidst shocking disturbances or unhealthy habits, as in *Caché* and *The Seventh Continent*. By immersing the viewer in a situation in which a film character mistakenly assumes a dogmatically fixed perspective, one that is inherently untrue to the flux and contingency of life itself, Haneke teaches the audience – via the error of the film character (and most especially the consequences of this error) – that other viewpoints are always possible, whether in judging one's own real-life situation or in interpreting a text such as a film narrative. Whether watching *The Seventh Continent* or *Caché*, the viewer almost cries out for the film characters to adopt a new perspective on their lives, one that will either allow for truthful and mutual communication and/or that will save them ultimately from suicidal despair.

Let us ponder a clear example of the kind of inauthenticity that arises from this delusion – i.e., the false conception of a seemingly fixed or unchanging perspective. In *Caché*, during a rare visit to his mother (Annie Girardot), Georges maintains that his life, at least on the surface, appears to be continuing in its normal tracks, with nothing happening that is dramatically better or worse than the last time he spoke with his mother. He and his wife work too much and hardly see one another anymore. His television talk show is going well, his son is battling with puberty, *et cetera*. Haneke is not afraid to give us a cinematic form of *"et cetera,"* especially in terms of his static long takes and use of repetition, since our feeling of continuing in the same rut lies at the heart of his critique of mainstream monotony and mediocrity. Haneke is willing to show us a dire need to reject the *"et cetera"* of contemporary bourgeois culture, much like his Viennese forebears of another age: Sigmund Freud, Arthur Schnitzler, Karl Kraus, Egon Schiele, Gustav Klimt, Arnold Schoenberg, and so forth.[16] This willingness on the part of the director is evident in this scene where Georges's mother senses that something is wrong and voices her concern, suggesting that he seems to be hiding or repressing a problem. But Georges insists that all is well, even though he and the audience know full well the reasons why this is a white lie (Fig. 24.2).

It is one of Haneke's most poignant scenes. Georges's mother conveys her concern through her eyes, but she also conveys her own pride. In response to Georges's own inquiry, she insists that she is not "unwell," as Georges believes

Fig. 24.2   Georges (Daniel Auteuil) confers with his mother (Annie Girardot) about a disturbing recent dream and a past childhood incident. *Caché* (2005), dir. Michael Haneke, prod. Andrew Colton and Veit Heiduschka.

she is. Her eyes tell all and she attempts to push a smile upon her face so that Georges will not feel any more of a burden than he is obviously already feeling. Mother and son are alike in that they resist any opportunity to communicate the truth, ensuring the other that "all is well" and that "life continues," whether through work or TV watching or whatever else makes up their (as they like to see it) conventional and traditional lives. They succumb to mutual deception in avoiding the creation of extra burdens and to ensure an inauthentic sense of well-being.

And yet Georges is not afraid to ask his mother about a childhood incident that ended rather badly and that may have come back to haunt him and his family. Perhaps he expects and even wishes that his mother will (as she does indeed do) attempt to return him to a sense that "all is well" and that there is no reason to have a troubled conscience over a childhood event at this point in his life. His mother tells him stoically – in the same reserved way in which Georges had previously refused to share any problems that were bothering him – that she does not think of it any more. It all happened so long ago and it is not a happy memory. She does not wish to relive it, despite her son's report of a recent dream about the subject and her brief curiosity about the dream. The sad story of young Majid has been buried for a long time, and, in their eyes, hopefully will continue to be. Georges calls his dreams "stupid," and that is that.

This is a scene whose primary theme is the repression of the truth, even amidst a half-hearted attempt to get at the truth. Repression may be viewed as the psychological attempt to conceal a true perspective on one's life by temporarily substituting a different and/or less-than-true perspective, thereby "burying" or "bottling up" the psychological energy associated with the concealed point of view. This occurs, for example, when many of Haneke's film characters continue their daily routines and try to tell themselves that things are fine as psychological problems nonetheless mount. This is a kind of repression that has negative and even fatal consequences.

Repression can easily lead to the attempt to establish the illusion of a permanent perspective when one chooses to stick with the status quo no matter what – which, again, ultimately does injustice to the fleeting, variable, and multifaceted nature of human existence. Georges's insistence that he and his family merely "chug along" with "no great highs or lows," despite trouble brewing below the surface, is a perfect illustration of the self-repressive willingness to create the illusion of a humdrum but inauthentic existence. And this is the kind of repression that characterizes the late nineteenth- and early twentieth-century European bourgeois culture against which writers and thinkers such as Nietzsche, Freud, Hesse, and the Viennese Secession artists reacted so furiously.[17] Haneke – like these intellectual and cultural forebears whom he knows well as a student of philosophy and the arts – is a critic of the superficiality and complacency bred by a materialistic consumer culture. And he is not afraid to reveal the dangers involved in such an existence.

Haneke as Anti-Nihilist

There is a final way in which Haneke persuades us to think about our attitudes toward the truth, and that is by depicting the consequences of the outright negation of the overall value of truth. This is a form of *nihilism* that has epistemological as well as moral dimensions, implying a loss of belief in the very goal of truth as something that is intrinsically good.

According to its most basic meaning, nihilism is the conviction that nothing matters and that nothing makes a difference. A genuine nihilist often adopts such a position due to an all-encompassing skepticism or feeling of indignation, most especially in the form of a lack of faith in traditional values and in conventional structures of meaning. By rejecting the need for truthfulness or truth-acquisition as an end-in-itself in our everyday lives, communication becomes a mere game at best and the philosophical debate over appropriate truth-models becomes moot. The negation of the value of truth itself may lead to a pathological form of life-denial according to which moral propositions become meaningless. Such an attitude or orientation often emerges when we begin to over-generalize after experiencing the sheer irrationality of others' acts (e.g., acts of arbitrary violence) and/or when we come to acknowledge the seeming contingency of our lives.

Now it would be too easy, from an overly quick survey of Haneke's films, to classify him as a nihilist because of his choices of subject matter as well as his willingness to undermine audience trust and narrative truth-telling. But a director who chooses subject matter that evokes reflection on the problem of nihilism is not necessarily one who maintains with consistent conviction that nothing makes a difference or that all moral propositions lack genuine meaning. By his very will to make such films and to build a career upon the continual choice of such subject matter, Haneke is indeed, I would argue, an *anti*-nihilist. Not unlike Stanley Kubrick, Haneke reveals the problem of nihilism in modern society and seeks to point beyond the problem. He makes us acknowledge the ugly truth of reality and also the real possibility of our own eventual numbness, detachment, and indifference. As Haneke once said in an interview:

> I think it can hardly be denied that each fictional story, no matter how cryptic or horrible, is a trifle compared with the horror that strikes against us in reality. In order to see this, one must not be a pessimist – it suffices if one is simply more-or-less awake . . . What is positive can only be the merciless demand for personal truthfulness. Only: The truth is no longer beautiful. As Nietzsche already said in the past century: "For a philosopher it is an indignity to say that the good and the beautiful are the same. He must add that one should clobber the truth. The truth is ugly."[18]

Haneke often evokes a nihilistic form of anxiety or horror: our dread, not of some specific object or threat, but of the very sense of meaninglessness or "nothingness" that may seem to pervade our lives at certain moments. For example, certain acts of violence in Haneke's films become nihilistic when they reveal that the human regard for reason and truth has been completely rejected – when it is the very failure to engage in rational communication that has occasioned the hatred or self-contempt that has led to such violence. Nihilistic horror is most evident in scenes where there is a rejection of the attempt at reasonable dialog, implying no desire whatsoever on the part of certain characters for truthfulness and mutual understanding.

Such a rejection is illustrated in the type of *seemingly* irresolvable conflicts between cultures and generations that is the primary theme of *Code Unknown*, whose very title may indicate a lack of mutual trust or understanding. In this film there is an unbridgeable chasm of silence (despite their love) between Jean (Alexandre Hamidi), the boy who comes to visit his brother in Paris, and his father, a stoic farmer. Attempts at communication and expressed affection have been forsaken, just as there is no conversation possible between those who know nothing of each other's language. There are indeed attempts at shared understanding in the film: Georges (Thierry Neuvic), a photojournalist, attempts to communicate the suffering in Kosovo to others through static images, just as Amadou (Ona Lu Yenke), an immigrant in Paris, tells the police officers that he will explain how his altercation with Jean has arisen. The attempts themselves are not nihilistic, since there is still faith here in the very will to communicate, but the context in which these attempts occur points to the possibility of an indifferent, perhaps meaningless world in which such endeavors are likely to fail. In the case of Georges, we do not see any immediate evidence of his photos resulting in any greater understanding of the happenings in Kosovo. Even more importantly, we even wonder what *he* has personally learned about suffering, since he is quite unsympathetic to Anne's concerns about the possibility that the girl living next door to her is being abused. In the case of Amadou, his attempt at communication falls on the deaf, biased ears of the policemen and they instantly escort him forcibly to jail.

In *Caché* a similar danger of nihilistic surrender is embodied in the confrontations between Georges and Majid, particularly in their final encounter. The opportunity for a genuinely redeeming conversation has been forsaken – ironically so, given that Georges is by profession a television talk-show host. Their acts of "mutual communication" have become a series of accusations, threats, and denials, all founded on lies and misperceptions. The only act of "closure" by which Majid sees fit to end their renewed "relationship" is a wordless act of self-destruction – a leap into the abyss.

Haneke presents us with worlds in which a belief in the positive nature of truthfulness and mutual understanding becomes jeopardized. In both *Caché* and *Code Unknown*, the fragility of human dialog is especially evident due to situations in which an implicit power imbalance exists. Non-first world immigrants are driven to forsake their attempts at forging reciprocal bonds of trust and communication with their first world counterparts. Prior attempts are greeted with derision and even hatred, and all that seems to remain is the act of surrendering one's very will to express the truth. For those who advocate a dialogical model of truth with a goal of universalizability in mind, Haneke shows us here that such a model may be inapplicable in situations where dialog is futile and even rejected. But once there is enough compassion, respectfulness, or simply tolerance to establish a situation in which different perspectives may be brought into conversation, the dialogical model may certainly be applied – though not without a corresponding recognition of its dependence upon a fragile and limited bond of trust between viewpoints that are otherwise self-contained and opposed.

And so, as with modernist European art cinema in general, Haneke's act of "secession" from the narrative and cinematic styles of mainstream Hollywood cinema is not the act of breaking away from rational civilized culture – just as Nietzsche was not merely some exuberant advocate of irrationalism. Here we must again remember the aims of many of Haneke's artistic forebears: the existentialists and the Secessionists. Haneke's acts of anti-conventionalism are those of departing from the deadening effects of the stagnant traditions of contemporary bourgeois culture – particularly today's industrialized, globalized, and technologized Western culture. Haneke attempts to show us that any surrender to the repressiveness and mediocrity of such a culture may in fact lead to senseless acts of deception and even violence. In his emphasis on the idea of perspectivism, the director reminds us that the trust we often place in abstract, dogmatic ideals and collectivized, impersonal goals results in forms of inauthenticity and mediocrity. By pointing to the need for creative individuality, thinkers like Nietzsche and artists like Haneke must sometimes violate our trust in conventional and traditional forms of truth-telling, and occasionally in ways that initially appear sadistic or even nihilistic. They are being truthful, even when creating illusions.

Acknowledgments

Many thanks to Roy Grundmann for his detailed, indispensable advice before I shaped my essay into its final form. And I thank him most especially for having interested me in Haneke in the first place.

Notes

1   And there are certainly other examples from *Caché*. During their dinner party for friends, the doorbell rings and Georges goes to answer it, finding a new tape and drawing in a plastic bag. When he returns, after putting these items in his coat pocket in the front hallway, Anna asks who it was, and Georges replies "Nothing . . . There was nobody." Later, when Georges talks to Majid in the latter's apartment, Georges asks: "What do you want?" Majid: "Nothing." After Georges finally confesses everything

to Anna, she inquires if he told his mother and asks what she said in response. Georges replies: "Nothing." And finally, after their son Pierrot is returned home after he worries his parents by staying away all night without any attempt at communicating where he is, Anna asks her son: "What's wrong?" Pierrot: "Nothing."

2   For example, in *Variation* (1983), Haneke's earlier production for Austrian/German television, the marriage of a couple slowly disintegrates as the husband cultivates an adulterous relationship. He then becomes highly resistant to discussing matters with his wife when she begins to suspect the truth and then demands some dialog about the issue. He refuses to respond, not merely because of a desire for deception but, more importantly, because of sheer indifference to his wife's emotional concerns.

3   Interview with Michael Haneke, Kino DVD version of his film *Time of the Wolf* (2003).

4   For example, the wife's visiting brother in *The Seventh Continent* (1989) breaks down crying at the dinner table with hardly a word uttered, and along with the silent responses of his sister's family, there is much "said" here in terms of what is *meant* when so little is actually *spoken*. On the other hand, the young hoodlums of *Funny Games* (both Austrian [1997] and American [2007] versions) *say* much more than they really *mean*, especially when their nonsensical play of idle chatter reveals an underlying core of utter irrationality, one than leads to random acts of sadistic violence. This "murder" of everyday meaningfulness or intelligibility begins with an intentional disregard of the truth.

5   The quotes here are taken from a printed insert in the Kino DVD version of Haneke's *Code Unknown* (on the reverse is the scene index) entitled "A Letter to Producer Marin Karmitz from Writer/Director Michael Haneke."

6   "Letter to Producer Marin Karmitz."

7   See, for example, Heidegger's landmark philosophical text *Sein und Zeit* (*Being and Time*) or his later *Gelassenheit* (translated as *Discourse on Thinking*). See also Gadamer's *Wahrheit und Methode* (*Truth and Method*).

8   Other examples of Haneke's "grace notes" may include the silent glimpses of a surreal coastline in *Benny's Video* (1992), the icily beautiful shots of natural landscapes in *Time of the Wolf,* or the stunning vision of the ghost-like donkey (recalling the title "character" of Haneke's admittedly favorite film, Robert Bresson's *Au hasard Balthazar,* 1966) at the end of his early TV production, *The Rebellion* (1992).

9   Serge Toubiana's interview with Michael Haneke, a special feature of the Kino Video DVD version of *Caché.*

10 See Seyla Benhabib (1990) and, in the same collection, Karl-Otto Apel and Jürgen Habermas.

11 Benhabib (1990: 337).

12 Benhabib (1990). For example: "And if I am correct that it is the process of such dialogue, conversation, and mutual understanding, and not consensus which is our goal, discourse theory can represent the moral point of view without having to invoke the fiction of the *homo economicus* or *homo politicus*" (358).

13 In his early film *71 Fragments of a Chronology of Chance* (1994), the inevitability of multiple perspectives is made emphatic in terms of the title itself and what it means in describing the very narrative format and accompanying style of the film. The movie is broken up into seventy-one fragmented scenes that, while presented in an ineluctably linear fashion, are connected at times in a mostly contingent manner.

14   *Funny Games* adopts self-reflexive (film-within-a-film) moves when the young hoodlums speak to the camera at times and then rewind the film at a later point in the film
to make us recognize in a jarring fashion that all that we have been watching has
been a video recording of the events taking place. This forces us into a realm of limbo
between reality and illusion and we question now even the filmmaker himself as a
truth-teller and as someone to trust. Is he simply playing funny games with us?

15   For the concept of Romantic irony, see for example Lilian R. Furst (1979), and especially her chapter "Romantic Irony and Narrative Stance."

16   Haneke explicitly depicts the aftermath of the grim turn-of-the-century (ca. 1900)
Viennese culture occasioned by Franz Joseph's obsessive conservatism in his earlier
production for Austrian television, *The Rebellion*, which was based on the novel by
Joseph Roth and which also (and most especially in its concluding section) forms a
kind of homage to F. W. Murnau's landmark silent classic *The Last Laugh* (*Der letzte
Mann*, 1924). The main character, Andreas Pum, is a former soldier who has sacrificed
one of his legs, not to mention years of opportunity for personal happiness, in military
service to the emperor during World War I. After the war he is now classified by
his society as an invalid, regardless of his wartime service and loyalty to the
emperor. He continues to live a drab and dreary existence by maintaining subservience
to almost everyone around him. When Pum finally explodes and protests against an
insulting injustice done to him by a "social superior" on the street tram, Andreas
is punished for his expression of sudden anger, a culmination of his long repressed
resentment against those who have looked down upon him.

17   The Viennese Secession (following in the wake of the Berlin and Munich Secessions)
was a group and movement of artists, founded by painter Gustav Klimt and architect Otto Wagner among others in 1897, who responded critically to a conservative
policy of traditionalism in the arts that had been advocated by leading schools and
museums. Haneke is in many ways a contemporary example of a "secessionist" who
seeks to break away from mainstream cinema.

18   This is my translation of the following excerpt from Franz Grabner and Michael Haneke
(2008): "Und ich denke, dem ist kaum zu widersprechen, denn jede erfundene
Geschichte, sei sie noch so abgründig und grauenvoll, ist eine Lächerlichkeit gegen
das Grauen, das uns aus und in der Realität entgegenschlägt. Um das zu sehen, braucht
man kein Pessimist zu sein – es genügt schon, wenn man einigermassen wach ist"
(11); "dieses 'Positive' kann nur die unbarmherzige Einforderung persönlicher
Wahrhaftigkeit sein. Nur: Die Wahrheit ist eben nicht mehr schön. Wie sagte
Nietzsche schon im letzten Jahrhundert: 'An einem Philosophen ist es eine
Nichtswürdigkeit, zu sagen, das Gute und das Schöne sind Eins. Fügt er gar noch
hinzu: und das Wahre!, so soll man ihn prügeln. Die Wahrheit ist hässlich" (12–13).

References and Further Reading

Apel, Karl-Otto: "Is the Ethics of the Ideal Communication Community a Utopia? On the
Relationship between Ethics, Utopia, and the Critique of Utopia," *The Communica-
tive Ethics Controversy*, ed. Seyla Benhabib and Fred Dallmayr (Cambridge, MA and
London: MIT Press, 1990), pp. 23–59.

Benhabib, Seyla: "Afterword: Communicative Ethics and Current Controversies in Practical Philosophy," *The Communicative Ethics Controversy*, ed. Seyla Benhabib and Fred Dallmayr (Cambridge, MA and London: MIT Press, 1990), pp. 330–69.

Furst, Lilian R.: *The Contours of European Romanticism* (London and Basingstoke: Macmillan, 1979).

Gadamer, Hans-Georg: *Truth and Method*, second revised edition, trans. Joel Weinsheimer and Donald G. Marshall (New York: Crossroad, 1990).

Grabner, Franz: " 'Der Name der Erbsünde ist Verdrängung': A Conversation with Michael Haneke," *Michael Haneke und seine Filme: Eine Pathologie der Konsumgesellschaft*, 2nd edition, ed. Christian Wessely, Gerhard Larcher, and Franz Grabner (Marburg: Schüren, 2008), pp. 11–24.

Habermas, Jürgen: "Discourse Ethics: Notes on a Program of Philosophical Justification," *The Communicative Ethics Controversy*, ed. Seyla Benhabib and Fred Dallmayr (Cambridge, MA and London: MIT Press, 1990), pp. 60–110.

Haneke, Michael: "A Letter to Producer Marin Karmitz from Writer/Director Michael Haneke," insert in *Code Unknown*, Kino Video DVD.

Haneke, Michael: Interview with Serge Toubiana, *Caché*, Kino Video DVD.

Haneke, Michael: Interview, *Time of the Wolf*, Kino Video DVD.

Heidegger, Martin: *Being and Time*, trans. John Macquarrie and Edward Robinson (New York, Hagerstown, San Francisco, London: Harper and Row, 1962).

Heidegger, Martin: *Discourse on Thinking*, trans. John M. Anderson and E. Hans Freund (New York: Harper Torchbooks, 1966).

25

The Unknown Piano Teacher

Charles Warren

I suspect that most if not all of us who want to think about Michael Haneke's films, and talk about them, feel ourselves to be beginners, tentative. We are impressed – perhaps feel provoked – by this still ongoing, evolving, and changing body of work. We want to find ways to approach it. More power to anyone who feels confident, feels that the riddle is solved, or is on the verge of being solved. But I sense that the feeling of being tentative is widespread. Perhaps this is a good thing. Perhaps the attitude is a good one for all film, for all art. Let us keep starting over. Let us make experiments in thinking. Perhaps the peculiar provocation of Haneke's work – taking hold of us, making us feel compelled to think, leaving us unsure whether we quite approve, making us willing, or hungry, for new approach after new approach – perhaps all this can show us, or remind us, how we really stand, or best stand, in regard to other work than Haneke's.

My own experience viewing Haneke's films, going back to an early stage, has been one of constantly being reminded of other films than his, other filmmakers, other film projects. Perhaps Haneke means to announce that he is ringing changes on concerns already in place, or that he means to disrupt or replace such concerns. Perhaps the allusions, or some of them, are not deliberate, something in film just taking over, the author dying not so much into his own work as into the very medium of the fictional feature film, which has its ways over time of wanting to go, its own drives to recurrence and transformation. In any case, the invocations of other films in Haneke seem to help to see more precisely what the Haneke films are doing. In what follows I take up a number of instances that help define, I think, the Haneke temperament. Then I turn more extensively to *The Piano Teacher* (*La Pianiste*, 2001), where my main topic is the film's affinity with the "unknown woman" material named and so eloquently described by Stanley Cavell.

There is more going on here, though, than clarification through comparison. Films talk to each other, in accord with T. S. Eliot's formulation in "Tradition and the Individual Talent" that "what happens when a new work of art is created is something that happens simultaneously to all the works of art which preceded it" (Eliot 1960: 5). Cavell, thinking of art and philosophy, speaks of the past as "unpredictably awaiting actualization" by what happens later (Cavell 2004: 356). What happens later is actualized, too, as we rethink, rediscover, what went before. Films, like other works of art, talk to each other, illuminate each other, re-form each other, and thus make film culture, something we know and engage with through the making of critical claims.

In *The Seventh Continent* (1989), with the sense of fragmentariness, the numerous brief shots of parts of actions, parts of human beings in action, objects without their context, a physical world seemingly more present than any human consciousness within it, one thinks of Resnais, of such a passage, say, as the brilliant opening of *Muriel* (1963), where the assault of images, the quick cuts, makes it hard to decipher the human encounter between Hélène (Delphine Seyrig) and her customer, in Hélène's apartment where everything is an antique for sale – objects marked by the past, by various pasts, and mixed together dressed up for new consumption – in all respects like the characters in the film. For Haneke, does Resnais's old project need to be revived in the 1990s? Is there a difference? Fragmentariness in Resnais suggests the difficulty of perceiving anything whole, perhaps because nothing is in fact whole, for the characters in the film or for us, if we will think about it, getting rid of our illusions. There does emerge in *Muriel* a sense of people with rich, if confused, human concerns. Relative to this, the people in *The Seventh Continent* are blank, and perhaps this indicates Haneke's sense that times have worsened, that Resnais's world where things and appearances – or habits of the work world, as in *Mon Oncle d'Amérique* (1980) – overwhelm human consciousness has degenerated to a condition of complete dehumanization. The only desire is for death, annihilation, figured as the longing for a beautiful utopia, Australia, the seventh continent, seen as a poster image. (I do not think so much of Bresson's fragmentariness, though clearly Haneke loves Bresson, and he alludes to him, or quotes him, often. The fragments in Bresson seem weighted with a meaning we cannot quite discern, like the weighted images of a dream. There is a sense that Bresson knows, or that his film knows, a whole, a greater entity than we see, of which we can have only intimations. Haneke's surfaces, relatively speaking, are just materiality.)

The prominent car wash in *The Seventh Continent*, where the physical and its maddening sounds press on the characters and on the viewer, recalls Godard's *Two or Three Things I Know About Her* (1967), a film about the sub-bourgeoisie, rather than the struggling middle class, as in *The Seventh Continent*. The car wash in these films is both the condensed provocation of the world as it is, its materiality and noise, and a baptism into new possibilities. Robin Wood has said that Haneke's use of the Alban Berg Violin Concerto in *The Seventh Continent*, when the father and child go to sell the family car, represents the director's wish to find a larger perspective, we might say a sublime and liberated alternative, to the condition of this world (Wood 2007: 48). The same might be said of Godard's use of the late Beethoven String Quartet, the F-major, opus 135, into which *Two or Three Things* explodes upon Juliette's car's emergence from the wash and its drive down a leafy Paris street. Godard manages to suggest a possible strong creative dimension even to acceptance of one's fate, the wife/mother/prostitute Juliette's fate in *Two or Three Things*, like the prostitute Nana's fate in *Vivre sa vie* (1962), or Ferdinand's fate in *Pierrot le fou* (1965), or the Virgin's fate in *Hail Mary* (1985). Godard is more a romantic than Resnais or Haneke. But perhaps *The Seventh Continent* suggests a beauty and a good to its family's rite of self-annihilation, preceded by the drawn-out ritual of destruction of worldly goods, cutting up of money and flushing it down the toilet, and so on. The fragment of Berg's Violin Concerto, this premier Austrian modernist's variation on a Bach chorale, itself derived from an older source than Bach, is not just an alternative to this family's world, but an epitome of their impulse to destroy and escape this world. The Berg, the beauty and orderliness of Haneke's shooting and editing (like Resnais's), the final actions of the family, all come together as a form of knowing and reacting that moves the viewer to a new place, washing over the viewer like those waves that come to life in the poster image of the Australian shore.

Haneke's dialog with other films and filmmakers goes on, for me, all but unendingly. His acknowledgment of lively human feeling in the child of *The Seventh Continent*, as when she cries out at the destruction of the fish tank, looks forward to a hope he seems to place in children and the young later – in Benny at the end of *Benny's Video* (1992), when he seems, unlike his parents, to regret all that has happened in violence and covering it up; or hope in the boy who would sacrifice himself near the end of *Time of the Wolf* (2003); or in the youths at the end of *Caché* (2005), who seem possibly the so-far unidentified accusers and punishers of the adult world's suppressed historical guilt. All this links Haneke to his contemporary in Iran, Abbas Kiarostami, who suggests repeatedly that children can come to life morally in ways impossible for their blinkered, wounded, sometimes authoritarian elders (and when Kiarostami leaves the world of children for that purely of adults, in *A Taste of Cherry* [1997], his theme is, of course, a disposition for suicide – remember that in *The Seventh Continent* it is not the child who desires to die; the plan, the order, comes from above, from the world of adults). The deaf children struggling to learn to communicate who appear in *Code Unknown* (2000) at the beginning and the end, framing the film, recall the stuttering boy and his therapy session at the start of Tarkovsky's *Mirror* (1975). If *Mirror* suggests that the past and reality of the Soviet Union can be spoken after all, *Code Unknown* answers with a bleaker picture of incomprehension in contemporary, prosperous, multi-ethnic Western Europe, though Haneke does acknowledge, most pointedly in the children, positive desire and struggle. Berg's Violin Concerto was offered as a tribute to a young woman who died of polio (Manon, the daughter of Walter Gropius and Alma, widow of Gustav Mahler, who wrote the *Kindertotenlieder*), and Haneke's use of the Berg in *The Seventh Continent* may be taken as a tribute to the little girl's feeling and possibilities in that film. This little girl, pretending at school to be blind, crying out there in a certain way, recalls the little boy pretending to be paralyzed in Antonioni's *Red Desert* (1964), another film about dehumanizing materiality. But *Red Desert* ends on a note of survival, the mother telling her child, who is now walking, of birds who learn to cope with poisonous gas, to recognize it and fly around it. Perhaps Haneke's films are more aimed at survival than is usually acknowledged. Allow yourself to be provoked in the right way, come into film as knowledge – a very Tarkovskian concept – and you may be saved.[1]

Resnais's fragmentariness comes to mind again with the narrative style of *71 Fragments of a Chronology of Chance* (1994) and *Code Unknown: Incomplete Tales of Several Journeys*. More pertinent perhaps is the American Robert Altman, who with films such as *Nashville* (1975) and *Short Cuts* (1993) began giving the picture of the complex life of a city, with many characters, many separate little worlds, the film moving from one to another and back and around seemingly at random. Life is characterized by miscomprehension and frustrated desires that issue in violence, as film itself seems to struggle to see, to comprehend, to keep up, and perhaps to wreak its own violence – on the film world and on viewers. Altman touches as deep a social and political despair as does Haneke. Yet there are differences. Altman takes a more mystical, fixated interest in death (even than Haneke does in *The Seventh Continent*, if in fact he does take such an interest, as I have suggested). There is a beauty that stops all thought, about McCabe in the snow at the end, about the Sterling Hayden writer character dying in the surf in *The Long Goodbye* (1973), Cookie in her ghost world in *Cookie's Fortune* (1999), the ruined empty room at the end of *Come Back to the Five and Dime, Jimmy Dean, Jimmy Dean* (1982), the dark that surrounds everything in *A Prairie Home Companion* (2006). And Altman's films touch forms of ecstasy, perhaps specifically American forms, not available to Haneke's world. McCabe and Mrs. Miller, the doomed lovers of *Thieves Like Us* (1974), the mad women of *Nashville* and *Come Back to the Five and Dime*, express themselves lyrically as their world devours them – something they almost seem to invite. Altman himself is lyrical. Sometimes taking hours, lingering over his material, he is an elegist. He is a disappointed idealist, mourning the loss of humanity. Haneke, more ordered, moving things along, is a critic, a teacher – this quality in him gives a nice resonance to the English-language title of *The Piano Teacher*.[2]

Altman's interest in the death wish has been linked by his more astute critics to Hitchcock's nihilism. The world needs and wants to die.[3] And Hitchcock figures very strongly in the Haneke mix. The cutting up of a dead body and cleaning away of a violent crime, from *Rear Window* (1954) and *Psycho* (1960), recur in *Benny's Video*; and *Psycho*'s subjection of everyday, familiar people to the annihilating wrath of a Norman Bates, rising up in their midst, recurs in *Funny Games* (1997). Robin Wood thinks of *The Birds* (1963) in regard to *Funny Games* – the universe taking revenge on the complacent (Wood 2004). Benny, overhearing his parents' discussion of the cutting up and cleaning up that they plan, is put in the position of *Rear Window*'s photographer L. B. Jefferies (James Stewart), aware of Thorwald's actions at a distance, across the courtyard, speculating, reacting. This link of Benny to Jefferies would go with Haneke's theme of the young coming to life morally. Benny has killed a young woman, suddenly and spontaneously, taunted by her. But Jefferies, too, something of an overgrown boy (as Erika in *The Piano Teacher* is something of an overgrown child), is implicated in the crime he wants to expose; Jefferies has projected his own violent impulses and resentment of a woman onto the screen, and thus behind the screen, of *that* window at a distance – so it feels in the film. Moral awakening goes with implication. Benny comes back in a sense – the same actor – to torment and destroy a well-off family in *Funny Games*. This is a more claustrophobic film than *Psycho* or *The Birds*. Norman Bates and the birds are other to, represent an alternative to, the everyday people and everyday world that they assault. Hitchcock suggests that the larger world than us holds strange recesses that we might venture into, or be forced to venture into, meeting dissolution. Haneke is more this-worldly, more purely the social critic. The tormenting and murderous duo in *Funny Games* seem part of the family in a way, well-bred young men who have run amok, something the world of the family has bred up radically to go against itself.

A dehumanized world, the power of music to suggest an alternative, the power of the child awakening morally through implication, a death wish that almost goes over the line from being, on Haneke's part, indirect social critique, into being just pure death wish, opening into mysterious realms – all this comes into play in *The Piano Teacher*. And indeed this film, Haneke's strongest in my view, echoes other films than Haneke's and those other films' concerns (with differences), finds itself involved with and enabled by other films, more than ever. Erika Kohut (Isabelle Huppert) lives with her mother, works as a highly respected teacher at the Vienna Conservatory, plays chamber music with other skilled musicians, and pursues perverse – by conventional standards – sexual interests, spying on others, viewing pornography in a private room in a video store, eventually getting involved with a younger man whom she entreats, by letter, to abuse her, sounding as if she is quoting the fantastic extended catalog of abuses from a Sade novel. For a time in the film, scenes and actions come as disconnected surprises, each seeming iconic, one more window into who this woman is. I believe the film is a character film, an attempt to get at, to evoke, a remarkable individual, and thus, becoming a moral project, to get at, to evoke, new realms of human possibility. Isabelle Huppert brings her own resonance to the film. But part of the resonance of Erika Kohut in this film is the film's connection to other women, other films.[4]

When I first saw *The Piano Teacher*, two scenes struck me as uncanny replayings of scenes from other films. When Erika/Huppert cuts her genitals with a razor blade, it seems a recurrence of the unnerving episode in Ingmar Bergman's *Cries and Whispers* (1972) when Karin (Ingrid Thulin) cuts herself with the shard of broken wineglass, and moments later, sitting in bed with a mad look on her face, reaches from her crotch to smear her face with blood, to the astonishment of her stuffy, difficult husband across the room. Karin/Thulin's act with the broken glass in *Cries and Whispers* is the rebellion of a narrow and unhappy character.

Erika Kohut is in ways frustrated and constricted in life, but her cutting of herself is private. She does not come out of the bathroom and make a demonstration to her mother, the way Karin in *Cries and Whispers* does to her husband. Erika's act seems in a way an experiment, a seeking for sensation, even for gratification of a sort (and in the film there is only this one incident; in the Elfriede Jelinek novel on which the film is based, Erika cuts herself frequently, in various places on the body – she is a familiar psychological type, the cutter, self-hating, self-punishing).

But if Erika is not quite Karin, Karin / Thulin in *Cries and Whispers* seems an extension or reincarnation of Ester (Thulin) in Bergman's earlier film *The Silence* (1963); and Ester there resonates with Erika Kohut. Thulin, with her unique deportment, links the women she plays in *Cries and Whispers* and *The Silence*, but also the scene with Karin's genital cutting recalls, answers, extends, the scene of Ester's masturbation in *The Silence*, just as both scenes come back in a way in *The Piano Teacher*. The strong scene, the strong image, is a main way for films to speak to us and to each other.[5] To go at one's genitals with a hand with a razor blade, with a shard of glass, with fingernails – for pain, for pleasure, for something that mixes the two – there is a blurring of these scenes or is about them a charge that leaps from one to another and invites reflection on who the women are and what it might mean that they are kin.

Ester in *The Silence* is an intellectual and professional woman, an artist in a sense – surely a translator can be an artist – formidable, bigger than her world. How many such portraits of a woman are there in film? Like Erika Kohut, Ester is often able to relate to others only through gestures of overbearing dominance or embarrassing abjection; and this seems not so much a fault as a necessity, or if a fault, the world's fault more than the woman's – she cannot break through to the stupid world, and resorts to extremes. The woman is not to be really known to her world, or to us as viewers – we are given only a strong intimation, made aware there is an endless more. Ester is ill in the superior way a Dostoevsky or Thomas Mann character is ill, her physical frailty manifesting an intellectual and spiritual superiority. Erika Kohut is not physically frail, but her obsessions and perverse behavior seem an equivalent. Ester seems middle-aged, her life turning downward, and Erika young, with a sense there is some future for her at the end – Haneke and Huppert find the child in Erika, in accord with Haneke's suggestion throughout his films that the child has a propulsive force that might save itself, might even save the world. In *The Silence* the measure of hope goes to Ester's little nephew, Johan, with whom she and the boy's mother are traveling and are situated in the strange hotel for most of the film. *The Piano Teacher* takes the formidable, artistic woman of *The Silence* and concentrates her in the child-woman, the seeker Erika, who might actually go somewhere, like little Johan on the train at the end of *The Silence*, leaving Ester behind in her room – and Johan, like Erika, has engaged in perverse sexual experiences, forming himself as he wandered the hotel's corridors over the course of the film – Erika is Ester in a way, but also this little boy. (Thulin was thirty-six years old at the time of *The Silence*, Huppert forty-six at the time of *The Piano Teacher* – the sense of age in the films is all a matter of the individual woman and her bearing.)

In *Cries and Whispers* Karin, her sister, and a woman servant stay in a country house, looking after a third sister in her dying days. The house has red walls, and all décor and clothes are black or white. It is an artificial world, a mental space, and all incidents have the suggestion of being fantasy. Thus Karin's scene with the broken glass, an address to her husband and a satisfaction of who knows what other stirrings in herself, has the air of a creative act, linking this high-bourgeois constrained Victorian wife to the women artist figures of *The Silence* and *The Piano Teacher*. One achievement of all the "unknown woman" material that Cavell describes, to which I am coming, is to declare the artist in the ordinary woman, or in the woman whom the world, and we, may not be disposed to see as an artist.

The second scene in *The Piano Teacher* that seems (to me) to replay another film is later, some time after the genital mutilation, when Erika gets into bed with her mother and appears to assault her sexually, saying in a childlike way at the end of it all when everything has calmed down, that she has glimpsed some of her mother's pubic hair. What this brings to mind is Chantal Akerman's *Meetings with Anna* (or *Anna's Meetings*, *Les Rendez-vous d'Anna*, 1978), where the lead character (played by Aurore Clément at age thirty-three) gets into bed, nude, with her mother for what turns out to be a warm, calm conversation, ultimately turning to the topic of sexual relations between women, recently experienced by this daughter for the first time. Akerman's Anne (she is called Anna only by the Italian woman friend with whom she had the affair, in a telephone machine voice message at the end of the film) is another portrait of a woman artist, in this case a filmmaker, decidedly young. She travels about Europe by train, meeting strangers and old acquaintances, listening to them, going to bed with a couple of men, talking to her mother, out of all this seeming to reflect, forming her identity, forming herself as an artist. We do not come to know her fully; what she takes in, and her quality of seeming to reflect, point to what she might be – and she is decidedly in flux. Anne's mother is not an antagonist like Erika Kohut's mother, and does not play a large part in her life – there is only the one scene, where Anne stops in her travels for a night. But the scenes in the two films stand out, women getting into bed nude with their mothers, in one case to enact sexual contact, in the other to talk about sex between women. Something leaps from one film to the other, as we find ourselves in the territory of the mother empowering the daughter, through antagonism or tolerance, through physical bonding incestuous or with overtones of incest. Who are these mothers, and what are they imparting? To savor this, the identities of the mothers as film actors need to come into play.

The mothers in both *Les Rendez-vous d'Anna* and *The Piano Teacher* are played by women who made a big impression in key roles in Italian film around 1960, and whom the later films seem to bring back from a certain obscurity, older, trailing certain clouds of glory with implications in that for what their daughters can gain from them. The mother in *Les Rendez-vous d'Anna* is Lea Massari, the girl (named Anna) who disappeared on the island in Antonioni's *L'Avventura* (1960), an alienated society beauty who has to give way, in narrative importance, to the Monica Vitti character (Claudia), a mature, charitable outsider to the film's social world, who becomes a traveler. Akerman's Anne is a version of the Vitti character, like her a traveler, looking for new bearings. Claudia/Vitti is Anna/Massari's best friend, her girlfriend, and loves her and wears her clothes after Anna's disappearance. But Claudia is born out of Anna's disappearance, and finds her own way. Akerman's Anne has left home and her mother's world of the dutiful wife and the traditional family, but draws strength from her mother's nonchalance about her lesbianism – the mother shows a little of the free spirit of Anna/Massari in *L'Avventura*. Erika Kohut will also both draw from and oppose the mother.

Of course, between *L'Avventura* and *Les Rendez-vous d'Anna* comes Louis Malle's *Murmur of the Heart* (1971), where Massari plays the mother who takes her teenaged son to bed. *Murmur of the Heart* plays into *Les Rendez-vous d'Anna* and also *The Piano Teacher* with the suggestion that a mother's nourishment of a child is unaccountable, unpredictable, tied to the mother's own independent nature and desires. In *Murmur of the Heart* the new growth, the counter-force, is not a daughter but a son, though a peculiar one, looking younger than his given age, sickly in a Thomas Mann way (murmur of the heart), treated as girlish by his older brothers, a reader of Camus and Proust, interested in self-defining existential acts, even suicide, and in lesbianism. Unaccountable mother love, unaccountable offspring. This is not the Freudian pattern where the son desires the mother but is made civilized (and unhappy) through conformity to the law of the father. Rather, independent-minded and whimsical Massari violates all law and later laughs it off with her son, presumably helping him on his strange way in life, as, in a different way, a quieter Massari does Anne/Clément in Akerman's film, and as, so I see it, Erika Kohut's mother imparts something to Erika, or is there for Erika to take it from her. We are in a world of powerful mother/daughter dynamics, but strangely Akerman's Anne and Erika Kohut are aligned also with those boys in *The Silence* and in *Murmur of the Heart*.

In *The Piano Teacher* the mother is Annie Girardot who was Nadia, the ill-fated prostitute and lover of two brothers in Visconti's *Rocco and his Brothers* (1960). Haneke's Erika Kohut is born of turbulence, even violence, a world of the displaced and the upward striving. Girardot as Erika's mother declares such a lineage for Erika. Nadia in *Rocco* was a victim caught in the counter-forces of her world (as could be said of Erika's mother, lacking the knowledge and power over her daughter's life that she would like, shut up behind a door when her daughter is raped). Erika is more comparable to the brothers, who are competitive, figures of transformation, in their case leaving behind the world of the peasantry of southern Italy and seeking a better life and admiration in the avenue of prizefighting, their form of art. And Rocco himself (Alain Delon) is an unanticipated figure, uncannily beautiful, gentle, in many conventional ways feminine, saintly – and yet the best prizefighter; this figure puts gender identity into question as all these films do, as the medium of film is so good at doing, so interested in doing, seeming in a way born to do this.

Rocco/Delon gives prizefighting the feel of art – a way of moving forward in life, of expressing the self, and a crystallized sublime image, something to contemplate – and art is what links Akerman's character Anne and Haneke's Erika, Anne a filmmaker and Erika a pianist. The films use these occupations to underscore both women's practice as artists of life, fashioners of their own lives (as the boy in *Murmur of the Heart* may come to be, as Rocco and his brothers ultimately fail to be). Anne is a listener, except when baring herself to her mother. She is one who reacts and remains polite. But she keeps moving, walking train corridors all through the night, traversing Europe, rejecting some forms of life, thinking, searching. Erika Kohut, thinking and searching, too, is more active, proceeding by fits and starts. Surely Anne as filmmaker is a figure for Akerman herself, making a creative act out of the observational, working with what is there. The art of a pianist and piano teacher is similar, bringing to new creative life the scores of Bach and Schubert, and forming the new generation of those who come to her for study. Perhaps Erika is a figure for Haneke, creating anew out of the stuff of film culture, focusing himself specifically as teacher, like Hitchcock not sparing the rod.

If Erika begins to seem caught in a hall of mirrors with these other films, other women, and young men, this is the very point. Rimbaud said, "I am another." Film has its own way of knowing and saying, within the one film and through interaction among films, that human identity is another – which is not to banish the idea of identity, but to reunderstand it, to redefine it.

Women who are artists of their lives, standing apart from others, battered by experience with others, at times seeming mad, to others and to themselves; a crucial and formative mother/daughter dynamic; alignment of the filmmaker and of the very medium and technique of film with the central woman, with her imagination; the film revealing, in what seems like self-revelation, more and more facets of the woman as it goes along, making clear that we will never get everything – all this puts us in the world of the films Stanley Cavell has named and described as "melodramas of the unknown woman," taking the name, of course, from Max Ophuls's 1948 Hollywood film *Letter from an Unknown Woman*, starring Joan Fontaine – as it happens, a film like *The Piano Teacher* in being set in Vienna, and, like the latter, not made in the German language (the linguistic dislocation seeming to compound film's endemic putting together of closeness and distance, absorption and critique); a film about the world of music and musicians, where music aligns itself with the imagination of the heroine, her imagination of her life; a film whose central woman's character is formed on an axis of masochism and sadism, where we are asked radically to rethink these dispositions.[6] Lisa/Fontaine (with overtones of Fontaine's uncertain personality in Hitchcock's *Rebecca* [1940] and *Suspicion* [1941]) brings harm on herself and others. As a teenager she leaves home to dedicate her life to loving a man, Stefan/Louis Jourdan, who does not know her and to whom she will not speak even after a one-night affair with him that leaves her with a child and very needy. On her deathbed she writes her lover a letter that gives us the film in flashback, and that so astounds him he fails to run away from a duel that will mean his life. Her paralyzing letter is her art, fully aligned with Ophuls's dark images, the film's all but palpable sound effects, the music, the elaborate crane and tracking shots. Or does Ophuls, does the film, stand at any distance and judge Lisa? Hard to say, we are so caught up in her poetic self-revelation, which can never fully come clear.

Cavell discusses *Letter from an Unknown Woman* and other melodramas – the Sternberg/Dietrich *Blonde Venus* (1932); *Stella Dallas* (King Vidor, 1937), with Barbara Stanwyck; *Now, Voyager* (Irving Rapper, 1942), with Bette Davis; *Gaslight* (George Cukor, 1944), with Ingrid Bergman, and still other films – as part of American film culture of the 1930s and 1940s, and American culture more broadly, and in specific relation, as opposite, to a line of romantic comedies he designates "comedies of remarriage," films that center on conversational breakthroughs, and women and men finding their equals.[7] The women in the melodramas remain essentially unknown. The women, and indeed the men, in the comedies are not exactly to be known, but the woman and the man in a comedy can *acknowledge* (not know, but acknowledge) each other, can acknowledge something in each other that is crucial to each, and can proceed together, talking, giving and taking, evolving, on an uncertain path, blessed by the optimism of comedy.[8] The film comedies seem especially American in their personalities and settings, and perhaps in their optimism. But Cavell notes that the interest of the melodramas goes back into European figures such as Greta Garbo in films of the 1920s and 1930s, and of course Dietrich, and back to nineteenth-century European stage drama and opera (*A Doll's House*, *La Traviata* . . .). And it is easy to see the interest of the unknown woman extending to the alienated women of Antonioni and Bergman, to figures in Rossellini or Mizoguchi, and to later material such as Akerman's films. The roots and branches run and spread.[9]

What is important about the melodramas of the unknown woman in connection with Haneke is that these films represent something that film wants to do: put the right actress together with certain material about constrictions on a woman and the drive toward eloquence, the drive to connect, and let the woman emerge; direct and embellish and photograph and shape it as this potent situation demands. The films go where they will, unfold as they must, each film, as it emerges, casting light on, even altering, the others and the whole that all the films go to make up – a whole that is a project to unveil (to some degree) an unacknowledged aspect of the human – a project asking our critical engagement, to see one film in light of others, and to see what they are as a whole after. Haneke wades into these waters, into this realm with its strong vibrations, taking up the story of Erika Kohut and casting the star Isabelle Huppert, with her distinctive air of innocence, seriousness, and thoughtfulness, her intensity, her believability as a person of depth. One comes away from this film with memories mainly of Huppert's face, of wonderful passages of music, and of physically or emotionally violent sex acts. All these go together to make, or to begin to suggest, this woman.[10]

After announcing the players, but before the title and full credits, *The Piano Teacher* gives us a protracted domestic scene as Erika comes home at night to her mother, and the two fight physically over a dress Erika has bought, eventually reconciling and retiring for the night, together. Toward the end of the episode the camera dwells on Annie Girardot's face, hurt, regretful seemingly of a lifetime's painful experiences, human, even warm. This mother is not the simple, pushing tyrant of Jelinek's novel. This opening can seem the matrix from which all the rest of the film is derived, projected as the daughter's fantasy or film or dream out of the dark and close interior spaces of this domestic world, just as the course of events in *Blonde Venus* or *Letter from an Unknown Woman* can seem the fantasy of the woman character at the center of it. As Erika and her mother settle into bed, turn off the light, become quiet, and, presumably, begin to dream, the screen announces the title, *La Pianiste*. Erika draws something from her mother, her capacity for feeling, her violence; and also needs to form herself in opposition, to liberate herself, to get out of this house, to spin something out of it. Erika/ Huppert will never let her face become as open as Annie Girardot's. She must draw herself together and take a stand. She insists to her mother in the pillow conversation here that music and musical judgment is her own field, and that her mother should stay out of these concerns. This drawing from and opposition to the mother on the part of the central woman is characteristic, Cavell says, of the unknown woman story, the unknown woman situation – this dynamic being played out most elaborately in *Now, Voyager*.

Cavell also says that a child or child substitute will be present, at once a burden and a field for creativity and self-realization. It is easy to think of Erika's piano students as her children in a sense, perhaps even Walter, her lover. But the crucial opening with her mother comes to focus on one student in particular, Anna (again) Schober, who Erika says has a talent for Schubert, and whom we come to see working on the accompaniment for Schubert's song cycle *Winterreise*. Erika is hard on this girl in lessons, as she is on everybody, but she is also encouraging at important junctures: When Anna is upset in the street, fearing she will not be good enough to play in the student concert, Erika tells her she may well be able to play, that she should keep working and try the piece with the singer; and when Anna is ill in the bathroom before the concert rehearsal and the (male) singer is harsh to her, Erika tells her not to take it all so seriously, they won't eat her, it's just a rehearsal. Of course, in one of the film's most disturbing acts, Erika puts broken glass into Anna's coat pocket during the rehearsal, causing her to injure her right hand badly. This is perhaps done out of jealousy, after Erika sees Walter giving Anna kind attention. But there is something perversely mentoring about it. Erika causes the girl, with her talent for Schubert as Erika has acknowledged it, to bleed, just as she has caused herself to bleed with that razor blade.

In an interview with Anna's mother, Erika sends Anna the message to take this opportunity to work hard on her left hand playing, which is needed and important. In the film's first episode after the credits, the musicale in a private apartment, Erika does her most extended bit of playing and establishes her musical identity, in the final movement fugue of Bach's C-major Concerto for two keyboards, where we see Erika play a passage for left hand. In a strange way, at some level, Erika would lead her child, the talented, nervous Anna, into the world of blood and the left hand, the hand of deviance, a deviance embraced in the sane insanity of music, of Bach.

After the opening domestic scene, while the credits come, intercut shots give us moments from Erika's piano instruction with various students. Several times, the camera looks straight down onto the keyboard and playing hands – the point of view of the person playing, or of the teacher – and at one point Erika takes over and plays for the student, Anna Schober, as it happens. Haneke in effect gives his camera to Erika, suggesting that the film is her projection, that she is its director, or that he is she – try thinking of every shot as Erika's, her point of view away from herself, or her self-regard – it is possible. (Sternberg said, "I am Miss Dietrich. Miss Dietrich is me," and by "Miss Dietrich" he meant the woman in the films.)

In the opening instruction scenes we hear, and see played, striking passages by different composers. Erika makes some comments on playing technique, but here and throughout the film her comments mostly go to the meaning and feeling of the music. Unlike the character in Jelinek's novel, the film's Erika is deeply interested in music. She identifies herself through it. The film is interested in music. Haneke is interested in music. Music is a presence in the film – like Huppert herself – as it is not in Jelinek's novel, which could just as well be about some other career (and music can be a presence in prose fiction, as it is in Mann's *Doctor Faustus* or *The Magic Mountain*). And it is part of the Huppert identity that she herself is interested in music, as we see in Werner Schroeter's documentary *Poussière d'Amour* (1996), where Huppert visits the great retired dramatic soprano Martha Mödl, gets a singing lesson from her, and the two listen to a recording of Mödl singing Leonora's big aria "Abscheulicher" from Beethoven's opera *Fidelio*. Catherine Clément's *Opera, or the Undoing of Women*, a crucial text for thinking about the crucial relation between opera and film melodrama, praises Carmen as the great exception among opera heroines, a woman who does as she likes and who says "no" and sticks to it; but Clément does not mention Beethoven's heroic, creative, successful Leonora. Huppert adores Leonora, channeled through the mother/teacher figure Mödl. Crucial, for me, to the Huppert identity is her appearance in Godard's *Passion* (1982). No musicians here, but the film is fairly bursting with music, as if Godard puts every emotionally moving passage he can think of onto the soundtrack to draw expression out of the frustrated characters – frustrated precisely in expressiveness – at the center of whom is Huppert, stuttering and struggling with speech, like Tarkovsky's child or those in *Code Unknown*. Setting the mood for *Passion* is Ravel's apocalyptic, soulful *Concerto for the Left Hand*, written for Ludwig Wittgenstein's brother Paul, who lost his right arm in World War I. The hand of deviance is all that is left – it can work wonders.

The views down onto the keyboard in *The Piano Teacher*'s credits sequence ultimately give way to wider views of the studio, first with Erika working with Anna under a portrait of Bach, the composer through whom Erika will principally announce herself; then a shot taking in much of the room with Erika standing at a window, looking out, a portrait of Robert Schumann on the wall to her left. Erika faces the large rectangle of the window and the bright world beyond as if giving her attention to a film screen, imagining her life, about to project it. We do not hear Schumann's music during the film, but Erika says that he is, along with Schubert, her favorite composer, and she mentions Adorno's remark that Schumann's *Fantasy in C Major* for piano represents the mind that holds sane while knowing that it is on the border of insanity. We do not hear Schumann's music in the film, but the film *is* in a sense Erika's C-major fantasy. Arnold Schönberg, dedicated atonalist, teacher of Alban Berg among others, and some of whose music we hear in the film, famously remarked that there is still much good music to be written in C major. And so we begin Erika's film, with the elaborate musicale scene where she, as it were, summons up her appreciator and lover, Walter Klemmer, and presents herself in the Bach C-major Concerto.

It is possible to take the story that follows in more than one way, which adds to its interest. Robin Wood has written that he identifies with, and sympathizes with, Erika entirely as someone whose desires cannot be fulfilled, someone whom upbringing, culture, the world as it is, and her tempestuous nature drive to a life of frustration, neurosis, loneliness, and self-destructive acts (Wood 2002: 55). Taking the film this way would see the complex unknown woman, larger than her world, as giving signs about herself with her every act, musical or sexual, crying out, declaring herself, never being fully read or rightly responded to.

But one can also see the relationship of Erika and Walter as the playing out of a dynamic that is just what Erika wants. Walter is rather a fantasy figure, striking in looks, multi-talented, immediately in love with Erika as a result of her Bach performance – and, perhaps like all fantasy figures, humanly lacking – one does think of Stefan/Louis Jourdan in *Letter from an Unknown Woman*. Of course, the fantasy quality of these men, ultimately shallow, is due in part to their being seen so much from the highly imaginative women's point of view. Ophuls and Haneke tap into one of the great powers of film, to render the human being as at once real and fantasy.

Erika and Walter's affair begins on the occasion of the rehearsal at the conservatory for the student concert. At first we hear a good deal of the same Brahms Sextet for strings that Louis Malle uses obsessively in *The Lovers* (1958), finally having it spark off and accompany Jeanne Moreau's night of abandoned love with the Walter Klemmer-like young man she has brought home off the highway. In the bathroom sex scene at the concert rehearsal in *The Piano Teacher*, Erika is all the master, Walter humiliated. In Erika's room at home, having Walter read her letter of instructions for abusing her, the tables begin to be turned, with Walter disgusted and self-righteous, or pretending to be, and Erika beginning to quail. Erika seeks Walter out at his ice hockey rink, and in the storeroom sex scene there he is all angry master and she submissive. Their declarations of love through all this seem genuine, though everything else can seem play-acting of a kind they desire, or something that blurs the border between play-acting and rough human interaction that is not exactly what is desired. In any case, perhaps the desirable is fully gone when Walter invades Erika's apartment near the end of the film, bloodies her face, and rapes her, and we watch her face in a very protracted shot while the rape goes on, she seeming only stoically to endure it, still, quietly asking him to stop – the intense, sustained close view of her face counters the wonderful one earlier where she listens to Walter audition various pieces to get into the conservatory. Can she have wanted it to come to this? I think it is impossible to say. All that is left of the film is, next day, Erika's taking of the kitchen knife and going off with her mother to the concert, meeting Walter briefly in the lobby, then, left alone, stabbing herself and walking away into the night (Jelinek's novel makes it clear that the wound is slight; in the film it is not clear). Perhaps this is one more melodramatic move in the game, the affair that began at a rehearsal and now comes to the concert for which the rehearsal was held. Perhaps there will be more.

The abundance of music in the first part of the film gives way to the playing out of the love affair in the second part. After the rehearsal, the only music we get is in Walter's lesson with Erika where she is trying to show him that a Schubert Sonata represents a wide scale of strong feeling and comes of a core experience of suffering such as Walter cannot know, with his charm, lack of depth, and fatedness to success in the world's terms. Erika seems to admit that Walter can never be her equal. The falling away of music as Erika gets more and more involved with Walter can seem both a turning-away from music on Erika's part, which is a mistake for her, or a playing-out of something implicit in the music. The music of this film – Bach, Schubert, and so on – is larger than all the world; it contains everything. Part of the teacher Haneke/Erika's lesson for us, something he/she wants to get us to think about, is that all the intense and subversive human drama we might imagine is there in Bach and Schubert, just as it is there in the culture of film, where, in some needful way, different in the case of every piece of music, every film, life is coped with and made livable, even if this means we must go from the music or film and be changed.

At last Erika walks off into the night, like Stella Dallas in the famous final shot at the end – and new beginning – of her story. But the camera does not track back before Erika, looking at her face, admiring her, wondering who she is now, as the camera does with Stella. Rather, Erika disappears from frame as the camera holds on the façade of the conservatory, the great mother (and Erika's mother is now inside, no doubt wondering where Erika is). Repeatedly Erika has been associated, has associated herself, with the journeyer in *Winterreise*, wounded, wandering, apart from and unlike all others, on the edge of madness. She ends here in motion, still going, walking alone, like Mann's Hans Castorp wandering in the snow, obsessed with a *Winterreise* song other than the three we hear in *The Piano Teacher*, namely, "Der Lindenbaum":

> By the well, before the gate,
> Stands a linden tree;
> In its shade I dreamt
> Many a sweet dream . . .

Substitute music conservatory for linden tree. The tree, and the snow, of course, hold the lure of death for Hans Castorp; but he goes on. Death and rebirth, violence and overcoming, imagination, projection, dreams, new life, film as such all come together in Haneke's Erika/Huppert, this film-being and person, who is Haneke, who takes over Haneke, that is, Haneke as director, as film, with her human depth and her boundless desire.

Notes

1   Film as knowledge is a major theme of Andrei Tarkovsky (1986).
2   Something of the Altman woman might be seen in Naomi Watts in the English-language remake *Funny Games U.S.* (2007). Watts's ecstatic, even sexualized, suffering once the horrors start opens a new dimension in the woman. She is expressive.
3   See, especially, Tom Hopkins (2003); William Rothman (2003); and Marian Keane (2003). Hopkins's essay, long unpublished after his untimely death in 1984, nevertheless circulated widely and provoked much discussion among people interested in Altman.
4   The film is doing something quite different from the Elfriede Jelinek novel on which it is based, a very bitter satire and social critique, not much interested in character. There are many differences between the book and the film, some of which I mention below. I am more interested in the film than in the book, and for me the film is born mainly of film culture, and is most illuminated by film culture.
5   The importance of the single scene or image, stirring a viewer, opening depths in a film and reaching out beyond the film in ways that the scene's context might not seem to allow, is the running theme of Murray Pomerance in *The Horse Who Drank the Sky* (2008).
6   The key text is Stanley Cavell's *Contesting Tears* (1996). The idea of the genre is further developed in Cavell, *Cities of Words* (2004).
7   Cavell's *Contesting Tears* follows on his *Pursuits of Happiness* (1981).
8   Acknowledgment, as opposed to knowing or knowledge, is a key concept in Cavell's philosophy, developed fully in Cavell (1976, 1979).
9   I discuss the relation of the melodrama of the unknown woman to some later American films in Warren (2006).
10   In Huppert's interview published with the commercial DVD of *The Piano Teacher*, she remarks on how close the director had been to her working on the film, listening

to what she as a woman was saying through the character; and says that Haneke as director, not as a man, identified with the character, who was his subject, not an object; and that her own actor's more intimate film, developing as she worked, was able to coincide with a director's film. She says, too, that in film she thinks of herself not as playing a character, but as playing/becoming a person.

One can feel that Haneke prepared for *The Piano Teacher* working with the Juliette Binoche character, another Anne, in *Code Unknown*. It is possible to come away from that film feeling that it centers on the soul in development of this woman artist – she is a professional actress. Everything can seem to come back to her, as she makes her way through the film, taking in its various worlds as her path crosses those of others, as she tries out roles – in life, on the stage, in films – the three areas blurring. Binoche's screen presence, with her distinctive air of psychological and moral uncertainty, rather takes over *Code Unknown*.

References and Further Reading

Cavell, Stanley: *Cities of Words: Pedagogical Letters on a Register of the Moral Life* (Cambridge, MA: Belknap Press of Harvard University Press, 2004).

Cavell, Stanley: *The Claim of Reason: Wittgenstein, Skepticism, Morality, and Tragedy* (Oxford: Oxford University Press, 1979).

Cavell, Stanley: *Contesting Tears: The Hollywood Melodrama of the Unknown Woman* (Chicago: University of Chicago Press, 1996).

Cavell, Stanley: *Must We Mean What We Say? A Book of Essays* (1969; Cambridge: Cambridge University Press, 1976).

Cavell, Stanley: *Pursuits of Happiness: The Hollywood Comedy of Remarriage* (Cambridge, MA: Harvard University Press, 1981).

Clément, Catherine: *Opera, or The Undoing of Women*, trans. Betsey Wing (Minneapolis: University of Minnesota Press, 1997).

Eliot, T. S.: "Tradition and the Individual Talent," *Selected Essays*, new edition (1919; New York: Harcourt, Brace, and World, 1960), pp. 3–11.

Hopkins, Tom: "Love, Death and the Mirror," *Film International* 6 (2003): 24–33.

Keane, Marian: "Posthumous Texts: Robert Altman's Films and Tom Hopkins's Criticism of Them," *Film International* 6 (2003): 34–49.

Pomerance, Murray: *The Horse Who Drank the Sky: Film Experience Beyond Narrative and Theory* (New Brunswick, NJ: Rutgers University Press, 2008).

Rothman, William: "Matters of Life and Death," *Film International* 6 (2003): 50–2.

Tarkovsky, Andrei: *Sculpting in Time: Reflections on the Cinema*, trans. Kitty Hunter-Blair (Austin: University of Texas Press, 1986).

Warren, Charles: "Cavell, Altman, Cassavetes," *Film International* 22 (2006): 14–20.

Wood, Robin: " 'Do I Disgust You?', or *Tirez pas sur La Pianiste*," *CineAction* 59 (September 2002): 55–61.

Wood, Robin: "Foreword: What Lies Beneath?," *Horror Film and Psychoanalysis: Freud's Worst Nightmare*, ed. Steven Jay Schneider (Cambridge: Cambridge University Press, 2004).

Wood, Robin: "Michael Haneke: Beyond Compromise," *CineAction* 73–4 (2007): 73–4.

26

Discordant Desires, Violent Refrains

La Pianiste (The Piano Teacher)

Jean Ma

I would like to be recognized for making in La Pianiste an obscenity, but not a pornographic film . . . Insofar as truth is always obscene, I hope that all of my films have at least an element of obscenity. (Michael Haneke[1])

Michael Haneke's 2001 film *La Pianiste* (known in English as *The Piano Teacher*), based on the 1983 novel *Die Klavierspielerin* by the Austrian writer and Nobel laureate Elfriede Jelinek, tells the story of a relationship between a middle-age piano professor at the prestigious Vienna Conservatory and her pupil, a young man from a privileged and cultured family who desires her affections as well as her tutelage.[2] The film's publicity at the time of its release included one widely circulated photograph of teacher and student, played respectively by Isabelle Huppert and Benoît Magimel, locked in a passionate embrace as they kneel on the floor of what appears to be a public lavatory. In a single glance the image encapsulates the predictably steamy allures of the romance narrative for the film's potential audience, a genre affiliation that remains familiar even as it is spiced with the transgression of pedagogical and generational propriety. *La Pianiste*, however, invites such expectations only to betray them, as the film vigorously and mercilessly deconstructs the very conventions of romance, critiquing both the signifiers of heterosexual love in which it traffics and the ideologies of sex and gender upon which its gratifications are founded. The significance of coupling here has less to do with the dissolution of differences and the contingencies of social position within the crucible of passion than with the inevitable and necessary failure of love to suspend such differences – a failure reflected in the disturbing outcome of the affair between the main characters. If the global history of the romance narrative encodes a utopic desire to heal a ruptured social order in the flights and fortunes of individual desire – as evidenced in the genre's marked investment in stories of crossing and passing, across racial, ethnic, national, religious, and class divisions

– then *La Pianiste* confronts desire with exactly that which it seeks to escape. What the film presents to the viewer is not melodrama, the director notes, but rather a "parody" of melodrama, an anti-romance (Foundas 2001).

Or, indeed, given the shocking turns of its story – replete with references to violence and pornography, brutal in both the acts it depicts and its effects upon the viewer – the film might more appropriately be described, as one commentator suggests, as an instance of "modernist, cerebral horror," centering upon the eponymous protagonist, Erika Kohut, as both monster and victim (Hoberman 2002).[3] The fastidious, severe, and austerely elegant Professor Kohut reveals a side of her persona incommensurable with her façade of respectability during her unusual nightly pursuits of sexual stimulus and her propensity for auto-mutilation. Her student Walter Klemmer's declaration of love prompts the full expression of her sexual idiosyncrasies: Erika curtails Walter's ardent outbursts of affection, instead setting forth the terms of their intimacy in a letter that minutely details a tableau of bondage, with Erika playing the role of the submissive and Walter that of her torturer and master. He in turn responds to her proposition with vehement repulsion and affront. The alternating frustrations that mark their courtship culminate in a harrowing climax that is at once difficult to watch and opaque in its implications vis-à-vis what has previously transpired between the couple: Walter charges into Erika's apartment in a state of rage, then beats and rapes her. The fantasy of escape held forth by romance ultimately collapses into a dystopic reality where sexual relations are inseparable from gendered dynamics of objectification and coercion, bearing out in a vivid fashion Jelinek's intractable insistence on the impossibility of authentic and reciprocal connection between men and women.[4] In view of this outcome, Christopher Sharrett locates the film within "a line of US and European cinema locating mental breakdown and social disorder precisely at the heart of Western bourgeois patriarchal civilization" (Sharrett, "Horror of the Middle Class").

La Pianiste further underscores the violence and perversity of erotic passion through a strategy of cognitive dissonance. Its disconcerting story is set to the sounds of Bach and Franz Schubert, and takes place in Vienna, the capital of the European classical tradition, with the relationship of the piano teacher and the student constituted through an aesthetic ideal of classical music as much as through an idiom of violation. Such a strategy does not reduce merely to a stylistic effect of ironic counterpoint, with sublime background music heightening the shock effect of base actions. Rather, music is foregrounded as a principal mechanism of enunciation, operating at multiple narrative levels throughout the film. As well as figuring the identity of the characters and mediating their desire for one another, music instantiates a tension between the ideal and the obscene, the ineffable and the corporeal, as a structuring polarity within the narrative. This polarity is crystallized in order to set the stage for Erika and Walter's affair but is also evaporated by an echo effect as it becomes difficult to distinguish the relationship of lovers from that of teacher and student, and to mark the boundary between the rarefied realm of high art and the more prosaic settings in which its promise of transcendence is pursued, summoned, actualized, and sometimes broken. On the one hand, the intrusions of the particularities of class and gender identity that differentiate Erika's and Walter's positions within the cultural economy of classical music serve to deflate the universalist claims of art, to cement it within concrete relations of power. On the other hand, something of the transcendent remains intact in the film's framing of the aesthetic, lingering in the beckon of a detached position from which to contemplate and critique these same relations of power. In *La Pianiste* classical music functions both diegetically in the description of repression and suffering and structurally as a key to comprehending the film's strategy of disrupting heterosexual romantic norms from within their cultural lexicon. If such a strategy can be described as a sort of subversive mimicry, the film escalates the political and ethical stakes of mimicry with its explicit representation of sexual violence aimed as an indictment of the very social mechanisms that give rise to sexual violence. In the conjunction of aesthetics, sexuality, and violence, then, we can begin to discern the distinction between obscenity and pornography, between the critical and affirmative valences of shock, a distinction that is crucial for a work that endeavors to condemn by showing.

The rape scene in *La Pianiste* can be considered alongside numerous other disturbing images of extreme violence that punctuate the films of Michael Haneke, images whose unsettling graphic effects issue directly from their pronounced eschewal of sensationalist or dramatizing effects. Such images are often framed within a gaze so deliberatively restrained as to border on clinical, captured in long static shots that allow the intensity of the profilmic to both build up and dissipate in real time, bringing together the before and after of the event in a single continuum that exerts unusual demands upon the tolerance of the audience while insisting upon the human face of pain and the subjectivity of the victim. The oftentimes startling visceral effect of such sequences is more readily associated with the excesses of the horror film than the art film, and in this regard Haneke's work participates in a recent turn toward explicit, at times gory, violence in European art cinema, exemplified in films by contemporaries such as Gaspar Noé, Marina de Van, and Catherine Breillat, to name only a few.[5] If this development suggests as much about the crossings of high and low genres – for instance, art film and horror – in contemporary film culture as about shifting boundaries between the obscene and the permissible, then what distinguishes Haneke's films and positions them decisively within a strategy of modernist reflexivity, as opposed to postmodern hybridity, is their investigation of the ways in which the effects of violence are inseparable from its forms of circulation and representation. Works like *Benny's Video* (1992), *Funny Games* (1997/2007), and *Caché* (2005) have addressed the complicit role of the mass media, in particular television, in the reproduction of violence as a commodity, while *La Pianiste* takes up such concerns in its scrutiny of the uneasy proximity between sexual violence, pornography, and film.

Pornography is introduced as a theme in the film's story when Erika, relishing some stolen hours of relief from her routine obtained through subterfuge to avoid the wrath of her hypercontrolling mother, visits a sex shop to watch videos in a private booth. The location of the sex shop in a shopping mall underscores the commodified character of the pleasure Erika seeks, the only pleasure available to her given her social isolation, as does the matter-of-factness with which Erika purchases tokens from the cashier. The setting of the booth, littered with the used tissues of its previous occupants, reminds us of the reality effect attendant to a class of representations that do not merely reproduce sexual acts onscreen but also aim to provoke a sexual response in the body of the viewer. The definition of pornography as a genre, that is, entails a slippage between the fictional and the actual, between depiction and realization, such that the social and moral anxieties surrounding it frequently respond less to its actual contents than to its ambivalent position between reality and image, its seeming suspension of the very function of mediation. (For this reason, critics of pornography frequently cite the real harm inflicted upon its performers during its production, as well as upon the consumer during viewing.) With the advent of representational technologies like film capable of producing images of unprecedented likeness to reality, such anxieties contaminate the medium itself. Thus Linda Williams notes that the 1986 Meese Commission on Pornography turns to André Bazin's essay "The Ontology of the Photographic Image" to build its case against pornography, citing his well-known assertion that the photographic image is existentially equivalent to "the object itself" (Williams 1989: 184–5). From this, she remarks, follows Stanley Cavell's assertion that the "ontological conditions of the cinema reveal it as inherently pornographic" (ibid.). If the heightened reality effect of film threatens to overwhelm the rational defenses of the spectator, as apparatus theory maintains, affecting her at the level of the unconscious, then that of pornography similarly overcomes the viewer's agency with its capacity to arouse somatic responses, as an example of what Williams terms "body genres," which are frequently stigmatized for "the perception that the body of the spectator is caught up in an almost involuntary mimicry of the emotion or the sensation of the body on the screen."[6] Thus while D. H. Lawrence could argue in defense of *Lady Chatterley's Lover*, "Culture and civilisation have taught us to separate the word from the deed, the thought from the act or the physical reaction. We now know that the act does not necessarily follow on the thought," it is this very intransitivity and interval of reflection upholding the inviolability of the written word that is obviated by the filmic image (Lawrence 1994: 307).

La Pianiste can in no way be considered a pornographic film, in the way that it might be a revisionist melodrama or horror film. But the issues raised by pornography concerning the unruly transitivity of representation are highly relevant to the film's reflexive commentary upon gender, sexuality, and violence. If the film touches on pornography, it is as a symptom of a set of social conditions to be brought to light, called into question, and critiqued. But by going further, in presenting the viewer with graphic configurations of sexuality and violence – lethal bursts of rage, cutting, masochism, rape – *La Pianiste* also provokes us to ask how a representation of violence can achieve an interrogation of, rather than a participatory reiteration of, violence. This question – whose answer is by no means self-evident given the extent to which, as Haneke persistently reminds us, contemporary mass media are complicit in the perpetuation of social violence – is articulated by the director in terms of a distinction between the obscene, or that which retains its capacity to outrage the audience, and the pornographic, which renders obscenity banal and anaesthetic. "Whether concerned with sexuality or violence or another taboo issue, anything that breaks with the norm is obscene," he maintains, while "by contrast, pornography is the opposite, in that it makes into a commodity that which is obscene, makes the unusual consumable, which is the truly scandalous aspect of porno rather than the traditional arguments posed by institutions of society . . . I think that any contemporary art practice is pornographic if it attempts to bandage the wound, so to speak, which is to say our social and psychological wound" (Sharrett, "The World That is Known"). How might the transgression of social and representational norms work to actually challenge those norms rather than to collude with them? Given that the very definition of obscenity as that which has been deemed unrepresentable reinscribes the validity of the law, with the act of prohibition entailing the frisson of the illicit instead of vice versa, then how can the shock effect of violation work to critique social norms and the ideologies they uphold?[7] Is it possible to speak of the obscenity of social norms themselves?[8]

Even if the mere presentation of certain actions and images threatens to exceed the narrative and rhetorical edifice of meaning in which they are situated, *La Pianiste* remains invested in the power of such images to elicit a critical response. Yet the film does not make good on this investment by offering its viewer the comfort of a morally unambiguous perspective from which to condemn the violence she sees. Rather, the film explores the murky territory between description and conflation – between the work *on* pornography and the work *of* pornography – by framing its representation of sexual violence in a way that renders it particularly difficult to interpret. Its climactic scene has been the subject of much debate, understood by some as a fulfillment of Erika's masochistic desires[9] and by others as a violation of her desire. While my own reading lies squarely and insistently in the second camp, in the remainder of this essay I will confront the ambiguities contributing to the misapprehension of this scene of rape as consensual sex in order to turn them in a different direction, insofar as these ambiguities uphold, rather than detract from, the film's effectiveness as a feminist denunciation of gendered violence.

The challenges that the rape scene poses for the understanding of the audience lie in its familiarity: What shocks is not only the sudden intrusion of violence into the realm of intimacy, but also the uncanny echoing of Erika's fantasies in Walter's actions. Slightly earlier in the film, Erika demonstrates her receptiveness to Walter's romantic overtures with the offering of a letter; its contents are relayed to us when he reads the letter aloud in her presence: "Then, gag me with some stockings I will have ready. Stuff them in so hard that I'm incapable of making any sounds. Next, take off the blindfold please, and sit on my face and punch me in the stomach to force me to thrust my tongue in your behind." Here Walter pauses to inquire incredulously, "Is this supposed to be serious?" and continues reading: "For that is my dearest wish. Hands and feet tied behind my back and locked up next door to my mother but out of her reach behind my bedroom door, till the next morning . . . If you catch me disobeying any of your orders, hit me, please, even with the back of your hand on my face. Ask me why I don't cry out for my mother or why I don't fight back. Above all, say things like that so that I realize just how powerless I am." Walter responds by storming out in disgust, but returns the next day and, upon entering Erika's apartment, slaps her face and asks, "Is this really what you had imagined?" As he continues to assault Erika, he recites the letter from memory over Erika's pleas to stop: "As for my mother, pay no attention to her. Yes? Am I quoting you exactly? Give me lots of slaps darling. Hit me hard, no, hit me around the face and hit me hard. At your service, dear lady." At this point, he strikes Erika's face. "Is that what you want?"

To take Walter's words at face value would be erroneous, as the two encounters present fundamentally different configurations of sexuality, violence, and power. At the same time, however, these differences become intelligible only against the backdrop of the film's various reiterations and resignifications of violence across shifting realms of fantasy and reality, private and public, inscription and enactment. Thus I propose to approach sexual violence in *La Pianiste* as Deleuze considers pain in his essay "Coldness and Cruelty," as a trope that "only acquires significance in relation to the forms of repetition which condition its use" (Deleuze and Sacher-Masoch 1991: 199). The troubling echoes of the one scene in the other disallow a reading that would insist upon a clear-cut distinction between fantasy and reality –

Fig. 26.1   "All my desires on paper for you to peruse at will." *The Piano Teacher* (2001), dir. Michael Haneke, prod. Veit Heiduschka.

Fig. 26.2   "Is this really what you had imagined?" *The Piano Teacher* (2001), dir. Michael Haneke, prod. Veit Heiduschka.

that would invoke theater as a metaphor for sexual "role-playing," for instance – even as these two scenes trace a trajectory from the perverse idiosyncrasy of individual desire (masochism) to the general social existence of violence against women (rape). They signal the operation of a structure of repetition and circularity that not only sets the film apart from conventional narratives of seduction and coupling, whether ending in fulfillment or failure, but also underwrites a critical strategy that works from within the idiom of power and domination rather than claiming a position that transcends ideology. In this regard, Haneke's description of the film in terms of parody takes on a heightened meaning: As well as mimicking the conventions of genre for the purpose of a meta-commentary on genre, *La Pianiste* further locates this meta-commentary within a series of mimetic reenactments that locate the possibilities of social critique within the language of the symptom itself.[10]

In the two scenes described above, violence marks both the moment of inter-subjectivity and the negation of its realization, inscribing a hierarchy of control that calls into question the very possibility of reciprocity. This uneven dynamic of control is not unique to the sexual encounter but rather pervades the routine of work and the mundane interactions between Erika and her students. The opening scenes in the film introduce her character in the context of her profession as a piano instructor and establish the remarkable stringency and loneliness of her daily schedule, which consists of eight hours conducting lessons at the conservatory, followed by privately commissioned rehearsals before retiring to the apartment she shares with her domineering mother. The images of Erika at work present a life dedicated to an aesthetic ideal whose rigor is directly proportional to its rigidity. The interpersonal relations that transpire within the space of the conservatory are oriented entirely toward the attainment of this ideal, informed as well

Fig. 26.3   At the conservatory. *The Piano Teacher* (2001), dir. Michael Haneke, prod.
Veit Heiduschka.

by an unambiguous hierarchy between the teacher who instructs, guides, commands, and the student who receives and internalizes her instructions in the process of training. Erika's place in this hierarchy is secured through expert knowledge and talent, sanctified by the institutional authority of the conservatory. A guardian of the gates of high culture, she exercises enormous control over the fate and mental health of the aspiring musicians who seek entrance through these gates.

At the same time, as a player as well as teacher of piano, Erika subjects herself to the same regime that she imposes upon her pupils, disciplining her own body in accordance with the standards demanded by the composition.[11] As *La Pianiste* makes clear, the very act of musical performance, as an interpretation and realization of a score that consists essentially of an encoded set of instructions, requires a negation of the will of the performer. Virtuosity entails at once a display of exceptional mastery and exceptional submission. Thus Carolyn Abbate notes the automatism that generally underlies the interpretation of a score: "Nowhere is our machinelike status more clear than in a musical performance in which someone plays someone else's work . . . musical performance exists in a performance network in which a master voice animates a medium, the human performer, to reproduce his thoughts. There is a puppet master, and there is a marionette" (1999: 477). For Erika, this dialectic of mastery and submission plays out most starkly in the rigorous challenge of playing Schubert, whom she describes as "no walk in the park," but her "favorite." And in a conversation regarding Schumann, another composer who holds a special place in her work, she extends the stratifications of control characterizing the social space of the academy and the situation of performance to artistic production itself. "Have you read Adorno on Schumann's Fantasia in C Major?" she asks Walter. "He talks of his twilight. It's not Schumann bereft of reason, but just before. A fraction before. He knows he's losing his mind. It torments him but he clings on, one last time. It's being aware of what it is to lose oneself, before being completely abandoned." In her anecdote, the relationship of performer and composer is internalized to the experience of the composer himself, as he oscillates between a loss and an assertion of control, between the limits of the body and the aesthetic overcoming of those limits.

Notably, this encounter represents Erika and Walter's first meeting, signaling the arousal of their interest in one another, and as this interest develops further, the problematic of control introduced by Erika to this discourse on music is transferred to their discourse as lovers. Their desires find expression for the first time after he interrupts his studies in engineering to enroll in her master class, during a tryst that takes place in the women's lavatory of the conservatory in the middle of a rehearsal of one of Bach's Brandenburg Concertos. After an initial outburst of passion between the two, Erika breaks up the embrace that supplies the image for the publicity photograph and imposes a deliberately distanced and awkward format upon their interactions, forcing Walter to stand at a distance from her with his arms at his side as she manipulates his penis while watching him impassively. When he attempts to talk to her, she cuts him off with a series of curt and authoritative commands, as the concerto continues to play in the background: "Be quiet"; "Look at me, not at your penis"; "Hands off"; "Don't move, or I'll leave"; "Face me"; "Now you can put it away." Erika ends by leaving Walter in a state of unconsummated arousal, deferring any further gratification by telling him, "I'll write down what you can do to me. All my desires on paper for you to peruse at will." The effect of her directions is to replace the spontaneity of their amorous entanglement with a pointedly denaturalized and formalized choreography of bodies. The scene replicates and heightens the dynamic of the piano lesson, with Erika playing the role of scenarist as well as teacher, asserting a disciplinary control over Walter's bodily expressions and making him into her marionette. Her interjection of the written word into their lovers' repartee in the promise of the letter heightens the delaying effect of her spoken commands, further dissolving the spontaneity of passion within the studious interval of writing and reading. The letter, as we soon discover, is a score for their affair, a notation of a sequence of commands to be enacted by Walter in a performative execution of mastery as submission.

Both of these encounters reveal the ways in which passion is mediated by the musical arts in *La Pianiste*. Indeed, during the private recital at the home of Walter's aunt Mrs. Blonsky, where the two are introduced to one another, the arousal of their feelings is indicated through a series of close-ups as each in turn listens to the other playing the piano. Erika's aesthetic approach to love, however, is deliberative and cold in contrast to Walter's heat. While he declares music to be something that "can bring us together," she eschews such romantic notions in her insistence upon the hierarchies that subsist in the realm of aesthetics, reflected not only in the relationship of teacher and student or of composer and performer but also in a cultural economy of music in which she is dependent upon the largesse

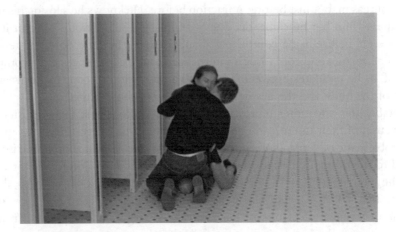

Fig. 26.4   Spontaneity and heat. *The Piano Teacher* (2001), dir. Michael Haneke, prod. Veit Heiduschka.

Fig. 26.5   Coldness and cruelty. *The Piano Teacher* (2001), dir. Michael Haneke, prod. Veit Heiduschka.

of Walter's wealthy family, whose dedication to the support of the classical tradition allows her to exist as an artist. That the perverse and unusual bent of her desires finds a precedent in these aesthetic hierarchies indicates the need for a discussion that goes beyond the psychobiography of perversion within which many commentators have situated her fantasies. To be fair, the character of Erika Kohut in many ways cries out for psychoanalytic interpretation as a paradigmatic case study of repression, exhibiting symptoms of neurosis, psychosis, narcissism, and frigidity, all pathologies that have been named in connection with her in the critical reception of *La Pianiste*.[12] To leave the question of her masochistic proclivities in the realm of pathology, however, would be to overlook the ways in which it holds up a mirror to and implicates the world surrounding it. Thus my reading of Erika's masochism turns away from a solely psychoanalytic framework in order to locate her symptoms within a constellation of formal, contractual, and social relations, drawing upon Deleuze's discussion of the aesthetics of perversion.

In "Coldness and Cruelty," Deleuze challenges the commonplace tendency to view masochism and sadism as related and complementary perversions, located upon a single continuum of aggression, in order to show that the two represent fundamentally different dispositions toward desire, knowledge, and the law. Turning to the writings of Leopold von Sacher-Masoch and the Marquis de Sade, he argues that to discern what is at stake in these dispositions we must look beyond the descriptive function of language to the patterns of repetition and enunciatory positions that organize the discourse of masters and victims.[13] Deleuze's elaboration of masochism finds several parallels in Erika's situation: Unlike the sadist who requires an unwilling victim, the masochist is a "victim in search of a torturer and who needs to educate, persuade, and conclude an alliance with the torturer in order to realize the strangest of schemes" (1991: 20). In this regard, the masochist is "essentially an educator" in the subject of his own victimization, who must seek out a consenting participant with whom to enter into "a system of reciprocal rights and duties" (21, 77). And insofar as the victim himself initiates and sets the terms of this contractual alliance, masochism involves acts of ventriloquism, with the victim speaking "through the mouth of his torturer, without sparing himself" and, conversely, with the torturer bound to the victim as a puppet, having consented to play a predetermined role (22). The contractual and scripted aspect of masochism effectively reverses the physical hierarchy of victim and torturer, instating the one as the master of the other. Recast within the terms of intimacy set forth by the masochist, then, are the relational constructs of teacher–student and composer–performer as these function to demarcate a set of fixed positions that enable the expression and enactment of desire and power, as well as their conversion and displacement between bodies. The masochist is essentially a scenarist, a composer of tableaux, whose fantasies transpire within the temporal duration of waiting, delay, and suspense, patterned upon "the immobile and reflective quality of culture" (70). Thus Deleuze describes the masochistic attitude as fundamentally aesthetic, driven by the faculty of imagination (in contrast to the pure reason that impels the sadist) and whose objective is not merely the satisfaction of carnal desire but also an "ascent from the human body to the work of art" (22).

In the fictive universe of Sacher-Masoch, the masochist is always a masculine subject held in thrall to the whip wielded by a "Venus in furs" or some such feminine icon of cold beauty. In its reversal of this schema, *La Pianiste* complicates the prismatic architecture of fantasy described in "Coldness and Cruelty" and forces us to dwell further on the status of violence within the masochistic scenario. If violence is to a certain degree neutralized by prior consent in the account given by Deleuze, which consistently paints the masochist as a male subject-victim in search of a female object-torturer, the film does not allow for a similar circumvention of its descriptive effects. For the figure of the *female* masochist, as many have noted, provokes a certain anxiety in view of the uncomfortable congruities between her position and the subordinate position of all women in a patriarchal world. As Williams points out, "Because women have so often been presumed not to have sexual agency, to be objects and not subjects of desire, masochism has in many respects been taken as the 'norm' for women under patriarchy" (1989: 213). Thus the female masochist appears to be complicit with her own disempowerment, having internalized the norm to such a degree that her pleasure depends upon it. She is, in the words of Lynda Hart, the woman who "asks for it," who assents to her own victimization, who crafts her desires as "an iconic reproduction of the oppressive model" (1998: 87, 85). If male masochism can aspire to the transfiguring condition of art, then it seems that its female counterpart can only lapse into the banality of femininity as a given social condition.

Despite the difficulties of mapping the female victim onto the masochist aesthetic described here, however, we find in Deleuze's view of masochism as an engine of "dialectical reversal, disguise, and reduplication" a useful starting point from which to approach the film's representation of Erika's sexuality. The masochistic scenario sets into motion a series of transpositions that do not only occur between victim and torturer, as "a scene being enacted simultaneously on several levels with reversals and reduplications in the allocation of roles and discourse," but also extend beyond the parameters of the fantasy itself (22). For Deleuze the violence that attends this scenario originates not from within the inner recesses of the individual psyche but rather from without: "With Sade and Masoch the function of literature is not to describe the world, since this has already been done, but to define a counterpart to the world capable of containing its violence and excesses . . . Thus eroticism is able to act as a mirror to the world by reflecting its excesses, drawing out its violence" (37). While sadism draws out the violence of the world in order to multiply it through a process of quantitative reiteration and accumulation, the dialectical spirit animating masochism reflects the excess of violence in order to reconstruct it in a different format that nonetheless still preserves this excess. In this regard, we can also understand masochism as a disposition toward reality, defined chiefly in terms of disavowal as a particular operation of knowledge. "Disavowal should perhaps be understood as the point of departure of an operation that consists neither in negating nor even destroying, but rather in radically contesting the validity of that which is," Deleuze writes, an operation that "neutralizes the given in such a way that a new horizon opens up beyond the given and in place of it" (31). It is therefore not only consent that neutralizes violence, but the artfulness of the refusal that does not deny, but instead displaces.

Such an account of masochism is striking for the way that it undermines the confidence with which we can define perverse or deviant sexuality in opposition to a norm, calling attention to the reverberations of normalized forms of violence within the realms of fantasy and desire. In *La Pianiste* we can begin to see how the ordinary world it portrays takes on a menacing cast when glimpsed through the reflecting lens of Erika's masochism, as it draws to the surface the subtle forms of coercion coursing through the interactions of men and women to reveal a ubiquitous undercurrent of everyday violence. This undercurrent emerges in the sidelines of the film's central drama, finding expression in moments illustrative of the details of Erika's existence. For instance, after she furtively trails Walter to an outdoor ice rink, she spies two young girls as they practice figure skating suddenly interrupted by the members of Walter's ice hockey team, who surround them and aggressively push them off the ice. In another scene, Erika cruises the lot of a drive-in movie theater and plays peeping tom to a young couple engaging in vehicular sex, drawing upon herself the fury of the man when he spots her and chases her through the lot yelling, "Stay there, cunt!" And when one of her students attempts to apologize to her after she has caught him browsing pornographic magazines with his friends at a bookstore, she firmly rejects his apology, demanding, "What for? Sorry isn't enough if I don't know why. Are you sorry because you're a pig, or because your friends are pigs? Or because all women are bitches for making you a pig?"

While the film contains numerous incidents where Erika seems as much a sadist as a masochist, particularly toward her students, one scene in which she vents her violent impulses on her own body is especially important as a prefiguration of her entanglement with Walter. Erika locks herself in the bathroom and perches at the edge of the bathtub with a razor in one hand and a mirror in the other. Her body is framed in a long shot, turned to the right, so that what she is doing as she holds the mirror between her legs is not apparent until bright red blood begins to flow down the side of the tub. When her mother calls her to dinner, she efficiently washes away the evidence of her activities, bandages her cuts with a sanitary napkin, and enters the living room to join her mother at the table. The two converse about Erika's day as the mother lays out their meal. She suddenly pauses and asks, "What's wrong with you?" pointing to the blood that is streaming down Erika's leg. "Is that why you're in a bad mood? You might be more careful. That's not very appetizing." What Erika's mother perceives is exactly what we as an audience have been shown, blood dripping from an imperceptible source, and she misconstrues this sign as menstruation. This misconstrual, along with Erika's choice of bandage, accomplishes a stunning deflation of the shock of this self-infliction of violence, referring its effects to the natural, and vaguely unappetizing, cause of female anatomy. At the same time, this juxtaposition of the shocking and the banal refracts back onto the female body in order to render it strange, uneasy, menaced. Their exchange frames Erika's auto-mutilation not as symptom of self-alienation but rather as a self-reference to the body, achieved by a violent mimicking of the biological processes that mark sexual difference. Erika's actions ultimately construe femininity as a wound, a wound that appears as a natural condition but whose origins in fact lie elsewhere.

This idea of violent reiteration similarly informs Erika's masochistic attitude as a way of negotiating the wound of femininity as it is exposed within the domain

Fig. 26.6   Auto-mutilation. *The Piano Teacher* (2001), dir. Michael Haneke, prod. Veit Heiduschka.

Fig. 26.7   "It's not very appetizing." *The Piano Teacher* (2001), dir. Michael Haneke, prod. Veit Heiduschka.

of sexual intimacy. The victimization that she demands for herself from Walter must be seen as a stance constituted in opposition to, as a refusal of, the gestures of chivalry that he continually offers, gestures that would deny difference and mask gender inequality to allow it to go unacknowledged and therefore unquestioned. Even as the masochistic fantasy scripted by Erika mirrors a relationship of power organized along the lines of sexual difference, it simultaneously transforms this relationship in the process of its reauthoring and contractual restaging. Erika's strategy is an attempt to construct intimacy as a space of freedom that is not thoroughly conditioned by power, yet without disavowing the existence of power. By contrast, Walter's insistence upon a normative notion of romantic love – succinctly captured in his entreaty to Erika, "Why destroy what could bring us together?" – amounts to a disavowal of the "natural law" of gender in the interest of collusion with the social order. This collusion is realized to its fullest extent in the rape scene, a parody of consummation in whose wake the full significance of Erika's masochism emerges as the standard of health against which her "sickness" is measured. If masochism registers a reaction against the subordination of femininity that preserves the very condition reacted against, then the literalism of Walter's act of violence, against the spirit of the letter, shuts down this dialectic of violence with abrupt finality.

Walter, however, is not the only monster in this horror film, and Erika's own capacity for brutality toward others renders her doomed from the start, suggesting the fragility of the illusion of control sustained by her appropriation of violence. This much is confirmed in the final scene, when Erika and Walter cross paths at the conservatory just before a recital in which she is to perform the day after the assault. Left alone in the lobby after their brief encounter, Erika removes a knife from her purse, weakly stabs herself in the heart, and leaves the building. The film offers no redemption for any of its characters as it traces a circular loop from condition to reaction wherein the compulsion to repeat violence trumps any possibility of transformation or escape beyond the given.[14] In view of this outcome, inconclusive in accordance with the logic of linear narrative exposition, how are we to make sense of *La Pianiste*'s edifice of interlocking repetitions of sexuality, power, and violence across the realms of word and image, notation and performative execution, fantasy and reality, and art and life? Does the film's lack of a resolution ultimately return us to the merely descriptive territory of pornography?

We can recall here how classical music serves as the engine of the film's brutal reproductions. This becomes apparent in the remarkable opening credit sequence that introduces Schubert's song cycle *Winterreise* as a sort of leitmotif within the film's narrative structure, to be repeated at key moments throughout the story, always in association with Erika's character. *Winterreise* consists of twenty-four songs, settings of poems by the minor German poet Wilhelm Müller, that detail the plight of a solitary wanderer who roams through an icy landscape of desolation and death, having abjured the comforts of human companionship. The film places an emphasis on the seventeenth song of the cycle, "In the Village," whose lyrics are sung at several points in the film:

Dogs are barking, rattling their chains. People are sleeping in their beds.
Dreaming of what they don't have, replenished of good and bad. And next morning, all flown away. So what? So what?
They've had their pleasure. And they hope that what they left behind might be waiting for them on the pillows.
Bark me away, you waking dogs. Don't let me rest in the sleeping houses.
I've reached the end of dreams. What will I do amongst the sleepers?

As Susan Youens points out, "In the Village" marks the moment when the wanderer recognizes the futility of dreams and illusion as "fantasy-deceptions incompatible with waking life" (1991: 60). His isolation is signaled by not only his exclusion from the domestic repose of the villagers as he wanders in the night but also his conscious rejection of the deceptive pleasure of dreams. The state of the wanderer invites comparisons with Erika, given her social alienation and her refusal of the illusions of romance. In the words of the director, "In the Village" encapsulates "the idea of following a path not taken by others" (Sharrett, "The World That is Known").

Beyond its allegorizing of an interior emotional state, however, *Winterreise* also reconveys the structure of repetition that frames the film's narrative, presenting a wanderer "walking around [a landscape] with no actual progress" (Adorno 2005: 10). Notable for its rejection of the motivic development that typically accompanies music's conventional phrase structure, the song cycle formally reinscribes the wanderer's obsessive reliving of the pains of his past in its circular design, the frozen vista of the winter journey in its brittle and paralytic arrangements. Adorno, in his 1928 essay "Schubert," invokes a series of crystalline metaphors – metal, mineral, stalagmites, magma, light – to not only describe the composer's work but also rescue his name from the kitsch appropriation that would equate its value with its sentimental resonance. In its crystalline divergence from organic musical forms, according to Adorno, resides the utopic value of Schubert's work: "Right from its origin it never had anything other than a nonorganic, erratic, brittle, mineral existence, so deeply steeped in death that death held no fears for it" (ibid.).[15] The pervasive presence of death and mourning in the work drags upon its temporal flow (accounting for, Adorno remarks, the composer's difficulty with endings and finales), yet this is also the means by which death moves beyond "inner pain" to become "the affect of sorrow about the human condition" (12). In its affective access to collective suffering the work becomes a medium of a truth not otherwise accessible to knowledge: "In jagged lines, like a seismograph, Schubert's music has recorded the tidings of man's qualitative change." The correct and only response to listening is tears, even as "we cry without knowing why . . . This is music we cannot decipher, but it holds up to our blurred, over-brimming eyes the secret of reconciliation at long last" (14).

Erika's mention of Adorno's name during her conversation with Walter about Schumann can hardly be viewed as coincidental given the film's *Winterreise* motif. Schumann's awareness of his incipient loss of mind finds a parallel in Schubert's knowledge of his impending death in the last years of his short life.[16] Erika's choice of favorite composers emphasizes the connections identified by Adorno between music and suffering, between art and "the affect of sorrow," connections that resurface in her own aestheticized approach to love as it rejects romantic idealism and strives at once to register and to overcome the contradictions of heterosexual love. Music as an art form is most effective when it confronts such contradictions, or "social antinomies," argues Adorno, availing its conceptual language to "express the calamities of the social condition and call for change in the cipher script of suffering. It does not behoove music to stare at society in helpless horror; its social function will be more exactly fulfilled if the social problems contained in it, in the inmost cells of its technique, are presented in its own material and according to its own formal laws" (1988: 70). The task of music and, indeed, of art itself is not to appease or to harmonize the frictions and tensions generated by social contradictions but rather to enunciate, reveal, and hyperbolize such tensions in order to render them available to consciousness. "Art imitates not the world, but its conditions of alienation and domination," and just as Schubert's compositions take in the disaster of death as part of a homeopathic reckoning with the fear of death, so art takes in and mimics the conditions of social misery – injustice, domination, pain – so that they may be experienced in a transformative way. For Adorno, the critical capacity of art lies in its mimetic relationship to a damaged social order, and it is only insofar as "art enunciates the disaster by identifying with it" that it can put us back in touch with the alienation to which we have become habituated (1997: 19).

The critical possibilities embedded within the aesthetic hinge upon a dual position of simultaneous determination and negation, of proximity and distantiation, wherein art preserves the very conditions that it protests. Contravening a Hegelian-romantic conception of aesthetic value that would leave behind the contingencies of material reality for the timeless, transcendent realm of universal truth and beauty, Adorno situates art in the position of a contradictory standstill between a desired utopia and fallen reality, at the locus of an unresolved tension between revelation and "the undifferentiated repetition of the status quo" (106). Recalling the language of his analysis of Schubert, he describes the non-progressive stance of the work of art in terms of "an immanent, crystallized process at a standstill" (180), which neither affirms the status quo by denying its supremacy nor reinstates it by extending its domain. The effect of aesthetic mediation can thus be understood as a kind of repetition *without* compulsion, whereby "space, time, and causality are maintained, their power is not denied, but they are divested of their compulsiveness" (138). Haneke alludes to such an understanding of aesthetics when he discusses *La Pianiste*'s use of music: "Great music transcends suffering beyond specific causes. *Winterreise* transcends misery even in the detailed description of misery. All important artworks, especially those concerned with the darker side of experience, despite whatever despair conveyed, transcend the discomfort of the content in the realization of their form" (Sharrett, "The World That is Known"). His words point to the potential of art to move beyond a "bandaging of the wound" in excess of its own descriptive function, and his film stakes a claim in this potential through its formally self-conscious representation of obscenity. If Haneke pursues such a critique by bringing together great music with a medium that Adorno rigorously excludes from his discussion of aesthetic theory, we can view his particular approach to modernism in terms of a further twist that binds the standstill of repetition ever tighter, in the complicit entanglement of an antidote composed of the poison itself.

Notes

1 In Sharrett, "The World That is Known." This interview is reprinted in this volume.
2 *La Pianiste* was released with the English title *The Piano Teacher*. This imprecise translation of both the film's French title and the unusual German term with which Jelinek titles her novel elides the derogatory and awkward undertones that play an important part in the presentation of the story's main character. (A more common term for the female piano player would be *die Pianistin*.) I will refer to the film by its French title throughout this essay because it more closely approximates Jelinek's original phrase and avoids the somewhat domesticating effect of the English translation.
3 Christopher Sharrett also describes *La Pianiste* as a work of "contemporary horror," comparable to *Psycho* (Alfred Hitchcock, 1960) in its "notion of the fractured subject, the 'monster,' as product of bourgeois family life" (Sharrett, "Horror of the Middle Class").
4 The authorship of *La Pianiste* is shared by Elfriede Jelinek and Michael Haneke. Jelinek is an outspoken socialist feminist who addresses the conditions of capitalist patriarchy in a number of her works. As Allyson Fiddler observes, "Nowhere in Jelinek's entire *œuvre* is sex presented as a mutually satisfying activity for both partners. It is generally violent and brutal" (Fiddler 1994: 47). Although a detailed consideration of the issue of adaptation would be illuminating in this context, in the remainder of this essay I will focus on the film, which deviates from the novel in its emphases even as it remains committed to its political vision.
5 For a discussion of this turn toward the graphic in French cinema, see Palmer (2006).
6 On the relation of involuntary affects and film genres, see Linda Williams (1991).
7 These questions can be asked of a number of contemporary independent productions and art films as well. An interesting point of comparison for *La Pianiste* is Noé's *Irréversible* (2002) – also containing a rape scene, one even more violent and disturbing – whose transgressive qualities ultimately affirm the bourgeois values that the film purports to violate.
8 To a certain extent, the problem of how to invoke obscenity in such a way that breaks with the logic of prohibition constitutes the obverse of the problem faced by those who would invoke obscenity with the aim of legislating prohibition, one that is clearly illustrated in legal debates on the censorship of pornography. The conundrum that confronts advocates of censorship is how to present the object that they deem to be unrepresentable; Anne M. Coughlin points out, "Every porn scholar must include in her work some references to prohibited images of conduct. At the moment of introducing the pornographic references into her own text, the scholar necessarily confronts the question of whether and how to comply with the prohibition that she purports to be evaluating, which forbids the very representations to which she is about to refer" (Coughlin 2002: 2146).
9 For example, Catherine Wheatley understands the significance of the rape scene in terms of the phrase, "Be careful what you wish for, it might come true" (2006: 126). Likewise, Wheatley's conclusions about the film's relationship to the genre of melodrama are very different from my own.
10 Such a strategy finds a certain parallel in Jelinek's tactics of hyperbolization throughout her writings, aimed at what one commentator describes as a Brechtian exaggeration

of contradiction, where "outlandish fictional terror is simply a caricature of the very real violence of everyday life" (Fiddler 1994: 47). This is especially apparent in her 1989 novel *Lust*, frequently compared to *Die Klavierspielerin* because of its interweaving of sexuality and violence. *Lust* is a work of socialist feminist pornography whose detailed and interminable descriptions of sexual acts aim to achieve an exorcism of pornography; some have described it as a work of "pornology," after Deleuze. For a discussion of this novel, see Fiddler (1994: ch. 5, "Sexuality and Subjectivity") and Strove (1994).

11 Amid the ever-expanding cycle of piano films, a pattern emerges in the representation of this musical instrument as a locus of the thwarted, muted, and repressed desires of female pianists, whose playing acquires the poignancy of a wordless expression of feelings otherwise inexpressible. More than an icon of sublimation mediating confinement and intensity, the piano figures as a prosthesis of feminine voice and sexuality, suggestive of interiority and secret depths. On the evidence of films like *La Pianiste* along with Jane Campion's *The Piano* (1993) and Dennis Dercourt's *The Page Turner* (2006), pianos have come to occupy a central place in the iconography of the "women's film."

12 For an example of a psychoanalytic reading of *La Pianiste* see Wyatt (2006). In discussions of both the film and the novel, the co-dependent relationship between Erika and her mother often figures centrally in the psychobiography of Erika's character. For instance, Sigrid Berka notes the relevance to the story of Jessica Benjamin's thesis that feminine masochism is rooted in the woman's failure to separate her identity from that of her mother (Berka 1994).

13 The term "masochism" was named by Krafft-Ebing as a class of perversion after Sacher-Masoch, author of works such as *The Fountain of Youth*, *The Fisher of Souls*, and, most famously, *Venus in Furs*.

14 Jelinek has stated that this ending, which is identical to that of the novel, was inspired by the conclusion of Kafka's *The Trial*.

15 "Schubert" was written by Adorno at the age of twenty-five, during a period spent in Vienna studying with Alban Berg. The value Adorno placed on Schubert's non-organic forms can be usefully considered in connection with his more well-known championing of the Second Viennese School's denaturalization of tonality as the dominant language of musical composition, reflected for instance in the compositions of Schönberg, which Adorno admired for the way in which their "internal tensions rend the mantle of tonality" (2002: 636). As Esteban Buch observes, Adorno invokes the idea of the crystalline structure in writings on both composers, notwithstanding the significant differences between their positions in music history. Somewhat counter-intuitively "for Adorno, at that time, both Schubert and Schoenberg represented alternatives to a musical canon centered on the organic, tonal sonata form" (Buch 2005: 29).

16 Schubert was diagnosed with syphilis in 1822 and died six years later at the age of thirty-one. In a letter of 1824 to his friend Leopold Kupelwieser, he writes: "Imagine a man whose health will never be right again, and who in sheer despair over this ever makes things worse and worse, instead of better; imagine a man, I say, whose most brilliant hopes have perished, to whom the felicity of love and friendship have nothing to offer but pain at best, whom enthusiasm for all things beautiful threatens to forsake, and I ask you, is he not a miserable, unhappy being?" (cited in Gibbs 1997: 42).

References and Further Reading

Abbate, Carolyn: "Outside Ravel's Tomb," *Journal of the American Musicological Society* 52:3 (1999): 465–530.

Adorno, Theodor: *Aesthetic Theory* (1970); trans. Robert Hullot-Kentor (Minneapolis: University of Minnesota Press, 1997).

Adorno, Theodor: *Introduction to the Sociology of Music* (1962); trans. E. B. Ashton (New York: Continuum, 1988).

Adorno, Theodor: "Schubert" (1928); trans. Jonathan Dunsby and Beate Perrey, *19th-Century Music* 29:1 (2005): 3–14.

Adorno, Theodor: "Toward an Understanding of Schoenberg" (1955/1967); trans. Susan Gillespie, *Essays on Music*, ed. Richard Leppert (Berkeley: University of California Press, 2002), pp. 627–43.

Berka, Sigrid: "D(e)addyfication: Elfriede Jelinek," *Elfriede Jelinek: Framed by Language*, ed. Jorun B. Johns and Katherine Arens (Riverside, CA: Ariadne Press, 1994), pp. 229–54.

Buch, Esteban: "Adorno's 'Schubert': From the Critique of the Garden Gnome to the Defense of Atonalism," *19th-Century Music* 29:1 (2005): 25–30.

Cavell, Stanley: *The World Viewed* (Cambridge, MA: Harvard University Press, 1979).

Chun, Wendy Hui Kyong: *Control and Freedom: Power and Paranoia in the Age of Fiber Optics* (Cambridge, MA: MIT Press, 2006).

Coughlin, Anne M.: "Representing the Forbidden," *California Law Review* 90:6 (December 2002): 2143–83.

Deleuze, Gilles and Sacher-Masoch, Leopold von: *Masochism* (Cambridge, MA: Zone Books, 1991).

Fiddler, Allyson: *Rewriting Reality: An Introduction to Elfriede Jelinek* (Providence, RI: Berg, 1994).

Foundas, Scott with Haneke, Michael: "The Bearded Prophet of *Code inconnu* and *The Piano Teacher*," *Indiewire* (December 4, 2001), www.indiewire.com/people/int_Haneke_Michael_011204.html (accessed November 2, 2006).

Gibbs, Christopher H.: *The Cambridge Companion to Schubert* (New York: Cambridge University Press, 1997).

Hart, Lynda: *Between the Body and the Flesh: Performing Sadomasochism* (New York: Columbia University Press, 1998).

Hoberman, J.: "Prisoner's Songs," *Village Voice* (March 27, 2002), www.villagevoice.com/film/0213,hoberman,33363,20.html (accessed October 16, 2006).

Johns, Jorun B. and Arens, Katherine, eds.: *Elfriede Jelinek: Framed by Language* (Riverside, CA: Ariadne Press, 1994).

Lawrence, D. H.: *Lady Chatterley's Lover/A Propos of "Lady Chatterley's Lover"* (New York: Penguin Books, 1994).

Palmer, Tim: "Style and Sensation in the Contemporary French Cinema of the Body," *Journal of Film and Video* 58:3 (Fall 2006): 22–32.

Sharrett, Christopher: "The Horror of the Middle Class," *Kinoeye* 4:1 (March 8, 2004), kinoeye.org/04/01/sharrett01.php (accessed November 19, 2004).

Sharrett, Christopher: "The World That is Known: An Interview with Michael Haneke,"

Kino-Eye: New Perspectives on Austrian Film 4:1 (March 8, 2004), www.kinoeye.org/04/01/interview01.php (accessed November 19, 2004). [Interview reprinted in this volume.]

Strove, Ulrich: "'Denouncing the Pornographic Subject': The American and German Pornography Debate and Elfriede Jelinek's *Lust*," *Elfriede Jelinek: Framed by Language*, ed. Jorun B. Johns and Katherine Arens (Riverside, CA: Ariadne Press, 1994) pp. 89–106.

Wheatley, Catherine: "The Masochistic Fantasy Made Flesh: Michael Haneke's *La Pianiste* as Melodrama," *Studies in French Cinema* 6:2 (2006): 117–27.

Williams, Linda: "Film Bodies: Gender, Genre, and Excess," *Film Quarterly* 44:4 (Summer 1991): 2–13.

Williams, Linda: *Hard Core: Power, Pleasure, and the "Frenzy of the Visible"* (Berkeley: University of California Press, 1989).

Wyatt, Jean: *"Jouissance* and Desire in Michael Haneke's *The Piano Teacher*," *American Imago* 62:4 (2006): 453–82.

Youens, Susan: *Retracing a Winter's Journey: Schubert's Winterreise* (Ithaca, NY: Cornell University Press, 1991).

27

Civilization's Endless Shadow

Haneke's Time of the Wolf

Evan Torner

A film that deliberately denies the viewer any escapism, *Time of the Wolf* (2003) appropriately begins with a thwarted vacation. The affluent, white European Laurent family arrive at their country cabin to find it occupied by a panicked refugee family. After the father, Georges (Daniel Duval), is killed during the encounter, the mother, Anne (Isabelle Huppert), travels with her two children, Eva (Anaïs Desmoustiers) and Ben (Lucas Biscombe), across the countryside seeking safety. They discover that some unnamed catastrophe has caused nearly all societal functions to cease, forcing them into a constant search for shelter and food. Their journey leads to a train station under the control of the gun-toting Koslowski (Olivier Gourmet), who barters with the Laurents and other refugees over their remaining goods while they wait for the train to come. After each family member is seen dealing with the stress and injustice of the situation in their own way, a jarring tracking shot at the end suggests that they might have caught the train after all.

Of all the films within Austrian director Michael Haneke's oeuvre, *Time of the Wolf* has been seen as the most inscrutable and the most impotent. Indeed, the nearly unified opinion in early 2004, maintained by reviewers on both sides of the Atlantic, was that the post-apocalyptic film delivered neither Haneke's usual aesthetic brilliance – as seen most notably in *The Piano Teacher* (2001) and *Code Unknown* (*Code inconnu*, 2000) – nor a particularly scathing critique of the post-apocalypse or *Endzeit* genre the film may be said to invoke, a deconstruction of the type Haneke performed with regard to the slasher film in *Funny Games* (1997) and the melodrama in *Fraulein* (1986). Stanley Kauffmann writes in his *New Republic* review of the film that "after Haneke has put his people in a fraught situation, their interactions during their wait are insufficiently interesting" (Kauffmann 2004: 33). The review of *Time of the Wolf* in the German news weekly *Der Spiegel* makes a similar point, claiming that the film's "cool, stylish minimalism – more illustrative than emotive – does not develop the emotional pull that gave earlier Haneke works their power" ("Kino in Kürze"). The film, then, seemed caught between an auteurist-influenced discourse of thwarted spectatorial and critical expectations and Haneke's own seemingly half-hearted commitment to the post-apocalyptic genre. Ironically, this curious situation has led to the fact that the film has been overlooked precisely as an *auteurist* work and as part of a sub-cycle of critically meditative and self-reflexive examples of the genre.

Perhaps the source of the ambivalence towards and, in some cases, open disdain for *Time of the Wolf* lies in its myriad conceptual, aesthetic, and narrative contradictions. It poses an eerie resistance to the patterns that guide conventional Hollywood narratives, yet it also refuses to resort to well-known filmic distantiation devices as found, for example, in Jean-Luc Godard's work – that is, until the final shot of the film. The title of the film is borrowed from Norse mythology – it is a direct reference to the Gylfaginning time of Ragnarök, a time of final violent conflict between all men left on Earth, although the film does not develop any further parallels to the myth. The film features prominent French actors such as Isabelle Huppert and Béatrice Dalle, but their talents appear squandered, as the histrionic range of the characters they play is largely confined to the register of panic, dismay, and dejectedness. The film's premise of global disaster is as much near-future science fiction as it is a record of the fairly mundane, microcosmic breakdown of modern societal comforts. Suffering is the thread that ties the film's characters together in moral ambiguity, but much of it does not arise from the conventional drama of direct human-on-human violence. Instead, viewers are confronted with the graphic portrayal of the slaughtering of helpless animals. Moreover, one of the film's prominent aesthetic features is an at times excruciating audio track of humans in despair. Haneke renounces the visually arresting, high-contrast deserts of post-apocalyptic films such as *A Boy and His Dog* (L. Q. Jones, 1975) and *Mad Max* (George Miller, 1979) for overcast European skies and virtually pitch-black night shots, going so far as to claim in the press release that *Time of the Wolf* is literally "one of the darkest films in cinema history." Thus, while the film develops its own visual style and intensity, it eschews commercial cinema's aesthetics of spectacle. In addition, the detachment from historical specificity that characterizes most of Haneke's theatrical feature films[1] takes on a unique character in *Time of the Wolf*. On the one hand, the film evinces an allegorical or parable-like dimension, whose frame of reference is broadly humanist, which is not uncharacteristic of the genre as a whole. On the other hand, the film also reflects on issues contextually bound to middle European politics of the 1990s – in particular the humanitarian crisis that developed in the wake of the breakup of Yugoslavia and the civil war that ensued.

Such contradictions actually serve to build the ambiguity and the discursive play into Haneke's film that is also characteristic of his other films. But the fact that *Time of the Wolf* deploys its apocalyptic *mise-en-scène* – near-total darkness, violence against animals, silence – alongside a post-apocalyptic story that dramatizes the crumbling of justice, the breakdown of the social order, and the characters' day-to-day struggle for survival makes the interplay of form and content almost tautological. This is where the film's departure from the genre is located. *Time of the Wolf* is a post-apocalypse film that, in contrast to many examples of the genre, resists hopeful hints at civilizational renewal. It refuses to end with a vision of the future, whether positive or negative.

I

As with most Haneke films, the plot of *Time of the Wolf* is not easily summarized. Indeed, part of the film's critique of conventional representations of catastrophes is that it eludes shorthand narrative description, just as the plight of suffering individuals around the world should not be summarized in headline news coverage or Diane Arbus-style snapshots of their physical state.

The opening credits present a contemplative anti-spectacle that one also finds at the beginning of Haneke's *Code Unknown*: a dark screen with no sound or music whatsoever, with small white letters presenting the film title and the names of the cast. This immediately codes *Time of the Wolf* as a serious European art film in Haneke's own tradition as well as that of Ingmar Bergman, Robert Bresson, or Chris Marker, but not as a self-consciously post-apocalyptic epic. Many films of the genre such as *Wizards* (Ralph Bakshi, 1977) and *Six String Samurai* (Lance Mungia, 1998) mediate the end of the world through an expository opening montage before turning to its post-apocalyptic consequences, cinematically distinguishing between the end of the world and the changed world to come. By contrast, *Time of the Wolf* suppresses the cause of the apocalypse, and the quiet intensity of the images emerges from the film's overall minimalism rather than partaking in the aesthetics of spectacle. Thus, the protagonists, whose fate we follow, are no more prepared for the events that unfold than we are as viewers.

The credit sequence is followed by a picturesque opening shot of a dense European forest. The white van of the Laurent family pulls into this thoroughly isolated space, reminiscent of Anna and Georg's vehicle trip to the Austrian vacation home in *Funny Games*. Soon after the Laurents arrive and unload their vehicle, Anne instructs Eva not to get dirty from the moist box she's carrying. Then the scene cuts to the dark interior of the house where Fred (Pierre Berriau), the head of the family of vagrants hiding in the cabin, will be revealed after a further cut to a Hitchcockian surprise establishing shot.

The significance of the preface to the confrontation with Fred should not be underestimated, for it foreshadows the rest of the film. Though there is no diegetic time or space that exists prior to the apocalypse in the film, the family exhibit a patterned set of behaviors that convey a vague sense of "normalcy." The brief establishment of this state and its subsequent disruption are part of the formula of the post-apocalyptic genre. In *Time of the Wolf*, this state is never regained or replaced by anything equivalent. The plentiful provisions and the van provide the unassuming presence of that which will soon become absent and coveted throughout the rest of the film. Anne's comment to her daughter can be seen as the film's attempt at social typing that tells viewers everything they need to know about the family: They possess bourgeois ideals about all aspects of life, and will continue to draw boundaries in Pierre Bourdieu's sense of the term – "the *discretio* (discrimination) demanding that certain things be brought together and others kept apart" (Bourdieu 1984: 473) – between themselves and the world. Class will structure all their experiences, whether the world ends or not. But it is the destabilization of borders and boundaries, as well as the breakdown of categories, codes, and rules, that Haneke's film is about both on the thematic and aesthetic level. It enacts this breakdown with a narrative determined by ambiguity and the withholding of crucial information, as well as by an aesthetic of murkiness and outright darkness. In this sense, the darkness of the cottage prefigures the darkness that comes to dominate the visuals of the film as a whole, as well as the shadow cast by civilization itself. The cabin is as much the family's retreat from the city as it is the site for a senseless murder, just as the train station is as much a shelter as it is an inhospitable, dangerous concrete purgatory. Just as a stable, purposive civilization narrative functionally determines the boundary between pre- and post-apocalyptic time, spaces like the cabin or train station only become post-apocalyptic when their former function suddenly becomes destabilized and, for better or worse, is put in flux.

After the vagrant family's appearance, Georges's sudden murder is the next shocking event. It demonstrates, in deadpan manner, the ineffectiveness of Enlightenment-style social negotiation and channels the macrocosmic violence of the offscreen apocalypse into the Laurent family's microcosm. Haneke constructs Georges's attempt to reason with Fred in a standard shot/reverse-shot conversation. He builds tension by adding Fred's wife (Valérie Moreau) and child (Ina Strnad) as a counterpoint to the man's rifle, allowing the scene to be both an object lesson in survival ethics and a confrontation between the helpless bourgeoisie and the firearm-empowered underclass. The child's greedy consumption of the soda can's contents initially registers as a kind of relief of the situation's tension, but in hindsight it takes on a decisively sinister, survival-of-the-fittest tone. Suddenly, as Georges is about to suggest both families put their differences aside, Fred shoots his rifle at point-blank range.[2] The viewer does not see Georges being shot, and interestingly, it is not Georges's wife, but Fred's, who subsequently breaks into hysterics, which is meant to signify that the killing is a traumatic event for all.

In contrast to mainstream variants of the genre, in which such scenes tend to simply illustrate the doom-and-gloom atmosphere, the implications of Georges's murder are richer and prove far more intriguing. To answer the question "Why did Fred shoot Georges?," one's impulse is to turn to explanations such as hunger, nervousness, desperation, Fred's wish to protect his family, or to see the weapon's firing as an accident; other speculations that may be entertained by viewers are class *ressentiment* and sheer malice. The stark material circumstances of the vagrants present a mild justification for the crime, but these are mitigated by the gunshot's sheer arbitrariness. The editing and camera framing also prove no help in discerning the root cause of Georges's murder. As Georg Seeßlen describes in his well-known essay on the structures of glaciation in Haneke's films, the lack of emotion and the characters' enigmatic motives and actions present the audience with merely an act, but no clue as to its cause:

> The characters on the screen are not performing emotions. It is not emotions that are enacted before us but, if anything, concrete gestures – attempts to retrieve via ritual that which was lost. It is just as difficult for the audience to condemn the figures for their lack of emotion, in a manner we know from classical cinema where the emotionless person is always the bad person and sooner or later will be punished. (Seeßlen 2008: 29)

Seeßlen indicates that nothing moral or psychologically significant is to be found in the characters' actions themselves; rather, these actions must be considered as objects within a larger framework that binds the characters to society and to the very vision we use to witness and judge these actions. Fred's wife's hysterics do not reveal any moral integrity, because it is not remorse that they signify. The characters' emotions are rendered incomprehensible by Haneke's formal distantiation from the gunshot, and yet the viewer nonetheless tries to comprehend the murder. The horror of the scene is not merely in its violence, but in how useless the powers of reason are in explaining it.

Following the murder, a significant cut is introduced: The children enter the cabin and close the door behind them, with the camera centering on the door before the family are seen from a distance walking their bicycle down the empty country road. The cut may be said to have allegorical implications in that it produces a surplus of connotations compared with relatively sparse narrative information. One presumes the opening and closing of the door to be a signal that the family are now officially cast from the violence of the apocalypse into the chaos of the post-apocalypse. There are several other such cuts in the film. One is the cut preceding the barn fire sequence that replaces the shot into the darkness over the fire with one of a raging inferno resulting from Eva's apparent carelessness. Another is a cut to the mysterious watercolor mushroom cloud seen in close-up while Eva is writing the letter to her dead father. What distinguishes these cuts from others is their self-conscious referencing of a greater signifier that, while not fully explained, seems to have something to do with the apocalypse itself. Because no specific information has been supplied about the nature, location, and time frame of the cataclysmic event, the closing of a door, the stare of a camera off into darkness, and the mushroom cloud introduced from an uncomfortably close proximity all take on a kind of contemplative function, as none of these shots yields any meaning about the time, space, and characters. Just as Haneke denies viewers the possibility to interpret scenes of violence in terms of narrative or sociological causality, these cuts, which stretch beyond a diegetic or narrative function, force the viewer to produce his or her own interpretations.

The rest of the film can be divided up into three thematically distinct sections: the Laurent family on the road seeking shelter, the initial days at the train station, and the inundation of the train station with refugees from the caravan. The first section poses the post-apocalyptic challenge in terms of the nomadic existence of Anne and her children, their struggle to stay alive, and their growing awareness of the irreversible loss of their secure, privileged bourgeois past. The second section expands the challenge by introducing a view of sociality via the representation of power relations within groups of human survivors, while the third section reformulates the challenge in terms of larger questions of loyalty, justice, and the long-term spiritual future of humankind. Not unlike mainstream films like *Dawn of the Dead* (Zack Snyder, 2004) that confront their protagonists with threats posed by a societal collapse before moving on to pondering larger philosophical dilemmas, *Time of the Wolf* follows the standard-issue presentation structure for post-apocalyptic cinema. But unlike such films, Haneke's film refuses to code any of the characters as heroes (no matter how flawed) capable of leading humanity into a new era.

The first post-murder scenes are characterized by a tension between several pairs of thematic and aesthetic opposites: warmth and cold, dark and light, shelter and exposure, food and hunger, and accessibility and barred entry. By the time the family arrive in the village from their cabin, it has grown dark. A resident whom Anne claims she knows refuses the family entry and asks them rhetorically, "Don't you know what's happened?" before closing the door on them. Detached from their bourgeois social networks and preoccupied with their own survival, Anne's acquaintances all prove unhelpful in her search for shelter, and her declarations that she "knows" them do not seem to matter. The family wander the streets in a quest for shelter and, in doing so, obliviously walk right past an indistinct burning pile of garbage and horse corpses. Arguably one of the most apocalyptic images in the film, the bonfire suggests animal-borne disease as a possible cause for the collapse of society. Moreover, it illustrates the reduction of the living and the inanimate in the cleansing flames of the end of the world. The treatment of humans and animals in death becomes an important point of comparison as the film evolves, and the horse corpses prefigure both the many more rotting animal corpses that will appear and the great onscreen suffering of animals to come. Though the Laurent family's anguish is acute and sympathetic, the pain they experience is incommensurate with that visited upon the hierarchically lower forms of life, the animals.

The Laurent family eventually settle down for the night in a wooden shed next to a secured stone building. They start a fire and consume canned goods very audibly in the firelight. Just before dawn, Anne leaves to forage for additional supplies, telling Ben to wait with Eva until she returns. Characteristically, conventional post-apocalyptic or horror films would at this point stage a personal encounter between the characters and some embodiment or instanciation of the monstrous realities of the apocalypse. Eschewing this cliché, the film shows that Anne in fact succeeds in procuring food and the children only encounter an issue with Ben's pet bird, a green parakeet who flutters around the shed looking for an escape route. Jürgen Jürges's handheld camera focusing on the bird empathizes with the animal's desperation before chronicling Ben and Eva's efforts to catch it. Ben is scratched by the bird while trying to catch it, spreading blood across his face as Georges's blood splashed on Anne's earlier, before Eva catches the bird for him. Ben puts the bird in his jacket, possessing it and thereby suffocating it. The post-apocalyptic struggle is not only between anonymous armed factions, but between master and pet.

The Laurents find a barn and build a pyre for the bird. Anne later knocks over this pyre when, in the middle of the night, Ben has gone missing. The reasons for his absence remain unexplained but the scene does serve to present the major scene of near-absolute darkness in the film. Eva lights a fire in the middle of the barn and is to keep the fire lit, so that Ben has a light to which to go; fire, which will later become part of his self-immolation attempt, is originally intended for his rescue. Meanwhile, Anne cries "Benny!" in a darkness lit only by her frequently extinguished torch. The painfully audible anguish of a mother who has lost her son is reinforced for the viewer by the darkness during this sequence.[3] The post-apocalyptic space becomes the vast void at night that swallows loved ones in the dark, but this is ironically juxtaposed to its conceptual correlative – the image of the barn in flames; Eva apparently let the fire go too long. Light-swallowing natural dark and an accidental inferno place the traditional dichotomy between dark and light, warmth and coldness, into an allegorically fraught context: Flames and, by extension, all manner of natural and artificial (i.e., civilizational) light require constant vigilance, while the dark is only threatening once someone needs to see in it.

When morning arrives, a psychologically damaged Ben is being held hostage a few yards away by a young Romanian runaway (Hakim Taleb), who introduces a few new dimensions into the Laurent family's survival story. There is a barter economy – Anne offers to treat the runaway's dog-bitten hand for a drink of water – and there is a train station to the south where the trains "sometimes come." The group discovers a sheep corpse. The sheep, as the young runaway claims, may have "died of thirst, or drank bad water. Or maybe the shepherds killed it to drink its blood." The dangers faced by the animals in the course of *Time of the Wolf* necessarily extend to the humans, too, and the collapse of the social order seems to have produced every epiphenomenon feared by Western Europeans accustomed to political stability and economic prosperity. In their efforts to flag down a train, the Laurents see that it bears refugees in-between its cars. Thus, their own situation is brought home to them even more dramatically.

At the point of the Romanian runaway's introduction in *Time of the Wolf*, the historical context suddenly lurches to the foreground. In 1993, when Haneke first conceived of the film,[4] an Eastern European boy hungrily scavenging for food would have immediately recalled the war raging in Bosnia that was, as Tony Judt describes it, "unfolding real time on the television screens of the world" (Judt 2006: 676). The conflict itself unraveled in such a way that it became extremely difficult to firmly establish the goals and allegiances of the dozens of different murderous factions involved, such that the day-to-day realities in Sarajevo or Foča may have resembled those of Haneke's chaotic post-apocalypse world.[5] Moreover, the Bosnian civil war ultimately produced over 1.8 million displaced people, refugees like the Laurent family fleeing unlivable circumstances and frequently at the mercy of armed men running makeshift camps like the one found at the train station in the film. And though Haneke's native Austria shared a border with the former Yugoslavia and accepted refugees from the crisis, it frequently sided with Serbian war criminals in international relations (Judt 2006: 786). The inability of the European Community to prevent the humanitarian crisis before it would escalate and assume genocidal features may have caused Haneke to consider how thoroughly *unsafe* for Europeans the present version of European civilization turned out to be. Though Haneke's films hardly ever explicitly address a specific historical topic, the young runaway serves as part of a cluster of iconically haunting allegorical references specifically for Western audiences to consider the apocalyptic circumstances found in the recent past on European soil.[6]

Haneke's allegorical treatment of contemporary historical material can certainly be called into question here. Allegories run the risk of slighting or eliding historical specificities – not a small risk, given the imperative to maintain the dignities of war victims and refugees, as well as the historian's obligation to avoid elision in the historiographic analysis. At the same time, however, allegories, particularly in an artistic representation of a complex and possibly taboo event, may serve to draw analogies to larger issues and between previously unrelated contexts. *Time of the Wolf* encourages such analogies to be drawn, and yet is preoccupied with its own characters' material suffering beyond the allegorical level: The Romanian runaway and the Laurents are archetypal refugees and yet also unique characters united in their flight.

From the time they meet the young runaway, the Laurents increasingly interact with a nascent post-apocalyptic society. The family discover the train station, only to find it occupied by a diverse array of individuals whose common goal is survival. The Laurents now share a space with the pistol-toting Koslowski, the Brandt couple (played by prominent French actors Béatrice Dalle and Patrice Chéreau), a Polish family with six children, the radio-listener Azoulay (Florence Loiret), an attractive woman from the city, Béa (Brigitte Roüan), and some desultory old men. The issues in this part of the film revolve around the moral practices of this community in the face of dangers and deprivation: They are presented in scenes that show the expulsion of the young runaway for theft, the merciless bartering for water with mercenary traders, and Béa having to trade sex with Koslowski for her place in the station. Young Eva is the principal witness to events ranging from the amoral to the unethical to the criminal. Meanwhile, the black-and-white vision of survival outside of the train depot becomes the endless gray of the cement walls and the ashen faces of the refugees. The suffering that was silently endured by the Laurent family is now drowned by the moans of the hungry, heavy breathing during the night, a sick baby's cries, a woman's prayer, and the bickering of the Brandt family.

Béa becomes the icon for any kind of preserved cultural memory amidst this suffering, as she recalls the tale of the Thirty-Six Just Men for Anne and sings the "Maikäfer flieg" song to soothe tensions, the original text of which merits further discussion: "Maikäfer flieg / Dein Vater ist im Krieg / Deine Mutter ist in Pommerland / Pommerland ist abgebrannt / Maikäfer flieg" ("June bug fly / Your father is in the war / Your mother is in Pomerania / Pomerania has burnt down / June bug fly"). The song originated in the Thirty Years' War and alludes not only to war, but also to a potential refugee problem. The forces of Wallenstein and Gustavus Adolphus of Sweden took turns invading the region between the years 1625 and 1648, destroying two-thirds of its populace, physically razing dozens of villages, and exposing future generations to cycles of plague and famine. Haneke is no doubt alluding to the June bug's journey as a flight from such certain death and misery toward an uncertain fate – which has also been the fate of many a refugee. Meanwhile, Eva becomes the refugee camp poet in her composition of a letter (read in voice-over) to her dead father. She talks to the young runaway about how he had to kill his own dog,[7] and a Polish child dies of disease. A kind of cinematic and narrative "normalcy" is established during this section: There is some mild unpleasantness and desperation, but also the establishment of a semi-functional society.

A caravan of refugees arrives as a child's funeral takes place. The arrival sparks a flurry of activities in the night. All of a sudden, the nighttime sequences begin to resemble the earlier ones, with plenty of human-generated light and noise. Familiar disputes over power and resources begin to surface: Koslowski becomes angry about the refugees using too much water, the Polish father is accused of murder by a gang of men and struggles with one of them on the ground, and Anne's space on the floor of the depot becomes an envied commodity. The characters have the opportunity to enjoy small pleasures, such as drinking milk from goats and listening to a tape recording of Ludwig van Beethoven's "Sonata for Piano and Violin No. 5, Op. 24 in F Major" – the only pre-recorded music in the film. A process of normalization, however fragile and tentative, sets in. The social world has realigned along many of its old lines of pleasure and prejudice. Suddenly, Fred's wife walks in front of the camera unprompted, and Eva's sense of surprise and horror may well be echoed by the audience.

The reappearance of the homicidal refugee family from the chalet provides a jarring reinsertion of the violent past into the formation of a new society, both a cautionary note about the beginning of any "new eras" and a subtle commentary on why post-communist Yugoslavia had difficulties in moving beyond religious and ethnic hatreds. While these are rooted in ideology, the bloodshed they caused left scars that made it difficult even for the middle class to move on. Anne is conspicuously reading Eva's letter to her dead father when Eva bursts into the room, dispersing any significance the letter may have held for the narrative. The cataclysmic, senseless murder still stands as the most shocking moment in the film, and Anne's paroxysm of outrage about the homicidal family's presence should effectively mirror that of the audience. She and the refugee family get into a yelling match near the boxcars, which is broken up by Azoulay. Suddenly, specific dates, locations, and facts tumble into the discussion and into *Time of the Wolf* itself. Anne cannot prove Fred or his wife's guilt to the men with guns in charge, but it is precisely her lack of power and her rage that have a rousing effect on viewers. Yet, here as in other Haneke films, the narrative will not resolve any conflicts or restore justice. Instead, the film amplifies the drama and the acrimony by pairing it with yet another scene of animal death. The refugees interrupt the fight with the shooting of a live horse, which is gutted in close-up. Haneke has positioned the Laurents' anguish over injustice against the merciless execution and onscreen desecration of a live animal. The film invites a comparison of states of suffering, followed by the elation of a sudden rain shower for a very thirsty populace. Though the scene is intended to pull the audience along an emotional roller coaster, there is no ideology for sale at the end of the ride. Viewers may dwell either on Fred's infuriating falseness or question why Haneke includes this on-camera killing. Their emotions may alternately seize on the relief provided by the rain, on the altruism of the young runaway providing Eva with a blanket, or on Ben's psychological collapse as he shivers under the boxcar, without being coerced to prioritize any of these aspects.

Two further events occur before the final two scenes provide an effective ending to the film. The first is the young runaway's theft of a goat; a theft immediately blamed on the Polish family, regardless of the fact that its logistics prove patently absurd. Ethnic prejudice clouds some refugees' sound judgment, just as Fred's presence clouds Anne's. While debate ensues about the goat's theft – justice having become a matter of material concerns rather than being a principle in its own right – the second event happens: The body of a woman who committed suicide is brought inside the station. The question is raised as to the precise circumstances and motivations for this woman – or anyone – to commit suicide. Another woman who helped carry her inside is at a loss. The central question that is raised by this scene in Haneke's film is one that has also preoccupied philosophers, and these have found a link between suicide and a specific aspect of war on the civilian population – the phenomenon of the refugee camp. During the UN peace-keeping missions in the former Yugoslavia, Jean Baudrillard commented in a 1995 *Libération* article that humanitarianism itself devalues life, and as such a concept helps give refugee camps their hopeless character:

> The only, necessarily negative, outlook for humanitarianism is the optimal management of waste that is by definition nondegradable. From the point of view of

survival – life superstitiously prolonged and sheltered from death – life itself becomes a waste product we can no longer rid ourselves of, one that falls under the spell of infinite reproduction. (Baudrillard 1996: 89)

Baudrillard's representation of the dark side of the humanitarian project also reflects the larger existential reasoning for suicide. There is not a moment where the young woman's suicide or Ben's attempt at suicide would be called into question by the audience: Under extreme circumstances, some human beings psychologically crumble. Yet, what is interesting is that the suicides only begin to happen at a point in the narrative when a larger community is beginning to develop and their food and water supply is about to stabilize. This is to say a materialist explanation for their desire to kill themselves is of very limited use. At issue are, rather, the overwhelming consequences of being trapped in a situation whose profoundly dehumanizing nature goes beyond the physical aspects of the fight for survival.

II

Given its high level of intertextuality and its formal consistency with Haneke's overall oeuvre, *Time of the Wolf* is best seen as a meditation not only on a possible apocalypse, but also on Haneke's recent work as a filmmaker. Intertextual references embellish the auteurist trappings of the film, as can be found, for example, in Haneke's frequent redeployment of similar dramatis personae in his films. The Laurent family are the embodiment of the bourgeois nuclear family that make their appearance in *Time of the Wolf* as well as in two other French-language productions by Haneke, *Code Unknown* and *Caché* (2005). Georges, Anne, Eva, and Benny's names have been used for representatives of the nuclear family in most of Haneke's feature films, from *The Seventh Continent* to *Caché* to the United States installment of *Funny Games* (2007). This "everyman"[8] approach to his characters allows Haneke to reinvoke archetypes from films past to place them in new, alienating contexts. Ben is once again the disaffected youth, Georges is the emasculated bourgeois intellectual, and Anne is the bourgeois housewife with a well-conditioned stiff upper lip who leaves the future of the family in the hands of Eva, the savvy daughter. Also making an appearance are the archetypes of the outsider and serious-looking men with authority, two groups that routinely pull on either side of the alienated bourgeois family in Haneke's work. The outsider, the young runaway, is played by a Romanian actor, who echoes Romanians cast as outsiders in *71 Fragments of a Chronology of Chance* (1994) (Gabriel Cosmin Urdes as Marian Radu, a very similar character) and *Code Unknown* (Luminita Gheorghiu as Maria). Koslowski could take the place of many a police officer in the Parisian or Viennese streets of Haneke's other films, though he possesses a quotidian sexual dimension in *Time of the Wolf* absent from these characters. All of these archetypes are as psychologically impenetrable as they are hopelessly mundane: They are "ordinary" people who, when encountering a threat to their materialist lives, adopt fierce defense mechanisms to protect the illusions and objects they possess.

Other connections to Haneke's oeuvre can be found within *Time of the Wolf*'s overarching thematic material and formal technique. Haneke still relies on a spare use of music, naturalistic lighting, and static shots that flatten characters into their social milieu and their physical environment. An advanced state of alienation of individuals in modern society from themselves and others can be seen in nearly every character written by Haneke. Most human relationships in the film rely on either obligation, guilt, or commodity exchanges to sustain them, and resentment builds among all the characters in each new situation in which they find themselves. In contrast to numerous examples from popular culture that imagine the apocalypse similarly to W. Wheeler Dixon, as "the simultaneously feared and anticipated . . . end of 'all,' the defining moment we all seek" (Dixon 2003: 4), *Time of the Wolf* depicts it as merely a series of endless moments of quiet and manic desperation already familiar from other Haneke films: Hans slapping his wife in *71 Fragments* or Georg closing out his accounts in *The Seventh Continent*. The unavailability of certain resources such as water or food pales in comparison to the already annihilated human interpersonal bonds.

The asymmetrical, visually horrific relationship between humans and animals has also been a subject of Haneke's film since the death of the goldfish in *The Seventh Continent* and the pig-slaughter footage in *Benny's Video* (1992). In contrast to depictions of human murder, suicide and animal slaughter earn the undivided attention of Haneke's camera, distinguishing between real animal deaths and (necessarily) play-acted human deaths – as well as between the graphic representation of animal slaughter and the oblique representation of human death. This is to avoid "pleasurable flinching" on the viewer's part.[9] In Susan Sontag's words:

> No moral charge attaches to the representation of these cruelties. Just the provocation: can you look at this? There is the satisfaction of being able to look at the image without flinching. There is the pleasure of flinching. (Sontag 2003: 41)

Haneke's principal critique of any established Hollywood genre, be it slasher film, romantic comedy, or post-apocalypse film, nearly always begins with the substitution of voyeuristic spectatorial pleasure for the possibility of a morally engaged spectatorial critique. Sontag's "flinching" dynamic is not transcended by *Time of the Wolf*'s onscreen killings of a goat and a horse, but it is rather exploited to draw attention to the violence that still makes an emotional impact on viewers and on the powerlessness of domesticated animals before the instrumental whims of humankind.

The final shot of the film, conceptually similar to the one in *Caché*, requires a more in-depth interpretation because of its relative independence from the film's content. Explicating it on the level of Haneke's cinematic language, this is one of the most optimistic shots within the director's career. The right-to-left tracking shot of a verdant middle or northern European countryside set to a soundtrack of gentle train noises functions on a narrative level as a self-evident answer to the question, "Will the train ever arrive?" Not only did it arrive but, as one may want to argue, the Laurent family and all the refugees are likely onboard, presumably heading south for a slightly better future than that offered by the cruel wait at the train station. Or are they? Haneke's final shot does not so much present a sudden refusal to provide narrative information, which he has been denying the viewer for the film's duration, as it liberates the viewer from the necessity of narrative itself. The process of slowly detaching the audience from the film's plotline begins with the shot emerging from the darkness of a forest to a scarcely inhabited stretch of forests and grass. In an era when one's chief view from a train consists of cement walls, fences, and graffiti, this presents a surprisingly idealized depiction not only of the European landscape itself, but also of the supposedly post-apocalyptic environment of the diegesis. The eye of the viewer is relieved from its nearly anthropological documentation of the film's characters and instead momentarily adopts their audiovisual perspective. Later, as the precisely two-minute duration of the shot and its quiet soundtrack begins to impose doubt about that perspective, the viewer is given contemplative space to reflect on the film's content and its trajectory.

This trajectory is encapsulated in the right-to-left motion of the shot. Against the left-to-right direction of Western reading, the linear progression of time, and the teleology of the Enlightenment, *Time of the Wolf* depicts the train moving right-to-left to agitate against the line of thinking that has led to the glut of apocalyptic fantasy in the first place. It's almost as if Haneke's unwillingness to further the self-generated future of such prophecies stands in response to John Berger's argument that the very prophecies of the apocalypse become the apocalypse itself (Berger 1999: 8). After all, it was the forward progression of left-to-right tracking shots and left-to-right movement that introduced the film's journey into darkness: Anne and her children wander in this direction along empty roads and wilderness paths, most notably during the nighttime shot of burning horses and assorted offal in town. Anne and company also run left to right to try to flag down the train as it passes them by, another gesture symbolizing the fruitlessness of that direction. The final shot seems to suggest that Western principles of progress, indeed, the concept of teleology itself, including its narrative and aesthetic renderings in cinema, may be part of the apocalypse, possibly even counting among its potential *causes*.

By the same token, however, the combination of two of the most enduring symbols of Western civilization's so-called "advancement," namely, the train and the camera, to record natural landscapes hints at Haneke's critical appraisal of the viewer's position in this environment. The notion that the refugees can now look with indifference on the next group of people running to catch the train should not be lost on the viewer, nor should one forget that their point of view would now be aligned with ours. Andrew Tracy asserts that, in this final shot, Haneke predicts "the world will end with neither a bang nor a whimper but with a look, the time of images which we ourselves have conjured, making us mere spectators to the destruction or salvation that awaits us" (Tracy 2004). Tracy's poetic statement demonstrates a precise understanding of Haneke's skepticism about the human gaze, which cautions the viewer against the power of their very attention. On the other hand, this skepticism is embedded in the shot's other connotation – which, by default, is optimistic when contrasted with the rest of the film. Human suffering has been eliminated – not even the whimper signifying the world's end is present – as has the human image altogether. The shot is thoroughly post-human, and suggests a simple-but-necessary dissolution of *any* expectation from the visual, particularly in relation to narrative. The viewer's look may be partially to blame in ending the world for progress-driven humanity and certainly ends the film, but the image of the landscape outside the train car may linger in the viewer's mind far beyond the end of *Time of the Wolf*, and so may a discourse on reality that transcends the anthropocentric gaze.

Though the post-apocalypse film has traditionally been construed as an American creation, *Time of the Wolf* holds a definitive place among – and draws upon – a larger tradition of distinctly European post-apocalypse fiction. The origins of American post-apocalypse film can be found within traditional and heavy-handedly allegorical Hollywood depictions of nuclear war in *Five* (Arch Oboler, 1951) and Roger Corman's *The Day the World Ended* (1956), whereas European post-apocalyptic film saw its beginnings in Bergman's existential depiction of the Middle Ages, *The Seventh Seal* (1957), and Marker's remarkable photo-film *La Jetée* (1962). Unsurprisingly, American and Australian post-apocalyptic films like *Mad Max* and *Waterworld* (Kevin Reynolds, 1995) have perpetuated the Hollywood focus on spectacles of war and unproblematic violence. The European tradition, on the other hand, tends to emphasize the existential and social implications of the end of the world, seen in films such as Rainer Erler's *Operation Ganymede* (1977), Andrei Tarkovsky's *The Sacrifice* (1986), and Alfonso Cuarón's *Children of Men* (2006).[10] Hollywood-styled post-apocalyptic cinema creates new, brightly lit frontiers of battle to be explored and defended by hardened, sexually charged men and women; take Australia's *Road Warrior* (George Miller, 1981), *A Boy and His Dog*, *The Postman* (Kevin Costner, 1998), *I Am Legend* (Francis Lawrence, 2007), and *Doomsday* (Neil Marshall, 2008) as some of many examples. The European iteration of the genre emasculates its male figures and/or contextualizes them as potential components of a still-existing power structure, denying the illusion of a true "zero hour" in which all is reborn anew and certainly denying the seductive quality of that ending. The European apocalypse signifies a dismantling of the social welfare state and a reconfiguration of social relations along familiar boundaries, whereas Hollywood prefers to set unrestricted warfare among competing dictators and fledgling democracies in the ruins of civilization. Very little scholarship has commented on the European auteur version of this tradition, with general film surveys of (post-) apocalyptic cinema by Kim Newman, Charles Mitchell, and Wheeler Winston Dixon wholly disregarding important entries to the genre such as *La Jetée*.[11] Indeed, Haneke's film does not so much critique the American mode of the genre as it adopts tropes from existential and post-apocalyptic films by other European auteurs.

In addition to Haneke's usual employment of Hitchcockian and Bressonian techniques, *Time of the Wolf* takes many stylistic and ideological cues from Tarkovsky, Bergman, and Marker. Outside of strictly post-apocalyptic narratives, echoes of Tarkovsky's masterpiece *Andrei Rublev* (1966) can be found in the film through the onscreen execution of the horse. The meandering visual storytelling of *Stalker* (1979) is also present, as characters in both films physically journey into landscapes into which they slowly merge, as their bourgeois identities come further into question. Bergman's *The Seventh Seal* also offers a family up to the merciless ravages of the times while providing some hope for the future at the end, while his horror genre classic *The Hour of the Wolf* (1968) not only shares Haneke's Ragnarök reference in the title – not to mention exceedingly spare opening credits – but also abandons a woman (Liv Ullmann's Alma Borg) to her fate before a kind of mystical apocalypse. Johan Borg's (Max von Sydow) suspenseful shooting of his offscreen wife mirrors Fred's startling murder of Georges.

But it is *The Sacrifice* and *La Jetée* that inspire the bulk of *Time of the Wolf*'s *mise-en-scène* and minimalist narrative style. Seen together in the category of spare, non-reflexive, socially critical post-apocalypse films by notable auteurs, the three films seem to share a kindred spirit across their four decades of separation. *La Jetée* may indulge in the visual pleasure of showing ruins of famous Parisian monuments, but the focus of the film quickly turns inward on the *reduction* of human faculties and frontiers, rather than their expansion. Indeed, *La Jetée* may be one of the few films in which time travel as an invention seems to present a regression – particularly if it produces the paradox featured at the end of the film – rather than an expansion of human understanding. Jean Négroni's voice-over statement after the apocalypse – "Many died. Some fancied themselves the victors. Others were made prisoners" – refuses to pronounce judgment on the circumstances, while acknowledging that the preservation of asymmetrical power relations yet again prevents the meek from inheriting the Earth. The darkness enveloping the survivors in the tunnels seems to situate their adaptation into curious mole-men with eye goggles, just as the near-absolute darkness in Haneke's film justifies why the survivors stick together even as they are at each others' throats in the train station. It is space and light that determine these characters' motivations, as opposed to some inherent nature or psychology.

In contrast to Marker's authoritative and testimonial photographs, *The Sacrifice* destroys the world on television and thereby engulfs its characters, who are located on an isolated island off Denmark, in depression. Taking a page from Pier Paolo Pasolini's *Theorem* (1968), Tarkovsky uses the apocalypse to knock a bourgeois family out of its accustomed orbit and have it spiral out of control into cinematically interesting acts of despair. Haneke's and Tarkovsky's respective films begin and end with shots of trees – though Tarkovsky's solitary tree on the beach is given much more expository philosophical weight than Haneke's vision-obscuring forests – and primarily concern themselves with problems of perception and perspective of the end of the world. Neither *Time of the Wolf* nor *The Sacrifice* give direct, unmediated pictures of the apocalyptic destruction as in *La Jetée*, but *The Sacrifice* does do the viewers the service of broadcasting news footage on television about impending nuclear war, while simultaneously introducing low-flying bombers over the island. Portentous conflict and destruction *somewhere else* are introduced by the synchronizing of television reality with diegetic reality, though the characters themselves remain physically untouched by said conflict. The hardship that the characters face is a psychological one. Haneke's characters, on the other hand, receive no word of the end of the world, but rather find its social epiphenomena invading their microcosmic reality.

Tarkovsky's film also bears the unenviable status of being philosophically incoherent, one reason why Haneke judiciously avoids the expository or overtly meta-textual dialog employed in *The Sacrifice* in favor of landscapes, people waiting, and audible cries of pain.[12] Nevertheless, both films align in style and purpose with their use of redemptive, sacrificial fire near the end to individualize – and exculpate humanity from – the horrors of an uncertain future. In both, flames emerge as monuments to faith and such faith's crippling shortcomings. In *The Sacrifice*, Alexander (Erland Josephson) makes a pact with God to have the world restored as it was in exchange for a sacrifice and his silence. Alexander offers his family's solitary coastal home on the island with all its bourgeois trappings in the flames and is rewarded for saving the world by being whisked away in an ambulance. In *Time of the Wolf*, Benny, who has become mentally unhinged since the night after his parakeet died, somnambulistically follows the tale of the Thirty-Six Just Men by building a flame on the railroad tracks – something that would inevitably stop any train that might pass – and resolving himself to throw his body on it to continue to make way for a new redeemer. As opposed to the human levitation and divine salvation seen in *The Sacrifice*, Ben's attempted suicide is framed as exactly that: a mixture of delusion and despair driving him to kill himself on the faith that it will improve his family's lot. In both films, the flames encompass a more personal, subjective apocalypse than the apocalypse of spectacle normally arrayed before cinema audiences, with the flames deliberately adopting multiple levels of meaning for the characters and the philosophical import of the film. *The Sacrifice* does a long take of the house slowly catching fire, and then tracks away from the fire in a second shot as Alexander runs away into the daylight to be caught several seconds later. The fire takes on not only the significance of micro-level sacrifice for the sake of the macro level, but the loss of identity that Alexander undergoes when he performs the act of destroying all of his and his family's possessions. Such behavior cannot be condoned in the first world, and thus he is labeled insane and carted away. The bonfire in *Time of the Wolf*, on the other hand, begins as the flame of a young man's despair and transforms into the firelight by which the guard who rescues him tells him an optimistic tale of the future: "Maybe a car will come by tomorrow. Someone will step out and say everything's alright." In this case, Ben's micro-level despair is also confronted with a healthy dose of escapism – this is just a slight setback within a wider progress narrative from which humanity can recover – but the tracking shot pulling out from Ben and the watchman frames the escapist hope itself as something worth enshrining. The self-built sacrificial fire becomes a blazing signal of hope in the darkness, which only truly stands out as such when given more darkness in context.

Time of the Wolf thus stands as a cautionary tale not only in its depiction of the existential outcome of a major disaster in an affluent country, but in what happens when a film deliberately complicates and contradicts too many normative discourses of transcendence and resolution for audiences to handle. The Enlightenment dies with Georges's reasoned argument being cut off by a rifle blast, with both Azoulay and the refugee leader's (Serge Riaboukine) later attempts at rational negotiation coming in-between the Laurent family and their justifiable retribution. Religion and superstition are similarly deconstructed, with the tale of the Thirty-Six Just Men providing a collective site of imaginary penance and a potential site for the senseless suicide of a young boy. Kindness in the film is rewarded with exploitation, but exploitation of the refugees at the train station leads to some recognizably stable social hierarchies. Narrative and communication reproduce the existing social conditions. Even bonds with the dead are put in contradictory terms, as neither the funeral rituals in the film seem to relieve the living of their grief, nor does Eva's letter to her dead father escape the demystifying gaze of her distraught mother. If one adds to this Haneke's abundant use of dim or no light whatsoever in shooting, one finds *Time of the Wolf* to be a film that perfectly foils the escapism of the eye and mind.

The hope contained within the film's final shot is that the viewer recognizes all of these impulses held in check by the film and, in response, develops a more sophisticated view of the world. Just as *Caché*'s final shot of a non-white character moving through a white crowd reveals our inherently race-inflected vision of reality, so does *Time of the Wolf*'s final shot prompt the viewer to reflect on how her vision itself shapes the end of the world and her expectations thereof. In this respect, I find Berger's call for a more responsible and humbling vision of the post-apocalyptic world reflective of Haneke's views on the matter:

> The world is new, therefore unconstrained. But the moral vision has, and should have, bifocals. Make the perception new, but recognize that the damage is long-standing, symptomatic, haunting, and historical. The damaged, post-apocalyptic world is sustained by powerful institutions that benefit from the world as it is. (Berger 1999: 218)

To free civilization from its dark and necessary post-civilization *Doppelgänger*, Haneke seeks to liberate representations of the end of the world from being easily imagined and consumed, the mystical from the unreflective, the Enlightenment from purely instrumental reason. Only by scrambling against age-old institutions in the darkness of a new age can the age-old humanist principles of justice, nurturing, and equality find new meaning. Only film viewers left without the comforts of a world framed in Hollywood genre expectations can begin to form new expectations of their culture.

Notes

1 From *The Seventh Continent* (1989) on, Haneke's theatrical feature films have taken place in the recent past or "the present," which is primarily established through sound-bites of concrete television news events. This actually constitutes a break with his earlier made-for-TV films, such as *Fraulein* and *The Rebellion* (1992), which maintain precise and explicit historical frames of reference in relation to the present.

2 Haneke's sequence is actually quite conventionally executed in its depiction of a surprising murder. Georges dies in a series of cuts similar to Kevin Spacey's abrupt demise in *L.A. Confidential* (Curtis Hanson, 1997), as Ruthe Stein points out in her 2004 *San Francisco Chronicle* review of the film.

3 Another contemporaneous film that exploits such a situation of extreme darkness to reorient perception is Gaspar Noé's *Irréversible* (2002), albeit for a far more nauseating purpose.

4 It took Haneke a decade and Huppert's additional efforts to secure funding for the film from Bavaria Film and Canal+.

5 The recently released *Grbavica* (2006), a ZDF and Arte-produced feature film concerning the mass rape of Bosnian women by Serb forces, highlights the human legacy of "rape camps" like the one at Foča, revealing a much grimmer European past than Haneke's near-future.

6 Dina Iordanova devotes chapter 2 of her book *Cinema of Flames* (2001) to the debate about whether or not the Balkans belong in Europe, or whether or not their experience with genocide is as "European" as the Holocaust.

7 The young runaway's story about the dog is likely a direct reference to – and a deconstruction of – the classic post-apocalyptic film *A Boy and His Dog*. In that film, the master–pet relationship is confirmed in the end. Here, such a relationship leaves a mistrustful boy with an infected bite on his hand.

8 Or more precisely, "every white, affluent Western European."

9 Haneke's essay entitled "Violence and the Media" further elucidates his position on this, in that certain forms of violence have become trivialized in order to sell films and, in turn, distort perceptions of wider violence in society. See Haneke (2008: 156–7; English translation in this volume).

10 Other films deserving mention as part of the European iteration of this genre include *No Blade of Grass* (Cornel Wilde, 1970), *The Element of Crime* (Lars von Trier, 1984), *Delicatessen* (Marc Caro and Jean-Pierre Jeunet, 1991), and *4* (*Chetyre*; Ilya Khrjanovsky, 2005).

11 It is noteworthy, however, that Newman mentions European post-apocalypse films that conform and prove palatable to American audience expectations, such as Luc

Besson's *Le Dernier Combat* (1984) and the intense cycle of Italian apocalypse movies of the early 1980s. See Newman (2000: 188–9).

12   The unnecessary *double* sacrifice that Alexander makes by sleeping with his virgin serving girl Maria *and* burning down his own house has been decried as weakening the philosophical core of a very philosophically self-important film (Johnson and Petrie 1994: 172).

References and Further Reading

Baudrillard, Jean: "Quand l'Occident prend la place du mort," *Libération*, July 17, 1995; "When the West Stands In for the Dead," trans. J. Patterson, *This Time We Knew: Western Responses to Genocide in Bosnia*, ed. T. Cushman and S. Meštrović (New York: New York University Press, 1996).

Berger, John: *After the End: Representations of Post-Apocalypse* (Minneapolis: University of Minnesota Press, 1999).

Bourdieu, Pierre: *Distinction* (Cambridge, MA: Harvard University Press, 1984).

Dixon, W. W.: *Visions of the Apocalypse: Spectacles of Destruction in American Cinema* (New York: Wallflower, 2003).

Haneke, Michael: "Gewalt und Medien," Thomas Assheuer, *Nahaufnahme Michael Haneke. Gespräche mit Thomas Assheuer* (Berlin: Alexander, 2008). [English translation in this volume.]

Hochhäusler, C.: "Interview – Michael Haneke," *Revolver: Kino muss gefährlich sein*, ed. Marcus Seifert (Frankfurt am Main: Verlag der Autoren, 2006).

Iordanova, Dina: *Cinema of Flames: Balkan Film, Culture and Media* (London: BFI, 2001).

Johnson, V. T. and Petrie, G.: *The Films of Andrei Tarkovsky: A Visual Fugue* (Bloomington: Indiana University Press, 1994).

Judt, T.: *Postwar: A History of Europe Since 1945* (New York: Penguin, 2006).

Kauffmann, S.: "Beyond Convention," *New Republic*, June 28, 2004, pp. 32–3.

"Kino in Kürze: Wolfzeit," *Der Spiegel*, December 29, 2003, p. 113.

Mitchell, C. P.: *A Guide to Apocalyptic Cinema* (Westport, CT: Greenwood Press, 2001).

Newman, K.: *Apocalypse Movies: End of the World Cinema* (New York: St. Martin's Griffin, 2000).

Seeßlen, Georg: "Strukturen der Vereisung: Blick, Perspektive und Gestus in den Filmen Michael Hanekes," *Michael Haneke und seine Filme: Eine Pathologie der Konsumgesellschaft*, ed. Christian Wessely, Franz Grabner, and Gerhard Larcher (Marburg: Schüren, 2008), pp. 25–44. [English translation in this volume.]

Sontag, Susan: *Regarding the Pain of Others* (New York: Picador, 2003).

Stein, R.: "Losing Their Sang-Froid When Disaster Strikes," *San Francisco Chronicle*, July 16, 2004, p. E5.

Tracy, A.: "If Looks Could Kill: Andrew Tracy on *Time of the Wolf*," *Reverse Shot* (Winter 2004), www.reverseshot.com/article/time_wolf.

28

The Intertextual and Discursive Origins of Terror in Michael Haneke's *Caché*

T. Jefferson Kline

My films are intended as an appeal for a cinema of insistent questions instead of false (because too quick) answers, for clarifying distance in place of violating close-ness, for provocation and dialog instead of consumption and consensus. (Michael Haneke, 1992)

Michael Haneke's *Caché* (2005) introduces a new twist to the cinema. Video images become in his film a form of terror. Indeed, the twenty-first century seems to be redefining the very concept of terror. And by introducing the idea of *video and film* as forms of terrorism, Haneke seems to be reopening another question: "What is cinema?" – one that lies at the heart of the rebirth of French film in the second half of the twentieth century. Whereas the question, posed famously by André Bazin in his book of the same title, is carefully limited to aesthetic and philo-sophical considerations, the advent of state terrorism, coupled with the advances in Internet imaging, have brought with them an increased awareness of the ways in which cinema itself might be defined as a form of terror. Our investigation of Haneke's film, then, will focus on the ways this director uses the story of a Parisian family's encounter with terror to pose some larger questions about the inter-connections between the politics of state terror and the very nature of the medium of film. *Caché* is a fictional account of a French television talk-show host, Georges Laurent (Daniel Auteuil), who begins to receive videotapes of his house accompanied by grotesque drawings of faces covered with blood. The series of tapes apparently leads him to an apartment on the outskirts of Paris. Believing "he knows who it is" but refusing to share his suspicions with his wife, Georges follows the clues to the apartment where he encounters Majid (Maurice Bénichou), an Arab man whom, it turns out, he'd known as a child. Upon entering the Arab's apartment, Georges will immediately accuse him of terrorizing the Laurent household with his videos and bloody drawings.

In the "present tense" of Haneke's film, then, Majid is now grown up and living modestly in Romainville with his teenage son. When confronted by Georges, Majid freely admits that he has recognized Georges on his TV talk show but calmly evinces stupefaction at the visit and is mystified by the accusation. Georges's (real or feigned) anger escalates rapidly and yet he ends up by admitting that he was the cause of Majid's forcible removal from Georges's parents' house. Georges ends his visit to his childhood friend by violently threatening that if Majid "continues to scare his family or damage him, he'll regret it." When Majid asks, "Are you threatening me?," Georges answers, "Yes, I'm threatening you and believe me, I mean it." He then stalks out of the apartment. Curiously, Georges lies to his wife, Anne (Juliette Binoche), about this visit, telling her there was nobody at home when he went to the apartment! And even more curiously, this visit turns up on videotape that is mailed to both Georges's wife and to his boss at the television station. What the video reveals in addition to the scene we have just witnessed, however, are the desperate tears shed by Majid after Georges's departure.

When Anne confronts Georges with this tape, evidence that he was lying, he responds, incredibly, "I lied to save you more stress. The world won't stop turning because of it!" This idea of lying for what the liar decides is to the benefit of the other is one we shall have reason to examine more closely in what follows. And then the bombshell, if I may be so aptly blunt: Georges confesses that the Arab's parents worked on the Laurent farm when he was a child; that his father liked them and that they were good workers. Then he says:

> In October '61 the FLN called all Algerians to a demonstration in Paris. They went to Paris. On October 17th, Papon, the police massacre. They drowned about 200 Arabs in the Seine. Majid's parents were probably among them. In any case they never returned. When my father went to Paris to search for them, the police told him that he should be glad to be rid of these "jigaboos." My parents decided to adopt the boy, I don't know why. They must have felt responsible in some way . . . It annoyed me. I didn't want him in the house. He had his own room. I had to share. I was six years old! . . . I told lies about him. Afterwards he was sent away, sick, to a hospital or a children's home. I don't know which. I was happy. I don't feel responsible for it. It's all absurd!

It is perhaps a mere coincidence, but in the same year that Michael Haneke was shooting Caché, Alain Tasma was in Paris directing a docu-fiction film of the events that Georges is describing here. The two films share so many concerns that a comparison of their narrative structure and discursive origins seems imperative. Whereas Haneke uses Caché to present a current (2005) perspective on events that happened almost a half-century previously, Tasma uses Nuit noire to provide a searing and unsettling account of those events as they unfolded at the time. We might say that Tasma's version presents a kind of graphic illustration of Georges's very elliptical account as told to his wife (above). In this other version, we learn the context of the FLN (National Liberation Front of Algeria) terrorism in Paris.

According to Tasma, North Africans were being routinely arrested and brutalized by the Parisian *forces de l'ordre* throughout the late summer and early fall of 1961. In September, the FLN staged several attacks on the police that the Algerians deemed to be retaliations for these many brutalities. The demonstration of October 17, however, was never intended to be a form of terror. As depicted in *Nuit noire*, the organizers of the protest issued a strict order that no weapons of any kind were to be carried and carefully instructed every participant that the demonstration was to be above all a peaceful one. The film portrays a police action, carefully orchestrated by the police commissioner Maurice Papon, in which some 7,500 persons resembling North Africans were swept up in police vans before they could reach the center of Paris.

Meanwhile, those who did march were met by brigades of CRS (riot control) forces wielding night sticks and automatic weapons. The situation in *Nuit noire* reaches a climax when the police confront the demonstrating Algerians on the Pont de Neuilly in Paris, shoot and/or brutally beat them and throw their bodies, whether dead or still alive, into the Seine. (The horror of this scene is no doubt magnified by its uncanny resemblance to another infamous massacre that took place on Saint Bartholomew's Day, August 24, 1572, when French Catholics murdered thousands of Protestants and threw so many of their bodies into the Seine that the river was dammed up by the sheer mass of their floating corpses.) In the aftermath of this police action, Papon was able to convince the great majority of the French press corps that the Algerians had fired on the police and that the number of deaths and arrests of the marchers was entirely justified. Tasma's purpose is quite clearly to paint a devastating picture of the racism, fear, and overreactions of the French *forces de l'ordre* in dealing with this Algerian "threat." According to *Nuit noire*, the French police staged an unprovoked massacre and then succeeded in covering it up. This contextualization of Georges's all-too-brief description will have important resonances for our understanding of his motivations later in the film.

But Tasma's film is important to our present discussion for two other reasons. First, the film depends heavily (as does Haneke's film) on images that are "borrowed" from Gillo Pontecorvo's famous docu-drama of the popular uprising in Algiers in 1962 that led to the ouster of the French from Algeria. Tasma repeatedly films events, both the bombs exploded by the Algerians at Paris police stations and the violence with which the police put down the FLN's demonstrations, in ways that are directly reminiscent of *The Battle of Algiers* (1966). The reasons for this homage to Pontecorvo will be extremely important for understanding both *Nuit noire* and, as we shall see, *Caché*.

The second connection between Tasma's and Haneke's films is the question of the control of the visual media. In *Nuit noire*, a member of the French press is able to capture on film some footage that directly contradicts Papon's "official" version of the night's events. When she attempts to show this film, however, it is impounded and destroyed by the police. One might say, then, that the real conflict in *Nuit noire* involves competing *images* of the night's events. In the end, Tasma suggests, whoever controls the media, controls the situation. This too will take on an important dimension in our discussion of *Caché*.

In Haneke's film, the content and authenticity of another set of films, in this case the "terrorist" videos, become the focal point of the narrative. When Georges finally reports to Anne the scene in Majid's apartment and denounces his child-hood friend's involvement in the "terrorist tapes," Anne counters, "I don't think he's lying," certainly echoing what the viewer has likely felt after seeing the video of Georges's first visit to Majid's apartment, which corroborates the film's initial representation of the visit, but supplements it by showing Majid's tears after Georges has left. Majid comes across as a gentle, peaceable person, genuinely surprised and upset by Georges's accusations.

When, subsequently, Pierrot, the Laurents' eleven-year-old son, fails to come home one night, Georges and Anne go to the police and, without producing a shred of credible evidence, Georges has Majid and his son arrested and carted off to spend a night in jail. A short while after that Georges responds to Majid's request to visit, reenters Majid's apartment, and watches horrified as his Arab friend calmly takes a razor blade from his pocket and slits his own throat, an act so graphic that he seems more to drown in his own blood than to die of his wound.

What is particularly unsettling about Haneke's film is our absolute inability to guess how or by whom any of the videos that are produced and sent to Georges, his wife, and his boss could have been shot. Each successive video has a quiet authen-ticity to it that we do not question. And *Caché* strongly suggests to us that each is taken from a point that should have been – rather, that *had to be* – visible to those being filmed. This is true not only of the tape of the Laurents' house, since Georges walks directly by the exact location in which the camera had to have been placed, but also of the video in which he threatens Majid, clearly taken inside the very apartment where their interaction takes place. At the film's end we are offered no solutions to this puzzle and must simply accept our inability to solve this mystery. It is indeed rare to leave a theater unable to account for an insoluble paradox presented by the film we have been watching!

Although we can never know who made these videos, what we *do* know is that Georges immediately becomes convinced, first, that these videos constitute an act of *terrorism* against himself and his family and, second, that they *must* originate at the hands of an Algerian man who once lived in his family's house. They very quickly offer him a reason to visit Majid, to threaten him, and to have him arrested, all of which will appear to push the Algerian to his death.

When we think of the film's events in the larger context of the French–Algerian conflict and the question of the authenticity and credibility of the media, we begin to feel that this story is not new, that it has its origins in other stories. Let us turn to what is perhaps the most celebrated version of this story known to French audiences. In the most crucial scene of *The Stranger*, arguably the most widely read French novel of the twentieth century, Albert Camus's absurdist hero, Meursault, walks along an Algerian beach in search of an unnamed Algerian, subsequently known only as "The Arab" in the novel. Meursault carries a gun, for reasons even he cannot name, and his purpose in pursuing this particular Arab is hazy at best. Raymond, the friend who invited Meursault to the beach and then provided him with a gun, has already demonstrated his hateful tendency to sexually exploit Algerian women and has artfully drawn Meursault into a nasty dust-up with a couple of Arabs encountered earlier on this same beach. Raymond's pattern is to provoke the Arabs through violence to their women, and then to blame and punish them if they react. Raymond is able to convince Meursault that their friendship obliges Meursault to join him in the unpleasant and violent business of teaching these Arabs a lesson about interfering in the "business interests" of the French. In other words, Meursault has no personal stake in this fight, yet participates in it out of some vague cultural duty to his fellow Europeans. As Meursault approaches his "man," Camus, who has until this passage of the novel written almost without any metaphoric language whatsoever, overwhelms the reader with a burst of violent images. As he walks along the beach toward his eventual victim, Meursault is assailed by "épées de lumière" – "swords of light" – from the early afternoon sun, and in the "halo" of light on the far rocks, he perceives the Arab boy's image as "dancing in the enflamed air" as if this boy were an incarnation of everything diabolical. As the Arab draws a knife, Camus's language transforms this pitiful weapon into "une longue lame étincelante qui m'atteignait au front" –"a long *blade* which shot upward and transfixed my forehead" – and then as "a keen *blade* of light flashing up from the knife . . . gouging my eyeballs" (Camus 1946: 93–6). In other words, the actual weapons are transformed metaphorically into a kind of epic sword battle, rendered all the more curious by the phrase, "Il y avait déjà deux heures que la journée n'avançait plus, deux heures qu'elle avait jeté l'ancre dans un ocean de métal bouillant" (Camus 1957: 93) ("For two hours the sun had stood still in the sky, two hours that it had been anchored in an ocean of molten steel," 1946: 74).

As if obeying some urgency that comes from without, Meursault fires once, and then after realizing he has upset "the equilibrium of the day" he fires four more bullets into the inert body of the defenseless Arab boy now lying in the pool of his blood flowing into the spring water before him. The rhetorical intensity of this passage is all the more inexplicable since the Arab in question will be virtually forgotten for the rest of the novel. What's more, as readers of this work can attest, Meursault will be condemned to the guillotine not because he has shot a defenseless North African boy, but because he failed to shed a tear at his mother's funeral the previous day. What Camus does so skillfully is to gradually efface this horrific murder and "hide" it behind the public outrage that greets Meursault's apparent indifference to his mother.

Those with a knowledge of French literature and history remain troubled, however, by Camus's rhetorical flourish here, for the insistent language of swords flashing, leading to the phrase "for two hours the sun stood still in the sky," evokes without doubt the most celebrated of all French texts, *The Song of Roland*. In that famous twelfth-century epic, we encounter another Frenchman in pursuit of an Arab foe: Charlemagne has just learned that his beloved Roland has fallen prey to a heinous ambush and, in his bereaved fury, he sets out after the Saracen Caliph, begging God to allow the sun to remain in the sky long enough for him to reach his enemy and kill him. God grants his wish and the Saracens are all massacred and, significantly, *thrown in the river to drown* (Jenkins 1924: stanzas 178, 179). Charlemagne's Christian God appears to endorse and even to abet this bloody massacre and drowning.

And so it is that pursuing Arabs and killing them by sword and by water belongs to a long and "noble" tradition in French culture – a history which subtly infiltrates Camus's absurdist novel, *The Stranger*, a work generally considered to be quite devoid of any concern with Franco-Arab relations. I would like to suggest that in this respect, *The Stranger* (and, by extension, *The Song of Roland*) constitute powerful sources for *Caché*.

We might say that one of the things that is hidden in *Caché* is a system of allusions to a set of books and films (*The Battle of Algiers* being principal among them) – thinly veiled references that spur us to meditate on the age-old history of Franco-Arab relations, and to reflect on the way our own interpretation of the images of the Franco-Arab conflict in this film may be manipulated and disseminated by powerful forces that we cannot see.

Or can we see them without really being aware of it?

Twice during the film, and at the height of their anxiety over the "terrorism" that afflicts them, Georges and Anne carry on a discussion sitting on their living room couch in such a way as to frame the large television in front of them. In the first instance, there is a newscast on an outbreak of an epidemic in China. Although this reportage at first seems entirely divorced from the Laurents' problems, the word "caché" emanating from the newscast suddenly bleeds through their conversation and becomes audible to the film's spectator. Alerted by hearing the film's title in the background, our attention is drawn to the newscast. We see men in germ-proof suits carrying a body on a stretcher into an ambulance.

What could be going on here? One way to think of this "invasion" of the word and the images of an *epidemic* is that Haneke has subtly but insistently included an apparently "innocuous" image stream that may provide a significant commentary on the so-called "terrorist" tapes mysteriously sent to the Laurent household. What would news of an epidemic have to do with the violence Georges is experiencing? Could there be a connection between violence and contagion?

Yes, certainly, argues René Girard, one of France's most influential cultural anthropologists. In *Violence and the Sacred*, Girard looked at the way the earliest ("primitive") societies coped with violence. By studying the myths of cultures the world over, Girard hypothesized that when violence broke out in primitive societies, there seemed to be no way to stop its spread. Once a member of one family had been slain by a member of another tribe, a *reciprocal* act was required, which itself called for a reprisal. In this way, members of the community knew that reciprocal violence had a way of spreading that no one seemed to be able to control. (The Hatfield–McCoy feuds during the nineteenth century in the United States and the feuds of the Kerrs and Scots in sixteenth-century Scotland are latter-day examples of such unstoppable violence.) For these reasons, Girard regards violence "as something eminently communicable . . . a contaminating process . . . There is something infectious about the spectacle of violence . . . The more men strive to curb their violent impulses, the more these impulses seem to prosper" (1977: 30–1). Ultimately, Girard argues, communities suffering from this "plague" of violence discover that the only solution involves what he calls "violent unanimity": an act in which all of the members of a community together discover a victim who is in some way marginal – that is to say, does not evoke a reciprocal act of revenge – and collectively murder that person. In this way, the community discovers the purifying value of sacrifice. This scapegoat, victim of a collective act, is instinctively recognized as the savior of the community and becomes revered as an emissary of their collective health. And so, the ritual of sacrifice (first of humans, later of animals) becomes institutionalized and repeated to ward off the "germs" of reciprocal violence.

However, the more communities evolve away from rituals of sacrifice, the more they are prone to what Girard calls "a sacrificial crisis" in which violence can reappear and rage seemingly without any form of "anti-virus." And the mythical evidence of this "sacrificial crisis" brings us eerily close to the central conflict in *Caché*. Citing the examples of Cain and Abel, Jacob and Esau, Eteocles and Polynices, Romulus and Remus, Richard the Lionheart and John Lackland, Girard notes that "[t]he proliferation of enemy brothers in myth and in dramatic adaptations of myth implies the continual presence of a 'sacrificial crisis' . . . rooted in the distinctive traits of fraternal strife" (61–3). The central *agon* of Haneke's film involves two boys forced to live as brothers, but whose relationship rapidly devolves into images of violence. This first TV allusion to contagion takes on even more significance when it is subsequently juxtaposed to a second intrusion of the Laurents' television into their own interaction.

Haneke repeats this "tele-intrusion" (at the seventieth minute of the film) when Anne arrives home late from work (and/or her adulterous affair) and finds Georges at his desk in the living room. Together they position themselves in such a way as to pointedly frame the television screen so that it occupies the focal point of the image, at the direct center of the screen. Even when Anne moves, she takes up a position across from Georges that reframes the TV. Interposed with their angry dialog about her lateness, we see a series of stories on *Euronews*: first of the Barbara Contini affair in which the Italian journalist was fired on by US troops in Iraq, an affront which led her to call for a unified set of "rules of engagement" for all the "occupying forces" in Iraq. This is followed by a long take of an American soldier next to an American flag; and finally, under the heading "Mid-East," a view of Palestinians rioting in the streets, protesting the death and injury of some of their countrymen. In this last story, we see several bloodied bodies of Palestinians being carried past the camera.

These images provide a significant contemporary commentary on Georges's violent reactions, and as they roll, we learn from the conversation between Georges and Anne, standing in the foreground of the shot, that the Laurents' son, Pierrot, has gone missing. The unexplained absence of Pierrot will lead Georges directly to the Gendarmerie, and, with a contingent of armed police, to Majid's apartment in Roumainville. The images of Majid and his son being roughly hauled out of their apartment by the police only add to a store of images that have an increasingly familiar feel to them. The television footage (almost occulted by the conversation between Georges and Anne) is crucial in the lead-up to Majid's arrest.

The combined set of images here, including, first, the rioting Palestinians, next the invasion of Majid's apartment and brutal arrest of the two Algerians, and finally Majid's blood-soaked, suicided body, are not "innocently" produced and they certainly do not belong solely to the private war between Georges Laurent and his boyhood rival, Majid. It turns out that, like many of the images in Tasma's *Nuit noire*, they all have a common origin in Pontecorvo's celebrated *Battle of Algiers*. That earlier film opens with a raid on the Arab quarter in Algiers. As the film's credits flow across the screen, jack-booted French paratroopers storm an unarmed housing complex, bang on apartment doors, rush the inhabitants of each unit onto the open-air landings, and herd them brutally toward the waiting paddy wagons. No explanation is provided (or needed) for this invasion, and it visually anticipates Georges's use of the police to conduct a similar operation on the unarmed and unprepared Algerians at Roumainville. The TV images of Palestinians rioting in the streets are also reminiscent of Pontecorvo's film where Algerians protesting French brutality are attacked by French tanks. Finally, the image of Majid's bloodied body echoes a stark and haunting image of torture in *The Battle of Algiers*.

Yet, in creating such a symbolic stream, Haneke seems to bring the film's fictional events into an interpretive arrangement not only with the long tradition of the Franco-Arab conflict, but also with the current dynamics of the "war on terror." But how are we to understand the connections between this larger context and Georges's particular problems with "terrorism?"

Certainly at the level of contemporary political allegory, it is evident that, whatever their origin, Georges has *used the appearance of the set of "terrorist" videos* to get back at an enemy from his childhood, whose sole crime was to have encroached on Georges's personal sense of his home(land). As an adult, Georges now discovers the means to inflict a terrible retribution on an Algerian who has no reason to suspect he is the target of such a crusade. For, as we know from the history of another George, the decision to launch a "crusade" against "the forces of evil" brought untold suffering upon both his enemies and his own people.[1] Surely, the inclusion of the television footage linking Georges Laurent with "contagion," the war in Iraq, and violence in the Middle East can now be understood allegorically.

But Michael Haneke raises the stakes in this film to a higher level. Perhaps we can appreciate this other-level interpretation if we turn back to the videos that arrive at the Laurent residence in Paris. Many viewers of *Caché* have expressed their frustration at the film's ultimate ambiguity. We simply can never know who has produced the videos that Georges immediately labels a form of terrorism: Could it be Majid? This is quite unlikely, not only given our (and Anne's) trust in his genuinely uncomprehending reception of Georges's first visit but also given the inclusion of the video that leads Georges to Majid's apartment – a nonsensical tactic if Majid is really attempting to terrorize his childhood friend.

Could the tapes have been filmed by Georges's son, Pierrot, in concert with Majid's son, since we see them leaving the school yard together at the end of the film? This suggestion derives some plausibility from the poster of Eminem prominently displayed in Pierrot's room, allowing us to consider the possibility that, like Eminem, the son may be one of those who "cross over" to identify with a racial minority. Perhaps the two sons are complicit, but even their "complicity" would not be sufficient to explain the existence of images of Georges's childhood home, mingled with Georges's own nightmares of events there. There are simply too many elements in the third and fourth videos that are known only to Georges and Majid.

Could it be Georges himself? This hypothesis is worth exploring on several grounds. The most compelling argument for suspecting Georges is that he is the only character in this film who has the capability to manipulate images in a way that possibly could produce "terrorist" videos of the kind he has been confronted with. This becomes clear when we are surprised that a scene purporting to be a broadcast of his talk show turns out (much like the terrorist tapes) to be a tape. Our experience of the talk show, thought to be in diegetic time but suddenly rewound, exactly replicates the viewer's uneasy experience of the "terrorist" videos. At no other point in the film, other than in those "terrorist" videos, are we, as spectators, subjected to this kind of uncertainty about the "real time" and origin of the images we are watching.

Certain aspects of Georges's behavior must also strike us as suspicious. Why does he hide from Anne his first visit to Majid's apartment? After all, she should be his primary ally in this struggle. Why does his repeated inability to rationalize his behavior lead to such violent misunderstanding with his wife? Why does he claim not to know that Pierrot is absent from the apartment where he has been working for hours? Why doesn't Georges call the police immediately when Majid takes a knife to his own throat, but, instead, *goes to the movies*? In sum, then, his behavior (feigning ignorance when he already has a suspect), his diffidence about involving the police until he can get an arrest on other grounds, and his general propensity to lie about his involvement with Majid would constitute solid grounds for suspicion.

But the fact is, *we cannot know for sure*. And the reason we cannot know is crucial, it seems to me, for the significance of Haneke's objectives in this film. For one thing, the "terrorist" images are absolutely indistinguishable from the "image maker's" presentation of the real time of *Caché*. The first "terrorist video," especially, carries imbedded in it the film's credits, legitimizing it as deriving directly from the film's image maker (i.e., Haneke himself). Secondly, all of the "terrorist" submissions are distinctly different from the televised images the Laurents view on their TV set. In contrast to the TV images, the mailed tapes, when played back on the Laurents' TV, have the look of 35 mm film rather than the pixilated video quality we would expect. We end up, as a result, anxious about our ability to distinguish between (the film's) reality and the images that are represented as "produced by terrorists." If, indeed, these images can only have been produced by the official image maker, then the question arises, who is producing terror? And is this not Haneke's intent after all? We *should* not be able to distinguish because, in "the war on terror," it is precisely in the interests of those with the power to control the media to confuse reality with ideology. In this sense, Haneke's *Caché* can be read as part allegory (the story of Georges and Majid repeats in its basic outlines the story of the massacre of Majid's parents, and *that* story eerily replicates in detail the "original" story of this conflict told in *La Chanson de Roland*). The film is also (and therefore) a searing critique of the way images are produced (and or repressed as they are shown to be in Tasma's film) – and why. If the production (by those who are deemed to be the objective and authoritative source) of "terrorist videos" allows Georges to pursue, arrest, and drive to suicide an Arab against whom he harbors an age-old grudge, then these videos have achieved their purpose.

I do not need to remind you how the United States government used a carefully concocted Arab threat of nuclear terror to justify war against an Arab nation. Few thought to question or disprove these positions, because the United States government, relying on its citizens' faith in the truth of its assertions, produced visual and discursive "evidence" of this Arab threat. If the production of images of an Arab threat in Iraq convinced many to believe in the justness of this war, then those images (like the "terrorist" videos in *Caché*) have also achieved their purpose. And, like the viewers of terrorist videos in *Caché*, the average Western viewer had no way to distinguish fictional from real images of Iraq's threats, nor any way to deviate from the interpretations given by the image makers. However skeptical we might be of Georges's manipulation of events, we simply have no way to step outside the diegesis of the film to critique the veracity of the images produced. The film helps us understand how the control, dissemination, and manipulation of images commonly assumed to be documentary and objective have become features of governance. That this control has been exercised (in both the France of 1961 and the United States of 2003) against a particular "threat" should not surprise us, given the millennial rehearsal of this crusade from the twelfth century forward. Its presence in Haneke's film constitutes a subtle and unsettling reminder of the control exercised by the media that surround us and the fragility of our hold on the truth.

What Haneke has achieved here, then, is a meditation on the nearly limitless power to present what the director himself calls "24 lies per second at the service of truth, or at the service of the attempt to find the truth."[2] Or, as we must sadly surmise in this case, at the service of an attempt to hide the truth.

Notes

1   The term "crusade" is borrowed from numerous articles in the American and French press beginning in 2002. See, for example, James Carroll (2004), citing President George W. Bush: "This crusade . . . this war on terrorism." See also Alexander Cockburn and Jeffrey St. Clair (2004). In France, see Monique Chemillier-Gendreau (2004); Eric Laurent (2003).
2   Comment made by Michael Haneke, Boston University Master Class, Wednesday, October 17, 2007.

References and Further Reading

Bazin, André: *What is Cinema? Volume I and II*, trans. Hugh Gray (Berkeley, Los Angeles, and London: University of California Press, 1967–71).

Camus, Albert: *L'Etranger* (1942; Paris: Gallimard, 1957); *The Stranger*, trans. Stuart Gilbert (New York: Vintage Books, 1946).

Carroll, James: *Crusade: Chronicles of an Unjust War* (New York: Holt, 2004).

Chemillier-Gendreau, Monique: "Sous le sceau des croisades," *Le Monde diplomatique*, December 2004.

Cockburn, Alexander and St. Clair, Jeffrey: *Imperial Crusades* (Petrolia, CA: Verso, 2004).

Girard, René: *Violence and the Sacred*, trans. Patrick Gregory (Baltimore: Johns Hopkins University Press, 1977).

Haneke, Michael: "Film als Katharsis," *Austria (in)felix: zum österreichischem Film der 80er Jahre*, ed. Francesco Bono (Graz: Blimp, 1992), p. 89.

Jenkins, T. Atkinson, trans.: *La Chanson de Roland*, Oxford version (Boston: D. C. Heath, 1924).

Laurent, Eric: *La Guerre des Bush* (Paris: Plon, 2003).

Michael Haneke Speaks

PART V

Michael Haneke Speaks

29

Terror and Utopia of Form

Robert Bresson's Au hasard Balthazar

Michael Haneke

> *"Must we, therefore, eat from the tree of knowledge once more, to fall back into the state of innocence?"*
> *"Most certainly, that is the last chapter of the history of the world."* (Heinrich von Kleist, *On the Puppet Theatre*)

The first film I can – dimly – remember going to see was Laurence Olivier's *Hamlet*. Since the film was shot in 1948, I must have been at least six years old. Of course I saw the film again several times, so I cannot exactly separate what I experienced that first time, and what I remember from later viewings. But I precisely remember the theater, already gloomy with its dark paneling, growing darker as the screening began, the majestic lifting of the curtain, and the gloomy images of the castle of Elsinore surrounded by surging waves, accompanied by similarly gloomy music.

I also remember that my grandmother, who was with me in the theater that day, told me years later that she was forced to leave with me after less than five minutes, because I was screaming in fright at those gloomy images and sounds.

Soon after – it must have been the same year, as I had not yet started school – I spent three months in Denmark for "recreation" as part of an aid program for children from countries that had lost the war. It was the first time I was away from home for an extended period, and I was miserable. In an effort to cheer me up, my Danish foster parents took me to the movies. It was a murky, rainy, late fall day, cold and cheerless, and the film, the title and plot of which I've forgotten, took place in the jungle and savannah of Africa. Here, too, I can exactly remember the long, narrow, gloomy theater with doors along the side that openend directly on to the street. The film comprised a number of traveling shots, obviously filmed from inside a jeep, before which fled antelopes, rhinoceroses, and other creatures I'd never seen before. I, too, was seated in that car, captivated with astonishment and joy.

Finally the film came to an end and the lights went on, the doors were opened to the twilit streets, outside rain was pouring down, the noise of traffic filled the theater, and the moviegoers opened their umbrellas and stepped out of the theater. But I was in a state of shock: I could not understand how I, who scant seconds before had been in Africa in the sun amidst the animals, had been transported back so quickly. How could the theater, which for me had been like a car I was traveling in, have driven back – and especially so quickly – to northern, cold Copenhagen?

When I think about the directness and intensity of these first two movie memories, I am always reminded of those remote tribes to whom, shortly after being "discovered" – that is, shortly after their initial confrontation with so-called civilization – films were shown with a screen and projector set up in the middle of the jungle. According to the projectionists' accounts, the savages fled in panic, and could barely be calmed down. When they asked the reason for this reaction, they learned after a long, terrified silence, that for the natives, the framing of the images was a real mutilation of the people shown in the film, who they perceived as actually being there: For them, the close-up of a head was really the talking, moving, amputated head of a person who was physically present, and who, given such dismembering, should have long been dead!

The knowledge of those magical living images, with their power to evoke horror and delight equally, has, in a world that accustoms even infants to the constant presence of virtual reality in their living-room television set, largely fallen into oblivion. (The question remains, to what extent magical fright, to which adults have long become oblivious, can still hold sway over the children's room when night falls.) I had grown up in a world in which television did not – yet – exist, and in which for the child, and, in subsequent years, for the youth, visiting one of our small town's three cinemas was always a rare, unusual, and thus precious experience. I don't know to what extent this experience can be conveyed at all to those who were born more recently and have grown up in a world unthinkable without the constant presence of competing floods of images.

Years later, during my last year in senior high school, I saw Tony Richardson's screen adaptation of Fielding's *Tom Jones*. The film relates the eventful story of an orphan boy growing to maturity in eighteenth-century England; it was fast-paced and directed with wit, and it succeeded in its efforts to make the viewer into an accomplice of its fun-loving [*sinnenfreudig*] hero. Suddenly, perhaps a third of the way into the film, in the middle of a breathtaking chase sequence, the protagonist stopped in his tracks, looked into the camera (that is, at ME!), and, before resuming his flight from his pursuers, commented on the difficulty of his predicament, thereby making me aware of mine.

The shock of recognition of this moment was in every way equal to the terror of my childhood movie experiences: Naturally I had long since grasped that the movies were not real, naturally I had long since distanced myself physically and probably mentally by ironic observations from the unnerving immediacy of a thriller's virtuality, but never before this shocking discovery of my constant complicity with film protagonists had I experienced the dizzying immediacy that separates fiction and reality; never before had I physically experienced to what extent I and my fellow humans – that is, the audience – were largely victims and not partners of those whom we paid to "entertain" us. Of course, I knew what the power of living images could achieve when put in the service of ideologies, but this knowledge was little more than abstract and, like anything abstract, merely prevented direct experience.

Weeks later I remembered those initial moviegoing experiences, whose overwhelming effect, whose fright and joy I had long since repressed. I had looked behind the mirror and began to see the cinema with different eyes, to distrust those storytellers who pretended to render unbroken reality. Nonetheless, my hunger for stories was not sated – I wasn't sure what I was looking for in the movies. It was no doubt a form of film art that still offered the experience of being directly touched, the wonderful enchantment of the films of my childhood, but which did not thereby turn me into the helpless victim of the story being told and its teller.

That I, in 1967, while already a university student, was able to see Bresson's film at all – if it screened publicly, it did so to no publicity – I owe to a film course at our university that gave students the opportunity to become familiar with some of the films that, as uncommercial "artworks," were very unlikely to reach our theaters. The film crashed into our seminar like a UFO fallen from a distant planet and divided us into fanatic supporters and fierce opponents: Provocative, foreign, and surprising, the film broke with all the golden rules of mainstream cinema on both sides of the wide ocean, as well as with those of so-called European "art film," and was at the same time uncannily perfect in its absolute unity of content and form. I grasped only later that this perfection had its own story of maturation behind it, when I had the opportunity to see Bresson's previous films. Nonetheless, and despite the masterpieces that came after it, *Au hasard Balthazar* remains for me the most precious of all cinematic jewels. No other film has ever made my heart and my head spin like this one. What was, what is so special about it?

What does the film tell? [*Was erzählt der Film?*] Balthazar is a donkey. The film tells the story of his life, his suffering, and his death. And it tells – in fragments – the story of those who cross Balthazar's path.

The beginning: The screen still dark, before the fade-in of the first image, the tinkling of the bells of a herd of sheep. Then the first shot. Close-up, the baby donkey drinks from between its mother's legs; in the background we sense the herd of sheep more than we see it; only their bells are heard ringing softly and serenely. Then a child's skinny arm wraps itself around the animal's neck, tugs it away from its mother, the camera pans along and we see the little girl tenderly hugging the donkey, a boy about the same age also bending over and patting it, and between them, in the background, a man. They are all dressed lightly, it is summer. "Can we have him? Please, Daddy!" "What do you want him for?"

Long shot: The children are running beside their father, who is pulling the little donkey behind him down into the valley from the mountain pasture. The sheep's bells have fallen silent.

Close-up: With a small pitcher one of the children pours water over the donkey's head and says, "Balthazar. I baptise you in the name of the Father and the Son and the Holy Ghost. Amen."

The ending: Balthazar carries the loot of a pair of smugglers – they are going over the border in the mountains. It's night. Suddenly the "Don't move!" of a border guard. The smugglers run back the way they came. As we hear shots, the camera lingers on Balthazar's face, then he, too, takes off, downhill, in the direction where his masters, who tormented him constantly, have just fled.

Daylight. Balthazar is standing quietly between the pine trees on the mountain. Close-up: his shoulder – blood is seeping from a bullet wound. He begins to move, wanders out from under the sheltering trees, into the pristine alpine pastures, still burdened with the smugglers' loot on his shoulders. The bells of a herd. We see sheep approaching, black sheepdogs jump around them, barking, the bells ringing. A shepherd. Individual dogs. Then the herd stands around Balthazar, we can barely make him out through all the sheep surrounding him, we hear the bells from up close. The black dogs. The sheep begin to move off, slowly revealing the donkey, who is now sitting on the ground. Again the dogs. Then the sheep have retreated into the background – Balthazar in the foreground. The music comes in – the deeply sad [tot-traurig] andantino from Schubert's A major sonata, which has accompanied Balthazar's life story through the film, offering pity and at the same time consolation. Slowly, very slowly, Balthazar's head sinks. Then, completely filling the frame, only the herd – it is in motion – leads us back to Balthazar, who is lying there, stretched out on the grassy pasture, not moving anymore. The music stops. Only the sound of the bells. The sheep wander off into the background, disappearing into the mountain landscape. In the foreground: Balthazar is dead. The bells become softer. The end.

In between lies a life that, in its sad simplicity, stands for those of millions, a life of small pleasures and great efforts, banal, unsensational, and because of its depressing ordinariness, apparently unsuitable for exploitation on the silver screen. In fact, the film is not about anyone, and thus about everyone – a donkey has no psychology, only a destiny.

The title is the precise reflection of the film's intention: "By chance, for instance, Balthazar." It could be anyone else, you or I. Bresson chose the name, he says, for its alliteration. That sounds arbitrary, like a platitude, but is actually just the opposite.

Bresson's "model" theory, his rigorous rejection of professional actors in favor of aptly chosen amateurs, has often been discussed and still more often criticized – it is also what prevented his films' financial success. Here, in *Balthazar*, the motive for this theory shapes up most clearly and coherently: The screen "hero" is not a character who invites us to identify with him, who experiences emotions for us that we are allowed to feel vicariously. Instead, he is a projection screen, a blank sheet of paper, whose sole task is to be filled with the viewers' thoughts and feelings. The donkey does not pretend to be sad or to suffer when life is hard on him – it is not he who cries, it is us, for an icon of imposed forbearance, precisely because he is not like an actor peddling his ability to exteriorize emotion. The animal Balthazar, along with the knights in the director's later *Lancelot du lac*, locked up in their clattering suits of armor to the point of being unrecognizable, are Bresson's most convincing "models" simply because they are by definition unable to pretend.

Not that Bresson's "model" concept has always worked well. Amateurs can be cast just as inappropriately as actors. (The otherwise wonderful *Procès de Jeanne d'Arc*, for example, suffers from its protagonist's lack of charisma.) That notwithstanding, the "non-acting" of his always painstakingly, even lovingly chosen amateurs, the monotony of their manner of talking and moving, their presence – reduced to mere existence – was and is a liberating experience (far more than the casual "naturalness" of the young actors in the cerebral fireworks and intellectual jokes of his younger colleague Godard); it gave back to the people in front of the camera their dignity: No one had to pretend anymore to make visible emotions that, because acted, could only be a lie anyway. It had always struck me as obscene to watch an actor portray, with dramatic fury, someone suffering or dying – it robbed those who were truly suffering and dying of their last possession: the truth. And it robbed the viewers of this professional repro-duction of their most precious possession as viewers: their imagination. They were forced into the humiliating perspective of a voyeur at the keyhole who has no choice but to feel what is being felt before him and think what is being thought. Cinema has missed out on the opportunity it has, new in comparison with literature, to represent reality as a total sensory impression, to develop forms that maintain and even for the first time enable the necessary dialog between a work of art and its recipient. The lie that pretense is reality has become the trademark of cinema – one of the most profitable in the annals of industry.

One senses in *Balthazar*, as in all of Bresson's films, its author's almost phy-sical aversion to any type of lie, especially to any form of aesthetic pretense. This passionate aversion appears to be the driving force behind his entire oeuvre. It leads to a purity of narrative means unique in the history of cinema.

While reading the description of the beginning and end of the film, for a reader unfamiliar with Bresson's films, the impression may creep in of "poetry," affected beauty, pretentious stylization. There is none of that in the film: Documentary simplicity in framing, an almost manic rejection of "beautiful," that is, pleasing images (as were occasionally to be found in his earliest films, and as are dominat-ing today's art cinema, as well as American A pictures and TV advertising) – indeed, one could venture to say that Bresson invented the "dirty" image in the field of art cinema. Alongside the ever palpable desire to show things as clearly and simply as possible, an infallible instinct saves him from the danger of sterile stylization; for all the precision of their framing, his pictures always give the impression of being frayed, open and ready for when reality breaks the rules. Herein lies the source, I think, of his well-known conflicts with his cameramen, such as De Santis, all famous for the "beauty" of their images.

Precision rather than beauty – each shot shows only what is absolutely essential, each sequence has been compressed to its most concise form and briefest duration possible. Even so, the length of the shots and cuts are – even for the period when the film was made (1965) – unusually calm. Never do pauses create room for sentimentality, in its simplicity everything gives the impression of having developed naturally and, while being in the service of a rigorous aesthetic concept, is never the victim of the latter. Bresson reportedly intended to personify the seven deadly sins in his characters – but against a declaration such as this can be placed a sentence from his *Notes sur le cinématographe*: "Hide the ideas, but in such a way that they can be found. The most important will be the best hidden." And at another spot he writes, "production of emotion obtained by resistance to emotion." And: "Emotion will emerge from a mechanics, from the compulsion towards a mechanical regularity." In support, he cites the pianism of Lipatti: "A great pianist, not a virtuoso (one like Lipatti) relentlessly hits the notes the same way: half-notes, the same duration, the same intensity; fourth-notes, eighth-notes, sixteenth-notes, etc., *idem*. He doesn't pound the emotion into the keys. He waits for it. It comes and takes over his fingers, the piano, him, the concert hall."

What does this mean for the film? One example: The village teacher, who has been dealt a rough blow both through his own pride (is it the embodiment of hubris?) and through the malice of others, dies, still young, without having been ill (from a broken heart?). How is this being told? The teacher's wife shows the priest into the house. When opening the door to the teacher's room, she says: "He is full of despair, perhaps you can help him." The priest goes through the door into the room. The teacher in his bed turns toward the wall. The priest doesn't know what to say. Then he sees the teacher's table with the Bible, goes to get it and, sitting down and opening it, says: "One must have forgiveness. For everyone. You will be forgiven a lot because you suffer so much." The teacher, turned away: "I suffer less than you think." The priest leafs through the Bible, finds something, reads it to the teacher: "The Lord does not forsake forever and when he sends us woes he is compassionate in his divine mercy. He does not like to humiliate mankind nor does he enjoy making them suffer." The teacher's wife had stopped at the partly open door, now she turns away, steps in front of the house, sits on the bench at the door, says: "My Lord, please do not take him away from me, too. Leave him for me. You know how painful my life will otherwise be." Knocks on the inside of the window. The wife looks. The hand behind the window disappears gradually. The wife gets up, goes inside. She enters the teacher's room, the camera follows her to his bed. Standing up, her torso blocks the view onto his upper body. We only see his hands. As he lies on his back, they lie still on both sides of his body. The woman kneels down, folds the man's hands. Offscreen the priest's voice: "Ego te absolvo peccatis tuis." His hand comes into the frame, blesses the deceased. "In nomine patri et filii et spiritus sancti." The woman leans forward to kiss her husband's hands. Quick dissolve. The woman is sitting in the garden next to a tree. We see her from behind. She has put her face into her hands.

The whole sequence takes less than two and a half minutes. The lines are spoken quickly and without emotion, the characters move with the monotony of marionettes. No motions driven by emotion, no tear relieves the pent-up sorrow. And yet, or precisely because of this do we as viewers sense the depth of despair in all characters more strongly than in any melodrama that pulls our heartstrings. All actions and events retain the polyvalence of real life – the author never takes sides, the spectator is always called upon to use his own personal judgment, free to choose, to find his own truth and interpretation. The priest's efforts to console find their counterpart in his insecurity and in the rigidification of the rites and phrases at his disposal; the teacher's despair stands in contrast to his pride that has devolved into hubris, the wife's fear to her passive suffering; and vis-à-vis all the neediness and misery there is the indifference or non-existence of a God who, when asked to grant life, imposes or permits death.

The polyvalence of plot and motifs creates distance. The often repeated charge is that Bresson makes it difficult for the viewer and that he prevents the possibility of identification, and that his films are cold, arrogantly elitist, and pessimistic. With regard to the latter charge he responded to an interviewer: "You are confusing pessimism with clarity," and he went on to say: "Take Greek tragedy – is that pessimism?"

I have a videotape of the awards ceremony from the 1983 Cannes Film Festival, where the Golden Palm was awarded jointly to the then seventy-six-year-old Bresson for his last film, *L'Argent*, and to Andrei Tarkovsky, for *Nostalghia*. As Bresson, called up by Orson Welles, stepped on to the stage, a tumult broke out, a furious acoustic battle between those booing and those acclaiming him; the audience was asked for calm a number of times – only as Tarkovsky was invited on stage did the storm of protest abate. (Himself an open admirer of Bresson, Tarkovsky may not have been happy with this. What he had extolled about the films of his idol was precisely their independence from audience tastes, for which Bresson was now being booed before his eyes, while he, who had likewise been vilified as a hermeticist, was being cheered.)

What, then, is so different about his way of using image and sound that Bresson found it necessary to resurrect for himself a term that had fallen into disuse, "cinematograph," because he no longer found a common language and a common meaning with that which is called and calls itself cinema?

A decade before *Au hasard Balthazar* was made, Adorno wrote, in his essay "Form and Content in the Contemporary Novel," with regard to Kafka: "His novels, if they still at all fall under that category, are prolegomena to a condition of the world in which the contemplative attitude has become bloody mockery, because the permanent threat of catastrophe no longer permits anyone to look on passively or to tolerate the aesthetic result of such passivity." And elsewhere, referring to Dostoevsky: "No modern work of art worthy of the name that would not take pleasure in the dissonant and the unbound. But inasmuch as such works of art embody terror uncompromisingly and invest all the bliss of observation in the purity of such expression, they serve freedom, which mediocre works only betray."

The illusion that reality can be depicted in an artifact rather than being only an agreement between the artist and his recipient had – since it had been questioned by Nietzsche – become obsolete at the very latest since the incommensurable horrors of the Nazi reign, the Holocaust and the world war for everyone who sought to participate even somewhat consciously in this field of activity. The verdict that no more poems could be written after Auschwitz demarcated the horizon of consciousness of the survivors and future generations as much as did the retraction of the Ninth Symphony together with all of Western culture in Thomas Mann's *Doktor Faustus*.

In German-speaking countries, the perturbed inheritors of guilt seized with wide eyes on the analysis of those words and signs that had turned out to be so corruptible. But even beyond the German language the faith in a solid and also stable relationship between art and its reception was dealt a blow at once devastating and productive.

Only the cinema, the most expensive form of artificial communication and the one most dependant on money, firmly withstood every reflective renewal. The new subjects, positions, or putative findings were presented in the old, long compromised forms. And the supposed distinction between the most presumptuously self-assured anaesthetizing schmaltz of right- as well as left-wing provenance and the so-called "progressive art film" remained but a self-justifying farce of the artists and actors who live off the film industry.

For the contents and crises of meaning of a shattered world, new forms had to be found, on behalf of the financiers, that betrayed these contents by making them fit for consumption – otherwise the films would not be made. Naturally such forms were found. They were refined and compiled, and in the course of this process the majority of those involved forgot why they had been undertaken in the first place.

A polemic oversimplification? I think this is required in order to express why Bresson, this scandal-monger, was and is such a provocation in the world of moving pictures. In order to be and to remain active in the feature film world (to avoid the term "film business"), even those who saw through and despised the rules of the game described above found themselves forced to subscribe to them, even to place themselves in their service. To what extent they did so while consciously distancing themselves from them, or were influenced unconsciously by them, is visible in their attempts to playfully circumvent these rules of the game. The strategies that film-producing countries of the so-called "free world" deployed to circumvent the rules differed from those of totalitarian countries only through their semantics. If individual works strayed from this unspoken agreement (which had been restored due to economic pressure) – namely, that artistic inconsistency was the result of exigencies – they were panned, shortened, reedited, castrated, regarded as a faux-pas of their makers, relegated to the realm of the experimental film (and thus no threat to the market), or at best half-heartedly tolerated by certain critics as exceptions that prove the rule. The most exciting and most truthful of what international cinema has to offer can be found in this category of exceptions: Pasolini's *Salò*, Tarkovsky's *Serkalo*, a few films by Ozu, Rossellini, Antonioni, and Resnais, Kluge's *Artists*, Straub's *Chronik*, and a handful of others.

What happens in them? The films are as different as their authors and the cultural circles from which they originated. What they have in common, and what differentiates them from the great mass of film production, and even from other films by the same author, is their successful unity of content and form. It shatters the dubious consent between representer and represented, and, like the optical torture chair in Kubrick's *A Clockwork Orange*, prevents us from closing our eyes, and forces us to gaze in the mirror: What a sight! The horror! Spectators accustomed to and luxuriously accommodated within the lies, leave the theater aghast. Starved for a language capable of capturing the traces of life, and with hearts and minds suddenly opened, the remaining spectators wait for a continuation of the stroke of luck that has unexpectedly taken place.

Few of the above-mentioned authors achieved more than once this unity of what is depicted and how it is depicted. They found their way back to more easily trodden paths – the storm warnings of failure must be heeded, the fidelity of one's fans rewarded. And the bigger the following, the wider and more well-worn the path. But it's the builders of freeways who earn the most.

In such a context, Bresson's continuity seems almost miraculous: After his two-and-a-half tentative first steps, which already contain the thematic catalog of his later works (a short, *Les Affaires publiques*, and his two first features, *Les Anges du péché* and *Les Dames du Bois de Boulogne*), his formal vocabulary is fully developed with *Le Journal d'un curé de campagne* in 1950, and he remains unwaveringly committed to it for the duration of his output (another ten films in thirty-three years).

Of almost all the great auteurs it is said that in all their works they have always made the same film over and over. Of none is this so accurate as of Bresson. To be addicted to truth – indeed, this leaves no choice. "Do not think of your film beyond the means that you have chosen for yourself," he writes in his *Notes*. And indeed, it is impossible to tell, while watching his films, if the means have determined the content, or the other way around, they are so very much one and the same. Their unity leaves no room for ideology or interpretation of the world, commentary or consolation. Everything dissolves into pure relationality, and it is up to the viewer to draw conclusions from the sum of the arrangements.

Reduction and omission become the magic keys to activating the viewer. In this respect, it is precisely the hermetic aspects of Bresson's oeuvre that seek to make the spectator's role easier: It takes him seriously.

What is omitted is the gesture of persuasion of models that invite emotional identification.

What is omitted is the (all too) coherent meaning of the explanatory contexts of psychology and sociology – as in our daily experience, chance and contradiction of fragmentary splinters of action demand their rights and our attention.

What is omitted is the pretense of any kind of wholeness, including that of man's representation – the torso and the extremities come together only for fleeting moments; they are separated, set equal to objects and at their mercy, the face becomes one part among many, a motionless, expressionless icon of melancholy for the loss of identity.

What is omitted is the unusual, because it would defraud the misery of every-day existence of its dignity.

What is omitted, finally, is happiness, because its depiction would desecrate suffering and pain.

And it is precisely this universal retraction (not so unlike that of Mann's *Faustus*), this tender respect for people's capacity for perception and personal respon-sibility, that harbor in their gesture of refusal more utopia than all the bastions of repression and cheap consolation.

The unity of content and form redeems a premonition of the interrelation of meaning that has been lost to the described world. In leaving out the portrayal of happiness, wishing grows wings, and for the happy moment of viewing, pain is caught in its own icon.

Translated by Robert Gray and Roy Grundmann

30

Violence and the Media

Michael Haneke

The topic of VIOLENCE AND THE MEDIA is typically brought up with the goal of placing a guilty party under arrest. Depending on the conviction of the debaters, either the media are that objective "mirror of society," reflecting nothing but reality itself, or the permanent presence of violence in the media is what really bears responsibility for the increasing violence in our daily interactions with each other. On the hunt for a scapegoat, this form of discourse quickly turns into a fundamental chicken-or-egg question. The inconclusiveness of this inquiry is productive for both discursive positions: Both are right.

Is this question incorrectly chosen? Should the media's critics cry for the censorship of bloody images in film and television, and those in charge of programming leave the brutality of everyday society to the popular press headlines, since we are less likely to be stirred to violence through articles and photos than through sequences of images and sounds?

It is not merely in light of the banal truth that information is also a commodity that such polarized alternatives debunk themselves. Debating whether violence in the media is necessary is a moot point in light of its existence. With respect to our topic – to debate the *right* kind of action, action, that is, which is both urgent and necessary on behalf of society – the question of the FORM of representation makes more sense, I think, because it is not directed at *institutions*, where responsibility is notoriously hard to personalize and accountability can rarely be demanded, but directly and demandingly at *individuals* – the editor, the journalist, the director.

It should be said in advance that *the representation of violence* is part and parcel of the history of moving images – pointedly formulated, it is part of their very essence. The Western, crime, war, adventure, and horror genres define themselves in no small part through violence, and the word ACTION, which precedes the filming of every take, has fused with the word FILM – at least in the minds of the consumers – as a synonym for violent spectacle.

The simultaneously eye- and ear-occupying intensity of the film medium, the monumental size of its images, the speed at which its images demand to be viewed, its capacity above all other art forms to render or simulate reality virtually in toto, to make it *tangible to the senses* – in short, the medium's capacity to *overwhelm* – downright predestine it for a narcotized, that is, an *anti-reflexive* reception. In contrast to literature and the fine arts, even the morally conscious and responsible depiction of acts of violence is bound to move into controversy. The moving image requires other criteria than the still image – from the image's viewer as well as its producers: The still image generally shows an action's *result*, whereas the film shows the *action itself*. The picture usually appeals to a viewer's solidarity with the *victim*, while film often puts the viewer in the position of the *perpetrator*. (Upon, say, looking at Picasso's *Guernica*, we see the suffering of the victims frozen for us to behold for all eternity. By virtue of the time allowed for becoming conscious of and contemplating the represented subject, our path towards solidarity with them is portrayed without any moral stumbling blocks. With the carnage in Coppola's *Apocalypse Now* supported by Wagner's "The Ride of the Valkyries," we are riding along in the helicopter, firing on the Vietnamese scattering in panic below us, and we do it without a guilty conscience because we – at least in the moment of the action – do not become aware of this role.) This guiltless complicity is also that to which violence in film owes its all-overpowering presence. The surrogate action banishes the terror of reality; a mythical narrative mode and an aestheticizing mode of representation allow a safe release of our own fears and desires. The hero on the screen transcends the helplessness and powerlessness of the viewer with his accomplishments. The salesman who defines and produces film as a commodity knows that violence is only – and particularly so – a good sell when it is deprived of that which is the true measure of its existence in reality: deeply disconcerting fears of pain and suffering. Except for the individual case of the pathologically sadistic voyeur, those fears remain non-consumable and are bad for business.

The vocabulary of forms used to exorcise reality that has evolved within violence-preoccupied film genres is enormous, and this is neither the time nor the place to analyze it in detail. But I think that we can by and large identify *three dramaturgical* premises, of which at least one must be satisfied in order to attain a large audience with the display of violence:

- First, the *disengagement* of the violence-producing situation from the viewer's own immediate life experiences that elicit identification (the Western, science fiction, horror genres, and the like).
- Second, the *intensification* of one's living conditions and their jeopardization, which allows the viewer to approve of the act of violence as liberating and positive – because it was the only acceptable solution (war and police films as well as vigilante dramas of American provenance (*Death Wish, Falling Down*)).
- Third, the *embedding* of the action *in* a climate of *wit and satire* – I refrain from using the word HUMOR here (from the slapstick of silent film to beat-them-up comedies with Bud Spencer and Terence Hill, from spaghetti

westerns right up to war grotesques based on the model of *Catch 22* and the postmodern cynicism of *Pulp Fiction*).

Each of these three categories has in turn developed its own canon of tropes, and each producer, screenwriter, and director of the respective genre is well advised to observe them with painstaking accuracy. The mixing of genres, as attempted every now and then by European films and American independent films, may be artistically fruitful, but inevitably leads to a drop in audience numbers and ratings.

The topic of VIOLENCE AND THE MEDIA – I already hinted at this earlier – certainly implies a danger, namely, that of an interplay between mediatized violence and the real existing violence of society. The criteria sketched out above, which have applied since the origin of film, are only indirectly related to this interplay. Murder, the atrocities of war, and bloody crimes were a matter of course in film long before the question of the danger of its effects – with all its present-day vehemence – was even suggested.

So what has changed?

Due to the enormous increase in the quantity and the distribution potential of the electronic media, has there been a spike in the *quality* of terror such that only now, and now too late, the eyes of those responsible are opening to the dangers of an atavistic thirst for destruction only seemingly contained by its depiction? Or did the *similarity between the forms* through which real and fictional violence are represented influence our perception and especially our sensitivity in such a way that we are no longer able to distinguish between the *contents* of either, so that the value of authenticity of the corpses of Grozny and Sarajevo approximate that of *The Terminator*, and that *Star Wars* can only be distinguished from the media event of the blitz invasion of Kuwait by the timeslot in which it goes on the air?

But how is such commingling and indistinguishability possible? Only a few years ago, it was not difficult for every passably intelligent adult to keep the levels separate. (To what degree children, who – at least in highly industrialized countries – experience the world primarily *via* the viewing screen, can still develop this capability to distinguish would have to be treated as a separate topic and is, among other things, also the subject of the film you're about to see.)

By what means did this indistinguishability come about?

As we all know, the cinema is celebrating 100 years of existence this year. For more than half of this time period, it was the sole ruler in the realm of moving pictures, a period during which it tried to develop a grammar intended to enable this completely new organ of speech to speak in its own terms. Two devices, the camera and the tape recorder, offered the possibility of reflecting and simulating an almost complete impression of reality. The reports of the incredible effect of the new medium are well known and range from the panic of the Parisian audience with regard to *Arrival of a Train at La Ciotat* by the Lumière Brothers to the terrified reactions of South American jungle inhabitants upon their first confrontation with film projections half a century later.

For the viewer, the boundary between *real existence* and *image* was difficult to establish from the beginning, which is precisely why the medium won a great deal of its fascination. The oscillation between the disconcerting feeling of being present at *a real event* and the emotional security of seeing only the *image* of an artificially created or a found reality was what enabled the emergence of the genre described above. Violence became domesticated in its image and the pleasant chill of horror administered in homeopathic dosages was quite welcome. The controlled invocation of evil permitted the hope for its controllability in reality.

The scene changed with the appearance of television. The documentary element entered the foreground. (In the cinema, it had become – at least with regard to its acceptance by viewers – a marginal area shortly after its inception.) The *speed* by which electronic media conveyed and *disseminated* information led to a shift in viewing habits. The impact of the impression exerted by the larger-than-life image on the screen during a single trip to the movies was matched and then eclipsed by the sheer *mass* of impressions and their permanent presence in the living room. Building on the dramaturgical and aesthetic forms of the cinema, television changed precisely these forms by permanently deploying them.

The cinema tried to counter the overwhelming omnipresence of the electronic media by intensifying its own means, which television – as much as it was technically able – then immediately integrated into its system again. The compulsion to trump one another led to the permanent paroxysm of attempted intensity and, thus, indirectly to the further blurring of the boundary between reality and image as well. (In the area of representing violence, the producers of *fictional* violence were forced to compete against the sensation of authentic terror by upping the visual appeal. In the battle against it, *journalistic* ambition shed the last remnants of respect for the dignity of the exposed victims.) An end to this process is not in sight – on the contrary: It seems as though it has only just begun – in the battle over market shares and viewer ratings, any innovation, whether of a technical or artistic kind, contributes to driving it on. The *form of representation* determines the *effect of its content*. In the course of implementing these mandates, a short-circuit has occurred with media competitors in that, for the sake of constantly increasing the impact of form, content has become an interchangeable variable. This applies to violence as much as it does to its counterpart, to the war victim as much as to the TV star, to the car as much as to toothpaste. The *absolute equivalency of all the contents* stripped of their reality ensures the *universal fictionality* of anything shown and, with it, the coveted *feeling of security* of the consumer. The form–content relation of classical aesthetics appears to have become obsolete. The morality of selling has little in common with that of a possible social contract.

So where is THE RIGHT which might be discussed here? And where might we look for it in the realm of media production? A solution of the suggested problem is – how could it be otherwise? – nowhere in sight.

Nevertheless: What is it that is worth trying?

I'm not talking here as a sociologist or a media critic, but rather as a filmmaker, as – in this discursive context, anyway – a representative of the art of film.

The word ART is difficult for me to say, since – in light of what I've just said – I would be hard-pressed to give a definition of it. What is it about an art form that emerged only a century ago as the newest and thereby most hopeful, and which – in its best minds – is barely fazed by its own mutation? Does it earn its name and, if so, what could be its mission?

Based on the premise that – at least within the realm of contemporary society – every art form reflects the conditions of its reception and does so not merely with regard to the economic aspect of its potential for distribution, but with regard to a human dialog, then what does this mean for the media artifact in light of everything said earlier? The horror that its recipient, the viewer, could degenerate or already has degenerated into a spineless consumer of empty, interchangeable forms also contains a slice of utopia, since it begs the question: How can the dialog that was interrupted be resumed, how can I return its lost value of authenticity to representation?

Or, put a different way: How do I give the viewer the chance to recognize this loss of reality and his own implication in it, thus emancipating him from being a victim of the medium to its potential partner?

The question is not: "What am I allowed to show?" but rather: "What chance do I give the viewer to recognize what it is I am showing?" The question – limited to the topic of VIOLENCE – is not: "How do I show violence?" but rather: "How do I show the *viewer* his *own position* vis-à-vis violence and its portrayal." *For this purpose*, one must find forms – if one wants to avoid having the Enlightenment's dedication to humanity, which the media so opportunistically parrot, degraded into cynical hypocrisy.

Yes, I would go so far as to speak of medial ART only when it contains this act of text-based self-reflection, an act that has long become a *sine qua non* condition of all other forms of modern art. The technical innovation of the electronic medium has changed the world and long since ousted the nineteenth-century conception of reality – now is the time for the heads of programming to react to this with regard to content.

Translated by Evan Torner

31

The World That Is Known

An Interview with Michael Haneke

Christopher Sharrett

Austrian filmmaker Michael Haneke has achieved major international prominence with *The Piano Teacher*, which won a Grand Prize and two best acting awards at Cannes 2001, became both a *bête noire* and *cause célèbre* for critics, and remained in urban art cinemas through much of 2002. With this film, Haneke fulfilled considerably the expectations produced by all of his early work – which has remained predictably marginal to current film culture – by provoking the viewer with an intelligence of extraordinary seriousness and significance. That many journalistic reviewers focused solely on *The Piano Teacher*'s graphic portrayal of masochism and other sexual acts, ignoring its complex analysis of the family and the politics of repression, is an emblem of the current media's reaction and intellectual bankruptcy. Fortunately, the Cannes awards and a few perceptive critical remarks sustained the film long enough for many to take notice. With extraordinary performances by Isabelle Huppert and Benoît Magimel (both of whom took best acting honors at Cannes), *The Piano Teacher*, based on a renowned novel by Elfriede Jelinek, achieves unusual power in its meditation on the interconnections of art and the forces of repression. A middle-aged Viennese pianist and piano instructor (Huppert) lives with her hopelessly possessive mother, able to connect with the sexual/social world only through voyeurism and masochism. Her encounter with a young prodigy (Magimel) of unusual artistic sensibility seems to offer the prospect of romance, until the very notion is exploded as the film explores the assumptions of heterosexual relations and the culture with which it is associated. The questions raised by the film seem very much part of the legacy of artistic modernism and, as handled by Haneke, demonstrate their power to provoke in the postmodern moment. Erika Kohut, Huppert's character rendered by the actor with devastating authority, manages to suggest both the precarious mental health of Western civilization at the end of the millennium and the hopeless state of women in a still-unrealized struggle for sexual liberation at the end of the twentieth century.

Born in 1942, Haneke entered filmmaking rather late in his career, after distinguished work in Austrian theater complemented by seriously engaged, ongoing study of philosophy and psychology. Haneke has established a position as one of the cinema's important *provocateurs*, a concept lost in an era where cultural/ political subversion is often seen as *passé*, or conceived with jaundiced, anti-humanist cynicism. His first feature, *The Seventh Continent* (1989), is a staggering work based on a news story about a family opting for collective suicide rather than continuing in the present alienated world. Unable to accept the notion that the family took their own lives (could the terrors of daily life override the life instinct?), relatives insisted that authorities pursue the case as a murder, despite all the evidence militating against such a conclusion. The film takes numerous deceptive turns as we expect the family, which goes through daily life in a set of rote behaviors relentlessly chronicled by Haneke's highly disciplined camera (using close-ups and slow intercutting forcing the viewer to consider the features of banal activities), to leave for the promised utopia of rural Australia, since a lush tourist ad for the country appears at regular intervals in the film. The film introduces altogether unanticipated questions about the nature of utopia, suggesting that the quietude of death may constitute a satisfactory promised land in the mind of the suicide. With its many silences, its interest in the alienating features of contemporary urban life, its remarkable sense of architecture as signifier of entrapment, *The Seventh Continent* introduced Haneke's kinship with forebears such as Antonioni. With each film – thus far *The Seventh Continent, Benny's Video* (1992), *71 Fragments of a Chronology of a Chance* (1994), *Funny Games* (1997), *The Castle* (1997), *Code Unknown* (2000), and *The Piano Teacher* (2001) [Haneke's title is *La Pianiste*] – Haneke affirms his presence as one of the key modernist directors at a time when modernist ambitions seem defunct. *71 Fragments, Benny's Video,* and *Funny Games* are among the most unsettling of the cinema's many meditations on television and other media, in particular their role in the erasure of conscience and emotion. These films are by far the most contentious – and perhaps because so least discussed at this writing – observations on the media and their relationship to violence, alienation, and social catastrophe. *Funny Games* in particular is the most disturbing remark on action cinema and those works pretending to comment on its social ramifications. Containing elements of Peckinpah and other directors, this tale of a young family besieged by two yuppie psychopaths becomes Brechtian, suddenly "rewinding" scenes, implicating the viewer, who is asked to choose an ending (the film opts for the bloodiest and least consoling). Unlike any number of self-reflexive films engaged with the study of media culture and the role of violence therein, *Funny Games* never becomes a strained position paper, nor does it participate, for all its relentlessness, in the excesses it criticizes.

Revisiting Kafka's *The Castle* may seem an odd gesture at this date, but Haneke's inflections of Kafka affirm his commitments to reexamination of some of the basic notions of modernity. Haneke's version is the least involved in narrativizing

Kafka, and is concerned more with a sense of disruption and dislocation, the structure of the film featuring literal breaks that foreground the novel's artifice. *Code Unknown*'s exploration of the collapse of language picks up concerns of Bergman, Resnais, and Antonioni, suggesting to us that the questions posed by such artists have been ignored as if they have been fully answered, even as the media age has only further complicated them. Using as its linchpin a discarded paper bag cruelly tossed into the lap of a beggar by an insolent, dissolute boy, whose off-hand action affects all the major characters of the narrative in a manner suggesting not the "six degrees of separation" connecting humanity but rather the ever-widening abyss absorbing it, *Code Unknown* displays Haneke's remarkable "applied theory," his use of semiotics and language theory in a deeply felt, harrowing exploration of the end of communication, and that failure's relationship to racism and economic/social injustice. In his complex commentary in *The Piano Teacher* on classical Western culture's legacy, in particular its relationship to the idea of the family and gender politics, Haneke establishes firmly his sensibility. He rigorously eschews the snide humor, affectlessness, preoccupation with pop culture, movie allusions, and moral blankness of postmodern art. Yet nothing about Haneke's work seems anachronistic, precisely because he recognizes that the crises that affected twentieth-century humanity, in particular alienation and repression, continue in the new millennium even if they are simply embraced as features of contemporary life in much postmodern artistic expression. His harrowing explorations of psychological and societal breakdown and the oppression of technological civilization evoke a yawn only from those who accept the terms of this civilization.

Haneke is currently working on two films, *Time of the Wolf* and *Hidden*. In the former, Haneke reunites with Isabelle Huppert of *The Piano Teacher*. This interview was conducted by conference telephone call in November 2002 and April 2003. I am most grateful to my colleague Jürgen Heinrichs, without whose skills as a translator the interview would have been impossible.

CS: Your work seems an ongoing critique of current Western civilization.

HANEKE: I think you can take that interpretation, but as I'm sure you know it is difficult for an author to give an interpretation of his or her own work. I don't mind at all that view, but I have no interest in self-interpretation. It is the purpose of my films to pose certain questions, and it would be counterproductive if I were to answer all these questions myself.

CS: I'm interested in your sense of the modern landscape, in particular your images of architecture and technology. In a film like *The Seventh Continent* the cityscape comes across as both alluring and deadly, somewhat in the manner of Antonioni.

HANEKE: I think that this landscape operates in both of the modalities you mention. It isn't my interest to denounce technology, but to describe a situation in a highly industrialized society, so in that sense my films are very much concerned with a predicament specific to this society,

European society, rather than, say, the third world. My films are aimed therefore more to an audience that is part of the conditions of Western society. I can only deal with the world that I know, to be a little more precise. As for Antonioni, I very much admire his films, no question.

CS: There seems to be some degree of competition in your films between classical culture and popular culture. I'm thinking in particular of the opening of *Funny Games*, where the music of Mascagni, Handel, and Mozart suddenly changes to John Zorn's thrashpunk music.

HANEKE: This question has been asked a great deal. I think there is a certain amount of misunderstanding here, at least in regard to *Funny Games*. That film is in part a parody of the thriller genre, and my use of John Zorn was also intended as parodical. Zorn isn't a heavy metal artist. I have nothing against popular music and wouldn't think of playing popular against classical forms. I'm very skeptical of the false conflict that already exists between so-called "serious" music and music categorized strictly as entertainment. These are totally absurd distinctions, especially if one insists that an artist such as John Zorn must be seen as either classical or experimental or pop, since his work cuts across all categories. I see in John Zorn a kind of *über* heavy metal, an extreme and ironic accentuation of that form just as the film is an extreme inflection of the thriller. I think Zorn's style tends to alienate the listener in a sense that heightens awareness, which was effective to the points I wanted to address.

CS: In that film it seems the first "funny game" is the guessing game that the bourgeois couple plays with their CD player, guessing the classical compositions. Is there some association here of the bourgeoisie possessing classical culture?

HANEKE: That wasn't my first concern. Of course there is a certain irony here in the way that the bourgeoisie has insinuated itself in cultural history. But I didn't intend for the Zorn music to be seen solely as the music of the killers, so to speak, with the classical music strictly as the theme of the bourgeoisie. This is too simplistic. But of course with the guessing game at the beginning of the film there is an irony in the way their music suggests their deliberate isolation from the exterior world, and in the end they are trapped in a sense by their bourgeois notions and accouterments, not just by the killers alone.

CS: The two yuppie psychopaths seem to be intellectuals, especially in their chatter when they dispose of the wife. They are rather unusual serial killers, at least when we look at the genre.

HANEKE: I think this may be true only of one of them, not Dickie, the fat, slow one. They really don't have names – they are called Peter and Paul, Beavis and Butthead. In a way they aren't characters at all. They come out of the media. The tall one who is the main "plotter" so to speak might be seen as an intellectual with a deviousness that could be associated with this type of destructive fascist intellect. I have no problem with that interpretation. The fat one is the opposite; there is nothing there on the order of intellect.

CS: *Funny Games* seems to be a contribution to the self-reflexive films about media and violence along the lines of *Natural Born Killers* or *Man Bites Dog*.

HANEKE: My goal there was a kind of counter-program to *Natural Born Killers*. In my view, Oliver Stone's film, and I use it only as example, is the attempt to use a fascist aesthetic to achieve an anti-fascist goal, and this doesn't work. What is accomplished is something the opposite, since what is produced is something like a cult film where the montage style complements the violence represented and presents it largely in a positive light. It might be argued that *Natural Born Killers* makes the violent image alluring while allowing no space for the viewer. I feel this would be very difficult to argue about *Funny Games*. *Benny's Video* and *Funny Games* are different kinds of obscenity, in the sense that I intended a slap in the face and a provocation.

CS: If we can return to music, it seems in *La Pianiste* that classical music, while embodying the best sensibility of Erika, is also implicated in her pathology.

HANEKE: Yes, you can see the music functioning in that way, but you need first to understand that in that film we are seeing a very Austrian situation. Vienna is the capital of classical music, and is therefore the center of something very extraordinary. The music is very beautiful, but like the surroundings can become an instrument of repression, because this culture takes on a social function that ensures repression, especially as classical music becomes an object for consumption. Of course you must recognize that these issues are not just subjects of the film's screenplay, but are concerns of the Elfriede Jelinek novel, wherein the female has a chance, a small one, to emancipate herself only as an artist. This doesn't work out, of course, since her artistry turns against her in a sense.

CS: Schubert's *Winterreisse* seems central to *La Pianiste*. Some have argued that there is a connection between Erika and Schubert's traveler in that song cycle. This goes back to the broader question as to whether music represents the healthy side of Erika's psyche or simply assists her repression.

HANEKE: Of course the seventeenth song holds a central place in the film, and could be viewed as the motto of Erika and the film itself. The whole cycle establishes the idea of following a path not taken by others, which gives an ironic effect to the film, I think. It is difficult to say if there is a correlation between the neurosis of Erika Kohut and what could be called the psychogram of a great composer like Schubert. But of course there is a great sense of mourning in Schubert that is very much part of the milieu of the film. Someone with the tremendous problems borne by Erika may well project them onto an artist of Schubert's very complex sensibility. I can't give a further interpretation. Great music transcends suffering beyond specific causes. *Die Winterreisse* transcends misery even in the detailed description of misery. All important artworks, especially those concerned with the darker side of experience, despite whatever despair conveyed, transcend the discomfort of the content in the realization of their form.

CS: Walter Klemmer seems to be the hero of the film, but then becomes a monster.

HANEKE: You need to speak to Jelinek [laughs]. All kidding aside, this character is actually portrayed much more negatively in the novel than in the film. The novel is written in a very cynical mode. The novel turns him from a rather childish idiot into a fascist asshole. The film tries to make him more interesting and attractive. In the film the "love affair," which is not so central to the novel, is more implicated in the mother–daughter relationship. Walter only triggers the catastrophe. In the book Walter is a rather secondary character that I thought needed development to the point that he could be a more plausible locus of the catastrophe.

CS: One comes away feeling that sexual relationships are impossible under the assumptions of the current society.

HANEKE: We are all damaged, but not every relationship is played out in the extreme scenario of Erika and Walter. Not everyone is as neurotic as Erika. It's a common truth that we are not a society of happy people and this is a reality I describe, but I would not say that sexual health is impossible.

CS: Images of television recur numerous times in your films. Could you address your uses of TV, and your understanding of media in the current world?

HANEKE: Obviously in *Benny's Video* and *Funny Games* I attempt to explore the phenomenon of television. My concern for the topic isn't quite so much in *The Seventh Continent*, *Code Unknown*, and *La Pianiste*, although the place of television in society influences these films as well. I am most concerned with television as the key symbol primarily of the media representation of violence, and more generally of a greater crisis, which I see as our collective loss of reality and social disorientation. Alienation is a very complex problem, but television is certainly implicated in it. We don't of course anymore perceive reality, but instead the representation of reality in television. Our experiential horizon is very limited. What we know of the world is little more than the mediated world, the image. We have no reality, but a derivative of reality, which is extremely dangerous, most certainly from a political standpoint but in a larger sense to our ability to have a palpable sense of the truth of everyday experience.

CS: In *The Seventh Continent* there is a privileged use of both TV and pop music in the moment just before the murder/suicide. The family watches a rock video of "The Power of Love" on their TV as they sit in the demolished apartment. There is a sense both of the song as a genuine plea as well as the inadequacy of pop culture.

HANEKE: There I asked the producer to supply me with certain types of songs. The issue of copyright was a problem of course. I chose a song, actually a series of songs, which appealed to me, not so much because of the text, but because of a certain sentiment. As you suggest, the moment generates a certain ironic counterpoint to the story.

CS: There is another very interesting piece of music in *The Seventh Continent*, where you use the Alban Berg violin concerto, suddenly interrupted, as the young girl watches a ship go by while her father sells the family car in the junkyard. She seems to possess a vision of utopia that her family can't realize.

HANEKE: You can certainly interpret it that way, or simply as the girl spotting a boat, a very banal moment. Of course the Berg piece is not accidental. There is also a citation of the Bach chorale which could be a motto of the entire film.

CS: In the same film, the series of shots showing the couple's destruction of the apartment recalled to me somewhat the end of *Zabriskie Point*. The shots of the destruction of the household goods are beautiful, but there is real anguish and horror as well. The color scheme, here and elsewhere in the film, is extraordinary.

HANEKE: I'm a little surprised that you found beauty in this sequence. You could look at the phenomenon of the destruction of one's own environment in terms of a German notion, which in translation is "destroy what destroys you." It can be seen as a liberation. But the way it is represented is rather the opposite. They carry out the destruction with the same constricted narrowness with which they lived their lives, with the same meticulousness as life was lived, so I see this as the opposite of the vision of total destruction in *Zabriskie Point*. The sequence is portrayed as work. I have tried to portray it as something unbearable. As the wife says, "my hands really hurt from all that *Arbeit*," so all this hard work of destruction merely precedes the self-destruction. As for the color, I have always tried for cool, neutral colors. I couldn't say that I tried for a rigid color schematic in *The Seventh Continent*. In this film, however, my aesthetic centered mainly on the close-up, the emphasis on enlarged faces and objects. From an aesthetic standpoint, much of the film could be said to resemble television advertising. I have many reservations about television, but saw a use for its style here. Of course if *The Seventh Continent* had been made for television it would have failed totally in my view. But in the cinematic setting, a close-up of shoes or a doorknob takes on a far different sense than a similar shot in TV, where that style is the norm. This was a very conscious choice, since I wanted to convey not just images of objects but the objectification of life.

CS: You seem very interested in the long take. There are a number of static shots in your films, like the final image of *La Pianiste*. I'm also thinking of shots like that of the blank bathroom wall just before Walter rushes in for Erika, the many shots of Erika's face, the long take of the bloody living room in *Funny Games*, or the numerous still lifes in *The Seventh Continent*.

HANEKE: Perhaps I can connect this to the issue of television. Television accelerates our habits of seeing. Look for example at advertising in that medium. The faster something is shown, the less able you are to perceive it as an object occupying a space in physical reality, and the more it becomes something seductive. And the less real the image seems to be, the quicker you buy the commodity it seems to depict. Of course this type of aesthetic has gained the upper hand in commercial cinema. Television accelerates experience, but one needs time to understand what one sees, which the current media disallow. Not just understand on an intellectual level, but emotionally. The cinema can offer very little that is new; everything that is said has been said a thousand times, but cinema still has the capacity, I think, to let us experience the world anew. The long take is an aesthetic means to accomplish this by its particular emphasis. This has long been understood. *Code Unknown* consists very much of static sequences, with each shot from only one perspective, precisely because I don't want to patronize or manipulate the viewer, or at least to the smallest degree possible. Of course film is always manipulation, but if each scene is only one shot, then, I think, there is at least less of a sense of time being manipulated when one tries to stay close to a "real time" framework. The reduction of montage to a minimum also tends to shift responsibility back to the viewer in that more contemplation is required, in my view. Beyond this, my approach is very intuitive, without anything very programmatic. The final image of *La Pianiste* is simply a reassertion of the conservatory, the classical symmetry of that beautiful building in the darkness. The viewer is asked to reconsider it.

CS: Would you speak to your conception of the family as it is portrayed *La Pianiste*?

HANEKE: I wanted first of all to describe the bourgeois setting, and to establish the family as the germinating cell for all conflicts. I always want to describe the world that I know, and for me the family is the locus of the miniature war, the first site of all warfare. The larger political-economic site is what one usually associates with warfare, but the everyday site of war in the family is as murderous in its own way, whether between parents and children or wife and husband. If you start exploring the concept of family in Western society you can't avoid realizing that the family is the origin of all conflicts. I wanted to describe this in as detailed a way as I can, leaving to the viewer to draw conclusions. The cinema has tended to offer closure on such topics and to send people home rather comforted and pacified. My objective is to unsettle the viewer and to take away any consolation or self-satisfaction.

CS: Porno and erotica play a role in *La Pianiste* that caused much controversy in America. There is an ongoing debate about whether or not porno has a liberating function.

HANEKE: I would like to be recognized for making in *La Pianiste* an obscenity, but not a pornographic film. In my definition anything that could be termed obscene departs from the bourgeois norm. Whether concerned with sexuality or violence or another taboo issue, anything that breaks with the norm is obscene. Insofar as truth is always obscene, I hope that all of my films have at least an element of obscenity. By contrast pornography is the opposite, in that it makes into a commodity that which is obscene, makes the unusual consumable, which is the truly scandalous aspect of porno rather than the traditional arguments posed by institu-tions of society. It isn't the sexual aspect but the commercial aspect of porno that makes it repulsive. I think that any contemporary art prac-tice is pornographic if it attempts to bandage the wound, so to speak, which is to say our social and psychological wound. Pornography it seems to me is no different from war films or propaganda films in that it tries to make the visceral, horrific, or transgressive elements of life consum-able. Propaganda is far more pornographic than a home video of two people fucking.

CS: I notice that the porno shop Erika visits is in a shopping mall, which is a little unusual to an American viewer.

HANEKE: That was shot on location, the original setting. That is the way porno is sold in Vienna. Maybe we are a tiny less puritanical than the Americans [laughs].

CS: Just before she goes to the mall and the porno shop we see Erika prac-ticing Schubert's "Piano Trio in E Flat" with her colleagues. The music stays on the soundtrack right up to the moment that she puts coins in the video booth to start the porno video, at which point the music stops, as if Schubert finally can't compete with this image.

HANEKE: I have no problem with that interpretation at all, but again, I don't want to impose my own views beyond what I have already committed to film.

CS: One of your concerns seems to be, at least as expressed in *Code Unknown*, that all communication, the linguistic code, has failed. The scene of the deaf children drumming toward the end of the film seems to emphasize this failure.

HANEKE: Of course the film is about such failure, but the scene of the children drumming is concerned with communication with the body, so the deaf children have hope after all, although the drumming takes on a differ-ent function at the conclusion when it provides a specific background. Yes, the failure of communication is on all levels: interpersonal, familial, sociological, political. The film also questions whether the image trans-mits meaning. Everyone assumes it does. The film also questions the purpose of communication, and also what is being avoided and prevented in communication processes. The film tries to present these questions in a broad spectrum.

CS: The world your film describes seems catastrophic. There is the family suicide of *The Seventh Continent*, the violence of *Funny Games*, the image of the media in *Benny's Video*, the collapse of meaning in *Code Unknown*, the tragedy of *La Pianiste*.

HANEKE: I'm trying as best I can to describe a situation as I see it without bull-shitting or disingenuousness, but by so doing I subscribe to the notion that communication is still possible, otherwise I wouldn't be doing this. I cannot make comedies about these subjects, so it is true the films are bleak. On the subject of violence, there are an increasing number of modal-ities with which one can present violence, so much so that we need to reconceptualize the whole concept of violence and its origins. The new technologies, of both media representation and the political world, allow greater damage with ever-increasing speed. The media contribute to a confused consciousness through this illusion that we know all things at all times, and always with this great sense of immediacy. We live in this environment where we think we know more things faster, when in fact we know nothing at all. This propels us into terrible internal conflicts, which then creates angst, which in turn causes aggression, and this creates violence. This is a vicious cycle.

CS: There seems to be some confusion about the title of your last film, which is actually *La Pianiste* although marketed in America as *The Piano Teacher*.

HANEKE: I was adapting the title of Jelinek's book, which in the original is *Die Klavierspielerin*, or *The Piano Player*, which is a deliberately awkward title and an uncommon term in German. This is to point to Erika's degraded situation. *Pianistin* is the German word for the female pianist, so the title of the novel in German is a put-down suggesting Erika's crisis. The English translation of the novel is *The Piano Teacher*, which isn't correct at all, and is of course a little nonsensical and even more devaluing of the protagonist. I left the German title of the book not quite as it is, to give her more dignity, which is simply my approach to the material.

CS: *La Pianiste* is the most popular and recognized of your films thus far. Do you feel that it best represents your sensibility and development as a filmmaker?

HANEKE: I wouldn't say this, since the idea isn't mine but based on a novel, whereas my other films come from my own ideas. I recognize myself a bit more in those films rather than in works based on other texts. Of course I chose the topic of *La Pianiste* because I was very much drawn to it, and what I could bring to this work. But in some ways it is a bit distant from me. For example, I couldn't have written a novel on the subject of female sexuality. The topic of the novel interested me, but my choice of other source material for a film will probably continue to be the exception.

CS: I notice that your recent films are in French, although the setting remains Austrian.

HANEKE: This is to accommodate the producers and actors. My principal source of support has come from France, and my casts have been largely French. Isabelle Huppert, Juliette Binoche, Benoît Magimel, Annie Girardot . . . they are wonderful. Austria's film industry is a bit more limited in resources. The French production industry has been very helpful to me, and I am very comfortable with the language.

CS: Could you speak a bit about your new projects?

HANEKE: I am making *Caché*, which is about the French occupation of Algeria on a broad level, but more personally a story of guilt and the denial of guilt. The main character is a Frenchman, with another character an Arab, but it would be incorrect to see it strictly as a story of the past but rather a political story that deals with personal guilt. So it might be seen as more philosophical than political. The second film I'm preparing is *The*

Time of the Wolf. This is about how people treat each other when electricity no longer comes out of the outlet and water no longer comes out of the faucet. I'm a bit concerned that after the events of September 11 this film will be read very specifically, but it takes place in neither America nor Europe, and focuses on very primal anxieties.

CS: Could I ask you for your views on the current international situation, the war on Iraq, the "war on terrorism" and the like?

HANEKE: I think that at least eighty percent of the people of Europe, and perhaps the United States, did not want war. The war is horrible. War is always the dumbest way of solving problems, as history clearly shows. My impression is that the American government made up its mind a long time ago, so I'm rather pessimistic as to the outcome. The war is insanity. The US government doesn't see it this way, because it represents powerful interests. But the people don't want it. Some may be nervous merely because of the economic consequences, and some seem to follow blindly, but my impression is that the people are very much against war.

CS: Thanks so much.

32

Unsentimental Education

An Interview with Michael Haneke

Roy Grundmann

Michael Haneke's cinema is best known for thematizing the challenges and dys-functions of contemporary European society. For the past two decades two sets of concerns have repeatedly intersected in his films: the decline of Western Europe's white middle class, whose moral and spiritual crisis he has described as a state of "glaciation," and the various repercussions of Europe's geopolitical restruc-turing, the latter caused by the collapse of the Eastern bloc and the European Union's stepped-up efforts at integrating the continent economically and politi-cally. In Haneke's films these issues typically converge on the site of the family. The absence of ethical values and teachings, a lack of communication, and pas-sively endured interpersonal alienation are often dramatized in conflicts between parents and their children. In fact, several of Haneke's films could be described as perversions of the *Bildungsroman*, the bourgeois literary genre that depicts a young protagonist's painful but instructive path to maturation. If the genre is not always immediately recognizable in Haneke's films, it is because they may use only certain elements from it that they turn inside out: A focus on psychology is substituted by an exterior portrait of the consequences and effects of characters' decisions and actions; inference takes the place of explicit description; and, most importantly, intellectual and moral development, rather than being celebrated, is identified through negative, even diabolical examples. In addition, as Haneke's narratives often take the form of puzzles or mind games, they themselves assume a curiously pedagogical mode of addressing the viewer.

Haneke's new film is no exception in this regard. It tells the story of how a small village comes under the spell of a series of violent incidents. The local doctor has a riding accident when his horse is felled by a rope clearly installed for this purpose; a woman crashes through the rotten wood floor of a barn and dies; the son of the Baron is found tied up and beaten; the barn of the Baron's estate burns down; the handicapped child of the local midwife is found stabbed in the eyes. Despite increasing suspicions and fingerpointing among the villagers, no culprit or culprits can be identified. But while most of the incidents remain unsolved, the film is nonetheless decidedly more explicit than Haneke's 2005 mystery thriller, *Caché*, in feeding the viewer certain clues. Two explicit scenes – one depicting the sons of the estate's foreman throwing the Baron's son into the pond despite the fact that he can't swim, the other showing the pastor's daughter seizing the pet bird that her father later finds "crucified" on his desk – suggest that at least some of the incidents may have been planned and perpetrated by children of the village. For the most part, the film depicts the children as listeners, bystanders, eavesdroppers, and receivers of commands. They are interviewed by the police and ordered about by their parents, who punish them for their reticence and force them to wear around their arms a white ribbon as a symbol of the moral virtue they are deemed lacking. But one can't help but sense that the children may have formed some sort of secret society. They seem to study their parents closely, realizing that their parents do not live by the morals they preach. We don't learn exactly how much they find out about their parents' secret infringements, but if it is a fraction of what the film reveals to us viewers – namely, acts of violence, adultery, and incest – it is not hard to see how the children are poised to behave like the eponymous protagonist of *Benny's Video* (1992). Rather than redeeming through their innocence the jaundiced adult world they are forced to absorb while growing up, their actions come to echo this world and its hypocritical righteousness in horrifically amplified form – which is what makes them appealing dramatic ploys for Haneke to mount his critique of the world.

It becomes clear this critique is more important for Haneke than concern with the whodunit format. *The White Ribbon* portrays the children as historical characters on the eve of World War I, whose actions are meant to prompt us to chart connections to the time by which they would have grown into adults – the Nazi period. Its period setting and overt concern with the historical parameters of the time it depicts put *The White Ribbon* closer to Haneke's television films than to his theatrical features. Several of these films engage with the concept of the nation as a historical and ideological construct, as well as with the trauma that may result from damage to or loss of this construct. The post-World War II reconstruction melodrama *Fraulein* (1986) depicted a mid-1950s Germany that might have attempted to come to terms with its past, but chose to buy into the illusory, fetishistic aspects of its collective phoenix-from-the-ashes self-image. The post-World War I drama *The Rebellion* (1992) tells the story of a returning war veteran's disenchantment with and failed integration into an impersonal, opportunistically organized Austria bereft of its monarchy and national pride. Austria's loss of its dual monarchy and the foundation of a republic that would later become annexed by Nazi Germany are more obliquely touched upon in *Three Paths to the Lake* (1976), which concerns itself with a photojournalist whose international success has been read as an indirect critique of post-World War II Europe's commerce-driven and disingenuous cosmopolitanism.

While the TV films and the theatrical features in their combined scope reference numerous key historical periods in Austrian, German, and European history (one may add the biting depiction of 1960s post-radicalism in *The Seventh Continent* [1989] and *Benny's Video* and the investigation of French colonial history in *Caché* [2005]), none of Haneke's films have dealt directly with the period of the Third Reich. In *Fraulein*, the Nazi period is the burdensome, taboo past, whereas in *Three Paths to the Lake*, it is the conspicuously missing link between Austria's pre-World War I multi-ethnic past and its post-World War II blandly bureaucratic modernization. In *The White Ribbon* the Third Reich is the not too distant future that the film never names but alludes to with rhetorical force. But this also becomes the vexing tension in the film – its attempt to showcase something typically, perhaps essentially, German and its simultaneous refusal to identify this essence as a manifest destiny.

The film's observation of its subject, the Wilhelminian combination of discipline, authority, and Protestantism, has been noted for its meticulous attention to detail, which, in any Haneke film, extends from the characterization of the protagonists and the depiction of cultural attitudes to the selection of music. Music in *The White Ribbon* is featured sparsely, but comes to an apposite climax with Martin Luther's Protestant hymn, "A Mighty Fortress is our God." The film sharply identifies Protestantism as effecting a double ideological transference from which Imperial German culture drew its fateful combination of efficiency and fervor. It secularized divine law through a series of paternal stand-ins (emperor, pastor, paterfamilias) who seemed to embody and enforce authority in inverse proportion to their rank. In turn, it sanctified the family and the nation as fortresses of unquestionable importance and divine standing. Rebellion against either was considered a form of treason. Compared to this pressure cooker of discipline, doctrine, and deeply engrained guilt, the repressive tolerance of the Catholic confessional takes on a downright liberating dimension.

Despite the distancing effects of the film's nuanced, richly shaded black-and-white cinematography and the voice-over narration, the film, on one level, is more realist than many of Haneke's other films. It invokes the period with the same careful detail as its main contemporary chronicler, Theodor Fontane. Indeed, Haneke's keen eye for the highly restrictive position of women – the unloved Baroness, the self-debasing midwife, the coy and cautious sweetheart of the village school teacher – makes *The White Ribbon* an interesting counterpart to Rainer Werner Fassbinder's adaptation of *Effi Briest* (1974). But the film does not focus on these characters. It is hypnotically drawn to the children, whom it nonetheless depicts as marginal to the world of the adults. The fraught gap between what we see of the children and what sorts of thoughts and actions we attribute to them is designated by Haneke as the space in which historiography is supposed to do its work. This is where the film, whose title is underscored by a subtitle written in Old German script as "A German Children's Story," purports to be about something much broader, or, depending on how one looks at it, something much more specific than early twentieth-century German history. Leaving things out is a standard *modus operandi* in Haneke's work – there are gaps and then there is a spine.

The directions for filling in the gaps at times come across as rather didactic. They threaten to remove Haneke's textual edifices from a comparison with what Theodor W. Adorno, whom he reveres, characterized as the open-ended forms of modern art. But in laying out the pieces and asking the viewer to put these together, Haneke usually ensures that the spine does get rattled.

Another feature that harks back to Haneke's work for television is the film's voice-over narration. It is spoken by German actor Ernst Jacobi, who does not appear in the film, but who is meant to intone the character of the village school teacher (Christian Friedel) in old age. To understand the significance of this device, this character deserves attention. Though Haneke rightfully characterizes the film as an ensemble achievement, the village school teacher is arguably its central protagonist. Indeed, despite his thirty years and his vocation, he is the one who receives the real education in the film. It is he who ends up confronting the pastor with the shocking possibility that it is the latter's own children who may be among those responsible for the violence. In the film's carefully observed drama-tis personae, the school teacher seems, on the face of it, the most contrived ele-ment. While not free of authoritarian lapses, he is a sympathetic character and someone who might be said to embody the Enlightenment's positive qualities; he has been spared by personal neurosis and has retained the impulse to second-guess himself and question received ideas.

In the film's carefully observed dramatis personae, the school teacher seems, on the face of it, the most contrived element. On the one hand, he serves as carrier of audience identification – a dynamic Haneke has deployed here to unprecedented degree. This role does not necessarily make him the most interesting character in the film, but it does ensure that he becomes the film's moral center as well as its narrator. On the other hand, if moral authority is constituted not by judging infraction and meting out punishment (which would merely replicate the oppres-sive dynamics of the environment depicted) but by recognizing and testifying to the existence of dysfunction, the village school teacher is a rather modern, perhaps even postmodern character. In the voice of his older person, he announces at the beginning of the film that his narrative authority is not to be trusted fully. It is true that the film shows us things beyond his knowledge, but these things do not exactly contradict his intuition or identify him as a victim of misperceptions. A self-reflexive narration, by virtue of admitting to its own partiality, gathers its own form of integrity and, thus, authority. But what is perhaps just as important is Haneke's very decision to reintroduce into his work the device of voice-over narration, which he last used in his made-for-TV adaptation of Franz Kafka's *The Castle* (1997), and which, in general, must be closely associated with his adapta-tions of works of modernist and postmodernist literature (examples of modernism, in addition to Kafka, are Ingeborg Bachmann's *Three Paths to the Lake* and Joseph Roth's *The Rebellion*; an example of postmodernism is Peter Rosei's *Who Was Edgar Allan?*). The use of a narrator in a film based not on a novel but on Haneke's own original script is in and of itself an important gesture. It not only implies the significance Haneke accords to the aesthetic tension between voice and image (no matter how supportive the contents of the voice may appear to be of the image), but to the implicit tradition of fragmentation, pluralism, and dissent embodied in various ways by modernist and postmodernist literature.

Does the teacher bear out these qualities as a historical figure or is he an idealist construct? The fact that he gets to leave the village and is given the privilege of narrating the story in hindsight when so many of his fellow villagers, twenty years later, would line the streets to cheer the rank-and-file parade of his erstwhile pupils would seem to indicate the latter. But this is ultimately a speculation and, as such, implicitly just as reductive as its alternative. In 1932, the state of Prussia held elections that produced a splintered array of political parties with no clear majority. Unable to form a viable coalition government, the old rulers were ordered to stay in power, but were placed under the authority of a commissary, who effectively disempowered them. This move curtailed the political power and influence of Prussia on Germany and made it significantly easier for Hitler to gain power six months later. The Weimar constitution was ill-equipped for this type of crisis, but the election result also showed the reality of a fledgling democracy – considerable political heterogeneity. No matter their individual political leanings, Prussia's civil servants would have had a vital interest in preserving the autonomy of their state against the Reich in the spirit of a federalist balancing of the power structure. The village school teacher from *The White Ribbon* might have been one of them. But even as someone who rejected the state education system and became a small business owner or who, in an alternative scenario, might have decided to emigrate from Weimar Germany to America, he would have been among Hitler's political opponents – that is, if one is prepared to let one's speculation follow Haneke's suggestions. I spoke with Haneke by phone in his apartment in Vienna in September 2009.

RG: *The White Ribbon concerns* itself with the roots of fascism, but not exclusively. As you have indicated in other interviews, the topic of the film is the roots of terrorism of any kind: When an idea becomes absolute and is turned into an ideology, it becomes inhuman and turns against everyone. Can you explain this in greater detail?

HANEKE: The intention of the film is to show what is, of course, a broader theme through its most prominent example, German fascism, and also through the representation of the children in the film. Today, one could make a film about the same theme in other countries. There is not only fascism from the right but also from the left – any kind of radical ideology. Those who get branded as enemies are oppressed or murdered. The initial ideas often intend to further the cause of humanity. Communism is a wonderful idea that every humanist is compelled to agree with. But it has cost millions of lives. The same is the case with Christianity. And with Islam. This is still evident today.

RG: This means you are pursuing a universal element?

HANEKE: This was my intention. But this is something every spectator must decide for him/herself. I want to avoid the misunderstanding that is incurred when critics receive the film exclusively as a film about German fascism. There are so many causes that led to this specific form that the film couldn't possibly name them all. It is something the film is unable to accomplish. Hence, this narrow reception would be a misinterpretation.

RG: But when one radically reduces a topic such as this one to a more general level, does this not downplay important differences between various totalitarian systems?

HANEKE: They aren't downplayed – they are simply not the topic of the film. Of course, if you make a film about Islamism today, economic and other immediate factors are of a different kind. But the basic model is the same: that people are unhappy and distraught because of whatever oppresses and humiliates them. Because they suffer pain and lack hope, they clutch at a straw that promises them that they will be able to overcome their misery. And in most cases, this straw turns out to be some kind of ideology that, however, looks different in different countries. No film can cover the full scope of all these differences. The only thing one can do is take one concrete example to point to the basic dynamics according to which this phenomenon has unfolded in history. This is what I have tried to do.

RG: The main protagonists in your film are children. Do you believe that one can identify this kind of universal situation particularly with children?

HANEKE: With children one can show the formation of character most efficiently. Of course, adults, too, can be coerced into following an ideology. But the younger we are the more manipulable we are.

RG: You have said that you have worked on the topic of this film for some time. Was there anything in particular that triggered your interest in it?

HANEKE: The screenplay for the film has already existed for ten years. And before the script was completed I had already spent quite a few years on developing the idea. It is difficult to name a specific impulse or point of origin. There is a risk of naming things retroactively, of rationalizing the biography, when the development of such a project always tends to be affected by many coincidences. What made a big impression on me was a documentary about Eichmann and his trial in Israel. I was stunned by this man, who completely lacked any conscience, and by his attempt at justification: that he was a dutiful civil servant, that he merely did his job for the benefit of the state, and that he was actually uncomfortable with the fact that he had to do what he did. This mentality dumbfounded me. This fanaticism – that people don't realize what kinds of things they cause.

Italian fascism was not exactly funny either, but the justifications of its criminals show that it articulated itself in very different ways. In Germany, it was the absolute belief in the "right thing" – the National Socialist ideology of the "*Volk*" – as well as a certain ideology of efficiency, which already has a lot to do with Protestantism, particularly with

Lutheranism. There is, of course, also the Protestantism of Thomas Münzer, which was different, closer to communism. Lutheran Protestantism has always very much identified itself with authority.

Consider the opposite end of the spectrum: the German left-wing terrorism of the Baader-Meinhof group. Gudrun Ensslin was the daughter of a pastor, Ulrike Meinhof also came from a Protestant and very religious home. In their moral rigor, they did not balk at committing crimes for a "good cause" – that is, a cause they deemed good. They were one hundred percent convinced that what they were doing, the crimes they were committing, aided humanity and were good. They, too, did not have a guilty conscience. I knew Ulrike Meinhof personally. She was a highly intelligent, socially very engaged woman, who acted with incredible energy on behalf of oppressed people. But this rigor went so far that it led to committing crimes. This story and that of Eichmann initially made me think about this whole complex.

RG: What seems to be poisoning the children in your film is the combination of discipline, authority, and religion. This is very German, don't you think?

HANEKE: If you look at the situation today in Arab countries, there are, of course, other details apart from religion. To what extent these have to do with discipline, strictness, and piety is beyond my knowledge. That's why I picked the German example. Because it is easiest to convey the problem through this constellation, which is, after all, the best known.

RG: This brings me back to your work with children. They seem to have a certain model character in your films. An example is *Benny's Video*. But many of your films deal with children. I know few directors of contemporary world cinema who have shown such a consistent interest in children.

HANEKE: But it is difficult. Filming with children is rather tedious.

RG: What were the problems in this film?

HANEKE: They primarily consisted of finding the children. We auditioned about seven thousand children in order to find the fifteen that we needed. They are different from the way children normally get used in a film, where they are simply nice and chatty. These were emotionally difficult roles that required finding talented children. A whole crew worked on this for half a year. The person in charge of this process was then also present during the complete shoot. He had prepared the children well, so that the work was relatively free of problems. With the very young it is, of course, tedious. A five-year-old concentrates for five minutes and then he is bored. Then you have to take a break and play with him, after which you can continue to shoot a bit more. Working with the older ones wasn't much more difficult than working with professional actors, because they had been very carefully selected and prepared.

RG: What was it like to work with the handicapped child?

HANEKE: Those were the most difficult scenes. You simply have to shoot until you happen to get it right. You cannot order the child to do anything.

He does what he feels like doing. The scene at the beginning, when the mother picks him up from school, was shot twice, on different days. Shot, viewed, shot again, all day, because he always did something different, and we had to find a sequence that was reasonably credible.

RG: If one considers that the children in the film grow up to live as adults in the Third Reich, which then self-destructs, the film does point towards a certain path of self-destruction.

HANEKE: This is your own interpretation. Everyone needs to make his or her own decision here. The film itself says nothing about fascism. We simply depict a group of children who absolutize the ideals preached to them by their parents. On the basis of these absolute ideals, the children judge their parents. And when they realize that the parents do not live by the rules they preach, the children punish the parents. This is the story that is being told. But because of the generation to which the children belong, it acquires another context, another meaning. But I deliberately steered clear of engaging with fascism in any way. This would open a can of worms. A single film cannot accomplish such a thing.

RG: And this determines the specific point in time when the story takes place, the period on the eve of World War I.

HANEKE: Of course. But this moment also constituted the great break in European culture. Up until then, there had been the feudal society that had maintained itself over centuries, with God at the top, followed by the emperor and the church. All this died once and for all with World War I.

RG: This is also the topic of *The Rebellion*, although the film deals with the Austrian perspective and does not engage with Protestantism. Would it be too simple to claim that if the children of *The White Ribbon* had lived in a Catholic village, they would have been spared?

HANEKE: That would be too simple. *The White Ribbon* is not a document but a metaphor. The education metaphor works anywhere. The rigor of Protestantism is highly exemplary. The question of education is one of the fundamental questions of society. I belong to the so-called '68 generation, which raised their children anti-authoritarian. This was not the best thing either, because the children, when they left the family and stepped into life, had tremendous problems adjusting. I know quite a few children of friends who, to this day, have not gained a footing in society. And looking at schools today, when teachers must fear their students, this may not be the ideal kind of education either.

RG: Another topic that pervades your films is the critique of the school as an educational institution.

HANEKE: Yes, but not only as that. The only thing you can do in your role as artist is thematize things. I don't suggest solutions. I don't know either how to raise a child the right way. Making a child into a responsible member of society who is not neurotic is one of the most difficult things in the world and, of course, the institutions invariably fail, because they measure everyone and everything by the same yardstick. There doesn't seem to be any other way, but this is dangerous. There is this nice word in English that I learned while making the new version of *Funny Games*. The boy who pees in his pants out of fear receives the comment: "He is not yet housebroken!" When this term, "housebroken," was explained to me, I found it to be a very enlightening word. It is the ideal term to describe the concept of bringing someone up. We break the young individual, so that he or she becomes tolerable for society.

RG: But if this is the case, the role of the village school teacher in your new film gives me pause.

HANEKE: Dramaturgically, I needed a figure who comes from the outside and who can narrate the events in retrospect. The Baroness is a similar character. She is the only one who announces her intention to leave the village. And the teacher's love interest also comes from the outside. These characters come from outside the universe of this village, which does function as a model. And through this, the teacher is given the opportunity to reflect critically upon the events in retrospect. At the end of the film he tells the audience that, after the war, he took over his father's tailor shop. Apparently, he no longer wanted to remain in the service of the kind of education he had been made to represent.

RG: He escaped the Wilhelminian world.

HANEKE: He escaped the system. At film festivals the film is shown with a completely subtitled print, and this print will also be shown at urban art cinemas. But in the print that will be shown in regular movie theaters, the narrator is going to be dubbed rather than subtitled. By the same actor who speaks the German text and who, of course, has a heavy German accent. Spectators then get to form their own interpretations. An American viewer might well imagine that the teacher emigrated from Germany. It doesn't have to mean that – the teacher could also simply have told the story to an American. But one could understand it this way, if one wanted to.

RG: The voice-over narration is also very important for your literary adaptations *Three Paths to the Lake* and *The Rebellion*. It introduces an element of alienation into the film.

HANEKE: Yes, just like the use of black-and-white film.

RG: But in comparison to these earlier films I found the alienation effect in the new film to be less strong. To be sure, the narrator at the beginning of the film admits that he is not fully reliable because he cannot remember every detail, but he does comment on the events more seamlessly than the narrator of *Three Paths to the Lake*.

HANEKE: Do you think so? I don't.

RG: That film had certain discrepancies between voice-over narration and image. What was talked about did not fully correspond to what one sees on the screen.

HANEKE: *Three Paths to the Lake* was my first attempt in this regard. I attenuated it in both the Roth and the Kafka adaptation, because I found it silly not to show what is being talked about. The narrator as such already constitutes the element of alienation. In the Bachmann adaptation we have a little bit of a double effect. In my opinion this is a bit inchoate. Besides, at the beginning of *The White Ribbon*, the narrator announces not only that he does not know whether everything he says corresponds to the truth and that some of it he only knows from hearsay. The film also shows things that the narrator cannot possibly have seen or heard – the conversation between the doctor and his midwife, for example, and also the sex scenes between the two. After all, herein lies the irony of deploying a narrator: That he says he isn't fully in the know and that some of it is based on hearsay immediately signals that one should distrust the reality of what is shown and claimed.

RG: Conventionally, the voice-over narration also has a certain authority, and a film that critiques authority must, of course, also proceed cautiously with the voice-over narration.

HANEKE: The use of black-and-white film is also in the service of alienation. On the one hand, it is meant to give spectators easier access to the time period. Any images we know about this period are black-and-white. This is one of the effects of its use in the film. But the other one is that the black-and-white always constitutes a certain stylization, which, rather than pretending to be a naturalist image of reality, emphasizes the prototypical character of the story. It is an artifact and is being presented as such.

RG: Have any of the images been treated digitally?

HANEKE: Of course. The horse accident, for example, and countless details, such as TV antennas, modern-style house roofs, and so on.

RG: Giving spectators access to the period was also a concern of yours when making *The Rebellion*, where you integrated historical footage into the film – the funeral of the Austrian emperor, for example, and battle scenes from the war. Was this something you also considered doing in the new film?

HANEKE: I considered it but then deliberately left it out for reasons I just explained. Because I don't want people to reduce the film to a German example.

RG: The film has been coproduced by Austria. Would this story have been possible in Austria? Does it have any validity with regard to Austria?

HANEKE: I hope so. Because I also hope that it has validity for America, France, and Italy – wherever. It is not exclusively about Protestantism. The latter is meant as an example. But if it had taken place in Austria, I would have had to think up a different story.

RG: Because the social structure and the religion are different.

HANEKE: And the way of life. But the basic social model, both in Austria and Germany, was the village. One mustn't forget that ninety percent of the population used to live in village-like structures. The number of urban dwellers was relatively marginal in relation to the rural population. If you go into any developing country today, you have the same structures.

RG: But I think the film depicts a certain tension. On the one hand, there is village life, which has remained the same for hundreds of years. But on the other hand, the film also clearly shows the "achievements" – the modernity of the Prussian state. For example, every child goes to school and learns how to read and write. Given the year is 1913, this was an achievement.

HANEKE: But this was historical reality. If I had set the story back by a hundred years, it would have looked different.

RG: But reading and writing can also be used as means of indoctrination.

HANEKE: Again, this is a question of interpretation. I don't believe that by teaching children reading and writing one necessarily prepares them for indoctrination. I believe the opposite – the less educated someone is, the easier it is to indoctrinate that person.

RG: I would like to return to the topic of acting. Your work with children in the new film has already been commented on. What interests me now is your work with actors in general. It has been neglected as a topic in the critical reception of your films. I believe that your experience in the theater is of considerable significance here.

HANEKE: Certainly. I always advise my own film students to do a theater production. You learn a thousand times more than working in film. You have to approach actors differently because they have much more freedom in the theater. If you fail to talk to the theater actor in a way that really convinces him, he will play whichever way he wants and not the way you want him to. This means you really have to engage with the actor, which is something you often don't do in film, due to time pressure. In this situation the actor has to do what the director wants, and if the director fails to get the actor to do what he is supposed to do, the director ends up calling the actor incompetent. But, truth be told, it is the director's fault, because he doesn't know anything about acting. The theater teaches you how to treat actors.

RG: But theater and film are very different media.

HANEKE: True enough, but skillful psychological engagement is required anywhere. As a conductor, too, you have to learn the full bag of tricks as to how to get an orchestra to stay dynamic in a way you would like it to be. Orchestra musicians tend to work under ever-changing conductors. You have to use energy and tricks to motivate them and to make an orchestra sound better than it tends to. It is the same with actors. This is a skill one has to acquire. And one acquires it more easily in the theater, even if the forms of acting are very different there.

RG: You once said that even a wonderful actor can be dreadful when he or she is miscast.

HANEKE: I always say that good casting is already half the success of the film, if not more. Rather than superstars, you need the right people in the right parts. In the case of the new film, these are people who are, in any case, not known in the US. They are, for the most part, German actors, though some of them have become well known in Germany through film and TV. What I am proud of is that I have nonetheless achieved a certain ensemble effect with the film. There are also no diverse acting styles among the cast.

RG: Would you say that the long take is very important for you in order to transpose acting from theater to film for the kinds of things you would like to see going into a performance?

HANEKE: Not to transpose from theater to film, because I don't even attempt this. No matter whether he or she has theater experience or is purely a film actor, it is more pleasant for the actor to be able to develop emotions over long sequences than piecemeal.

RG: The editing of *The White Ribbon* seems a bit different. Can this be related to your claim that the form of a film has to be adjusted to the respective project?

HANEKE: It was clear that the dialog scenes with the small children, for example, could not be filmed in a long take, because they cannot memorize their lines. We had to do shot/countershot. Knowing this in advance is part of the craft of directing, so one doesn't have to improvise.

RG: Shot/countershot was also used in other sequences in this film.

HANEKE: This is stipulated by the form of the individual scene. If the scene is about a conflict that is mainly verbal, shot/countershot is the optimal solution because it allows you to register most of what transpires. Scenes involving a lot of physical motion can under certain circumstances also be shot in long takes, but scenes that involve an exchange of words in which you have two people facing each other, shot/countershot is the most apposite solution. But this film, like almost every one of my films, contains all kinds of aesthetic solutions. Only *Code Unknown* was shot entirely in long takes. This was an exception, because the focus itself was on fragmentation, the fragmentation that I had already thematized in *71 Fragments of a Chronology of Chance*. But I was dissatisfied with it, because if I claim there are seventy-one fragments, there technically should not be more than seventy-one takes. But this is something I did not yet do with this film, and that was the reason to do it in *Code Unknown*.

RG: How important was it to create a romance for the village school teacher? Is this a concession to entertainment cinema or a minor detail?

HANEKE: There is such a large number of characters in this film – like in a Russian novel – that it would simply be a lie if one or the other is not a sympathetic figure whose life has positive aspects. And that a love story can happen under terrible circumstances is certainly not new.

RG: The village school teacher has certain implications that fascinated me. As you say, he certainly is an outsider who eventually gets to leave. But if viewed as a historical figure, he would technically have been – or eventually have become – a civil servant of the Prussian state. This state was characterized by political heterogeneity in the final stage of the Weimar Republic.

HANEKE: One shouldn't forget that there were also a great many people from within the Protestant church who fought against fascism. It is too simple to equate Protestantism with the furthering of fascism. I have never claimed this.

RG: Yes, Dietrich Bonhoeffer was among them.

HANEKE: There are many examples. And in this way, one can, of course, counter Gudrun Ensslin's example by saying there have been many visionaries in German history, who came from parishioners' families. It would be a fatal misunderstanding to claim the film wants to draw a negative picture of Protestantism.

RG: The doctor is a negative figure.

HANEKE: He is not a very sympathetic figure. But such characters apparently do exist in the world.

RG: But he is not a stereotype.

HANEKE: He is very nice to the handicapped child. But he is severely neurotic. The midwife says to him: "You must be very unhappy to be so mean." He reacts very sensitively to this observation, because it touches a sore spot. He, too, has some secret wound that he compensates. But this is life. This also goes back to the issue of the love story: The larger the dramatis personae, the more one is obligated to reference the contradictory nature of life. Within this contradictoriness there is something bright within the darkest darkness and something dark within the brightest brightness.

RG: But this is ironic with regard to the doctor, because as a scientist he is an Enlightenment figure.

HANEKE: Yes, but just because someone is enlightened or an intellectual does not mean that he or she is automatically a good person.

RG: This is certainly true. With the other characters in the film I have the impression that they contain elements from characters in some of your other films. What emerges is an impression of the Haneke universe, to which new characters are being added all the time, but which also returns other characters in modified form. The Baroness, for example, has something from Erika Kohut, the protagonist of *The Piano Teacher*. The discipline and aggressiveness with which she plays the piano . . .

HANEKE: . . . against the house teacher, I know, but that was the standard way of dealing with the staff. And playing the piano was her joy.

RG: This brings me to the next topic. Music is very important for your films. It is used very deliberately and often very sparsely. In this film, too, which is relatively long, but which has only three or four music pieces. How did you select the music?

HANEKE: The Baroness and the house teacher were supposed to play together because this makes the village school teacher mention that he, too, used to play together with the Baroness, but that he wasn't good enough for her. The Schubert variations for flute and piano that she plays at the beginning are based on a song from "Die Schöne Müllerin," which is called "Trockene Blumen." This is, of course, a nice metaphor for this somewhat neglected woman. Then there is the "Sicilienne" by Bach, which is played by the village school teacher when his future lover comes to his school. Before that, he plays a little piano piece by Robert Schumann during which he is interrupted. It is called "Liedchen." To a certain extent I had to follow the musical capabilities of the actors. The actress who plays the Baroness can play the piano, actually quite well. She could have played this live. But the actor playing the house teacher had to practice the flute for months. The actor playing the village school teacher can improvise. He has a pretty voice and sings pop, but I had to find something he was able to play himself. I searched for a long time. The "Sicilienne" is a particularly intimate piece, which he plays to console her, whereas the initial piece is an easy exercise that every beginner is required to play.

RG: Why does Schubert have such significance for you?

HANEKE: Because he always affects me personally, when I listen to his music. Like Bach and Mozart. They are my house gods. At the end of the film there is "A Mighty Fortress is our God." This is the Protestant hymn, so to speak. I learned it when I was a young student and I know it by heart. It was played on such occasions, because it strengthens the feeling of community. Of course, the text, "A mighty fortress is our God, a bulwark never failing; our helper He, amid the flood of mortal ills prevailing," has a general meaning – as a fortress against evil and Satan, who appears in the second verse of the song, which is not in the film. But it also has a second meaning, in relation to the outbreak of the war. Evil is now understood as the enemy of the nation. As soon as there is an image of an enemy, the lyrics fit really well. The last scene, which takes place in the church, shows four young lads walking to the front with little bouquets in their lapels. These are the first enlistees.

RG: I know the song, too. I also was raised Protestant. I have read that you once wanted to become a pastor.

HANEKE: Yes, when I was fourteen. Mischievous people say that one can still see this in my films today. [Laughs]

RG: But other films of yours also engage with Catholicism. Your films frequently deal with religion.

HANEKE: Religion is a topic one cannot ignore as a dramatist. It has always been one of the pillars of civilization and it will always remain one in one form or another, even though God has been declared dead for over a hundred years. But since then, we have simply turned to various kinds of gurus. Religion is simply the yearning for additional spiritual worth and, as such, it is something characteristic of humans.

RG: In one of your early films, *Lemmings*, the priest is a weak figure. His equivalent in the new film is rather a tyrant.

HANEKE: Perhaps this is what it appears like from our perspective today. But he is highly representative of the period's attitude towards education. He is a father who loves his children and is one hundred percent convinced that his way of raising them is right because this is how he was raised.

RG: But he is fully defined by authority.

HANEKE: Of course. That's what it was like. I did a lot of research for this and have read dozens of historical education manuals in preparation for this film. The white ribbon is something I did not invent either. It is from one of those books, from an educational manual that advises parents to use it on their children.

RG: The priest in *Lemmings* has no authority and does not pretend to be able to help.

HANEKE: He is a modern intellectual. A classic priest of modernity who no longer believes and is without hope – and, thus, he boozes. There are several examples like this one in modern literature. But the pastor in the new film still believes. He is really a tragic figure, because he sees his faith being destroyed. Take the scene towards the end, in which the village school teacher articulates the suspicion against the children. The reason for the pastor's reaction is that, a few weeks or months earlier, he had found the dead bird lying on his desk. It is not as though he can't figure out who is behind this. And so this is an incredibly tragic position. He wanted to achieve the best and now he stands before the shards of his existence.

RG: So this is the same loss of authority that Andreas Pum, the protagonist of *The Rebellion*, experiences a few years later, right after the end of World War I.

HANEKE: Actually, Pum never really had any authority. He always lacked privilege.

RG: But he believed in authority.

HANEKE: Yes, that's true.

RG: You were saying that the dead bird on the desk is a hint for the pastor as to who is behind the violence. Of course, this is also the case for the spectator. This brings me to the last question, which is about the dramatic structure of your films. As in other films of yours, the spectator of *The White Ribbon* receives a few specific and highly controlled bits of information. Never enough to explain the whole story. This way, spectators are given a certain leeway for interpretation. It is now their job to establish contexts of meaning. But how do you decide from film to film how much leeway viewers should be given? In *Caché* the amount of information is very restricted. We don't know exactly what causes Majid to commit suicide. The film does not tell us who made and mailed the videotapes. In *Benny's Video* we don't find out what it is that makes Benny report his parents to the police as accessories after the fact. How do you decide from film to film what kind of information should be given to spectators and what should be withheld? And why is the amount of information in *The White Ribbon* relatively large in comparison to *Caché*?

HANEKE: For years, I have been trying to restore to spectators a little bit of the kind of freedom they have in the other arts. Music, painting, the fine arts give recipients breathing space in their consideration of the work. The language-bound arts already circumscribe this freedom considerably, because they are forced to name things by their name. But what is named by its name is artistically dead, has stopped breathing, and can only be recycled in discussion. Film exacerbates this further. Whereas the reader forms an image in his or her head, the image that the spectator forms is replaced by the one issued by the director. In other words, film has, from the outset, a tendency towards disenfranchising the recipient. But if film aspires to be an art, it must take its addressee seriously and, as much as possible, attempt to restore the lost freedom to the latter. By what means? I think this is a very decisive question, with which all serious filmmakers engage. I always say, a film ought to be like a ski jump, but it is the viewer who must do the jumping. But to enable the viewer to do so, the jump has to be constructed in a certain way. One has to find a construction that lets the viewer fly – in other words, that stirs the viewer's imagination. And this provocation is constituted by all the gaps, the things that are not shown to viewers, that are not put into the image, but that the image alludes to; by the questions that get posed but not answered by the story and that enable viewers to bring their own thoughts and imaginations to the film. Every single time, this turns out to be a complicated construction. Because you first of all have to create several possibilities of interpretation, which is, of course, tedious in comparison to having a clear solution. This is what I have tried to do in various ways with various films. There is no set principle for me to follow. It is determined by the exigencies of the individual story.

Filmography

1974
    After Liverpool (***Und was kommt danach . . .***) (**TV**)
West Germany, color, 89 minutes
A Production by Südwestfunk (SWF)
Script: Michael Haneke (after a radio play by James Saunders, in German by Hilde Spiel)
Cast: Hildegard Schmahl, Dieter Kirchlechner
Cinematography: Gerd E. Schäfer, Jochen Hubrich, Günter Lemnitz
Sound: Wilhelm Dusil
Editing: Christa Kleinheisterkamp
Set design: Jörg Höhn
Assistant Director: Gerda Orlowski

1975
    Bulk Garbage (***Sperrmüll***) (**TV**)
West Germany, 16mm and video, color
A Production by Zweites Deutsches Fernsehen (ZDF)
Script: Alfred Bruggmann
Cast: Ernst Fritz Fürbringer (Johannes Gander), Tilli Breidenbach (Gerda Gander), Karl Heinz Fiege (Helmut Gander), Suzanne Geyer (Eva Gander), Susi Engel, Oliver Linnow, Else Quecke, Fritz Strasser, Ludwig Thiesen
Cinematography: Henric von Barnekow, Alois Nitsche
Set design: Peter Scharff

1976
    Three Paths to the Lake (***Drei Wege zum See***) (**TV**)
West Germany/Austria, 16mm, color, 97 minutes
A Production by Rolf von Sydow from Südwestfunk (SWF) and Österreichischer Rundfunk (ORF)
Script: Michael Haneke, after a short story by Ingeborg Bachmann

Cast: Ursula Schult (Elisabeth Matrei), Guido Wieland (Mr. Mattrei), Walter Schmidinger (Trotta), Bernhard Wicki (Branko), Yves Beneyton (Philippe), Udo Vioff (Manes), Dieter Wernecke, Rainer von Artenfels, Jane Tilden, Michael Gspandl, Pamela White, Mathieu Chardet, Pierre Brechignac, Geoffrey Keller, Suzannah Dijan
Narration: Axel Corti
Cinematography: Igor Luther
Assistant Director: Gerda Orlowski
Sound: Wilhelm Dusil, Harald Lill
Music: Arnold Schönberg, W. A. Mozart, Henry Purcell
Editing: Helga Scharf
Set design: Friedheim Boehm
Costumes: Barbara Langbein
Makeup: Erika Elfert

1979   *Lemmings (Lemminge)*
Part One: *Arcadia (Arkadien)*
Austria/West Germany, 16mm, color, 113 minutes
Produced by Schönbrunn Film Production Company: Head of Production: Robert Siepen; Commissioning Editors/Executive Producers: Wolfgang Ainberger at Schönbrunn-Film/Österreichischer Rundfunk (ORF), Jens-Peter Behrend at Sender Freies Berlin (SFB)
Script: Michael Haneke
Cast: Regina Sattler (Evi Wasner), Christian Ingomar (Christian Beranek), Eva Linder (Sigrid Leuwen), Paulus Manker (Sigurd Leuwen), Christian Spatzek (Fritz Naprawnik), Hilde Berger (Anna the Servant Girl), Walter Schmidinger (Professor Georg Schäfer), Elisabeth Orth (Gisela Schäfer), Bernhard Wicki (Mr. Leuwen), Gustl Halenke (Mrs. Leuwen), Kurt Sowinetz (Mr. Naprawnik), Grete Zimmer (Mrs. Naprawnik), Rudolf Wessely (Mr. Wasner), Ingrid Burkhard (Mrs. Wasner), Kurt Nachmann (Dr. Aigner), Helma Gautier (Mrs. Aigner), Lena Stolze (Gertraud Aigner), Zoltan Paul (Letscho), Elisabeth Schwarzbau (Bettina Rabenstein), Manfred Neuböck (Hans Malecz)
Cinematography: Jerzy Lipman, Walter Kindler
Assistant Director: Gusti Brünjes-Goldschwend
Sound: Johannes Paiha
Music: Franz Schubert, Ludwig van Beethoven, Alexander Steinbrecher
Editing: Marie Homolkova
Set design: Peter Manhardt
Costumes: Barbara Langbein
Makeup: Adolf Uhrmacher, Edda Hackenberg

Part Two: *Injuries* (*Verletzungen*) (TV)
Austria/West Germany, 16mm, color, 107 minutes
Produced by Schönbrunn Film Production Company: Head of
Production: Robert Siepen; Commissioning Editors/Executive
Producers: Wolfgang Ainberger at Schönbrunn-Film/Österreichischer
Rundfunk (ORF), Jens-Peter Behrend at Sender Freies Berlin (SFB)
Script: Michael Haneke
Cast: Monika Bleibtreu (Eva Beranek), Elfriede Irrall (Sigrid
Leuwen), Rüdiger Hacker (Christian Beranek), Wolfgang Hübsch (Fritz
Naprawnik), Norbert Kappen (Minister), Guido Wieland (Gröhlinger),
Vera Borek (Bettina), Wolfgang Gasser (Peter), Julia Gschnitzer
(Neighbor), David Haneke
Cinematography: Jerzy Lipman
Assistant Director: Gusti Brünjes-Goldschwend
Sound: Johannes Paiha
Music: J. S. Bach
Editing: Marie Homolkova
Set design: Peter Manhardt
Costumes: Barbara Langbein
Makeup: Adolf Uhrmacher, Edda Hackenberg

1982   *Variation* (TV)
West Germany, 16mm, color, 98 minutes
A Production by Christa Vogel at Sender Freies Berlin (SFB)
Script: Michael Haneke
Cast: Elfriede Irrall (Anna Beranek), Hilmar Thate (Georg Leuwen),
Suzanne Geyer (Kitty), Eva Linder (Sigrid), Udo Samel (Peter), Celso
Adrian, Jens-Peter Behrend, Kurt Hübner, Tobias Meister, Edith
Robberts, Dietrich Streuber, Ilse Trautschold, Monica Bleibtreu
Cinematography: Walter Kindler
Sound: Klaus Vogler, Joachim Prokesch
Music: Egberto Gismonti, Jan Garbarek, Charlie Haden
Editing: Barbara Herrmann
Set design: Roger von Möllendorff
Costumes: Reinhild Paul
Makeup: Brigitta Wehrend

1984   *Who Was Edgar Allan?* (*Wer war Edgar Allan?*) (TV)
Austria, 16mm, color, 83 minutes
A Production by Wolfgang Ainberger at Neue Studio Film for the
Österreichischer Rundfunk (ORF) and Alfred Nathan at Zweites
Deutsches Fernsehen (ZDF)
Festival Premiere: Berlin 1985

Script: Hans Broczyner and Michael Haneke, after a novel by Peter Rosei
Cast: Paulus Manker (The Student), Rolf Hoppe (Edgar Allen), Guido Wieland (The Lawyer), Otella Fava (Carlo), Renzo Martini (Clerk), Walter Corradi (Kumpan), Roberto Agazzi (Dealer), Sonia Bovo, Ermanno Bullo, Delio Campelli, Gian Campi, Raul Costantini, Massimo Del Rio, Primo Senigallia, Eros De Simone
Cinematography: Frank Brühne
Sound: Walter Amann
Music: Ennio Morricone
Editing: Lotte Klimitschek
Set design: Hans Hoffer
Costumes: Annette Beaufays
Makeup: Otello Fava, Christiana Bettini
Assistant Director: Gusti Brünjes-Goldschwend

1985   *Fraulein (Fraulein – Ein deutsches Melodram)* (TV)
West Germany, 35mm, B&W and color, 108 minutes
A Production by Ulrich Nagel at Telefilm Saar for the Saarländischen Rundfunk (SR)
Festival Premiere: Munich 1986
Script: Bernd Schröder and Michael Haneke
Cast: Angelica Domröse (Johanna Kersch), Peter Franke (Hans Kersch), Lou Castel (André), Mareile Geisler (Brigitte Kersch), Michael Klein ("Mike" Kersch), Hans Werner Kraehkamp (Karl), Cordula Gerberg (Gisela), Margret Homeyer (Mother Kersch), Bob Anderson (John), Paulus Manker (Hotel Porter), Lisa Hellwig, Axel Ganz, Guylaine Péan, Chris Howland, Suzanne Geyer, Dieter Steinbrink
Cinematography: Walter Kindler, Karl Hohenberger
Sound: Wolf-Dieter Spille, Peter Paschinger
Editing: Monika Solzbacher, Monika Schreiner
Set design: Roger von Möllendorff, Karl-Heinz Andes
Costumes: Annette Beaufays
Makeup: Elke Naujoks, Stephanie Speicher
Assistant Director: Paulus Manker

1988   *The Seventh Continent (Der Siebente Kontinent)* (TV)
Austria, 35mm, color, 111 minutes
A Production by Veit Heiduschka at Wega-Film (Vienna)
Festival Premiere: Cannes 1989 (Directors' Fortnight)
Festival Prizes: "Bronze Leopard," Locarno 1989; Prize for Best Music and Sound in Film, Ghent 1989; Award for Film Art in Belgium, Brussels 1989; Austrian Prize for Film Art (awarded through the National Ministry for Education and Art, Vienna)

Script: Michael Haneke
Cast: Birgit Doll (Anna), Dieter Berner (Georg), Leni Tanzer (Eva), Udo Samel (Alexander), Silvia Fenz (Optometrist's Customer), Robert Dietl (Oertl), Elisabeth Rath (Teacher), Georges Kern (Bank Clerk), Georg Friedrich (Postal Clerk)
Cinematography: Toni Peschke
Sound: Karl Schlifelner
Editing: Marie Homolkova
Set design: Rudi Czettel
Costumes: Anna Georgiades
Makeup: Ernst Dummer
Assistant Director: Gebhard Zupan

1991   *Obituary for a Murderer* (*Nachruf für einen Mörder*) (**TV**)
Austria, video, color, 110 minutes
A Production by Wolfgang Ainberger and Evelyn Itkin at Österreichischer Rundfunk (ORF Art Pieces)
Festival Prizes: Special Honor from the National Ministry for Education and Art, Vienna
Script: Michael Haneke
Editing: Brigitte Pevny
Assistant Director: Hanus Polak, Jr.

1991/1992   *Benny's Video*
Austria/Switzerland, 35mm, color, 105 minutes
A Production by Veit Heiduschka at Wega-Film (Vienna), Bernhard Lang AG (Zürich)
Festival Premiere: Cannes 1992 (Directors' Fortnight)
Festival Prizes: "FIPRESCI Prize," Thessaloniki 1992; Vienna Film Prize, Viennale 1992; "FIPRESCI Prize," European Film Award 1993; Jury Prize for the Best Lighting, Festival de L'Images de Film, Chalon-sur-Saône; "Goldener Kader" Prize for Best Film 1994
Script: Michael Haneke
Cast: Arno Frisch (Benny), Angela Winkler (Mother), Ulrich Mühe (Father), Ingrid Stassner (Girl), Stephanie Brehme
Cinematography: Christian Berger
Sound: Karl Schlifelner
Music: J. S. Bach
Editing: Marie Homolkova
Set design: Christoph Kanter
Costumes: Erika Navas
Makeup: Giacomo Peier
Assistant Director: Hanus Polak Jr.

1992   *The Rebellion (Die Rebellion) (TV)*
            Austria, 16mm and video, B&W and color, 90 minutes
            A Production by Veit Heiduschka at Wega-Film (Vienna) for the
            Österreichischer Rundfunk (ORF)
            Festival Prizes: "Best TV Play," Television Prize for Austrian
            Education, 1994; "Best German-language TV Play," Television Prize
            of the German Academy of the Dramatic Arts, 1994; "Goldener Kader"
            Prize for Best TV Film 1994
            Script: Michael Haneke, after the novel by Joseph Roth
            Cast: Branko Samarovski (Andreas Pum), Judith Pogány (Kathie
            Blumich), Thierry van Werveke (Willi), Deborah Wisniewski (Anna
            Blumich), Katharina Grabher (Klara), August Schmölzer (Vinzenz
            Topp), Marinus Brand (Small Man), Götz Kauffmann (Arnold),
            Georg Trenkwitz (Schaffner), Karl Paryla (Prison Doctor), Johannes
            Silberschneider (The Commissioner), Karl-Ferdinand Kratzl (Prison
            Guard), Ulrich Reinthaller (Engineer), Christian Spatzek (Criminal
            Agent Huber), Markus Thill (Policeman), Georges Kern (Policeman),
            Josef Kemr (Music Cart Salesman), Justus Neumann, Haymon
            Maria Buttinger
            Narrator: Udo Samel
            Cinematography: Jiri Stibr
            Sound: Karl Schlifelner
            Music: Franz Schubert
            Editing: Marie Homolkova
            Set design: Christoph Kanter
            Costumes: Erika Navas, Darina Suranova, Jana Jankova
            Makeup: Paul Schmidt, Claudia Herold, Marta Doktorova
            Assistant Director: Hanus Polak Jr.

1993/1994   *71 Fragments of a Chronology of Chance (71 Fragmente einer
            Chronologie des Zufalls)*
            Austria, 35mm, color, 96 minutes
            A Production by Veit Heiduschka at Wega-Film (Vienna) for the
            Österreichischer Rundfunk (ORF) in cooperation with Zweites
            Deutsches Fernsehen (ZDF)/ARTE
            Festival Premiere: Cannes 1994 (Directors' Fortnight)
            Festival Prizes: "Gold Hugo" Award: Best Film, Chicago Film Festival
            1994; "Prix L'age d'or" Cinémathèque Royale de Belgique 1994;
            Festival Internacional de Cinema Fantástic de Stiges 1994, Best Film,
            Best Script, and Critics' Prize
            Script: Michael Haneke
            Cast: Gabriel Cosmin Urdes (Romanian Boy), Lukas Miko (Max the
            Student), Otto Grümandl (Tomek, the Old Man), Anne Bennent (Inge

Brunner), Udo Samel (Paul Brunner), Branko Samarowski (Hans), Claudia Martini (Maria), Georg Friedrich (Bernie the Soldier), Alexander Pschill (Hanno), Klaus Händl (Gerhard), Corinna Eder (Anni), Dorothee Hartinger (Kristina)
Cinematography: Christian Berger
Sound: Marc Parisotto
Editing: Marie Homolkova
Set design: Christoph Kanter
Costumes: Erika Navas
Makeup: Ilse Weisz-Stainer
Assistant Director: Ramses Ramsauer

1995   *Lumière and Company* (segment "Michael Haneke/Vienne")
France/Spain/Sweden, 35mm, B&W and color, 88 minutes
A Production by Fabienne Servan-Schreiber, Cinétrevé (Paris)
Artistic Direction: Anne Andreu
Direction: Sarah Moon, Anne Andreu
Cinematography: Philippe Poulet, Didier Ferry, Sarah Moon, Frederic Le Clair
Sound: Bernard Rochut, Jean Casanova
Music: Jean-Jacques Lemetre
Editing: Roger Ikhlef, Timothy Miller

1996/1997   *The Castle (Das Schloß)* (TV)
Austria, 35mm, color, 131 minutes
A Production by Veit Heiduschka at Wega-Film (Vienna) with cooperation from Österreichischer Rundfunk (ORF), Christina Undritz at Bayrischer Rundfunk (BR), and ARTE
Festival Premiere: Berlin 1997 (International Forum of New Cinema)
Festival Prizes: Television Prize for Austrian Education 1998
Script: Michael Haneke, after the novel by Franz Kafka
Cast: Ulrich Mühe (K.), Susanne Lothar (Frieda), Frank Giering (Artur), Felix Eitner (Jeremias), Nikolaus Paryla (The Chief), Dörte Lyssewski (Olga), Inga Busch (Amalia), André Eisermann (Barnabus), Norbert Schwientek (Bürgel), Birgit Linauer (Pepi), Hans Diehl (Erlanger), Branko Samarowski (Herrenhof Landlord), Ortrud Beginnen (Bridge Landlady), Otto Grünmandl (Bridge Landlord), Johannes Silberschneider (Teacher), Paulus Manker (Momus), Martin Brambach (Schwarzer), Wolfram Berger (Gerstäcker the Coachman), Monika Bleibtreu (Teacher), Conradin Blum (Hans), Ulrike Kaufmann, Joachim Unmack, Lisa Schlegel, Hermann Fritz
Narrator: Udo Samel
Cinematography: Jiri Stibr

Sound: Marc Parisotto
Editing: Andreas Prochaska
Set design: Christoph Kanter
Costumes: Lisy Christl
Makeup: Waldemar Pokromski, Isabella Gasser
Assistant Director: Hanus Polak, Jr.

1997   **Funny Games**
Austria, 35mm, color, 103 minutes
A Production by Veit Heiduschka at Wega-Film (Vienna)
Festival Premiere: Cannes 1997 (Competition)
Festival Prizes: FIPRESCI Prize, Flanders International Film Festival,
Ghent 1997; Silver Hugo Award: Best Director, Chicago 1997; 13th Prix
Trés Communiqué de Presse, Paris 1997; Konrad-Wolf Prize for his
Lifetime Achievement, Awarded through the Academy of Art, Berlin 1998
Script: Michael Haneke
Cast: Susanne Lothar (Anna), Ulrich Mühe (Georg), Arno Frisch (Paul),
Frank Giering (Peter), Stefan Clapczynski (Schoschi), Doris Kunstmann
(Gerda), Christoph Bantzer (Fred), Wolfgang Glück (Robert), Susanne
Meneghel (Gerda's Sister), Monika Zallinger (Eva)
Cinematography: Jürgen Jürges
Sound: Walter Amann
Music: W. A. Mozart, Giuseppe Verdi, John Zorn
Editing: Andreas Prochaska
Set design: Christoph Kanter
Costumes: Lisy Christl
Assistant Director: Hanus Polak, Jr.

1999/2000   **Code Unknown (Code inconnu: Récit incomplet de divers voyages)**
France/Germany/Romania, 35mm, color, 117 minutes
A Production by Marin Karmitz, MK2 Productions and Alain Sarde,
Les Films Alain Sarde in Co-Production with Arte France Cinéma,
France 2 Cinéma, Bavaria Film International, ZDF, Romanian Ministry
of Culture, Filmex Romania in cooperation with Canal+
Festival Premiere: Cannes 2000 (Competition)
Festival Prizes: Prize of the Ecumenical Jury, Cannes 2000
Script: Michael Haneke
Cast: Juliette Binoche (Anne), Thierry Neuvic (Georges), Sepp
Bierbichler (The Builder), Alexandre Hamidi (Jean), Hélène Diarra
(Aminate), Ona Lu Yenke (Amadou), Djibril Kouyate (The Father),
Guessi Diakite-Goumdo (Salimata), Luminita Gheorghiu (Maria),
Crenguta Hariton Stoica (Irina), Bob Niculescu (Dragos), Bruno
Todeschini (Pierre), Paulus Manker (Perrin), Didier Flamand (The

Director), Walida Afkir (The Young Arab), Maurice Benichou (The Old Arab), Carlo Brandt (Henri), Philippe Demarle (Paul), Marc Duret (The Policeman), Arsinée Khanjian (Amadou's Girlfriend), Nathalie Richard (Mathilde), Andrée Tainsy (Mrs. Becker)
Cinematography: Jürgen Jürges
Sound: Guillaume Sciama, Jean-Pierre Laforce
Music: Giba Gonçalves
Editing: Andreas Prochaska, Karin Hartusch, Nadine Muse
Set design: Manuel de Chauvigny
Costumes: Françoise Clavel
Assistant Director: Alain Olivieri

2000/2001   *The Piano Teacher (La Pianiste)*
A Production by Marin Karmitz, MK2 Productions and Alain Sarde, Les Films Alain Sarde in Co-Production with Arte France Cinéma
Festival Premiere: Cannes 2001 (Competition)
Festival Prizes: Jury's Grand Prize, Cannes 2000; Best Actress for Isabelle Huppert, Cannes 2001; Best Actor for Benoît Magimel, Cannes 2001; Best European Actress for Isabelle Huppert, European Film Awards, Berlin 2001; Best Supporting Role for Annie Girardot, Paris 2002; Critics' Award for the Best Foreign Film, Moscow Kinotawr 2002; Best Female Actress for Isabelle Huppert, Moscow Kinotawr, 2002; ROMY (Best Austrian Film), Vienna 2002; German Gold Prize for the Best Foreign Film, Berlin 2002; Best Female Actress for Isabelle Huppert, Seattle Film Festival 2002
Script: Michael Haneke, after the novel by Elfriede Jelinek
Cast: Isabelle Huppert (Erika Kohut), Annie Girardot (Mother), Benoît Magimel (Walter Klemmer), Susanne Lothar (Mrs. Schober), Anna Sigalevitch (Anna Schober), Udo Samel (Dr. Blonskij), Cornelia Köndgen (Mrs. Blonskij), Thomas Weinhappel (Bariton), Philipp Heiss (Naprawnik), Rudolf Melichar (Director), Gabriele Schuchter (Margot), Georg Friedrich (Man in Drive-In Movie), Vivian Bartsch (Girl in Drive-In Movie), Volker Waldegg (1st Male Professor), William Mang (2nd Male Professor), Michael Schottenberg (3rd Male Professor), Dieter Berner (Singing Teacher), Martina Resetarits (1st Female Professor), Annemarie Schleinzer (2nd Female Professor), Karoline Zeisler (3rd Female Professor), Liliane Nelska (Secretary), Luz Leskowitz (Violinist), Viktor Teuflmayr (Pianist), Florian Koba (Student)
Cinematography: Christian Berger
Sound: Guillaume Sciama, Jean-Pierre Laforce
Music: Frédéric Chopin, Joseph Hadyn, Franz Schubert, Ludwig van Beethoven, J. S. Bach, Arnold Schönberg, Sergei Rachmaninoff, Johannes Brahms

Editing: Monika Willi, Nadine Muse
Set design: Christoph Kanter
Costumes: Annette Beaufays
Makeup: Thi Loan Nguyen, Ellen Just, Françoise Andrejka
Assistant Director: Hanus Polak, Jr.

2002   *Time of the Wolf (Le Temps du loup)*
France/Austria/Germany, 35mm, color, 113 minutes
A Co-Production by Veit Heiduschka at Wega-Film (Vienna), Bavaria Film, Centre National de la Cinématographie (CNC), Eurimages, France 3 Cinéma, Les Films du Losange, Arte France Cinéma, and Canal+
Festival Premiere: Cannes 2003 (Competition)
Festival Prizes: Best Film, Festival International de Cinema Stiges, 2003; Critics' Prize, Festival International de Cinema Stiges, 2003
Script: Michael Haneke
Cast: Isabelle Huppert (Anne Laurent), Béatrice Dalle (Lise Brandt), Patrice Chéreau (Thomas Brandt), Rona Hartner (Arina), Maurice Bénichou (Mr. Azoulay), Olivier Gourmet (Koslowski), Brigitte Roüan (Béa), Lucas Biscombe (Ben), Hakim Taleb (Young Runaway), Anaïs Demoustier (Eva), Serge Riaboukine (The Leader), Marilyne Even (Mrs. Azoulay), Florence Loiret (Nathalie Azoulay), Branko Samarowski (Policeman), Daniel Duval (Georges Laurent), Thierry van Werveke (Jean), Michael Abiteboul (Armed Man), Pierre Berriau (Fred), Costel Cascaval (Constantin), Luminita Gheorghiu (Mrs. Homolka), Franck Gourlat (Water Seller), François Hauteserre (The Music Lover), Maria Hofstätter (Quarrelling Woman), Valérie Moreau (Fred's Wife), Claude Singeot (Razor-Blade Man), Ina Strnad (Child at Chalet), Adriana Tranafir (Marya), Roman Agrinz, Alexander Bárta, Peter Bartak, Gabriela Bauer, Ileana Brancau, Georg Friedrich, Simon Hatzl, Alexandra Höftmann, Edmund Jäger, Silke Jandl, Dorothea Kocsis, Natascha Kuhskova, Carmen Loley, Andreas Lust, Huttová Margita, Marian Mitas, Martin Najalka, Klaus Ortner, Maria Esperanza Paraschiv, Petru Pecican, Andreas Puehringer, Sonja Romei, Christoph Theußl, Sophie Wimmer-Lieb, Christian Wlach, Werner Wultsch, Mira Zeichmann
Cinematography: Jürgen Jürges
Sound: Guillaume Sciama, Jean-Pierre Laforce
Editing: Monika Willi, Nadine Muse
Set design: Christoph Kanter
Costumes: Lisy Christl
Assistant Director: Hanus Polak, Jr.

2004   *Caché*
France/Austria/Germany/Italy/USA, 35mm, color, 117 minutes
A Co-Production by Veit Heiduschka at Wega-Film (Vienna),
Bavaria Film, Les Films du Losange, BIM Distribuzione
Festival Premiere: Cannes 2005 (Competition)
Festival Prizes: Best Director, Cannes 2005; FIPRESCI Prize, Cannes
2005; Prize of the Ecumenical Jury, Cannes 2005; Best Foreign
Language Film, British Independent Film Awards 2006; Best Foreign
Language Film, Chicago Film Critics Association Awards, 2006; Best
Feature Film, Diagonale Austria 2006; Best Actor for Daniel Auteuil,
Best Director, Best Film at European Film Awards, 2005; Best Foreign
Language Film, Film Critics Circle of Australia Awards, 2006; Best
Foreign Language Film, Los Angeles Film Critics Association Awards,
2005; Best Screenplay, Lumiere France 2006; Best Foreign Language
Film, San Francisco Film Critics Circle 2005
Script: Michael Haneke
Cast: Daniel Auteuil (Georges Laurent), Juliette Binoche (Anne
Laurent), Maurice Bénichou (Majid), Annie Girardot (Georges'
Mother), Bernard Le Coq (Georges' Editor-in-Chief), Walid Afkir
(Majid's Son), Lester Makedonsky (Pierrot Laurent), Daniel Duval
(Pierre), Nathalie Richard (Mathilde), Denis Podalydès (Yvon), Aïssa
Maïga (Chantal), Caroline Baehr (Nurse), Christian Benedetti (Georges'
Father), Philippe Besson (TV Guest), Loic Brabant (Police Office #2),
Jean-Jacques Brochiet (TV Guest), Paule Daré (Orphanage Attendant),
Louis-Do de Lencquesaing (Bookstore Owner), Annette Faure
(Georges' Mother, Young), Hugo Flamigni (Young Georges), Peter
Stephan Jungk (Writer), Dioucounda Koma (Cyclist), Marie Kremer
(Jeannette), Nicky Marbot (Orphanage Driver), Malik Nait Djoudi
(Young Majid), Marie-Christine Orry (Housekeeper), Mazarine
Pingeot (TV Guest), Julie Recoing (Georges' Assistant), Karla Suarez
(Novelist), Laurent Suire (Police Officer #1), Jean Teulé (TV Guest)
Cinematography: Christian Berger
Sound: Jean-Paul Mugel, Jean-Pierre Laforce
Editing: Michael Hudecek, Nadine Muse
Set design: Christoph Kanter, Emmanuel de Chauvigny
Costumes: Lisy Christl
Assistant Director: Alain Olivieri

2007   *Funny Games U.S.*
USA/France/UK/Austria/Germany/Italy, 35mm, color, 111 minutes
A Production by Celluloid Dreams, Halcyon Pictures, Tartan Films,
X-Filme International, Lucky Red, and Kinematograf

Festival Premiere: London Film Festival 2007
Script: Michael Haneke
Cast: Naomi Watts (Ann Farber), Tim Roth (George Farber), Michael Pitt (Paul), Brady Corbet (Peter), Devon Gearhart (Georgie Farber), Boyd Gaines (Fred Thompson), Siobhan Fallon (Betsy Thompson), Robert LuPone (Robert), Susanne Hanke (Betsy's Sister-in-Law), Linda Moran (Eve)
Cinematography: Darius Khondji
Sound: Nadise Muse, Jean-Pierre Laforce
Editing: Monika Willi
Set design: Kevin Thompson, Hinju Kim
Costumes: David C. Robinson
Assistant Director: Urs Hirschbiegel

2009   **The White Ribbon (*Das weisse Band*)**
Austria/Germany/France/Italy, 35mm, B&W, 144 minutes
A Production by Veit Heiduschka at Wega-Film (Vienna), X-Filme Creative Pool, Les Films du Losange, and Lucky Red
Festival Premiere: Cannes 2009
Festival Prizes: Palme d'Or, FIPRESCI Prize, and Cinema Prize of the French National Education System, Cannes 2009; FIPRESCI Prize, San Sebastian International Film Festival 2009
Script: Michael Haneke
Cast: Susanne Lothar (Midwife), Ulrich Tukur (Baron), Burghart Klaußner (Pastor), Josef Bierbichler (Steward), Marisa Growaldt (Farmhand), Christian Friedel (Teacher), Leonie Benesch (Eva), Ursina Lardi (Baroness Marie-Luise), Steffi Kühnert (Anna), Gabriela Maria Schmeide (Emma), Rainer Bock (Doctor), Maria-Victoria Dragus (Klara), Leonard Proxauf (Martin), Janina Fautz (Erna), Michael Kranz (Tutor), Levin Henning (Adolf), Johanna Busse (Margarete), Yuma Amecke (Annchen), Thibault Sérié (Gustav), Enno Trebs (Georg), Theo Trebs (Ferdinand), Sebastian Hülk (Max), Kai-Peter Malina (Karl), Aaron Denkel (Kurti), Anne-Kathrin Gummich (Eva's Mother)
Cinematography: Christian Berger
Sound: Guillaume Sciama, Jean-Pierre Laforce
Editing: Monika Willi
Set design: Christoph Kanter
Costumes: Moidele Bickel
Assistant Director: Hanus Polak, Jr.

Index

Page numbers in italics indicate illustrations.